Casebook of Child and Pediatric Psychology

Casebook of Child and Pediatric Psychology

Edited by

MICHAEL C. ROBERTS
The University of Alabama

C. EUGENE WALKER
University of Oklahoma

THE GUILFORD PRESS
New York   London

© 1989 The Guilford Press

A Division of Guilford Publications, Inc.

72 Spring Street, New York, NY 10012

Printed in the United States of America

Last digit is print number: 9 8 7 6 5 4 3 2 1

Library of Congress Cataloging-in-Publication Data

Casebook of child and pediatric psychology / edited by Michael C.
  Roberts, C. Eugene Walker.
      p.   cm.
    Includes index.
    ISBN 0-89862-739-7
    1. Child psychiatry—Case studies.   2. Child psychology—Case
studies.   I. Roberts, Michael C.   II. Walker, C. Eugene (Clarence
Eugene), 1939–
    [DNLM: 1. Child Psychology—case studies.   2. Mental Disorders—in
infancy & childhood—case studies.   WS 105 C338]
R J499.C282   1989
618.92′8909—dc19
DNLM/DLC
for Library of Congress   88-37197
                                                              CIP

To Our Children,
   Erica and Alicia—M.C.R.
   Chad, Kyle, and Cass—C.E.W.

Contributors

THOMAS M. ACHENBACH, Ph.D. Department of Psychiatry, University of Vermont, Burlington, Vermont.

DARLENE M. ATKINS, Ph.D. Departments of Adolescent Medicine and Psychiatry, Children's Hospital National Medical Center, George Washington University Medical School, Washington, District of Columbia.

STEPHEN R. BOGGS, Ph.D. Department of Clinical and Health Psychology, University of Florida, Gainesville, Florida.

ANDREW S. BRADLYN, Ph.D. Department of Behavioral Medicine and Psychiatry, West Virginia University Health Sciences Center, Morgantown, West Virginia.

MICHAEL P. CAREY, Ph.D. Department of Psychiatry and Behavioral Sciences, Medical University of South Carolina, Charleston, South Carolina.

DONNA R. COPELAND, Ph.D. Department of Pediatrics, The University of Texas, M.D. Anderson Cancer Center, Houston, Texas.

DANITA CZYZEWSKI, Ph.D. Department of Psychiatry, Baylor College of Medicine, Texas Children's Hospital, Houston, Texas.

LYNNDA M. DAHLQUIST, Ph.D. Department of Psychiatry and Behavioral Sciences, Baylor College of Medicine, Houston, Texas.

EDWARD R. DAVIDSON, Ph.D. Department of Pediatrics, The University of Texas, M.D. Anderson Cancer Center, Houston, Texas.

STEPHEN J. DOLLINGER, Ph.D. Department of Psychology, Southern Illinois University, Carbondale, Illinois.

KAREN DURNIAT, R.N., B.S.N. Department of Nursing, Medical College of Ohio, Toledo, Ohio.

SHEILA M. EYBERG, Ph.D. Department of Clinical and Health Psychology, University of Florida, Gainesville, Florida.

A. J. FINCH, Jr., Ph.D. Department of Psychiatry and Behavioral Sciences, Medical University of South Carolina, Charleston, South Carolina.

BEVERLY W. FUNDERBURK, M.A. Department of Clinical and Health Psychology, University of Florida, Gainesville, Florida.

GARY R. GEFFKEN, Ph.D. Departments of Psychiatry, Pediatrics, and Clinical and Health Psychology, University of Florida Health Science Center, Gainesville, Florida.

BETTY N. GORDON, Ph.D. Department of Psychology, University of North Carolina, Chapel Hill, North Carolina.

LEILANI GREENING, M.A. Psychology Internship, UCLA Neuropsychiatric Institute, Los Angeles, California.

LAURA J. HEWETT, B.A. Psychology Department, Northwest Passages Adolescent Hospital, Boise, Idaho.

HONORE M. HUGHES, Ph.D. Department of Psychology, University of Arkansas, Fayetteville, Arkansas.

SUZANNE BENNETT JOHNSON, Ph.D. Department of Psychiatry, Pediatrics, and Clinical and Health Psychology, University of Florida Health Science Center, Gainesville, Florida.

PATRICK C. KELLY, D.O. Department of Pediatrics, Developmental Pediatrics Section, Madigan Army Medical Center, Tacoma, Washington.

ANNETTE M. LA GRECA, Ph.D. Department of Psychology, University of Miami, Coral Gables, Florida.

JAMES E. MADDUX, Ph.D. Department of Psychology, George Mason University, Fairfax, Virginia.

STEPHANIE H. McCONAUGHY, Ph.D. Department of Psychiatry, University of Vermont, Burlington, Vermont.

LEONARD S. MILLING, Ph.D. Department of Psychiatry, Medical College of Ohio, Toledo, Ohio.

KEVIN C. MOONEY, Ph.D. Department of Psychology, Valparaiso University, Valparaiso, Indiana.

JAMES M. NELSON, Ph.D. Department of Psychology, Valparaiso University, Valparaiso, Indiana.

ARLENE NORIEGA-GARCIA, M.S. Department of Psychology, University of Miami, Coral Gables, Florida.

PAMELA G. OSNES, M.A. Florida Mental Health Institute, University of South Florida, Tampa, Florida.

STEVEN C. PARKISON, Ph.D. Clinical Psychology Service, Department of Psychiatry, Madigan Army Medical Center, Tacoma, Washington.

MICHAEL C. ROBERTS, Ph.D. Department of Psychology, The University of Alabama, Tuscaloosa, Alabama.

CAROLYN S. SCHROEDER, Ph.D. Chapel Hill Pediatrics and Departments of Psychiatry and Pediatrics, University of North Carolina, Chapel Hill, North Carolina.

WILLIAM J. SHAW, Psy.D. Oklahoma City Clinic, Oklahoma City, Oklahoma.

TREVOR E. STOKES, Ph.D. Florida Mental Health Institute, University of South Florida, Tampa, Florida.

WENDY L. STONE, Ph.D. Department of Pediatrics, Vanderbilt University School of Medicine, Nashville, Tennessee.

STEVEN THURBER, Ph.D. Psychology Department, Northwest Passages Adolescent Hospital, Boise, Idaho.

C. EUGENE WALKER, Ph.D. Department of Psychiatry and Behavioral Sciences, University of Oklahoma Health Sciences Center, Oklahoma City, Oklahoma.

DONALD WERTLIEB, Ph.D. Eliot–Pearson Department of Child Study, Tufts University, Medford, Massachusetts.

DALE W. WISELY, Ph.D. The Vaughan Clinic, Birmingham, Alabama.

Contents

1
Clinical Cases in Child and Pediatric Psychology: Conceptualization and Overview

MICHAEL C. ROBERTS
C. EUGENE WALKER

The overlapping specialties of clinical child and pediatric psychology presently evidence tremendous growth in clinical practice opportunities and in applications of psychological knowledge to a variety of behavioral and health problems. There currently exists a shortage of professionals qualified to work with children, youth, and families in both clinical child and pediatric psychology (Tuma, 1981, 1985). It has been estimated there will be an unfilled requirement of around 5,000 additional professionals in these specialties by 1989 (VandenBos, Nelson, Stapp, Olmedo, Coates, & Batchelor, 1979).

Concomitantly, there is renewed emphasis on training students to become mental health professionals to work with children, youth, and families as well as on continuing the education of those already in the field. The specialties of pediatric and clinical child psychology increasingly require specialized training efforts (Roberts, 1982). In recent years, considerable attention has been given to formalizing training efforts especially given the special aspects of work with children and families. The Division of Child, Youth, and Family Services of the American Psychological Association formulated a statement of minimal training components for professionals in this area (Roberts, Erickson, & Tuma, 1985). These elements included: child development and lifespan developmental psychology; child

Michael C. Roberts. Department of Psychology, The University of Alabama, Tuscaloosa, Alabama.

C. Eugene Walker. Department of Psychiatry and Behavioral Sciences, University of Oklahoma Health Sciences Center, Oklahoma City, Oklahoma.

1

and adult psychopathology; mental retardation and developmental disabilities; specialized child assessment techniques; child psychotherapy and behavior change; parent, family, and school intervention techniques; specialized clinical practica; research methods; and ethical and legal issues. These were basically endorsed and elaborated upon by the National Conference on Training Clinical Child Psychologists (Tuma, 1985). Additionally, considerations of training have been discussed with regard to pediatric psychology for interventions in medical settings and with problems associated with medical conditions (La Greca, Stone, Drotar, & Maddux, 1988; Roberts, Fanurik, & Elkins, 1988a). The increased attention to training experiences for practitioners in pediatric and clinical child psychology reflects the growth in these related fields. There are special aspects of clinical practice in these areas relative to general clinical psychology.

The breadth of applications in these fields can be seen in the statement of coverage for the *Journal of Pediatric Psychology* (sponsored by the Society of Pediatric Psychology, the organizational home for professionals in this area):

> Pediatric psychology is an interdisciplinary field addressing the full range of physical and mental development, health, and illness issues affecting children, adolescents, and families. [It encompasses] . . . a wide variety of topics exploring the relationship between psychological and physical well-being of children and adolescents including: understanding, assessment, and intervention with developmental disorders; evaluation and treatment of behavioral and emotional problems and concomitants of disease and illness; the role of psychology in pediatric medicine; the promotion of health and development; and the prevention of illness and injury among children and youth. (Roberts, La Greca, & Harper, 1988b, p. 2)

Clearly, the fields of interest cover the study of psychological–behavioral aspects of emotional disturbances, school/learning problems, child rearing/development, physical illness/handicap, and health/medical procedures as well as psychological intervention for all of these as they relate to children and their families. La Greca et al. (1988) dichotomize the two areas by noting that "clinical child psychologists may focus to a greater extent on traditional mental health issues, problems, and settings; whereas pediatric psychologists may emphasize health, assessment, and consultation/liaison areas (Tuma, 1980)" (p. 137). The types of problems presenting in pediatric and clinical child psychology practices are significant and varied. Specialized training is needed for competent practice (Roberts et al., 1985; Roberts et al., 1988a). Increasingly, critical elements of practice and research are being examined to influence training sequences for generic child-related work (Roberts et al., 1985), clinical child psychology (Tuma, 1985), and pediatric psychology (Roberts et al., 1988a).

As these overlapping areas have grown in recent years, a number of texts and written materials have been produced for the didactic training of students and as resources for practicing clinicians. For example, in pediatric psychology a number of books are available such as the volumes edited by Phyllis Magrab (1978a, 1978b), the *Encyclopedia of Pediatric Psychology* (Wright, Schaefer, & Solomons, 1979), the *Handbook for the Practice of Pediatric Psychology* (Tuma, 1982), and *Pediatric Psychology: Psychological Interventions and Strategies for Pediatric Problems* (Roberts, 1986). Most recently, the Society of Pediatric Psychology sponsored the publication of the *Handbook of Pediatric Psychology* (Routh, 1988). These didactic resources have complemented more general books on clinical child psychology such as *Handbook of Clinical Child Psychology* (Walker & Roberts, 1983) and *Clinical Child Psychology* (Pfeiffer, 1985). The wealth of these resources reflects the significant growth of the specialties for practice and research.

Much material exists as resources for didactic training in clinical child and pediatric psychology. What is lacking in the published literature are illustrations of the actual application of the techniques taught in academic courses or outlined in books. Generally, scientific journals do not provide the student or clinician with exposure to clinical work per se because their focus tends to be more on research rather than on the *application* of the research or theory. Occasionally, journals in some areas report case studies. The primary goal in scholarly reports is on the scientifically validated inferences. These published case examples typically leave out details on the decision-making process in diagnosis and treatment—that is, the art of implementation. In addition, clinical case reports in the published literature almost invariably report successful interventions and imply an ease in implementation that is not always true in practice. The restrictions on journal space preclude elaboration and discussion of false starts, blind alleys, and so forth. In a similar vein, Hayes (1981) has argued that "there are few outlets for on-line clinical research. On-line single case evaluations, modified as they frequently are by realities of clinical practice, may meet a severe reception in most clinical journals" (p. 194).

Finally, the orientation of most journals tends to be focused on the theoretical implications and the "hard" data of a case, that is, the diagnosis and treatment must illustrate a theory-driven approach and present it in a scientific framework (Lazarus & Davison, 1971). We have found that many published cases are "too clean" because of the need for experimentlike data and the theory–approach relationship. There is an almost "made up" quality to the many reports such that they are unreal examples of clinical work. Published case reports seemingly convey the idea that clinical practice moves smoothly from predetermined assessment strategies through smartly implemented interventions to easily discernible success. This does not happen in many cases in "real" clinical practice. Professionals are often puzzled by such neat reports, while students are confused and intimidated.

Trial and error changes in intervention as the clinician proceeds characterize true clinical work with a great deal of problem solving, gathering of
data, decision making at various points, and use of a variety of techniques.

In sum, those who conduct training and those in clinical practice often
find that the complexity of child assessment and treatment are not conveyed
when relying upon case studies published in the research and professional
literature. Techniques and cases are all too frequently presented as completed products with the decision points obscured by the therapist-authors'
knowledge of the end result. Nevertheless, the use of case illustrations can
expose students to a larger variety of clinical problems and approaches than
would be possible in direct experience through clinical practica.

The case study method is a frequently invoked method of teaching both
formally (in grand rounds and case conference presentations) or informally
("I once had a case that . . ."). Case presentations demonstrate while also
presenting facts. This method is important for illustrating applications of
techniques and for conveying the clinical process. Case examples truly
"exemplify." Slater and Thomas (1983) have noted that:

> Often faculty has been forced to sort through its client files or to resort to
> data from colleagues' files. . . . Problems may be encountered if the faculty
> member does not have extensive enough files to provide the students with a
> good cross-section of children. (p. *xv*)

Training in many professional disciplines relies upon analyses of case
examples for conveying significant aspects of a profession and its practice.
For example, business schools traditionally use case analysis to illustrate
good and bad decision making in corporate management. Because of the
principle of stare decisis (precedence), legal training utilizes case law and
descriptions to transmit knowledge of the judicial process and to enhance
critical thinking in aspiring lawyers. Throughout its history medicine has
based its training in diagnosis and treatment on individual case presentations. Medical professionals have given considerable attention to the process
of teaching problem solving through case formulations (e.g., Eddy & Clanton, 1982; Engel, 1971; Kassirer, 1983; Kassirer & Gorry, 1978).

The case study also has a long and rich history in psychology and "has
played a central role in clinical psychology" (Kazdin, 1981, p. 183). The
importance of case studies in psychological applications was recognized by
the first clinical psychologist, Lightner Witmer, who published case reports
from the first psychological clinic at the University of Pennsylvania
(McReynolds, 1987). In the earlier years of the profession, the case study
approach to presenting and understanding clinical interventions was used
widely to illustrate psychopathology, assessment, and therapy as well as to
provide basic data for scientific inquiry. By the 1940s and 1950s, the case
study was recognized as a formalized method of organizing and interpreting

various types of information (e.g., observations, test results, communications from a variety of sources) following some plan or theoretical framework (Garfield, 1957; Weinberg & Hire, 1956). Although case reports and summaries often remain the most important mechanism of information organization and communication about clients and their problems, scientific inferences drawn from uncontrolled case studies are limited (Hayes, 1981; Kazdin, 1981). Although used more or less formally in training mental health professionals, the educative process of case analysis of problem solving, diagnosis, and treatment has been neglected by psychology more recently. Case analyses are used more in certain areas of professional literature to demonstrate the scientific control and efficacy of theoretically driven interventions (e.g., in the behavioral literature) than to train clinical processes.

The National Conference on Training Clinical Child Psychologists stated that "case management conferences should be utilized to integrate assessment, treatment, and consultation with ethical considerations and an increased awareness of [the need for] evaluating the success of our chosen interventions" (Tuma, 1985, p. 5). In many respects, the case studies published in this volume serve as case conferences. Although they are not as formal as the "Case Records of the Massachusetts General Hospital: Weekly Clinicopathological Exercise" published in the *New England Journal of Medicine*, they attempt to capture the richness of case material in the clinical learning process.

Lightner Witmer appears to be the first clinical child and pediatric psychologist as he practiced and published in the area of psychological applications to children's problems in collaboration with physicians, teachers, and parents. There have been many changes in the field over time. Pediatric and clinical child psychology now possesses a stronger data base, justifying the applications many clinicians now employ routinely. The published literature, even with the limitations noted here, helped promote the move from an intuitive base of clinical practice to a more empirical one (Roberts, 1986). Nonetheless, clinical practice remains both an art *and* a science.

We set out to develop the present casebook to do something different from the typical case study reported in the journal format and, we hope, meet some of the training needs of students and clinicians. We sought to publish case reports that portray the richness of clinical work while also maintaining the necessary linkage to the research and theoretical aspects of psychology. To accomplish this, we wrote to about 100 practicing psychologists across the country to inquire if they or one of their associates would be interested in preparing a case based on their own practice. We noted in our inquiry letter that the case problem need not be unique or necessarily a theoretically important intervention. The cases could be unique, but we were more interested in the typical referrals (even if mundane and seemingly unexciting), which are the bulk of clinical practice. Typical cases with twists in the process and those with changes at various points were solicited. We asked that the cases be good illustrations with high educative value which included information on the critical points in the assessment and treatment process through a discussion of the clinical method. We noted that the pertinent research literature would need to be covered and integrated in the case discussion. From this initial inquiry, we received over 100 brief case descriptions—an overwhelming, positive response.

When reviewing these case briefs, we selected those that represented various aspects of practice in clinical child and pediatric psychology. We were particularly guided by tabulation reports of clinical problems referred to various pediatric psychology services. Problem categories were defined initially in an article by Mesibov, Schroeder, and Wesson (1977). Later, Walker (1979) collected data on presenting problems in a pediatric psychology clinic serving a large children's hospital. Over a long term period, Kanoy and Schroeder (1985) compiled parental concerns and common referral problems for a practice of psychologists working in a private pediatric practice with a "call in/come in" component. Ottinger and Roberts (1980) tallied pediatricians' referrals to a pediatric psychology practicum in a clinical training program. Finally, Roberts (1986) made a composite of these three reports in Table 1-1.

More than anything, the variety of clinical cases evaluated and treated by pediatric and clinical child psychologists epitomizes the diversity of the field. This tabular summary, then, guided selection of cases for inclusion in this volume. As can be seen, the starred referral problems (indicating coverage in this book) represent the most frequent cases seen in these practices. Also, a fairly consistent pattern of practice emerges with negative behaviors, school-related problems, and personality disorders having a high degree of frequency. Also well represented in the presenting problems are physical complaints, adjustment to disease, developmental delays, toileting, and infant management problems.

As other selection criteria, we tried to choose cases that had potential to demonstrate (1) what assessment tools were used (or not used) and why, (2) based on the evaluation, how the intervention was determined for the particular characteristics of the case, (3) how the therapist initially chose one treatment over another (with documentation from the literature), (4) how treatment procedures changed as events in the progress of the case dictated, (5) what additional decisions were made as to whom to include in treatment, whether to change interventions, when to terminate, and (6) how the effects of the interventions were evaluated. Of course, given the large number of case responses, we unfortunately had to decline many cases with great potential in order to limit ourselves to the 20 cases included in this volume, which is all even a very understanding publisher would permit in a single volume.

As the authors embarked on writing their case reports, we provided them only with a minimal set of guidelines for coverage in the chapters. First, we asked the authors to use the first person when referring to themselves as clinicians rather than the abstract third person. We felt this personalized approach was more honest and reflected our belief that the therapist is an active element in therapy (regardless of theoretical orientation). In the science of psychology, an experimenter may be viewed more as an objective collector of data: Third person reports are fairly standard in publication styles. In clinical practice, however, the therapist directly interacts with the child, family, and other systems in a personal and subjective manner. The first person conveys this better. However, in some cases treatment was done by a team of professionals, and it posed some problems to differentiate contributions. Also, on occasion the authors felt compelled to step back in order to analyze their cases. In such instances, they used their own discretion on which form to employ.

In their chapters, we asked the authors to utilize the growing research base, and integrate theory with their clinical presentations. We requested that they describe the case, the data gathered in assessment, and the diagnosis based on either the third edition of the *Diagnostic and Statistical Manual of Mental Disorders* (DSM-III; American Psychiatric Association, 1980) or on the revision of DSM-III, DSM-III-R (APA, 1987). Incidence and prevalence, related diagnoses, and theories of etiology were also to be covered. Background information, as relevant, and a brief summary of procedures used in assessment with results and interpretation, as would be done with most clinical practice, were to be provided. In a discussion of the case formulation, we asked the authors to explain the probable basis of symptoms and indicate their decision-making process as they approached the case. We asked the authors to provide an outline of the initial treatment protocol with a description of the course of therapy. Outcome information on progress, status at termination, follow-up, and so forth were to be incorporated as well. Finally, we asked the authors to reflect on the case in terms of the main points illustrated, comparisons with other cases of the specific type, and additional clinical experiences useful to understanding the clinical process with the particular case. These guiding thoughts were presented a priori to the authors, but not as a definitive outline for each section in the case chapter.

We deliberately allowed the authors great latitude in describing their own case or cases because each problem, each child and family, required different expositions. The problem or case often dictated the organization of the report. Forcing a rigid protocol with all cases would have compromised the cases' illustrative value. Thus, in some instances the chapter presents one important aspect of a clinical case, as in Chapter 2 by Wertlieb about using test reports in advocating for children, or in Chapter 3 on assessment procedures outlined by McConaughy and Achenbach. On the other hand, a

TABLE 1-1. Referral Problems to Three Pediatric Psychology Services

	Kanoy & Schroeder (1985)[a]	Ottinger & Roberts (1980)	Walker (1979)
*Negative behaviors Toward parents—doesn't obey, has tantrums, demanding, cries, whines	15	10	10
*Toileting Toilet training, encopresis, enuresis	10	8	5
*Developmental delays Perceptual–motor problems, speech problems, slow development, school readiness, overactivity	7	10	16[b]
*School problems Dislikes school, poor performance, reading or math problems, child aggression toward teacher	9	15	9
*Sleeping problems Resists bedtime, nightmares, naps	8	2	1
*Personality problems Lacks self-control, motivation; irresponsible; overly lies, steals; dependent	10	5	4
*Sibling/peer problems Has no friends, aggressive toward peers, sibling fighting	7	1	<1
*Divorce, separation, adoption Custody decisions, appropriate visitation schedule, how tell child	8	1	2
*Infant management Feeding, nursing, cries all the time ("colic"), stimulation	3	6	<1
*Family problems Mother feels isolated, conflict over discipline, parents arguing, child abuse	4	3	10
Sex-related problems Opposite-sexed parents' clothing, no same-sexed friends, lack of sex-appropriate interests	2	1	2
*Food/eating problems Picky eater, eats too much or too little	1	4	2
*Specific fears Dogs, trucks, dark	2	—	<1
Specific bad habits Thumb sucking, nail biting, tics	3	2	2
Parent's negative feelings toward child Dislike child, no enjoyable interactions	2	—	<1

TABLE 1-1. *(continued)*

	Kanoy & Schroeder (1985)[a]	Ottinger & Roberts (1980)	Walker (1979)
*Physical complaints Headaches, stomachaches, fainting	2	16	23
*Parent's concerns about school Is child getting what's needed? Does teacher understand child?	2	—	—
Moving Preparation for moving and problems of adjustment afterwards	1	—	<1
Death Understanding and adjusting to death	1	—	1
Guidance of talented child Special programs, proper stimulation	1	1	<1
*Adjustment to disease, handicap	—	13	—
Drug/alcohol abuse	—	2	—
Miscellaneous	1	—	11[c]

Note. Blanks (—) indicate category was not used in compilation. Asterisks (*) indicate chapters in casebook. Percentages were rounded to nearest whole number. From *Pediatric psychology: Psychological interventions and strategies for pediatric problems* by M. C. Roberts, 1986, New York: Pergamon. Copyright 1986 by Pergamon. Reprinted by permission.

[a]A totaled categorization based on Mesibov et al. (1977), Schroeder (1979), and new data from Kanoy and Schroeder (1985).

[b]Combines category with mental retardation and hyperactivity.

[c]Includes depression, hallucinations, suicide, instability.

number of chapters illustrate the complexity of information and factors in the clinical cases (e.g., Chapter 6 on personality disorders by Gordon and Schroeder and Chapter 20 on anorexia nervosa by Atkins). Several chapters juxtapose two or more cases—the first illustrating a typical case handled fairly routinely, the others containing unforeseen difficulties or complexity (e.g., Chapter 18 on pain management by Dahlquist and Chapter 13 on feeding disorders by Czyzewski). The cases include those seen by individual therapists in a variety of settings (e.g., Chapter 14 on outpatient treatment of enuresis by Geffken and Johnson in a medical setting and Chapter 5 on sleep disorders treated in a psychological clinic by Greening and Dollinger), and others managed by an interdisciplinary team (e.g., Chapter 15 on encopresis by Parkison and Kelly and Chapter 21 on inpatient approaches by Thurber and Hewett).

Several of the chapters contain less than optimal information gathered in assessment. That is, in retrospect, many of the clinician–authors noted how they wished that they had gathered certain information earlier. This aspect is clearly reflective of the way clinical practice is. Slater and Thomas (1983) suggested that, in the field, kinds of data "vary both in extent and in quality of presentation. The frustration that one may experience in attempting to interpret incomplete data will likely be met in the field" (p. *xvi*). The perfect protocol or assessment is often impeded by a variety of factors. To indicate otherwise would be to whitewash the realities of the art of clinical practice. In some cases, additional information which could have been obtained might have changed the approach to therapy. In other cases, the information would have been difficult or impossible to obtain. In many instances, information that would have been of great utility later had it been gathered did not seem necessary at the time. Often clinicians efficiently and effectively forgo comprehensive evaluations because total information is not necessary in every situation. Only after difficulties arise or new data enlighten the clinician does the need for having such information become clear. In situations in which the information was not needed, the clinician's decision was validated. Cases in the current volume are successful in exemplifying these circumstances in clinical work. As the saying goes, "Only hindsight has 20/20 vision."

Similarly, some case reports indicate that the therapeutic approach changed during the course of treatment. This reflects the changing nature of the problems, conceptualization, and success or failure of attempted interventions. This, too, reflects real clinical practice rather than the typical journal report that presupposes or preordains the outcome.

The field of pediatric and clinical child psychology represents a diversity of theoretical opinions. June Tuma conducted a series of surveys on professional psychologists who were members of the two primary identity groups for these fields—Section I of the Division of Clinical Psychology of the American Psychological Association (known as the Clinical Child Section) and Section V of this division (known as the Society of Pediatric Psychology). Tuma and Pratt (1982) found that clinical child psychologists claimed psychodynamic and behavioral theories as major influences. About half of the respondents ascribed their actual clinical practice to one theory and the other half to the other. The survey of pediatric psychologists found more emphasis on behavioral than psychodynamic orientations (Tuma & Cohen, 1981, cited in Tuma & Pratt, 1982). Similarly, Tuma and Grabert (1983) reported that internship training programs in those areas typically provide coverage in a broad range of techniques for assessment and treatment.

We have tried to capture the diversity of fields in the types of cases we selected and in the theoretical underpinnings of the authors' clinical approaches. As clinicians ourselves, we might not have approached each case in the same manner as the chapter author. Thus, by including the chapter we do not imply endorsement of all the procedures used by all authors, just as they might not agree with all of our interventions, nor with those of their fellow authors. This is the essence of psychological practice at this point of discipline development. We did ask the authors to describe their decision making and thinking by also including alternative approaches and by explaining the reasons these were not used in the particular case. Thus, the authors provide their thinking and rationale at the time *and* in retrospect. The cases presented here *were* handled in ways consistent with a theoretical or clinical framework accepted by a number of professionals. The authors cite the appropriate literature base. The authors are clearly competent clinicians operating well within ethics and standards for providers of psychological services (American Psychological Association, 1977, 1981). This is true not only when the outcome was successful but even in the face of assessment error or treatment failure. Where one disagrees with a diagnosis or approach, that can be a critical point for discussion and information gathering to further the instructive process.

Our intention is not to demonstrate the efficacy of treatment through the modalities used by the clinician-authors. Additionally, we do not intend for the chapters to provide definitive evidence for the precise variables responsible for change (cf. Kazdin, 1981) or for all of those factors impeding therapeutic change to be enumerated. Our purpose is to elucidate the clinical process as it *is* in practice. In many of the cases reported here, the process mirrors or confirms the empirical–clinical perspective (Goldfried & Davison, 1976). Other cases reflect what some might call "flying by the seat of the pants," but they actually seem more to be a healthy eclecticism in which the clinician relied upon several basic theoretical notions and tested their utility for particular clients. This, too, is the nature of clinical practice. More often than not, practicing clinicians appear to hold implicit rather than explicit theories of psychological disorders and appropriate treatment. However, they need flexibility to shift conceptually when the need arises. A diagnosis does not lead automatically to a single treatment approach. Blind application of a set procedure or protocol may result in inappropriate treatment and failure in too many cases. After noting that behavioral interventions are frequently implemented by pediatric psychologists because they meet the requirements of the medical setting in being demonstrably effective, brief, and targeted, Roberts (1986) proposed:

> . . . pediatric psychological practice may be classified more as multitheoretical or "theoretically ambidextrous" because many practitioners and researchers function within many various theoretical orientations. The flexibility of such eclecticism allows the practitioner to respond more appropriately to individual patients with particular problems and situations. (p. 12)

Although they do not purport to provide scientific validation, the chapter authors do manifest the scientific approach to the practice of psychology in formulating hypotheses, testing them by gathering data, evaluating and checking their interventions, and using a self-correcting process upon feedback (Zaro, Barach, Nedelmann, & Dreiblatt, 1977). The term *empirical–clinical methodology* has been invoked to convey this process (e.g., Kiesler, 1981). Kendall and Norton-Ford (1982) describe this approach:

> Clinical psychologists gather data from multiple perspectives and then draw on their professional knowledge to formulate, implement, and evaluate intervention programs for each unique client. In these efforts, clinical psychologists are hypothesis testers who utilize *empirical* data from both their assessments and their acquaintance with prior research and theory, and *clinical* data from both their inferences in assessment and their past experiences with clients. They then develop and carry-out *clinical* interventions to aid each client, as well as conducting *empirical* evaluations of the effectiveness of these strategies. Although the specific data sources, inferences, interventions, and evaluations may vary from psychologist to psychologist, all clinical psychologists aspire to reach the ideal that this *empirical–clinical methodology* represents. . . . (p. 415)

To a more or less degree, the chapter authors demonstrate this approach in their clinical enterprises. The key points for the present volume are the clinical processes illustrated, not the scientific validation, although that is also a worthwhile goal.

This book is not a set of procedures to be followed, but it should serve to illustrate the way actual clinical practice goes on (as opposed to some abstraction about the way it *might* or *should* proceed). In presenting the diversity of approaches in this volume, we are attempting to demonstrate the breadth of actual practice in pediatric and clinical child psychology, rather than advocating a particular approach.

In order to obtain a more comprehensive background on the disorders covered in this volume, we urge the reader to follow up the reference citations provided by the chapter authors and to consider chapters in such relevant handbooks as the *Handbook of Clinical Child Psychology* (Walker & Roberts, 1983), the *Handbook of Pediatric Psychology* (Routh, 1988), and others (e.g., Gross & Drabman, in press; Karoly, 1988; Matson, 1988).

Finally, it should be noted that the clinician-authors have been sensitive to the special nature of clinical practice with children and families. We asked each to disguise the names and change the nonessential referral information to protect the identity of the child and family. We asked the authors to provide documentation that their report had been examined and cleared with the appropriate authorities for ethics review. For example, some cleared their case report with their institutional review board, others with department heads or clinic directors and clinic ethics committees. The authors are active clinicians who exemplify the best in psychology in that they utilize research and professional literature in their clinical work.

We intend for these chapters to provoke thinking, discussion, and information seeking by their case illustration as well as to stimulate greater involvement in psychological interventions with children. We hope that we and the authors have produced a useful volume that captures the excitement and the essential dynamics as well as the problems and pitfalls of clinical work with children and families.

REFERENCES

American Psychiatric Association. (1980). *Diagnostic and statistical manual of mental disorders* (3rd ed.). Washington, DC: Author.

American Psychiatric Association. (1987). *Diagnostic and statistical manual of mental disorders* (3rd ed. revised). Washington, DC: Author.

American Psychological Association. (1977). *Standards for providers of psychological services*. Washington, DC: Author.

American Psychological Association. (1981). *Ethical principles of psychologists*. Washington, DC: Author.

Eddy, D. M., & Clanton, C. H. (1982). The art of diagnosis: Solving the clinicopathological exercise. *New England Journal of Medicine, 306*, 1263-1268.

Engel, G. L. (1971). The deficiencies of the case presentations as a method of clinical teaching: Another approach. *New England Journal of Medicine, 284*, 20-24.

Garfield, S. L. (1957). *Introductory clinical psychology*. New York: Macmillan.

Goldfried, M. R., & Davison, G. C. (1976). *Clinical behavior therapy*. New York: Holt, Rinehart & Winston.

Gross, A. M., & Drabman, R. S. (Eds.). (in press). *Handbook of clinical behavioral pediatrics*. New York: Plenum.

Hayes, S. C. (1981). Single case experimental design and empirical clinical practice. *Journal of Consulting and Clinical Psychology, 49*, 192-211.

Kanoy, K. W., & Schroeder, C. S. (1985). Suggestions to parents about common behavior problems in a pediatric primary care office: Five years of follow-up. *Journal of Pediatric Psychology, 10*, 15-30.

Karoly, P. (Ed.). (1988). *Handbook of child health assessment: Biopsychosocial perspectives*. New York: Wiley.

Kassirer, J. P. (1983). Teaching clinical medicine by iterative hypothesis testing. *New England Journal of Medicine, 309*, 921-923.

Kassirer, J. P., & Gorry, G. A. (1978). Clinical problem solving: A behavioral analysis. *Annals of Internal Medicine, 89*, 245-255.

Kazdin, A. E. (1981). Drawing valid inferences from case studies. *Journal of Consulting and Clinical Psychology, 49*, 183-192.

Kendall, P. C., & Norton-Ford, J. D. (1982). *Clinical psychology: Scientific and professional dimensions*. New York: Wiley.

Kiesler, D. J. (1981). Empirical clinical psychology: Myth or reality? *Journal of Consulting and Clinical Psychology, 49*, 212-215.

La Greca, A. M., Stone, W. L., Drotar, D., & Maddux, J. E. (1988). Training in pediatric psychology: Survey results and recommendations. *Journal of Pediatric Psychology, 13*, 121-139.

Lazarus, A. A., & Davison, G. C. (1971). Clinical innovation in research and practice. In A. E. Bergin & S. L. Garfield (Eds.), *Handbook of psychotherapy and behavior change* (pp. 196-213). New York: Wiley.

Magrab, P. (Ed.). (1978a). *Psychological management of pediatric problems: Vol. 1. Early life conditions and chronic diseases.* Baltimore, MD: University Park Press.

Magrab, P. (Ed.). (1978b). *Psychological management of pediatric problems: Vol. 2. Sensorineural conditions and social concerns.* Baltimore, MD: University Park Press.

Matson, J. (Ed.). (1988). *Child and adolescent psychopathology: A handbook.* New York: Plenum.

McReynolds, P. (1987). Lightner Witmer: Little known founder of clinical psychology. *American Psychologist, 42,* 849–858.

Mesibov, G. B., Schroeder, C. S., & Wesson, L. (1977). Parental concerns about their children. *Journal of Pediatric Psychology, 2,* 13–17.

Ottinger, D. R., & Roberts, M. C. (1980). A university-based predoctoral program in pediatric psychology. *Professional Psychology, 11,* 707–713.

Pfeiffer, S. I. (Ed.). (1985). *Clinical child psychology.* Orlando, FL: Grune & Stratton.

Roberts, M. C. (1982). Clinical child programs: What and where are they? *Journal of Clinical Child Psychology, 11,* 13–21.

Roberts, M. C. (1986). *Pediatric psychology: Psychological interventions and strategies for pediatric problems.* New York: Pergamon.

Roberts, M. C., Erickson, M. T., & Tuma, J. M. (1985). Addressing the needs: Guidelines for training psychologists to work with children, youth, and families. *Journal of Clinical Child Psychology, 14,* 70–79.

Roberts, M. C., Fanurik, D., & Elkins, P. D. (1988a). Training the child health psychologist. In P. Karoly (Ed.), *Handbook of child health assessment: Biopsychosocial perspectives* (pp. 611–632). New York: Wiley.

Roberts, M. C., La Greca, A., & Harper, D. (1988b). *Journal of Pediatric Psychology:* Another stage of development. *Journal of Pediatric Psychology, 13,* 1–5.

Routh, D. K. (Ed.). (1988). *Handbook of pediatric psychology.* New York: Guilford.

Schroeder, C. S. (1979). Psychologists in a private pediatric practice. *Journal of Pediatric Psychology, 4,* 5–18.

Slater, B. R., & Thomas, J. M. (1983). *Psychodiagnostic evaluation of children: A casebook approach.* New York: Teachers College Press.

Tuma, J. M. (1980). Training in pediatric psychology: A concern for the 1980s. *Journal of Pediatric Psychology, 5,* 229–243.

Tuma, J. M. (1981). Crisis in training pediatric psychologists. *Professional Psychology, 12,* 516–522.

Tuma, J. M. (Ed.). (1982). *Handbook for the practice of pediatric psychology.* New York: Wiley-Interscience.

Tuma, J. M. (Ed.). (1985). *Proceedings: National Conference on training clinical child psychologists.* Baton Rouge, LA: Section on Clinical Child Psychology, American Psychological Association.

Tuma, J. M., & Grabert, J. (1983). Internship and postdoctoral training in pediatric and clinical child psychology: A survey. *Journal of Pediatric Psychology, 8,* 245–260.

Tuma, J. M., & Pratt, J. M. (1982). Clinical child psychology practice and training: A survey. *Journal of Clinical Child Psychology, 11,* 27–34.

VandenBos, G. R., Nelson, S., Stapp, J., Olmedo, E., Coates, D., & Batchelor, W. (1979). *APA input to NIMH regarding planning for mental health personnel development.* Washington, DC: American Psychological Association.

Walker, C. E. (1979). Behavioral intervention in a pediatric setting. In J. R. McNamera (Ed.), *Behavioral approaches to medicine: Applications and analysis* (pp. 227–266). New York: Plenum.

Walker, C. E., & Roberts, M. C. (Eds.). (1983). *Handbook of clinical child psychology*. New York: Wiley-Interscience.

Weinberg, H., & Hire, A. W. (1956). *Case book in abnormal psychology*. New York: Knopf.

Wright, L., Schaefer, A. B., & Solomons, G. (1979). *Encyclopedia of pediatric psychology*. Baltimore, MD: University Park Press.

Zaro, J. S., Barach, R., Nedelmann, D. J., & Dreiblatt, I. S. (1977). *A guide for beginning psychotherapists*. Cambridge, England: Cambridge University Press.

2
The Psychological Test Report: An Instrument of Therapy and Advocacy for the Child with Learning Problems

DONALD WERTLIEB

Only the family exceeds the school in terms of impact and influence on the life of a child. Many of the child's waking hours are devoted to adaptation to the school environment and the pressures of academic performance and achievement. The school also provides the context for the negotiation of a broad range of socioemotional issues of relating to one's self, one's peers, and the adults and institutions beyond one's family. Not surprisingly, then, is the substantial proportion of energy that the pediatric or clinical child psychologist must devote to understanding and influencing schooling. Epidemiological data suggest that as many as 20% of the current school-age population experience difficulties that compromise their success in school. A confused and confounded muck of diagnostic labels such as learning disability, underachievement, and learning disorder identify these children (Kistner & Torgesen, 1987). Seventy to eighty percent of children referred for mental health services have poor schoolwork reported among their behavior problems (Achenbach & Edelbrock, 1981). In terms of the day-to-day professional activity of many pediatric and clinical child psychologists, assessment and psychodiagnostic work in these areas is among their central commitments.

Historically, our parent profession, clinical psychology, is rooted in the art and science of psychological testing. Contemporary professional practice continues to rely heavily on the skills, technology, and slowly maturing

Donald Wertlieb. Eliot–Pearson Department of Child Study, Tufts University, Medford, Massachusetts.

database of the psychological testing enterprise. Despite continual controversy and debates, at least in academic circles, psychological testing continues as a usual, sometimes even predominating, professional enterprise. The reader interested in the debate can see it in its most eloquent forms in juxtaposition to contributions by Brooks (1983), Gittelman (1980), and Applebaum (1976).

This chapter addresses psychological assessment as one of the key professional activities of the pediatric or clinical child psychologist engaged in meeting the needs of children encountering difficulties in school. More specifically, the focus is on the psychological test report as a potentially crucial intervention in a child's life. An overview of some general considerations for psychological test reports is presented first. Next, a case example is offered, followed by comments articulating the particular and nontraditional considerations posed in the discussion and implications for practice.

There are numerous textbooks available to the student or professional seeking direction on the administration and interpretation of psychological tests. Some are traditional, even classic (e.g., Holt, 1968; Rapaport, Gill, & Schafer, 1968; Schafer, 1954). Some are the current standards for the field (e.g., Exner & Weiner, 1982; Palmer, 1983; Sattler, 1988). Many are rich in case examples, often including sample test reports (Goldman, Stein, & Guerry, 1983; Klopfer, 1982; Knoff, 1986; Palmer, 1983; Sattler, 1988). Fischer's (1978) and Tallent's (1988) contributions are especially valuable in providing good examples of how not to report psychological findings. Those texts using extensive case study formats are especially instructive in modeling sophisticated clinical processes (e.g., Hirsch, 1970; Schwartz & Eagle, 1986). Among the more recent contributions to the literature that are most concordant with some of the main emphases of this chapter (to be articulated subsequently) are the discussions by Brooks (1979, 1983), Dana (1986), Knoff (1986), Sanders (1979), Schectman (1979), and Simeonsson (1986). Wodrich (1984) has recently provided a "consumers' guide" to psychological testing aimed at an audience of parents and other nonpsychologists.

If compiled in accordance with our professional standards (American Psychological Association, 1985), the manual that accompanies each specific test should certainly be a major resource to the psychologist. To complement the reliability and validity data contained in any manual, there is often a body of empirical research quite heterogenous in terms of size and quality. Among the journals most directly useful to pediatric and clinical child psychologists involved in the assessment of school and learning problems are the *Journal of Clinical Child Psychology*, the *Journal of Psychoeducational Assessment*, the *Journal of Pediatric Psychology*, the *Journal of Learning Disabilities*, and the *Journal of Personality Assessment*, as well as several other school psychology journals.

In terms of the specific focus of this chapter, there are very few volumes and papers on the technical aspects of test reports. Tallent (1988) and

Klopfer (1960, 1982) present the basics, the "how to" and the "do's and don'ts" without succumbing to a mechanical cookbook orientation. They, as well as Shellenberger (1982), provide reviews of some interesting empirical work on the use of and satisfaction with reports by various consumers, especially other mental health and education professionals. Many of the textbooks mentioned above consider the mechanics of report writing, and others also offer relevant guidelines (Garrick & Stotland, 1982; Huber, 1961; Seagull, 1979). Neither the textbooks, manuals, nor how-to-write-a-report books will be comprehensively reviewed here. A number of points made by these sources will be reiterated below, but for the most part the emphasis will be upon an often ignored, sometimes implicit, and sometimes precluded or denigrated aspect of the psychological testing enterprise: the test report as an instrument of therapy and advocacy.

TOWARD THE GOOD-ENOUGH TEST REPORT

According to some authorities, "there are no ironclad rules to follow about reports, in terms of form or style" (Goldman, Stein, & Guerry, 1983, p. 11). Other authorities proposed "commandments" such as Salvia and Ysseldyke's (1981) reference to the Psychological Corporation Test Bulletin #54 (1959) dicta on parent's rights to know what their school knows and the school's obligation to communicate usable knowledge or Hudgins and Schultz's (1978) four commandments for report writing: "Thou shalt first enter the referral agent's frame of reference, thou shalt personalize the evaluation, thou shalt write about behavior, and thou shalt respond to the referral question" (pp. 57–58). These constitute good advice, if not laws to live by, and several other suggestions on form, style, and content are offered here.

The good test report will consist of "lean, disciplined prose with a minimum of objectives and a commitment to brevity" (Smith, 1976, p. 168). Although directed to pediatric psychologists' special concerns, Roberts' advice is compelling, that

> . . . Targeted, to-the-point psychological reports are more likely to be read and utilized . . . than are lengthy, esoteric reports containing great quantities of psychological jargon. Walker (1979) suggests tightly worded, action-based reports communicating what should be done about a patient's problem. Typical reports from pediatric psychologists do not ramble on and on about background information; they do not elaborate test data and personality descriptions. These reports by necessity usually indicate the problem and referral question, give a brief exposition of what was done and what was found, and place the greatest emphasis on what is recommended to be done." (1986, p. 12)

The writing style will reflect a balance of the literary, clinical, and scientific biases explicated by Tallent (1988). "The interpreter must be able to translate from the language of the test to a language that an intelligent lay person can understand" (Exner & Weiner, 1982, p. 436). Tailoring a report for the audience is particularly challenging in work with children, given the wide range of potential "users" for any report—other mental health professionals, other health care providers, schools, courts, parents, and so forth. Usually the audience is obvious and explicit; sometimes an eventual audience is less obvious, for example, a court in a custody hearing 2 years later or an insurance company deliberating on a claim.

"The consultee is seeking an expert opinion as well as one that he or she can understand and apply" (Garrick & Stotland, 1982, p. 851). To include in one's test report that the child's Rorschach F+ % was 82%, to specify fabulized combinations, or to substantiate a child's performance as "two standard deviations below the mean" is rarely to fulfill one's professional obligation as a tester. As accurate, impressive, or crucial to one's formulation such a "fact" might be, its appearance in a test report indicates that much of your task remains to be done. You have administered, scored, and interpreted the tests and perhaps begun to understand the child, but communication of that understanding in a useful way—the task of the report—remains unfinished.

To distinguish data, inference, and speculation, clarity for the tester, as well as for the audience, is crucial. Indeed, the certainty we can convey is often limited. Exner and Weiner (1982) correctly noted that virtually all statements of psychological test findings are really probability statements, and they urge minimal speculative and predictive statements. Klopfer (1982) warns that

> . . . a psychologist who acts as if his or her written report were a document engraved in stone rather than a series of probability statements will eventually lose his or her audience. Clinical psychology remains an inexact science, and appropriate humility about our degree of certainty will always be a respectable rather than a weak position. (p. 505)

TOWARD A BETTER TEST REPORT

In his foreword to one of the earlier "how-to-write-a-report" manuals, Bellak (cited in Klopfer, 1960) suggests that the development of the field could be well inferred and elucidated through examination of reports written over the years. He applauds our progress from the primitive, "rather naive, shotgun type of ill-assorted tests based upon the 'sign-approach'" to the "slow emergence of ego-psychological thinking, an awareness of the

limitations of our instruments, and a sophistication concerning the different levels of inference in the clinical interview and test material" (p. *vii*).
More recently, psychologists' abandonment of a solipsistic stance in regard
to their test reports is even more profound. We are moving above and
beyond even the early promotion of considering the intended audience for a
report. The contextual–transactional aspects of the assessment enterprise are
more widely acknowledged both in terms of the therapeutic implications
and the potential for advocacy.

Heralding this more sophisticated perspective on the psychological test
report was Appelbaum's (1970) statement on "Science and Persuasion in the
Psychological Test Report," wherein he outlined the multiple roles of the
tester as sociologist, politician, diplomat, group dynamicist, salesman, and
artist, as well as psychologist. It was against this backdrop that viewing the
test report as a "guide to practical action" (Appelbaum, 1976) emerged. Some
of this practical action has been carried out in very traditional psychotherapeutic avenues, with recognition of the therapeutic potential of a patient's or
client's involvement in the assessment process (e.g., Sattler, 1988; Sundberg,
Taplin, & Tyler, 1983) or explicit use of psychological test material in more
innovative treatment processes (e.g., Cerney, 1978; Mortimer & Smith, 1983;
Santostefano, 1980). As our sensitivity to children's rights and the ethical
aspects of diagnosis heightened, so did our appreciation of the impact of our
reports. In substantiating the child's right to be informed of test findings,
LoCicero (1976) recognized the direct therapeutic impact of "conveying a
sense of concern and hope" (p. 14), as well as an indirect therapeutic impact
obtained by modeling such interaction for the parents, whether in an informing conference or a written report. Dana's (1986) and Klopfer's (1982) reformu-
lation of assessment practice in terms of "feedback" processes is an especially
promising model for exploiting the therapeutic potential of the psychological
test report. Simeonsson (1986) noted the importance of the psychological test
in the evaluation of progress and outcome of a child's intervention program.
This function is increasingly salient in the context of demands by public
policies such as PL 94-142 and PL 99-457 for accountability and cost-effective-
ness in the provision of psychological services for children and families with
special educational needs.

In fact, it is our involvement as psychologists in the implementation of
federal policy guaranteeing educational opportunity to all children that has
stimulated our appreciation of the advocacy burden and potential now
carried by any test report we pen. Sanders (1979) foreshadows this in the
closing sentences of her important book on the clinical assessment of children's learning problems:

> The clinician plays a critical, though not solitary, role in determining what
> program is likely to be most appropriate for a child, in monitoring the
> accuracy of that determination over time, and in recommending changes as

they become necessary. While the individual clinician cannot make significant changes in the capacity of society to implement large-scale federal
programs such as PL 94-142, he or she can help see to it that the opportunities afforded by such programs are used to the best advantage by those
children and families for whom the clinician has professional responsibility. (p. 262)

In submitting a psychological test report, the psychologist can, even
must, be advocating for the child. Seagull (1979) casts the report in terms of
"helping the reader understand and take appropriate action on behalf of the
child" (p. 39). Conoley (1981) emphasizes "writing persuasively" (p. 167).
Exner and Weiner (1982) duly warn against the dangers of creating professional "sets," as with the use of certain jargon or labels. In implementing the
therapeutic and advocacy potential of test reports, the deliberate creation of
such "sets" becomes an intervention. The psychologist's responsibility as a
child advocate is increasingly recognized as a necessary albeit sometimes complicating component of his/her clinical potential and effectiveness (Fischer,
1978; Knoff, 1986; Mearig, 1978; Melton, 1983; Ysseldyke & Algozzine, 1983).

Are therapy and advocacy inconsistent enterprises, as some have suggested (e.g., Conoley, 1981)? The psychological test report represents a
vehicle for coordinated intervention comprised of both therapy and advocacy, as illustrated in the case example that follows.

CASE EXAMPLE

Mr. and Mrs. C sought a psychological assessment of their 10-year-old son
Robert after having heard from his teachers for the third year in a row: "He's
such a bright boy, we just don't think he's working up to his potential."
Heightening their concern and stimulating them to now act on the school's
repeated suggestions that "we take a closer look at the problem" was
Robert's recent complaining, even despondency, about school, including
accusations that his teacher was mean and that the other kids disliked him
because he was a "dummy." Mother and father agreed that it was a problem
ascertaining whether Robert "wouldn't" or "couldn't" do better schoolwork, although father was inclined to chalk the problem up to Robert's
"laziness." The family had been advised by the school that the school's own
staff could execute a comprehensive evaluation, but on the advice of a
friend, they opted for an independent evaluation at their own expense. The
following report was provided to Mr. and Mrs. C, representing a crucial, but
not final, stage in the evaluation and consultation. The superscript numer-
als are imposed in the presentation to key into specific comments that
follow the report (see "Commentary" below) concerning its rationale or
illustrations of statements made elsewhere in the chapter.

Assessment

Dear Mr. & Mrs. C:[1]

I am writing to review the findings and recommendations of my psychological assessment of your son Robert, as we discussed at our conference on June 15, 1987. This evaluation was undertaken in your effort to clarify concerns about Robert's academic achievement and adjustment. You were especially concerned about Robert's distress, evident in his unhappiness about school. Robert's teachers over the years have complained that his performance, in math especially, seems less and less consistent with what they perceive as his strong capabilities and potential. Robert himself expressed interest in improving his school situation, both in terms of "getting easier work" and in terms of "getting more friends." It is the intention of all involved—you, Robert, and the school professionals— that this evaluation contribute to educational planning for next year.[2]

The impressions and recommendations that follow are based on the social and developmental history you provided at our June 1, 1987 meeting; a battery of psychological tests administered to Robert in individual testing sessions on June 7, 8, and 9; a review of school records and classroom work samples; and telephone consultations with Robert's previous and current classroom teachers, Mrs. J and Mrs. M.[3]

The battery of psychological tests included the following instruments: Wechsler Intelligence Scale for Children—Revised (WISC-R), Beery-Buktenica Developmental Test of Visual–Motor Integration (VMI), Wide Range Achievement Test—Revised (WRAT-R), Spache Diagnostic Reading Scales, Rorschach Inkblot Test, Thematic Apperception Test (TAT), Conger Sentence Completion, Draw-A-Person, and Kinetic Family Drawing. Robert and I also spent a portion of our time in more open-ended interview. This battery is helpful in assessing a child's academic, intellectual, social, and emotional development, especially in terms of his particular strengths and weaknesses relevant to these developmental tasks. In addition, it suggests potential solutions to particular problems a child might be experiencing. I remain available to you, Robert, or the school to discuss the specifics of any particular test if there is interest or concern.[4]

Robert related and cooperated well in the interview and testing situation. Initial apprehension about the testing quickly evaporated as we engaged in spontaneous conversation about his interests in sports and oceanography. His pronouncements that "I'm real good at this" conveyed a generally confident stance, but one that was all too easily shaken as tasks became more challenging, or as he detected his own mistakes. When I steered conversation to more emotionally charged topics such as encounters with friends or teachers, or when test materials stimulated such issues, Robert's initial tack was to reclaim control of the interchange, using his considerable charm in a pleasant and engaging way. At one point he struggled valiantly, but unsuccessfully, to contain his tears as we discussed the school situation. At moments, under the stress of the more taxing, challenging, and less structured test demands, Robert's stance of confidence, competence, and positive involvement gave way to worry, preoccupation, and distraction, reflecting too-high levels of poorly managed anxiety and painful insecurities. He generally responded well to the structure and support I provided, suggesting a good capacity to make use of such intervention. In general, Robert was a fine collaborator in this evaluation, committed to our task of better understanding the concerns shared by you and the school and eager to participate in changing matters for the better.[5]

According to standardized intelligence testing, Robert is indeed a very bright youngster, functioning in the high average and superior ranges in many areas assessed, especially those reflecting verbal reasoning and abstraction capacities. Under optimal circumstances, his school achievement should be above grade level, even in the context of high performance typical at his particular school. On the standardized achievement tests administered as part of his assessment, Robert demonstrated reading, spelling, and mathematics skills at the sixth grade level.[6]

Several aspects of Robert's problems with math were highlighted in our work together. Although Robert's test scores indicate very high skill levels, some significant gaps in specific skills and, perhaps more important and pervasive, some variability or inefficiency in his information-processing style, contribute to the discrepancy between his potential and his actual day-to-day performance. Robert's basic computational skills are well consolidated, but when operations must be organized and sequenced in more complex problems, such as long division or reduction of fractions, problems arise.[7]

Robert's inattentiveness to detail accounted for some of his errors, for instance, when he continued to add, although the sign for the test item instructed him to subtract. Another aspect of his problem of attention and organization became evident in Robert's execution of long division problems where his failure to maintain neat rows and columns for his step-by-step calculations resulted in errors. At no point did Robert spontaneously or automatically show evidence of verbally or visually monitoring or checking his work. When instructed to do so, he was usually able to detect and correct his errors whether in reading, spelling, math, or in replicating designs with blocks. However, it was at these moments that overt embarrassment and anxiety distracted Robert and compromised the quality of our working relationship. Robert was quite able to observe this behavior and acknowledge some frustration and unhappiness.

The roots of some of this frustration and unhappiness were most poignantly revealed in Robert's pronouncement that his dad was a "champion math whiz kid." Robert wants desperately to impress and please those for whom he cares, including family members and teachers. He recognizes that success in school, especially in math, is one way to please. He seems unsure what other avenues are available or acceptable and needs help in perceiving and appreciating his own particular strengths and weaknesses.[8]

Recommendations

In summary, Robert is a youngster with considerable interpersonal and intellectual strengths whose academic and socioemotional development are compromised by an inefficient learning style and less-than-optimally re-solved psychological concerns. He is in need of psychoeducational and mental health services aimed at modifying his learning style so that his approach to academic tasks will better and more consistently yield perfor-mance reflecting his capacities and skills.[9]

Psychoeducational services should include small group and individual tutorial aimed at modifying his learning style, as described previously; strengthening and generalizing his self-monitoring orientation; and improv-ing his skills at controlling his attention and managing his anxiety. A diag-nostic–prescriptive approach with highly structured success-guaranteed steps should facilitate better skill acquisition and performance more consonant with his capacities. Teachers and tutors must remain vigilant and sensitive to the emotionally charged tension Robert brings to the learning situation. A "therapeutic tutoring" approach is likely to engage and help Robert by including a focus on his feelings about the learning situation and his style of managing the tasks and feelings, as well as the actual task. Both at home and in school, as well as in the psychotherapy to be recommended subsequently, Robert can be helped to perceive and experience his successes in terms of his own active efforts, rather than experiencing them according to his current framework of feeling at the mercy of luck, or the mood or behavior of others.

If individualizing the curriculum for Robert, creative adaptation of high-interest materials should yield progress. For instance, Robert's love of oceanography and sports may provide avenues for addressing a wide range of math and language arts objectives. I would be available to consult further with you or the school team to articulate additional implications and specifications for classroom and tutorial approaches.[10]

Psychotherapy should complement this modification of his learning style and facilitate the mastery of the issues he is currently struggling with. In particular, Robert needs help in developing a more adaptive and flexible range of coping mechanisms with which to manage his current dilemmas and future challenges. A major psychotherapeutic task facing Robert is the formu-lation of a positive and comfortable sense of himself that incorporates a realistic appraisal of his strengths and weaknesses as well as resources within himself and family. Thus, management of self-esteem and insecurities associated with his role in the family and peer group will be a major focus of psychotherapy. Whether such work is best addressed in individual therapy with concurrent parent guidance and/or family therapy remains a diagnostic question best addressed by you and the mental health clinician you retain. In either event, the likelihood of Robert resolving his school and personal concerns would be enhanced through active collaboration and consultation among parents, school, and psychotherapist. It would be advisable to insure that one member of the team, perhaps the psychotherapist, take responsibility for coordination, monitoring, and periodic evaluation of the efforts to improve Robert's situation. By 6-months time you will probably have some good information on which aspects of these recommendations are most helpful.[11]

It would be important for Robert to be informed of the findings of this evaluation in a way most conducive to the solution of the problems presented. I briefly discussed some of these impressions with Robert at the close of our last session.[12]

I hope these comments are useful to you and the school in planning for Robert. I remain available to you, Robert, and the school to clarify or elaborate these impressions and to discuss avenues and resources for meeting Robert's needs. Please do not hesitate to contact me with any questions or concerns.[13]

Sincerely,

Donald Wertlieb, Ph.D.

Commentary

1. The letter format is chosen as a more "user-friendly" vehicle than the typical, more mystifying structure beginning with identifying information, reason for referral, tests administered, behavior during exam, intellectual findings, emotional findings, and recommendations. Much of the same information is similarly sequenced in the letter format, although some compromise in explicit structure might be involved. The gains in terms of readability, coherence, and a child-centered rather than test-centered report outweigh these losses. Klopfer (1982) and Groth-Marnat (1984) reviewed several formats for organizing reports and strongly urged "person-oriented" presentations that are neither overly "test-linked" nor overly "theory-linked." (See also Note 5.) An explicit heading is employed later for *"Recommendations,"* given that this detailing of the action plan is so crucial to the effectiveness of the report, whether traditionally conceived or, as viewed here, an instrument of therapy and advocacy.

2. The report is a summary and review of massive, complex, and potentially difficult-to-understand, hear, or convey information. Especially when the therapy/advocacy approach proposed here is adopted, comprehensiveness is rarely the top priority. Comprehensiveness is especially to be eschewed when it becomes a limiting influence on comprehensibility. Brev-

ity and focus are virtues. At three to four pages a report is almost always long enough.

Robert's parents are seeing this information in print after hearing much of it at a face-to-face conference. This sequencing, also endorsed by Sanders (1979) and consistent with the practices proposed by Dana (1986), enhances the therapeutic potential of the assessment consultation and allows the clinician an opportunity to include consideration of the parents' response to his/her impressions in preparing the written document—identifying areas in need of clarification, emphasis, or deemphasis. Given the present view that in order to be the best advocacy instrument possible, whether as "contribution" or "ammunition" at subsequent stages of the change process involving the school, the test report is now more likely to be a joint statement issued by the psychologist and the parents as well as an invitation to others wishing to join the partnership on behalf of Robert. Robert's own views as well as the shared goal of the evaluation are succinctly and explicitly stated in the first paragraph.

3. This paragraph details the sources and extent of the database employed by the clinician to arrive at his impressions and recommendations with a commitment to comprehensiveness and a systemic–ecological orientation. Alternative and traditional approaches allowed a child's learning problems to be diagnosed in a vacuum, without consideration of day-to-day schoolwork and behavior as only teacher reports and work samples can reveal. Although not employed in Robert's case, an actual classroom observation period is often well worth the added expense of time and money.

The "blind analysis" approach to test interpretation has been abandoned. There is limited fear that reading reports and talking to teachers will compromise some elusive objectivity and somehow bias or invalidate the assessment. "When people's lives and futures are at stake, where important decisions concerning their welfare are to be made, every possible source of information should be exploited" (Klopfer, 1960, p. 62). The parents sought a psychologist not solely because they wanted a technician to administer tests; they needed and wanted a clinician to participate with them in a problem-solving process. The tests are useful and powerful tools; the clinical processing of the data they contribute to the larger pool is but one of the psychologist's resources for this role.

4. The parents, and certainly the other educational and mental health professionals who will use this report, do need to know some of the specifics of the test battery. To a certain extent this is a fairly standard basic battery relevant to presenting problems such as Robert's. The psychologist must have available a range of more specialized instruments that might be called for either at the time of understanding the presenting problem or as a formulation unfolds suggesting additional specific tests. Some of the more specialized procedures may be within the competence and repertoire of the particular psychologist; others may involve immediate or subsequent refer-

ral to colleagues in neuropsychology, neurology, speech and language pathology, psychopharmacology, and so forth.

The string of test names and acronyms that comprises this section risks confusing or alienating the reader. Robert's parents are offered a bottom-line summary reminder of the rationale for the battery and reassurance of the continued availability of the clinician for clarification or elaboration of test-centered questions.

5. Traditionally, behavior during the exam has been used both as data for hypothesis building and hypothesis testing much like other test data and for assessing the quality of motivation or involvement presumed to affect the validity of test performance. Already in this first highly selective presentation of general and specific aspects of Robert's behavior, illustration and reiteration of the formulation shared at the parent conference and allusions to implications for intervention are evident. Beginning here, and continuing throughout the remainder of the report, "to the clinician, the data (and the report) will reflect the nature of the child" (Schwartz & Eagle, 1986, p. 15, parentheses added).

Also evident in this paragraph is a beginning process of reframing the problem and relabeling Robert in more positive and adaptive terms. Alternatives are suggested for earlier views of Robert's "laziness" or hostile willfulness. An old problem in clinical psychology is the tendency toward "pathologizing" (labeling behavior with a bias toward the abnormal and maladaptive). Emphasis on adaptive intents or accomplishments of even "bad" or "sick" behavior may have therapeutic impact in an assessment.

6. This paragraph along with subsequent paragraphs presents a relatively focused and concise formulation describing and explaining Robert's problem as manifested in the test data. Although based on test data, the discourse is more about Robert than about the tests or his scores. Further, the familiar, traditional, and topical headings such as cognitive/intellectual functioning, emotional functioning, and so on, are eschewed. These narrow compartmentalizations are overcome in the effective therapy/advocacy test report for two related reasons. First, consideration of the test data on a test-by-test, even item-by-item, basis is a necessary stage in the assessment process; however, the psychologist's skills and his/her contribution to the well-being of the child is in the synthesizing and integrating of these technical bits into an understanding and an action plan. Second, especially with learning problems such as Robert's, a test-by-test scorecard or a statement on his intellectual strengths and weaknesses followed by a statement on his somehow separable emotional assets and liabilities is unlikely to capture the complexity of the child or his needs. (Brooks, 1979).

For similar reasons it is usually unnecessary, even inadvisable, to include specific test scores in a report because of the technicality and sensitivity of interpretation. At times a parent or school makes explicit requests for scores, and they can be provided along with an explanation of their meaning, implications, and limitations. Scores as well as "official" diagnostic labels may be important to include, especially when such a designation is warranted and/or a prerequisite for the provision of needed services. For instance, a statement that "Robert's problems can be understood as a learning disability" might be considered and documented in terms of local educational definitions such as a 20-point discrepancy between WISC-R Performance and Verbal IQ or a 12-month lag in achievement, and so forth. Insurance reimbursement usually requires use of a diagnostic label. Even in conveying interpretations of scores such as "high-average" intelligence or "grade-level" achievement, Robert's parents are reminded of the generally higher level or higher capacity children who populate Robert's school.

7. The psychologist will recognize that Robert's assessment involved more than a standard "by-the-book" administration of tests. Rather, Robert had the benefit of an active diagnostic interchange such as that advocated by Brooks (1979), which included an emphasis on processes and strategies rather than simply on specific skill areas, and used limit-testing and diagnostic teaching aimed at generating bases for recommended interventions. Robert's own level and degree of awareness of his learning style were among the specific elements of concern.

8. Inferences conveyed in this paragraph therapeutically reframe some of Robert's behavior in terms that may enhance parents' and teachers' ability to sympathize, empathize, and help. Frustrations that they had begun to experience as Robert acted against them are now open for reconsideration as are his efforts to respond and comply. Some direction for facilitating a better match in viewpoints is simultaneously provided, acknowledging that important work lies ahead. There were several other interesting and important motivational issues or conflicts for Robert that might have been presented; this single "core" issue was highlighted as most likely to enhance the report's value as a therapy/advocacy instrument.

9. The summary and recommendations are the most often read section of a report, sometimes the only read section. Their clarity, comprehensiveness, and coherence are thus of special importance.

In cases where one can anticipate the consultation as a step in the process of Individualized Educational Planning (IEP) prescribed by PL 94-142, it is useful to approximate the content and format of the recommendations to that of the IEP documentation employed by the particular school system, thus facilitating more timely and accurate integration of the psychological component into the plan. Specificity and clarity in terms of goals and objectives are crucial. As with the report as a whole, the recommendations should be directly responsive to the referral questions, in both their manifest and latent content (Cohen, 1980).

10. These two paragraphs suggest particular strategies, structures, and technologies for addressing Robert's special needs. In order to most effectively advocate for Robert, balancing notions of optimal and realistic or

practical expectations and demands must precede the written report. Besides a school's orientation toward providing services, the psychologist needs to consider Robert's and his parents' attitudes and concerns about services, especially in terms of complex issues of entitlement and stigmatization.

Psychologists working with children such as Robert need to be competent and current in special educational theory and practice and in the realities of life in the school and classroom. At times it can be helpful to direct parents or teachers to very specific readings or curricula. It is rarely helpful to recommend material that is overly dense, technical, obtuse, or far removed from practical application. Part of being competent, as well as ethical, is to know the limits of one's expertise, and this is especially so in making psychoeducational recommendations, appreciating and using the competence and expertise of allied professionals, and respecting boundaries and "turf." Among recent discussions likely to be useful to psychologists in this regard see Brooks (1979), Mann and Sabatino (1985), Kistner and Torgeson (1987), and Salvia and Ysseldyke (1981).

11. Recommendations for psychotherapy that are overly vague, perfunctory, obligatory, or telegraphic should be avoided. If the child is a good candidate for psychotherapy, then the specification of type and goals increases the likelihood of his/her getting and benefiting from appropriate intervention. The psychologist and his/her test data are in a very advantageous position for making such specifications given that in many instances a test battery can yield a virtual roadmap for initial phases of productive psychotherapy. Failure to specify the types or nature of therapy (and sometimes therapists most likely to meet the child's needs) can leave parents and some less-sophisticated school professionals at the mercy of their own, often misinformed, stereotypes of psychotherapy. One of the more typical and pernicious of these "mass-media," "kernel-of-truth" stereotypes is the view of psychotherapy as "getting your feelings out." Many, perhaps most, children such as Robert or children with other forms of pathology associated with learning disorders, are better served with an orientation toward psychotherapy as a process aiming at better management of feelings; "getting feelings out" is but one possible step or dimension in such a process.

Recommendations are not the final word. When remaining diagnostic questions can be more clearly stated as a result of a psychological assessment, then progress has been made in both the therapy and advocacy mission. Sometimes, clarification of the need for further consultation is accomplished. For instance, referral for a speech and language evaluation to clarify the extent to which a problem is developmental and/or responsive to speech therapy might be recommended. Sometimes a recommendation aims at initiating the information seeking and weighing of pros and cons for certain psychopharmacological interventions or special school placements. In Robert's case, a commitment to individual versus family therapy seems premature prior to a more formalized family therapy assessment.

The additional feature of these recommendations lies in the explicit demand for coordination of care and program evaluation. In Robert's case, given my prior experience with breakdowns in these processes with this particular school system, the recommendation is posed in terms of the mental health professional assuming the liaison-coordination responsibility. Sometimes a parent is especially adept at such work. It is especially helpful if a school-based professional can carry this crucial burden.

12. Too often, a child is subjected to extensive and intensive psychological scrutiny and provided with virtually no feedback, direct or indirect. Such practice is highly inconsistent with the therapy/advocacy orientation advanced here. Sanders (1979) urged feedback "even if only a few sentences at the end of the last testing session" (p. 255) that can provide reassurance, support, a rationale for help, and facilitate the child's active involvement in helping himself/herself. As noted previously, LoCicero (1976) emphasizes "conveying a sense of concern and hope" (p. 14) and recognizes the therapeutic aspects of the report to the child as a model for parents. Furthermore, as indicated previously, in providing the rationale for a parent conference preceding the written report, additional data bearing on both formulation and recommendations are presented in the feedback process.

13. A concluding comment such as this reiterates the alliance among Robert, parents, school, and me, as psychologist. It is important to emphasize "next steps" of action on Robert's behalf and the continuing availability of the psychologist's understanding and skill.

Effectiveness and Follow-Up

In urging clinical and pediatric psychologists to emphasize their test reports as instruments of therapy and advocacy, data from systematic empirical evaluation research would, of course, be most compelling. Such data are yet to be generated, but the need and demand for demonstrations of the effectiveness of our health service efforts loom ever larger. At present, single-case studies and clinical impressions provide guideposts for shaping clinical practice, and in Robert's case some initial support for the approach might be gleaned. As an instrument of advocacy and therapy, the test report had several goals for Robert, as articulated in the recommendations and the commentary. Steps toward each of these goals were evident in a reexamination of Robert's situation 6 to 8 months after the assessment in the report.

Robert's parents presented the report to the school's Child Study Team, which was soon to convene to consider his special educational needs. Although some defensiveness was anticipated, little emerged. In fact, the school urged the parents to have me attend the team meeting where decisions would be made about programming for the next school year. The parents' financial responsibility for my consultation was duly emphasized. Several factors may have accounted for the receptivity of the school to the report and consultation. For one, there was a very limited focus in the exchange upon past mistakes, failures, or faults on the part of Robert, the parents, or the school. Rather, emphasis was on problem solving to enhance the likelihood of next year's success. Two, there was sufficient shared view of the situation as held by most of the school staff and as portrayed in the test report such that a common ground was immediately available. Three, it seemed as if the connection and initial alliance established in my brief telephone consultations with Robert's teachers contributed to the report's effectiveness and the constructive mode and mood of the team meeting.

Both in the team meeting and in the Individualized Educational Plan (IEP) document generated by the team, reliance upon the organization and content of the test report was evident. Phrases and paragraphs were virtually lifted from the report to the IEP, and even in some instances, effectively integrated with perspectives articulated by members of the school staff. Among the specific plans adopted were inclusion of a daily "resource-room" period for Robert to be used for remedial work in math along with study skills interventions that might address some of the information-processing and learning-style issues noted in the report. The plan also called for the guidance counselor to consider involving Robert in a weekly social-skills group he might run and for a monthly review of Robert's school progress with the guidance counselor coordinating the involvement of teachers, parents, Robert, and the outside psychotherapist. At follow-up, four of the six scheduled meetings had taken place, with a generally constructive process. The social-skills group had yet to begin. Neither at the initial child study team meeting nor at subsequent progress meetings was there much follow-up to the offer made in the report for discussion of specific curricular modifications. Both regular and special educators seemed to feel satisfied or adequately equipped with the methods and tools they were already using. Robert's improving status, including acceptable academic progress, responsiveness to the tutor and tutoring, and a lightening in his mood at home and at school, suggested change in a positive direction. One additional index of effectiveness to consider is the referral of two additional families to me by the school at midyear, one for an initial assessment and the other for an assessment of how and why the current plan being implemented for the child was failing.

One should stay alert to possible "co-opting" dynamics either in terms of an outside report being too-readily adopted or in terms of shifting alliances among school, parents, and psychologist. This is particularly a concern if there is not a positive change in the child's status. In the context of positive change in the child's status, the concern is minimized, although of continuing interest in terms of generalizing, understanding the effectiveness of the intervention, and clarifying intended effects and side-effects.

Effectiveness of the test-report approach suggested here was also evident in the family's decision to pursue psychotherapy, as recommended. Further evaluation quickly identified family therapy as the preferred mode. The initial weeks were devoted to fairly focused discussion of sections of the test report and probably aided the parents in their participation in the Child Study Team meetings mentioned previously. As family therapy progressed, the dominant theme was the father–child relationship. Robert and his father have begun a constructive struggle. Their efforts aim to sort out the mixture of Father's memories of his own student days of uncertainty about whether he could or would meet academic expectations, the harsh parental and school reaction to these anxieties, and the discrimination of that historical experience and role from the current experience and role with Robert. On a regular basis, a segment of each family therapy session is devoted to updating one another on any parent–school–psychologist exchange. It is anticipated that an addditional 3 to 4 months of weekly family therapy will be conducted. Reassessment of the mental health intervention will be coordinated with end-of-year school evaluation and planning.

FURTHER CONSIDERATIONS

The preceding case example of a test report may contrast sharply with the psychologist's training of clinical psychologists. The report template and rationale are offered as options for the professional to consider in his/her practice, complementing or supplementing traditional techniques and conceptual frameworks for assessment and intervention. The divergence is rooted in a broader, more differentiated view of the psychologist's role in providing services to children. In exaggerated form, the traditional or classic role emphasizes the psychologist as an independent consultant, born expert, and/or member of a multidisciplinary mental health team often headed by a psychiatrist. In this narrow, classic role, there is often a press for the more traditionally structured, test-centered and driven, lab report-oriented and psychopathology-oriented documentation of a psychological assessment. A medical model is operative and "diagnosis" is emphasized. The opportunities for feedback, therapy, or advocacy illustrated in this chapter are generally minimal—unrecognized, unexploited, even negatively sanctioned.

As a psychologist's interests and practice venture beyond these traditional roles and as appreciation of the impact on child and family of institutions such as schools, courts, and human and social service agencies increases, the psychologist must elaborate and reconfigure his/her understandings and tools. One such set of elaborations is inherent in the suggestions of this chapter that the test report be viewed and constructed as an instrument of therapy and advocacy. A parent comes to you or is sent by the school for a diagnosis of his/her child's learning problems. You perform an assessment, provide some of the diagnosis, but act as therapist and advocate. Alarm bells and red flags materialize.

When one approaches or crosses a boundary of traditional practice in terms of function or role, bells and red flags ought to go up to insure appropriate, explicit reflection upon ethical and legal considerations. The practice of psychological assessment even in its traditional form is fraught, even mired, with pressing and difficult ethical and legal conflicts and parameters. The discussions by Bersoff (1984), DeMers (1986), Koocher (1976), Dana (1986), Hays (1984), and Drake and Bardon (1978) are especially helpful in mapping these issues. By taking on therapy and advocacy as part of one's assessment practice, many of these issues are even further complicated. Some can be quickly framed, even resolved. For instance, do parental consent and child assent for assessment constitute consent/assent for therapy or a contract for advocacy services? Not necessarily. The psychologist practicing in the framework posed in this chapter includes a presentation to the family of how even the assessment they are requesting can be helpful or therapeutic and how facilitation of action responsive to their request and on behalf of the child is part of the psychologist's professional interest and responsibility. As another example of an ethical issue, recall that as a clinical child psychologist you have certainly participated in training and achieved competence in interpretation of test protocols, but may never have had a course or supervised experience in how to influence a school system to provide appropriate services. This training gap should be addressed through appropriate supervision and/or continuing education.

Other ethical and legal issues may be more subtle and elusive. For instance, consider the extent to which the suggestion of therapeutic potential inherent in an assessment might be in and of itself an unsolicited strategic intervention. The student or professional is particularly obligated to struggle with the morass of ethical and legal dilemmas should he or she find some merit in the approach to test reports offered in this chapter. The field and the children and families we serve are likely to benefit.

Acknowledgment. The author gratefully acknowledges Tillie Nelder and Rose Chioccarriello for preparation of the manuscript.

REFERENCES

Achenbach, T., & Edelbrock, C. (1981). Behavioral problems and competencies reported by parents of normal and disturbed children aged 4 through 16. *Monographs of the Society for Research in Child Development, 46* (1, Serial No. 188).

American Psychological Association. (1985). *Standards for educational and psychological tests.* Washington, DC: Author.

Appelbaum, S. (1970). Science and persuasion in the psychological test report. *Journal of Consulting and Clinical Psychology, 35,* 349–355.

Applebaum, S. (1976). Objections to diagnosis and diagnostic psychological testing diagnosed. In P. Pruyser (Ed.), *Diagnosis and the difference it makes* (pp. 161-166). New York: Jason Aronson.

Bersoff, D. (1984). Psychological assessment in the schools. In N. Repucci, L. Weithorn, E. Mulvey, & J. Monahan (Eds.), *Children, mental health and the law* (pp. 259-287). Beverly Hills, CA: Sage.

Brooks, R. (1979). Psychoeducational assessment: A broader perspective. *Professional Psychology, 10,* 708-722.

Brooks, R. (1983). Projective techniques in personality assessment. In M. Levine, W. Carey, A. Crocker, & R. Gross (Eds.), *Developmental-behavioral pediatrics* (pp. 974-989), Philadelphia: Saunders.

Cerney, M. S. (1978). Use of psychological test report in the course of psychotherapy. *Journal of Personality Assessment, 42,* 457-463.

Cohen, L. (1980). The unstated problem in a psychological test referral. *American Journal of Psychiatry, 137,* 1173-1176.

Conoley, J. C. (1981). Advocacy consultation: Promises and problems. In J. Conoley (Ed.), *Consultation in schools* (pp. 157-178). New York: Academic.

Dana, R. H. (1986). Clinical assessment. In G. S. Tryon (Ed.), *The professional practice of psychology* (pp. 69-87). Norwood, NJ: Ablex.

DeMers, S. T. (1986). Legal and ethical issues in child and adolescent personality assessment. In H. M. Knoff (Ed.), *The assessment of child and adolescent personality* (pp. 35-55). New York: Guilford.

Drake, E. A., & Bardon, J. I. (1978). Confidentiality and interagency communication: Effect of the Buckley Amendment. *Hospital and Community Psychiatry, 29,* 312-315.

Exner, J., & Weiner, I. (1982). *The Rorschach: A comprehensive system. Vol 3. Assessment of children and adolescents.* New York: Wiley.

Fischer, C. (1978). Dilemmas in standardized testing. In J. Mearig (Ed.), *Working for children: Ethical issues beyond professional guidelines* (pp. 115-134). San Francisco: Jossey-Bass.

Garrick, J., & Stotland, N. (1982). How to write a psychiatric consultation. *American Journal of Psychiatry, 139,* 849-855.

Gittelman, R, (1980). The role of psychological tests for differential diagnosis in child psychiatry. *Journal of the American Academy of Child Psychiatry, 19,* 413-438.

Goldman, J., Stein, C., & Guerry, S. (1983). *Psychological methods of child assessment.* New York: Brunner/Mazel.

Gorth-Marnat, G. (1984). *Handbook of psychological assessment.* New York: Van Nostrand Reinhold.

Hay, J. (1984). Legal aspects of psychological testing. In S. J. Weaver (Ed.), *Testing children: A reference guide for effective clinical and psychological assessments* (pp. 197-208). Kansas City: Test Corporation of America.

Hirsch, E. (1970). *The troubled adolescent as he emerges on psychological tests.* New York: International Universities Press.

Holt, R. (Ed.). (1968). *Diagnostic psychological testing—Revised edition.* New York: International Universities Press.

Huber, J. (1961). *Report writing in psychology and psychiatry.* New York: Harper.

Hudgins, A. L., & Schultz, J. L. (1978). On observing: The use of the Carkhuff model in writing psychological reports. *Journal of School Psychology, 16,* 56-63.

Kistner, J., & Torgesen, J. (1987). Motivational and cognitive aspects of learning disabilities. In B. Lahey & A. Kazdin (Eds.), *Advances in clinical child psychology* (Vol. 10, pp. 289-334). San Francisco: Jossey-Bass.

Klopfer, W. G. (1960). *The psychological report: Use and communication of psychological findings.* New York: Grune & Stratton.

Klopfer, W. G. (1982). Writing psychological reports. In C. E. Walker (Ed.), *Handbook of clinical psychology: Theory, research and practice.* Homewood, IL: Dow-Jones-Irwin.

Knoff, H. (Ed.) (1986). *The assessment of child and adolescent personality.* New York: Guilford.

Koocher, G. (Ed.). (1976). *Children's rights and the mental health profession.* New York: Wiley.

LoCicero, A. (1976). The right to know: Telling children the results of clinical evaluations. In G. Koocher (Ed.), *Children's rights and the mental health professions* (pp. 13–21). New York: Wiley.

Mann, L., & Sabatino, D. (1985). *Foundations of cognitive process in remedial and special education.* Rockville, MD: Aspen.

Mearig, J. (1978). *Working for children.* San Francisco: Jossey-Bass.

Melton, G. (1983). *Child advocacy.* New York: Plenum.

Mortimer, R., & Smith, W. (1983). The use of the psychological test report in setting the focus of psychotherapy. *Journal of Personality Assessment, 47,* 134–138.

Palmer, J. (1983). *The psychological assessment of children.* New York: Wiley.

Psychological Corporation. (1959). *Test Service Bulletin #54: On telling parents about test results.* New York: Author.

Rapaport, D., Gill, M., & Schafer, R. (1968). *Diagnostic psychological testing.* New York: International Universities Press.

Roberts, M. C. (1986). *Pediatric psychology.* New York: Pergamon.

Salvia, J., & Ysseldyke, J. (1981). *Assessment in special and remedial education* (2nd ed.). Boston: Houghton Mifflin.

Sanders, M. (1979). *Clinical assessment of learning problems: Model, process and remedial planning.* Boston: Allyn & Bacon.

Santostefano, S. (1980). Cognition in personality and the treatment process. *Psychoanalytic Study of the Child, 35,* 41–66.

Sattler, J. (1988). *Assessment of children* (3rd ed.). San Diego, CA: Sattler.

Schafer, R. (1954). *Psychoanalytic interpretation in Rorschach testing: Theory and application.* New York: Grune & Stratton.

Schectman, F. (1979). Problems in communicating psychological understanding: Why won't they listen to me? *American Psychologist, 34,* 781–790.

Schwartz, L., & Eagle, C. (1986). *Psychological portraits of children: An integrated developmental approach to psychological text data.* Lexington, MA: D. C. Heath.

Seagull, E. (1979). Writing the report of the psychological assessment of a child. *Journal of Clinical Child Psychology, 8,* 39–42.

Shellenberger, S. (1982). Presentation and interpretation of psychological data in educational settings. In C. Reynolds & T. Gutkin (Eds.), *The handbook of school psychology* (pp. 51–81). New York: Wiley.

Simeonsson, R. (1986). *Psychological and developmental assessment of special children.* Boston: Allyn & Bacon.

Smith, S. (1976). Psychological testing and the mind of the tester. In P. Pruyser (Ed.), *Diagnosis and the difference it makes* (pp. 167–174). New York: Jason Aronson.

Sundberg, N., Taplin, J., & Tyler, L. (1983). *Introduction to clinical psychology.* Englewood Cliffs, NJ: Prentice-Hall.

Tallent, N. (1988). *Psychological report writing* (3rd ed.). Englewood Cliffs, NJ: Prentice-Hall.

Walker, C. E. (1979). Behavioral intervention in a pediatric setting. In J. R. McNamara (Ed.), *Behavioral approaches to medicine: Applications and analysis* (pp. 227–266). New York: Plenum.

Wodrich, D. (1984). *Children's psychological testing: A guide for nonpsychologists.* Baltimore, MD: Brooke.

'Ysseldyke, J., & Algozzine, B. (1983). On making psychoeducational decisions. *Journal of Psychoeducational Assessment, 1,* 187–195.

3

Empirically Based Assessment of School Learning and Behavior Problems

STEPHANIE H. McCONAUGHY
THOMAS M. ACHENBACH

School learning and behavior problems are reported for many children referred to psychologists and mental health services. Teachers report, for example, that 76% of referred 10- to 11-year-old boys have difficulty learning and that 81% are doing poor schoolwork (Achenbach & Edelbrock, 1986). Although the initial referral complaints often sound simple, such as "can't follow directions" or "doesn't pay attention," school learning problems can be complex to assess. First, many factors can lead to learning problems, including developmental lags, lack of appropriate cultural experiences, specific learning disabilities, general cognitive deficits, social immaturity, and emotional problems arising from stressful experiences in the home or school. Because multiple risk factors are often present, it may be difficult to isolate a single cause for poor learning. Second, as children develop, their problems assume different forms and outcomes that vary with the age of onset and the type of intervention used. Third, children's behavioral competencies and problems often vary from one situation and interaction partner to another, sometimes producing conflicting reports from different people (Achenbach, McConaughy, & Howell, 1987). Finally, children seldom decide that they need professional help. Instead, help is sought for them by adults, especially parents and teachers. As a result, adults rather than the children are the main sources of information about the problems.

Administrative concepts of children's problems often involve categorization according to diagnostic criteria or service distinctions that fail to capture the multifaceted nature of the problems. The tendency to think of

Stephanie H. McConaughy and Thomas M. Achenbach. Department of Psychiatry, University of Vermont, Burlington, Vermont.

children in terms of mutually exclusive categories has been reinforced by administrative criteria for special education required by Public Law 94-142 (Education of the Handicapped Act, 1977, 1981) and by the American Psychiatric Association's third edition and revised third edition, *Diagnostic and Statistical Manual of Mental Disorders* (DSM-III and DSM-III-R; American Psychiatric Association, 1980, 1987).

To receive special education services, a child must meet legally defined criteria for an eligibility category such as mental retardation, specific learning disability, serious emotional disturbance, or another specific handicapping condition. When a child exhibits characteristics of more than one category, administrative rules still require determining which problems are primary and which are secondary. Certain categories are also considered mutually exclusive, such as mental retardation and learning disabilities.

Like Public Law 94-142, the DSM requires categorical distinctions between disorders based on present versus absent judgments of criterial features. The DSM, however, recognizes the need for considering multiple aspects of functioning by providing axes for personality and developmental disorders, physical conditions, psychosocial stressors, and global assessment of functioning.

MULTIAXIAL EMPIRICALLY BASED ASSESSMENT

To take account of the multifaceted nature of children's problems, we have proposed a model called multiaxial empirically based assessment (Achenbach, 1985; Achenbach & McConaughy, 1987; McConaughy & Achenbach, 1988). This model emphasizes that assessment should utilize standardized procedures to identify strengths and weaknesses in multiple areas based on data from multiple sources. Because children's functioning often varies from one situation and interaction partner to another and there can be multiple causes for problems, the goal is to use what each procedure reveals about needs for help in different contexts. In some cases, multiaxial assessment may reveal that certain interaction partners, such as a parent or teacher, need changing more than the child does. In other cases, multiaxial assessment may show that one type of intervention is needed for one context but a different type is needed for another context.

Table 3-1 outlines our model in terms of five assessment axes applicable from preschool through high school: *I. Parent Reports, II. Teacher Reports, III. Cognitive Assessment, IV. Physical Assessment,* and *V. Direct Assessment of Child.* Examples of assessment procedures are listed that have promising reliability, validity, and/or normative data. Procedures are also included for obtaining relevant history and other important information not addressed through standardized assessment. Axes III and IV present

TABLE 3-1. Examples of Multiaxial Assessment

Age range	Axis I Parent reports	Axis II Teacher reports	Axis III Cognitive assessment	Axis IV Physical assessment	Axis V Direct assessment of child
2–5	Child Behavior Checklist (CBCL) Developmental history Parent interview	School records Teacher interview	Intelligence tests (e.g., McCarthy [1972] Scales of Children's Ability) Perceptual–motor tests Speech and language tests	Height, weight Medical exam Neurological exam	Observations during play interview Direct Observation Form (DOF)
6–11	CBCL Developmental history Parent interview	Teacher's Report Form (TRF) School records Teacher interview	Intelligence tests (e.g., WISC-R [Wechsler, 1974]) Achievement tests Perceptual–motor tests Speech and language tests	Height, weight Medical exam Neurological exam	DOF Clinical interview
12–18	CBCL Developmental history Parent interview	TRF School records Teacher interview	Intelligence tests (e.g., WISC-R, WAIS-R [Wechsler, 1981]) Achievement tests Speech and language tests	Height, weight Medical exam Neurological exam	Youth Self-Report (YSR) Clinical interview Self-concept measures Personality tests

Note. From *Empirically-Based Assessment of Child and Adolescent Psychopathology: Practical Applications* (p. 27) by T. M. Achenbach and S. H. McConaughy, 1987, Newbury Park, CA: Sage. Copyright by T. M. Achenbach. Reprinted by permission.

examples of procedures for assessing children's cognitive functioning, physical development, and medical needs. The particular tests listed on Axis III represent only a small sample of the standardized instruments that have been developed to assess children's cognitive functioning and school achievement.

Axes I, II, and V include measures we have developed for assessing children's competencies and behavioral/emotional problems: the Child Behavior Checklist (CBCL), Teacher's Report Form (TRF), Direct Observation Form (DOF), and Youth Self-Report (YSR). These procedures represent a family of standardized, empirically based instruments for obtaining data from multiple informants, including parents, teachers, observers, and the children themselves. Details of the development, reliability, validity, and applications of the instruments are presented in manuals by Achenbach and Edelbrock (1983, 1986, 1987). Hand-scored and computer-scored profiles are available for all the instruments. We will describe each instrument as we present our case study of a boy with school learning problems. Before proceeding to our case study, however, we will outline some general features of empirically based assessment as described by McConaughy and Achenbach (1988).

Empirically Derived Syndromes

The first general feature concerns the empirical derivation of syndrome scales. All four instruments are scored on profiles of behavioral/emotional problems that were derived from factor analyses of informants' ratings on clinically referred children. That is, rather than deciding a priori which items would make up various scales, we used empirical procedures to identify the problems that actually occur together to form syndromes. This avoids restricting scales to diagnostic categories that may in fact lack empirical support.

Systematic Organization

A second feature is the aggregation of problems into two levels of scales: (1) *narrow-band* scales derived from factor analyses of individual items; and (2) *broad-band* scales derived from second-order factor analyses of the narrow-band scales to produce groupings designated as Internalizing and Externalizing problems. The organization into narrow-band and broad-band scales facilitates evaluation of children's problems at relatively differentiated and more global levels. This approach enables the evaluator to organize information in a systematic and useful way. It is then possible to focus on syndromes of problems found to co-occur rather than dealing with separate problems one by one.

Multiple Informants

A third feature is the use of multiple informants to obtain ratings on children's behavior. As pointed out previously, there are separate instruments for four different types of informants: parents, teachers, direct observers, and children themselves. Separate factor analyses were performed on each instrument for these different informants. The narrow-band scales, therefore, vary across instruments, reflecting variations in the types of data obtained from different informants.

Some of the scales are similar across informants, reflecting consistency in syndromes across different situations. An Aggressive syndrome, for example, was found for both boys and girls in all age ranges across the four instruments. A Depressed syndrome was found in ratings on all four instruments, but not for all sex/age groups. A Delinquent syndrome was found in CBCL, TRF, and YSR ratings, but not in DOF ratings. Other syndromes varied more across the four instruments, reflecting greater situational and informant differences.

Comprehensive Assessment

A fourth feature is the comprehensiveness of assessment. The diverse items on the four instruments enable the evaluator to obtain information on a broad range of potential problems rather than focusing only on the referral complaints or problems that seem most salient at the time. This comprehensive approach also makes it possible to examine potential differences in judgments across different informants.

Normative Data

A fifth feature is the provision of normative data for the profile scales. Separate norms have been constructed for each instrument for different sex/age groups. Standard scores (normalized T scores) and percentiles show how a child compares with normative samples of the same sex and age on each scale of the relevant profile of the CBCL, TRF, and YSR. The DOF also provides T scores and percentile cutoffs for the total problem score. However, only raw scores and percentile cutoffs are computed for DOF Internalizing, Externalizing, and narrow-band scales, because variance in these scores is limited.

The normative data enable the evaluator to judge the degree of deviance in reported behavior in relation to what is reported for randomly selected nonreferred children. It is then possible to identify areas in which the reports indicate functioning in the normal versus clinical range. The profiles of scales highlight strengths and weaknesses in behavior, just as high and low subtest scores on intelligence tests highlight patterns of cognitive functioning. A broken line on each scoring profile indicates cutoff points between the normal and clinical range.

Efficient and Economical

A final feature is the efficiency and low cost of this approach. The CBCL and TRF take parents and teachers approximately 15 minutes to complete. The YSR can be completed in about the same time by adolescents with fifth grade reading skills. Clerical workers can hand-score profiles in about 10 to 15 minutes or score them on microcomputers in 3 to 5 minutes. They are thus much less costly than psychological testing or clinical interviewing. By having the checklists completed prior to an appointment, an evaluator can use face-to-face contacts more efficiently to follow up on the main problems revealed by the profiles. The empirically based measures are not intended to replace other forms of assessment, but to make assessment more focused and cost-effective.

Our case study illustrates the application of multiaxial empirically based assessment to Richard, a boy with school learning and behavior problems who was evaluated at age 10 and then again at age 15. The case demonstrates how the multiaxial model easily lends itself to a multidisciplinary team approach to assessment. Richard's evaluation was a cooperative effort between the psychologist and school staff. The psychologist served on a multidisciplinary school team that included special educators, guidance counselors, the school nurse, and the principal. Child psychiatrists from an outpatient clinic also consulted with the team when appropriate for individual cases. Classroom teachers referred cases to the team for assessment of learning and behavioral/emotional problems. The team developed an evaluation plan and determined who would conduct each component of the assessment after parental permission was obtained.

CASE BACKGROUND

When Richard was 10 years old, he was referred to the school multidisciplinary team by his fifth grade teacher. Richard was the older of two children in a middle class family. His teacher complained that he was inattentive, often failed to complete assignments, and seemed unmotivated and sullen much of the time. She described him as disorganized and messy, often losing materials and assignments, even though he appeared to have normal ability. He also seemed to have few friends and recently had begun fighting with other children on the playground. An evaluation was requested to determine whether learning disabilities and/or emotional problems were contributing to his poor school performance.

ASSESSMENT PROCEDURES

Because school problems were in question, the team needed assessment procedures that would meet federal and state criteria for determining whether or not Richard was eligible for special education services under one of the handicapping conditions defined by Public Law 94-142. Based on the referral complaints, the two most relevant conditions were "specific learning disability" and "serious emotional disturbance." PL 94-142 defines specific learning disability (SLD) as follows:

> . . . a disorder in one or more of the basic psychological processes involved in understanding or in using language, spoken or written, which may manifest itself in an imperfect ability to listen, think, speak, write, spell, or to do mathematical calculations. The term includes such conditions as perceptual handicaps, brain injury, minimal brain damage, dyslexia, and developmental aphasia. The term does not include children who have learning problems which are primarily the results of visual, hearing, or motor handicaps, of mental retardation, or of environmental, cultural, or economic disadvantage. (Education of the Handicapped Act, 1977, p. 42478)

The regulations stipulate further that the team may determine that a child has a specific learning disability if the child "has a severe discrepancy between achievement and intellectual ability in one or more of the following areas: (i) oral expression; (ii) listening comprehension; (iii) written expression; (iv) basic reading skills; (v) reading comprehension; (vi) mathematics calculation; or (vii) mathematics reasoning" (Education of the Handicapped Act, 1977, p. 65083). To meet these requirements in evaluating Richard, the team utilized a variety of standardized measures for cognitive assessment (Axis III of the multiaxial model). These included the Wechsler Intelligence Scale for Children—Revised (WISC-R; Wechsler, 1974), the Bender Gestalt Test (Koppitz, 1975), the Peabody Individual Achievement Test (PIAT; Dunn & Markwardt, 1970), the Test of Written Language (TOWL; Hammill & Larsen, 1983), and other standardized individual language and achievement tests.

PL 94-142 defines eligibility criteria for serious emotional disturbance (SED), but does not stipulate specific procedures for determining the severity of disturbance. (We will discuss the definition of SED later in this chapter.) Assessment of Richard's behavioral/emotional problems utilized our empirically based measures listed on Axes I, II, and V for obtaining parent reports, teacher reports, and direct observations. A clinical interview and personality testing of Richard, along with interviews with his mother and teacher, supplemented the empirically based procedures.

The psychologist and school staff conducted the assessment over the course of 3 weeks following Richard's initial referral to the multidisciplinary team. As a first step, the Child Behavior Checklist (CBCL) and a form covering medical and developmental history were mailed to Richard's mother, and the classroom teacher completed the Teacher's Report Form (TRF). These forms were sent to the psychologist for scoring. An independent observer rated Richard's behavior in school on the Direct Observation Form (DOF), and interviewed the classroom teacher. The special educator and speech pathologist administered individual achievement and language tests at school over several days. After these procedures were completed, the psychologist interviewed Richard and his mother and conducted cognitive and personality testing. We will now present the results of the multiaxial assessment for each of the five axes listed in Table 3-1.

Parent Reports

Richard's mother completed the Child Behavior Checklist (CBCL) to provide an assessment of his social competence and behavior. On the CBCL, parents provide information for 20 competence items covering their child's activities, involvement with social organizations, social relations, and school performance. Parents also rate their child on 118 behavior problem items using a 0-1-2 scale for how true each item is now or within the past 6 months. Parents' responses to the CBCL are scored on the Child Behavior Profile, which consists of three social competence scales and a variety of empirically derived problem scales.

Richard's total competence score on the CBCL was in the clinical range ($T = 36$; below the 10th percentile) compared with norms for nonreferred 6- to 11-year-old boys. This was largely due to low scores on the School scale, although his mother also reported some problems on the Social scale by rating him as "worse" than other children in terms of how well he gets along with other children, behaves with parents, and plays and works by himself. His low score on the School scale reflected the fact that he had repeated first grade, was receiving remedial help in math and reading, and was below average in all subjects except science.

Richard's total problem score was in the clinical range for 6- to 11-year-old boys ($T = 73$; above the 90th percentile), as were his scores on both the Internalizing ($T = 65$) and Externalizing scales ($T = 80$). Figure 3-1 shows the pattern of Richard's problems on the narrow-band scales of the CBCL. The Social Withdrawal, Hyperactive, Aggressive, and Delinquent scales were all in the clinical range (above the 98th percentile). The Social Withdrawal scale included scores for items such as *25. Doesn't get along with other children*; *34. Feels others are out to get him*; and *48. Not liked by other children*. The Hyperactive scale included items such as *1. Acts too young for his age*; *8. Can't concentrate, can't pay attention for long*; *10. Can't sit still, restless, or hyperactive*; and *41. Impulsive or acts without thinking*. The Aggressive and Delinquent scales included scores for many items reflecting

verbal and physical aggression and violations of social rules, such as
3. Argues a lot; *22. Disobedient at home*; *37. Gets in many fights*; *43. Lying
or cheating*; *81. Steals at home*; *94. Teases a lot*; *95. Temper tantrums or hot
temper*; and *106. Vandalism.*

No Internalizing narrow-band scale scores were in the clinical range,
although Richard's mother did report a number of problems on the Depressed
scale, such as *12. Complains of loneliness*; *14. Cries a lot*; and *45. Nervous,
highstrung, or tense*, as well as problems on the Obsessive–Compulsive scale,
such as *9. Can't get his mind off certain thoughts, obsessions*; *47. Nightmares*;
and *84. Strange behavior.* As shown by intraclass correlations (ICC) with profile
types identified via cluster analyses (Edelbrock & Achenbach, 1980), the overall pattern of Richard's problems was most like that of clinically referred boys
with Hyperactive (ICC = .497) and Delinquent (ICC = .646) profile types.

The psychologist's interview with Richard's mother focused on his
early development and current family circumstances. Richard's mother reported a normal pregnancy and birth, but described him as very active,
unpredictable, and moody as a young child. He was easily frustrated and
had frequent temper tantrums. He repeated first grade because of learning
problems and "social immaturity." Although he participated in small remedial reading groups at school, Richard had never received special education
services. When asked about family circumstances, Richard's mother reported considerable stress at home. The father suffered from a chronic
illness. Although he was employed full time, his condition was deteriorat-
ing and his moods fluctuated. There was much conflict between Richard
and his father and between the two parents. The mother worried that
Richard was becoming more rebellious and difficult to discipline.

Teacher Reports

The Teacher's Report Form (TRF) was completed by Richard's fifth grade
teacher. The TRF is designed to obtain teachers' reports of children's school
performance, adaptive functioning, and behavior problems. School performance is rated on a 5-point scale ranging from 1 (far below grade level) to 5
(far above grade level) for each academic subject. For adaptive functioning,
teachers rate children on 7-point scales in four areas: how hard the child is
working; how appropriately he/she is behaving; how much he/she is learning; and how happy he/she is. The TRF also includes 118 behavior problems items scored 0-1-2 like those on the CBCL. Ninety-three items have
counterparts rated by parents, while the remaining items concern school
behaviors that parents would not observe, such as difficulty following
directions, failing to finish things, and disrupting class discipline. The base
rating period for the TRF problems is 2 months, rather than the 6 months
requested on the CBCL, in order to avoid restricting teachers' ratings to the
last months of the school year.

Internalizing

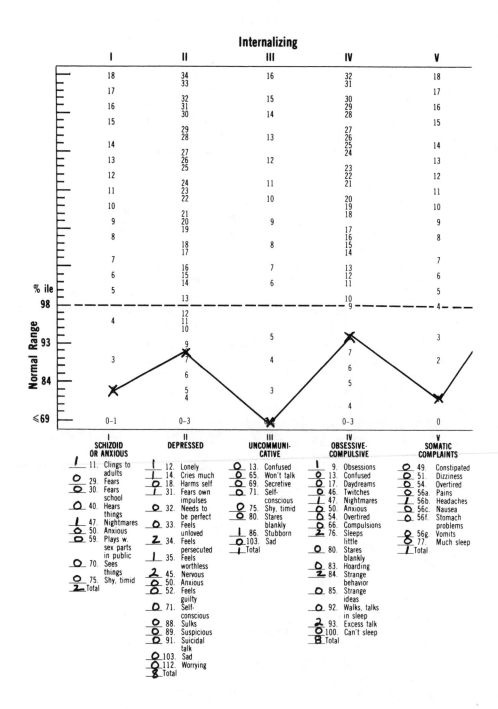

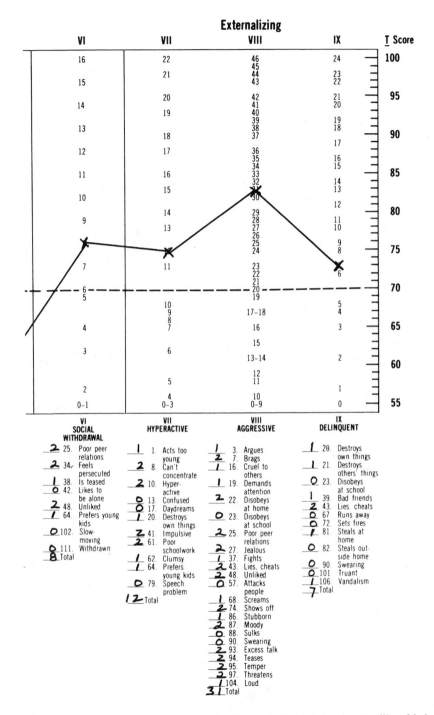

FIGURE 3-1. Parent's ratings on the Revised Child Behavior Profile of behavior problems (for boys aged 6 to 11) for Richard at age 10. Copyright 1978 by T. M. Achenbach. Reprinted by permission.

Richard's total adaptive functioning on the TRF was in the clinical range ($T = 34$; below the 13th percentile) for boys 6 to 11. His teacher rated him below the typical student on school performance, working hard, behaving appropriately, and learning. The only average rating was for happiness. Richard's total problem score was in the clinical range ($T = 69$; above the 89th percentile), as were his Internalizing ($T = 66$) and Externalizing ($T = 69$) scores. As Figure 3-2 shows, Richard scored near or above the clinical cutoffs on all scales except the Anxious scale. The Social Withdrawal scale was in the clinical range (above the 98th percentile), similar to the CBCL, showing scores for items such as *60. Apathetic or unmotivated*; *65. Refuses to talk*; *88. Sulks a lot*; and *103. Unhappy, sad, or depressed*. The Obsessive–Compulsive scale was at the clinical cutoff, while scores on the Self-Destructive, Aggressive, Inattentive, and Nervous–Overactive scales were just below the cutoffs.

Cognitive Assessment

Intelligence testing by the psychologist showed low average ability on the WISC-R (Verbal IQ = 84; Performance IQ = 91; Full Scale IQ = 86), with especially low scores on subtests related to distractibility and acquired information. The Bender Gestalt Test showed low average visual motor integration, with an age equivalent score of 9 years and soft signs of neurological dysfunction. The PIAT administered by the special educator showed low average achievement in mathematics, spelling, and general information (age standard scores = 82, 81, and 85, respectively), but below average scores in reading recognition and reading comprehension (age standard scores = 77 and 72, respectively). Additional testing at school produced similarly low scores in reading and language skills, and a below average score for written expression on the TOWL (Written Language Quotient = 76).

During the testing with the psychologist, Richard was very cooperative and seemed to enjoy the one-to-one attention and use of the stopwatch to time himself on tasks. Although he was sullen at first, he soon warmed up so that, by the end of the session, he asked if he could be tested again sometime. He was not unusually restless or overactive, but did have problems concentrating on auditory tasks. He frequently asked for feedback on his performance, had difficulty understanding directions, and needed encouragement to continue trying on difficult items. He had particular difficulty with writing and drawing tasks, performing very slowly and erasing many times.

Direct Assessment of Child

An independent observer rated Richard's behavior in school on the Direct Observation Form (DOF) prior to his appointment with the psychologist. The DOF is designed for recording behavior problems observed over

10-minute intervals. The observer writes a narrative description of the child's behavior and interactions over the 10 minutes, keeping the items to be rated in view and then making the actual ratings at the end of the observation session. There are 96 items on the DOF, of which 73 have counterparts on the CBCL and 85 on the TRF. Each item is rated on a 0-1-2-3 scale. The addition of one more point on the DOF rating scales (as compared with the 0-1-2 scales of the CBCL and TRF) allows the observer to include a rating for slight or ambiguous occurrences of a behavior (scored 1), as well as occurrences with mild-to-moderate intensity or less than a 3-minute duration (scored 2), and severe intensity or more than a 3-minute duration (scored 3). A total problem score is computed by summing the scores on all 96 items. An on-task score is also computed by summing ratings of on-task behavior made at 10 one-minute intervals. The scores on the DOF are to be averaged over several observational sessions to obtain a stable index of behavior. Comparisons with one or two "control" children are also recommended to provide a standard of comparison within the target child's own classroom.

Richard was observed on three occasions, as were two control boys in the same classroom. The observer chose two boys who were seated at opposite ends of the room from Richard and rated each separately on the DOF. Results showed that Richard was on-task an average of 75 percent of the time, compared with 90 percent for the control boys. Richard's total problem score was in the clinical range ($T = 70$; above the 93rd percentile), while the average of the control boys' scores was in the normal range. His Internalizing and Externalizing scores were also in the clinical range. Figure 3-3 shows the pattern of Richard's scores on the narrow-band scales of the DOF (solid line) compared with those of the control boys (broken line). Richard's scores were in the clinical range on the Withdrawn–Inattentive and Nervous–Obsessive scales, and at the clinical cutoff on the Depressed scale. His score on the Hyperactive scale was also higher than that of the control boys, but not above the clinical cutoff. (The DOF narrow-band scales are scored only by computer, because of the complexity of averaging scores for every item across multiple observation sessions.) Curiously, the mean score for the control boys was in the clinical range on two scales, indicating that Richard was not the only child in the classroom displaying problem behavior. However, the mean total problem score for the control boys was in the normal range, in contrast to Richard's much higher score, which was in the clinical range.

FORMULATION AND PROPOSED TREATMENT

Richard's mother and his teacher both reported poor school performance and behavior problem scores in the clinical range, indicating that his problems at home and at school were well beyond those typical of 6- to 11-year-old boys.

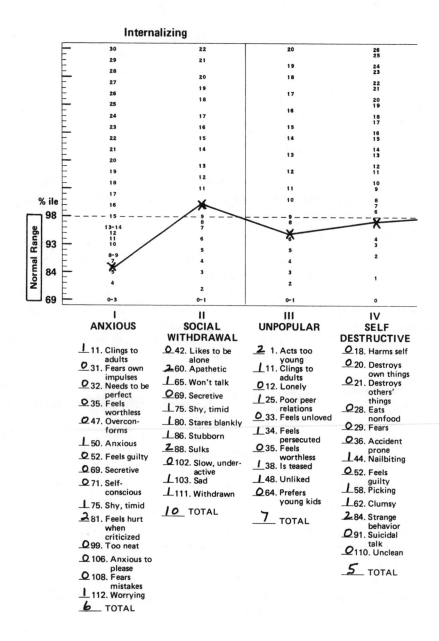

Internalizing

	I ANXIOUS	II SOCIAL WITHDRAWAL	III UNPOPULAR	IV SELF DESTRUCTIVE

I — ANXIOUS

- _1_ 11. Clings to adults
- _0_ 31. Fears own impulses
- _0_ 32. Needs to be perfect
- _0_ 35. Feels worthless
- _0_ 47. Overconforms
- _1_ 50. Anxious
- _0_ 52. Feels guilty
- _0_ 69. Secretive
- _0_ 71. Self-conscious
- _1_ 75. Shy, timid
- _2_ 81. Feels hurt when criticized
- _0_ 99. Too neat
- _0_ 106. Anxious to please
- _0_ 108. Fears mistakes
- _1_ 112. Worrying
- **_6_ TOTAL**

II — SOCIAL WITHDRAWAL

- _0_ 42. Likes to be alone
- _2_ 60. Apathetic
- _1_ 65. Won't talk
- _0_ 69. Secretive
- _1_ 75. Shy, timid
- _1_ 80. Stares blankly
- _1_ 86. Stubborn
- _2_ 88. Sulks
- _0_ 102. Slow, underactive
- _1_ 103. Sad
- _1_ 111. Withdrawn
- **_10_ TOTAL**

III — UNPOPULAR

- _2_ 1. Acts too young
- _1_ 11. Clings to adults
- _0_ 12. Lonely
- _1_ 25. Poor peer relations
- _0_ 33. Feels unloved
- _1_ 34. Feels persecuted
- _0_ 35. Feels worthless
- _1_ 38. Is teased
- _1_ 48. Unliked
- _0_ 64. Prefers young kids
- **_7_ TOTAL**

IV — SELF DESTRUCTIVE

- _0_ 18. Harms self
- _0_ 20. Destroys own things
- _0_ 21. Destroys others' things
- _0_ 28. Eats nonfood
- _0_ 29. Fears
- _0_ 36. Accident prone
- _1_ 44. Nailbiting
- _0_ 52. Feels guilty
- _1_ 58. Picking
- _1_ 62. Clumsy
- _2_ 84. Strange behavior
- _0_ 91. Suicidal talk
- _0_ 110. Unclean
- **_5_ TOTAL**

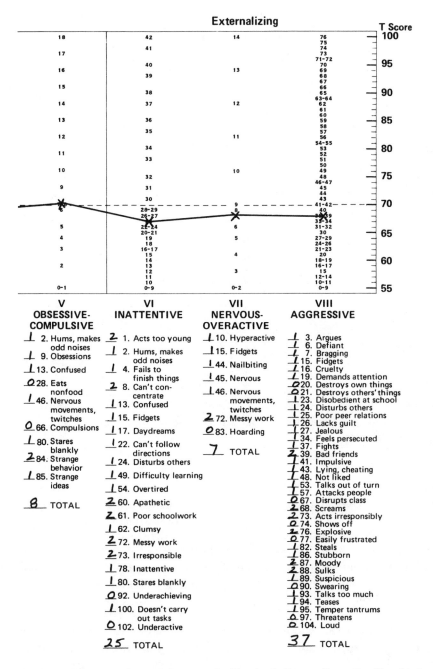

FIGURE 3-2. Teacher's ratings on the Teacher's Report Form Profile of behavior problems (for boys aged 6 to 11) for Richard at age 10. Copyright 1982 by C. S. Edelbrock and T. M Achenbach. Reprinted by permission.

DIRECT OBSERVATION FORM OF THE CHILD BEHAVIOR CHECKLIST
PROFILE FOR NARROW BAND SCALES

```
--------------------INTERNALIZING------------------------------------------------------------EXTERNALIZING----------
-I   15.0+           15.0+              15.0+    I    15.0+     I    15.0+         15.0+    I-
-I                                               I              I                          I-
-I                   14.0               14.0     I    14.0      I    14.0          14.0     I-
-I   X ——— X  RICHARD                            I              I                          I-
-I   X --- X  CONTROLS                  13.0     I    13.0      I    13.0          13.0     I-
-I                                               I              I                          I-
-I                   12.0               12.0     I    12.0      I    12.0          12.0     I-
-I                                               I              I                          I-
-I   11.0            11.0               11.0     I    11.0      I    11.0          11.0     I-
-I                                               I              I                          I-
-I·  10.0            10.0               10.0     I    10.0      I    10.0          10.0     I-
-I                                               I              I                          I-
-I   9.0             9.0                9.0      I    9.0       I    9.0           9.0      I-
-I                                               I              I                          I-
-I   8.0             8.0                8.0      I    8.0       I    8.0           8.0      I-
-I                                               I              I                          I-
-I   7.0             7.0                7.0      I    7.0       I    7.0           7.0      I-
-I                                               I              I                          I-
-I   6.0             6.0                6.0      I    6.0       I    6.0           6.0      I-
-I                                               I              I                          I-
-I   5.0             5.0                5.0      I--------5.0-------I    5.0           5.0      I-
-I   I                                           I              I                          I-
-I   4.0             4.0                4.0      I    4.0       I    4.0           4.0      I-
-I                                               I    I         I                          I-
-I   C                3.0               3.0      I    3.0       I    3.0           3.0      I-
-I                                               I              I                          I-
-I------2.0-----\         I                 C        I         2.0        \---------2.0------I-98%ILE
-I              \                                I              I---1.5------\            I-
-I   1.0          \---    1.0------------   I ----I         1.0    I                   1.0      I-
-I                                               I    C---        I                          I-
-I____0.0_____C_____0.0___I____0.0_____I___C_____C_____I-
   WITHDRAWN-INATTN  NERVS-OBSESSIVE   DEPRESSED   HYPERACTIVE  ATTENTION DEMANDING  AGGRESSIVE
```

FIGURE 3-3. Observer's ratings on the Direct Observation Form Profile for Richard at age 10.

High scores on the CBCL Hyperactive, TRF Inattentive and Nervous–Overactive, and DOF Withdrawn–Inattentive scales all supported a DSM-III diagnosis of Attention Deficit Disorder with Hyperactivity (ADDH). At the same time, the empirically based measures also identified deviance in aggressive and delinquent behavior reported by Richard's mother and social withdrawal at home and school, thus showing serious conduct and social problems accompanying the ADD/H. Cognitive assessment showed a low average FSIQ and VIQ, but an average PIQ. Richard's achievement was below average in reading and written expression. Low scores on the CBCL School scale and TRF School Performance scale and adaptive functioning provided further evidence that Richard's school functioning was below that of typical students.

Based on the results of psychoeducational testing and the empirically based measures, Richard was deemed eligible for special education services in school under the learning disability category. Though his test scores did not meet the state criterion of a 1.5 standard deviation discrepancy between full-scale IQ and achievement, the multidisciplinary team concluded that his low achievement test scores, combined with evidence of deviance on the CBCL, TRF, and DOF, justified special education services. This decision opened opportunities for much more intensive educational interventions that had been available in the past.

An intervention plan was developed that combined an Individual Education Plan and treatment with stimulant medication for the Attention Deficit Disorder. Richard was placed on Ritalin (10 mg twice daily) by a child psychiatrist. The psychologist monitored his behavior by obtaining parent and teacher ratings on the Conners checklists (Goyette, Conners, & Ulrich, 1978) over a 6-week trial period. The results showed a substantial reduction in the hyperkinesis score after medication was begun. Special education instruction was initiated in the Resource Room twice daily to improve reading and writing skills and develop better organizational strategies and study skills. Richard's classroom teacher cooperated with the special educators by reducing the length of individual assignments and presenting only one or two tasks at a time to maximize Richard's attention span.

Because Richard responded well to feedback and encouragement during testing, a behavior contract was developed to increase on-task behavior and completion of assignments. A daily point system was established whereby Richard could choose from a menu of rewards when he met daily and weekly goals of completed work. Negative consequences were specified for uncompleted assignments below minimum standards. The behavior plan also incorporated points for appropriate school behaviors, such as having materials ready (pencil, book, etc.), working quietly, and asking for help when he did not understand something. In addition, Richard participated in small group sessions with peers, conducted by the school guidance counselor, addressing social relations and problem solving. His parents also agreed to seek counseling from a family therapist for coping with behavior management and discord at home, but they failed to keep appointments after the first few sessions.

REASSESSMENT AT AGE 15

When Richard was 15, he was again referred to the school multidisciplinary team because he not only continued to show learning problems, but now seemed unhappy and angry in school much of the time. He was in ninth grade and was failing many of his courses despite continuing special education services. His teachers reported that he refused to do school work even in the special education class and often isolated himself from other students. His behavior problems had escalated over the past few years, leading to several school suspensions. The teachers expressed concerns to Richard's parents that he had begun associating with bad companions, and they suspected the he was experimenting with alcohol and drugs. Treatment with Ritalin had continued over the past 5 years, but Richard was becoming more resistant to taking the medication.

Since the initial evaluation, several changes had occurred in the family. When Richard was 13, his father died after a 6-month hospitalization. The mother remarried 1 year later, adding two stepchildren to the household, one of whom was older than Richard. Richard had difficulty getting along with his stepfather, and there were frequent arguments among the siblings. An evaluation was requested to assess Richard's academic progress and behavioral/emotional problems. The evaluation again included parent and teacher ratings on the CBCL and TRF along with psychoeducational testing. Richard's self-ratings on the YSR added an important new perspective as part of the direct assessment.

Parent Reports

On the CBCL completed by his mother, Richard's total competence score was again in the clinical range, and was even lower than at age 10. His scores on the Activities and Social scales were just above the clinical cutoff, while his score on the School scale remained below the cutoff.

Richard's total problem score remained in the clinical range, as did his Internalizing and Externalizing scores, compared with norms for boys aged 12 to 16. As Figure 3-4 shows, his scores were in the clinical range on the Hostile–Withdrawal, Delinquent, Aggressive, and Hyperactive scales, and at the clinical cutoff on the Obsessive–Compulsive scale. This pattern resembled the one obtained at age 10, but was now scored on the profile for boys aged 12 to 16. Richard's profile pattern was most similar to the Uncommunicative–Delinquent (ICC = .546) and Delinquent (ICC = .537) profile types, but was also similar to the Hyperactive (ICC = .423) type.

Teacher Reports

Three of Richard's teachers completed the TRF. His total adaptive functioning was in the clinical range on all three reports, with low ratings for working hard, behaving appropriately, learning, and happiness. His scores for school performance were also in the clinical range. Richard's total problem, Internalizing, and Externalizing scores from two teachers were in the clinical range, and just below the clinical cutoff from the third teacher. As Figure 3-5 shows, scores were in the clinical range from one or more teachers on the Social Withdrawal, Obsessive–Compulsive, Immature, Self-Destructive, Inattentive, and Aggressive scales. The teachers described Richard as angry, unhappy, withdrawn, and having an extremely poor attention span. Two teachers scored him on item *84. Strange behavior,* describing odd noises, odd facial expressions, and hiding under the furniture. Compared with the fifth grade teacher's ratings at age 10, the new TRFs at age 15 showed a more differentiated pattern of problems, including poor peer relations, immaturity, inattentiveness, and aggression. The dotted line represents the teacher who scored him lowest in problems—the vocational education teacher who taught woodworking.

Cognitive Assessment

The WISC-R showed a low average full-scale IQ (FSIQ = 84), but below average verbal IQ (VIQ = 73) with a drop of 9 points from the previous testing. Richard's performance IQ, on the other hand, increased 9 points (PIQ = 100). Despite many school-based interventions, Richard was failing most of his academic subjects and was often in trouble for violating school rules. His achievement test scores in reading and written language were well below average, making it hard for him to keep up with the high school curriculum. His scores on the Test of Written Language (Hammill & Larsen, 1983) (Written Language Quotient = 60) and the Test of Reading Comprehension (Brown, Hammill, & Wiederholt, 1978) (Reading Comprehension Quotient = 59) were both more than 1.5 standard deviations below his full-scale IQ score, thus meeting state special education criteria for learning disabilities.

Direct Assessment of Child

The Youth Self-Report (YSR) added a new dimension to the evaluation at age 15 by giving Richard an opportunity to rate himself on many of the same items rated by his mother and teachers. The YSR is designed to obtain an assessment of social competence and behavior problems as perceived by adolescents. It is intended for 11- to 18-year-olds with a mental age of at least 10 years and fifth grade reading skills. (The YSR can be read aloud to those with reading skills below the fifth grade.) The YSR has most of the same competence and problem items as the CBCL, but the items are stated in the first person. A total of 16 CBCL items considered inappropriate to ask adolescents are replaced with 16 socially desirable items that enable respondents to say something favorable about themselves. The favorable items are omitted from the total problem score. There are 103 problem items corresponding to items on the CBCL and 90 corresponding to items on the TRF. The scoring profiles are standardized separately for each sex for ages 11 to 18.

Richard's self-ratings on the YSR produced scores on the Activities and Social scales in the normal range—a sharp contrast to the low competence scores from the CBCL and low adaptive functioning scores on the TRFs. The total problem and Externalizing scores were in the clinical range

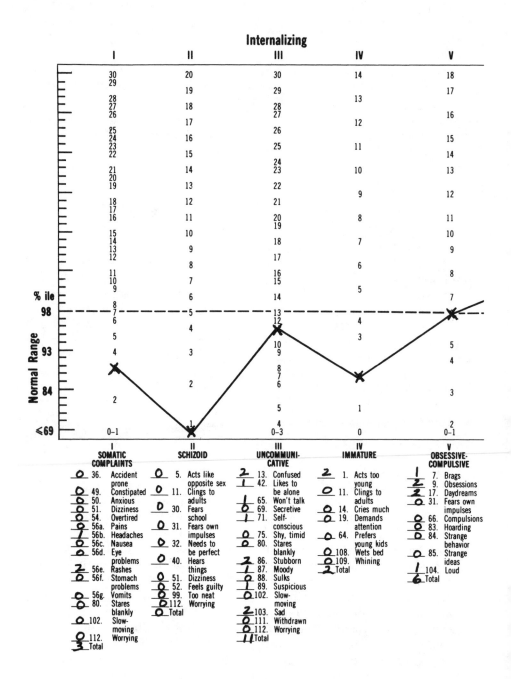

Internalizing

	I	II	III	IV	V
	30	20	30	14	18
	29	19	29		17
	28	18	28	13	
	27		27	12	16
	26	17	26		
	25	16		11	15
	24		25		
	23	15	24		14
	22	14	23	10	13
	21	13	22		
	20			9	12
	19	12	21		
	18	11	20	8	11
	17		19		
	16	10	18	7	10
	15				
	14	9	17	6	9
	13				
	12	8	16		8
	11	7	15	5	
	10		14		7
	9	6	13		
	8	5	12	4	
	7				
	6	4	10	3	5
	5		9		4
	4	3	8		
			7	X	3
		2	6	1	2
			5		
			4		
	0-1	1	0-3	0	0-1

% ile — 98 — Normal Range — 93 — 84 — ≤69

I SOMATIC COMPLAINTS	II SCHIZOID	III UNCOMMUNI-CATIVE	IV IMMATURE	V OBSESSIVE-COMPULSIVE
0 36. Accident prone	**0** 5. Acts like opposite sex	**2** 13. Confused	**2** 1. Acts too young	**1** 7. Brags
0 49. Constipated	**0** 11. Clings to adults	**1** 42. Likes to be alone	**0** 11. Clings to adults	**2** 9. Obsessions
0 50. Anxious		**1** 65. Won't talk		**2** 17. Daydreams
0 51. Dizziness	**0** 30. Fears school	**0** 69. Secretive	**0** 14. Cries much	**0** 31. Fears own impulses
0 54. Overtired		**1** 71. Self-conscious	**0** 19. Demands attention	
0 56a. Pains	**0** 31. Fears own impulses			**0** 66. Compulsions
1 56b. Headaches	**0** 32. Needs to be perfect	**0** 75. Shy, timid	**0** 64. Prefers young kids	**0** 83. Hoarding
0 56c. Nausea		**0** 80. Stares blankly		**0** 84. Strange behavior
0 56d. Eye problems	**0** 40. Hears things	**2** 86. Stubborn	**0** 108. Wets bed	
2 56e. Rashes		**1** 87. Moody	**0** 109. Whining	**0** 85. Strange ideas
0 56f. Stomach problems	**0** 51. Dizziness	**0** 88. Sulks	**2** Total	
	0 52. Feels guilty	**1** 89. Suspicious		**1** 104. Loud
0 56g. Vomits	**0** 99. Too neat	**0** 102. Slow-moving		**6** Total
0 80. Stares blankly	**0** 112. Worrying	**2** 103. Sad		
0 102. Slow-moving	**0** Total	**0** 111. Withdrawn		
0 112. Worrying		**0** 112. Worrying		
3 Total		**11** Total		

56

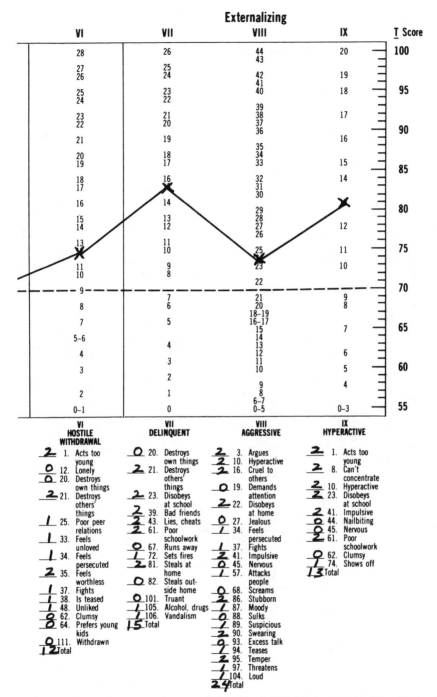

Externalizing

	VI	VII	VIII	IX	T Score
	28	26	44 43	20	100
	27 26	25 24	42 41 40	19 18	95
	25 24	23 22	39 38 37 36	17	90
	23 22	21 20	35 34 33	16 15	85
	21	19	32 31 30	14	
	20 19	18 17	29 28 27 26	12	80
	18 17	16			
	16	14			
	15 14	13 12	25 23	11	75
	13 11 10	11 10 9 8	22	10	
	9	7 6	21 20 18–19 16–17	9 8	70
	8	5	15 14 13 12 11 10	7	65
	7 5–6 4	4 3 2	9 8	6 5	60
	3 2	1	6–7	4	
	0–1	0	0–5	0–3	55

VI HOSTILE WITHDRAWAL	VII DELINQUENT	VIII AGGRESSIVE	IX HYPERACTIVE
2 1. Acts too young	**0** 20. Destroys own things	**2** 3. Argues	**2** 1. Acts too young
0 12. Lonely	**2** 21. Destroys others' things	**2** 10. Hyperactive	**2** 8. Can't concentrate
0 20. Destroys own things	**2** 23. Disobeys at school	**2** 16. Cruel to others	**2** 10. Hyperactive
2 21. Destroys others' things	**2** 39. Bad friends	**0** 19. Demands attention	**2** 23. Disobeys at school
1 25. Poor peer relations	**2** 43. Lies, cheats	**2** 22. Disobeys at home	**2** 41. Impulsive
1 33. Feels unloved	**2** 61. Poor schoolwork	**0** 27. Jealous	**0** 44. Nailbiting
1 34. Feels persecuted	**0** 67. Runs away	**1** 34. Feels persecuted	**0** 45. Nervous
2 35. Feels worthless	**1** 72. Sets fires	**1** 37. Fights	**2** 61. Poor schoolwork
1 37. Fights	**2** 81. Steals at home	**2** 41. Impulsive	**0** 62. Clumsy
1 38. Is teased	**0** 82. Steals outside home	**0** 45. Nervous	**1** 74. Shows off
1 48. Unliked	**0** 101. Truant	**1** 57. Attacks people	**13** Total
8 62. Clumsy	**1** 105. Alcohol, drugs	**0** 68. Screams	
0 64. Prefers young kids	**1** 106. Vandalism	**2** 86. Stubborn	
0 111. Withdrawn	**15** Total	**1** 87. Moody	
12 Total		**0** 88. Sulks	
		1 89. Suspicious	
		2 90. Swearing	
		0 93. Excess talk	
		1 94. Teases	
		2 95. Temper	
		1 97. Threatens	
		1 104. Loud	
		24 Total	

FIGURE 3-4. Parent's ratings on the Revised Child Behavior Profile of behavior problems (for boys aged 12 to 16) for Richard at age 15. Copyright 1982 by T. M. Achenbach. Reprinted by permission.

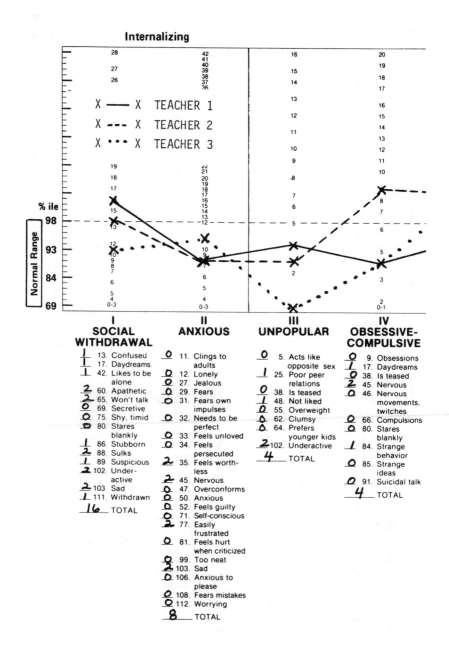

Internalizing

X —— X TEACHER 1
X --- X TEACHER 2
X ••• X TEACHER 3

% ile
Normal Range
98
93
84
69

I **SOCIAL WITHDRAWAL**	II **ANXIOUS**	III **UNPOPULAR**	IV **OBSESSIVE- COMPULSIVE**
_1_ 13. Confused	_0_ 11. Clings to adults	_0_ 5. Acts like opposite sex	_0_ 9. Obsessions
_1_ 17. Daydreams	_0_ 12. Lonely	_1_ 25. Poor peer relations	_1_ 17. Daydreams
_1_ 42. Likes to be alone	_0_ 27. Jealous		_0_ 38. Is teased
_2_ 60. Apathetic	_0_ 29. Fears	_0_ 38. Is teased	_2_ 45. Nervous
_2_ 65. Won't talk	_0_ 31. Fears own impulses	_1_ 48. Not liked	_0_ 46. Nervous movements, twitches
_0_ 69. Secretive	_0_ 32. Needs to be perfect	_0_ 55. Overweight	
_0_ 75. Shy, timid	_0_ 33. Feels unloved	_0_ 62. Clumsy	_0_ 66. Compulsions
_0_ 80. Stares blankly	_0_ 34. Feels persecuted	_0_ 64. Prefers younger kids	_0_ 80. Stares blankly
_1_ 86. Stubborn	_2_ 35. Feels worthless	_2_ 102. Underactive	_1_ 84. Strange behavior
_2_ 88. Sulks	_2_ 45. Nervous	_4_ TOTAL	_0_ 85. Strange ideas
_1_ 89. Suspicious	_0_ 47. Overconforms		_0_ 91. Suicidal talk
_2_ 102. Underactive	_0_ 50. Anxious		_4_ TOTAL
_2_ 103. Sad	_0_ 52. Feels guilty		
_1_ 111. Withdrawn	_0_ 71. Self-conscious		
_16_ TOTAL	_2_ 77. Easily frustrated		
	_0_ 81. Feels hurt when criticized		
	_2_ 99. Too neat		
	_2_ 103. Sad		
	_0_ 106. Anxious to please		
	_0_ 108. Fears mistakes		
	_0_ 112. Worrying		
	_8_ TOTAL		

58

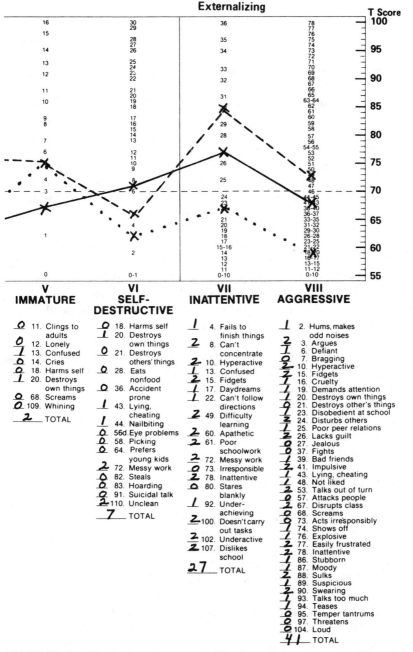

FIGURE 3-5. Teacher's ratings on the Teacher's Report Form Profile of behavior problems (for boys aged 12 to 16) for Richard at age 15. Item scores for each scale are those of Teacher 1. Copyright 1984 by C. S. Edelbrock and T. M. Achenbach. Reprinted by permission.

59

($T = 64$ and 67, respectively; above the 89th percentile), similar to those from the parent and teacher ratings. Figure 3-6 shows that Richard's score on the Thought Disorder scale was in the clinical range, whereas scores on all other YSR scales were below the cutoffs. Richard scored as "sometimes true" items *84. I do things other people think are strange* and *85. I have thoughts that other people would think are strange,* as well as several other items on the Thought Disorder scale indicating fears, nightmares, repetitious acts, seeing things that aren't there, and storing up unneeded things. Richard did not indicate what he meant by strange behavior or ideas. Interestingly, he did not report as much aggressive behavior as did his mother and teachers, but he did acknowledge a number of delinquent behaviors, including having bad companions and using alcohol and drugs.

The empirically based measures and cognitive assessment demonstrated that Richard's learning and behavioral/emotional problems exceeded those of normal 12- to 16-year-old boys. With this evidence in mind, the psychologist conducted additional testing and interviewing to probe further into Richard's emotional functioning and the possibility of disturbed thinking, as suggested by the YSR and TRF ratings. The clinical interview revealed extreme unhappiness, poor self-esteem, and adjustment issues underlying overt behavioral problems. Richard's anger and grief over the death of his father remained unresolved, with denial as his main defense. He was also experiencing new adjustment problems with his mother's remarriage and the fact that he was no longer the oldest sibling in the family. He had developed very negative feelings about school as a result of his long-standing learning problems, although he did express interest in vocational courses. When asked about his reports of strange ideas and behavior on the YSR, Richard said other students think he is "weird" and he "clowns around" in school.

FORMULATION AND PROPOSED TREATMENT

The reevaluation showed that Richard continued to experience severe learning and behavioral/emotional problems at age 15 despite the previous interventions. Parent and teacher ratings on the empirically based measures showed low competence and extreme problems compared with normal 12- to 16-year-old boys. The vocational teacher's more positive ratings, however, suggested that Richard functioned better in this type of class than in academic courses. Richard's self-ratings also indicated that he saw himself as having many problems and disturbed thoughts, but not being as low in competence as reported by his mother and teachers. The clinical interview further highlighted his unhappiness and the nature of concerns about school and family relations.

The pattern of Richard's problems continued to warrant a DSM-III-R diagnosis of Attention-deficit Hyperactivity Disorder, now accompanied by more delinquent behavior, unhappiness, and adjustment problems in the new family structure. The teacher reports showed that his behavioral/emotional problems in school had actually worsened despite his having received special education services for the past 5 years to address his learning problems. These results indicated that previous educational interventions and stimulant medication were not sufficient to address all of his needs. The multidisciplinary team concluded that new stresses in the family and Richard's behavioral/emotional problems had become primary factors contributing to his poor school performance. They concluded that he not only met special education criteria for specific learning disabilities, but he also now met criteria for serious emotional disturbance (SED), defined by PL 94-142 as follows:

> (i) The term means a condition exhibiting one or more of the following characteristics over a long period of time and to a marked degree, which adversely affects educational performance: (a) an inability to learn which cannot be explained by intellectual, sensory, and health factors; (b) an inability to build or maintain satisfactory interpersonal relationships with peers and teachers; (c) inappropriate types of behavior or feelings under normal circumstances; (d) a general pervasive mood of unhappiness or depression; or (e) a tendency to develop physical symptoms or fears associated with personal or school problems. (ii) The term includes children who are schizophrenic. The term does not include children who are socially maladjusted, unless it is determined that they are seriously emotionally disturbed. (Education of the Handicapped Act, 1977, p. 42478; amended 1981, p. 3866)

The multiaxial assessment provided substantial evidence of serious emotional disturbance under the PL 94-142 definition as we will discuss shortly. Classification of Richard as SED, as well as SLD, provided opportunities for expanding his Individual Education Plan (IEP) to address both learning and behavioral/emotional problems. Richard's school program was shifted to emphasize vocational training, since this was the area in which he showed the most interest and success. His IEP included a paid job placement first within the school setting and the following year within the community. He continued to receive daily special education services in the Resource Room for reading and writing skills. His high school courses, however, were adapted to focus more on practical and vocational/occupational skills. He was given textbooks with lower readability levels, and less written work was required to earn credit. A special SED tutor was provided to help Richard complete academic assignments and to develop his social problem-solving skills. The tutor acted as an advocate for Richard in deal-

PROBLEM SCALES

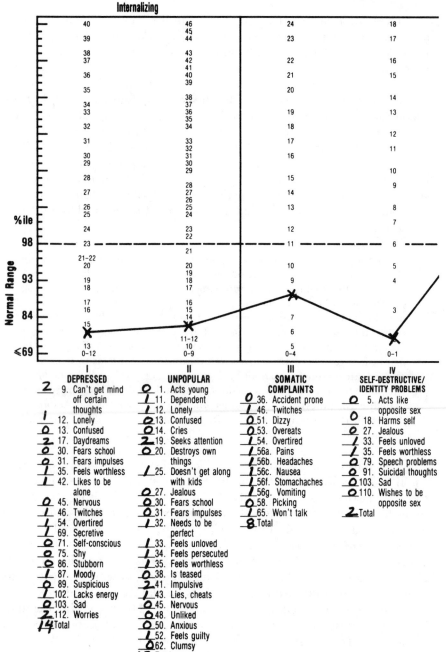

Internalizing

%ile

98

Normal Range

93

84

≤69

I	II	III	IV
DEPRESSED	**UNPOPULAR**	**SOMATIC COMPLAINTS**	**SELF-DESTRUCTIVE/ IDENTITY PROBLEMS**
_2_ 9. Can't get mind off certain thoughts	_O_ 1. Acts young	_O_ 36. Accident prone	_O_ 5. Acts like opposite sex
_1_ 12. Lonely	_1_ 11. Dependent	_1_ 46. Twitches	_O_ 18. Harms self
_O_ 13. Confused	_1_ 12. Lonely	_O_ 51. Dizzy	_O_ 27. Jealous
_2_ 17. Daydreams	_O_ 13. Confused	_O_ 53. Overeats	_1_ 33. Feels unloved
_O_ 30. Fears school	_O_ 14. Cries	_1_ 54. Overtired	_1_ 35. Feels worthless
_O_ 31. Fears impulses	_2_ 19. Seeks attention	_1_ 56a. Pains	_O_ 79. Speech problems
_1_ 35. Feels worthless	_O_ 20. Destroys own things	_1_ 56b. Headaches	_O_ 91. Suicidal thoughts
_1_ 42. Likes to be alone	_1_ 25. Doesn't get along with kids	_1_ 56c. Nausea	_O_ 103. Sad
_O_ 45. Nervous	_O_ 27. Jealous	_1_ 56f. Stomachaches	_O_ 110. Wishes to be opposite sex
_1_ 46. Twitches	_O_ 30. Fears school	_1_ 56g. Vomiting	_2_ Total
_1_ 54. Overtired	_O_ 31. Fears impulses	_O_ 58. Picking	
_1_ 69. Secretive	_1_ 32. Needs to be perfect	_1_ 65. Won't talk	
_O_ 71. Self-conscious	_1_ 33. Feels unloved	_8_ Total	
_O_ 75. Shy	_1_ 34. Feels persecuted		
_O_ 86. Stubborn	_1_ 35. Feels worthless		
_1_ 87. Moody	_O_ 38. Is teased		
_O_ 89. Suspicious	_2_ 41. Impulsive		
_1_ 102. Lacks energy	_1_ 43. Lies, cheats		
_O_ 103. Sad	_O_ 45. Nervous		
_2_ 112. Worries	_O_ 48. Unliked		
_14_ Total	_O_ 50. Anxious		
	_1_ 52. Feels guilty		
	_O_ 62. Clumsy		
	_13_ Total		

62

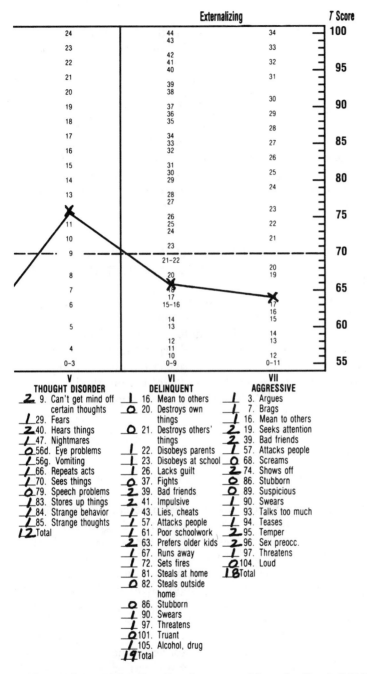

FIGURE 3-6. Richard's self-ratings at age 15 on the Youth Self-Report Profile of behavior problems (for boys aged 11 to 18). Copyright 1986 by T. M. Achenbach and C. S. Edelbrock. Reprinted by permission.

ings with teachers and school administrative staff. These changes allowed Richard to remain in a mainstream environment for much of his school day, rather than being transferred to a more restrictive placement.

Outside of school, Richard and his family began therapy with a psychologist specializing in child and family problems. Seeing the high scores on the empirically based measures, particularly the YSR, helped convince the family of the severity of Richard's problems and thus strengthened their commitment to continue with therapy this time. The psychologist worked individually with Richard and met intermittently with the family on behavior-management issues. Treatment with stimulant medication was also continued, monitored by a child psychiatrist working in the same clinic as the psychologist seeing the family.

RELATIONS BETWEEN EMPIRICALLY BASED ASSESSMENT, THE DSM, AND SPECIAL EDUCATION CLASSIFICATIONS

Richard's case illustrates the comprehensiveness of our multiaxial empirically based model of assessment and its compatibility with other systems for classifying child and adolescent psychopathology. Justification for psychiatric treatment and school services for Richard depended on his qualifying for a DSM diagnosis and meeting administrative criteria for special education services according to PL 94-142. The results of the multiaxial empirically based assessment were applied to these classification systems in the following ways.

Diagnostic and Statistical Manual

Richard was initially diagnosed at age 10 as having an Attention Deficit Disorder with Hyperactivity according to DSM-III. The empirically based measures and developmental history documented problems in inattention, impulsivity, and hyperactivity thereby warranting this diagnosis. His pattern of problems at age 15 continued to meet criteria for a similar DSM-III-R diagnosis of Attention-deficit Hyperactivity Disorder (ADHD) with at least 10 of 14 criteria listed for ADHD. The empirically based measures also showed that Richard was exhibiting severe aggressive and delinquent behavior and disturbed thinking, along with ADHD, thus providing a more comprehensive picture of his problems than indicated by a single DSM diagnosis. Several of the empirically derived syndromes have approximate counterparts among the child and adolescent disorders of the DSM. Table 3-2 summarizes the similarities among the empirically derived syndromes and the DSM-III-R categories. (See Achenbach & Edelbrock, 1983, 1986, 1987; Achenbach & McConaughy, 1987; McConaughy & Achenbach, in press, for further discussion of relations between DSM-III-R and the CBCL system.)

TABLE 3-2. Approximate Relations between DSM-III-R and Empirically Derived Syndromes

DSM-III-R	CBCL	TRF	YSR	DOF
Solitary Aggressive Conduct Disorder	Aggressive	Aggressive	Aggressive	Aggressive
Oppositional Defiant Disorder				
Group Delinquent Disorder	Delinquent	Delinquent	Delinquent	—
Attention-deficit Hyperactivity Disorder	Hyperactive	Inattentive Nervous–Overactive	—	Hyperactive
Overanxious Disorder	Anxious–Obsessive Schizoid–Anxious	Anxious	—	Nervous–Obsessive
Gender Identity Disorder for Males	Sex Problems (boys 4–5)	—	Self-Destructive/ Identity Problems (boys only)	—
Schizoid Personality	Social Withdrawal	Social Withdrawal	—	—
Schizotypal Personality	Schizoid	—	Thought Disorder	—
Somatization Disorder	Somatic Complaints	—	Somatic Complaints	—
Obsessive–Compulsive Disorder	Obsessive–Compulsive	Obsessive–Compulsive	—	—
Major Depression Dysthymia	Depressed	Depressed (girls only)	Depressed	Depressed

Note. From *Empirically-Based Assessment of Child and Adolescent Psychopathology: Practical Applications* (p. 154) by T. M. Achenbach and S. H. McConaughy, 1987, Newbury Park, CA: Sage. Copyright by T. M. Achenbach. Reprinted by permission.

65

Specific Learning Disability

The multidisciplinary team at school determined that Richard at age 10 qualified for special education services as a learning disabled child. Although Richard's test scores at that time did not meet state statistical criteria for a discrepancy between overall ability and achievement, the team concluded that Richard's attentional and learning problems significantly limited his school performance, particularly in areas related to reading and written expression. Low scores on the CBCL School scale and TRF Adaptive Functioning scale provided normative comparisons supporting this conclusion. The scores on reading and writing tests at age 15 were even lower than at age 10, and did meet the state criteria for learning disabilities, indicating that Richard's learning problems continued to have a significant detrimental impact on his achievement.

Serious Emotional Disturbance

At age 15, the school multidisciplinary team determined that Richard exhibited serious emotional disturbance (SED) in addition to specific learning disabilities. As outlined by Slenkovich (1983), the PL 94-142 definition specifies the following criteria for a determination of SED:

1. There must be a condition which produces one or more of five defined characteristics of serious emotional disturbance.
2. The child must manifest at least one of five defined characteristics or have a diagnosis of schizophrenia.
3. The characteristic must exist over a long period of time.
4. The characteristic must exist to a marked degree.
5. The condition must adversely affect educational performance.
6. The term SED does not include children who are socially maladjusted unless they are also seriously emotionally disturbed.

The findings on the empirically based measures for Richard showed marked deviance in behavioral and emotional functioning from all perspectives: parent, teachers, and Richard himself. As Table 3-3 shows, there was evidence from the CBCL, TRFs, and YSR supporting several of the criteria for SED:

1. Inability to learn was indicated by deviant scores on the Inattentive scale of the TRF profiles from several teachers.
2. Inability to build or maintain relationships was indicated by deviant scores on the Withdrawal scales of the CBCL and TRF profiles.
3. Inappropriate types of behavior and feelings was indicated by deviant scores on the Obsessive–Compulsive, Hyperactive, Self-

TABLE 3-3. Findings of Empirically Based Assessment for the Case of Richard, Age 15

PL 94-142 Components of SED	CBCL	TRF	YSR
Inability to learn	—	Inattentive	—
Inability to build or maintain relationships	Hostile Withdrawal	Social Withdrawal	—
Inappropriate types of behavior or feelings	Obsessive–Compulsive Hyperactive Aggressive	Obsessive–Compulsive Self-Destructive Aggressive	Thought Disorder
General pervasive mood of unhappiness	—	—	—
Tendency to develop physical symptoms or fears	—	—	—
Schizophrenic	—	—	—
Long period of time	Clinical range scores at ages 10 and 15	Clinical range scores at ages 10 and 15	—
Marked degree	Total, Internalizing, and Externalizing scores > 90th percentile	Total, Internalizing, and Externalizing scores > 89th percentile	Total and Externalizing scores > 89th percentile
	Narrow-band scores > 98th percentile	Narrow-band scores >98th percentile	Narrow-band scores > 98th percentile
Adversely affects educational performance	School scale < 2nd percentile	School scale < 2nd percentile	—
		Adaptive functioning < 13th percentile	

67

Destructive, and Aggressive scales of the CBCL and TRF profiles, and a deviant score on the Thought Disorder scale of the YSR.

4. The persistence of poor learning and behavioral/emotional deviance from age 10 to age 15 added evidence that problems had existed for "a long period of time," in spite of special education interventions.

5. Scores in the clinical range for total problems and broad-band and narrow-band scales on all three empirically based measures indicated problems of "a marked degree."

6. Low scores on the CBCL School scale, TRF School Performance scale and adaptive functioning scales indicated that these behavioral/emotional problems "adversely affected educational performance," a conclusion further supported by extremely low achievement test scores. (See Achenbach & Edelbrock, 1987; Achenbach & McConaughy, 1987; McConaughy & Achenbach, in press, for further details on relations between SED criteria and the CBCL system.)

REFLECTIONS AND IMPLICATIONS

While federal and state special education laws define specific learning disabilities and serious emotional disturbance as separate categories, the overlap between learning and behavioral/emotional problems makes such absolute distinctions difficult. Richard's case is an excellent example of how learning and behavioral/emotional problems often occur together. Though Richard exhibited behavioral deviance on the empirically based measures when he was first evaluated at age 10, it was not until age 15 that he was considered eligible for special education services as a seriously emotionally disturbed student. This cautious approach was probably appropriate, since research has shown that learning disabled children often exhibit behavioral/emotional problems, although not usually as severe as those of emotionally disturbed children.

Three recent studies have used the CBCL and TRF to assess behavioral/emotional problems of 6- to 11-year-old learning-disabled (LD) and seriously emotionally disturbed (SED) boys (Harris, King, Reifler, & Rosenberg, 1984; Mattison, Humphrey, & Kales, 1986; McConaughy & Ritter, 1986). McConaughy and Achenbach (in press) compared these studies for similarities and differences between LD and SED children. The combined results showed that both LD and SED boys had scores well above the normative samples on all of the CBCL and TRF scales. CBCL and TRF total problem scores were above the clinical cutoffs for both groups. Other research has also shown that deviant behavioral/emotional problems characterize 12- to 16-year-old LD and SED boys as well as younger boys (Mattison, Forness, Hotchkiss, Russell, & Sinclair, 1986; McConaughy, 1986).

The limited research to date suggests that the main feature distinguishing SED from LD boys is greater severity of problems. The 6- to 11-year-old SED boys in the studies cited previously showed significantly higher total problem, Internalizing, and Externalizing scores than the LD boys on both parent and teacher ratings. On the syndrome scales, SED boys showed more severe problems than LD boys in several areas, but LD boys also showed more problems than the normative samples. Parents rated SED boys higher than LD boys on scales measuring anxiety, uncommunicativeness, somatic complaints, social withdrawal, hyperactivity, aggression, and delinquency. Parents of LD and SED boys reported equally high levels of hyperactivity but lower levels of depression on the CBCL. Teachers rated SED boys significantly higher on social withdrawal, inattention, and nervous–overactivity, but unlike parents, teachers rated both LD and SED boys equally high on aggression. The finding that both parents and teachers rated SED boys higher than LD boys on social withdrawal suggests that this may be an additional distinguishing feature across home and school environments.

The presence of behavioral/emotional deviance in both LD and SED groups warrants a caveat to practitioners about using cutoff scores on behavioral rating scales as the sole criterion for serious emotional disturbance. As with all eligibility decisions, the final determination of whether a child meets LD or SED criteria for special education services requires integration of information across multiple assessment axes. Within this context, the empirically based measures provide objective, standardized information on the nature and severity of a child's behavior and emotions, which can then serve as a framework for evaluating other information on cognitive, academic, and social functioning. Such a multiaxial assessment should, in turn, lead to more comprehensive Individual Education Plans and therapeutic interventions addressing both learning and behavioral/emotional needs for children with school problems.

REFERENCES

Achenbach, T. M. (1985). *Assessment and taxonomy of child and adolescent psychopathology.* Newbury Park, CA: Sage.

Achenbach, T. M., & Edelbrock, C. (1983). *Manual for the Child Behavior Checklist and Revised Child Behavior Profile.* Burlington, VT: University of Vermont Department of Psychiatry.

Achenbach, T. M., & Edelbrock, C. (1986). *Manual for the Teacher's Report Form and Teacher Version of the Child Behavior Profile.* Burlington, VT: University of Vermont Department of Psychiatry.

Achenbach, T. M., & Edelbrock, C. (1987). *Manual for the Youth Self-Report and Profile.* Burlington, VT: University of Vermont Department of Psychiatry.

Achenbach, T. M., & McConaughy, S. H. (1987). *Empirically based assessment of child and adolescent psychopathology: Practical applications.* Newbury Park, CA: Sage.

Achenbach, T. M., McConaughy, S. H., & Howell, C. T. (1987). Child/adolescent behavioral and emotional problems: Implications of cross-informant correlations for situational specificity. *Psychological Bulletin, 101*, 213-232.

American Psychiatric Association. (1980). *Diagnostic and statistical manual of mental disorders* (3rd ed.). Washington, DC: Author.

American Psychiatric Association. (1987). *Diagnostic and statistical manual of mental disorders* (3rd ed., revised). Washington, DC: Author.

Brown, V. L., Hammill, D. D., & Wiederhot, J. L. (1978). *The Test of Reading Comprehension*. Austin, TX: PRO-ED.

Dunn, L. M., & Markwardt, F. C. (1970). *Peabody Individual Achievement Test*. Circle Pines, MN: American Guidance Service, Inc.

Edelbrock, C., & Achenbach, T. M. (1980). A typology of child behavior profile patterns: Distribution and correlates for disturbed children aged 6-16. *Journal of Abnormal Child Psychology, 8*, 441-470.

Education of the Handicapped Act. (1977). *Federal Register, 42*, 42478, 65083.

Education of the Handicapped Act. (1981). *Federal Register, 46*, 3866.

Goyette, C. H., Conners, C. K., & Ulrich, R. F. (1978). Normative data on revised Conners Parent and Teacher Rating Scales. *Journal of Abnormal Child Psychology, 6*, 221-236.

Hammill, D. D., & Larsen, S. C. (1983). *The Test of Written Language*. Austin, TX: PRO-ED.

Harris, J. C., King, S. L., Reifler, J. P., & Rosenberg, L. A. (1984). Emotional and learning disorders in 6-12-year-old boys attending special schools. *Journal of the American Academy of Child Psychiatry, 23*, 431-437.

Koppitz, E. M. (1975). *The Bender Gestalt Test for young children* (Vol. 2). New York: Grune & Stratton.

McCarthy, D. (1972). *McCarthy Scales of Children's Abilities*. New York: Psychological Corporation.

McConaughy, S. H. (1986). Social competence and behavioral problems of learning disabled boys aged 12-16. *Journal of Learning Disabilities, 19*, 101-106.

McConaughy, S. H., & Achenbach, T. M. (1988). *Practical guide to the Child Behavior Checklist and related instruments*. Burlington, VT: University of Vermont Department of Psychiatry.

McConaughy, S. H., & Achenbach, T. M. (in press). Contributions of developmental psychopathology to school services. In T. Gutkin & C. Reynolds (Eds.), *The handbook of school psychology*. New York: Wiley.

McConaughy, S. H., & Ritter, D. (1986). Social competence and behavioral problems of learning disabled boys aged 6-11. *Journal of Learning Disabilities, 19*, 39-45.

Mattison, R. E., Forness, S. R., Hotchkiss, R., Russell, A., & Sinclair, E. (1986). *Educational placement of children and adolescents with psychiatric disorders*. Paper presented at the meeting of the American Academy of Child and Adolescent Psychiatry, Los Angeles, CA.

Mattison, R. E., Humphrey, F. J., & Kales, S. N. (1986). An objective evaluation of special class placement of elementary schoolboys with behavior problems. *Journal of Abnormal Child Psychology, 14*, 251-262.

Slenkovich, J. E. (1983). *PL 94-142 as applied to DSM-III diagnoses*. Cupertino, CA: Kinghorn.

Wechsler, D. (1974). *Wechsler Intelligence Scale for Children—Revised*. New York: Psychological Corporation.

Wechsler, D. (1981). *Wechsler Adult Intelligence Scale—Revised*. New York: Psychological Corporation.

4

Separation Anxiety Disorder and School Phobia

TREVOR F. STOKES
STEPHEN R. BOGGS
PAMELA G. OSNES

Childhood fears are common difficulties that confront families during a child's development. Developmental studies suggest that there is some consistency across children in the stimulus events which most commonly elicit behaviors labeled as "fearful" at various ages. For example, Miller (1983) noted that the most common sources of fear for children under 6 months of age are excessive or unexpected sensory stimuli, loss of support, and loud noises; whereas children from ages 1 to 2 years frequently exhibit fear responses to separation from parents, physical injury, and toilets. Most fears occurring in childhood usually diminish without requiring treatment, but some become so problematic that professional assistance is required (Johnson, Rasbury, & Siegel, 1986).

DIAGNOSIS OF SEPARATION ANXIETY DISORDER AND SCHOOL PHOBIA

One of the most prevalent fear-related problems of childhood which may require professional intervention is Separation Anxiety Disorder of Childhood (Anderson, Williams, McGee, & Silva, 1987). This disorder is described as one in which the predominant disturbance is excessive anxiety developing whenever the child is separated from parents or familiar surroundings (American Psychiatric Association [APA], 1987).

Trevor E. Stokes and Pamela G. Osnes. Florida Mental Health Institute, University of South Florida, Tampa, Florida.

Stephen R. Boggs. Department of Clinical and Health Psychology, University of Florida, Gainesville, Florida.

Historically, children who experienced extreme states of anxiety and panic when separated from a parent were often labeled "school phobic" due to the frequent occurrence of problematic behaviors when these children were left in the school setting. This term was first used by Johnson, Falstein, Szurek, and Svendsen (1941) to distinguish these children from those who avoided school to participate in other activities or because of dislike of the learning environment ("truants").

"School phobia" remained the most commonly used term in the psychological literature to describe children experiencing separation difficulties until the 1980 publication of the third edition of the *Diagnostic and Statistical Manual of Mental Disorders* (DSM-III, APA, 1980). This classification system recognized the pervasive nature of the separation problems of these children and included the diagnostic category "Separation Anxiety Disorder of Childhood." DSM-III-R lists nine criteria, three of which must be satisfied, for diagnosis of the disorder. The criteria describe a broader disorder than the one implied by the term "school phobia." They suggest that separation from parents is the event eliciting fear responses rather than some aspect of the school situation.

Gardner (1985) described the clinical presentation of separation anxiety disorder in detail. He stated that the majority of these children demonstrate a persistent refusal to go to school and argued that the older term, "school phobia," may still be relevant as the child and parents will often focus on the school environment as the source of their distress. Gardner points out that frequently the child is abnormally dependent upon the mother. These children may also refuse to play outside, attend parties, or engage in any other activities away from the home (Walen, Hauserman, & Lavin, 1977).

PREVALENCE OF SEPARATION ANXIETY DISORDER AND SCHOOL PHOBIA

In a survey of children selected from the general population in Dunedin, New Zealand, Anderson et al. (1987) found that 3.5% of the 792 children studied presented as separation anxiety disorder. It was the third most prevalent disorder, following attention deficit disorder and oppositional disorder. Earlier research on school phobia reported incidence data ranging from 2 to 17 per 1,000 school children per year (Kahn & Nurstein, 1962; Kennedy, 1965). Trueman (1984b), however, suggested that past studies of the incidence of school phobia may have been methodologically inadequate and advised caution in the use of these estimates. Smith (1970) studied a group of school-phobic children in London and found that the peak incidence occurred between the ages of 11 and 12 years, with a smaller peak between 5 and 6 years of age. Walen et al. (1977) indicated that although intelligence, gender, and socioeconomic status did not appear to be correlated with school phobia the disorder seemed to be more prevalent among youngest siblings and only children.

Separation anxiety disorder presents a significant problem for service providers of children and their families. For example, Schmitt (1971) describes anxiety over separation from parents as "the great imitator." It has been observed that many pediatricians and other specialists complete diagnostic medical workups of children who complain of such physical symptoms as abdominal and chest pain, sore throats, headaches, and insomnia only to find that no physical cause for these symptoms exists. Instead, the child's complaints result from an anticipated or actual separation from the parents at school.

ETIOLOGY OF SEPARATION ANXIETY DISORDER AND SCHOOL PHOBIA

Separation anxiety disorder and school phobia can be conceptualized as the result of maladaptive, learned behavior. The central process involved is the child's avoidance of particular situations. In school phobia, specific aspects of the school environment can sometimes be identified as the feared stimuli, e.g., interactions with peers or teachers. In the more global separation anxiety disorder, the feared situations are well generalized and the child actively seeks the presence of the parents. When confronted with events which elicit fear and anxiety, such as separation from a parent, these children behave in ways that encourage, almost force, the parent's return. For example, crying, clinging, and tantrumming may lead to a parental response of comforting attention. Each time these child behaviors are successful, the operations of positive and negative reinforcement may come into action (Stokes, 1985). In negative reinforcement, the frequency of maladaptive child behavior increases as a function of the termination of the event that precipitates the escape, such as absence of the parent. Positive reinforcement operates when the frequency of the behavior increases as a function of the added consequences, such as the parental affection and statements of concern. In combination, these are a powerful set of circumstances which with repetition serve to strengthen and maintain seriously maladaptive behaviors.

TREATMENT OF SEPARATION ANXIETY DISORDER AND SCHOOL PHOBIA

Treatment reports involving children diagnosed as displaying separation anxiety disorder or school phobia have described traditional psychoanalytic, medical, and behavioral management of these problem behaviors. Psychoanalytic approaches stress uncovering the unconscious dynamics underlying the neurotic symptoms of anxiety and require lengthy therapy. For example, Gardner (1985) advocates use of such traditional strategies during ongoing individual and family therapy, but also recommends forcing an immediate return to school while ignoring the child's protests. Empirical support for the effectiveness of purely psychodynamic approaches is lacking.

Gittelman-Klein and Klein (1971) described the successful use of imipramine, a tricyclic antidepressant, in the medical management of school phobia. They found that children given relatively large doses of this medication returned to school more readily than those given a placebo. However, in their review of the few studies available regarding the use of antidepressant and anxiolytic medications for the treatment of separation anxiety and school phobia, Simeon and Ferguson (1985) concluded that further research was necessary to support the use of these drugs, particularly given the possibility of undesirable side effects.

In comprehensive reviews of the literature about school phobia, most authors suggest that behavioral treatment approaches have provided the most effective strategies for dealing with this complex problem (Atkeson & Forehand, 1978; Gordon & Young, 1976; Johnson, 1979; Trueman, 1984a; Walen et al., 1977). Walen et al. (1977) conclude that the prognosis for behavioral treatment of school phobia is good, even if the child has been experiencing problems over an extended period of time.

Behavioral studies of school phobia may recommend either a prompt, complete return to the normal school environment or a more gradual, desensitization approach. For example, Kennedy (1965) treated 50 school-phobic children with no previous history of this problem. The program involved an immediate return of the child to the classroom setting. Parents were instructed to ignore all inappropriate behavior and school personnel were recruited to retain the child in the classroom. Parents were also encouraged to reward the child for attending school without tantrumming. In addition, the child was not allowed to engage in pleasurable home-based activities if school was successfully avoided. Kennedy reported 100% success using this technique, with treatment gains maintained at a 2-year follow-up.

Other brief interventions using similar strategies have also been reported. Hersen (1968) instructed a mother to rearrange environmental contingencies which were maintaining the school refusal of her 12-year-old son and then implement reinforcement programs for school attendance. Success was achieved after only 10 sessions. A similar case study was reported by Hersen (1970) with treatment consisting of training the mother of another 12-year-old boy to reinforce appropriate behavior and to ignore crying and begging while also involving the child in individual sessions designed to reinforce school attendance. This program was successful after 15 weeks of treatment. Numerous other studies provide additional examples of rapid treatment gains with the school-phobic child after the child is firmly assisted in returning to school and carefully designed differential reinforcement programs are implemented (e.g., Edlund, 1971; Gresham & Nagel, 1981; Rodriquez, Rodriquez, & Eisenberg, 1959).

In her review of the school phobia literature, Johnson (1979) commented that the brief treatment approaches, such as those described previously, appeared to be most effective with the young, acute onset school phobic. Walen et al. (1977) also found that treatment studies involving children who appeared to have more generalized separation problems took a more gradual approach in alleviating the children's fears. Perhaps such studies, although still focused mainly on school attendance problems, included children who would more broadly fit the revised third edition of the *Diagnostic and Statistical Manual of Mental Disorders* (DSM-III-R) diagnosis of separation anxiety disorder.

One study that described a gradual desensitization to separation was reported by Montenegro (1968). Montenegro treated two children aged 6 years and 2½ years who refused to separate from their mothers in any setting by using a reciprocal inhibition technique. He instructed the mothers to withhold breakfast from the children, but to bring favorite foods to the individual therapy sessions. By having the children eat their preferred snacks during increasingly longer times of separation in the treatment room, he was able to decrease fear responses and reported a generalized effect to other settings as well (e.g., babysitter's home and preschool). Montenegro commented that the feeding responses counteracted the physiological anxiety state in the children, allowing gradual extinction of the fears.

More traditional approaches to systematic desensitization of school phobia involve the construction of hierarchies of increasingly more anxiety-producing situations, and pairing presentation of these situations with responses incompatible with fear. Miller (1972) presented an example of this treatment strategy that involved pairing deep muscle relaxation with imagined school-approach scenes from a hierarchy developed prior to treatment. In addition, Miller implemented an in vivo desensitization strategy subsequent to this treatment in which a 10-year-old boy approached the school in gradual steps along a similar hierarchy. This treatment program was successful in returning the child to school after 5 weeks. Follow-up at 18 months indicated no further school attendance difficulties. Other researchers reported success with similar desensitization techniques used to treat school phobia (e.g., Chapel, 1967; Croghan, 1981; Garvey & Hegrenes, 1966), and it seems reasonable to expect that such methods will prove useful with separation anxiety disorder as well.

In the case presented in this chapter, a child diagnosed as experiencing separation anxiety disorder of childhood was briefly treated with medication, with partial success, prior to referral for psychological treatment. The child was attending school, but only with the mother present and readily available for contact. One study in the literature presented a similar situation. Neisworth, Madle, and Goeke (1975) treated a preschool child who exhibited extreme anxiety (screaming, crying, social withdrawal) when left at school by her mother. A plan was implemented in which the mother would attend school with the child, but leave for gradually increasing periods of time. The child was rewarded each time she met the goal established for the separation trial. Since this shaping procedure began with very short periods of time which were acceptable to the child (seconds), few fearful behaviors were ever emitted during the course of treatment.

CASE EXAMPLE

Barry, a 10-year-old male, attended the fifth grade in a rural school 40 miles from the university hospital where he received treatment. He was the second of two children, and lived on a small farm with his parents and his brother, Wayne, a 19-year-old college student. His father, Jack, age 41 years, had been a miner for 14 years. He had been unemployed for 4 months prior to Barry's treatment. Barry's 38-year-old mother Pat did not work outside the home. Unemployment compensation and farming provided the family's income.

Barry was first seen by a child psychiatrist at the emergency room of the hospital 1 month prior to his referral to us for psychological treatment. He had been seen briefly at a community mental health center before his contact at the emergency room. His parents, however, had been dissatisfied with the services provided there and sought further assistance. At the hospital, Barry initially received outpatient treatment from a child psychiatrist, while concurrent psychological testing was conducted. After 4 weeks, the psychiatrist referred Barry to a hospital child psychologist (T. S.) because he felt that specific assessment and clinical programming in behavior management techniques might be advantageous. The psychological treatment as described in this chapter was conducted and conceptualized by us, with Trevor Stokes taking the major responsibility. All references to the psychologist in this chapter, therefore, are to "he" or "I."

Intake Evaluation

Barry was taken to the emergency room after he displayed uncontrolled shaking at school. His parents said that Barry cried excessively and resisted going to school. They were concerned about Barry being happy at school and overcoming his problems. Additionally, Barry exhibited eating problems, weight loss, sleep disturbances, and nail-biting. Barry's teacher had told his parents that he shook so badly "his legs would go 50 miles an hour." Discussion with the parents showed that the mother's pregnancy and Barry's development had been normal.

During his psychiatric interview, Barry was cooperative and friendly, showing no evidence of affective problems or thought disorder. He accepted separation from his mother to enter the psychiatrist's office. Barry reported that the beginnings of school years had been the only times when he had any difficulty going to school. He described that he had been "okay" until the third grade when he had cried some and in the fourth grade he had cried for the first week. Now in the fifth grade, he had no problems until the last day of the first week. Barry reported that when he felt like crying at school, he would respond by thinking that he would be back home soon and everything would be all right. He could not describe any specific classroom events that made him feel like crying. His goal was to become a veterinarian someday.

The diagnosis given by the psychiatrist was "Separation Anxiety Disorder (309.21) as manifested by excessive anxiety concerning separation, specifically from his mother with unrealistic worry and reluctance or refusal to go to school." No specific physical disorder had been detected during recent physical examinations. The severity of psychosocial stressors was probably mild and the highest level of adaptive functioning during the past year had been good, according to DSM-III-R guidelines.

Barry met the following DSM-III-R criteria for Separation Anxiety Disorder of Childhood:

> (1) unrealistic persistent worry about possible harm befalling major attachment figures or fear that they will leave and not return; (2) unrealistic and persistent worry that an untoward calamitous event will separate the child from a major attachment figure, e.g., the child will be lost, kidnapped, killed, or be the victim of an accident; (3) persistent reluctance or refusal to go to school in order to stay with major attachment figures or at home; (5) persistent avoidance of being alone, including "clinging" to and "shadowing" major attachment figures; (7) complaints of physical symptoms, e.g., headaches, stomachaches, nausea, or vomiting, on many school days or on occasions when anticipating separation from major attachment figures; and (8) recurrent signs of complaints of excessive distress when separated from home or major attachment figures, e.g., wants to return home, needs to call parents when they are absent or when child is away from home. (APA; 1987, p. 61)

Summary of Psychological Testing

Psychological testing occurred a week after the emergency room visit. Barry started the testing in a cooperative manner. Midway through the testing, he began to cry and refused to participate further. He turned sideways in his chair, then left the room and stood in the hallway. Testing resumed when he returned with his mother who stayed with him throughout the remainder of the appointment.

The Wechsler Intelligence Scale for Children—Revised (WISC-R) revealed a verbal IQ below average and a performance IQ above average. According to an administration of the Peabody Individual Achievement Test, Barry's basic school skills were about mid-third-grade level. Performance on Connors Parent and Teacher Rating Scales, when completed by his parents and his teacher, showed no evidence of attention deficit disorder. The evaluator commented that Barry seemed manipulative and likely would respond to stress through avoidance or inappropriate behavior.

Initial Psychiatric Treatment

In the emergency room, a regimen of Benadryl, 25 mg taken once or twice per day as needed with one to two additional capsules at bedtime, was prescribed by the child psychiatrist. At the first psychiatric appointment, it was reported that Barry was calmer but he still refused ïo allow his mother to leave him at school. Some mild gastrointestinal discomfort was reported, so the medication was changed to imipramine hydrochloride (Tofranil), 10 mg three times daily (t.i.d.). Progress was reported at the next visit, but Barry continued to attempt to manipulate his parents by crying. For example, he had prevented his parents from attending a football game by crying when they tried to leave.

Treatment focused on relaxation with visual imagery, using the parents to provide relaxation instructions to Barry, practicing responding appropriately to criticism by parents, and teaching Barry that parental criticism was independent of their feelings for him. By the third appointment, Barry was attending school, but was experiencing more severe shaking at home. He tantrummed if even minor events did not go smoothly, for example, if he was unable to find his socks. Tofranil was increased to 25 mg t.i.d. (which was less than 2.5 mg of medication per kg of weight).

It was reported on the subsequent visit that he was going to school regularly if taken by a parent, but he refused to ride the bus. Shaking had decreased considerably. At his next visit, it was reported that Barry still resisted his parents' attempts to leave him at school or home. Barry said that he was afraid if his parents left him they might not come back. Tofranil was reduced to 25 mg twice daily (b.i.d.). In the week prior to the sixth appointment, Barry's mother occasionally left the school for brief time periods (i.e., 15 minutes). School grades were variable and remained above failing. At the sixth appointment, Tofranil was increased to 25 mg t.i.d., and concurrent treatment with the psychologist began. At subsequent appointment days, Barry and his family were seen by the psychiatrist for a brief review of progress and a medication check and then by the psychologist for ongoing psychological treatment. From this point, psychiatric treatment consisted only of medication checks. The parents arranged for appointments to be at intervals of 2 weeks because the family had to travel a long distance to the hospital.

Child Psychology Assessment

Three assessment appointments were scheduled. After discussing the general problems with Barry and his family, each family member was interviewed separately.

Appointment 1. Barry refused to separate from his parents so he waited outside the clinic with his father during his mother's interview. Pat (his mother) cited the following as Barry's problems: crying, nervousness, lack of expression of feelings, stubbornness, noncompliance, and arguing. Pat reported previous management strategies to include spanking; pleading with him; sending him to his room; removal of television privileges; promising rewards for engaging in desired activities; ignoring his inappropriate behaviors; praising; and giving physical affection. At times, she had reacted angrily to Barry's inappropriate behaviors by harshly telling him to stop behaving in that manner. None of the management strategies seemed to have worked well for her, so she had discontinued their use or had used them intermittently.

The parents were asked to keep Antecedent–Behavior–Consequence (ABC) records to bring to the next appointment. This involved keeping notes on the occurrence of appropriate and inappropriate behaviors, as well as the events prior to and following those behaviors (Stokes, 1985; Stokes & Osnes, 1985).

Appointment 2. After some general discussion about the events of the past 2 weeks with the family together, Jack (the father) was interviewed alone. He cited Barry's problems at school as his primary concern. They included crying during the first weeks of school which had occurred for the previous 4 years, refusing to ride the school bus, refusing to eat lunch on school days, complaining about school, shaking of the legs, and decreased academic progress. He recalled that other classroom problems, including noncompliance and avoidance of the classroom, had begun when the teacher had placed Barry in the hallway after noncompliance. Following this, whenever Barry became upset, his teacher allowed him to leave the room to sit in the hallway so he could calm down. Barry's mother was present in that hallway, so she would try to help calm him. Peer relationships at school were good, however. At home, Jack reported crying and pouting to be the primary problems. These were especially prevalent at times when Barry was not given what he wanted. Because Barry's crying made Jack feel anxious, he attempted to calm him by talking to him.

The ABC records, which the parents had been keeping for the previous 2 weeks, were reviewed. They were thorough and complete, leading me to conclude that the parents would likely be cooperative in other aspects of Barry's programming. The records regarding school performance reported that sometimes Barry left class to show papers to his mother and said he did not want to return. When this happened, he returned to the classroom after talking briefly with his mother. The parents' record-keeping continued to be excellent throughout treatment.

Appointment 3.   Barry's parents reported that he had made progress since the last appointment, remaining separated from them for as long as 40 minutes at school and 30 minutes at home. On one day when Pat returned after a 30-minute absence, Barry was crying. Pat's reaction was to give him a hug, after which he returned to the classroom.

Barry consented to leave the clinic to go for a walk around the hospital with me, something he had previously refused to do. This allowed me to make an assessment of Barry's behavior while separated from his parents. It also allowed me to interview Barry. Although he had expressed concern that he might get lost, Barry consented to sit in the cafeteria and have a soft drink for 20 minutes before returning to the clinic. Barry was friendly, had good eye contact with me, spoke frequently, and smiled often during the interview. He talked about his likes and dislikes, his daily schedule, friends at school, and his teachers. He reported liking to play soccer, to eat beans and macaroni, and one teacher in particular who he felt explained things clearly to him. However, he felt another teacher was unhelpful when he had problems and made him "figure things out for himself."

During the psychiatric appointment, the Tofranil was reduced to 25 mg in the morning and 10 mg in the evening.

Assessment Summary and Treatment Plan

I concluded that Barry's problems focused primarily on the parents' management strategies instead of being confined to the school setting alone. Many of the consequences the parents reported using seemed generous and disproportional given the behaviors performed. For example, Barry had been promised a pellet gun on one occasion to prompt him to return to class. He received the gun that evening, and was given unlimited access to it afterwards. On another occasion, Barry was promised a colt if he would allow his mother to go home from school. After receiving it, he separated from his mother at school for a few days before separation became problematic again. There was evidence of a history of inconsistent, ineffective management by the parents. As a result, Barry's inappropriate behavior at times of separation was extreme and persistent. The consequence was that Pat stayed at school most of each day to remain accessible to Barry. Initially, she sat at the back of his classroom, but had begun sitting in the hallway or assisting in the nearby school office until Barry experienced difficulty. This availability provided positive consequences for Barry's avoidance of the classroom and his manipulative behaviors. Both positive and negative reinforcement contingencies possibly were in operation at school and home, maintaining the behavior of Barry and his parents (Stokes, 1985). The majority of Barry's inappropriate behaviors seemed to result from misapplied consequences and maladaptive interactions within the family. Therefore, I considered the clients to be both parents as well as Barry. Separation from the parents at home and school required treatment. Changes in the parents' interactions with Barry were targeted, so that his positive behavior would be reinforced and his manipulative behavior would decrease. In both settings, treatment involved the parents' use of attention, affection, and inexpensive rewards that the assessment indicated were likely to function as positive reinforcers for Barry's appropriate behavior. Barry's active participation in his own treatment was incorporated by the use of self-recording, goal-setting, and negotiation procedures.

Psychological Treatment

Barry and his parents attended twelve treatment appointments, with more concentrated changes programmed early and fading out of my active participation coming later in the series of appointments. Progress is summarized next.

Appointment 1. The parental report indicated some increased separation time over the prior 2 weeks. With Barry and his parents present, I gave Barry stickers and positive attention for his improvement. Because Barry had done well, he received my attention and time at the beginning of the appointment. If he had not done well, the parents would have received the major part of my attention. Such a practice was employed because Barry seemed to enjoy my attention. If he had shown appropriate treatment progress, he was told, "You have done well, I want to spend extra time with you today." If the assessment had been that Barry had preferred to avoid me, however, avoidance of, or escape from, me would have been allowed only if Barry had done well in the previous week and during the time with me in the clinic. Barry accompanied me on a walk around the hospital, ending at the cafeteria. There, Barry agreed to return to the clinic unaccompanied. Although he had expressed concern that he might get lost, he found his way back. I did not respond to his expressions of fear so that there would be no social attention to such comments. Additional attention would have been provided had he tried to do well on his own.

Appointment 2. The records showed Barry had spent as much as 2 hours per day away from his parents during the preceding 2 weeks. Time with the parents centered on practicing giving positive attention when Barry was doing well and decreasing the amount of corrective attention, which primarily consisted of telling him what he had done poorly.

Because he had done so well, I spent 30 minutes alone with Barry. We discussed how successful Barry had been during the previous week and engaged in friendly conversation about activities at home and school, his parents, and his brother. This time was also used to assess Barry's reaction to various playful physical consequences, for example, a handshake, tickling, and arm wrestling. These activities served multiple functions. It was important to continue to assess what interactional consequences Barry reacted to in a positive manner. These consequences became prime candidates for use as potential positive reinforcers which could be incorporated into the treatment program. I was also trying to provide a positive history of experiences for Barry during his interactions with me. This would facilitate my becoming a source of social reinforcement. These interactions also allowed continuing assessment of Barry's behavior away from his parents and during situations that might provide some frustration for him, e.g., not winning in arm wrestling.

A self-recording program was set up. The initial agreement between Barry and me was as follows:

> Barry has agreed to keep notes for Dr. Stokes. Every day, he will record how much time mom spends away from school each day and how much time Barry spends away from mom and dad at home each day. If Barry does this, Dr. Stokes will be very nice to him.

| _____ | _____ | _____ |
| Barry | Trevor | Date |

Variations of this simple agreement were made with each addition or revision of Barry's program. They were always written in my notebook, which we reviewed together.

Appointment 3. It was reported that Barry played well with relatives and visitors over the Christmas holidays. He also spent time with his older brother away from his parents. He went back to school after the holidays without serious behavior problems such as crying and excessive shaking. After discussion with the parents, it was agreed that they would provide stickers and attention for "good" behaviors that were not specified to Barry in advance. This provided an opportunity for the parents to give unpredicted positive consequences to Barry. They were also told to pair social approval with all such consequences because that would enhance the potency of their social attention. The parents kept records of the giving of these consequences and the behaviors they followed. Barry's compliance with instructions had improved.

Barry's self-recording was excellent. His records were informally compared with the parental reports and with information provided by the school teacher during telephone contact. This allowed me to assess the reliability of Barry's reporting, which was acceptable. In this session, goal-setting was discussed and Barry set school and home goals for the next 2 weeks: 40 minutes away from school for his mother and 60 minutes away from parents at home. After discussion it was also decided that if Barry met his school target 8 of the 10 days and his home targets 10 of the 14 days he would get a special treat at the next appointment. The treat was unspecified in order to increase the possible novelty effect. On the record sheets, Barry started to note when he met his goals for the day by placing a checkmark next to the times the goal was met. I talked to Barry about his activities over the holidays, such as riding his new motorcycle. A few things I had done over the break were also mentioned by me as a social consequence for Barry's progress. We also engaged in some art work, drawing portraits of one another in my notebook. Another function this served was to let Barry see that what was in the notes was available to him to look at.

Appointment 4. Barry continued excellent self-recording. Home goals were met on 11 of 15 days. Paradoxically, the parents now were concerned that Barry might start to spend too much time away from them at home. They were reassured that the goal was for Barry to spend only a reasonable amount of time away. After discussion, a limit on the home goal of 2 hours per day was set.

In contrast with his encouraging home performance, Barry failed to meet his school goal on any day. After discussion, Barry increased his home goal to 65 minutes per day and left the school goal at 40 minutes. Barry left the clinic with me for 30 minutes to go to the cafeteria. This allowed a comparison between Barry's separation from his parents at the clinic and their reports of his separations at home.

Differential attention was discussed with the parents and role playing used examples of interactions which had been observed previously in the clinic. I routinely noted interaction examples that occurred in the clinic that I used later as relevant examples for treatment. For example, the subtlety of Barry's noncompliance was discussed, including his delays in answering his parents' questions, which led to entrapment of his parents' attention. Reported home interactions were also discussed. Occasions when his parents responded to his complaining and crying with positive consequences, for example, increased interactions and hugs were highlighted.

In the session with the parents, they agreed to take daily 30-minute samples of the distribution of their attention. In the evening, they would track each time they attended to Barry, i.e., talked to, instructed, reprimanded, etc. They would then note whether that attention followed appropriate or inappropriate behavior. This attention was recorded on a piece of paper divided into a positive and a negative side (attention following appropriate and inappropriate behavior, respectively).

Appointment 5. Barry spent between 65 minutes and 3 hours away from his parents at home every day. Progress at school was slower. More time was spent considering parental use of differential attention, i.e., attending positively to appropriate behavior and limiting attention to inappropriate, manipulative behavior.

The fact that Pat always waited for Barry to tell her if it was "okay" to leave school was considered as another example of how Barry frequently attempted to control situations. It was decided that as progress had already been made at school it was time for Pat's presence to fade. Previously, she had always let Barry know when she was leaving. It was agreed among Barry, Pat, and myself, that Pat would leave unannounced twice per day and would talk to Barry only after she returned. In order to continue Barry's active involvement in his own treatment, he agreed to participate in the fading procedure by asking his mother twice daily to leave the school. Barry's understanding was that if he "did well," his parents would be "very nice" to him. By leaving the dimensions of "being nice" unspecified, the family was given the problem-solving task of defining the conditions under which Barry would earn positive consequences. I used these types of procedures to dissuade the family from becoming unduly dependent upon me for specific behavior management guidelines. The outcome of the family's assignment was reviewed by me at a later appointment.

The parents continued to keep records of the distribution of attention. At best, only 50% of their attention followed appropriate behavior. The role of attention as a potential reinforcer of Barry's inappropriate, as well as appropriate, behavior was described. That is, a reprimand may function as a reinforcer in the same way as praise and recognition. Therefore, parental attention needs to be used carefully. I used examples of interactions in the clinic to emphasize that attention seemed important to Barry. Also discussed were: the parents' reactions to Barry's tears and crying and to his expressions of concern about his mother's absence from school; their repeated attempts to get Barry to talk or answer questions; and the way their sympathetic feelings toward Barry's behavior problems sometimes resulted in their use of maladaptive management strategies. Specific guidelines for the parents were discussed, written down, and then practiced with me taking the role of Barry while Barry waited outside. At home, they were not to talk about Barry's problems. They were not to wait longer than 5 seconds when Barry failed to talk to them. They were not to talk to him for 30 seconds when he made rude remarks, pouted, or was noncompliant. Instead, they were to attend positively and enthusiastically when Barry behaved in ways that were incompatible with his presenting problems. When the mother was at school, similar guidelines were in effect. She was to talk with Barry only during recess and lunch breaks, and focus her attention on Barry's successful attempts at establishing independence from her.

The parents were now asked to note instances where Barry had displayed an inappropriate behavior that they ignored. Furthermore, during the day, each parent was asked to note that they attended positively to appropriate behavior at least 10 times. Both recordings required the parent to focus on their own successes in management.

At the appointment with the psychiatrist, medication was reduced to 10 mg in the morning and evening.

Appointment 6. Excellent progress was made over a period of 2 weeks. The parents reported giving considerable attention to Barry's positive behavior and infrequent attention to inappropriate behavior, as well as successfully refraining from falling into negative attention traps. The parents noticed appropriate changes. Barry met the goal of being away from his parents every day at school (40 minutes) and at home (65 minutes). The average was 85 minutes per day for school and 120 minutes per day for home. Pat was able to leave school unannounced for 20 or 30 minutes twice a day. On separate occasions, Barry told his mother to leave for 20 or 30 minutes twice a day. Among themselves, the family negotiated that Barry could extend his bedtime by an extra 30 minutes in the evening if he met his school goal for that day. I recommended that such a negotiation should occur following continuing progress at school so it would be an extra consequence for Barry's performance.

The parents expressed that they were very pleased with Barry's progress. Barry exhibited no problems when he left the clinic with me. After discussion, he increased his school goal to 50 minutes. Barry was not asked to change his home goal and it was not increased even though his separation times ranged from 65 to 180 minutes. He took considerable pleasure in the days he exceeded his goals. Consistently, his performance was better than his goals, so increasing the goals more quickly under my direction was not considered important. It was also agreed that if Barry met his goals again before the next appointment, other unspecified consequences could be discussed. In the meantime, Barry's parents told him that they would be "really nice to him if he did well."

Barry continued to see the psychiatrist briefly prior to each appointment with me. The psychiatrist and I remained informed about all aspects of Barry's treatment so that it was well coordinated. At this time, medication was discontinued. The psychiatrist remained available to consult with me or the family if needed.

Appointment 7. Barry showed a range of 60 to 180 minutes away from parents at home (mean of 140 minutes) with a goal of 65 minutes. Barry spent time alone in the car with his grandfather which was the first time in 6 months. He met his goal on 11 of the 13 days. With a 60-minute goal, a range of 65 to 120 minutes that Pat was away from school per day (mean of 85 minutes) was shown. He met his school goal every day. Barry continued to improve despite being in a motorcycle accident the previous week. He missed 2 school days but his physical condition was now satisfactory. He went to have x-rays by himself at the local hospital's emergency room following the accident. Barry was staying up an extra 30 minutes in the evening when he met his school goal. An additional positive consequence for meeting the school goal, a milkshake, was negotiated by Barry during discussion with his parents. I did not participate in this negotiation.

Barry went for a 20-minute walk with the psychologist without problem. He reported that he was doing fine away from his parents, then qualified the statement by saying, "At least I'm doing better." He enjoyed keeping the records and graphing them with me. He reported he had no problem being without the medication.

Pat and Jack continued to record their attention to appropriate behavior and maintained their quota of at least 10 instances daily of attention contingent on appropriate behavior. The parents agreed to keep notes on instances where they wanted to talk or argue with Barry following inappropriate behavior but did not, as well as similar situations when they did debate issues with Barry. This recording provided me with information about successful occurrences of the parents' appropriate management of their interactions as well as information regarding the areas or situations in which they were not being successful. The parents reported that they were much more relaxed about Barry and with themselves. Previously cited problems regarding eating, weight, and sleep were now not a concern.

The use of other kinds of consequences for managing Barry's behavior were considered. Ironically, access to outside play was a focus of discussion. In the beginning, Pat and Jack were interested in Barry going outside and spending time away from them. Now, he seemed to be spending too much time outside and not getting his homework done on time. A natural contingency recommended was that Barry complete his homework first and then go out to play (and work toward his goal of separating appropriately from parents).

Appointment 8. At school the average time Pat was away from school was 158 minutes, with a range of 140 to 240 minutes. At home, Barry was away from his parents an average of 142 minutes, with a range of 40 to 540 minutes. Barry also took the bus home from school one day for the first time in 6 months. As was planned, Pat's time away from the school was increased 30 minutes per day each afternoon until she was not present in the afternoon at all. Pat and Jack continued to keep records of their differential attention. They showed that they were not attending to inappropriate behavior and were still responding to the appropriate behavior of Barry.

Barry was now graphing his own records daily instead of doing it weekly with me. He received his milkshake and 30 minutes evening time consistently. He also received stickers from me and from his parents when he did well. These were usually given without any warning or prior contingency. Barry decided that Pat did not need to come into his class anymore to announce she was leaving or was back. She could just do it. A new school target was "negotiated": 180 minutes, which was a considerable increase over the previous target of 50. Although the increase was large, it was still well within Barry's demonstrated performance. Therefore, I did not try to keep it at a lower level. Barry reported that he was playing better with his friends, and peers were including him in their games more frequently. Time with me continued to be a mixture of task-oriented activity and relaxed talk and play, for example, eating an apple, arm wrestling, shooting paper wads (basketballs) into the clinic trash can.

Appointment 9. Barry's records showed he was spending 1 to 6 hours away from his parents each day, with an average of 3 hours per day. School performance was going equally well, with Pat spending at least 3 hours away every day, sometimes whole days. The grandparents were also reporting improvements such as an increased willingness to talk to them. Barry and his parents reported that Barry was getting along better with his peers at school, for example, the children were more accepting of him and no longer teased him. Barry said he was going to go to school on the school bus the next day, something he had not done for many months. He was going to ride with his friends. Barry was very pleased with his progress and success and made a notation to that effect ("I am very happy with how well I am doing") in my notebook and signed it.

Appointment 10. Barry rode the bus to school every day except 1 during the past 2 weeks. He stayed at school every day by himself. Including the bus trips, this totaled over 8 hours per day. His grades showed some improvement, with better grades in three subjects. Barry's self-recording continued to be excellent and his behavior had improved considerably. Therefore, contingent on his performance and dependent upon the maintenance of the improvements, Barry was released from the requirement of self-recording. The structure of the program was diminished while still requiring a verbal report that could be substantiated by the parents. It was essential that Barry did not become dependent on me. Thus it was important that I fade my role in the program as soon as was feasible.

The treatment had progressed well, except Barry was now calling home at least three times per day. This had been arranged between the school and the parents, but the parents now wanted to know how to fade the telephone calls. Barry would call to make sure they were home and find out what his parents were doing. In essence this transferred the parents' captivity from school to home. The parents were not home 2 or 3 hours each day and were concerned about what would happen if they were not at home if Barry called. As described subsequently, this problem was modified using goal-setting and contingent attention procedures.

Appointment 11. Barry continued to go to and from school on the bus and stay at school all day by himself. There were no teacher reports of inappropriate behavior. The parents said Barry was definitely doing better without medication. As I suggested, Pat and Jack had provided minimal attention to Barry's calls home, and they had been very positive about Barry's coping on the one day he had not called home. The parents also did not increase their time at home. Barry usually called home twice per day. There were no problems concerning separation from parents at home. Barry even stayed overnight at his grandmother's house, 75 miles away from home.

Barry went to the hospital cafeteria by himself and returned later with a soft drink without problem. In the meantime, Barry's oppositional behavior was discussed with the parents. He was being told three or four times to do things. He was occasionally arguing with his parents, and threatening that he would not go to school. He was still engaging some attention traps by not answering questions, for example, when asked a question, he would say to his father, "you tell," and Jack would say, "no, you tell me." This interaction would continue until Barry finally started talking. He would engage in negative conversation at dinner and sometimes turn in his chair to avoid facing his family. Minimizing attention to inappropriate behavior, not arguing with Barry, and not trying to entice Barry to do things were emphasized and role played with me. Furthermore, providing positive consequences when Barry did well was presented as the best strategy for handling these behaviors.

Barry continued to report he was pleased with his progress. He set a goal for calling home of one call per day. The goal was set without input from me. It was decided that it would be "good" if he called no more than twice, "very good" if he called only once, and "the very best" if he did not call at all.

Appointment 12. During the last 2 weeks, Barry always rode on the bus and stayed at school all day without his mother. He called home zero times on 7 days and one time on 3 days. This was a significant improvement over the previous visit. Barry was congratulated and spent most of the appointment with me talking about his successes and his daily life. Telephone calling goals were not changed.

Follow-Up Maintenance Program

There were three maintenance appointments over a period of 2 months as the school year came to an end. In the parents' sessions, there was continuing emphasis on the controlling effects of their attention in avoidance and positive situations. The parents reported that they were spending more time together, which they enjoyed. Barry continued to do very well, riding to and from school in the bus, staying at school without calling home, and spending time away from parents at home. He would now stay in the house with anyone, but would not stay in the house by himself. After general discussion of the problems, I asked, "What do you think would be a good management strategy here?" They suggested that Barry be left by himself for short times and the time be increased, both announced and unannounced. In addition, the parents said they should be sure to praise Barry and attend positively to him when he was doing well. I agreed with their plan and encouraged the parents to continue working with Barry by applying similar principles and procedures with these as well as other behavior problems that Barry might exhibit now and in the future.

I was moving to a new position in another state. Therefore, I told the parents not to hesitate to contact the psychiatrist if further problems arose. In addition, I met with the psychiatrist to inform him of the progress of treatment. I also set up a follow-up program with Barry. This involved Barry's keeping some notes on his progress at home and school in the next year, for example, activities at school, whether there were calls home, whether mom went to school, and how everything was going at home. After receiving these notes in the mail, I wrote back to the family.

At the beginning of the next school year, there was some continuation of the problems Barry had displayed the previous year but his parents never stayed at school with him. He began calling home about once a day. The frequency decreased across the school year. Barry had no problems separating from his parents at home. The parents reported that he was able to leave them in public places, which was progress that they enjoyed, they could go to the games room at a shopping mall for an hour. Manipulative behavior continued, although not with the extreme outcome seen the previous year. Barry complained that some of his teachers were not being nice to him. The parents went to a conference in a city 150 miles from home. The previous year Barry would not allow his parents out of sight: He successfully manipulated them by crying continuously until they agreed not to leave. In contrast, Barry was hardly seen by his parents at this year's conference. He spent most of his time with friends.

About halfway through the school year, I wrote to the parents to emphasize that they continue the management procedures and to attend particularly to interactions with Barry. For example, I suggested that if Barry whined or cried, his parents should not talk to him for 5 minutes. If Barry chatted nicely to his parents, however, they should make a special effort to talk to him and be friendly. I also suggested that any day Barry did well at school and did not call home, the parents should tell him how proud of him they were and provide a special treat such as a milkshake. If Barry did not have a good day, his parents should not talk to him about it because he had not been acting "like a big person." The parents should also refrain from criticizing Barry on days when things had not gone well. If Barry studied hard and showed his parents what he had learned, they should show great interest in what he is doing and talk about it. Whenever Barry showed improvement in grades or maintained a good grade his parents should let him know how proud they were and take him out for a special treat, e.g., ice cream, hamburger.

At the start of the next school year, now 2 years after the initial presentation at the emergency room, Barry stayed in school with minimal distress. Jack occasionally stayed for a while in his car in the parking lot, but this was faded out. His parents wrote that he seemed to have a better disposition. If he pouted, they said they ignored it and "he gets over it." The teachers reported to the parents that Barry was making "great progress." At the end of the school year, Barry's parents wrote that he had a very good year. He would occasionally call home at noon and talk for a minute or two. At home he was doing well also.

Summary

Barry, a 10-year-old student in the fifth grade, was diagnosed as displaying Separation Anxiety Disorder of Childhood. He evidenced problems during separation from his parents at both school and home. Assessment showed that the problems seemed to be related to maladaptive parental management during interactions with Barry. In particular, contingencies of positive and negative reinforcement were related to the inappropriate, manipulative behaviors at school and home. The parents and Barry were seen as the most important clients and all were targeted for treatment by me. Active participation in the treatment by the clients was facilitated through self-management strategies such as self-recording, goal-setting, and family negotiation (Blount & Stokes, 1984; Kelley & Stokes, 1982, 1984). The manipulation of the contingencies of attention and affection and the use of inexpensive activity consequences were emphasized (Stokes & Osnes, 1985). Generalization was programmed during treatment by fading my role to facilitate client independence during the self-management procedures and during follow-up/maintenance contact and consultation (Stokes & Baer, 1977; Stokes & Osnes, 1986, in press). Barry successfully showed appropriate separation from his parents at home and school, his parents showed improved child management skills, and these effects maintained across subsequent school years.

The parents and Barry all showed themselves to be astute observers of their own behaviors, careful recorders of information requested by me, and cooperative and systematic implementors of the procedures outlined and practiced with me. The motivated involvement of the family was due, at least in part, to the severity of the stress for the family as initially presented and the management by me in maintaining active participation. Initially the family was quite distressed by the presenting problems, and anything that could be done by me to reduce that stress was seized upon by the family. In addition, it was necessary to provide some context and expectation regarding the likely course of the problems. It was made clear that these problems would take some time to change, perhaps over the school year, but some initial changes should be noted relatively quickly, within the first month. With the initial severity of the problem behaviors, compliance with the procedural directions was high. We practiced the various skills in the clinic, and I provided feedback in a positive and constructive manner. I also responded positively and enthusiastically to the clients' actions at home and school by my positive attention and explanation of how such conscientious involvement would contribute significantly to Barry's progress. I was also relying on the fact that Barry's and his parents' participation would be associated with some prompt and positive improvements in Barry's behaviors. This natural consequence of significant behavior change is the factor that I depended upon as the more tangible payoff for compliance. It was a more difficult task to maintain the active participation later in the course of treatment, when the highest stress levels were reduced and the family started to relax and returned to a more balanced lifestyle that did not focus dramatically on the problems of the child. It is at this point when initial changes have been made, but there are still serious interactional and consequences components of treatment to be considered that I need to have established enough credibility with the family that my judgement was trusted and the family will follow through because I told them it was very important. In these circumstances the clients did what I asked because it had worked for them in the past and there was no reason to believe there would not be a similar positive outcome now. At this point in treatment, I was also careful to continue to recognize successes to date and the essential role that the family played in contributing to their own progress.

Acknowledgments. Trevor Stokes and Pamela Osnes thank the Department of Psychology, University of Western Australia, Perth, for support during the writing of this chapter. Preparation of this chapter was also supported in part by U.S. Department of Education Grants #G008630340 and #H024A80037.

REFERENCES

American Psychiatric Association. (1980). *Diagnostic and statistical manual of mental disorders* (3rd ed.). Washington, DC: Author.

American Psychiatric Association. (1987). *Diagnostic and statistical manual of mental disorders* (3rd ed., revised). Washington, DC: Author.

Anderson, J. D., Williams, S., McGee, R., & Silva, P. A. (1987). DSM-III disorders in preadolescent children: Prevalence in a large sample from the general population. *Archives of General Psychiatry, 44*, 69–76.

Atkeson, B. M., & Forehand, R. (1978). Parents as behavior change agents with school-related problems. *Education and Urban Society, 10*, 521–583.

Blount, R. L., & Stokes, T. F. (1984). Self-reinforcement by children. In M. Hersen, R. M. Eisler, & P. M. Miller (Eds.), *Progress in behavior modification* (Vol. 18, pp. 195–225). Orlando, FL: Academic.

Chapel, J. L. (1967). Treatment of a case of school phobia by reciprocal inhibition. *Canadian Psychiatric Association Journal, 12*, 25–28.

Croghan, L. M. (1981). Conceptualizing the critical elements in a rapid desensitization to school anxiety: A case study. *Journal of Pediatric Psychology, 6*, 165–169.

Edlund, C. V. (1971). A reinforcement approach to the elimination of a child's school phobia. *Mental Hygiene, 55*, 433–436.

Gardner, R. A. (1985). *Separation anxiety disorder: Psychodynamics and psychotherapy.* Cresskill, NJ: Creative Therapeutics.

Garvey, W. P., & Hegrenes, J. R. (1966). Desensitization techniques in the treatment of school phobia. *American Journal of Orthopsychiatry, 36,* 147–152.

Gittelman-Klein, R., & Klein, D. (1971). Controlled imipramine treatment of school phobia. *Archives of General Psychiatry, 25,* 204–207.

Gordon, D. A., & Young, R. D. (1976). School phobia: A discussion of etiology, treatment, and evaluation. *Psychological Reports, 39,* 783–804.

Gresham, F. M., & Nagle, R. J. (1981). Treating school phobia using behavioral consultation: A case study. *School Psychology Review, 10,* 104–107.

Hersen, M. (1968). Treatment of a compulsive and phobic disorder via a total behavioral therapy program: A case study. *Psychotherapy: Theory, research and practice, 5,* 220–225.

Hersen, M. (1970). Behavior modification approach to a school-phobia case. *Journal of Clinical Psychology, 26,* 128–132.

Johnson, A. M., Falstein, E. I., Szurek, S. A., & Svendsen, M. (1941). School phobia. *American Journal of Orthopsychiatry, 11,* 702–711.

Johnson, J. H., Rasbury, W. C., & Siegel, L. J. (1986). *Approaches to child treatment: Introduction to theory, research, and practice.* New York: Pergamon.

Johnson, S. B. (1979). Children's fears in the classroom setting. *School Psychology Digest, 8,* 382–396.

Kahn, J. H., & Nurstein, J. P. (1962). School refusal: A comprehensive view of school phobia and other failures of school attendance. *American Journal of Orthopsychiatry, 32,* 707–718.

Kelley, M. L., & Stokes, T. F. (1982). Contingency contracting with disadvantaged youths: Improving classroom performance. *Journal of Applied Behavior Analysis, 15,* 447–454.

Kelley, M. L., & Stokes, T. F. (1984). Student–teacher contracting with goal-setting for maintenance. *Behavior Modification, 8,* 223–244.

Kennedy, W. A. (1965). School phobia: Rapid treatment of 50 cases. *Journal of Abnormal Psychology, 70,* 85–289.

Miller, L. C. (1983). Fears and anxiety in children. In C. E. Walker & M. C. Roberts (Eds.), *Handbook of clinical child psychology* (pp. 337–380). New York: Wiley.

Miller, P. M. (1972). The use of visual imagery and muscle relaxation in the counterconditioning of a phobic child: A case study. *Journal of Nervous and Mental Disease, 154,* 457–460.

Montenegro, H. (1968). Severe separation anxiety in two preschool children successfully treated by reciprocal inhibition. *Journal of Child Psychology and Psychiatry, 9,* 93–103.

Neisworth, J., Madle, R., & Goeke, K. (1975). "Errorless" elimination of separation anxiety: A case study. *Journal of Behavior Therapy and Experimental Psychiatry, 6,* 79–82.

Rodriquez, A., Rodriquez, M., & Eisenberg, L. (1959). The outcome of school phobia: A follow-up study based on 41 cases. *American Journal of Psychiatry, 116,* 540–544.

Schmitt, B. D. (1971). School phobia—the great imitator: A pediatrician's viewpoint. *Pediatrics, 48,* 433–438.

Simeon, J. G., & Ferguson, H. B. (1985). Recent developments in the use of antidepressant and anxiolytic medications. *Psychiatric Clinics of North America, 8*(4), 893–907.

Smith, S. (1970). School refusal with anxiety: A review of sixty-three cases. *Canadian Psychiatric Association Journal, 15,* 257–264.

Stokes, T. F. (1985). Contingency management. In A. S. Bellack & M. Hersen (Eds.), *Dictionary of behavior therapy techniques* (pp. 74–78). Elmsford, NY: Pergamon.

Stokes, T. F., & Baer, D. M. (1977). An implicit technology of generalization. *Journal of Applied Behavior Analysis, 10,* 349–367.

Stokes, T. F., & Osnes, P. G. (1985). Self-abuse. In M. Hersen & C. G. Last (Eds.), *Behavior therapy casebook* (pp. 342–356). New York: Springer.

Stokes, T. F., & Osnes, P. G. (1986). Programming the generalization of children's social behavior. In P. S. Strain, M. J. Guralnik, & H. Walker (Eds.), *Children's social behavior: Development, assessment, and generalization* (pp. 407–443). Orlando, FL: Academic.

Stokes, T. F., & Osnes, P. G. (1988). The developing applied technology of generalization and maintenance. In R. H. Horner, G. Dunlap, & R. L. Koegel (Eds.), *Generalization and maintenance: Life-style changes in applied settings.* Baltimore, MD: Brookes.

Stokes, T. F., & Osnes, P. G. (in press). An operant pursuit of generalization. *Behavior Therapy.*

Trueman, D. (1984a). The behavioral treatment of school phobia: A critical review. *Psychology in the Schools, 21,* 215–223.

Trueman, D. (1984b). What are the characteristics of school phobic children? *Psychological Reports, 54,* 191–202.

Walen, S., Hauserman, N. M., & Lavin, P. J. (1977). *Clinical guide to behavior therapy.* Baltimore, MD: Williams & Wilkins.

5
Treatment of a Child's Sleep Disturbance and Related Phobias in the Family

LEILANI GREENING
STEPHEN J. DOLLINGER

INTRODUCTION

Childhood sleep disturbances are well documented in clinical and epidemiological surveys. At any given time from one-third to one-half of the children referred to pediatricians and clinical psychologists experience dream-related sleep disturbances (Dollinger, 1986). A much smaller percentage report other types of distressing events during sleep or at bedtime (parasomnias) including nightmares (7%–30%), night terrors (1%–4%), and sleepwalking (1%–6%) (American Psychiatric Association, 1987; Dollinger, 1986).

Although sleep disorders are documented in the literature and third revised edition of the *Diagnostic and Statistical Manual of Mental Disorders* (DSM-III-R), empirical research has not consistently shown childhood sleep disturbances to be a distinct dimension. Rather, factor analytic studies suggest that sleep problems load on such dimensions as anxiety or fears and somatic complaints. This finding indicates that childhood sleep disturbances fall within the broad-band "internalization dimension" of childhood psychopathology found repeatedly in the factor analytic literature (Achenbach & Edelbrock, 1978; Quay, 1979). Such a conclusion necessitates two cautions for the clinician. First, careful assessment is necessary to understand whether and how other internalization problems are function-

Leilani Greening. Psychology Internship, UCLA Neuropsychiatric Institute, Los Angeles, California.

Stephen J. Dollinger. Department of Psychology, Southern Illinois University, Carbondale, Illinois.

ally related to the sleep disturbance. And second, even with careful assessment, the clinician must be aware of side issues that are not immediately apparent with the referral statement.

Formal diagnostic procedures can include methods especially applicable to sleep problems (e.g., all night physiological recording, Coates & Thoresen, 1981; sleep logs or diaries) and procedures used in more general assessment such as interviews and behavior checklists (e.g., the Sleep scale of the Missouri Children's Behavior Checklist; Sines, Pauker, Sines, & Owen, 1969). Our own preference is to emphasize a broader assessment of the child's personality style and family interactions (Dollinger, 1986). This approach is grounded in a view of psychotherapy that respects the individual child (Reisman, 1973), utilizing what is unique to the child, family, or situation in the treatment (Gardner & Olness, 1981).

The formal literature on treatment of childhood sleep disturbances generally consists of behavioral interventions and family therapy for incidental problems that include sleep. The few single-case studies reported indicate that contingency management and relaxation, alone and in combination, have been used successfully for treating insomnias and nightmares (Anderson, 1979; Bergman, 1976; Weil & Goldfried, 1973; Yen, McIntire, & Berkowitz, 1972). Other behavioral approaches, including systematic desensitization (to precipitating events or feared objects) and response interruption early in the chain of behaviors, have been effective in treating night terrors, sleepwalking, and nightmares (Cavior & Deutsch, 1975; Clement, 1970; Kellerman, 1979; Roberts & Gordon, 1979; Silverman & Geer, 1968).

Treatment packages (Graziano & Mooney, 1980; Graziano, Mooney, Huber, & Ignasiak, 1979; Kellerman, 1980) that include a combination of such interventions as relaxation, pleasant imagery, competence statements about sleeping, and reinforcement for appropriate sleeping behavior (e.g., bravery tokens, praise) have also yielded impressive results for childhood nighttime fears.

Competence is also the focus in suggestions and ego-enhancing imagery in which the child reexperienced the disturbing nightmare except with a new ending that emphasizes self-mastery. Taboada (1975) reported improvement using a hypnotic induction about swimming for a 7-year-old boy who developed night terrors after being frightened on a boat ride. This case is especially impressive because the child's fear remitted after one session. The apparent similarity between emotive imagery and such behavioral techniques as muscle relaxation, desensitization, and cognitive restructuring suggest that these approaches are more alike than different.

Like the behavioral studies, reports on other treatment approaches, including psychodynamic and family therapies, are single-case studies and largely anecdotal. In psychodynamic psychotherapy the child works through his/her fears either with play or insight, depending on the child's cognitive skills (Kurtz & Davidson, 1974; Rosenthal & Levine, 1971). Family systems theorists view the child's disturbance as a mechanism for maintaining the status quo in the family dynamics. Shifting the dynamics by means of suggestion or family therapy will cause the problem to become unnecessary (Hoffman, 1981; Madanes, 1980; Papp, 1980). Family therapy, in our opinion, is especially appropriate for clinicians presented with familial problems that perpetuate the sleep disturbance.

The present case began as a rather typical representation of a child's night fears and bedtime resistance—what Kanner (1972) called "spoiled child insomnia." Over the course of treatment, the nature of this problem and the identity of the problem-bearer(s) repeatedly changed course necessitating successive changes in treatment. Thus, the case illustrates a number of possible "moves in the game," albeit a case that was neither a clear victory nor a draw. Regardless of changes in the problem and therapy tactics, our underlying philosophy consistently called for attempting to maintain and enhance the child's sense of self-efficacy in handling his difficulties.

CASE BACKGROUND

The client, who will be called Bradley A, was a 9-year-old boy referred by his parents to a university psychology clinic. The presenting complaints included fears of the dark and sleeping alone in his bedroom. Because of the clinic's intake procedures, the parents were first interviewed by a social worker to obtain background information about the problem.

Bradley lived with his parents and his 12-year-old sister, Janet, in a rural Midwestern town. The family appeared to be a typical, conservative working class family. Mr. A was employed at a potentially dangerous blue-collar job that required him to work the nightshift. He also worked part time operating a small family farm. Mrs. A, who had a college degree in school psychology, had worked in the past when Mr. A was laid off from work. At the time of referral she was unemployed but expressed an interest in working part-time. Individual family members engaged in some extra-curricular activities such as the Kiwanis Club, little league baseball, and church activities. Yet, they preferred to do things as a family and had no close friends.

According to Mrs. A, Bradley's fears were first noticed when he was 6 years old. Mr. A had taken Bradley and his sister to see the movie *Jaws*. Bradley was frightened by the movie and would not sleep in his bedroom alone at night. His sleep disturbance continued intermittently and then intensified the following summer when he began to complain of nightmares about monsters in his room and people trying to kill him. He would refuse to go to sleep unless a light was left on in his room. Mr. and Mrs. A attributed Bradley's sleep disturbance to the movie he had seen recently and felt his fears would dissipate with time. An improvement in his sleep problem was noticed when he returned to school in the fall. However, the following summer Bradley's fears recurred and were more intense than the previous year. He would fall asleep and wake up during the night crying and yelling for his parents because he was scared. Mr. or Mrs. A would comfort Bradley until he fell asleep and then return to their bedroom, only to be awakened a few minutes later by Bradley's screaming. It is noteworthy to mention that the family was also burdened with financial difficulties during this time because Mr. A was laid off from work.

The problem continued with intermittent relapses and remissions over a 3-year period. The family had tried various tactics to deal with the problem including providing verbal reassurances, having someone sleep on a cot in Bradley's room, and "praying to God for guidance." At the time of referral, Janet was sleeping on a cot in Bradley's room to appease him. These tactics provided only a temporary reprieve, if any at all, until the next episode and clearly suggested family enmeshment in the problem and attempts to solve it. Inevitably the family would get involved in each episode which typically resulted in everyone yelling at each other. The shouting matches were so distressing that one night 3 months prior to the referral Bradley cried and said, "I would do anything in the world not to be like this." Bradley's statement consequently prompted Mrs. A to consult a psychiatrist who referred Bradley to the clinic for psychological treatment.

ASSESSMENT

After the initial interview, the case was referred to us for treatment. First, we interviewed the family for a 50-minute session. In addition to inquiring about the nature of the problem, we observed nonverbal reactions, interaction patterns, and obtained more detailed information about bedtime rituals and the family's perception of the problem. Such information provided impressions about the family dynamics in general. In a second 2-hour session we administered the following standardized tests: an expanded version of the Sleep scale from the Missouri Behavior Checklist (Sines et al., 1969), the California Child Q-Sort (Block & Block, 1980), the Personality Inventory for Children (PIC; Wirt, Lachar, Klinedinst, & Seat, 1977), and the Harter Perceived Competence Questionnaire (Harter, 1982)—which measures self-competence in such areas as social, athletic, cognitive, and overall self-esteem. The PIC is a standard protocol administered to all children referred to the clinic. Like the Q-Sort, it provided data about Bradley's personality style. The Harter Questionnaire was included for a research project at the clinic and complemented the personality measures for this case.

A medical examination by Bradley's physician revealed that he was in good health. The parents reported that there was no family history of sleep disturbances. A relative in Mr. A's extended family had been hospitalized for an emotional problem. However, Mr. A did not know the nature of the illness.

During the interview Mr. and Mrs. A described Bradley as a fearful child who worried about harm befalling his family. Such worries included fear of robbery or his parents' dying. He was particularly afraid that his father would be killed at work or on the long drive to work during the night. Interestingly, his parents shared the fear that someone in the family would be fatally injured in an accident. Mrs. A worried that her husband would be killed at work and related stories about workers who were killed on the job. Furthermore, she kept a loaded pistol in the house because she and the family were afraid of being robbed while the father was working. Mr. A worried about his children's safety to the extent that Bradley could not ride his bicycle off of their property. The parents described Janet (in her presence) as anxious also, especially about her school performance and social acceptability.

On the California Q-Sort the parents stated that Bradley is sulky and whiny; overreacts to minor frustrations; is eager to learn; is energetic, fearful, and anxious; cries easily; and is stubborn. On a sleep questionnaire (Dollinger, 1982), they noted several problems indicating anxiety, including difficulty going to sleep, refusing to go to bed, afraid of the dark, refusing to sleep without a light or door open, bad dreams, wants to sleep with parents or vice versa, and bedtime rituals (e.g., long good nights, organizing things). They also noted the anxiety-related behavior of nail-biting, which was observed by us during the assessment. On the Personality Inventory for Children (PIC)—a parent report MMPI-type inventory—Bradley obtained a single significant elevation, that of being on the Anxiety scale.

Bradley's perception of himself as assessed by the Harter Perceived Competence Questionnaire was below average for physical competence in comparison to other children at his fifth-grade level. His self-esteem in the social, cognitive, and general areas were all within normal limits.

Based on the personality tests Bradley manifested an anxious personality. This observation fits the finding from factor analytic studies that childhood sleep disorders load on the broad-band internalization dimension. His parents also exhibited anxiety as evidenced by their fears (e.g., being robbed, father being killed at work). This feature is similar to a case presented by Madanes (1980) of a boy with night terrors and his phobic mother. Madanes conceptualized the child's symptom as benevolent helpfulness to distract his mother from her own fear of being attacked by a burglar. Similarly, Bradley's sleep problem "protected" his parents from their worries and as long as the parents were distracted by attempting to change the symptom, Bradley's protective behavior was maintained. Although different in conceptualization, the systemic and behavioral perspectives are similar in that the family's attention reinforces the problem. Both frameworks propose that Bradley's fears should dissipate once the family's attention to the problem changed.

While we conceptualized Bradley's sleep disturbance as symptomatic of his parents' fears, the symptom first warranted direct intervention (Bergman, 1985). We started with a simple suggestion followed by several additional approaches as needed. Regardless of the technique, the focus of treatment was to enhance Bradley's sense of self-mastery. Treatment consisted of a total of 28 sessions. One of us (L.G.) was the therapist and the other (S.D.) supervised the therapy.

TREATMENT

Initial Therapeutic Steps

We started treatment with a suggestion to see if the simplest approach would be effective. I (L. G.) told Bradley that because he was about to begin adolescence he was becoming capable of coping with stressful situations and demonstrating independence. Furthermore, it was not necessary or appropriate for his sister, who was entitled to her privacy, to continue sleeping on a cot in his room at night. Therefore, he would sleep in his own room alone tonight and every night thereafter. We intended for this suggestion to carry the message of confidence in his ability to observe if enhancing his feeling of self-efficacy would produce changes in the problem (and perhaps his family's perception of him). Bandura (1977) proposed that changes in self-efficacy can effect changes in behavior.

Bradley appeared to accept the instruction and the rationale given in the session. His parents were instructed to reinforce his sense of competence at home by expressing confidence in his ability to comply with the instruction. Bradley, however, refused to sleep in his room alone. Mrs. A reported in the next session that he called out for her during the night and came to sleep in her bed. Mr. A was not home at the time because he worked the nightshift. The therapist encouraged Bradley and his family to follow the initial instructions for another week. Yet, the parents reported in the third session that Bradley continued to show fear at bedtime.

Bradley's response to the initial instructions indicated that more intensive treatment was necessary. We elected for systematic desensitization because of its effectiveness with phobias in general (Rimm & Masters, 1979; Ross, 1981). Bradley first learned relaxation exercises which involved successively tensing and relaxing voluntary muscles in an orderly sequence until all the main muscle groups of the body were relaxed (Rimm & Masters, 1979). The premise of the procedure is that muscle tension is related to anxiety and that marked reduction in anxiety is experienced with muscle relaxation. Bradley practiced the relaxation exercises for four sessions. He also practiced the exercises for 20 minutes every night at bedtime. After demonstrating mastery we then proceeded with systematic desensitization in the sixth session.

Bradley participated in devising a hierarchy of sleep-related imagery for desensitization. The imagery involved three broad categories that included getting ready for bed, sleeping alone in the dark, and hearing such noises outside his bedroom window as a stray cat or a passing car. The scenes were ranked in order from least to most anxiety-provoking. After establishing a hierarchy composed of 10 scenes, I proceeded to systematically desensitize Bradley to the scenes. The sessions began with 10 minutes of relaxation exercises, followed by 10 to 15 seconds of visual imagery of the scenes, and then 10 seconds of relaxation. The conditioned effect anticipated from pairing relaxation with anxiety-arousing imagery was expected to generalize to actual sleep situations for Bradley (Rimm & Masters, 1979).

After three sessions Bradley's response to treatment was not entirely satisfactory. He either became so relaxed that he fell asleep in the session, or he became disturbed by the imagery. We tried varying the procedures including presenting less anxiety-provoking scenes as intermediary steps leading up to the disturbing scene (Miller, Barrett, Hampe, & Noble, 1972). Regardless, the setback persisted for the three sessions without improvement. It appeared the imagery had a sensitizing effect. In order to overcome these obstacles and still enhance Bradley's sense of self-mastery we used a variation of systematic desensitization, guided emotive imagery (Lazarus & Abramovitz, 1962), in place of the desensitization hierarchy. We tailored the imagery after Bradley's interest in space travel and used a successful space mission as the theme. The imagery involved self-mastery in dark unfamiliar situations, much like sleeping alone in the dark. The following is a condensed excerpt from the "space trip":

> . . . as you turn around, you notice the pilot's chair. It is a tall straight-back leather chair seated before a panel of brightly-colored lights and a large picture window. You walk confidently over to the chair. As you sit in it you feel very comfortable and secure, as if the chair was made to suit you. Now that you are comfortable you examine the panel of lights and confidently locate the various switches and buttons for operating the ship. You decide to start the engine and locate the main power switch on the panel. You reach to turn it on and can hear the soft humming sound of the engines starting up. As you confidently prepare for takeoff, you firmly place your hands on the throttle in front of you. You feel competent and in command as you pull the throttle toward you slowly and steadily. The ship starts to vibrate as it slowly rises above the ground. You can feel the vibration through your hands on the throttle. As the ship rises so does your confidence. You gaze out the window and can see how you are rising above the ground, above the trees, the hills, and now you can see the entire country-

side below you. You feel so calm and secure above it all. It looks so peaceful and pretty in the dark with a few small flickering lights. You continue to pull the throttle forward as the ship rises higher and higher and the view below grows dimmer and darker. As you sit back in the pilot's chair and admire the view you feel confident and relaxed. With your hands still in command of the throttle you glide it forward and the ship shifts forward and proceeds to sail through space. Now Bradley I'd like you to describe to me what you see, how you feel, and what you hear as you travel through space.

Bradley was asked to participate by using all his senses to describe the journey in order to check on the vividness of imagery (Miller et al., 1972).

Bradley responded positively to this technique in therapy. After four sessions of guided emotive imagery his parents reported a definite reduction in bedtime resistance. However, based on parental report Bradley continued to show periodic relapses including calling out to his mother and sleeping in his parents' room. On one occasion Bradley's father slept on a cot in his room. This not only provided diagnostic information about Bradley, but about the father's method of handling the problem.

Middle Stages of Therapy

Although Bradley's fears had subsided, guided emotive imagery was continued in individual sessions to reinforce the initial therapeutic gains. And now that the crisis stage of therapy had passed we also included family conferences for the succeeding six meetings. After Bradley's hour-long sessions, I met with the family for another hour. The purpose of the family sessions was to address the parents' fears and how they contributed to Bradley's phobia. These fears were evident from the family's descriptions of ritualistic behaviors. For example, before the father departed for work the family engaged in long good-byes as if each was their last good-bye. Both Bradley and his father reported that each time Mr. A left for work they felt that they would never see each other alive again. Mr. A related his fear to his feelings of guilt regarding the death of his younger brother, who died as a child after being hit by a truck while riding Mr. A's bicycle.

We drew upon Madanes' (1980) treatment of the boy with night terrors and in the first family meeting prescribed a nightly ritual for the family. The prescription involved an instruction for the family to formalize their ritual by selecting a signal symbolizing "take care" when the father left for work. Bradley suggested that they snap their fingers and the family agreed. We added that Bradley and his mother be responsible for checking the locked windows and doors before bedtime. Bradley's role as the competent protector in this instruction was emphasized because we followed Madanes' (1980) conceptualization that a child's disturbance protects the parents from being troubled by their own deficiencies. In effect, the symptom is the result of "an incongruity in the hierarchical organization of the family" (p. 84). Although the parents are in a superior position by virtue of their role as parents, the child is in a superior position by protecting them. If these dynamics are made overt by a paradoxical instruction, in this case Bradley protecting his mother, both the parents and child will resist the overt inappropriate hierarchical organization and reorganize appropriately. The symptomatic behavior will be abandoned as a result.

In general, such paradoxical interventions are reserved for long-standing, repetitious patterns of interaction that are more resistant to more direct interventions (Papp, 1980). We caution against using paradoxical interventions in cases involving violence and abuse because of the potential for misuse (Madanes, 1980). (See Rohrbaugh, Tennen, Press, & White [1981] for more information about the use of paradoxical instructions.)

In the following family meeting Mr. and Mrs. A reported that the instructions generated much insight about the absurdity of their phobic behavior. In recognizing the humor in their rituals, the parents voluntarily abandoned them 1 week after the assignment. Bradley, however, seemed intrigued with the novelty of the signal and periodically snapped his fingers when he left home for school or when his father left for work. The parents also recognized how they (or more accurately how the other spouse) displaced their fears on the children. This insight led to a discussion with the parents about their fears and suggestions to take steps toward trusting their children's judgment. For example, I encouraged Mr. A to allow Bradley to ride his bicycle off of their rural property, a practice he had prohibited and one Bradley desired. This was a significant step for the father because his brother was killed while riding his bicycle across a highway. A month later, in the last family meeting, Mr. A reported that he had allowed Bradley to ride his bicycle to a neighbor's house. We do not know what therapeutic process contributed to this change—insight, suggestion, his wife's encouragement, or a combination of factors. Given that Mr. A had been overprotective for a long period of time, we believe that the suggestion to trust his children initiated a small change which was reinforced by natural consequences.

While working on the family's phobia, we did not lose sight of Bradley's sleep problem. As indicated we continued with emotive imagery in individual sessions with Bradley. Interestingly, Bradley seemed concerned that we were neglecting his problem and complained once during a family conference that he was no longer the focus of the family meetings. Bradley's comment revealed the secondary gain he garnered from his phobia. I relied on parent verbal reports to monitor Bradley's sleep problem. Mr. and Mrs. A reported continued improvement with some minor disturbances. For example, Bradley still requested that a hall light be kept on during the night and he frequently called out to check that his mother was awake in the living room. On several occasions he woke up during the night and asked to sleep in his parents' room. I recommended specific behavioral suggestions to the parents to extinguish these minor disturbances.

First, I instructed Mr. and Mrs. A to return Bradley to his room when he came to them during the night. By changing the contingencies for going to his parents' bedroom, I speculated that Bradley's nighttime problem would dissipate (Bergman, 1976). Although strongly recommended, the parents did not comply consistently with the instruction because it was more convenient for them to let Bradley sleep in their room rather than to wake up and return him to his bedroom. The parents were either not motivated to change the problem or the task was more inconvenient than the problem was distressing.

As for the problem of Bradley insisting that a hall light be kept on, I suggested that Bradley keep a flashlight by his bed (cf. Dollinger, 1983). Easy access to the flashlight was intended to instill a sense of control and a feeling of power in the dark. The flashlight was a novelty for about 2 weeks then once it seemed unnecessary, it was eventually misplaced. Unfortunately, however, the sense of control (and "deconditioning trials" of not seeing a monster) did not effect any greater therapeutic gain; and upon inquiry Bradley and his parents reported that he continued to call out to his mother during the night or asked to sleep in his parents' bedroom.

It appeared that treatment had reached a plateau and it was difficult to progress beyond this point. The parents were reporting that Bradley's sleep problem had improved but that he continued to have difficulties sleeping alone in his room. When we made recommendations for handling these minor disturbances, the parents did not comply with them. In order to step back from the present therapy and plan yet another therapeutic approach, further assessment of Bradley's sleeping habits was considered the most appropriate step. Up until this point, the parents' verbal reports had been the method used to assess change. We decided that a more objective report of Bradley's bedtime behavior was needed to validate the parents' subjective impressions. We did not use monitoring before this time because the verbal accounts were sufficient for assessing the parents' concern about the problem.

During the fourth family meeting, Bradley and his mother were instructed to record the number of nights Bradley went to bed without incident (Rimm & Masters, 1979; Ross, 1981). In the 2 weeks that Bradley and his mother kept records Bradley showed marked improvement. On one occasion Bradley called out to his mother and slept in her bedroom. Overall, though, he slept through the night with little or no disruptions. Mrs. A and Bradley discontinued record-keeping after 2 weeks repeatedly claiming that they forgot (not an uncommon problem with behavioral assignments).

It appears that the monitoring either provided an objective and more favorable assessment than the parents' general impressions or the assessment process itself caused changes in Bradley's behavior. Tracking the desired positive response seemed to be itself a useful factor because Bradley was pleased that his mother noted the number of nights he went to bed without incident rather than her usual practice of noting how often he had problems. Regardless of the reason for improvement Bradley demonstrated considerable mastery over his fears and his parents praised him for his success. Individual treatment with Bradley ended upon mutual agreement between Bradley and his parents. However, Mrs. A requested family therapy for yet another problem, her daughter's math anxiety.

Family Therapy

Janet's problem contained many of the same qualities as Bradley's phobia. For example, Janet would cry about not understanding her math home-work, which elicited attempts from Mr. A to help. However, Janet's anxiety would escalate because her father had difficulties solving the problems quickly. Invariably an argument would ensue between Mr. A and Janet with Bradley and Mrs. A interfering and yelling. This scenario illustrates well the family's enmeshment and indicates that family therapy was the appropriate treatment.

After exploring such practice options as a tutor and a study partner, Janet's math anxiety was countered with a paradoxical prescription in the first family therapy session after which the problem was no longer a family conflict. Other family problems were then presented in therapy including Mrs. A's desire to work part-time and the parents' communication pattern. Family therapy continued for four sessions followed by three sessions of marital therapy to address the parents' communication. Treatment of these issues will not be elaborated here because of our wish to focus on childhood sleep disturbance.

In the third session of the marital therapy, Mr. and Mrs. A reported satisfaction with their progress in therapy and asked to terminate treatment. Both spouses had shown progress in the sessions, and I agreed to end treatment. However, Mrs. A did not wish to end contact completely and requested resuming treatment for Bradley. According to Mrs. A, Bradley had requested further treatment for his fear of scary movies. I agreed to meet with Bradley because he had hinted at this problem while in individual therapy. Surprisingly, rather than discuss or treat his fear, Bradley preferred to use the two sessions that we met to discuss other personal concerns such as peer pressure. His apparent anxiety about social problems clearly illus-trated his general internalized personality style.

Clinically, Bradley's fear of scary programs was not much of a problem. His parents handled it by encouraging Bradley to watch programs he felt comfortable watching. Kellerman (1980) had suggested this same response for a similar type of phobia. I suggested that the parents continue encourag-ing Bradley to watch programs he wished and to praise him for independently demonstrating mastery over his fears. Given that there did not appear to be a problem, I recommended that further treatment was unnecessary.

Follow-Up

Five months after termination I called the family to follow up on Bradley's progress for a closing summary required by the clinic. Mrs. A indicated that it was not a convenient time to bring me up-to-date because her father had died, and she was in the process of making funeral arrangements.

Two months later, Mrs. A called requesting that treatment be resumed for Bradley because she believed that Bradley had relapsed. She indicated that Bradley was complaining of dreams both about his grandfather and his pet dog which had died recently. Consistent with our conceptualization of family processes, Mrs. A reported having similar dreams about her deceased father. Although an appointment was scheduled, Mrs. A canceled because she felt ambivalent about resuming therapy. Moreover, her husband's opinion was that therapy was unnecessary. Bradley also refused to return because he did not want to be stigmatized as the problem child.

Two months after the cancellation, Mrs. A called again and requested an appointment. I asked that only the parents come for the appointment because, based on the telephone conversation, the problem appeared to be the mother's worries about Bradley. During this meeting the mother expressed concern about what she perceived to be a relapse in Bradley's sleeping problem; Bradley was falling asleep on the sofa in front of the television! Both parents believed he did this to avoid going to bed and trying to fall asleep in a dark room. However, Mr. A did not perceive Bradley's behavior as problematic and was not worried about it. Mrs. A, on the other hand, perceived Bradley's sleeping behavior as indicative of a chronic emotional problem. I reframed Bradley's sleeping behavior as an indicator of stress and remarked that it should be useful for gauging Bradley's feelings. Furthermore, I added that Bradley's sleeping habits were not necessarily an indicator of psychopathology. I instructed Mrs. A not to make an issue of Bradley's sleeping habits and to rely on her husband for support when she felt worried.

The mother's own fears seemed to us to be a manifestation of unresolved feelings about her father's death. This was evident during the meeting as Mrs. A talked about her feelings of loss and concerns about her own mortality. Her husband also expressed similar feelings. The parents were encouraged to talk about the loss of Mrs. A's father and especially their feelings, and to rely on each other for support. The parents accepted the recommendation and ended the session by talking about how their children were maturing.

In order to provide a long-term follow-up report on this case I called the family 2 years later and was updated by Mrs. A on the telephone. She reported that since our last contact Bradley's sleep disturbance had been in remission. Bradley continued to fall asleep on the sofa while watching television, but he would go to his room to sleep. Mrs. A regarded this ritual as a habit rather than as an indication of fear as she had in the past. I commented that watching television before going to bed seemed to help Bradley to relax and perhaps feel less anxious about forcing himself to sleep. Mrs. A added that occasionally Bradley would sleep with her when he had a bad dream or was restless.

Bradley also continued to do well in school. He had graduated from junior high school with academic honors and received honors in choir. Although he excelled academically, he continued to lack confidence in his athletic abilities. As reported by Mrs. A, Bradley's self-esteem in regard to his physical competence was noticeably low while in the seventh grade because his peers ridiculed him for being a "nerd." His confidence increased in the eighth grade after his family joined a country club and Bradley became friends with a clique of boys at the club. These boys also attended Bradley's school and thus provided a social network for him at school.

Bradley was expressing some apprehension about starting high school. Interestingly, Mrs. A identified with Bradley's feelings because she too was shy and awkward as an adolescent. Bradley's sister, who was going to be a senior in high school, was looking forward to Bradley starting high school so that she could help him adjust. Janet, as described by Mrs. A, was doing very well and was assuming the big sister role with Bradley. Janet no longer displayed math anxiety, in fact, she was considering taking a calculus class her senior year. Mrs. A was proud of her daughter as she spoke about Janet's academic achievements and extracurricular activities. As for the future, Bradley had his sights set on joining the air force and pursuing his interest in aeronautics.

There were other signs indicating improvement in the family. Most notably Mr. A had bought Bradley a motorbike and had allowed him to ride it on the highway. Even Janet expressed surprise at her father's action. Nonetheless, there was still some stress and irritation in the family, especially about Mr. A working the nightshift. Mrs. A reported that every night Bradley still tells his father to be careful driving to work, and driving home.

The parents' marriage also seemed to be under some strain. Mrs. A reported feeling irritated and argumentative toward her husband but could not pinpoint the reasons for her feelings. She also reported spending little time relaxing with her husband. She seemed to spend most of her time focused on her children.

DISCUSSION

The present case illustrates a process of trial and error or move and counter-move in the therapeutic process. It also illustrates a slippery problem that would not "sit still and let itself be treated." Just when things seemed to be improving, the problem would resurface in a new form (or an earlier one); and just before reaching the point of exasperation, the problem would appear to be resolved. Although unnerving to the scientist/practitioner who likes to document what works, this situation makes the case more true to life than the cases typically published by clinicians in journal articles.

In discussing the salient points for clinical practice, three questions about this case deserve consideration. First, what kind of problem was this, and why did it keep shifting in how it was manifested? Second, to the extent that treatment helped, how did it help? And third, why did a behavioral assessment task seem to produce a dramatic change for the better in Bradley's sleep disturbance?

Why Did the Problem Keep Shifting?

The nature of the problem and the nature of the shifting in its manifestation are two facets of the same issue. From a behavioral perspective, one can note that a specific traumatic event—a scary movie—precipitated the initial occurrence of the problem. And one might point to clearly inappropriate social reinforcement contingencies that could easily have helped to maintain Bradley's fearfulness at bedtime. Furthermore, the fact of problem recurrence might be explained by these reinforcement contingencies, particularly by the intermittent schedule of reinforcement which increases resistance to extinction. One can also point to a very powerful social learning factor in parental modeling of the kinds of anxieties that seem especially salient to youngsters when they go to bed at night (being separated from the security of their parents by the dark and by physical proximity). Such factors will also have been noted by psychodynamically oriented readers who will view Bradley's overall adjustment as reflective of a mechanism of regression exacerbated by the secondary gain of attention from an overprotective mother. This regression can be viewed as precipitated by a stressor—the family's financial difficulties and the father's unemployment. We might also note, from the dynamic perspective, the son's identification with his parents (e.g., their death and separation anxiety) and particularly the father as seen by their mutual fear that a family member would be killed in an accident. It was also observed that Mr. A targeted his son for some of his own emotional conflicts (e.g., his reluctance to allow Bradley the privilege of riding a bicycle off their property because Mr. A's brother was killed while riding a bicycle).

The shifting nature of the problem would fit the concept of symptom substitution fairly well (albeit with rather quicker reappearances of the problem than might be expected from this theory). As such, it would be taken as a sign that the core conflict had not been addressed. One might hypothesize that the core issue in this case is Bradley's anxiety about death and dying. In support of this issue one can cite the facts that the problem appeared following a movie that graphically depicted several horrifying deaths; that he constantly feared his father's death; and that Bradley's problems recurred following the deaths of his grandfather and his dog. Although this hypothesis seems plausible, we viewed the death anxiety not so much as the core issue, but rather as one element in the family's enmeshed relations which, in our view, needed to be resolved to allow greater individuation of family members. Specifically, we regarded it as dysfunctional for this family to share the worldview that one is safe only when in the presence of one's own family. Based upon this conceptualization of the problem, we worked within a loosely systemic–strategic framework to try to affect some small changes (Madanes, 1980; Papp, 1980).

Let us discuss from this framework how the problem may have started and why it shifted. In accord with the many systems theorists, we do not pretend to know much about causality. Rather, we offer the tentative hypothesis that, for unknown reasons, the family was having difficulty in growing from a family with children to a family with teenagers, and this was happening at a time of financial stress. Viewed systemically, the shifting back and forth in problems signifies a dynamic often noted in family therapy in which one member's improvement co-occurs with another family member's problem development (Hoffman, 1981; Palazzoli, Cecchin, Prata, & Boscolo, 1978; Watzlawick, Weakland, & Fisch, 1974). It is as if the family needs a problem-bearer (or sacrificial victim) to keep it in balance. Bradley seemed particularly willing to be this victim (recall his disappointment when he was no longer the focus in family therapy).

How Did Therapy Help?

In attempting to address this question, we need to make clear our belief that it is nearly impossible to make strong inferences from case studies. What we have to offer is speculation biased somewhat by our roles in the case.

Granting this limitation, we believe that two processes were influential in affecting change—an individual process and a group or family process. First, the treatment was devised in various ways to increase Bradley's sense of competence or self-efficacy (Bandura, 1977). Although we cannot document a smooth linear increment in that quality, we feel that the treatment did work to enhance Bradley's feelings of competence and self-control. Mrs. A reported after treatment that Bradley would go into dark rooms alone and outside at night to get his pets, behaviors he was afraid to do before treatment. Perhaps of primary importance for the success was the parents' recognition of Bradley's competence rather than his failures.

Second, we believe that the family sessions did produce some changes in terms of increased individuation of the family members, particularly the children. Bradley became more involved in extracurricular activities such as martial arts. Janet took up acting in school plays, and the mother worked part-time outside the home. None of these would have been accomplished without the family's commitment to change.

Why Did the Behavioral Assessment Task Have Its Effect?

Perhaps most surprising in this case was the impression that the behavioral self-monitoring task produced a dramatic improvement in Bradley's sleep problem. Why might this have happened? Several possibilities must be considered—what might be called the "reactive effects," "awareness," and "perceptual change" explanations.

First, it has been known for over 10 years that behavioral self-monitoring can produce reactive effects (Rimm & Masters, 1979). Could this case be yet another example? We think not because such effects tend to be found for behaviors that are more operant in nature (e.g., studying, smoking, overeating), and because a reactive effect seems most likely at the beginning of treatment. Moreover, when the problem is presented in a negative light by the client, the reactive effect could just as easily have produced data showing that the problem was much worse than before.

Second, one might wonder if the task merely documented a *real* improvement but that the family had not spontaneously noticed that improvement until data were collected. In other words, perhaps the family members had a new awareness of the problem resolution that had occurred, as it were, when they weren't looking. A variation on this explanation is that the behavioral assessment task caused a perceptual change such that the problem was no longer viewed as a problem but as a minor difficulty that could be lived with (Watzlawick et al., 1974). Restated in a cognitive–behavioral way, Bradley's focusing on the positive behavior of sleeping without incident may have reinforced and enhanced his growing sense of self-competence. Although both of these explanations seem plausible to us, we have the impression that the awareness explanation is more appropriate for Mrs. A, and the perceptual-change explanation is a better fit for Bradley.

In any case, the result of the task was a pleasant surprise for the family, therapist, and supervisor. And it nicely illustrates some of the paradoxes that occur in therapy, not to mention life itself.

In conclusion, this case illustrates well the twists and turns often encountered, but rarely published, by clinicians. We do not wish to overlook our own feelings of exasperation throughout this roller coaster of a case. Hoffman (1981) described so eloquently the frustration of dealing with the constant shifting of the problem in the following excerpt:

> The therapist may find himself feeling like those princes who keep going off and completing tasks against great odds to win the hand of the princess,

only to be told there is one more task and yet more. The therapist feels like the unhappy prince. Here I have solved one problem, only to be confronted by ten others. (Sotto voce: Is this princess really worth it?). (pp. 323–324)

Bradley and his family taught us what many novice clinicians should consider: A life problem is not cured by sophisticated therapeutic interventions but rather coping skills are learned to deal with the inevitable problems in life.

REFERENCES

Achenbach, T. M., & Edelbrock, C. S. (1978). The classification of child psychopathology: A review and analysis of empirical efforts. *Psychological Bulletin, 85,* 1275–1301.

American Psychiatric Association. (1987). *Diagnostic and statistical manual of mental disorders* (3rd ed., revised). Washington, DC: Author.

Anderson, D. R. (1979). Treatment of insomnia in a 13-year-old boy by relaxation training and reduction of parental attention. *Journal of Behavior Therapy and Experimental Psychiatry, 10,* 263–265.

Bandura, A. (1977). Self-efficacy: Toward a unifying theory of behavioral change. *Psychological Review, 84,* 191–215.

Bergman, J. S. (1985). *Fishing for barracuda: Pragmatics of brief systemic therapy.* New York: W. W. Norton.

Bergman, R. L. (1976). Treatment of childhood insomnia diagnosed as "hyperactivity." *Journal of Behavior Therapy and Experimental Psychiatry, 7,* 199.

Block, J. H., & Block, J. (1980). *The California Child Q-Sort.* Palo Alto, CA: Consulting Psychologists Press.

Cavior, N., & Deutsch, A. (1975). Systematic desensitization to reduce dream-induced anxiety. *Journal of Nervous and Mental Disease, 161,* 433–435.

Clement, P. W. (1970). Elimination of sleepwalking in a seven-year-old boy. *Journal of Consulting and Clinical Psychology, 34,* 22–26.

Coates, T. J., & Thoresen, C. E. (1981). Sleep disturbances in children and adolescents. In E. J. Mash & L. G. Terdal (Eds.), *Behavioral assessment of childhood disorders* (pp. 639–678). New York: Guilford.

Dollinger, S. J. (1982). On the varieties of childhood sleep disturbance. *Journal of Clinical Child Psychology, 11,* 107–115.

Dollinger, S. J. (1983). Childhood neuroses. In C. E. Walker & M. C. Roberts (Eds.), *Handbook of clinical child psychology* (pp. 524–542). New York: Wiley.

Dollinger, S. J. (1986). Childhood sleep disturbances. In B. B. Lahey & A. E. Kazdin (Eds.), *Advances in clinical child psychology* (Vol. 9, pp. 279–332). New York: Plenum.

Gardner, G. G., & Olness, K. O. (1981). *Hypnosis and hypnotherapy with children.* New York: Grune & Stratton.

Graziano, A. M., & Mooney, K. C. (1980). Family self-control instruction for children's nighttime fear reduction. *Journal of Consulting and Clinical Psychology, 48,* 206–213.

Graziano, A. M., Mooney, K. C., Huber, C., & Ignasiak, D. (1979). Self-control instruction for children's fear reduction. *Journal of Behavior Therapy and Experimental Psychiatry, 10,* 221–227.

Harter, S. (1982). The perceived competence scale for children. *Child Development,* *53,* 87–97.

Hoffman, L. (1981). *Foundations of family therapy: A conceptual framework for systems change.* New York: Basic Books.

Kanner, L. (1972). *Child Psychiatry* (4th ed.). Springfield, IL: Thomas.

Kellerman, J. (1979). Behavioral treatment of night terrors in a child with acute leukemia. *Journal of Nervous and Mental Disease, 167,* 182–185.

Kellerman, J. (1980). Rapid treatment of nocturnal anxiety in children. *Journal of Behavior Therapy and Experimental Psychiatry, 11,* 9–11.

Kurtz, H., & Davidson, S. (1974). Psychic trauma in an Israeli child: Relationship to environmental security. *American Journal of Psychotherapy, 28,* 438–444.

Lazarus, A. A., & Abramovitz, A. (1962). The use of "emotive imagery" in the treatment of children's phobias. *Journal of Mental Science, 108,* 191–195.

Madanes, C. (1980). Protection, paradox, and pretending. *Family Process, 19,* 73–85.

Miller, L. C., Barrett, C. L., Hampe, E., & Noble, H. (1972). Comparison of reciprocal inhibition, psychotherapy, and waiting list control for phobic children. *Journal of Abnormal Psychology, 79,* 269–279.

Palazzoli, M. S., Cecchin, G., Prata, G., & Boscolo, L. (1978). *Paradox and counterparadox.* New York: Aronson.

Papp, P. (1980). The greek chorus and other techniques of paradoxical therapy. *Family Process, 19,* 45–57.

Quay, H. C. (1979). Classification. In H. C. Quay & J. S. Werry (Eds.), *Psychopathological disorders of childhood* (2nd ed., pp. 1–42). New York: Wiley.

Reisman, J. M. (1973). *Principles of psychotherapy with children.* New York: Wiley.

Rimm, D. C., & Masters, J. C. (1979). *Behavior therapy: Techniques and empirical findings* (2nd ed.). New York: Academic.

Roberts, R. N., & Gordon, S. B. (1979). Reducing childhood nightmares subsequent to a burn trauma. *Child Behavior Therapy, 1,* 373–381.

Rohrbaugh, M., Tennen, H., Press, S., & White, L. (1981). Compliance, defiance, and therapeutic paradox: Guidelines for strategic use of paradoxical interventions. *American Journal of Orthopsychiatry, 51*(3), 454–467.

Rosenthal, A. J., & Levine, S. V. (1971). Brief psychotherapy with children: Process of therapy. *American Journal of Psychiatry, 128,* 141–146.

Ross, A. O. (1981). *Child behavior therapy: Principles, procedures, and empirical basis.* New York: Wiley.

Silverman, I., & Geer, J. H. (1968). The elimination of a recurrent nightmare by desensitization of a related phobia. *Behaviour Research and Therapy, 6,* 109–111.

Sines, J. O., Pauker, J. D., Sines, L. K., & Owen, D. R. (1969). Identification of clinically relevant dimensions of children's behavior. *Journal of Consulting and Clinical Psychology, 33,* 728–734.

Taboada, E. L. (1975). Night terrors in a child treated with hypnosis. *American Journal of Clinical Hypnosis, 17,* 270–271.

Watzlawick, P., Weakland, J., & Fisch, R. (1974). *Change.* New York: Norton.

Weil, G., & Goldfried, M. R. (1973). Treatment of insomnia in an eleven-year-old child through self-relaxation. *Behavior Therapy, 4,* 282–294.

Wirt, R. D., Lachar, D., Klinedinst, J. K., & Seat, P. D. (1977). *Multidimensional description of child personality: A manual for the Personality Inventory for Children.* Los Angeles: Western Psychological Services.

Yen, S., McIntire, R. W., & Berkowitz, S. (1972). Extinction of inappropriate sleeping behavior: Multiple assessment. *Psychological Reports, 30,* 375–378.

6

Evaluation and Treatment of a Child with a Schizotypal Personality Disorder

BETTY N. GORDON
CAROLYN S. SCHROEDER

After reviewing the literature on personality disorders in children, we were sorely tempted to change the topic of this chapter and thus avoid dealing with the multitude of problems we encountered. Problems exist in the definition and, therefore, the diagnosis of personality disorders as applied to children, and in the epidemiological studies which gave us little information on prevalence. (If one cannot agree on a definition or even if such a disorder exists in childhood, how can one count it?) We began to feel strongly, however, that it was important to set forth these issues, in part because the term "personality disorder" is frequently and often carelessly used in clinical discussions and practice with children.

In this chapter, we will first discuss problems in the definition and diagnosis of personality disorder. Next, what little empirical data we uncovered on its prevalence in childhood will be presented. We will then present a case study which we feel is an example of a child with a personality disorder, and finally we will reflect on some of the issues raised by this case and why we considered a diagnosis of personality disorder for this child.

DEFINITION

In order to define disorders of personality, one must necessarily begin with the question of what constitutes personality. Philosophers and theorists

Betty N. Gordon. Department of Psychology, University of North Carolina, Chapel Hill, North Carolina.

Carolyn S. Schroeder. Chapel Hill Pediatrics and Departments of Psychiatry and Pediatrics, University of North Carolina, Chapel Hill, North Carolina.

were struggling with this question long before psychology was recognized as a discipline, and the controversy has continued to the present (Phares, 1981). While there is general agreement that personality (and by implication, disorders of personality) exists, the many definitions extant reflect the wide variety of perspectives that are brought to this complex construct. All seem to have in common, however, some notion that personality consists of those characteristics which define us as individuals, that these characteristics are stable over time, and are consistent to some extent across situations (Phares, 1981). Understanding a particular person's personality then, should enhance our ability to predict (at least theoretically) how that person will behave in a variety of situations throughout his or her life.

While the study of personality and personality disorders has focused primarily on adults, our understanding of personality development in infants and young children has come primarily from research in the area of temperament (Thomas, Chess, & Birch, 1968). The term "temperament" is commonly used to refer to an individual's characteristic responses to his/her environment or the "how" of behavior rather than the "what," "why," or "how much" of behavior (Chess & Thomas, 1986). Also commonly accepted are the ideas that temperament is relatively stable, consistent across situations, and largely inherited (Plomin, 1983). Empirical evidence is rapidly accumulating that supports this view of temperament (Buss & Plomin, 1975; Plomin, 1983; Plomin & Dunn, 1986).

While authors such as Chess and Thomas deny that they are advocating a temperament-based theory of personality (Chess & Thomas, 1986), the similarities between personality and temperament are hard to ignore (McCall, 1986). Is temperament the same construct as personality? Can we consider disorders of temperament, say extremely temperamentally "difficult" children (Thomas et al., 1968), to be disorders of personality? Or do children with extremes of temperament become "personality-disordered" only when the environments in which they live fail to adapt and nurture their healthy growth and development over time?

Definitions of personality disorders also include notions of stability and consistency. Consider, for example, the revised third edition of the *Diagnostic and Statistical Manual of Mental Disorders* (DSM-III-R) definition (American Psychiatric Association, 1987).

> Personality *traits* are enduring patterns of perceiving, relating to, and thinking about the environment and oneself, and are exhibited in a wide range of important social and personal contexts. It is only when *personality traits* are inflexible and maladaptive and cause either functional impairment or subjective distress that they constitute *Personality Disorders*. (p. 335)

The meaning of these ideas for children must be carefully considered. Can this definition of personality disorder appropriately be applied to children? Is it reasonable for children, who through the natural process of growth and development are constantly changing, to be diagnosed as having a personality disorder? It is interesting to note that neither the *International Classification of Diseases—9th Revision* (ICD-9; World Health Organization, 1978) nor DSM-III-R, the two most commonly used systems of classifying childhood psychopathology, include personality disorder as a category to be applied to children (see Yule, 1981, for a summary). Rather, DSM-III-R suggests that there are specific disorders of childhood that are related to or may lead to adult personality disorders (for example, conduct disorder in childhood and antisocial personality disorder in adulthood). DSM-III-R states that a diagnosis of child personality disorder should be made only if "the particular maladaptive personality traits appear to be stable" (APA, 1987, p. 336). The caveat is added, however, that one can not be certain that a personality disorder will persist into adulthood, if it is diagnosed before age 18 years.

A recent review article by Nagy and Szatmari (1986) reported considerable evidence for the diagnostic validity of one particular type of adult personality disorder, called schizotypal personality disorder, for children. The DSM-III-R criteria for this disorder in adults involve having at least five of the following symptoms: (1) excessive social anxiety, (2) ideas of reference, (3) odd beliefs and magical thinking, (4) unusual perceptual experiences, (5) odd or eccentric behavior or appearance (unusual mannerisms, talks to self), (6) no close friends or confidants, (7) odd speech without loose associations (impoverished, inappropriately abstract, or digressions), (8) inappropriate or constricted affect (APA, 1987, pp. 341–342). Nagy and Szatmari note that descriptions of children with schizotypal symptoms appeared in the literature as early as 1944 but that the diagnostic labels given these children have varied by author (e.g., schizoid, autistic psychopathy). In a review of nine articles which gave a clear description of symptoms, Nagy and Szatmari concluded that the diagnostic validity of schizotypal disorders in childhood is supported by a consistent clinical picture and a relatively uniform prognosis.

In an attempt to identify specific criteria for the diagnosis of schizotypal personality disorder in children, Nagy and Szatmari (1986) reviewed the charts of 20 cases (18 boys and 2 girls). These cases were selected on the basis of symptoms of *both* social isolation and oddities of behavior or thinking, in order to distinguish them from the DSM-III diagnoses of avoidant (socially isolated) and schizoid (oddities of thinking) personality disorders. All 20 children had been identified as abnormal before the age of 5 years and had the following symptoms: (1) excessive fears and extreme anxiety, (2) severe and persistent difficulties with peer relationships, and (3) coordination problems. The majority of the children also had (1) extreme overreactions to change, (2) preoccupation with fantasy or objects, (3) deviant language development, (4) significant verbal-performance discrepancies on the Wechsler Intelligence Scale for Children—Revised (WISC-R), in either direction, and (5) severe academic problems. They also found a high frequency of neurodevelopmental markers of brain dysfunction (i.e., history of pregnancy or birth complications, clumsiness, speech delays, EEG abnormalities, left or mixed handedness, and psychometric test deficits). Nagy and Szatmari (1986) concluded that the DSM-III diagnostic criteria for schizotypal personality disorder in adults had acceptable validity for children, although illusions, ideas of reference, and suspiciousness were unusual in children.

PREVALENCE

The problems of defining personality disorders are reflected in the lack of studies on prevalence of personality disorders in children. We found only one epidemiological study of child psychopathology that included the diagnosis of personality disorder. Roghmann, Zastowny, and Babigian (1986) examined all child cases seen by mental health clinicians in an urban county of New York State for the period 1960 to 1977 ($N = 26,007$ cases). Of these, approximately 14% were diagnosed as the equivalent of the DSM-I and DSM-II category of personality disorder. One can not really determine if this over- or underestimates the actual prevalence of personality disorders today since (1) not all children with psychopathology receive mental health services, (2) it is not clear how the authors actually arrived at the diagnosis of personality disorder for these children, and (3) diagnoses based on DSM-I and DSM-II may not be relevant to current conceptualizations of personality disorders in children. It is interesting to note, however, that two-thirds of the personality disorder cases were boys and that only 29% were judged improved at termination of treatment.

As a result of their review of the literature on schizotypal personality disorder, Nagy and Szatmari (1986) suggest that this disorder is not uncommon in children. DSM-III (APA, 1980) indicates that as many as 3% of the population (adults included) may be so diagnosed. Of the more than 1,000 children seen in our practice over 5 years, only five cases fit this description.

The prognosis for children with schizotypal personality disorder appears to be guarded at best. In a controlled follow-up study of 22 males so diagnosed in childhood, Wolff and Chick (1980) found that 18 of the 22 were schizoid 10 years later. Five of these had attempted suicide and two were schizophrenic.

The complexities of defining and determining the prevalence of personality disorders in children are directly related to the diagnostic process. How does the clinician decide, for any individual child, what constitutes a personality disorder?

DIAGNOSTIC PROCESS

Wolff (1984) points out that in order to diagnose personality disorders in children, it is imperative to distinguish normal personality variation from personality characteristics that are disordered or deviant. This is never an easy task. For children especially, deviance is relative (Lewis & Rosenblum, 1981), and the distinction between what is abnormal and what is normal is, in large part, arbitrary (Yule, 1981). Rutter and Sandberg (1987), for example, encapsulate the essential issue: "What is the distinction between 'ordinary' misery and fearfulness and the psychiatric conditions characterized by depression and anxiety?" (p. 564). Yule (1981) suggests that children's abnormal behavior should be regarded as psychopathological only when it is *handicapping*, defined as interfering in some way with the child's functioning.

Clarke and Clarke (1984) point out the complexity of both normal and abnormal development. Development, they suggest, is a function not only of the individual's biological makeup (perhaps including temperamental characteristics), the social environment, and transactions between the two, but also of chance events. Chance events (such as parental death or divorce, birth of a sibling, etc.) are unpredictable but have an important impact (either positive or negative) on the course of development.

The DSM-III-R definition of personality cited in a preceding section leaves the clinician with the not inconsequential task of deciding what constitutes "inflexibility," "maladaptive," "functional impairment," and "subjective distress," as well as whether or not the traits in question are stable. Thus, in order to appropriately diagnose any child psychopathology, the clinician must have a solid basis of knowledge of normal child development; must carefully assess the child's behavior (its persistence, intensity, frequency, situation specificity, and age appropriateness) relative to the norm; must assess the environmental and cultural context in which the behavior occurs; and must account for recent life events. In order to make a diagnosis of personality disorder, an additional assessment of the stability of the behavior over time and situations must be made.

As a result of the essential diagnostic criteria of stability, a diagnosis of personality disorder implies a degree of "prognostic gloom" (Wolff, 1984, p. 5). The possibility of this diagnosis becoming a self-fulfilling prophecy is great and the diagnostic process must not be taken lightly. Thus, before making a diagnosis of personality disorder for a child, it would be critical to gather information about his or her behavior in relation to the environment over an extended period of time. The case which we will present illustrates the complex interaction of a child's temperamental and physical characteristics with environmental factors over a period of several years. It was only through the extended observation of this interaction that we came to a diagnosis of personality disorder.

The following case example began as an attempt to help a very anxious boy deal with court-ordered visitation with an estranged father. Evaluation of the problem, however, revealed a history of medical, behavioral, temperamental, and physical problems. Previous evaluation of these problems had repeatedly cited the parents' marital conflict as the likely cause of the child's behavioral and emotional problems. The persistence of the child's disordered behavioral responses over time and across situations became clear only after the intensity of the parents' conflict was decreased and after 3 years of treatment. It was only at this later time that we were able to reconceptualize the case as a personality disorder. That is, we realized that the child's characteristic and persistent maladaptive responses hindered his adjustment to his parents' divorce and the resultant visitation, rather than these being the cause of his problems.

To fully appreciate the persistence of this child's adjustment problems, the reader will have to bear with us through a description of the variety of intervention techniques we used in the attempt to change the course of this child's development. The approach taken was basically behavioral in the sense that behavior was defined, interventions planned, and outcomes evaluated. The intervention strategies, however, can only be viewed as eclectic, reflecting a willingness to try anything that "might work" (defined as a positively viewed and measurable change).

BACKGROUND INFORMATION

Referral

Bryan was a 7-year, 9-month-old boy, living alone with his mother, a 32-year-old teacher. He was referred to the psychology clinic by his pediatrician because of his mother's concern about his ability to handle extended visitation with his father, a 30-year-old salesman, who lived in another state, 200 miles from Bryan and his mother.

Family History

The father, Mr. S, was the youngest of three children in a family that had a history of psychiatric disturbances, although the exact nature of these was not clarified. When Bryan was 6 months old, his father reportedly had an acute psychotic episode that resulted in a diagnosis of paranoid schizophrenia. Mr. S refused to remain hospitalized at that time and subsequently refused outpatient treatment.

Mrs. S, Bryan's mother, was the only child of older parents who were reported to be very supportive of her. There was no history of mental illness or other significant problems in her family.

Bryan's parents were married in their early 20s. They separated when he was 3½ years old, after Mr. S reportedly had a homosexual affair.

History of Referral Problem

Following the parents' separation, visits between Bryan and his father occurred every Sunday, in the family home, until Bryan was 4½ years old. His relationship with his father was described as appropriate during this time. From age 4½ to 5½ years, visits with his father occurred about every 4 months for a few hours at a time, again in the family home.

When Bryan was 5½ years old, Mrs. S and Bryan moved to another state. All contact between Bryan and his father ceased at this time and Bryan next saw his father at age 7 years, 2 months. This visit was described as very difficult. Bryan locked himself in his room and refused to come out. After 2 days, Bryan was able to visit his father at his hotel, but expressed fears of being kidnapped.

Following that visit, Mr. S telephoned and wrote letters to Bryan on a weekly basis for about 2 months. This contact then stopped for another 2 months, at which time Mrs. S received a court order to allow Bryan to spend every other weekend and three 2-week-long periods during the summer with his father. This new schedule of visitation was to begin in 1 month with a 2-week visit at his father's home. Bryan became increasingly upset over this impending visit. His progress in school declined significantly, sleep problems and nightmares increased, and he began to express fears of being separated from his mother.

Developmental History

Bryan was the 7-lb, 10-oz result of an uncomplicated pregnancy and delivery. During his first year he was described as a colicky baby and a poor sleeper. Bryan had a history of minor medical problems, including jaundice, surgery for pyloric stenosis, an episode of unconsciousness associated with diarrhea and dehydration, recurrent middle ear infections with possible periodic conductive hearing losses, and a significant bone age delay which subsequently resolved.

As a toddler, he was described as very active and prone to temper tantrums. A neurological evaluation at age 3 years, 3 months suggested adjustment problems related to parental separation rather than hyperactivity. He was noted to have delayed gross motor skills at that time. At age 4 years, 3 months, further evaluation revealed delayed fine motor skills, articulation problems, normal hearing, and advanced language skills. Persistent concerns regarding his high activity level led to an EEG evaluation at age 4½ years, the results of which were normal.

Bryan began preschool at age 4½ years, where his activity level was reported to compromise his adjustment. At age 5½ years continued concerns regarding his poor motor skills, articulation deficits, and inconsistent hyperactivity led to a psychological evaluation. Results revealed high average intelligence as measured by the Stanford-Binet, with weaknesses in the visual–motor area. The Vineland Social Maturity Scale revealed below average scores because of motor awkwardness and related problems with self-help skills. The hyperactivity was noted but not seen as a major contributing factor to his difficulties in school.

Bryan attended kindergarten with no reported problems. In first grade he had a scattered academic profile, very poor penmanship, and periodic behavior problems. He frequently did not complete his work. He began receiving speech therapy in first grade and was also seen by the school occupational therapy consultant, who found significant problems with motor execution, postural control, and possible tactile defensiveness. Changes were made in the demands for written work, and private weekly occupational therapy sessions were begun. The school counselor also saw Bryan occasionally concerning "behavioral" issues (undefined).

Mrs. S's continuing concerns about Bryan's hyperactivity and her need for help in understanding Bryan's past evaluations prompted a referral to a developmental pediatrician when Bryan was 7 years, 4 months. The results of this evaluation were consistent with the previous evaluations and documented a diagnosis of mild neurologic dysfunction. A neurophysiologically based attention deficit disorder with hyperactivity was ruled out. Rather, his behavioral style was thought to be the result of emotional concerns and anxiety related to unresolved family issues and frustrations over his very real motor handicaps. Bryan was also described as overweight and as having chronic allergies and upper respiratory infections.

EVALUATION OF THE CURRENT REFERRAL PROBLEM

Procedures

Bryan and his mother were seen by a psychologist (C. S. S.) at a pediatric psychology clinic associated with a group of pediatricians. Three sessions were scheduled to assess his emotional status and resources for coping with extended visitation with his father. More formal psychological evaluation was not done at this time because of the time constraints, the need to resolve the immediate crisis quickly, and the previous extensive testing.

The initial three sessions included three extensive individual interviews with Mrs. S and Bryan and observation of Mrs. S and Bryan together. Time with the mother included gathering historical information (presented previously), as well as current behavioral data. She completed an Achenbach Child Behavior Checklist (Achenbach, 1982), an Eyberg Child Behavior Inventory (Eyberg & Ross, 1978), and a questionnaire focusing on developmental/behavioral issues, which is routinely completed by all parents who come to the pediatric psychology clinic. The time with Bryan included the use of the Children's Sentence Completion task, drawings, Piers–Harris Self-Concept Inventory (Piers & Harris, 1969), and talking with him about his school, home, neighborhood, and current concerns. Time with Bryan and his mother together involved observation of their interaction while drawing and playing a game.

Results

Bryan presented as a physically large, overweight, overactive, and socially immature child who appeared quite anxious, frequently laughing loudly and inappropriately. He was very vocal about his fear of spending time with his father and particularly of being separated from his mother. When discussing the visits or even any change in his daily routine, Bryan would jump up from his chair, shake, and say: "I just can't do it. I just can't handle it. I'll go crazy."

Bryan's responses to the sentence completion task indicated concerns about his father, strange sentence structures, and unusual expressive language. For example, to the stem "My father is . . ." Bryan responded "My #1 enemy." To the stem "My father should . . ." Bryan responded: "be more careful. It's very upsetting to my whole balance and too hard being stretched and stretched. My father is not a relative but he has ownership of me." To the stem "I get mad when . . ." Bryan responded: "I'm pushed down in the swampy area of my premises."

The Piers–Harris indicated significantly low self-esteem in general, with some acknowledgment of problems in fine motor work and getting along with peers. Bryan's drawings were very concrete and all were of his house. He refused to draw himself or any other people. Bryan was preoccupied with sleep during these sessions, stating "I wish I could go to sleep right now," and he often pretended to sleep during the interviews.

His mother gave him an intensity score of 126 and a frequency score of 13 on the Eyberg Child Behavior Inventory, indicating significant conduct problems. The Achenbach was above the 98th percentile for fears, obsessive-compulsive behavior, hyperactivity, and aggression. While he was described as a generally anxious youngster, Bryan also had specific fears of hypodermic needles, injections, and dental work. Mrs. S's interactions with Bryan, both from report and by observation, were quite supportive and sensitive to his complex needs, yet she was firm and reasonable in her expectations for him.

Impressions and Recommendations

Bryan's complex learning, motor, and speech problems, in combination with a difficult developmental history, made him a child naturally more vulnerable to stress. He was quite fearful of the unknown, obviously very worried about visiting his father, and appeared to have few emotional resources to cope with any new situations. At the time of this assessment, he was handling his fears by clinging to his mother, vacillating between very active and lethargic behavior, and refusing to do things.

Our assessment suggested that forcing Bryan to go to his father's home would unduly upset Bryan and probably damage any chance for a positive relationship with his father. We recommended that several weekend daytime visits in Bryan's community be scheduled no more than a month apart for Mr. S. The goal would be for Bryan to gradually get to know his father and be able to tolerate more extensive visits at his father's home. We also recommended that Bryan and his father be seen regularly by a psychologist who would monitor Bryan's response to visitation, help to reduce his fears, and also help Mr. S more fully understand Bryan's special needs.

A letter was written to the mother's attorney summarizing this assessment and giving the recommendations. The court did not fully accept our recommendations, ordering overnight visits on alternate weekends, with the first one in Bryan's home (with mother absent). The father was ordered to see a psychologist (C. S. S.) with his son at least once. The psychologist was to write a full summary and recommendations to the court in 1 year.

At this stage we recognized that Bryan would require some help dealing with environmental stresses in general because of his physical and temperamental vulnerability. We did not suspect, however, that his maladaptive responses were so pervasive as to warrant a diagnosis of personality disorder. In retrospect, we believe a diagnosis of personality disorder at the time of this evaluation would not have changed our approach to treatment. Our expectations for successfully altering this child's responses might have been more realistic, however, thus diminishing the feelings of frustration we experienced from time to time. On the other hand, a diagnosis of personality disorder might have decreased the amount of effort we, the mother, and the school expended on his behalf.

INTERVENTION PROCESS

Intervention in this case occurred in three distinct phases, each with a different focus and each utilizing different techniques. Each phase will be described with goals, treatment strategies and progress sections.

Phase I: September 1984 to June 1985

Goals

The focus of intervention during the first phase of treatment was on helping Bryan visit with his father without anxiety and helping them to develop a positive relationship. Helping the parents deal with difficult transition times was a second major issue. A third issue was to improve communication between the parents, and a fourth was ways to decrease Bryan's anxiety. As intervention progressed it also became clear that both parents needed to learn consistent behavior management skills.

Treatment Strategies

For the first 3 weeks Bryan and his mother were each seen individually for half-hour sessions. Bryan became increasingly concerned about the issues being discussed with his mother as he sat in the waiting room, so individual half-hour appointments were scheduled for them on different days.

Mr. S had an initial individual session. Thereafter he agreed to meet with us before going to pick up Bryan at his home, and then he and Bryan met with us at the end of the visits which occurred in Bryan's home community. Even though this meant seeing them on Sunday afternoons, we felt it important to observe Bryan with his father immediately after their time together, and before Bryan returned to his mother.

The transition times at pickup and dropoff were initially exceedingly difficult, with Bryan kicking and hitting his father. Mr. S clearly did not know how to handle Bryan, and Mrs. S simply removed herself from the scene. After the third visit, we decided that the transitions would occur in our office where Bryan's behavior could be observed and the father coached on management techniques.

The parents' difficulty in communicating with each other and with their lawyers was handled by our writing to Mr. S after each of his visits, summarizing what was discussed, what went on during the visits, and the plans for the next visit. Progress reports on Bryan in therapy and at home and school were also sent to the father. Copies of all correspondence to the father went to mother and to both parents' attorneys. Mr. S was encouraged to take increasing responsibility for planning his visits and communicating this directly to Bryan and Mrs. S.

Bryan's teacher was contacted shortly after visitation began. She was sent behavior recording forms that asked her to record any behavior that she considered problematic, what preceded the behavior, how it was handled, and Bryan's reaction. Stamped, addressed envelopes made it easy for her to mail these forms back to us. Phone contact with her occurred every 3 months with the understanding that she could call as needed.

As treatment progressed, we made two phone calls to Mr. S's lawyer to provide an update. While attempts were made to contact Mrs. S's attorney, he did not return any of the calls.

To help Bryan decrease his anxiety about visits, the following work was done:

1. We informed Mr. S of Bryan's needs by giving him copies of all previous evaluations and discussing the implications of these findings with him. We also talked with Mr. S about the needs of children Bryan's age, and discussed his expectations and goals for their relationship.

2. We helped Mr. S plan visits that would meet his goals yet decrease Bryan's anxiety and improve their relationship. This included helping Mr. S structure the visits with activities in the community, some quiet time, and ways of developing a history of their relationship. For example, Bryan and Mr. S got together a "weekend bag" where Bryan kept books, games, and toys that he and his father used on their weekends together. This was kept in Mr. S's car. Mr. S was encouraged to take pictures during the weekends, and the next time they were together he and Bryan put these in an album. We had Mr. S discuss plans for the visits ahead of time and consistently return Bryan home on time as a way of diffusing Bryan's fears of being kidnapped. Mr. S was also encouraged to write letters and phone on a regular basis between visits.

3. Strategies used in individual sessions with Bryan included having him rate the positiveness of his visits with his father on a scale of 1 to 10 (with 10 being fantastic), allowing him to express angry feelings toward his father by dictating letters which were never sent, and drawing pictures of feelings.

4. We taught Mr. S how to use timeout when Bryan kicked, hit, and pushed him at transition times.

5. We encouraged Mrs. S to ventilate her anger toward Mr. S with us or with friends, but not when Bryan was around. She was also informed of some of the weekend events so she could talk positively about them with Bryan.

6. We also taught Mrs. S some standard parent-training techniques (positive attention for appropriate behavior and use of timeout for inappropriate behavior), so she could maintain consistent discipline at home. A behavioral chart system was implemented wherein Bryan could earn 45 points each day for doing his chores, complying with requests, and speaking politely. Points were exchanged for 1 cent each at the end of the day. This system was adjusted over time to include such things as completing school work. The chart was also shared with Mr. S, and consistency between parents in discipline was encouraged.

Progress

At the beginning of treatment, Bryan was extremely angry and upset by his contact with his father. In the second session, he wrote the following letters to his father:

Dear Dad, I wouldn't like you to visit. Please stay at home. Hateful,
Bryan

Dear Dad, Please don't visit. I just get scared of you. Keep me at my
house, don't come within one foot of me. Bryan

Bryan's teacher reported that he was initially very upset the day after a
visit with his father, refusing to do his work, and having unprecipitated temper outbursts, aggression, and excessive crying. By the fifth visit his teacher
was not recording any dramatic changes in behavior following the visits.

Over time, Bryan developed a neutral, somewhat resigned attitude toward
visits with his father and was even able to cope with unexpected events such as
last minute cancellations. By the end of this phase of treatment, Bryan was
able to spend up to a week with his father, away from home, with little
anxiety. At home his behavior improved dramatically with the chart system
and consistency on his mother's part. General anxiety and emotional lability
persisted, however, with Bryan at times appearing quite depressed.

Mr. S proved to be very difficult to work with because of his unpredicta-
bility. He had great difficulty following through with recommendations for
consistency in visits and in planning ahead. For example, on the third
weekend visit with Bryan, he arrived for what was to be an "in-town" visit and
announced that he was going to take Bryan to another state for the weekend.
In addition, he had brought his girlfriend with him, a person unknown to
Bryan. Our letter to him following this visit outlines some of the problems he
presented and the attempts to deal with them (condensed here).

October 11, 1984

Dear Mr. S:

This past weekend was obviously a difficult one for you, but I do
feel that some progress was made in your relationship with Bryan. I
would like to briefly review with you my concern about the weekend. In
our sessions on September 21 and 23 we discussed at length the impor-
tance of establishing a routine with Bryan on your visits, allowing him
to help you plan some of the activities, and we covered many ways to
help the two of you develop a history, for example, picture, weekend
bag, etc. We also discussed Bryan's psychological, learning, and physi-
cal problems. I believe from our discussions that you understand that
Bryan is a fearful youngster who has difficulty with transitions. He will
need a great deal of consistency on your part to help him manage longer
visits and visits at longer intervals.

Given our previous discussions and my letter to you on September
30th, reviewing Bryan's needs, you can imagine my extreme surprise and
concern when you told me at 4:00 on Friday that you planned to take

Bryan out of state when you picked him up at 6:00. On September 23rd, Bryan expressed to you his continuing concerns about "being kidnapped" and, in my opinion, you would have terrified Bryan by your change in plans, a long nighttime trip to an unknown place in another state, and having a strange (to Bryan) woman make the trip with you. As we discussed, your weekend plan flew in the face of all the careful preparation that had been done on your first two visits. I was pleased that you were willing to consider other options and that we were able to secure money from the Department of Social Services to allow you to stay at the Holiday Inn and have money for food. While I know that you were emotionally exhausted by this process and the weekend was not as pleasant for you as you had hoped, it was obviously the best choice for Bryan.

Mr. S, I know you have many pressures, but it is very important for us to work together regarding Bryan, and it is important for you to take responsibility in planning visits that support Bryan and allow the two of you to develop a trusting relationship. He is a young child who needs more than two good visits to know that he is safe with you and can trust you.

We need to continue to make plans for future visits, especially those at Thanksgiving and Christmas. Our goal in all of this should be for you and Bryan to develop a relationship that is long lasting. Being a parent often does mean negating one's own needs to serve the best interests of one's child.

Sincerely,
Carolyn S. Schroeder, PhD
Pediatric Psychologist

It soon became clear that Mr. S had no intention of ever fully exercising his visitation rights. He admitted that his mother initiated the legal proceedings to begin visitation. Visits occurred approximately once a month but at uneven intervals and often with no planning, despite all efforts to the contrary. Mr. S did develop better behavior management skills and a better understanding of Bryan's emotional needs. At one point he said that Bryan reminded him of himself, "very difficult." A letter sent to the court after one year of treatment summarizes the visits, Bryan's behavior, and recommendations (condensed here):

CONFIDENTIAL
      Case: Mrs. S versus Mr. S
            Civil Action #23-56-537
  Regarding: Bryan S
            Date of Birth 9/14/77
      Date: July 27, 1985
Psychologist: Carolyn S. Schroeder, PhD

Bryan's visits with his father have been monitored by me since September 21, 1984 through June 1985. This has been done through contacts with Mr. S and Bryan before and/or after the majority of the visits, sessions with Mrs. S and Bryan, and through letters to Mr. S concerning Bryan's emotional and physical status and needs. My contacts with this family have included 20 sessions with Bryan and Mrs. S, 10 sessions with Mr. S, and 6 sessions with Mr. S and Bryan. Dates of visitation were as follows (specific dates of visitation were listed here to emphasize the sporadic nature of the visitation):

Findings:

Bryan, now 8-years-old, is a youngster with complex learning, motor, and physical problems which naturally make him more vulnerable to stress. A physical examination by his pediatrician in January 1985 and psychoeducational testing by his school system in April 1985 confirm these findings. My contacts over the past year indicate that Bryan is an overly anxious child with few emotional resources to cope with new situations. The focus of my work has been to help him to reestablish a positive relationship with his father and, consequently, deal with visiting his father outside his home territory.

Since September 1984, Bryan has shown marked improvement in his reactions to visits with his father. However, his fear over visits has increased as the time between visits has increased (from 4 to 9 weeks between the January and April visits and 7 weeks between the April and June visits).

While Bryan's relationship with his father has shown improvement, his emotional status, in general, continues to be tenuous. Even though both Mrs. S and the school have persisted in providing structured support and care for Bryan, he continues to exhibit many extreme anxiety and phobic reactions. Most recently he became so upset at YMCA Day Camp he threatened to kill himself. It is, therefore, imperative that the visitation issue be resolved so the focus can be turned to Bryan's other needs. To this end the following recommendations regarding visitation are made:

1. Bryan's visits with Mr. S should be no farther than 6 weeks apart. *Additionally, Bryan needs to know as far as possible in advance the dates and places where he will be seeing his father.*

2. Summer visitation with Mr. S should be limited for the next 2 years to a maximum of two 2-week periods versus the ordered two 3-week periods of time. *Given Bryan's emotional status and age a longer period of time is not recommended. As Bryan's psychological status improves and he grows older, an increased length of time with his father in the summer should be considered.*

3. Transitions between the parents at the Christmas visits should occur on the 26th of December versus the 25th *so Bryan will not have to deal with the transition at an already highly stimulating time.*

4. Alternating Thanksgiving and spring break vacations between parents versus Mr. S having both of these times. *Given the pressures*

> *Bryan faces in school, he needs some uninterrupted vacation time at*
> *home during the school year.*
>
> *Carolyn S. Schroeder, PhD*
> *Pediatric Psychologist*

Mrs. S continued to express very angry feelings about her exhusband throughout this phase of intervention. Since her anger had the potential to interfere with both her and Bryan's adjustment, she was referred for individual therapy but was unable to continue because of financial constraints. She did, however, learn to manage Bryan at home more effectively and proved to be quite flexible and creative in implementing the behavioral charting system.

Although strategies to set up a consistent visitation schedule failed, the parents were eventually able to take responsibility for transitions. They were also able to communicate well enough to set dates and times for visits to everyone's satisfaction. In spite of this progress, Bryan's problems persisted, especially at school. He continued to have difficulty completing his work, had trouble with "bullies" on the school bus, and was described by his teacher as being lonely and having no friends. Bryan expressed considerable anxiety about his school problems, saying "I don't think fast enough in school" and "I don't have friends there." He said the kids teased him and thought he was a "nerd." Thus, in the spring of 1985, at age 8 years, 4 months, another full psychoeducational evaluation was done by the school psychologist. The results are summarized here.

On the WISC-R, Bryan was found to have very superior verbal skills and average performance skills, the latter being compromised by his motor problems and documented mild neurologic dysfunction. Reading and written language were areas of strength and arithmetic, while at grade level, was a relative weakness. The significance of the third factor on the WISC-R, a measure of attention/distractibility, was noted. Classroom observation revealed significant distractibility and continuing frustration with written work. An occupational therapy reevaluation revealed (1) continuing problems in vestibular processing and bilateral coordination, (2) postural control and endurance problems, (3) choreiform movements, (4) refusal to participate in fine motor tasks, (5) behavior outbursts related to poor self-esteem, and (6) embarrassment over poor performance.

It was recommended that Bryan receive learning disability resource help for math and typing instruction, continue in occupational therapy, have increased contact with groups such as Boy Scouts, and continue psychological treatment for behavior problems.

Phase II: August 1985 to August 1986

This most recent evaluation clearly indicated that Bryan's neuropsychological problems were significant and persistent. While our treatment efforts which had focused on helping Bryan cope better with his father were somewhat successful, we became increasingly aware that his characteristic maladaptive responses to change, new situations, and everyday pressures were interfering with his functioning at home and at school. Bryan's social anxiety, hypersensitivity to criticism, difficulty in understanding social rules, odd speech, and inappropriate affect were of concern. We considered a diagnosis of personality disorder at this point, but felt that we had not done enough individual work with Bryan to determine the malleability of his behavior.

Goals

Focus of intervention during this phase changed from case management and visitation issues to improving Bryan's self-esteem, peer relationships, and his behavior and attitude in school. The specific issues dealt with were decreasing his distractibility, helping him to express emotions more appropriately, getting his needs met in more appropriate ways, and getting along better with his teacher and the other children in school. Desensitization of his hypodermic needle/injection and dental phobias was also a goal.

Treatment Strategies

Bryan was referred to a pediatric neuropharmacology clinic to evaluate the appropriateness of medication to reduce distractibility and increase on-task attention. He was placed on 10 mg Ritalin during the school day, with drug holidays on weekends and during school vacations.

We began individual treatment sessions with Bryan using Elizabeth Crary's series on problem-solving skills (Crary, 1982) and cognitive–behavioral techniques, including role play of problem-solving solutions, demonstration, practice, and positive contingencies for his attempts. Table 6-1 gives a sample problem-solving session. We also set up a chart system in school (see Table 6-2). This provided a way for Mrs. S and the teacher to keep in daily contact as Bryan was rewarded through a point system at home for his performance in school. We also monitored Bryan's behavior in school through letters and telephone contacts with the teacher. Mrs. S was seen at the end of each of Bryan's individual sessions and had eight other sessions in which her concerns about Bryan and the school were discussed and plans made to help resolve them.

Following eight individual sessions with the psychologist, Bryan began a social skills group with four other children at the psychology clinic. This decision was made, in part, because of his resistance to dealing with significant issues in individual treatment and problems with generalization of skills to his peer group. The social skills group met weekly for sixteen 1½-hour sessions that included the introduction of a skill (such as how to enter

TABLE 6-1. Sample Problem Solving Session

I. The problem: Kids beat me up on the bus and at lunch

II. How you feel about it: Scared and exhausted

III. Possible solutions:
1. Try to go to sleep
2. Tell a grown-up
3. Ask why they are hitting you and being mean
4. Stay away from them
5. Do something unexpected
6. Hit them back

IV. Evaluation of possible solutions:
1. Try to go to sleep
   + Will discourage them   − I'd be a sitting duck
   + Not letting them get you mad − They'd increase their attack
   + Give me something to do
2. Tell a grown-up
   + Would make me feel better for   − It would happen before I could get
      the time being   help
                                      − No one on the bus to help
3. Ask why they are being mean
   + It would surprise them   − Might process the question in a
   + Make them think a little   few seconds
   + Gives me 5 minutes to
      recuperate
4. Stay away from them
   + Can't hit you   − Nearly impossible to do
5. Do something unexpected
   + Gives you time   − They'll say "you're stupid"
6. Hit them back
   + Feels good   − Could get worse
   + Turns the bullet around

V. Selection of a strategy: Bryan chose to do something unexpected and to let them hit him three times before he hit them back. He agreed to try this for one week and report the results in our next session.

a group, accepting and giving criticism and positive feedback, tuning into nonverbal social cues), role play and practice of the skill, practicing techniques such as relaxation and cognitive restructuring for reducing anxiety, and free play. Parent groups and homework assignments were a regular part of the sessions and were designed to enhance generalization of skills.

Treatment Progress

While Bryan was taking Ritalin, improvement was noted in his attention and activity level, and he did better academically. His behavior in school, however, continued to deteriorate, in large part because his teacher was

TABLE 6-2. Chart System for Behavior in School

Date: _____

	Monday	Tuesday	Wednesday	Thursday	Friday
I. Completing work in class					
A. Spelling					
B. Writing					
C. English					
D. Math					
E. Reading (SRA)					
F. Social Studies					
G. Science					
H. Art					
I. P.E.					
II. Respect					
A. Does work without complaint — A.M.					
P.M.					
Bonus					

B. Pleasant face (no hate looks)	A.M.				
	P.M.				
	Bonus				
C. No nasty statements Example: "You lied to me"	A.M.				
	P.M.				
	Bonus				
III. Group participation Stays with class and tries to participate	A.M.				
	P.M.				
	Bonus				
IV. Homework A. Writes own homework assignments					
B. Brings books and assignments home					
C. Completes homework in an hour					
V. Brings charts in					

quite rigid and unwilling to think of him as having real learning and motor problems. He became quite disrespectful to his teacher and at one point, when the principal attempted to paddle him for this, he went berserk and began screaming hysterically. At another time, Bryan was suspended from riding the school bus because when he thought he had been unfairly criticized, he screamed at the bus driver and at the teacher who tried to calm him down. At this point we implemented the behavior chart in school and these problems were resolved.

Bryan was somewhat open to individual therapy and actively participated in the problem-solving process, but generalization outside the sessions was almost nonexistent. Emotional lability within the sessions also persisted, ranging from lethargic, sad, and negative moods with tears, to angry and hostile interactions, to cheerful, open, and pleasant interactions. Some of these mood changes could be attributed to his physical status; when he had a respiratory infection or was suffering from allergies, he was always more lethargic and had a pessimistic attitude. This was significant, given his frequent illnesses (50% to 60% of the time). These negative moods also occurred, however, when he was physically well. Allergy testing was ruled out because of Bryan's extreme fear of hypodermic needles and shots. The allergist also felt that testing would ultimately lead to only minimal relief. Bryan absolutely and resolutely refused to even consider working on his needle/injection fears or his dental phobia. Even trying to do vicarious desensitization with his mother met with little success. Bryan simply refused to stay in the room or covered his eyes and ears.

Bryan did reasonably well in the social skills group. Although he was never able to interact easily with the other children, he did improve significantly in his conversational skills and in his ability to give and receive criticism and positive feedback. He also became more open to sharing his ideas and accepting the ideas of others. He began to accept responsibility for his own behavior and was somewhat more willing to compromise in order to get along better with others. Generalization of skills continued to be a major problem, however, and he rarely entered into practicing the anxiety-reducing techniques in the group meetings.

After the social skills group ended, we made a major effort to find a therapeutic summer camp for Bryan, but none existed that could provide a scholarship. Mrs. S elected to discontinue treatment at this time. Bryan's medical, psychological, and occupational therapy treatment had become a major financial burden, and Mr. S had contributed no support for the past year. Mrs. S also felt that Bryan was doing reasonably well. Although his father kept contact by telephone or letter on a monthly basis, Bryan had seen him only twice in 9 months. Bryan did well during the summer, but experienced no stresses that might precipitate anxiety or behavioral problems.

At this point we recognized that Bryan displayed an increasing number of symptoms that are characteristic of a schizotypal personality disorder. He had excessive specific fears, consistently overreacted to change and to criticism, and exhibited extreme anxiety in stressful situations. Additionally, he continued to have severe and persistent difficulties relating to his peers. We recognized that although Mrs. S had terminated treatment, we would likely have to remain available to her and Bryan to help them deal with new situations and stresses as they arose.

Phase III: September 1986 to Present

Early in the next school year Bryan's teacher, with Mrs. S's permission, contacted us to discuss Bryan's unmanageable behavior. Apparently he had had trouble getting a book out of his desk and handled his frustration by turning over the desk and screaming. Both teacher and classmates were described as "intimidated." There was no aide in this fourth-grade class, and the teacher felt she could not give him the attention he needed. He was suspended from school for 3 days. Mrs. S was told that if Bryan's behavior was not consistently acceptable over a 6-week period, he would be placed in the self-contained classroom for emotionally handicapped (EH) children. This class consisted primarily of conduct-disordered children and several autistic children. After much discussion with us, Mrs. S decided that Bryan's erratic behavior was very likely to continue, that his school was not able to adequately meet his needs in the classroom, and that the EH classroom was not appropriate. She decided to move to a different school district, one that offered more services in general and if necessary had an EH class that appeared more appropriate for Bryan.

Goals

Treatment in Phase III shifted from teaching Bryan ways to adapt more easily to the demands of his environment, to changing his environment in order to facilitate his adaptation (Berkson, 1981). Simply put, we were not successful in changing Bryan to fit the school environment, so we looked for a school environment which was more flexible in adapting to his particular needs. The goals for this phase of treatment included helping Bryan make the shift to a new setting and helping the setting adapt to meet his special needs.

Treatment Strategies

We began by visiting the new school to set up a situation that would enhance positive behavior. Bryan was provided with learning disabilities resource help for math, placed in the academically gifted resource room, and in a regular classroom with a structured, kind, and rather "unflappable" teacher. We then began a series of nine individual sessions with Bryan to help him make the change. Strategies used in these sessions included helping him use some of the problem-solving skills and social skills learned the previous year, having him and his mother keep a daily log of at least one positive thing he did and one thing he enjoyed doing every day, and mutual storytelling about friendships. After 2 months in the new school, Bryan also returned to the pediatric neuropharmacology clinic for a reevaluation of his medication. Mrs. S was seen briefly for updates each time Bryan was seen.

Progress

While Bryan was viewed by both his teacher and classmates as "different," the structure of the classroom and the resource classes offered Bryan a great deal of support. The teacher ignored his initial impudent statements (e.g., "Does *that* satisfy you?" as he turned in homework), since she rightfully attributed these to his anxiety. Bryan soon began completing his work and with resource help did well academically.

Social relationships continued to be a primary concern as Bryan rarely interacted with children. When he was approached by other children he typically responded in "weird" ways. His voice quality was described as strange and he often offered irrelevant information. All attempts to change his social responses, even putting him in a friendship group in school, failed.

While taking Ritalin, Bryan's activity level and attention to tasks were observed to be within normal limits, but Mrs. S noted that he was much more depressed. He was very weepy and on occasion made suicidal statements such as "I wish I could eat cyanide." When he returned to the pediatric neuropharmacology clinic for a reevaluation, his medication was changed to Dexedrine. After 3 days, he began to exhibit an increasing number of facial and arm tics. Dexedrine was discontinued. Because the psychiatrist at the clinic was concerned about Bryan's persistent depressive moods, Bryan was placed on an antidepressant, Norpramin. Bryan's activity level did increase but the frequency and intensity of his depressive moods decreased. He was generally calmer and more willing to follow the classroom routine.

While respiratory infections persisted throughout the winter and spring and Bryan continued to be hyperreactive to his environment, he generally kept himself under control. A follow-up visit in May 1987 with Mrs. S and Bryan indicated that he was doing better in peer relations, had better self-control and manners with adults, and was making good progress academically. Bryan continued to complain that the other kids did not like him and called him a "nerd." He did not want to continue therapy, however, and said he would ask for it if he needed it.

REFLECTIONS

When Bryan was initially referred for treatment, he presented with a long list of high-risk characteristics including (1) a number of mild medical problems in his first year of life, (2) mild neurological deficits which were sufficient to interfere with fine and gross motor skills, speech, and academic performance, (3) hyperreactivity to environmental stimulation with general anxiety and a number of specific fears, (4) a family history of schizophrenia, and (5) a single-parent family which had experienced significant emotional turmoil early in his life. He was also physically overweight and had chronic respiratory and allergy problems. Temperamentally, he had many of the characteristics of a "difficult" child as described by Chess and Thomas (1986), including high activity level, intense responses, negative moods, inflexibility, and poor adaptability to change. Intervention helped him manage the initial crisis of visits with his father, but his adjustment to home, school, and the community continued to be problematic.

With time it became increasingly evident that Bryan's social and emotional deficits were significant. We realized that attempts to increase his adjustment through modifying his emotional and social deficits so that he could better meet the expectations of his environment would be limited in their success. For Bryan, the theme of his development seemed to be the constancy or stability of his characteristic ways of responding rather than the usual developmental theme of "inconstancy of characteristics" (Thomas & Chess, 1977).

Throughout the long treatment process, we did question the possible value of long-term, psychodynamically oriented treatment, more extensive psychological testing (i.e., projectives), and/or residential treatment. Given the lack of evidence to support the effectiveness of psychodynamic treatment approaches, we could not justify such a recommendation, although it was discussed with Mrs. S. There seemed little need to do more extensive testing, since we had good observational data plus a child who was very "up front" and vocal about his concerns. We did recommend a residential camp experience in the hope of enhancing his opportunity to learn to deal more effectively with peers, and residential treatment is still a possibility for Bryan. At this point, however, there is no reason to assume that removing Bryan from his natural environment would improve his skills, especially given his poor record of generalization.

In considering the appropriateness of a personality disorder diagnosis for this case, it is necessary to reflect back on the criteria set forth in the section on the diagnostic process. We considered the frequency, persistence, intensity, situational specificity, age appropriateness, and stability over time of Bryan's behavior; the environmental and cultural context in which the behavior occurred; and the impact of recent life events. In Bryan's case, recent life events and environmental and cultural factors did not account for the persistence of his maladaptive behavior, although they certainly did contribute to his level of distress. In our opinion, it was his characteristic patterns of responding that continually interfered with his ability to make an adequate adjustment. This style of responding appeared to have been present from birth. By Chess and Thomas' (1986) criteria, he would be described as a temperamentally difficult child. His physical, behavioral, and emotional profile, however, went beyond what one would expect from even the most temperamentally difficult child. In addition, Bryan's maladaptive response patterns persisted in spite of a supportive environment and rather intensive attempts to provide him with alternative responses. Thus, while temperament may be one aspect of personality, in Bryan it did not account for the extent of his "functional impairment and subjective distress" (APA, 1987, p. 335).

Bryan's psychological profile is strikingly similar to those children described by Nagy and Szatmari (1986) in their study of schizotypal personality disorder. He displayed the three symptoms characteristic of all the children in their sample: excessive fears and extreme anxiety, coordination problems, and severe and persistent difficulties with peers. Bryan also exhibited four of the five other characteristics often seen in these children: extreme overreaction to change, deviant language development, a significant WISC-R verbal-performance discrepancy, and severe academic problems. According to the DSM-III-R criteria for adult schizotypal personality disorder, Bryan had five of the eight symptoms: excessive social anxiety, odd or eccentric behavior, no close friends or confidants, odd speech (inappropriately abstract), and inappropriate affect. Thus, we gave Bryan the following DSM-III-R diagnosis:

Axis I: 314.00 Undifferentiated Attention Deficit Disorder
Axis II: 301.22 Schizotypal Personality Disorder with anxiety and emotional
           lability (Primary diagnosis)
           315.10 Developmental Arithmetic Disorder
           315.40 Developmental Coordination Disorder
Axis III: Chronic respiratory infections and allergies
Axis IV: Psychosocial stressors: Parental divorce and conflict over visitation
           Severity: 2—Mild (acute event)
Axis V: Current Global Assessment of Functioning (GAF): 60
           Highest GAF past year: 40

You may ask, as we did, why give Bryan a diagnosis at all, especially one that has a very guarded prognosis and could hinder treatment efforts? Given our need for more research, the label schizotypal personality disorder should clearly be used sparingly with children. However, diagnostic labels help to structure us in important ways, enhancing empirical inquiry and record-keeping from which our understanding of childhood psychopathology grows (Wolff, 1984).

While children such as Bryan are extremely frustrating to treat, they are also very intriguing and challenging. One must continually dig deeper into one's bag of clinical techniques in the attempt to help them. Economic issues must also be considered. Mrs. S had invested about one-fifth of her gross income into medical and psychological treatment, and occupational therapy for Bryan. Additionally, Mr. S never paid for his and Bryan's treatment, and no charges were made for the considerable time devoted to writing letters, telephone calls, and consultations with colleagues. Thus, until more treatment outcome studies are available to guide us, a realistic view of the efficacy of various treatment approaches is essential to the mental health of the clinician (and the pocketbook of the parents).

What is our role as child clinicians in Bryan's future? Our plan is to continue to monitor his progress and to be available to intervene through environmental changes or training as the need arises and the situation dictates, an approach very similar to that taken in our work with developmentally disabled children.

REFERENCES

Achenbach, T. M. (1982). *Revised Child Behavior Checklist*. Burlington, VT: University of Vermont, Department of Psychiatry.

American Psychiatric Association. (1980). *Diagnostic and statistical manual of mental disorders* (3rd ed.). Washington, DC: Author.

American Psychiatric Association. (1987). *Diagnostic and statistical manual of mental disorders* (3rd ed., revised). Washington, DC: Author.

Berkson, G. (1981). Traits, environments, and adaptation. In M. Lewis & L. A. Rosenblum (Eds.), *The uncommon child* (pp. 9–30). New York: Plenum.

Buss, A. M., & Plomin, R. (1975). *A temperament theory of personality development.* New York: Wiley.

Chess, S., & Thomas, A. (1986). *Temperament in clinical practice.* New York: Guilford.

Clarke, A. D. B., & Clarke, A. M. (1984). Constancy and change in the growth of human characteristics. *Journal of Child Psychology and Psychiatry, 25,* 191–210.

Crary, E. (1982). *Children's problem solving book series.* Seattle, WA: Parenting Press.

Eyberg, S. M., & Ross, A. W. (1978). Assessment of child behavior problems: The validation of a new inventory. *Journal of Clinical Child Psychology, 7,* 113–116.

Lewis, M., & Rosenblum, L. A. (1981). The uncommon as the common: A relative view. In M. Lewis & L. A. Rosenblum (Eds.), *The uncommon child* (pp. 1–8). New York: Plenum.

McCall, R. B. (1986). Issues of stability and continuity in temperament research. In R. Ploman & J. Dunn (Eds.), *The study of temperament: Changes, continuities and challenges* (pp. 13–26). Hillsdale, NJ: Lawrence Erlbaum.

Nagy, J., & Szatmari, P. (1986). A chart review of schizotypal personality disorders in children. *Journal of Autism and Developmental Disorders, 16,* 351–367.

Phares, E. J. (1981). *Introduction to personality.* Columbus, OH: Charles E. Merrill.

Piers, E. V., & Harris, D. B. (1969). *The Piers–Harris Children's Self-Concept Scale.* Los Angeles: Western Psychological Services.

Plomin, R. (1983). Childhood temperament. In B. B. Lahey & A. E. Kazden (Eds.), *Advances in clinical child psychology* (Vol. 6, pp. 45–92). New York: Plenum.

Plomin, R., & Dunn, J. (Eds.). (1986). *The study of temperament: Changes, continuities and challenges.* Hillsdale, NJ: Lawrence Erlbaum.

Roghmann, K. J., Zastowny, T. R., & Babigian, H. M. (1986). Mental health problems of children: Analysis of a cumulative psychiatric case register. In S. Chess & A. Thomas (Eds.), *Annual progress in child psychiatry and child development 1985* (pp. 475–495). New York: Brunner/Mazel.

Rutter, M., & Sandberg, S. (1987). Epidemiology of child psychiatric disorder: Methodological issues and some substantive findings. In S. Chess & A. Thomas (Eds.), *Annual progress in child psychiatry and child development 1986* (pp. 561–586). New York: Brunner/Mazel.

Thomas, A., & Chess, S. (1977). *Temperament and development.* New York: Brunner/Mazel.

Thomas, A., Chess, S., & Birch, H. G. (1968). *Temperament and behavior disorders in children.* New York: New York University Press.

Wolff, S. (1984). The concept of personality disorder in children. *Journal of Child Psychology and Psychiatry, 25,* 5–13.

Wolff, S., & Chick, J. (1980). Schizoid personality in childhood: A controlled follow-up study. *Psychological Medicine, 10,* 85–100.

World Health Organization (1978). *Mental disorders: Glossary and guide to their classification in accordance with the Ninth Revision of the International Classification of Diseases.* Geneva. Author.

Yule, W. (1981). The epidemiology of child psychopathology. In B. B. Lahey & A. E. Kazdin (Eds.), *Advances in clinical child psychology* (Vol. 4, pp. 2–52). New York: Plenum.

7
Social Skills Intervention:
A Case Example with
a Learning Disabled Boy

ANNETTE M. LA GRECA
WENDY L. STONE
ARLENE NORIEGA-GARCIA

In recent years there has been considerable interest in developing and evaluating procedures for enhancing children's friendships and peer relationships (see Conger & Keane, 1981; Ladd & Mize, 1983; Wanlass & Prinz, 1982, for reviews). This concern about children's peer interactions received much of its impetus from developmental literature that underscored the importance of peer relationships for psychological adjustment and emotional health (Cowen, Pederson, Babigian, Izzo, & Trost, 1973; Roff, Sells, & Golden, 1972).

For example, in one prospective study of children's emotional adjustment (Cowen et al., 1973), elementary school children were evaluated and followed for several years. Of all the measures that were gathered on the children (e.g., teacher ratings, grades), only the negative peer nominations (i.e., a measure of peer rejection) were found to be significant predictors of later adjustment. Similarly, others have noted that children with few or no friends, or who are actively rejected by peers, are more likely to be dropouts from school (Ullmann, 1957), or to display delinquent behavior (Roff et al., 1972), or to develop other adjustment problems (Roff, 1961, 1963). (See McConnell & Odom, 1986, for a review.) These compelling data on peer relationships and adjustment have raised our clinical awareness of the importance of children's social functioning.

Annette M. La Greca and Arlene Noriega-Garcia. Department of Psychology, University of Miami, Coral Gables, Florida.

Wendy L. Stone. Department of Pediatrics, Vanderbilt University School of Medicine, Nashville, Tennessee.

In response to this concern about the quality of children's peer relationships, clinical investigators began to develop specific interventions to improve the social skills and social status of children who were primarily in the elementary school grades. Initial work in this area focused on children who had low peer acceptance. However, we have come to appreciate that it is children who are actively rejected by their peers, not merely low in acceptance, who are most at risk for future problems.

THE NATURE OF CHILDREN'S SOCIAL PROBLEMS

There are a multitude of factors that may contribute to peer relationship problems. In order to intervene effectively, it is imperative to understand the specific nature of peer difficulties for the individual child. Broadly speaking, peer difficulties may fall into one of three categories: problematic characteristics of the child, deficits in the child's positive social interaction skills, and excesses in the child's negative behaviors that impede social functioning. (The reader is referred to several additional resources for more information on the nature of children's peer relationship problems: Asher, Oden, & Gottman, 1977; Gresham, 1981; Hartup, 1983; La Greca, 1987; La Greca & Mesibov, 1979.)

Child characteristics refer to aspects of the individual child that may be viewed negatively by peers, independent of the child's actual social behavior. These characteristics include, but are not limited to: low academic achievement, physical disabilities, obesity, and unattractiveness. When a problem is evident in one of these areas, intervention may take the form of trying to modify the child characteristic (e.g., improving appearance) or modifying other children's attitudes (e.g., improving peers' acceptance of handicapped children). For example, academic achievement has been found to be related to peer acceptance and adjustment in children of elementary school age (Dodge, Coie, & Brakke, 1982; Gottman, Gonso, & Rasmussen, 1975; Green, Forehand, Beck, & Vosk, 1980). Many children with academic problems such as learning disabilities and mental retardation may be ostracized by peers because of their poor academic skills. For such children, educational intervention may be a necessary adjunct to any social intervention.

Children with deficits in *positive social interaction skills* are those who lack the positive social behaviors that are necessary for successful social functioning. Such children may have difficulty cooperating and sharing with others, may lack good communication skills, or may be at a loss regarding how to make friends with others. These children may profit from learning more appropriate ways to interact with peers. Many social skills programs have been developed for this type of social problem (e.g., Gresham & Nagle, 1980; La Greca, 1981a; La Greca & Santogrossi, 1980; Oden & Asher, 1977).

Finally, in some instances, children's *excessive aggressive, impulsive, or intrusive behaviors* may elicit negative reactions from others, interfering with successful peer relations. Peers dislike others who display high rates of negative and intrusive behaviors (Coie & Kupersmidt, 1983; Dodge, 1983). Children who have difficulty controlling these behaviors may need to learn more effective self-control strategies in order to improve their interactions with peers (Bierman, Miller, & Stabb, 1987).

For many children, peer difficulties fall into one of these three categories, and require interventions that are targeted at the appropriate area. However, others exhibit problems in several areas, and require multiple interventions.

ADAPTING INTERVENTIONS TO SPECIAL POPULATIONS

Several investigators have examined the effectiveness of social skills training interventions with special child populations. Most of the initial social skills work was conducted with "normal" elementary school students (Gresham & Nagle, 1980; La Greca & Santogrossi, 1980; Ladd, 1981; Oden & Asher, 1977), and later extended to special child populations, such as children with learning disabilities, mental retardation, or aggressive behavior (e.g., Bierman et al., 1987; La Greca & Mesibov, 1979, 1981; La Greca, Stone, & Bell, 1983; Vaughn, Lancelotta, & Minnis, in press). Most investigators have recognized the importance of making adaptations in the procedures and methods used in the original social skills protocols when working with these special children (La Greca, 1981b).

One group that is at special risk for peer relationship problems, and that will be the focus of discussion in this chapter, is children with learning disabilities. Studies that have examined the sociometric status of children with learning disabilities (Bruininks, 1978; Bryan, 1974, 1976; Gresham & Reschly, 1986; Scranton & Ryckman, 1979) found that these children were less accepted and more actively rejected than their nondisabled classmates. Moreover, in one study (Bryan, 1976), the children were followed for a 12-month period. Despite the fact that the composition of the peer group had changed by 75%, the learning-disabled (LD) children still retained their poor social status. This underscores the need for intervening with LD children who are not well accepted by their peers.

Based on our earlier discussion of factors affecting peer relationships, it is not surprising that many children with learning disabilities have difficulties with peer interactions. By definition, children with learning disabilities display academic problems, a child characteristic that is viewed negatively by others. Moreover, LD children have also been found to demonstrate problems in some areas of positive social skills, such as social communication (see Vaughn & La Greca, 1988).

Although the presence of a learning disability may place a child at risk for peer relationship problems, it should be noted that many LD children display satisfactory peer relationships, and some may be well-liked by peers (Scranton & Ryckman, 1979). Not all LD children are in need of social interventions. Researchers are just beginning to examine subgroups of the LD population that appear to exhibit more severe social difficulties.

One such subgroup of interest is LD children who display concomitant problems with attention deficits and hyperactivity. Several investigators have noted the overlap between learning disabilities and attention deficit disorders with hyperactivity (ADDH) (Ackerman, Oglesby, & Dykman, 1981; Lambert & Sandoval, 1980). In one study (Lambert & Sandoval, 1980), 40% of the children in a large elementary school sample that evidenced ADDH also met criteria for the diagnosis of a learning disability. This overlap between learning disabilities and ADDH is of interest, as children with ADDH have also been found to display severe peer relationship problems (see Milich & Landau, 1982; Pelham & Bender, 1982, for reviews). It appears that the negative, intrusive, and sometimes aggressive behaviors that ADDH children may display have been linked to problems with peer rejection.

It is only very recently that some studies have examined the behavioral and social functioning of the subgroup of LD children who also display ADDH. These investigations strongly suggest that behavior problems and social deficits are most obvious in the LD/ADDH group, as compared with children with either diagnosis alone (Breen & Barkley, 1984; Flicek & Landau, 1985).

Based on existing research, one would anticipate that many LD/ADDH children would experience great difficuties in their peer interactions. Most likely, an effective social intervention for such children should begin with an appropriate educational setting for attending to academic problems. Beyond a suitable academic environment, however, intensive efforts to teach positive social behaviors as well as strategies for controlling aggressive, impulsive, or intrusive behaviors would also be highly desirable. The present case example will elucidate some of these issues.

CASE BACKGROUND

Gary is a 12-year-old Caucasian male who was referred for treatment by his parents due to concerns about his inability to maintain satisfactory social relationships. Although this was his first treatment referral, his parents described a long-standing history of difficulty with peers.

At the time of the referral, Gary had no friends at all due to his verbally aggressive and controlling behaviors. His parents' immediate concern was preparing Gary for summer camp, which had been a disastrous experience for him the previous summer. Behavior problems and peer rejection had necessitated a return home before the end of the session. In an effort to prevent another camp disaster, Gary's parents initiated contact with us approximately 10 weeks before he was due to leave for camp.

Gary lived at home with his parents. He had an older brother who was married and lived out-of-state. The family can be described as upper middle class. Gary's father was a lawyer, and his mother was a full-time homemaker.

In addition to social difficulties, Gary had a history of learning problems. Intellectually, Gary was functioning within the average range, with learning disabilities in the areas of visual–motor skills and auditory attention. He also had been diagnosed as having an attention deficit, for which he took Ritalin twice daily. At the age of 7, Gary began receiving special educational services. Gary was enrolled in a public school until the fourth grade, when his parents transferred him to a private school specializing in learning disabilities. At the time of the referral, Gary was in the sixth grade, performing average to low average work.

ASSESSMENT

Assessment information was obtained from Gary, his parents, and his school. The parents' interview revealed that there were few children of Gary's age in the neighborhood. His social contacts were further limited by the distance between his home and school, which restricted his opportunities for interacting with classmates after school. Gary's parents described some of his specific peer problems to be: bossiness, arguing, interrupting, teasing, and cheating during games. Peer situations reported to be particularly problematic were those involving activities with two or more children (i.e., joining and playing cooperatively). Conflicts with parents were described as occurring most about issues related to completing chores, taking medication, and doing homework.

In addition to an interview, Gary's parents also completed the Revised Behavior Problem Checklist (RBPC; Quay & Peterson, 1987) and an abbreviated version of the Social Skills Rating Scale (SSRS; Gresham & Elliott, 1985). While the RBPC focuses on behavior problems, the SSRS assesses positive as well as negative interpersonal behaviors. The abbreviated SSRS was comprised of 30 items: 10 items described behavior problems, and 20 tapped positive social behaviors in the areas of peer initiation and reinforcement, compliance with parents, and cooperation with peers.

The RBPC scores revealed elevations on the scales assessing anxiety–withdrawal, attention deficits, conduct disorder, and motor excess. The SSRS revealed the following high-frequency problem behaviors: excessive motor movements or fidgeting, arguing, acting lonely or unhappy, exhibiting anxiety about being with a group of kids, and complaining that nobody likes him. The only high-frequency positive social behavior reported for Gary was "initiating conversations." Together this information depicted a boy with externalizing behavior problems, but who also lacked self-confidence and could be withdrawn and shy at times.

Gary was interviewed prior to treatment. During the interview, Gary was observed to be an attractive boy, who had difficulty sitting still. He was fidgety, often changed the topic of conversation, and rarely made eye contact. Gary denied that there were any problems or difficulties in any sphere of his life. Negative interpersonal behaviors observed included bragging and repeatedly challenging the interviewer. However, it soon became clear that as much as Gary feigned disinterest, many of his behaviors were designed to impress the interviewer.

School contacts were made in order to obtain additional information. The assistant principal, who was quite familiar with Gary, reported similar concerns with Gary's negative peer relationships, and offered the further observation that Gary was beginning to be ostracized by his classmates. Behavioral contracting systems for Gary's work-related behaviors had been instituted recently at school.

CASE FORMULATION AND PROPOSED TREATMENT

In formulating a treatment plan for Gary, it was important to consider the assessment information as well as the immediacy of Gary's parents' needs. On the one hand, the assessment information revealed that Gary had difficulties in a number of areas. In addition to peer relationship problems, he demonstrated learning disabilities, attention deficits, and behavior problems. This is not unusual, as it is common for social difficulties to be seen in conjunction with other problems in preadolescent children. Moreover, the presence of learning disabilities and attention deficits place children at greater risk for peer problems (La Greca, 1981c, 1987; Milich & Landau, 1982). On the other hand, despite the presence of these other difficulties, his parents were requesting help with the circumscribed problem of social skills due to their concerns about his adjustment at camp. Furthermore, this need was immediate, as Gary's departure for camp was less than 3 months away.

The decision was made to work with Gary for the 10 weeks prior to camp, with the goal of facilitating his ability to interact appropriately with peers. Based on the assessment information, it appeared that Gary's social problems were of two types: He demonstrated low levels of appropriate peer relationship skills and high levels of aversive and intrusive behaviors. Therefore, the treatment plan was designed to both promote positive social skills as well as to reduce his noxious social behaviors.

The optimal situation would have been his participation in a structured social skills training program with one or more peers. The presence of other children can serve many functions, such as: providing the opportunity for peer feedback and reinforcement, enabling children to practice social skills with other same-age peers, and increasing the likelihood of observing peer difficulties first-hand, so that they may be addressed directly rather than hypothetically. However, no appropriately "matched" peers (i.e., boys of similar age with comparable treatment goals) were available at the time. Consequently, individual treatment was initiated, with the hope that peer pairing would become possible at a later point.

COURSE OF THERAPY

Individual Treatment

Gary was seen for individual treatment at a facility specializing in the assessment and treatment of children with developmental disabilities for four sessions. The individual social skills sessions with Gary were 50 minutes in duration, preceded by 10 minutes of discussion with Gary's mother. Because of Gary's attention problems, individual sessions had to be very structured and activity oriented in order to secure his involvement; he quickly lost interest during long verbal exchanges. The structure that was most effective in sustaining his attention consisted of switching activities every 10 to 15 minutes. A kitchen timer was utilized to signal the end of each activity period.

In order to secure Gary's interest and attention, material was presented in a game-like format whenever possible. One game that was used frequently was a modified form of the *Talking, Feeling, and Doing Game* (Gardner, 1975) that was previously developed by one of the authors (W. L. S). This game focused specifically on behavioral, affective, and cognitive components of children's social functioning. It included three sets of task cards: (1) *role-play cards* (e.g., "Pretend you're in a store with a friend and he/she suggests that you steal some candy," "Pretend your friend is visiting you and wants to play a game that you don't like."); (2) *sentence completion cards* (e.g., "I felt proud when _____," "Sometimes I worry about _____."); and (3) *problem-solving/feelings cards* (e.g., "Name one thing that makes you sad," "What is one thing you can do when you feel angry?"). Specific items had been developed for the purpose of eliciting information and providing discussion material relevant to interpersonal situations. During play with Gary, game pieces were moved around the board by throwing dice, and points could be earned for completing the task on the card. The use of a spinner (for extra points) and game cards with a selection of tasks and points introduced elements of chance into the game. This capitalized on Gary's competitive nature and motivation to win, as well as his need for activity. Gary's cooperation during the session was rewarded with a few minutes of unstructured time at the end of the session.

The content of the sessions focused on social skills such as understanding nonverbal behaviors and signs of annoyance (i.e., facial expressions, body postures) and learning appropriate peer initiation strategies. Role-plays were found to be especially effective for teaching and rehearsing behaviors such as inviting, responding to invitations, joining ongoing peer activities, and starting conversations (Cartledge & Milburn, 1980; Jackson, Jackson, & Monroe, 1983; La Greca, 1981a; La Greca & Mesibov, 1979). Situations that were related to anticipated camp experiences were emphasized.

The 10-minute parent meetings were implemented to keep Gary's parents apprised of the general nature of the treatment activities. During these meetings, we provided general information regarding Gary's goals and progress, and Gary's mother reported on his progress at home and discussed relevant events that occurred during the week.

Despite efforts to engage Gary in therapy activities, he generally was resistant to this form of intervention. For example, he often slumped in his chair with his arms folded and complained about having to attend the sessions.

After four individual sessions, we received a treatment referral for another boy in need of similar treatment. Chuck was a 12-year-old boy who also had learning disabilities and social difficulties. Given this opportunity for peer pairing, Gary's final 6 weeks before camp were spent in dyadic sessions with Chuck. The length of the sessions was extended from 50 to 60 minutes, which was the maximum time judged to be appropriate given the boys' observed and documented attention deficits.

Peer Pairing

During this phase of treatment, which lasted for six sessions, Gary's problematic peer interaction skills became much more apparent. In addition to his general negativistic behavior, Gary was initially very "bossy" and controlling with Chuck. For example, Gary would take charge during social skills games and activities and tell Chuck what he should be doing.

A token system was instituted to provide the boys with the high degree of structure that they required in order to function optimally. The system was based upon the provision of a "store," which was kept well-stocked with items of various expense ($0.25 to $6.00), ranging from packages of bubble gum, to Nerf basketballs, to plastic model assembly kits. The token value of these store items ranged from 5 to 100. The boys' input was critical in obtaining suggestions for store items that were motivating for them. Time was allotted at the end of each session for the boys to "purchase" desired items.

The boys' purchasing power was determined by the number of chips they earned during the sessions. The boys received tokens for each positive interpersonal behavior, such as giving suggestions and showing concern for the other child, as well as for behaviors that facilitated the group process, such as paying attention and staying on-task. These behaviors were rewarded immediately after they occurred on an intermittent reinforcement schedule. In addition, each boy had one or more individualized behavioral goals for which he could receive up to five chips per session. Individual goals were selected at the beginning of each session and determined on a week-to-week basis. The initial goals were intended to enhance the boys' participation and cooperation in the treatment sessions. For instance, due to Gary's attentional problems, his initial individual goal was to remain seated during the session to improve his attention and involvement. Later in training, his individual goals were more socially focused; for example, Gary's dominating behaviors led to an individual goal of asking Chuck if he needed help before intervening. In some cases, individual goals were continued in subsequent sessions, and new goals were added. Table 7-1 contains a list of Gary's individual goals for the peer-pairing sessions.

At the end of the session, the total number of chips earned by each boy was converted to points and added to his balance from previous weeks. In an average session, the boys each earned approximately 20 to 25 points. Each week the boys had the option of spending their points or saving them up for some of the more "expensive" store items. It should be emphasized that there were always items in the store that could be purchased with a minimum of points.

As with Gary's individual sessions, the format of the dyadic sessions was very structured. Each meeting began with an informal weekly update and a review of the previous session (abut 10 minutes). This was followed by the primary theme for the week (e.g., joining, starting a conversation,

TABLE 7-1. Peer-Pairing Sessions: Sequence of Gary's Individual Goals and Content of Sessions

Week	Individual goals	Content of sessions
1	Remain seated Pay attention when others talk	Introduction Description of procedures and "ice-breaker" activities
2	Ask Chuck if he wants help	Initiating conversations
3	Interrupt appropriately	Continuing conversations
4	Ask Chuck if he wants help Stay on topic Interrupt appropriately	Joining an ongoing conversation or peer activity
5	Same as all above	Giving positive feedback (complimenting)
6	Same as all above	Continuation of positive feedback Closure activities

inviting, etc.), which constituted the major portion of the session. During this time (about 30 minutes), specific skills were taught and practiced using role-play techniques. The next 15 minutes of the session were designated as "activity time." This was a relatively unstructured period, during which time the boys were able to select games to play together (e.g., Hangman, Uno). During the final 5 minutes the boys went to the "store."

The content of each session was determined by the assessment information as well as by the particular needs demonstrated by the boys during their interactions. Table 7-1 describes the sequence of training content for the six dyadic sessions. The training format used with the roleplays was similar to that reported in La Greca et al. (1983) and La Greca (1981a).

1. Describe a problematic situation that illustrates a specific skill (e.g., You see a group of kids playing ball and would like to join them).
2. Demonstrate an inappropriate response to the situation (e.g., approaching the children and grabbing the ball).
3. Discuss what was wrong with the response, and what its likely consequences would be (e.g., might make others angry).
4. Model an appropriate response (e.g., approaching a familiar child and asking to play).
5. Discuss what was better about this approach.
6. Have the children act out responses to the same situation and receive feedback on their performance from each other. The roleplays are repeated until the children's performances are satisfactory.

Overall, Gary responded quite well to this new format. Although he was initially negativistic (as before), his level of cooperation quickly increased, presumably reflecting his motivation to accumulate tokens. The structure of the sessions also helped him control his impulsivity and increased his ability to remain on-task. Gary enjoyed the roleplays and learned to give feedback to Chuck in an appropriate and positive manner. Although he had some initial difficulty, Gary gradually demonstrated some improvement in his ability to accept feedback from others. By the sixth and final session, Gary became better able to anticipate the effect of his behaviors on others, and was able to utilize new ways of initiating and sustaining interactions with Chuck. However, we felt that in less structured situations his impulsivity and long-standing maladaptive interaction patterns might place him at risk for continued difficulties.

Parent contacts were less formalized during this phase of treatment. Parents were consulted briefly before each treatment session, and individual appointments with parents were scheduled on an as-needed basis.

Unfortunately, the extent to which Gary's behavioral improvements carried over into more naturalistic peer interactions was unknown. Despite many efforts, it was not possible to obtain reports of his social functioning from his teachers. For example, numerous phone calls were made to his teachers, but none of the calls or messages were returned. Moreover, Gary's parents had little opportunity to observe his peer interactions over this 6 week period. Consequently, in light of these concerns, we recommended to his parents that Gary be placed with a younger age-group in camp. In this way, he would spend most of his time with boys who were more similar in terms of social and emotional development.

Summer Outcome

According to parental and child reports, Gary had a good time at camp and was able to remain for the entire 8-week session. No serious incidents of social problems were reported. In light of this success, Gary's parents were interested in continuing his social skills training. Since we were in the process of recruiting more children for social skills groups, they decided to wait until a larger treatment group could be formed. We felt that a larger group would present Gary with a greater challenge in applying his new skills and controlling his impulsivity within a more "stimulating" environment.

Group Treatment

Children with social skills problems were recruited for group treatment through an article in the newspaper describing social skills training. For each referral, a 30- to 40-minute screening interview (with child and parent seen separately) was scheduled. The purpose of the interviews was to form a group of four to six children evidencing peer problems who were similar in terms of their cognitive maturity. Children with severe behavioral or affective disorders (e.g., very depressed), severe family problems, or thought disorders were excluded and referred for other types of treatment. Based on this procedure a group of five boys was formed, heterogeneous with respect to the nature of their social difficulties (i.e., some had problems with aggression and others were shy or withdrawn). This group met for a total of 26 sessions.

The structure of the group drew heavily on descriptions provided by Rose (1975) and Urbain (1985). The format was similar to that used for peer pairing, with several modifications. We added a second trainer/therapist, in order to help with role-play demonstrations, to manage the children's behavior within the group, and to maintain parent and school contacts. The length of group sessions was extended to 90 minutes, and a behavioral contracting system (i.e., homework) was instituted to facilitate generalization of skills from group to home and school. Children were given specific "homework" assignments to practice certain behaviors.

Initial homework goals were monitored by parents, and were nonsocial (e.g., be dressed by 7:15 A.M.; feed dog without reminder), in order to familiarize the parents with the process of behavioral contracting. Social goals, at home and school then were initiated after approximately 6 weeks (see Table 7-2 for examples of goals used in the social skills group). In most cases, the contracts were more successful at home than in school, because the parents were more accessible and better able to monitor them in a consistent manner.

Homework was integrated into the group format by reviewing the contracts in the beginning of the session and awarding points (exchangeable in the "store") contingent upon performance. The other methods of earning chips used during the peer-pairing sessions were also maintained.

As anticipated, Gary had more difficulty exerting self-control with the increased activity and stimulation of four other boys in the same room. In this situation, however, his inappropriate behaviors were addressed by providing him with peer feedback, by having peers model appropriate responses, and by having him practice and roleplay more acceptable behaviors. When he became too bossy, for example, other children often spontaneously verbalized their disapproval by telling him to stop. At that time, we often asked group members how they felt when Gary was bossy, invited them to demonstrate alternative ways of making requests, and encouraged Gary to practice these more appropriate behaviors in impromptu roleplays.

During this phase of intervention, parent involvement was maintained through regularly scheduled meetings with one of us. These sessions were arranged at 6- to 8-week intervals and scheduled to last approximately

TABLE 7-2. Examples of Homework Goals Used during Group Sessions

Social	Nonsocial
Home	
Joining neighborhood kids after school	Come to dinner first time called
Take turns using Atari with sibling	Get dressed by 7:00 A.M. on school days
Call friend on telephone	Begin homework without reminder
Invite friend over	Practice piano for at least ½ hour each day
School	
Greet two classmates each morning	Bring completed homework to class
Spend 10 minutes of outdoor time playing with classmates	Raise hand before speaking
Start conversation with classmate during free time	Avoid making noises during seatwork
Refrain from teasing and name-calling	Attempt class assignments before asking teacher for help

30 minutes. One topic discussed with Gary's mother over the course of the year was the importance of creating more opportunities for peer interactions. At our suggestion, Gary was enrolled in a karate class, for the purpose of providing him with a peer group experience outside of school.

In addition, weekly parent contact was made to elicit feedback regarding the appropriateness of each child's homework goals. Furthermore, near the end of the treatment period, one group session was scheduled with all the parents. The purpose of this session was to discuss plans for the summer months; however, the meeting also provided a forum for the parents to share their concerns about their children's transition to adolescence, provide each other with support, and exchange information regarding the management of specific behavior problems. This session was so productive and well-received that we plan to institute parent group meetings as a regular adjunct to future social skills treatment programs.

OUTCOME

The group ran on a weekly basis from October through May, for a total of 26 sessions. The decision to disband the group for the summer was based upon the realization that summer camp and family vacations would result in erratic attendance for many of the boys. However, parents were informed that the group would resume in the fall if they wished to continue. Assessment instruments were administered prior to the termination of the group.

Gary's attendance was excellent; he missed only three group sessions. Although he demonstrated considerable behavioral variability on a week-to-week basis, he did show slow but steady improvements in his group behaviors as well as his performance on home and school goals. Within the group, Gary became less domineering, and better able to include others in decision making. He showed an improved ability to use problem-solving strategies to control his impulsivity, and received a great deal of group support for his efforts in this area. He participated well in group activities, and often attempted to provide helpful and constructive suggestions to others. While Gary retained his tendency to "clown around," the other boys became quite good at resisting and ignoring his efforts to engage them in his antics. As a result, Gary's disruptive behaviors decreased steadily throughout the year.

A posttreatment interview with Gary's parents revealed some improvements in his peer relationships outside of the group as well. For instance, Gary's experience in karate class had been a generally positive one. Although there were no same-age boys in the class, his mother reported that Gary was able to interact appropriately, and seemed to be well liked. His parents also reported that he had made a friend at school, and had been spending some time with him on the weekends. A further benefit of training, they mentioned, was that the implementation of behavioral goals at home had reduced nagging and conflicts with Gary related to chores. These improvements were reflected in positive changes in the parent responses on the behavioral checklists that were readministered following group training.

Gary's parents completed the same measures (RBPC, SSRS) as they had at the pretreatment. As before, the RBPC scores revealed elevations on the scales assessing anxiety–withdrawal, attention problems, conduct disorder, and motor excess, with little or no change noted from pretreatment levels. Although this was disappointing, it probably was not realistic for us to expect changes in long-standing behavior patterns as a result of an intervention that focused on social skills. For the SSRS, which we expected to be more sensitive to intervention efforts, improvements were noted for the scales measuring peer initiation and reinforcement, and compliance with parents. Specifically, Gary reportedly increased his participation in peer activities, and improved his ability to get along with other children. His parents additionally noted an improvement in his completing chores and the straightening up of his belongings.

Since Gary was in a new classroom situation, we were more successful in obtaining feedback from his teachers than had been the case the previous school year. Overall, Gary's teachers reported improvements in his behavior. His verbal aggression had decreased, and his self-control had increased. However, they remarked that his classmates generally continued to respond to him as before (i.e., his behavior changes had not resulted in noticeable changes in peer acceptance). It would have been helpful to have peer sociometric ratings to provide an independent assessment of Gary's classroom peer status, although this was not feasible.

REFLECTIONS

In this section, we will discuss several issues that were germane to the present case study, and which also have implications for social skills interventions more generally.

Generalization of Training to the School Setting

Although Gary's teachers reported behavioral changes in the classroom (less aggression, greater self-control), Gary continued to be rejected by his classmates. Similarly, other investigators have noted that social skills interventions may produce positive changes in the child, but may not alter the way the children are perceived by peers (Bierman & Furman, 1984; La Greca & Santogrossi, 1980). As a consequence, it may be important to consider intervention strategies that promote children's and teachers' acceptance of and responsiveness to the target child's behavior change.

One strategy for changing peers' perceptions of a given child is to involve peers in the intervention process. For instance, Vaughn and colleagues (Vaughn et al., in press) paired LD children with popular peers for social skills training. Afterwards, the popular peers were found to change their perceptions of LD children more so than the peers who were not involved in training. Another method may be to teach children to be more sensitive to and tolerant of handicaps in others; this may be appropriate, especially with children from special education programs who are mainstreamed in regular classrooms. Still another possibility is to pair a child with a classmate who may be responsive to the child's positive behavior change. (See Strain & Fox, 1981, for additional ideas on peer involvement.) Little attention has been devoted to developing strategies for involving peers and teachers in the intervention process, yet this seems like a very important endeavor if we wish to have children's behavior change accepted by peers.

Although classroom interventions are a desirable adjunct to social skills training, they may be easier to implement when the social skills training takes place in the school setting, rather than in a clinic. In Gary's case, it was very difficult to extend the intervention to the classroom for a number of reasons. First, his social problems were of more concern to his parents than to his teachers. Second, our initial intervention began near the end of the school year, a difficult time to begin a classroom intervention. Third, his teachers found it difficult to implement behavioral contracting due to the time constraints posed by large class size. Furthermore, it was difficult to manage the classroom components of training with five boys in treatment, as this meant coordinating five different classroom intervention programs with five different teachers who were often quite difficult to reach by telephone. (This type of teacher involvement becomes even more complex at the junior high level, when each student usually has several different teachers.) Perhaps a reasonable alternative would be to arrange periodic conferences with the classroom teachers, for the purpose of providing ideas and suggestions for how they might facilitate the goals that were promoted in social skills training. Another possibility might be to conduct the training groups within a single school setting, so that teachers could be more intimately involved in the treatment process.

In addition to strategies for promoting greater peer acceptance of problem children, it is often helpful to prepare the children in training for the possibility of continued negative responses from peers. This serves to prevent them from becoming too discouraged when their initial efforts are not rewarded by peers. One way of integrating this approach into training is to set up roleplays that specifically deal with handling rejection.

Regardless of whether the intervention takes place in a clinic or a school, it may be critical to help the child find another peer group—one that is not hampered by a history of negative interactions. For most children, this means developing peer contacts outside the school setting. In Gary's case, the summer camp and the karate class both filled this role. Other interest groups, such as scouts, a baseball team, or science club, might serve a similar function for other children. It is very important that some peer situations outside of school be available, to enable children to use their social skills successfully.

The Role of Parents in the Intervention Process

We have found it critical to involve parents in the intervention process, to the extent that is possible. In many cases, the parents may be quite concerned about their child's social functioning, although they may not possess the resources to help their child without guidance. Parent involvement is desirable for several reasons: to keep them appraised of specific social goals for their children; to have them reinforce and recognize positive changes in their children; to assess the appropriateness of home contact goals; to reinforce their efforts to monitor the home contracts; and to provide encouragement and feedback, especially when changes occur slowly. At the very least, brief, regularly scheduled parent conferences are recommended as an important means of involving parents in the treatment process.

The social skills literature does not provide guidelines or suggestions for involving parents as social change agents. In some cases the parents themselves may not be good role models for social skills. For the most part, however, parents can be invaluable allies in the treatment process if provided with some helpful suggestions and instructions. Based on our own experience, we would expand the degree of parent involvement in the future by incorporating more frequent parent groups.

One method of conducting individual or group parent sessions is to run them concurrently with the child sessions, and to coordinate the content with that of the child groups. For example, when children are learning how to extend invitations to others, these skills can also be reviewed with the parents, and suggestions provided for: prompting and reinforcing children's inviting skills; supporting their children's attempts to initiate peer contacts (i.e., offering to drive or pick up another child who lives far away); and engaging in coaching and problem solving with their children when initiation attempts go awry.

Presence of Concurrent Behavior Problems

Another interesting and challenging aspect of working with Gary was the fact that he was experiencing multiple problems. In addition to academic and social problems, Gary evidenced an attention disorder and problems with behavioral control. For many children, social skills deficits are just the tip of the iceberg; many other problems may exist concurrently, and require some professional attention. In our social skills group, for example, two of the five boys received additional individual treatment for behavioral problems, and one set of parents was involved in collateral treatment for behavior management counseling.

As discussed previously, children with learning disabilities often demonstrate concomitant problems with attention deficits and hyperactivity. Furthermore, these children with multiple symptoms generally present more severe social and behavioral problems than children with learning disabilities or attention deficits alone. Given the chronic nature of the cognitive problems of LD children, and the attention problems of ADDH children, one might anticipate that social remediation with these children would require intervention efforts over extended time periods. This was evidenced in our case example. Although Gary made some very positive progress in social skills training, it required 1 year of intervention to bring about this change, and there were additional social goals that remained at the time treatment was terminated.

Another implication of the LD/ADDH problem, in particular, is the need to consider interventions that promote positive social skills, as well as control or reduce negative, aversive behaviors. Clinically, we feel certain that Gary would not have been able to bring about any positive changes in his ability to get along with others had he not also been working toward controlling his intrusive behaviors. Many of the individual goals that were implemented during the early parts of the social skills training focused on helping Gary control his annoying habit of interrupting others and telling them what they should do. In Gary's case, it was important to institute procedures for controlling his noxious behaviors immediately, otherwise it would have been very difficult for him to participate in peer and group activities in a productive manner. When children display concomitant behavior problems, these problems need to be addressed within the training sessions, and often with supplementary therapeutic assistance as well.

Importance of Adapting Training Procedures to Children's Needs

Another implication of the multiproblem status of many children with social skills deficits, such as Gary, is the necessity of adapting existing social skills programs to meet the special needs of such children. In Gary's case, we designed the training to take into account his attentional difficulties. Specific adaptations included: shortening the length of the sessions; changing activities frequently to insure his attention and interest; and incorporating "structure" into the treatment sessions by using a timer to signal activity changes, a standard format each week, a token reinforcement system, and so forth. Basically, the content and format that had been used in previous social skills programs were altered to fit this particular child's needs. In the group treatment, skill areas were covered until Gary and the other group members appeared to master them sufficiently; the length of training was based on mastery rather than a predetermined number of sessions. Most likely, other clinicians will need to make similar modifications in existing social skills training protocols in order to adapt them to the needs of the children with whom they are working.

Motivational Level

One very important issue for any clinical intervention is the individual's motivation to be actively involved in the treatment process. In the case of social skills training with children, gaining the child's interest, cooperation, and involvement is critical to the treatment's success.

Initially Gary was very reluctant to participate in the individual training. We worked extremely hard to make the sessions as pleasant, positive, and reinforcing as possible. Gary's motivation seemed to improve when another peer was incorporated into the session, a strategy that may be helpful with other children as well.

In our opinion, the most critical strategy for improving treatment motivation was instituting a reinforcement system (i.e., tokens and a "store"). This provided a direct incentive for Gary (and Chuck, as well as the other boys who later joined the group) to practice and become involved in the treatment process. Reinforcement for completing homework assignments was also provided to encourage the children to practice appropriate peer interaction skills outside of the therapeutic setting.

What would have happened if our reinforcement system did not work, and Gary continued to resist treatment? That is a difficult question to answer. Indeed, there are some children who are not concerned about improving their interactions with others and for whom social skills interventions would be very difficult if not impossible to implement. In general, the level of interest and enthusiasm generated by the group leaders/therapists is extremely important for gaining children's participation and cooperation. However, with more resistant children, contracts for participating in a fixed number of sessions (e.g., four) can be established. The contracts may be helpful in securing the involvement of children who are initially reluctant or apprehensive.

Group Composition

Although we favor group interventions for the teaching of social skills, we also recognize that few, if any, successful formulas exist for structuring the composition of social skills groups. In terms of the number of participants, it is our clinical observation that groups of four to six members work best with two leaders/therapists. When all the children have multiple problems, however, six children can be too many. The advantage of a smaller group size is that each child will have more opportunities to roleplay and practice skills, with less time spent waiting their turn. In addition, if school contacts are a part of the extended treatment plan, the smaller group size enables the clinician to accomplish this goal more effectively, and in a less time-consuming manner. The advantage of a larger group clearly is the greater variety of children available for practice, the greater possibilities for modeling of appropriate peer behaviors, and the greater number of accumulated group ideas for how to handle problematic social situations.

With respect to the types of social problems children display, we have found it helpful to include children with diverse social difficulties rather than having very homogeneous groups. If the children's social skills are complementary, it provides everyone in the group with opportunities to learn as well as to model appropriate behaviors. If children with very severe problems are to be included, we attempt to limit the number to one such child per group.

In our experience, social skills groups work best when the children are fairly comparable in terms of their age, cognitive level, and physical maturity. For example, it is difficult to mix one 13-year-old who is concerned with dating issues with another same-aged child whose social problems relate to immaturity and impulse control. Likewise, we have found it problematic to include children with more than a 2-year age span in the same group. Sometimes groups combining elementary and junior high school students (i.e., sixth and seventh graders), even if they are the same chronological age, do not work well because of different developmental issues. Moreover, it also can be problematic when one child in the group is markedly slower than others cognitively. Although this may teach others to be patient and accepting of those with limitations, it often impedes the progress and completion of group activities. Considerations such as these have led us to the practice of composing groups that are roughly homogeneous with respect to age. Furthermore, throughout the elementary and junior high school years our groups are always homogeneous with respect to gender.

CONCLUSIONS AND SUMMARY

In closing, we will offer several brief comments regarding the nature of this case and of social skills training in general, to put the present case study in perspective. We selected this particular case for discussion because we felt that it illustrated some of the issues in social skills training that confront clinicians yet are not adequately addressed in the social skills treatment literature. For instance, Gary's need for structure and reinforcers in the treatment sessions, the difficulties that arose in coordinating the school and home aspects of his treatment, the importance of involving parents in the treatment process, and the need for adapting existing treatment procedures to fit an individual's needs, were all issues that arose in the course of Gary's treatment. However, few if any guidelines can be found in these areas within the social skills literature. Perhaps by raising these issues, we will inspire others to consider them more fully, and to research them more carefully.

We also selected this particular case because it represented a child who had multiple problems in addition to social skills difficulties. In our clinical experience, many referrals for social skills intervention are children who actually have multiple problems rather than circumscribed social skills deficits. For example, children with learning disabilities and/or with attention deficits constitute a disproportionately large number of referrals for social skills training. Because of this, we have found that interventions are often more complex, time consuming, and longer in duration than one might expect from reading treatment studies. On the average, students who are selected for treatment outcome studies from "normal" classroom situations do not have the multiple and long-standing social difficulties that are typical of children who are referred for clinical intervention. This is important to bear in mind; otherwise, it can be very discouraging to work with clinical populations demonstrating social deficits, especially those within older age ranges (i.e., with more long-standing and intractable problems).

On the positive side, however, we have been very encouraged by the changes we have noticed in children as a result of social skills training. It is exciting to observe improvements in children's social behaviors, and it is even more gratifying to know that there are many short- and long-term benefits for the children who work so hard to bring about these changes.

REFERENCES

Ackerman, P. T., Oglesby, D. M., & Dykman, R. A. (1981). A contrast of hyperactive, learning disabled and hyperactive-learning disabled boys. *Journal of Clinical Child Psychology, 10*, 168–173.

Asher, S. R., Oden, S. L., & Gottman, J. M. (1977). Children's friendships in school settings. In L. G. Katz (Ed.), *Current topics in early childhood education* (Vol. 1, pp. 33–61). Norwood, NJ: Ablex.

Bierman, K. L., & Furman, W. (1984). The effects of social skills training and peer involvement on the social adjustment of preadolescents. *Child Development, 55*, 151–162.

Bierman, K. L., Miller, C. L., & Stabb, S. D. (1987). Improving the social behavior and peer acceptance of rejected boys: Effects of social skill training with instructions and prohibitions. *Journal of Consulting and Clinical Psychology, 55*, 194–200.

Breen, M. J., & Barkley, R. A. (1984). Psychological adjustment in learning disabled, hyperactive, and hyperactive/learning disabled children as measured by the Personality Inventory for Children. *Journal of Clinical Child Psychology, 13*, 232–236.

Bruininks, V. L. (1978). Actual and perceived peer status of learning disabled students in mainstream programs. *Journal of Special Education, 12*, 51–58.

Bryan, T. (1974). Peer popularity of learning disabled children. *Journal of Learning Disabilities, 7*, 621–625.

Bryan, T. (1976). Peer popularity of learning disabled children: A replication. *Journal of Learning Disabilities, 9*, 307–311.

Cartledge, G., & Milburn, J. F. (1980). *Teaching social skills to children: Innovative approaches.* New York: Pergamon Press.

Coie, J. D., & Kupersmidt, J. (1983). A behavioral analysis of emerging social status in boys' groups. *Child Development, 54,* 1400–1416.

Conger, J. C., & Keane, S. P. (1981). Social skills intervention in the treatment of isolated or withdrawn children. *Psychological Bulletin, 50,* 478–495.

Cowen, E. L., Pederson, A., Babigian, H., Izzo, L. D., & Trost, M. A. (1973). Long-term follow-up of early detected vulnerable children. *Journal of Consulting and Clinical Psychology, 41,* 438–446.

Dodge, K. A., (1983). Behavioral antecedents of peer social status. *Child Development, 54,* 1386–1399.

Dodge, K. A., Coie, J. D., & Brakke, N. P. (1982). Behavior patterns of socially rejected and neglected preadolescents: The roles of social approach and aggression. *Journal of Abnormal Child Psychology, 10,* 389–410.

Flicek, M., & Landau, S. (1985). Social status problems of learning disabled and hyperactive/learning disabled boys. *Journal of Clinical Child Psychology, 14,* 340–344.

Gardner, R. A. (1975). *The Talking, Feeling, and Doing Game.* (Available from Creative Therapeutics, P.O. Box R, Cresskill, NJ 07626-0317)

Gottman, J. M., Gonso, J., & Rasmussen, B. (1975). Social interaction, social competence, and friendship in children. *Child Development, 46,* 709–718.

Green, K. D., Forehand, R., Beck, S. J., & Vosk, B. (1980). An assessment of the relationship among measures of children's social competence and children's academic achievement. *Child Development, 51,* 1149–1156.

Gresham, F. M. (1981). Social skills training with handicapped children: A review. *Review of Educational Research, 51,* 139–176.

Gresham, F. M., & Elliott, S. (1985). *The Social Skills Rating Scale.* Unpublished manuscript. (Available from authors at Department of Psychology, Louisiana State University, Baton Rouge, LA 70803)

Gresham, F. M., & Nagle, R. J. (1980). Social skills training with children: Responsiveness to modeling and coaching as a function of peer orientation. *Journal of Consulting and Clinical Psychology, 48,* 718–729.

Gresham, F. M., & Reschly, D. J. (1986). Social skills deficits and low peer acceptance of mainstreamed learning disabled children. *Learning Disability Quarterly, 9,* 23–32.

Hartup, W. W. (1983). Peer relations. In P. H. Mussen (Ed.), *Handbook of child psychology* (Vol. 4, pp. 103–195). New York: Wiley.

Jackson, N. F., Jackson, D. A., & Monroe, C. (1983). *Getting along with others: Teaching social effectiveness to children.* Champaign, IL: Research Press.

Ladd, G. W. (1981). Effectiveness of a social learning method for enhancing children's social interaction and peer acceptance. *Child Development, 52,* 171–178.

Ladd, G. W., & Mize, J. (1983). A cognitive-social learning model of social-skill training. *Psychological Review, 90,* 127–157.

La Greca, A. M. (1981a). Social skills training with elementary school students: A skills training manual. *JSAS Catalogue of Selected Documents in Psychology,* #2194.

La Greca, A. M. (1981b). Children's social skills: An overview. *Journal of Pediatric Psychology, 4,* 335–341.

La Greca, A. M. (1981c). Social behavior and social perception in learning-disabled children: A review with implications for social skills training. *Journal of Pediatric Psychology, 6,* 395–416.

La Greca, A. M. (1987). Children with learning disabilities: Interpersonal skills and social competence. *Journal of Reading, Writing, and Learning Disabilities, 3,* 167–186.

La Greca, A. M., & Mesibov, G. B. (1979). Social skills intervention with learning disabled children: Selecting skills and implementing training. *Journal of Clinical Child Psychology, 8,* 234–241.

La Greca, A. M., & Mesibov, G. B. (1981). Facilitating interpersonal functioning with peers in learning disabled children. *Journal of Learning Disabilities, 14,* 197–199, 238.

La Greca, A. M., & Santogrossi, D. A. (1980). Social skills training with elementary school students: A behavioral group approach. *Journal of Consulting and Clinical Psychology, 48,* 220–228.

La Greca, A. M., Stone, W. L., & Bell, C. R. (1983). Improving the interpersonal skills of mentally retarded individuals in a vocational setting. *American Journal of Mental Deficiency, 88,* 270–278.

Lambert, N. M., & Sandoval, J. (1980). The prevalence of learning disabilities in a sample of children considered hyperactive. *Journal of Abnormal Child Psychology, 8,* 33–50.

McConnell, S. R., & Odom, S. L. (1986). Sociometrics: Peer-referenced measures and the assessment of social competence. In P. S. Strain, M. J. Guralnick, & H. M. Walker (Eds.), *Children's social behavior* (pp. 215–286). Orlando, FL: Academic.

Milich, R., & Landau, S. (1982). Socialization and peer relations in hyperactive children. In *Advances in learning and behavioral disabilities* (Vol. 1, pp. 283–339). Greenwich, CT: JAI Press.

Oden, S., & Asher, S. R. (1977). Coaching children in social skills for friendship making. *Child Development, 48,* 495–506.

Pelham, W. E., & Bender, M. E. (1982). Peer relationships in hyperactive children: Description and treatment. In *Advances in learning and behavioral disabilities* (Vol. 1, pp. 365–436). Greenwich, CT: JAI Press.

Quay, H. C., & Peterson, D. R. (1987). *Manual for the Revised Behavior Problem Checklist.* (Available from the author, P.O. Box 248074, University of Miami, Coral Gables, FL 33124)

Roff, M. (1961). Childhood social interactions and young adult bad conduct. *Journal of Abnormal Social Psychology, 63,* 333–337.

Roff, M. (1963). Childhood social interactions and young adult psychosis. *Journal of Clinical Psychology, 19,* 152–157.

Roff, M., Sells, S. B., & Golden, M. M. (1972). *Social adjustment and personality development in children.* Minneapolis: University of Minnesota Press.

Rose, S. D. (1975). *Training children in groups.* San Francisco: Jossey-Bass.

Scranton, T. R., & Ryckman, D. B. (1979). Sociometric status of learning disabled children in an integrative program. *Journal of Learning Disabilities, 12,* 49–54.

Strain, P. S., & Fox, J. J. (1981). Peer social initiations and the modification of social withdrawal: A review and future perspective. *Journal of Pediatric Psychology, 6,* 417–433.

Ullmann, C. A. (1957). Teachers, peers, and tests as predictors of adjustment. *Educational Psychology, 48,* 257–267.

Urbain, E. S. (1985). *Friendship Group Manual for Social Skills Development (Elementary Grades).* (Available from Wilder Child Guidance Center, 919 Lafond Avenue, St. Paul, MN 55104)

Vaughn, S., & La Greca, A. M. (1988). Social interventions with learning disabled children. In K. Kavale (Ed.), *Learning disabilities: State of the art and practice* (pp. 123–140). Iowa City: University of Iowa Press.

Vaughn, S., Lancelotta, G., & Minnis, S. (in press). Teaching a metacognitive social strategy to LD students. *Learning Disabilities Focus.*

Wanlass, R. L., & Prinz, R. J. (1982). Methodological issues in conceptualizing and treating childhood social isolation. *Psychological Bulletin, 92,* 39–55.

8

Parent–Child Interaction Therapy: Issues in Case Management of Early Childhood Conduct Problem Behaviors

JAMES E. MADDUX
SHEILA M. EYBERG
BEVERLY W. FUNDERBURK

The majority of children (up to 80%) (Thomas, Chess, & Birch, 1968), seen by clinical child psychologists are referred for a cluster of problems behaviors known by a variety of names such as "acting out," "uncontrollable," "noncompliant," and "conduct problem behavior" (Eyberg & Robinson, 1982; Peterson, 1961). This pattern of behaviors has been isolated repeatedly in empirical studies with both clinical and normal populations (Achenbach & Edelbrock, 1978), and studies have shown that such behavior problems are predictive of problems in adolescence and adulthood (Robins, 1966; Quay, 1986). For these reasons, the development of effective methods of intervention with childhood conduct problems has been the focus of much effort and energy.

The most common and well-researched interventions for childhood conduct problem behaviors consist of teaching parents to be more effective "behavior modifiers" with their children (Dangel & Polster, 1984; O'Dell, 1974). These interventions are usually referred to as "parenting skills training" or simply "parent training." A large number of parent training programs have been developed and shown to be successful in dealing with childhood conduct problems (e.g., Barkley, 1981; Forehand & McMahon,

James E. Maddux. Department of Psychology, George Mason Univeristy, Fairfax, Virginia.

Sheila M. Eyberg and Beverly W. Funderburk. Department of Clinical and Health Psychology, University of Florida, Gainesville, Florida.

1981). The program described in this chapter, Parent–Child Interaction Therapy (PCIT), is designed for intervention with *preschool-age* children (approximately ages 2 through 6) and their parents. Its uniqueness stems from its practical virtues and suitability for the private clinical child psychology practice and its blending of the concepts and strategies of operant learning (i.e., behavior therapy) with the general principles of traditional play therapy, particularly the development of a warm and safe therapeutic relationship that allows the child to experiment with change (Eyberg, 1988). The goals of this chapter are to describe PCIT, describe an assessment strategy for preschool-age conduct problem behaviors, and present a case history that describes many of the problems and issues that arise in the treatment of these problems among preschool-age children.

DIAGNOSTIC ISSUES

The problems of concern in this chapter are similar to the problems described in the revised third edition of the *Diagnostic and Statistical Manual of Mental Disorders'* (DSM-III-R; American Psychiatric Association, 1987) criteria for "Oppositional Defiant Disorder" in that the parents' concern in the vast majority of cases is the child's noncompliance with, or opposition to, the parents' or other adults' instructions, directions, and rules. In addition, we recognize that childhood behavior problems cannot be defined without reference to the situations in which the problematic behaviors occur. Most children display behavior problems such as noncompliance and opposition in a variety of situations and with a variety of adults, but some children may display such problems with one parent but not the other or may be less manageable in some situations than others. Therefore, we assume that a referral for conduct problem behaviors is the result of a combination of factors, including the child's behavior, the parents' behavior management skills, the parents' frustration tolerance, the parents' expectations about child development and behavior, and the parents' emotional state (e.g., anxiety and/or depression). It makes little, if any, sense to say that a young child referred for behavior problems "has" a conduct disorder or an oppositional disorder since such terminology implies that the locus of the problem is *within* the child rather than in the situation or the interaction.

AN INTERACTION MODEL
OF CONDUCT PROBLEM BEHAVIORS

Consistent with the basic tenets of social learning theory, PCIT assumes that conduct problems exhibited by young children are established in the earliest interactions between parent and child. Although evidence supports a biological etiology for some conduct problem behaviors (e.g., difficult temperament, neurological problems, infantile autism), the child's vulnerability for behavior problems is nonetheless influenced by his or her early interactions with the parents.

PCIT assumes that the conduct problems displayed by preschool children are essentially parent–child interaction problems. The problematic parent–child interaction is typically characterized by habitual aversive behaviors on the part of both parent and child. Each party in this problematic relationship attempts to control the behavior of the other through behaviors that are maintained by intermittent positive and negative reinforcement. For example, a parent may terminate a child's tantrum in the short run by giving the child the toy he or she wants; the child may terminate the parent's yelling by temporarily not coloring on the wall or table or by intensifying his/her own crying or screaming. Thus both parent and child are encouraged to use these strategies again in different situations, causing these behaviors to be resistant to change.

PCIT attempts to change this interaction pattern from one characterized by aversive attempts at control to one characterized largely by positive, pleasant interactions (e.g., attention or praise by the parent of the child's appropriate behavior). Thus, a major goal of PCIT is to break the "vicious circle" of continually escalating aversive behaviors by teaching the parent skills that will interject a more positive note into the parent–child interaction and diminish the likelihood of the escalation of aversive behaviors. A result of this change is improvement in the parent–child relationship and a reduction in the child's anger: The child appears more relaxed and calm, and the oppositional behavior decreases. This sets the stage for decreased resistance to the introduction of the consistent and predictable discipline procedures also taught in PCIT.

Training Components of PCIT

PCIT involves the sequential training of parents in two distinct types of parent–child interactions, Child-Directed Interaction (CDI) and Parent-Directed Interaction (PDI). Each interaction is taught to the parents through description and modeling of its basic rules. Parents are then coached as they interact with the child in play situations.

The goals of the CDI are (1) to create or strengthen a positive and mutually rewarding relationship, and (2) to teach the parent to use praise and attention to elicit appropriate behavior from the child. During CDI, the parent is taught to listen attentively; respond at the child's level of understanding with enthusiasm, warmth, and genuineness; support the child's problem-solving efforts; and encourage creativity. The parent is taught to follow the child's lead in play and not to direct the child's activities, question the child, or criticize and punish the child. The parent also is taught to describe the child's activities to the child, reflect (repeat or paraphrase) the child's statements, answer the child's questions, praise the child for appropriate behavior, and ignore deviant or inappropriate behavior.

PDI focuses on increasing compliance with the parent's directions and instructions. The rationale for focusing on compliance with parental directions is that an increase in compliance can produce significant changes in a broad range of child behavior problems in a wide variety of situations. When new and appropriate behaviors do occur, they can be rewarded and strengthened. The parent continues to attend to the positive behaviors exhibited by the child and to otherwise practice the skills taught in CDI, but also learns to direct the child's activities by giving clear instructions, by following compliance consistently with praise, and by following noncompliance consistently with use of timeout. (A more detailed description of CDI and PDI can be found in Eyberg, 1974.)

The parent is not allowed to progress to PDI until he or she has mastered CDI skills.[1] A potential advantage of teaching the relationship-building skills of CDI before the "disciplinary" skills of PDI concerns the difference between mere compliance and the child's adoption and internalization of the values underlying prosocial behavior. In a review of the effects of firm parental control on effective socialization of children, Lewis (1981) proposed that "the least pressure that is sufficient to obtain a child's compliance will promote the greatest internalization of values by the child" (p. 548). CDI clearly involves less "pressure" to behave appropriately than does PDI and therefore may have a greater chance of eliciting from the child a desire to please the parent and engage in behaviors that are rewarding for their own sake rather than eliciting simply a desire to avoid punishment.

Research on Parent–Child Interaction Therapy

Most of the controlled studies designed to evaluate the treatment of conduct problem behaviors in preschool children have used the parenting skills training model developed by Constance Hanf (e.g., Forehand & McMahon, 1981) or modified versions of her original model (e.g., Barkley, 1981; Eyberg, 1979, 1988; Hamilton & MacQuiddy, 1984; Webster-Stratton, 1982, 1984, 1985). In these studies, the effectiveness of the general principles and techniques employed in PCIT has received good empirical support.

---

1. To be considered to have mastered CDI skills sufficiently to proceed to PDI, parents are typically expected to meet several criteria during a 5-minute observation period. First, a parent should give 25 to 50 descriptive or reflective statements, about equally divided between descriptions and reflections. (This criterion assumes the child is verbal and presents the parent with something to reflect.) Second, the parent should ask no questions, give no commands, and make no critical statements. Third, the parent should make at least 15 praise statements, 8 of which must be labeled praise statements (e.g., "I like the way you picked the truck up off the floor.") rather than unlabeled praise statements (e.g., "That was nice.").

Concerning PCIT specifically, Eyberg and Robinson (1982) studied its effects on seven referred children, their untreated siblings, and the psychological functioning of their parents using multiple process and outcome measures. Results following an average of nine sessions revealed high rates of attendance, home practice, cooperation, and satisfaction with treatment; significant pre- to posttreatment changes in child and sibling behavior; and improvement in parental adjustment. Following treatment, the target children demonstrated a decline in deviant behavior, a lower ratio of noncompliance to commands, and a higher ratio of compliance. Parental attitudes toward the target child improved markedly during treatment. Treatment effects generalized to the untreated sibling's behavior and to the target child's behavior at home. After treatment, measures of rate of deviant behavior and parent reports of home behavior problems were within normal limits for target children and siblings.

Eyberg and Robinson (1982) examined the effects of the overall PCIT program without examining the effects of CDI and PDI independently. Recent unpublished data (Maddux, Sledden, Way, & Eyberg, 1987), however, show that CDI alone can produce clinically significant improvements on standardized measures of parent–child interactions and home behavior problems. In many cases, PDI resulted in additional reductions in reported home behavior problems. Follow-up data taken from several months to over a year after treatment provide evidence for the effectiveness and durability of PCIT.

Assessment in Parent–Child Interaction Therapy

A considerable body of literature exists on psychological assessment of children and on behavioral assessment in particular. This chapter can not review this work in full, and the reader is referred to other sources for additional information (e.g., Ollendick & Hersen, 1984). Our goal, instead, is to describe a procedure for assessing noncompliance that has proven useful in determining the suitability of PCIT as an intervention for these children and for assessing treatment outcome. The procedure consists of three components: (1) interviews with the parent and child, (2) completion of behavioral inventories and checklists, and (3) observation of the parent–child interaction.

Behavioral Interview

An interview with the parent(s) is indispensable. Four important goals of this interview are: (1) to establish rapport; (2) to determine the parents' perceptions of the nature and extent of the child's problems and the parents' management techniques; (3) to determine the parents' ability and willingness to participate in the child's treatment; and (4) to determine the suitability of PCIT in addressing the family's problems. The interview strategies employed in gathering this information are the same as those employed in general behavioral assessment interviews. (For more detail, see Ollendick & Hersen, 1984; Roberts & La Greca, 1981.)

A brief interview with the child is also important. By interacting with the child alone, the clinician can observe how the child interacts with an adult other than the parents and can assess the child's responsiveness to techniques such as praise or directions. Building rapport with the child is helpful in eliciting positive feelings toward future therapy visits. In addition, parents may feel more confident about treatment if they believe the therapist actually knows their child. (For a more complete description of the child interview, see Boggs & Eyberg, in press.)

Inventories and Checklists

The following inventories have been found useful in assessing conduct problems in preschool children. For a complete review of other behavioral checklists and inventories, the reader is referred to McMahon (1984).

Eyberg Child Behavior Inventory. The Eyberg Child Behavior Inventory (ECBI; Robinson, Eyberg, & Ross, 1980) is a single-factor measure of conduct problem behaviors in children between the ages of 2 and 17. It consists of 36 typical home problem behaviors reported by parents of conduct problem children. Each behavior is rated on a 7-point scale for frequency of occurrence and a "yes–no" problem identification scale. Cutoff scores for treatment selection have been established, and scores on both scales of the ECBI discriminate conduct problems from other clinical problems and from normal children (Eyberg & Robinson, 1983a; Eyberg & Ross, 1978; Robinson et al., 1980). Normative data have shown consistency in ECBI scores across age and socioeconomic levels (Eyberg & Robinson, 1983a). ECBI scores have been shown to correlate significantly with parent–child interactions observed in the clinic (Robinson & Eyberg, 1981). Treatment outcome studies of PCIT and other treatments have shown the ECBI to be a sensitive measure of change in conduct problem behavior of children (Eyberg & Matarazzo, 1980; Eyberg & Robinson, 1982; Eyberg & Ross, 1978; Hamilton & MacQuiddy, 1984; Webster-Stratton, 1985).

Sutter–Eyberg Student Behavior Inventory. The Sutter–Eyberg Student Behavior Inventory (SESBI) has the same format and scoring procedures as the ECBI, but was designed for ratings by teachers rather than parents. Standardization with a normal preschool sample (Funderburk & Eyberg, in preparation) has demonstrated that the SESBI is also a single-factor instrument of conduct problem behaviors in preschool children. Good test–retest and interrater reliability for both scales of the SESBI have been established, and normative data are highly consistent with mean scores on the ECBI. Comparison of clinic-referred preschool children and the normative sample shows highly significant differences (Funderburk & Eyberg, in preparation).

Behavioral Observation

Observations of the parent–child interaction is an essential aspect of the assessment of conduct problems in preschool children (see Eyberg, 1985, and Ollendick & Hersen, 1984, for reviews of behavioral observation methods). Because home observation is very costly, observation in the clinical setting is a practical and viable alternative. Fortunately, research suggests that observation of semistructured parent–child interactions in a clinical setting can discriminate reliably between problematic and normal parent–child interactions and can identify specific problem behaviors (Robinson & Eyberg, 1981). Data obtained from the observation are used to determine the parent's present level of parenting skill, to assess the child's current degree of deviant behavior and noncompliance, and to understand how the present parent–child interaction serves to maintain the dysfunctional pattern. Observational data also serve as a measure of treatment outcome.

The observation method used in PCIT is the Dyadic Parent–Child Interaction Coding System (DPICS; Eyberg & Robinson, 1983b). Using the DPICS, observations are conducted with one parent–child dyad at a time in a playroom containing several toys. The clinician may observe the interaction from a corner of the room or from behind a one-way mirror, if one is available. The parent and child are observed in three standard situations that vary in the degree of parental control required. In the first situation, the Child–Directed Interaction, the parent is instructed to allow the child to choose any activity and to play along with the child according to the child's rules. In the second situation, the Parent–Directed Interaction, the parent is instructed to select an activity and keep the child playing according to his/her rules. In the third situation, Clean-Up, the parent is instructed to get the child to put away all the toys without assistance. The structure of the three situations allows both the parent and the child to proceed naturally in situations with increasing requirements for parental control. This maximizes the possibility of observing problematic interactions. Coding of behaviors is continuous and results in a record of the total frequency of each behavior during each 5-minute observation. A data recording sheet is used to record all data by a single observer.

The DPICS provides the therapist with data on a number of important parent behaviors that have been shown to discriminate between conduct problem and normal families (Robinson & Eyberg, 1981). Also coded are a number of deviant child behaviors, such as whining, sassing, aggressive behaviors, and compliance or noncompliance with parents' commands. A detailed coding manual operationally defines each behavioral category

(Eyberg & Robinson, 1983b). Studies have documented the reliability of the coding categories (Aragona & Eyberg, 1981; Eyberg & Matarazzo, 1980; Robinson & Eyberg, 1981), and normative data have been presented (Robinson & Eyberg, 1984). Results from discriminant function analysis of the DPICS showed this coding system to correctly classify 100% of the normal families, 85% of the treatment families, and 94% of all families. Using multiple linear regression, DPICS predicted 61% of the variance in parent report of home behavior problems. In addition, several studies demonstrated significant changes in the behaviors of parents and children following treatment (e.g., Eyberg & Matarazzo, 1980; Eyberg & Robinson, 1982; Webster-Stratton, 1985).

CASE EXAMPLE

Five-year-old John M was referred to our clinic by his pediatrician in response to John's parents' concern over his difficulty relating appropriately to other children. John's private kindergarten teacher reported that John refused to participate in group activities and avoided playing with other children. She reported that he sought the attention of adults by repeatedly asking the same question, and that his contributions to class discussions were often irrelevant or off the topic. The teacher described John as bright and inquisitive but noted that he had difficulty paying attention and frequently seemed confused by simple directions unless he received individual instruction.

Mr. and Mrs. M presented as concerned and involved parents. Mr. M owned a successful small business, and Mrs. M had not worked outside the home since John's birth. They also had a 3-year-old daughter, Beth, for whom they initially reported no behavior problems. John's parents first became concerned about him when he was slow to develop speech. At the age of 2, they discovered that John had fluctuating hearing sensitivity due to chronic ear infections. This problem was corrected by the placement of tubes in his ears, and John was given remedial speech therapy until the age of 3.

Mrs. M. said she remained concerned about John's failure to make friends. She reported that when children came to visit, he usually left the room to play with his toys alone. She expressed fear that when he entered first grade in a public school he would be teased and ostracized because of his failure to join in group activities. Mr. M expressed fewer concerns about John, but appeared equally committed to participating in treatment. Methods of discipline used in the home included verbal reprimands, sending John to his room, and occasional spanking. Mrs. M reported being inconsistent with discipline at times due to her uncertainty about what she should expect John to do, and whether he clearly understood her expectations. She reported that John was often noncompliant and would sometimes (about twice a week) throw tantrums when she tried to get him to do things he did not want to do or when she did not comply with his requests.

Assessment

Initial assessment revealed that John was of normal intelligence and was achieving above his age level in academic tasks. Mild attention deficit was noted, as were social skills deficits. The mother's ECBI scores (Intensity 136; Problem 11) indicated mild conduct problems. The father's ECBI scores (Intensity 116; Problem 4) and the teacher's SESBI scores (Intensity 108; Problem 9) were within normal limits for a child John's age. Many of the teacher's concerns were about social withdrawal, therefore were not measured by the SESBI, which measures externalizing rather than internalizing behaviors (cf. Achenbach, 1982).

In the baseline behavioral observations using the DPICS (Child-Directed Interaction, Parent-Directed Interaction, and Clean-Up), Mrs. M's interactions with John were generally warm and nondirective. There were frequent periods of silence, and John tended to play separately from his mother. In all three situations, approximately two-thirds of Mrs. M's statements were questions or descriptions. Mrs. M gave 4 commands during CDI, 14 during PDI, and 12 during Clean-Up. Of the 30 commands, 10 were direct, and John complied with all of these. Direct commands were typically instructions to "Look at this" or similar nonconfrontive requests. John complied with approximately 50% of his mother's indirect commands.

Mr. M was more directive and verbal with John, and although warm, his manner was brisk and task-oriented. He asked 48 questions and gave 11 commands during the 5 minutes of CDI. Of his 77 total commands, 34 were above John's capabilities or were repeated before John had an opportunity to comply. Of the 43 commands with which John was given an opportunity, he complied with 70%. Each parent praised John five times during 15 minutes of interaction. When asked how closely the interactions with John in the playroom resembled those at home, Mr. M stated that the similarity was very close, while Mrs. M indicated that John was more compliant at the clinic than at home.

We (S. E. and B. F.) described PCIT to Mr. and Mrs. M, and they responded with enthusiasm. In the CDI teaching session, they participated actively and complied well with the request to practice CDI skills for 5 minutes per day. During the second week of treatment, Mrs. M attempted to completely master the program by practicing CDI with John every waking moment. She appeared quite anxious to perform perfectly at that week's session and expressed frustration and guilt when she did not reach criterion. At that point Mrs. M was encouraged to be less demanding of herself, and was reassured that progress could be made with 5 minutes of daily practice. Mrs. M expressed a lack of self-confidence regarding her competence as a parent and often wondered aloud what she might have done to cause John's problems.

Toward the end of the first month of treatment, Mrs. M began reporting behavior problems which she said were not noticeable before. These problems included whining, bossiness, and contradicting the parents. The parents also noted that John seemed at times to "tune them out." Uncertain of how to respond to this latter behavior, they had tended to leave John to himself. They were advised to actively engage John's attention rather than allowing him to tune them out. John continued to refuse to participate at school during the first month of treatment. On the one occasion he brought a friend to his house, John spent much of the day restricted to his room for uncooperative behavior.

Both parents now reported that Beth actually displayed more "acting out" problem behaviors than John but that they were less concerned about Beth's behavior because she was an outgoing child who interacted appropriately with peers. They also described her as a strong-willed child who rebelled against their attempts at discipline more often than John. They used CDI with Beth at times and reported that she enjoyed the special attention.

During the treatment sessions, John became increasingly provocative, particularly with his mother (e.g., flicking the lights on and off, eating clay, and covering his mother with chalk dust). He changed activities approximately every 3 minutes. The parents were coached on ignoring low-level problem behaviors and praising cooperation and appropriate play. During the second month of treatment, reports from school became more variable. For example, during 1 week John had 2 "perfect days" at school and his worst day ever when he deliberately flooded the restroom by turning on all the water faucets. However, the teacher also reported an increase in on-task behavior. This was also noted during treatment sessions. John continued to test his parents during the sessions. His bossy statements (e.g., "Don't touch the red crayon.") and contradictions (e.g., "It is not!") occurred several times per session with each parent.

At the fifth session, Mrs. M requested a trial of medication for John with the goal of making him "calmer and better able to relate to other children." It was explained that while medication might increase John's ability to concentrate, it was not likely to improve his social skills. A decision was made to continue the treatment program without medication for another month and then reevaluate the desirability of a trial of medication.

Mrs. M had virtually mastered CDI by week 4, and by the sixth session both parents met the criterion for progressing to PDI. Mr. M had vastly improved his ability to follow John's play rather than directing it. John now remained on a single activity for up to 10 minutes. At this point the parents were asked to begin labeling John's bossy and contradictory statements at home. This was done to ensure that John would understand what behavior was unacceptable when an intervention program was initiated. About this time, Mr. M realized that he had a habit of teasing John and others by contradicting what they said. Believing that this behavior may have contributed to John's behavior problems, Mr. M began to work on reducing his own use of contradictions and negations.

Both parents completed ECBIs, and the teacher completed a SESBI after completion of CDI and prior to the first PDI session. The mother's ratings had moved into the normal range (Intensity score of 96; Problem score of 9), while the father and teacher now reported Problem scores of 10 and 19, respectively. The new problems reported by the teacher were indicative of increased conflict with peers such as teasing, making noises, and verbally fighting. These changes were interpreted to the parents as an indication that John was beginning to approach other children, although he had not yet developed the social skills necessary for successful interactions. The intensity of attentional problems and negative attention-getting behaviors with adults was generally lower.

Mr. and Mrs. M learned the rules of PDI quickly and practiced regularly. John also paid close attention to the rules when we outlined them for him at the beginning of the first PDI coaching session. During the session, he obeyed 20 commands from his father with only 5 warnings, and 16 from his mother with only 3 warnings. John did not have to go to the timeout chair during this session.

Mrs. M. expressed finding some difficulty using direct commands with John because she thought she sounded harsh. She was assured that she could use a pleasant tone of voice and say "please" as long as she kept her commands direct. By the third PDI session (week 10), she felt comfortable using direct commands throughout the day at home. She observed, herself, that John responded much better to her direct commands than to her indirect ones. She also notes that she now felt much less tense and worried about dealing with John. The parents described his behavior as dramatically improved at home. Mrs. M no longer wanted to pursue a trial of medication when that issue was discussed at Session 11.

Both parents began to use PDI with Beth as well. She had to be sent to the chair more often than John and several times stubbornly sat on the chair, refusing to comply, for up to half an hour. She soon learned to respond to most warnings without going to the chair, and Mr. and Mrs. M noted significant improvement in Beth's behavior over the next weeks.

Between Sessions 10 and 15, John moved from requiring warnings with an estimated 75% of commands given at home to less than 5%. Beth continued to require more warnings than John, but now averaged going to the chair once or twice per week rather than daily. House rules were established requiring John and Beth to automatically sit on the chair whenever they bossed or contradicted. When these rules were enforced consistently for a week, the problem behaviors quickly diminished in frequency. At this point the parents also again expressed their concern to us about John's repetitively asking the same question. We encouraged the parents to discuss how the techniques they had mastered might apply to this problem, and they decided (in John's presence) that they would first try ignoring all questions that had been answered once. This behavior rapidly diminished once it was ignored, and a neighbor spontaneously remarked several weeks later that John no longer questioned her repetitively.

One joint session was held with both children present so that we could observe and coach the parents interactions with both children simultaneously, since both parents had previously reported finding that situation particularly difficult. Upon observation, however, we noted that each parent handled both children together in a manner that was warm, consistent, and marked by good judgment. During feedback with the parents, they acknowledged that the children had responded very well when they applied their interaction skills to both children simultaneously. In subsequent sessions, they reported having had no further difficulty in managing joint activities.

The school teacher continued to report improvements in John's behavior. The parents also noted that John was very interested in making friends, although he preferred to play with 4-year-olds instead of his own classmates. Since the school year was ending, we encouraged John's parents to enroll John in a summer program which would allow him continued daily interaction with peers. Mrs. M expressed the fear that John would be unpopular and that summer camp would be a traumatic experience for him. In order to help prepare herself and John, she made a concerted effort to invite playmates over regularly. She noted that John played more cooperatively and that children began inviting him to their homes. The parents also noted with pleasure that neighbors and relatives spontaneously commented on the positive changes in John's behavior.

Despite the progress that had been made, Mr. and Mrs. M remained apprehensive about their ability to maintain and continue progress after termination of therapy. They continued to rely on us for guidance regarding generalization to new problems, such as how to modify use of the chair for noncompliance in public situations. Following Session 16, the family missed a session when they went on vacation. When they returned after 2 weeks, they had initiated and enforced two new house rules on their own, and expressed much more confidence in their own abilities to deal with problem behaviors. A final treatment session was scheduled for 2 weeks later, after John's first week of summer camp.

The teacher had completed a final SESBI during the last week of school, which corresponded to Session 15. The Intensity score of 92 was within normal limits for children John's age. The Problem score had dropped from a midtreatment high of 19 to 12, also within normal limits. The teacher indicated that John was less distractible and no longer "overactive." She also noted that he had less difficulty entering groups of other children. Several problem behaviors continued, although these showed improvement as well. These included demanding teacher attention and acting frustrated with difficult tasks. Peer interaction problems cited at midtreatment, but no longer present at the final rating, included teasing other students, verbally fighting with other students, and making noises in class.

Each parent completed the ECBI prior to their final session, and all scores were within normal limits (Mother's Intensity score, 93, Problem score, 9; Father's Intensity score, 100, Problem score, 4). Final behavioral observations demonstrated that both parents were consistently applying the techniques of CDI and PDI. John was immediately compliant with 85% of his mother's 26 commands and 95% compliant with his father's 39 commands. In instances of noncompliance, both parents appropriately issued warnings, which in all cases elicited John's compliance. John did not make any bossy or contradictory statements during the session, and the parents indicated that at home he had to be sent to the timeout chair for these behaviors only once in the past 2 weeks. They observed that he seemed to be "catching himself" and would sometimes stop in midsentence to rephrase his statement as a polite request, which they praised.

During their final session, Mr. and Mrs. M expressed delight with John's adaptation to summer camp. They reported that he was participating in all group activities except team sports and that he was reluctant to leave camp at the end of each day. During this session the family viewed the pre- and posttherapy videotapes of DPICS interactions. They commented on how much happier John seemed and on how attuned he was to them in the recent tape, while in the old tape he appeared to isolate himself and not listen when they spoke. They attributed these changes to their own behavioral changes. A follow-up session was scheduled for 6 weeks later.

No significant problems were reported for John or Beth at follow-up. The parents still had some concerns about John's peer relationships, but they noted continuing progress as they praised and supported John's increasingly appropriate interactions with peers. John stated that he was looking forward to beginning first grade with some friends he made at summer camp.

REFERENCES

Achenbach, T. M., & Edelbrock, C. S. (1982). The classification of child psychopathology: A review and analysis of empirical efforts. *Psychological Bulletin, 85,* 1275–1301.

American Psychiatric Association. (1987). *Diagnostic and statistical manual of mental disorders* (3rd ed., revised). Author.

Aragona, J., & Eyberg, S. (1981). Neglected children: Mothers' report of child behavior problems and observed verbal behavior. *Child Development, 52,* 596–602.

Barkley, R. A. (1981). *Hyperactive children: A handbook for diagnosis and treatment.* New York: Guilford.

Boggs, S. R., & Eyberg, S. (in press). Interviewing techniques and establishing rapport. In A. M. La Greca (Ed.), *Childhood assessment: Through the eyes of a child.* New York: Allyn & Bacon.

Dangel, R. F., & Polster, R. A. (Eds.). (1984). *Parent training: Foundations of research and practice.* New York: Guilford.

Eyberg, S. M. (1974). *Rules and rationale for the child-directed interaction and parent-directed interaction.* (Available from S. M. Eyberg, Department of Clinical Psychology, Box J-165, JHMHC, University of Florida, Gainesville, FL 32610)

Eyberg, S. M. (1979, April). *A parent–child interaction model for the treatment of psychological disorders in young children.* Paper presented at the annual meeting of the Western Psychological Association, San Diego, CA.

Eyberg, S. M. (1985). Behavioral assessment: Advancing methodology in pediatric psychology. *Journal of Pediatric Psychology, 10,* 123–139.

Eyberg, S. M. (1988). Parent–child interaction therapy: Integration of traditional and behavioral concerns. *Child and Family Behavior Therapy, 10,* 33–46.

Eyberg, S. M., & Matarazzo, R. G. (1980). Training parents as therapists: A comparison between individual parent–child interaction training and parent group didactic training. *Journal of Clinical Psychology, 36,* 492–499.

Eyberg, S. M., & Robinson, E. A. (1982). Parent–child interaction training: Effects on family functioning. *Journal of Clinical Child Psychology, 11,* 130–137.

Eyberg, S. M., & Robinson, E. A. (1983a). Conduct problem behavior: Standardization of a behavioral rating scale with adolescents. *Journal of Clinical Child Psychology, 12,* 347–354.

Eyberg, S. M., & Robinson, E. A. (1983b). Dyadic parent–child interaction coding system: A manual. *Psychological Documents, 13,* 24.

Eyberg, S. M., & Ross, A. W. (1978). Assessment of child behavior problems: The validation of a new inventory. *Journal of Clinical Child Psychology, 7,* 113–116.

Forehand, R., & McMahon, P. (1981). *Helping the noncompliant child.* New York: Guilford.

Funderburk, B., & Eyberg, S. M. (in preparation). Standardization of a school behavior rating scale with preschool children. University of Florida.

Hamilton, S. L., & MacQuiddy, S. L. (1984). Self-administered behavioral parent-training: Enhancement of treatment efficacy using a time-out signal seat. *Journal of Clinical Child Psychology, 13,* 61–69.

Lewis, C. C. (1981). The effects of parental firm control: A reinterpretation of findings. *Psychological Bulletin, 90,* 547–563.

MacMahon, R. J. (1984). Behavioral checklists and ratings forms. In T. H. Ollendick & M. Hersen (Eds.), *Child behavioral assessment: Principles and procedures* (pp. 80–105). New York: Pergamon.

Maddux, J. E., Sledden, E. A., Way, J. H., & Eyberg, S. M. (1987). [Parent–child interaction therapy: Effects of relationship training plus compliance training.] Unpublished raw data.

O'Dell, S. (1974). Training parents in behavior modification: A review. *Psychological Bulletin, 81,* 418–433.

Ollendick, T. H., & Hersen, M. (1984). An overview of child behavioral assessment. In T. H. Ollendick & M. Hersen (Eds.), *Child behavioral assessment: Principles and procedures* (pp. 3–19). New York: Pergamon.

Peterson, D. R. (1961). Behavior problems of middle childhood. *Journal of Consulting Psychology, 25,* 205–209.

Quay, H. C. (1986). Conduct disorders. In H. C. Quay & S. Werry (Eds.), *Psychopathological disorders of childhood* (pp. 35–72). New York: Wiley.

Roberts, M. C., & La Greca, A. M. (1981). Behavioral assessment. In C. E. Walker (Ed.), *Clinical practice of psychology: A practical guide for mental health professionals* (pp. 243–346). New York: Pergamon.

Robins, L. N. (1966). *Deviant children grown up.* Baltimore, MD: Williams & Wilkins.

Robinson, E. A., & Eyberg, S. M. (1981). The dyadic parent–child interaction coding system: Standardization and validation. *Journal of Consulting and Clinical Psychology, 49,* 245–250. (Ms. No. 2582)

Robinson, E. A., & Eyberg, S. M. (1984). Behavioral assessment in pediatric settings: Theory, method, and application. In P. R. Magrab (Ed.), *Psychological and behavioral assessment: Impact on pediatric care* (pp. 91–140). New York: Plenum.

Robinson, E. A., Eyberg, S. M., & Ross, A. W. (1980). The standardization of an inventory of child conduct problem behaviors. *Journal of Clinical Child Psychology, 9,* 22–28.

Thomas, A., Chess, S., & Birch, H. G. (1968). *Temperament and behavior disorders in children.* New York: New York University Press.

Webster-Stratton, C. (1982). Teaching mothers through videotaped modeling to change their child's behavior. *Journal of Pediatric Psychology, 7,* 279–294.

Webster-Stratton, C. (1984). Randomized trial of two parent training programs for families with conduct disordered children. *Journal of Consulting and Clinical Psychology, 52,* 666–678.

Webster-Stratton, C. (1985). Predictors of treatment outcome in parent training for conduct disordered children. *Behavior Therapy, 16,* 223–243.

9
Child Custody Evaluation

KEVIN C. MOONEY
JAMES M. NELSON

During the last 25 years, American society has witnessed an explosive growth in divorce rates, as well as an increased conviction that society should play a more active role in promoting the safety and well-being of children. As a result, psychologists have found increasing opportunities to become involved in the legal process with regard to child custody disputes. This chapter presents the thinking and decision making of two psychologists as they prepared a report that was submitted in a custody evaluation case and outlines many of the practical, legal, and ethical issues faced by psychologists conducting custody evaluations. Identifying details, including names, have been changed to protect confidentiality.

A body of literature has emerged in the last 10 years describing the theoretical and practical issues involved in child custody evaluations. For a more thorough guide to the preparation and writing of child custody evaluations, we suggest *Child Custody Evaluations: A Practical Guide* (1985) by Dianne Skafte. We also highly recommend Joseph Goldstein, Anna Freud, and Albert Solnit's (1979) landmark book, *Beyond the Best Interests of the Child,* as a starting point for many of the psychological issues and ethics involved in child placement. Although many may disagree with its psychoanalytic bias, it remains a work of vital interest to psychologists of all orientations. Given the variety of practices across states, anyone interested in the technical details of custody law should also consult a local law library. For a general legal reference regarding custody, we suggest Ann Haralambie's (1983) *Handling Child Custody Cases.*

The guidelines and procedures for conducting a child custody evaluation differ very little from those of other types of psychological evaluations. The following are some of the standard rules that apply.

Kevin C. Mooney and James M. Nelson. Department of Psychology, Valparaiso University, Valparaiso, Indiana.

1. *Obtain a clear referral question.* Exactly what does the person making the referral want to know? The evaluator should spend time discussing the referral question with the person making the referral to ensure that the question is as specific as possible, and to make certain that there is agreement that a psychological evaluation is the appropriate means for answering the question.

Forensic cases such as child custody cases differ from many psychological evaluations in that the referral source often has a vested interest in how the referral question is answered. Professional ethics, scientific objectivity, and concern for the best interests of the child, all suggest that the evaluator cannot agree to provide an evaluation that will automatically support the position desired by the referral source.

2. *Survey all the behavior–ability domains relevant to the referral question.* The exact domains to be included in the evaluation will depend on the referral question. For example, if information about intellectual development and school performance is needed, assessment of cognitive achievement and ability will be a necessary part of the evaluation. Information-gathering in most domains will include investigation of both past and present behaviors. Assessment of cognitive achievement and ability would thus involve consideration of past academic and developmental history in addition to examination of the present level of functioning.

3. *Gather information on each relevant behavior–ability domain using multiple sources and/or methods.* At least two methods of data collection and/or sources of information should be utilized in the evaluation of each behavior–ability domain. Traditionally, one data collection method has involved standardized psychological testing. Thus, if cognitive achievement and ability are to be assessed, the evaluator will want to include intelligence and achievement testing in addition to other sources of information such as teacher and parental reports.

4. *Present the results in an effective manner.* Results of the psychological evaluation should be conveyed in such a way as to directly address the referral question, and should do so in language that will be understood by those who are to hear or read the findings. A report for a lawyer and judge who are concerned with legal issues will differ from one that might be written to a physician with a similar referral question.

Another issue in effective presentation of results involves what the psychologist hopes to accomplish with the report. Most referrals will provide an opportunity to make recommendations concerning the treatment and disposition of the case. Recommendations that are made should be clearly stated and achievable within the constraints of the situation. Vague recommendations or unrealistic proposals will reduce the psychologist's ability to have a positive impact on the situation.

This chapter will present each section of a child custody evaluation report followed by a "Discussion" section in which we present our perceptions/observations and rationale for the decisions made.

CASE BACKGROUND

At the time of this evaluation report, one of us (K. C. M.) was associated with a training clinic for psychology graduate students, and the other (J. M. N.) was a graduate student in a clinical psychology program and a clinical assistant in the training clinic. Our involvement in the case began when we were contacted by the attorney hired by Jody E, the mother of the child involved in the custody decision. The attorney obtained our assistance because she was acquainted with K. C. M. through joint involvement with local social service agencies, and because the training clinic's sliding fee scale was within the client's limited financial means.

The child involved in the custody dispute was John H, a 5½-year-old boy whose parents had been divorced for about 1 year. Since the divorce, John had been in a temporary joint custody situation, living 1 week with his father in one town and the next week at the maternal great-aunt's in a town 60 miles from the other. Over the previous 6 months, the boy's mother had been involved in several live-in relationships and had been living at the great-aunt's between them. The boy's maternal grandmother was also a frequent visitor to the great-aunt's house. The mother felt that her son was extremely unhappy while he was at her ex-husband's house, and wanted to take advantage of a prearranged review of the custody arrangements so that her son could reside primarily at the great-aunt's. At the time of the original custody order, a judicial review of the case had been scheduled for later that summer, prior to the beginning of the school year.

The attorney solicited a psychological evaluation because of her concerns about the appropriateness of the child's current living situation. The current arrangements had been ordered at the time of the divorce by the judge, with no formal home or psychological evaluation. The father declined to participate in the present evaluation after a request was made by the mother, her attorney, and ourselves. The authors had no prior contact with the presiding judge.

Discussion

Before accepting any custody case, a psychologist should have familiarity with the following concepts common to most state laws: best interests of the child, psychological parent, parental integrity or rights, substantial and material change of circumstances, opinion of the child, and unfit parent. Many of these issues were factors in this case. It was clear from the outset that there would soon be a substantial and material change of circumstances since the child's present custody arrangement prevented him from attending one school system. The presence of John's great-aunt as a significant parental figure also raised the issue of "psychological parent," since she had filled that role and was thus the natural choice of custodian. On the other hand, both parents desired custody of John, and "parental rights" would support the notion that custody should continue to be a joint arrangement between them.

The issues of one parent being more "fit" than another and of the preference of the child were of secondary focus in this evaluation due to the circumstances of this case. Given that from the outset we were dealing directly only with the child's maternal caretakers, we could not judge the father's "fitness" as a parent nor the relative merits of the maternal and paternal homes. Although John had expressed the desire to live with his maternal caretakers, legal and psychological opinion gives little, or at least qualified, weight to the opinion of the child before he reaches the age of 14 (Ehrenreich & Melton, 1983; Lyman & Roberts, 1985).

A major problem in this case and other child custody disputes is that the various factors involved in making a custody decision conflict with one another. The legal system has traditionally sought to maintain parental integrity and rights in its child custody decisions. An alternative goal is provided by the psychological parent model (Goldstein et al., 1979) which states that sole custody should be given to the parent who provides the child with the most nurturance and overall attention. Although the psychological parent may also be a natural parent, at times the psychological parent model may support giving custody to an individual who is not a natural parent. In the case of John, it was possible that at some point the best interest of the child, to live with a psychological parent, would be pitted against parental integrity and rights of the father to have custody of the son. In such cases the issues of psychological parent and best interests of the child, while factors in custody decisions, typically do not take precedence over parental integrity and rights, except when there is considerable improper parental conduct (i.e., an unfit parent) or other unusual circumstances (such as abdication of parental responsibilities for a considerable period of time) (Haralambie, 1983). Factors such as material and cultural advantages are insufficient in and of themselves to abrogate parental rights and integrity.

This case presented a number of additional potential pitfalls, foremost being the difficulty in conducting an evaluation in which all parties were not involved. Many psychologists (e.g., Gardner, 1982; Skafte, 1985) refuse to be involved with cases unless appointed by the court (as part of the court's role of "parens patriae") so that they can consider all relevant factors in making their decisions (i.e., a "friend of the court") or unless both parties agree to be fully involved in the evaluation. In fact, we take that issue one step further in our practice by urging attorneys to bypass judicial decision making except on a pro forma level. In its place we advocate custody mediation prior to the formal legal custody proceedings in order to defuse hostile interactions, promote constructive alternatives, etc. However, given that there are times when this advice is ignored or impossible to implement, we are often left with many of the complex ethical, professional, and moral issues of forensic psychology in a family court. These issues include, but also exceed, the obvious conflict-of-interest dilemma summed up in the adage, "He who pays the piper calls the tune." (To be more blunt, a family court judge who is a friend of the authors claims that most of his colleagues view such "hired-gun" psychologists as prostitutes, with the lawyer acting as pimp.) Even more problematic is that, except when one is acting as a "guardian ad litum" or a "friend of the court," the child lacks legal standing. As a result, there is no forum to present the "best interests of the child." Consequently, we may be deluding ourselves by believing that we serve in the "best interests of the child." For example, if a psychologist's assessment opposes the hiring parent's position, he/she may be dismissed. Once dismissed, even if we had discovered in the process of our evaluation that the parent who had hired us was unfit and that staying with this parent would, in our opinion, certainly be in the worst interest of the child, we have no legal forum and hence no legal or professional recourse. Unless we are a "friend of the court," we cannot share this knowledge or opinion with anyone. If we share our information with the judge, he/she would have to disqualify himself/herself from the case. If we present our information to the opposing attorney, it is doubtful whether that attorney would be allowed to present that information in court, and we would be vulnerable to a lawsuit, as well as to disciplinary action by our state psychology licensing board for disclosure of confidential infor-mation. Given this state of affairs, why would any psychologist (for reasons other than greed) agree to practice and abide by the rules of such a potentially exploitative and harmful system? In our opinion, we, as psychologists, have a social responsibility to work in and with an imperfect judicial system which has, whether we like it or not, a major impact on the welfare of children, all the while attempting to promote change in that very same legal system. We, as psychologists, have a personal and social respon-sibility to use our professional expertise to benefit children, families, and society, and not, between now and the dawning of a "new age" of fairness and justice in the courts, to leave forensic work to the unqualified and unethical.

We decided to accept this case, despite the less than ideal evaluation situation, because we felt we could benefit the child. Further conversation with the attorney revealed a genuine concern that the child was at risk for learning, emotional, and/or behavioral problems. In fact, the attorney ex-pressed concern that she was representing the child instead of her client. This, in addition to our previous knowledge of this attorney and her ethical standards, laid to rest many of our fears of being exploited.

INITIAL CONTACT

We contacted the mother to arrange for the evaluation. We clearly stated to her that ours was a circumscribed initial evaluation that would focus on John's needs and best interests relative to his maternal living situation. We requested that all three of the maternal relatives come in with John for an interview and in order to complete some questionnaires. We estimated that the evaluation would likely involve a couple of 2- or 3-hour sessions during the following week.

Discussion

A major concern of all custody evaluations is losing perspective, given the variety of intentional and unintentional ways that information can be distorted. This was a primary concern in the case, given that we were not yet including the parental family. The opportunity to gain four perspectives on the situation (child, mother, grandmother, and great-aunt) was seen as potentially very helpful for the validity of our conclusions.

PSYCHOLOGICAL EVALUATION

Instructions about how to begin the Herculean task of writing a psychological evaluation have been discussed elsewhere (cf. Palmer, 1983). In the legal system the task is exacerbated by pressure upon the psychologist to make absolute pronouncements in a world full of incomplete knowledge and judgment calls. In this case, we decided to focus on the following areas: the child's current adjustment and attachment (see the Behavioral Assessment section), the child's social relationships (see the Social Relationships section), the child's academic potential (see the Intellectual Assessment section), and the strengths and weaknesses of the maternal family in raising this child (see the Family Information section). We strove in our final section, Recommendations, to give realistic, concrete, and specific advice.

All psychologists who intend to testify in court should be aware that they must return on other days, with other cases, to testify in that same courtroom. Hence, one's personal/professional goals of "covering one's self" and protecting one's credibility and reputation are major factors in forensic testimony and evaluation. We make a conscious effort to remain fair and even-handed, to include both the strengths and weaknesses of those involved, and to see that we are not "pigeonholed," i.e., seen as fixed on one recommendation, regardless of the circumstance. This attempt to be "objective," however, does not imply that we deny or cover up our ethics, values, and even our personalities in our report and testimony. In fact, we practice the opposite by developing a relationship with the local presiding judges, so that we become aware of each others' predilections and limitations. For instance, a judge in our area is philosophically opposed to joint custody. While that judge is aware that we do not share his position, he is also aware that with him we typically provide alternatives he can work with and base his decisions on. Because our convictions are on the table, we can disagree in one area and yet work together in other areas. (In fact, we occasionally convince the judge to make an exception and allow joint custody in particular cases.)

NAME: John H
AGE: 5 years, 6 months
DATE OF BIRTH: 11/20/80
DATES OF EXAMINATION: 5/19/86 and 5/21/86
DATE OF REPORT: 5/23/86
FAMILY PARTICIPANTS: Jody E (mother); Judy W (maternal grandmother); and Clarice L (maternal great-aunt)
TESTS ADMINISTERED:
    Child: Kaufman Assessment Battery for Children (K-ABC)
        Draw a figure and draw-a-family tasks
    Maternal relatives:
        Achenbach Child Behavior Checklist (CBCL)
        Minnesota Multiphasic Personality Inventory (MMPI)
        Rotter Incomplete Sentences Blank (ISB)
    All participants: Individual interview and family behavioral assessment.
TESTER: James Nelson   INTERVIEWER: Kevin Mooney

Discussion

In this case, the second author (J. M. N.) of the evaluation team administered and scored all the tests (under the first author's supervision) while the first author conducted all interviews. Hence, only the first author could be requested to provide courtroom testimony.

As psychologists, our task was to make recommendations based on our observations of individual and family functioning (a task that is also shared by social workers and psychiatrists) and on our interpretation of testing results (a task that exclusively rests with psychologists). Our task is not to make specific predictions regarding one custody arrangement or another (unless specifically requested by the court). We leave diagnosis per se to physicians or psychiatrists, although we have been known to use the phrase "our diagnostic impression. . . ." In custody situations we are acutely aware that everything we do is subject to scrutiny in a critical and adversarial light. Hence, a significant portion of our findings will always include instruments with standardized procedures and appropriate normative data, such as the K-ABC, MMPI, and CBCL.

More specific rationales for the tests administered are:

1. The K-ABC is a standardized intelligence or mental processing test particularly useful for children who may be culturally deprived (there are separate sociocultural norms) or verbally deficient (Kaufman & Kaufman, 1983). Furthermore, its sequential and simultaneous processing division provides useful information for screening for learning problems.

2. The MMPI was chosen as a screening instrument to detect serious pathology (Hathaway & McKinley, 1951). Its wide acceptance in the field, extensive research base, and validity scales contribute to its value.

3. The CBCL has a number of advantages as a standardized screening instrument (Achenbach & Edelbrock, 1983). It covers a wide variety of childhood behavior problems, some of which might be overlooked in an interview, and it is normed according to age and sex. In addition, administering the test to multiple respondents makes possible statements with consensual validity.

4. Figure drawings. We personally have great concerns about the reliability and validity of figure drawings as measures of personality or family dynamics. However, they have the advantage of both breaking up the interview with the child, promoting conversation, and focusing the child on his/her perceived position in the family. In our opinion, "projective" measures in court evaluations are valid primarily as starting points for further hypothesis testing.

5. The ISB was used with the maternal realtives following a rationale similar to the figure drawing tasks (Rotter & Rafferty, 1950). As we were not particularly interested in using the ISB as a global measure of conflict and adjustment, we did not use the standardized scoring.

6. Behavioral assessment. We know of no well-normed observational assessment instruments for parent–child interactions in an office or playroom setting. However, the available data do indicate that "problem families" have difficulty "faking good" in such a situation (Lobitz & Johnson, 1975). This should give the examiner some confidence in his/her assessment of the situation. We used one of many coding systems available—Barkley's (1981) Response Class Matrix—to assist us in attending to relevant aspects of parent–child interactions. Our general format is to observe the parent and child in unstructured play, then in play directed by the child, and then in play directed by the parent. Given John's living situation, which involved contact with all three maternal relatives, we chose to conduct the actual behavioral observation with all four persons in the room, observing how each interacted with John.

7. Clinical interviews. We used a fairly unstructured clinical interview, with the exception that we presented each caretaker with a number of hypothetical instances of how she might handle a variety of relevant problem situations. We particularly attended to the parental figures' awareness of current and future "developmental" problem areas and their ability to

enumerate alternative solutions to handling problems (including seeking appropriate social support).

Presenting Problem

John was referred to the ———— ———— clinic by Emily M, an attorney in ————. She requested an evaluation and recommendations concerning (1) John's living situation and (2) his prospective school performance.

Discussion

We wish to explicitly state that ours was neither an individual psychological evaluation nor a full-scale custody evaluation.

Behavioral Assessment

During the initial interview, John became extremely upset when asked to leave his maternal caretakers, evidenced by his whining and clinging to his great-aunt. After separation was achieved, he adjusted fairly rapidly, and good rapport was established. During the second interview there were no noticeable separation problems. All three caretakers appeared to be able to communicate clearly and relate in a positive manner to John. The mother was best able to play with John, but had difficulty structuring the situation; the grandmother could structure the situation well, but was clearly uncomfortable playing with John; and the great-aunt could attend to him well and watch him interact, but seemed to have difficulty redirecting him.

All three of the Child Behavior Checklists indicated that John was immature and had some somatic complaints (e.g., stomach problems, doesn't eat well). In addition to these problems, the checklist of the great-aunt's indicated that he was aggressive.

The behavioral assessment and observations were consistent. Emotionally, John appeared quite close and "connected" to all of his maternal relatives. The somatic and immature problems noted on the CBCL were predictable given that John seemed to be getting attention and nurturing in response to immature behaviors and that he might not be getting sufficient guidance, stimulation, and structure from his maternal caretakers.

Discussion

One's values and beliefs about what is central in a child's development play a key role in how one summarizes a child's behavior with his/her parents and, indeed, in all evaluations of children. There has been a strong tradition in psychology and the courts of advocating a "tender years doctrine." This has resulted in a preference to award the mother custody during the child's early years. During the last decade, APA and various states have argued that this practice of discriminating against men because of their sex in the assignment of child custody is psychologically unfounded, as well as in violation of human rights (Salk, 1977), although courts are still biased in this regard (Scherman, 1983). An aspect of the "tender years doctrine" that is widely held by psychological theorists (and, hence, often argued in court) is that a psychological parent is critical to a child's healthy development (cf. Goldstein et al., 1979).

Throughout a custody evaluation, we focus on what we consider to be the two major themes in the parenting literature: 1) the ability to nurture the child, that is to care for the child's emotional needs with sensitivity, acceptance, and accessibility; and 2) the ability to structure a child's experience, that is to provide appropriate discipline and stimulation, to protect the child, and to be neither rigid nor laissez-faire. In accord with a variety of psychological theorists, we believe that as the child grows, the relative importance of nurturance and structure is likely to shift, with nurturance given more relative weight in a decision involving young children and structure seen as relatively more important with older children and adolescents.

Social Relationships

According to John's self-report and those of all the maternal relatives, John lacked friends or peers with whom he consistently interacted. The few peer encounters he did have appeared to not be particularly successful.

Discussion

Typically, in a custody evaluation, we would involve neighbors and/or teachers. In this case, John was not in school, and his isolated life in the country gave him limited contact with neighbors or other social contacts. Given the unanimity of the evidence from John and his maternal relatives (John did not appear to know the last name of anyone he had played with and the maternal relatives cited no consistent playmate), further investigation at this time did not seem warranted.

Intellectual Assessment

John seemed interested and involved in the testing process, and applied himself to all of the tasks. Hence, the test results are likely an accurate indication of his intellectual ability. On the K-ABC, he achieved a standard score of 87 on the Global Sequential Processing scale, 71 on Simultaneous Processing, and 75 on the Mental Processing Composite (MPC). His MPC score exceeded only 5% of those in the sample with the same sociocultural background. His overall standard score on the achievement tests was also low at 76, exceeding only 5% of those with comparable racial background and parental education. These test results suggested that John fell in a borderline category of intellectual functioning just superior to that of mild mental retardation.

John showed significant strengths and weaknesses on the various parts of the K-ABC. He did significantly better on sequential than simultaneous tasks, that is, he had a relative problem with being able to look at a number of things at one time and put them together. He was especially strong in the Hand Movements task, which involves coordination, the ability to follow directions, and short-term memory. He scored especially low on the Magic Window test, which can be affected by a number of factors, including early language development problems and inability to synthesize information.

The cause or causes of John's intellectual weaknesses were unclear. The pattern of deficits was consistent with early language development and environmental deprivation problems, while his speech problems might have been indicative of the presence of organic problems. Further evaluation would be necessary to reach a decision on this.

Discussion

The K-ABC results are given in reasonable detail. Given what appears to be the importance of remedial assistance for John, we wanted our recommendations to have weight in the report.

Family Information

The MMPI, ISB, and interview suggested that Clarice L, the great-aunt, is conventional and stable, possibly bordering on rigid, as well as somewhat sensitive and suspicious, and generally uncomfortable with other people.

Judy W, the grandmother, stood out as a very conventional and rigid individual, to the point that she might have considerable difficulty dealing successfully with change. Her MMPI indicated a defensive person who might have some tendency to abuse substances.

Jody E's testing and interview suggested that she is suspicious, sensitive, angry, irritable, unconventional, and has a tendency to blame others for her difficulties. Since she scored very high on the Familial Discord subscale of the MMPI, it is possible that some of her anger and suspiciousness might have been a reaction to familial conflict. Her MMPI and her past history make substance abuse an ever-present possibility in her life.

John's current living situation with the great-aunt needed improvement. Neither the mother, the grandmother, nor the great-aunt were currently providing the structure, social experiences, or long-term planning that would best benefit John. This was evidenced by their inability to cope with his clinging and whining behavior, the limited social relationships to which he was exposed, and their extremely vague responses in accepting or dealing with John's potential learning and social difficulties. Furthermore, the mother has a high potential for substance abuse and is currently involved with and had a history of abusive and unstable relationships which provided very poor role modeling for John.

On the positive side, all three women quite evidently care for John, and John did appear to have established a strong and positive, almost amorphous, mother-son relationship with all of them. As a group they provide John with love, stability, and support, and there is no doubt that John needed this very much at this time. Of the three, Clarice L, the great-aunt, is probably the best single current caretaker for John, but the combined contributions of all three appeared considerably greater than any one of them alone.

Finally, this evaluation was obviously incomplete without a concurrent assessment of John's father and his home. However, some tentative statements seem warranted. First, John considered Clarice L's house to be home. Second, John and the maternal relatives' perception that John remained ignored by or at least uninvolved with his father, step-mother, and step-siblings while living with them needed investigation.

Discussion

All sources of information agreed that, with the exception of the mother's history of substance abuse, none of the caretakers exhibited behavior particularly dangerous to John. However, all three caretakers had significant personal weaknesses and John's living situation there, in our opinion, ranged from less than ideal to inadequate. As in many custody cases, the principle suggested by Goldstein et al. (1979) of making decisions in light of "the least detrimental available alternative for safeguarding the child's growth and development," rather than the more positively focused principle of "best interests of the child," seemed the most appropriate.

In some cases a direct listing of likely weaknesses might be viewed as jeopardizing our relationship with either the attorney or maternal family. However, the mother and her attorney were well aware of a variety of shortcomings and both appeared sincere in wanting what was best for John given the poor situation. Furthermore, we were convinced, as is reflected in our recommendations, that John was "at risk" for a number of emotional/behavioral/social/academic difficulties, and the factors that contributed to this needed to be clearly documented and stated or else they would continue to go unaddressed.

On a more positive note, John seemed to receive from all three of the maternal relatives, at different times and in different situations, much of the nurturance, satisfaction of physical needs, and support that an adequate caretaking situation includes. While it was unlikely that any of the maternal caretakers would change markedly, we hoped that their concern for John would motivate them to follow through on specific recommendations.

The Family Information section was also notable for what it did not include. Foremost was our decisions regarding how much information to include about John's father and step-family. In addition to what was documented in the report, John indicated considerable hostility and dislike of his father. The maternal relatives indicated a history of current alcohol and spouse (but not child) abuse by the father. We chose not to include the maternal relatives' information since it was secondhand and possibly biased. John's opinions were also not mentioned in the report because John had been living with his maternal relatives at the time the complaints were voiced. The inclusion of any possibly biased material in our report would have been contrary to our goals of working in the best interests of the child. It would also work against obtaining full cooperation from the father, if further evaluation is warranted.

Recommendations

1. John should be referred to a qualified speech and hearing therapist for assessment of his speech and potential language difficulties. Two referral sources are Mary Ellen K, a speech therapist in private practice in ——— , and the Communication Disorders Clinic at ——— .

2. We strongly suggest that John begin school at the kindergarten level, as opposed to the first grade (kindergarten is optional in this state). Given John's speech and language difficulties, performance on mental testing, and his limited social and structured experience, he will assuredly have difficulties in school. A copy of the K-ABC results should be sent to the school he will attend, and the school should be contacted to arrange appropriate screening for the special programs available that might increase John's chances of success. Given the lack of structure and educational opportunities at his maternal home (and possibly his paternal home), the structure and opportunities provided by the school will likely be critical to John's continued development.

3. We feel that the great-aunt, grandmother, and mother are within the broad limits of adequate parental figures for John, and that John is clearly attached to all three of them. Our tentative conclusion is that the love, stability, and support provided by the home of Clarice L, along with support from Jody E and Judy W, constitutes an acceptable, potentially positive living situation for John.

4. Regardless of John's placement, we feel strongly that he needs to be given vastly increased opportunities to spend time with other children his age. When he begins school, every effort should be made to see that his peer

contact extends beyond school hours. This will enable him to improve his social skills and establish an appropriate degree of independence.

Discussion

The rule of providing specific behavioral recommendations in evaluations is nowhere more important than in forensic evaluations and courtroom testimony. If one provides all possible alternatives to a judge, the judge may make any decision he/she wishes. A major function of a forensic psychologist and a client's attorney is to present to the judge a small set of reasonable alternatives upon which she/he can act. In this case, recommendations 1, 2, and 4 are very specific and deal with what will be a significant issue in John's life—his adjustment to school. Recommendation 4 leaves open the option of living with his father, but responds to the attorneys' concern that the mother, grandmother, and great-aunt provide an acceptable home for John.

We did not include a particular counseling recommendation, as we believed that John needed an enriched environment more than anything else. As we considered a specific recommendation, we also gave weight to our impression that the caretakers were poor candidates at best for therapy.

We did not mention the need for one stable home environment, as it seemed likely that the necessities of school would end the current situation of one week at one home and the other week at the other home. In addition, such a recommendation could have been seen as critical of the judge's current ruling.

FOLLOW-UP

According to a follow-up conversation with the attorney at the time of the custody hearing, the father did not contest the mother's attorney's suggestion to allow John to live with Clarice L (the great-aunt), with support from Jody E and Judy W (the mother and grandmother, respectively). The written psychological evaluation was never entered into the court records. We have received no follow-up on the child's progress in school or whether our recommendations were followed. Neither the father nor the maternal relatives sought out counseling or social service support.

REFLECTIONS

In retrospect, we view this case as successful in that we may have played a role in averting a costly custody battle that would almost certainly have worked against John's welfare and best interests. Also, in our professional opinion John is now in a custody situation that meets many of his needs, albeit imperfectly. One result of advising is that one's advice can be ignored. We never heard whether John's family followed through on our educational program recommendation. We wonder whether a recommendation for therapeutic support for John would have been acted upon by the family and been a useful safeguard for the meeting of John's needs. This lack of final control is one frustration all court evaluators must deal with. The court may choose, because of additional information, points of law, or merely because of different values, to accept, modify, or reject an evaluator's opinion. Parents may choose to ignore us. We are only one part of a larger legal process. We have the opportunity to educate, interpret, and (very selectively and occasionally) persuade, but not to coerce.

This participation in the legal process is done in an adversarial context ill designed for subtle interpersonal issues and the needs of children. In fact, the skills and understanding and often personal compassion of psychologists and other mental health professionals necessary for therapy may clash with the process and goals of the legal system. Nevertheless, it is under these adverse circumstances that we must express our findings, work toward the welfare of the child, and, as Skafte (1985) writes, attempt to bring "a higher level of understanding and decision making to a legal process that urgently needs it" (p. 11).

REFERENCES

Achenbach, T. M., & Edelbrock, C. S. (1983). *Manual for the Child Behavior Checklist and the Revised Child Behavior Profile*. Burlington, VT: University Associates in Psychiatry.

Barkley, R. (1981). *Hyperactive children: A handbook for diagnosis and treatment*. New York: Guilford.

Ehrenreich, N. S., & Melton, G. B. (1983). Ethical and legal issues in the treatment of children. In C. E. Walker & M. C. Roberts (Eds.), *Handbook of clinical child psychology* (pp. 1285–1305). New York: Wiley.

Gardner, R. A. (1982). *Family evaluation in child custody litigation*. Cresskill, NJ: Creative Therapeutics.

Goldstein, J., Freud, A., & Solnit, A. J. (1979). *Beyond the best interests of the child*. New York: The Free Press.

Haralambie, A. H. (1983). *Handling child custody cases*. Colorado Springs, CO: Family Law Series, McGraw-Hill.

Hathaway, S. R., & McKinley, J. C. (1951). *Manual for the Minnesota Multiphasic Personality Inventory* (rev.). New York: The Psychological Corporation.

Kaufman, A. S., & Kaufman, N. L. (1983). *Kaufman Assessment Battery for Children: Administration and scoring manual*. Circle Pines, MN: American Guidance Service.

Lobitz, W. C., & Johnson, S. M. (1975). Parental manipulation of the behavior of normal and deviant children. *Child Development, 46*, 719–726.

Lyman, R. D., & Roberts, M. C. (1985). Mental health testimony in child custody litigation. *Law and Psychology Review, 9*, 15–34.

Marcus, R. F. (1983, August). *Custody decisions in the courts: A review of criteria related to the concept of "psychological parent."* Paper presented at the annual convention of the American Psychological Association, Anaheim, CA.

Palmer, J. O. (1983). *The psychological assessment of children.* New York: Wiley.

Rotter, J. B., & Rafferty, J. E. (1950). *Manual: The Rotter Incomplete Sentences Blank.* San Antonio, TX: Psychological Corporation.

Salk, L. (1977). On the custody rights of fathers in divorce. *Journal of Clinical Child Psychology, 6,* 49-50.

Scherman, A. (1983, August). *Child custody—Legal and court decision implications.* Paper presented at the annual convention of the American Psychological Association, Anaheim, CA.

Skafte, D. (1985). *Child custody evaluations: A practical guide.* Beverly Hills, CA: Sage.

10

Psychological Assessment
of Physical Child Abuse

A. J. FINCH, JR.
MICHAEL P. CAREY

Physical abuse and neglect are not recent phenomena. As early as 1874, litigation was used as a tool to protect children from being terrorized and beaten by their caretakers (Fontana, 1971). By 1965, legislation required mandatory reporting of child abuse in all 50 states. This legislation and the resulting increase in the number of reported cases accelerated the increased interest in child maltreatment. In recent years one result of this legislation has been an upsurge of interest pertaining to the protection of children from physical child abuse. However, the literature on child maltreatment frequently has not differentiated physical abuse from other forms of child maltreatment such as neglect, emotional abuse, and sexual abuse. The result has been the development of a voluminous literature which has failed to employ operationally defined constructs and consequently has often led to conflicting and inconsistent findings. Similarly, the literature on physical child abuse has lacked a consensual operational definition of the essential characteristics of physical child abuse (Friedman, Sandler, Hernandez, & Wolfe, 1981). Therefore, considerable controversy has existed regarding what constituted physical child abuse.

Friedman et al. discussed three approaches which had been used to define physical child abuse. One approach stressed the infliction of an injury to a child, such as bone fractures or contusions. The weakness of this approach was that it did not provide a means of discriminating accidental from nonaccidential injuries. A second approach added the dimension of intent to injure the child. Although it offered an improved definition of physical abuse, it lacked the qualities needed for an operational definition. Specifically, it relied solely on the subjective appraisal of intentionality,

A. J. Finch, Jr. and Michael P. Carey. Department of Psychiatry and Behavioral Sciences, Medical University of South Carolina, Charleston, South Carolina.

which was highly unreliable. A third approach, proposed by Parke and Collmer (1975), emphasized the importance of culture in determining abuse. This approach acknowledged that abusive behavior occurred on a continuum. Additionally, it attempted to take into account the individual's cultural heritage when making a social judgment as to the presence or absence of abuse. However similar to the second approach, the culturally determined label also expanded the degree of subjectivety involved in the determination as to whether physical child abuse was present or absent.

In an effort to unify and organize the area on psychological maltreatment, the International Conference on Psychological Abuse of Children and Youth convened in 1983 (International Conference on Psychological Abuse of Children and Youth, 1983). The conference drafted a generic definition of child maltreatment which stated:

> Psychological maltreatment of children and youth consists of acts of omission and commission which are judged by community standards and professional expertise to be psychologically damaging. Such acts are committed by individuals, singly or collectively, who by their characteristics (e.g., age, status, knowledge, organizational form) are in a position of differential power that renders a child vulnerable. Such acts damage immediately or ultimately the behavioral, cognitive, affective, or physical functioning of the child. (p. 2)

Furthermore, the generic definition went on to specify a number of examples of psychological maltreatment of children and youths including their rejection, terrorization, isolation, and exploitation. Unfortunately, the generic definition failed to adequately define the specific examples.

Brassard and Gelardo (1987) attempted to provide further clarification of the examples of maltreatment reported at the conference. Of particular importance for physical abuse was their definition of "terrorizing." Specifically, they stated that terrorizing was: "Threatening to physically hurt or kill; forcing a child to observe violence directed toward loved ones; leaving a young child unattended" (p. 128). Although their explication of terrorizing does not meet all the required prerequisites of a true operational definition, it increased the objectivity of the term "terrorizing" while still allowing sufficient flexibility.

The preceding discussion of the definitions of physical child abuse indicates the continued need for refinement in the definitions that are employed. Currently, the definitions tend to be overly subjective without adequate examples and illustrations to aid in the identification and reporting of child abuse. Without these clearly defined definitions, it is unlikely that our knowledge is going to advance in the area. Consequently, the following sections of this chapter should be regarded as tentative since the studies discussed are based upon different criteria and definitions rather than on one agreed upon and clearly identifed by everyone.

EPIDEMIOLOGY

Incidence Rates

Generally, the lack of a clear operational definition of physical child abuse has contributed to the reporting of widely discrepant incidence rates. In addition, the incidence rates usually have relied on government-reported statistics and have not separated the rate of physical abuse from other forms of child maltreatment. One exception was a study conducted by Gelles (1978) which employed a self-report interview of 1,146 two-parent families with children between the ages of 3 and 17. Gelles concluded that between 3.1 and 4.0 million children were subjected to coercive behavior (kicked, punched, or bitten) by their parents during their life. Moreover, Gelles projected that from 1.4 to 2.3 million children had been beaten by their parents during their development. Gelles's estimates have been considered as the upper bound estimates of child abuse.

Another issue that confounds accurate incidence rates of physical child abuse is the differences between reported and actual physical child abuse cases. For instance, in Louisiana roughly 40% of the child abuse cases that are reported are substantiated (R. Bouxdreau, personal communication, March 7, 1988). Nonetheless, there appears to have been a marked increase of reported child abuse within the last 10 years (Wolfe, 1987). For instance, from 1976 to 1982 there was 123% increase in documented cases of child abuse and neglect (American Humane Association, 1984). Furthermore, the recent development of the 24-hour child abuse hotline also appeared to have contributed to the rise of reported child abuse. However, it is widely believed that in comparison with the past there has been a decrease in the rate of child abuse in modern times (Walker, Bonner, & Kaufman, 1988).

At this time it would appear that our best estimates of physical child abuse are inaccurate. However, there are clear indications that the incidence of reported physical child abuse are increasing, and that the actual incidence rate is greater than the reported rate. Exactly how we can obtain accurate estimates of the incidence awaits the clearly defined definition of physical child abuse and the development of a methodology to obtain the information.

ETIOLOGY

Theoretical Models

In spite of problems operationalizing child abuse, three primary models have been proposed to account for the onset and maintenance of child abuse. Historically, the first proposed model was the "Psychiatric Model." This particular model emphasized the etiological importance of the psychopathology of the parents. Essentially, the Psychiatric Model proposed that child abusers were psychologically deranged (Belsky, 1978), and that their psychopathology was responsible for child abuse. Proponents of this model were often of a psychodynamic orientation and attempted to identify a distinct personality type which characterized child abusers. However, a number of investigations have indicated that child abusers do not exhibit a single severe psychiatric disorder (Kempe, 1973; Spinetta & Rigler, 1979).

Another conceptualization of child abuse is the "Sociological Model." The Sociological Model attempted to place primary importance on societal factors, such as socioeconomic status, marital discord, social isolation, family size, housing conditions, and unemployment (see Parke & Collmer, 1975). Despite these sociological factors having found considerable support, these societal factors in isolation have not proven to be great predictors of child abuse.

A third conceptualization is the "Social-Interactional Model" (Burgess, 1979). This model focuses on parent–child interactions within the family and also within society. Unlike the Psychiatric Model, this approach has emphasized a bidirectional relationship between the parent and child, and that each member plays a part in the interaction. For instance, social learning theorists such as Patterson (1982) and Wahler (1980) have stressed the importance of negative reinforcement in the escalation and maintenance of coercive behavior. Specifically, the child engages in some behavior that is aversive to the parent, which results in the parent abusing or severely punishing the child. This results in the child stopping the aversive behavior and subsequently negatively reinforcing the parent for their abusive behavior.

In summary, all three of the models have received limited support; however, none of the individual models have been able to satisfactorily differentiate abusive versus nonabusive parent–child dyads. Therefore, Belsky (1980) proposed that since each model seems to have some merit, they should be combined into a single model in the hopes of increasing the level and degree of discrimination. The usefulness of this combination has not been evaluated, and the contribution of Belsky and others (Garbarino, 1977) await the results of future studies.

Predisposing Risk Factors

Part of the literature on child maltreatment has focused on the identification of high-risk factors related to the parent or child which have been associated with child abuse. The general strategy has been to assess a set of variables (e.g., demographic, personality characteristics) within a group of identified abusive parents or abused children. These studies have usually focused on unidimensional relations between the variable of interest to the researcher and child abuse. In recent years there has been a rise in the number of experimental studies comparing abusive and nonabusive samples of parents or children (e.g., Gelardo & Sanford, 1987; Wolfe, 1987). These high-risk factors generally have been subdivided into what appeared to be factors which predisposed the child or parents to abuse or abusive situations.

Parent Factors

A number of high-risk factors have been identified with abusive parents. One factor which has received considerable support is a positive history of the perpetrator having been abused or neglected (Silver, Dublin, & Lourie, 1969). Other studies have indicated that, according to rating scales, abusive parents have lower self-esteem (Gelardo & Sanford, 1987), a high incidence of emotional problems, such as depression (Lahey, Conger, Atkeson, & Treiber, 1984), and marital discord. Wolfe (1987) has suggested that multi-variate studies of the psychological characteristics of abusive parents have indicated the presence of three distinctive patterns of behavior. The first subgroup of abusive parents was described as "emotionally detached," often exhibiting a lack of interest in the activities of their children. A second subtype was described as exhibiting "harsh/intrusive behaviors." Although parents in this subgroup were attentive to their child's behavior, they employed harsh means to express their disapproval of the child's inappropriate behavior. The third subtype was termed "covert/hostile." Parents within this grouping displayed higher rates of humiliation along with little positive behavior when compared with the other two subgroups. It would seem likely that additional multivariate research in this area may prove very useful.

Child Factors

Until recently, few studies had examined the role of the child's behavior in predicting abusive behavior by the caretaker. One reason for the recent upsurge of interest in high-risk factors of the child has been the application of reciprocal interaction conceptualizations as an explanation of abusive behavior. A number of studies have indicated perinatal risk factors of child abuse. One of the more resilient findings has been the overrepresentation of low-birth-weight or short-gestation babies. This finding was not surprising in light of recent studies which have indicated that abusive parents appear to have a lower threshold for aversive child behavior, such as crying (Frodi, 1981), and stressful parent–child interactions (Wolfe, Fairbanks, Kelly, & Bradlyn, 1983). Other studies have indicated that abused children may have a tendency to engage in more oppositional, dangerous, and aggressive behavior (Herrenkohl, Herrenkohl, & Egolf, 1983; Kadushin & Martin, 1981). Those of us who have worked clinically with abused children have seen too many children who seemed to engage in self-defeating behaviors.

ASSESSMENT

The assessment of physical child abuse offers a challenge to the professional's ability to discover the antecedents, behavior, and consequences of behavior which often occurs in private and at a low base rate. Readers are referred to Friedman et al. (1981) for a more detailed discussion of the issues related to the assessment process of child abuse. An added feature which complicates the assessment process is the frequent unwillingness of the parents of caretakers to actively disclose the occurrence of physical abuse, often from fear of litigation or the prospect of removal of the children. Another factor which effects the assessment process is the purpose for the evaluation. For instance, assuming that the evaluation was conducted by a child protection agency the intent is usually to determine if abuse has occurred and whether the child requires immediate removal from the caretaker's household in order to protect the child. In contrast, referral to a mental health professional is more likely to focus on intervention and secondary prevention of subsequent incidents of physical abuse. Friedman et al. (1981) outlined the major content areas which might be involved in the evaluation, specifically assessment of the abusive parent, assessment of the abused child, and a functional analysis of the abusive situations.

Regarding the assessment of the abusive parent, it should include an evaluation of how the parent attempts to promote or increase new behaviors and decrease aversive or inappropriate behaviors (i.e., parenting techniques). This information also requires the concurrent assessment of the parents' understanding of age-appropriate child development. A third content area includes a screening for psychopathology of the parent, which often can be accomplished by a standardized personality inventory, such as the Minnesota Multiphasic Personality Inventory (MMPI). Other parent-related content areas include an evaluation of the marital relationship and degree of social support available to the parents. Also, information is needed which addresses how the parents cope with stressful situations as well as the amount and chronicity of stressors to which the family has been exposed, such as economic hardship, physical illness, unemployment, etc. The aforementioned content areas can be accomplished using a number of strategies, including but not limited to information gathered through the clinical interview; administration of self-report measures of parenting style, parenting techniques, child development, adult psychopathology, and marital interactions; and observation of the parent and parent–child interactions within the routine clinical interview and contrived marital interaction situations.

A second area which requires assessment is the status and condition of the child. Initially, a detailed developmental history should be obtained from the parents (Friedman et al., 1981). Of course, in cases where there are indications of physical injury, referral to a physician is essential. One area of particular interest is the identification of factors which might have placed the child at greater risk for physical abuse, such as birth weight, prematurity, developmental delays, chronic physical illness, and the temperament of the child. Another factor which requires particular attention involves the assessment of the child's appropriate and inappropriate behavior within the home environment. This information can be obtained from the parents as well as the child. Methods of assessment include the use of standardized objective parent and child ratings such as the Child Behavior Checklist (Achenbach & Edelbrock, 1983), interviewing the parent and child, home and school observations, and consulting the child's school record.

The final area of assessment involves a detailed evaluation of the situations where physical abuse has occurred and the circumstances surrounding the occurrence of the incidents. This component of the assessment process involves the identification of events which precipitate the onset of physical abuse, the identification and description of the abusive behaviors, and the consequences to the child and parent. However, since physical abuse occurs at a low-base rate, the assessment is frequently focused on observing parent–child interactions for aversive or coercive interactions. Although these interactions are best observed in the natural environment, observations within the clinic offer a viable alternative.

INTERVENTION

A number of intervention strategies have been employed with physical child abuse. These strategies have ranged from the immediate removal of the child from the parent or caretaker's home to intensive psychotherapy (Denicola & Sandler, 1980; Katz, Hampton, Newberger, Bowles, & Snyder, 1986). Although there are a number of outpatient interventions available, there appears to be a bias toward institutionalization of physically abused and neglected children (Katz et al., 1986). In light of recent social policy changes and the recent work of advocacy groups (e.g., National Alliance of the Mentally Ill), it seems likely that the social service and mental health systems will increasingly move toward a model of home-based services.

One of the more common intervention methods has involved the removal of the child from the parents' custody by child protection agency workers and his/her subsequent placement in a foster home, group home, residential facility, or psychiatric hospital for a limited or extended period of time. This approach assures that the child will be physically protected from further physical abuse. However, this approach also results in considerable disruption to the family situation and the emotional development of the child. Moreover, those children which are removed from their caretakers most frequently are moved to more than one foster care placement (Knitzer & Allen, 1973), which further decreases the likelihood that the child is provided with a stable, nurturant environment. Recent studies also have indicated that the decision to place a child in an out-of-home placement is biased. For instance, McPherson and Garcia (1983) found that those children that were removed because of abuse or neglect were more likely to be from poor minority families. Moreover, the type of abuse has also been linked to decisions to remove the child from the home. Katz et al. (1986) found that abused children from homes where the mother was involved in the abuse were more likely to be removed from the home. Interestingly, children whom had suffered physical injuries were less likely to be placed in an out-of-home placement than were neglected children.

Another problem with the removal of abused children from their home has been the lack of guidelines outlining when the abused child should be returned to the home (Katz et al., 1986). Therefore, Katz et al. provided four recommendations for determining placement decisions. First, Katz et al. proposed that a multidisciplinary team composed of a pediatrician, psychiatrist, psychologist, social worker, nurse, and lawyer should be used to make placement decisions, thus guarding against decisions based primarily on emotional reactions by a single clinician. Second, members who represent racial minorities should be included in all placement decisions. Third, a more integrated network of social agencies is needed to enhance the likelihood of appropriate services being rendered in a timely fashion. Finally, Katz et al. suggested that clinicians serve as service advocates for abused clients.

A second group of interventions involves the use of traditional psychotherapy to promote intrapsychic change. Cohen (1979) evaluated 11 federally funded demonstration projects and found a high incidence (30%) of continued abuse during the time that psychotherapy was instigated. Moreover, a study by Herrenkohl, Herrenkohl, Egolf, and Seech (1979) found an extremely high incidence of relapse of abuse following the termination of traditional psychotherapy.

A third group of interventions has been the development and application of behavioral interventions (see Wolfe, 1987). These interventions have usually included some combination of the instruction of the parents in child management skills, stress inoculation or anger control training, and parental education. Preliminary data concerning these interventions have been encouraging (Denicola & Sandler, 1980; Wolfe, Lawrence, Graves, Brehony, Bradlyn, & Kelly, 1982). One limitation has been that the aforementioned interventions have not examined their long-term effectiveness in promoting continued secondary prevention of physical child abuse.

Finally, another type of intervention involves the use of intensive home-based interventions for abused children. Kinney, Madsen, Fleming, and Haapala (1977) described an intensive home-based intervention in Tacoma, Washington. The target population was families who were likely to dissolve, and the goal of the intervention was to maintain the child in the home. The intervention involves the use of a team of clinicians who are experienced with family therapy, crisis intervention, assertiveness training, and parent effectiveness training going into the home, rather than removing the child and placing him/her in foster care. At least one of the three-member team is available on a 24-hour basis for a 6-week period. In addition, similar programs also facilitate referrals to day-care centers, employment assistance, and housing needs (e.g., Families Inc., West Branch, IA). Initial results have been encouraging. For instance, in the homebuilders program, 121 of 134 children were able to remain within the home without reported child abuse incidence and at a substantial financial savings. Currently, similar programs exist in Iowa (Families, Inc., West Branch, IA), New Hampshire (Family Strength, Concord, NH), Wisconsin (Home and Community Treatment, Madison, WI), New York (Intensive Family Support, Rochester, NY), and Oregon (Oregon Intensive Services, Portland, OR). Four of the programs have achieved better than a 90% success rate (i.e., maintaining the child in the intact family at termination), whereas the other two programs have reported a success rate ranging from 66% to 75% (Child Welfare League of America, 1986). Although the results for home-based interventions appear encouraging, additional work is needed delineating appropriate outcome criteria for home-based interventions.

CASE EXAMPLE

The case that we have chosen to present is fairly typical of the physical abuse cases that we see in the Youth Division of the Department of Psychiatry and Behavioral Sciences at the Medical University of South Carolina. The Youth Division is the Division of Child and Adolescent Psychiatry that operates two inpatient units (an adolescent and a child), an outpatient clinic, and a consultation/liaison service with the Department of Pediatrics. Faculty members in the division are psychiatrists, psychologists, social workers, and nurses. Most of the physical abuse cases referred by the Department of Social Services to our service are referred after the alleged physical abuse has been investigated, and the child has been removed from the home. This procedure means that the child is usually in foster care at the time. Thus, the child has suffered not only the stress of abuse but also the stress of having been removed from his/her home. In fact, approximately 45% of the cases that we see are those in which the child is in at least his/her second foster home. Although this situation is not ideal for research in the area, we believe that it is not at all atypical of the circumstances under which many physically abused children are seen by psychologists.

Chip (not his real name) was an 11-year-old caucasian male referred by the attending physician on our child inpatient unit for a psychological evaluation following his attempt to hang himself. This attempt occurred 3 weeks after Chip had been returned to the custody of his mother. Prior to his being returned to his mother's custody, he had been in six different foster homes and two emergency shelters over an 18-month period. Originally Chip had been removed from the custody of his parents by the Department of Social Services because of repeated physical abuse by his father. Chip was the oldest of four children born to his parents shortly before their marriage. Both parents had been the victims of abuse themselves.

According to the Department of Social Services record, Chip's parents had a stormy marriage including many separations and alcohol abuse by both. Although a psychological evaluation was not available on the parents, there were extensive records available from the Department of Social Services indicating that both parents had a history of labile behaviors. In addition, both had a history of having been in considerable trouble with the law since their youth. It was evident from the histories that both parents had emotional difficulties of their own.

Reportedly, all of the children were the victims of physical abuse, and one of the children had suffered a skull fracture under suspicious circumstances. Following a violent outburst by the father which resulted in his being arrested, Chip and his siblings were taken under protective custody by the Department of Social Services. Chip's behavior during his various foster care placements was characterized by hyperactivity and aggressiveness directed mainly toward younger children and himself. Chip's mother divorced and remarried while Chip and the other children were out of the home. As a result of this increased stability, the decision was made for the children to return home. Although Chip appeared fearful of his new stepfather, their interactions were not overtly unpleasant, consisting of few actual interactions.

During the course of three interviews, Chip readily discussed his attempted suicide, stating the he was mad because of having had his radio taken away from him as a punishment. Interestingly, this punishment had taken place several days before the suicide attempt, and prior to the attempt Chip had not exhibited any major reaction at the time to the discipline. There was not a great deal of affect associated with his discussions of his attempted suicide, and the details were presented in a very matter-of-fact manner. During the interview, it was obvious that Chip was attempting to please the examiner by being overly solicitous in his interactions.

Given the confusing clinical picture that Chip presented, a complete psychological evaluation was requested by the attending psychiatrist on the unit to aid in treatment planning and diagnosis. The first author administered an extensive battery of tests involving visual–motor and behavioral ratings scales, and achievement, intelligence, and personality tests (both objective and projective). Table 10-1 presents a list of the tests administered.

During the evaluation, Chip was very cooperative and eager to please the examiner. He worked in a goal-directed manner and did not appear to be overly concerned about his failures.

TABLE 10-1. List of Tests Administered

Wechsler Intelligence Scale for Children—Revised (WISC-R)
Peabody Individual Achievement Test
Bender Visual–Motor Gestalt Test with Recall
House–Tree–Person Technique
Kinetic Family Drawing
Rorschach Psychodiagnostic
Thematic Apperception Test (TAT)
Children's Depression Inventory
Revised Children's Manifest Anxiety Scale
State–Trait Anxiety Inventory for Children
Children's Inventory of Anger
Nowicki–Strickland Locus of Control Scale for Children
Achenbach Child Behavior Checklist (Parent and Teacher Forms)

Intellectually, Chip had a Verbal scale IQ of 98, a Performance scale IQ of 102, and a resulting Full scale IQ of 100. All of these scores were in the average range of intellectual ability. According to the Kaufman's (1979) approach to interpretation, his major strengths were on Similarities and Picture Completion (superior range), while his weaknesses were in Digit Span and Coding (borderline to low average range). His Freedom From Distractibility factor was well below his other scores suggesting difficulty with sustained attention.

Personality testing was very enlightening with his case. On all self-report measures (see Table 10-1 for list), Chip obtained very low scores and did not endorse any anxiety, depression, or anger. These findings were not surprising since we have found that many abused children have a difficult time either admitting or reporting negative affect. A significant number of the children we see who are clearly depressed, anxious, or angry seem to be unable to endorse these items on self-report measures, despite the obvious presence of these feelings to the casual observer. We are not sure if this is an inability or an unwillingness on their part. We suspect that this may be their way of protecting themselves from the painful experiences associated with previous affective experiences. Regardless of the reason, this has been a frequent clinical finding for us with these children and appeared to apply to Chip's case.

The Rorschach also was administered and coded according to the Comprehensive System (Exner, 1986) and proved to be very useful with this case. Although the Rorschach is not well researched in pediatric settings (Krahn, 1985), we have elected to discuss it here because it has been useful at our facility in aiding in treatment planning. A detailed discussion of the

Comprehensive System is beyond the scope of this chapter, and the interested reader is directed to Exner (1986). Briefly, the Comprehensive System for the Rorschach is an empirically based nonprojective approach to dealing with the material generated by the subject. It is an evolving system which rests on a strong research base and has served to bring the Rorschach back into the arena of empirically based clinical psychology. For our purposes, we will provide a brief summary of the information obtained from a review of Chip's Rorschach. Table 10-2 presents the sequence of scores, and Table 10-3 presents the structural summary.

Chip gave an average number of responses for his age and seemed to approach the test in a nondefensive manner. There was no reason to suspect the validity of his testing. Chip distorted his environment and tended to interpret it in an overly personalized manner. This distortion tended to be particularly evident when Chip attempted to integrate and synthesize complex responses, which he did frequently. It was evident that this young man needed to organize and integrate his environment in a meaningful manner

TABLE 10-2. Sequence of Scores

Card	No	Loc	#	Determinant(s)	(2)	Content(s)	Pop Z	Special scores
I	1	W+	1	Mao	2	(H), H	6.0	MOR, AG
	2	Wo	1	Fu		A	1.0	INC, MOR
	3	Wo	1	Fo		A	P 1.0	MOR
II	4	Dd+		FMa−	2	A	3.0	AG
	5	D+	6	Ma−	2	H	3.0	AG
III	6	D+		Ma.FY−	2	H, Hd, Id	P 3.0	AG, FAB
	7	Do		Fo		A		
	8	Do	2	Fo		A		
IV	9	Wo	1	Fu		(A)	2.0	PER
V	10	Wo	1	FMao		A	P 1.0	
VI	11	W+	1	FMa.FYu		A, Ad	2.5	
VII	12	W+	1	Mau	2	H, Ay	2.5	
VIII	13	W+	1	FMau	2	A, Bt, Ls	P 4.5	
IX	14	W+	1	Mp.FDu	2	(H), Bt, Ls, Ad	P 5.5	FAB
X	15	Do		Fo	2	A		
	16	D+	6	FMau	2	A	4.0	FAB
	17	Do		F−		Ad		MOR, PER
	18	Do	7	Fo	2	A		

Note. Explanation of abbreviations: DQ: "/" = v/+; Contents: "Id" = idiographic content; Special Scores: "CFB" = CONFAB; "CON" = CONTAM; "FAB" = FABCOM; "INC" = INCOM. Adapted from *Rorschach Interpretation Assistance Program* (p. 25) by J. E. Exner, 1985 (originally published in 1976), Asheville, NC: Rorschach Workshops. Copyright 1985 by John E. Exner. Adapted by permission.

TABLE 10-3. Structural Summary

R = 18	Zf = 13	ZSum = 39.0	(2) = 10	P = 5	Fr + rF = 0

Location features

W = 9
(Wv = 0)
D = 8
Dd = 1
S = 0

DQ
.... (FQ-)
+ = 9 (3)
v/+ = 0 (0)
o = 9 (1)
v = 0 (0)

Form quality

FQx	FQf	M Qual.
+ = 0	+ = 0	+ = 0
o = 7	o = 5	o = 1
u = 7	u = 2	u = 2
− = 4	− = 1	− = 2
none = 0		none = 0

Determinants

Blends

M.FY
FM.FY
M.FD

Single

M	= 3
FM	= 4
m	= 0
C	= 0
Cn	= 0
CF	= 0
FC	= 0
C'	= 0
C'F	= 0
FC'	= 0
T	= 0
TF	= 0
FT	= 0
V	= 0
VF	= 0
FV	= 0
Y	= 0
YF	= 0
FY	= 0
Fr	= 0
rF	= 0
FD	= 0
F	= 8

Contents

H	= 3, 1
(H)	= 2, 0
Hd	= 0, 1
(Hd)	= 0, 0
A	= 11, 0
(A)	= 1, 0
Ad	= 1, 2
(Ad)	= 0, 0
Ab	= 0, 0
Al	= 0, 0
An	= 0, 0
Art	= 0, 0
Ay	= 0, 1
Bl	= 0, 0
Bt	= 0, 2
Cg	= 0, 0
Cl	= 0, 0
Ex	= 0, 0
Fi	= 0, 0
Fd	= 0, 0
Ge	= 0, 0
Hh	= 0, 0
Ls	= 0, 2
Na	= 0, 0
Sc	= 0, 0
Sx	= 0, 0
Xy	= 0, 0
Idio	= 0, 1

S-Constellation (child)

NO .. $FV + VF + V + FD > 2$
NO .. Col − Shd Bl > 0
NO .. $3r + (2)/R < .35$
NO .. Zd > +− 4.0
NO .. Afr < .40
YES .. X+ < .70
NO .. L < .35, L > 1.20
NO .. PureH = 0

1 . . . . . Total

Special Scorings

DV	= 0
INCOM	= 1
DR	= 0
FABCOM	= 3
ALOG	= 0
CONTAM	= 0
WSUMG	= 14
AG	= 4
CONFAB	= 0
CP	= 0
MOR	= 4
PER	= 2
PSV	= 0

Ratios, percentages, and derivations

ZSum − Zest = 39.0 − 41.5

Zd = −2.5

:EB = 5:0.0   EA = 5.0:

:eb = 5: 2   es = 7 :   > D = 0

(FM = 5 : C' = 0 T = 0)   (Adj D = 0)
(m = 0 : V = 0 Y = 2)

a : p = 9: 1

Ma : Mp = 4: 1

SCZI = 4

FC:CF + C = 0: 0
(Pure C = 0)

Afr = 0.50

3r + (2)/R = 0.56

L = 0.80

Blends:R = 3:18

X + % = 0.39
(F + % = 0.63)
X − % = 0.22

DEPI = 1

W:M = 9: 5

W:D = 9: 8

Isolate:R = 4:18

Ab + Art = 0

An + Xy = 0

H(H) : Hd(Hd) = 5: 0
(Pure H = 3)
(HHd) : (AAd) = 2: 1

H + A : Hd + Ad = 17: 1

S − CON = 1

Note. Adapted from *Rorschach Interpretation Assistance Program* (p. 25) by J. E. Exner, 1985 (originally published in 1976), Asheville, NC: Rorschach Workshops. Copyright 1985 by John E. Exner. Adapted by permission.

but was not very accurate in doing this. This difficulty likely resulted in behaviors inconsistent with the environmental demands since they were based on his own misperceptions and interpretations. His perceptions of the stimuli in the environment likely markedly differed from the typical individual, and these differences might have resulted from his unique learning history.

Further examination of his record indicated that Chip tended to be rather imprecise in his decision making. He tended to respond without careful evaluation of his environment and based his decisions on incomplete information. It is noteworthy that such children frequently are described as responding before they think and persist in making the same mistakes. In Chip's case, this impulsive and negligent response style probably contributed to his inaccurate perceptions of his environment and was consistent with his low score on the Freedom from Distractibility factor of the WISC-R.

As might be expected from his history, Chip's interpersonal perceptions were markedly distorted and characterized by aggressiveness. Chip saw the social environment as marked by aggressiveness and had come to expect aggressiveness in his world. In addition, many of his more positive cooperative responses involved aggressiveness. For example, two individuals pulling someone apart occurred twice in his record. Consequently, it seems that even when Chip perceived interpersonal relations as more cooperative in nature, there was the probability of these interactions being characterized by aggressiveness. In addition, it seems that Chip no longer expected to have his emotional need for closeness and warmth met by others. These findings suggest that initiating therapy with Chip would be difficult since he did not expect others to be able to meet his needs and tended to see interpersonal interactions as being characterized by aggressiveness. On a more positive note, Chip did appear to have an interest in people and in interacting with them. Frequently, this interest can be used to involve the individual in therapy to help modify their distortions.

Chip's perceptions of himself were extremely poor. Although he showed a normal amount of self-focus for his age, he did not have a good opinion of himself, saw himself as damaged, and tended to be overly critical in his self-evaluation. He was generally pessimistic about the future and about his ability to cope with the demands that were placed on him. He tended to lack appropriate assertiveness which was probably related to his poor self-concept. Consequently, it seemed likely that traditional therapy might be very difficult for Chip since he might find it very uncomfortable to introspect.

Chip also had a very difficult time dealing with affect. He tended to avoid it and to deny its expression. In attempting to integrate how Chip dealt with affect, it was evident that he dealt with it through social withdrawal and denial. In therapy it would be difficult to have him discuss his feelings and to deal with affectively loaded material, since this discussion would result in a tendency to withdraw and avoid the topic. He was fearful of these topics and expected to be harmed by them. Therapy would have to proceed slowly and in a reassuring manner. Affectively loaded topics would need to be addressed directly in therapy but not pushed too quickly.

In his thinking Chip tended to be very rigid. His thinking tended to be somewhat narrow and not really open for debate. Once he had an idea in his mind, it was very difficult to change it. He simply was more likely to accept his ideas as fact and not listen to reason. Consequently, it appears that therapy would be difficult and slow, since Chip has his own ideas about the world and these ideas are fairly rigidly held by him.

In summary, testing indicated that this young man was of average intellectual ability. On self-report measures, Dale denied excessive feelings of anxiety, depression, and anger. On the Rorschach he tended to distort reality, possibly because of the nature of his reality. His distortions were more likely to be associated with his excessive strivings to synthesize and produce more complex responses. He tended to be negligent in his decision making by not considering all of the available alternatives. Interpersonal relations were very distorted and characterized by aggressiveness. Closeness and warmth were no longer expected. However, he remained interested in others. Chip's perceptions about himself were negative, and he was pessimistic about his future and his ability. Affect was difficult to deal with for Chip, and he tended to flee situations involving it. He tended to be somewhat rigid in his thinking and had a difficult time changing his mind once he had an idea.

What are the treatment implications of this evaluation? First, Chip has average intellectual ability, which is usually mentioned as a good indicator. In addition, he has an interest in other people and, although he does not expect them to meet his needs, he could be expected to respond to the positive attention of an adult. However, this initial interest might be offset by his perception of interpersonal relations as being aggressive. He might be fearful of forming a close relationship with the therapist. In addition, because his perceptions of reality were distorted, he might misinterpret the therapist's interest if threatened. Chip tended to be rigid in his thinking, making it unlikely that he would be "talked out of" many of his misperceptions easily. Changes in attitudes and beliefs would come slowly, and Chip's therapist should not expect otherwise. In addition, the self-focus associated with more traditional therapies will be painful for Chip since he saw himself in an overly critical manner. Another difficult area in therapy would be affect. Chip had a difficult time dealing with affectively loaded material, thus would attempt to avoid it in treatment. His therapist would need to be patient and gentle in dealing with this type of material.

Given these findings, it was concluded that therapy with Chip would be more long term and difficult. The therapist would need to be patient but persistent in helping Chip deal with his conflicts. He would be slow to respond and would misinterpret many aspects of therapy. Changes in Chip's environment would also be necessary. Given his history with an abusive father and his tendency to misread the environment in an aggressive manner, it would be expected that he would have a more difficult time adjusting to the presence of his new stepfather. It might be necessary to introduce him more gradually and attempt to arrange their interactions in a way to maximize their positive quality. However, even given all of the above cautions and safeguards, the prognosis for Chip is not good and treatment would be difficult.

Now we will address how this description of Chip fit with what the literature tells us about children who have been abused. In examining the theoretical models of child abuse, it is evident that Chip's case tends to support all three models. First, there are indications that his parents had psychiatric problems, thus supporting the Psychiatric Model of physical child abuse. Both parents were in juvenile detention homes as adolescents, both parents abused alcohol and had a history of violence. For the Sociological Model, support comes from the fact that there were socioeconomic problems, marital discord, and a poor employment history. Finally, for the Social–Interactional Model, Chip tended to be somewhat hyperactive and distractible, and it would not take much imagination to visualize him exhibiting disruptive behaviors at home that were aversive to his parents. These aversive behaviors then might be controlled by abusive behaviors which served to reduce the rate of Chip's aversive behaviors, thus reinforcing the parents' abusive behaviors. Thus, we would have to conclude that our case data would support Belsky's (1980) proposal to combine the three models into a more comprehensive one. Applying this model to Chip, we see a youngster who was born to parents with emotional problems of their own, who abused alcohol, and who had been abused themselves as children. In addition, there were a number of sociological factors which complicated their life such as socioeconomic difficulties, marital problems, and employment difficulties.

Turning to predisposing risk factors we find that according to the records of the Department of Social Services, both of Chip's parents were abused as children themselves, thus adding further support to this consistent finding. In addition, although there was not any psychological testing of the parents, we know that both abused alcohol and that alcohol abuse is frequently associated with depression and affective disorders. If we are willing to take this logical leap, there would seem to be support for Lahey et al. (1984), who reported that parental depression was frequently associated with abuse.

In exploring potential predisposing risk factors of the child, it is noteworthy that Chip did seem to have an attention deficit disorder with hyperactivity. This condition had been noted in the previous psychological evaluation and by school history. Those of us who have been around children who exhibit hyperactivity and attention deficit disorder are familiar with the potential difficulties that they can present for even the most patient of parents. In addition, in the psychological testing there were a number of other factors which might contribute to Chip's potential for abuse. Although it could be argued justifiably that many of the problems may have their origins in his disturbed parent–child interactions, it seems likely that his misperceptions of his environment, his impulsiveness and lack of precision in decision making, his needs to achieve and be perfect, his view of human interactions as aggressive, and his poor opinion of himself may all have been factors in his abuse.

In summary, it would appear that Chip's case is fairly consistent with the literature. It should be noted that this case was selected without specific knowledge of the material to be discussed in the first portion of this chapter dealing with the research literature, and represented a typical case from our records. Consequently, we would be led to suspect that much of the information in the literature is based on similar cases and that Chip is fairly representative of physically abused children seen by psychologists working in medical settings. Unfortunately, his case is probably more typical than we would like to admit. Given the distance between our facility and his home, Chip and his family were not followed by us but were referred to a mental health clinic for treatment. However, upon return to home he continued to have difficulty adjusting to school and to his new family setting. Subsequently, he was admitted to another psychiatric hospital shortly after his discharge. From that hospital he was placed in a residential treatment program and has had adjustment difficulties there.

Of what value was our evaluation? Those of us conducting psychological evaluations on children frequently feel that we have some answers but that no one is asking the correct questions. Such feelings have led many to question the usefulness of psychological testing. However, we continue to conduct tests and have increasingly come to appreciate their potential usefulness. The major problems we have encountered have been the lack of trained personnel in the community to treat children and their families. There simply are too few resources devoted to disturbed children and their families, and they go underserved.

REFERENCES

Achenbach, T. A., & Edelbrock, C. S. (1983). *Manual for the Child Behavior Checklist and Revised Child Behavior Profile*. Burlington, VT: Department of Psychiatry, University of Vermont.

American Humane Association. (1984). *Highlights of official child neglect and abuse reporting 1982*. Denver, CO: Author.

Belsky, J. (1978). Three theoretical models of child abuse: A critical review. *Child Abuse and Neglect, 2*, 37–49.

Belsky, J. (1980). Child maltreatment: An ecological integration. *American Psychologist, 35*, 320–335.

Brassard, M. R., & Gelardo, M. S. (1987). Psychological maltreatment: The unifying construct in child abuse and neglect. *School Psychological Review, 16*, 127–136.

Burgess, R. L. (1979). Child abuse: A behavioral analysis. In B. Lahey & A. E. Kazdin (Eds.), *Advances in clinical child psychology* (Vol. 2). New York: Plenum.

Child Welfare League of America. (1986). *Family preservation project.* New York: Author.

Cohen, A. H. (1979). Essential elements of successful child abuse and neglect treatment. *Child Abuse and Neglect, 3*, 491–496.

Denicola, J., & Sandler, J. (1980). Training abusive parents in child management and self-control skills. *Behavior Therapy, 11*, 263–270.

Exner, J. E., Jr. (1986). *The Rorschach: A comprehensive system: Vol. 1. Basic foundations* (2nd ed.). New York: Wiley.

Fontana, V. J. (1971). *The maltreated child* (2nd ed.). Springfield, IL: Charles C. Thomas.

Friedman, R. M., Sandler, J., Hernandez, M., & Wolfe, D. A. (1981). Child abuse. In E. Mash & L. Terdal (Eds.), *Behavioral assessment of child disorders* (pp. 221–253). New York: Guilford.

Frodi, A. M. (1981). Contributions of infant characteristics to child abuse. *American Journal of Mental Deficiency, 85*, 341–349.

Garbarino, J. (1977). The price of privacy in the social dynamics of child abuse. *Child Welfare, 56*, 565–575

Gelardo, M. S., & Sanford, E. E. (1987). Child abuse and neglect: A review of the literature. *School Psychological Review, 16*, 137–155.

Gelles, R. J. (1978). Violence toward children in the United States. *American Journal of Orthopsychiatry, 48*, 580–592.

Herrenkohl, R. C., Herrenkohl, E. C., & Egolf, B. P. (1983). Circumstances surrounding the occurrence of child maltreatment. *Journal of Consulting and Clinical Psychology, 51*, 424–431.

Herrenkohl, R. C., Herrenkohl, E. C., Egolf, B. P., & Seech, M. (1979). The repetition of child abuse. How frequently does it occur? *Child Abuse and Neglect, 3*, 67–72.

Kadushin, A., & Martin, J. (1981). *Child abuse: An interactional event.* New York: Columbia University.

Katz, M., Hampton, R., Newberger, E., Bowles, R., & Snyder, J. (1986). Returning children home: Clinical decision making in cases of child abuse and neglect. *American Journal of Orthopsychiatry, 56*, 253–262.

Kaufman, A. S. (1979). *Intelligent testing with the WISC-R.* New York: Wiley.

Kempe, C. H. (1973). A practical approach to the protection of the abused child and the rehabilitation of the abusing parent. *Pediatrics, 51*, 804–812.

Kinney, J. M., Madsen, B., Fleming, T., & Haapala, D. A. (1977). Homebuilders: Keeping families together. *Journal of Consulting and Clinical Psychology, 45*, 673–677.

Knitzer, J., & Allen, M. (1973). *Children without homes: An examination of public responsibility to children in Out-of-Home care.* Washington, DC: Children's Defense Fund.

Krahn, G. L. (1985). The use of projective assessment techniques in pediatric settings. *Journal of Pediatric Psychology, 10*, 179–193.

Lahey, B. B., Conger, R. D., Atkeson, B. M., & Treiber, F. A. (1984). Parenting behavior and emotional status of physically abusive mothers. *Journal of Consulting and Clinical Psychology, 52,* 1062–1071.

McPherson, M. C., & Garcia, L. (1983). Effects of social class and familiarity on pediatrician's responses to child abuse. *Child Welfare, 62,* 387–393.

Parke, R. D., & Collmer, C. W. (1975). Child Abuse: An interdisciplinary analysis. In E. M. Hetherington (Ed.), *Review of child development research* (Vol. 5). Chicago: University of Chicago Press.

Patterson, G. R. (1982). *Coercive family process.* Eugene, OR: Castalia.

Proceedings of the International Conference on Psychological Abuse of Children and Youth. (1983). Indianapolis, IN: Office for the Study of the Psychological Rights of the Child, Indiana University.

Silver, L. B., Dublin, C. C., & Lourie, R. S. (1969). Agency action and interaction in cases of child abuse. *Social Casework, 52,* 164–171.

Spinetta, J. J., & Rigler, D. (1979). The child abusing parent: A psychological review. *Psychological Bulletin, 77,* 296–304.

Wahler, R. G. (1980). The insular mother: Her problems in parent–child treatment. *Journal of Applied Behavior Analysis, 13,* 207–219.

Walker, C. E., Bonner, B. L., & Kaufman, K. L. (1988). *The physically and sexually abused child: Evaluation and treatment.* New York: Pergamon.

Wolfe, D. A. (1987). *Child abuse.* New York: Sage.

Wolfe, D. A., Fairbanks, J. A., Kelly, J. A., & Bradlyn, A. S. (1983). Child abusive parents' physiological responses to stressful and nonstressful behavior in children. *Behavior Therapy, 5,* 363–371.

Wolfe, D. A., Lawrence, J. S., Graves, K., Brehony, K., Bradlyn, D., & Kelly, J. A. (1982). Intensive behavioral parent training for a child abuse mother. *Behavior Therapy, 13,* 438–451.

11
A Child-Oriented Approach to the Treatment of Intrafamilial Sexual Abuse

HONORE M. HUGHES

INTRODUCTION

The purpose of this chapter is to acquaint the reader with the general dynamics which are involved in child sexual abuse and describe one approach to treating the child who is the survivor of such maltreatment. Basic information related to child sexual abuse will be briefly presented, followed by a description and history of the family of the girl involved in this case. Next, a formulation of the situation and proposed treatment will be presented, then the general course of services provided will be outlined, along with a discussion of the outcome of the intervention. Following that will be a wrap-up section consisting of my conjectures and reflections given the benefit of hindsight.

The focus of difficulties described in the present case report is problem-focused, rather than centered upon a specific diagnosis. Children who have suffered from sexual abuse are likely to receive a number of different diagnoses describing the child's behavior; these reactions may have some commonality across children but also vary from child to child. (The effects of sexual abuse will be covered shortly.) In order for the readers to better understand the problem, a definition of child sexual abuse will be provided first, along with estimates of incidence and prevalence. Then, etiology will be discussed, and descriptions of some recommended interventions will be provided.

Honore M. Hughes. Department of Psychology, University of Arkansas, Fayetteville, Arkansas.

DEFINITION AND PREVALENCE

The definition of sexual abuse adopted by the National Center on Child Abuse and Neglect (1978) is: "contacts or interactions between a child and an adult when the child is being used for the sexual stimulation of the perpetrator or another person when the perpetrator is in a position of power or control over the victim" (p. 42). However, different investigators often use varying definitions of sexual abuse which contribute to difficulties in obtaining accurate information regarding child sexual abuse. In addition, experts speculate that this type of maltreatment is underreported to the point where only one-fifth to one-third of all the abuse that occurs comes to the attention of an agency or someone in authority (Finkelhor, 1986).

Regarding prevalence, one of the more carefully drawn estimates of sexual abuse is that girls are abused in approximately a 2.5:1 ratio to boys, while men are the sexual abuse perpetrators in about 95% of the cases of abuse of girls and 80% of the abuse experienced by boys (Finkelhor, 1984). Whereas "incidence" refers to the number of new cases occurring in a year, "prevalence" studies are those which attempt to identify the number of children who have been sexually abused at some point during their childhood or adolescence. Since both types of figures are largely underestimates, and difficult to obtain, most researchers focus on prevalence. In a recent review, Finkelhor (1986) points out that there is considerable variation in the prevalence rates derived from different North American studies, with rates ranging from 6% to 61% for females and from 3% to 31% for males. He attributes the large range in estimates to differences among studies, including variations in definitions, samples, and methods of obtaining the information. Excluding noncontact sexual abuse (e.g., exposure), his best estimate of sexual abuse for girls is that from 22% to 38% of all females have been sexually abused at some point in their life before the age of 18. In approximately 75% of the cases the child knew the perpetrator; in 47% of the cases the perpetrator was a family member.

ETIOLOGY

The etiology of child sexual abuse is currently under extensive investigation, and discussions in the area mostly consist of identification of characteristics frequently found associated with child sexual abuse (e.g., Mrazek, 1983; Sgroi, Blick, & Porter, 1982; Waterman & Lusk, 1986). When the sexual abuse is intrafamilial, especially involving a father or stepfather, family dynamics are frequently included in the etiology, dynamics which are usually formulated from a psychodynamic or family systems perspective (e.g., Waterman, 1986). Factors associated with children who are at high risk for sexual abuse include characteristics of both the children and the family. As previously stated, girls are at the highest risk for abuse, and preadolescents appear to be at greater risk than preschool or adolescent girls (Finkelhor, 1986). The increase in vulnerability to sexual abuse rises at ages 6 to 7 years, and then dramatically increases again at about age 10 years.

According to Finkelhor (1986), the variables which were the most strongly and consistently associated with risk status were those related to the parents of abused children. He found that girls who were victimized are (1) more likely to have lived without their natural fathers, (2) more likely to have mothers who were employed outside the home, (3) more likely to have mothers who were disabled or ill, (4) more likely to witness conflict between their parents, and (5) more likely to report a poor relationship with one of their parents. In addition, girls who lived with stepfathers were at greater risk for abuse. Girls from lower socioeconomic status families were found to be at no greater risk than others.

However, the emphasis on studying victims and their families can lead to overemphasizing the victims' roles in the experiences, and blaming the victim. Finkelhor (1984) points out that "the most immediate and relevant 'cause' of the victimization was a decision made by the offender" (p. 30), and emphasizes that knowledge regarding both child and perpetrator must be brought together to better understand the phenomenon. Based on his and others' research, Finkelhor presents a model, which he calls the Four Preconditions Model of Sexual Abuse, in which the two perspectives are juxtaposed in order to combine the knowledge gained from focusing on the victim and on the offender.

His model is a comprehensive one, bringing together knowledge about offenders, victims, and families, and incorporating explanations at both the psychological and sociological levels, while concomitantly it is general enough to account for many different types of sexual abuse ranging from father–daughter incest to compulsive molesting. The four preconditions that need to be met before sexual abuse can occur are: first, "potential offender had to have some motivation to sexually abuse a child"; second, "a potential perpetrator had to overcome internal inhibitions against acting on that motivation"; third, "the potential offender had to overcome external inhibitions to sexually abuse"; and fourth, the potential offender or some other factor had to undermine or overcome a child's possible resistance to the sexual abuse" (Finkelhor, 1984, p. 54). Finkelhor suggests that this model can be very useful in the assessment and treatment of children and families by helping clinicians organize the facts in the case and plan strategies for intervention.

IMPACT

One assumption that many clinicians make regarding a child's experience of sexual abuse is that the impact is detrimental to the child's psychological functioning. However, while there is a reasonable amount of literature describing the behaviors which seem to be related to sexual abuse, no longitudinal, prospectively gathered evidence exists supporting the belief that the experience of sexual abuse causes later difficulties. Nevertheless, a number of reviews support the notion that children who are survivors of sexual abuse manifest both initial and longer-term reactions (e.g., Finkelhor, 1986; Green, 1988; Haugaard & Reppucci, 1988; Lusk & Waterman, 1986; Mrazek, 1983).

Browne and Finkelhor (1986) present a review of the research regarding initial and long-term effects, and point out the problems in the literature. Their critique includes sample, design, and measurement difficulties, all problems which temper the conclusions from those studies. The authors conclude their review by stating that the presence of fear, anxiety, depression, anger and hostility, and inappropriate sexual behavior in some portion (one-fifth to two-fifths) of girls who are victimized is supported by the literature, although the findings are sketchy. When studied as adults, female victims as a group tend to demonstrate more impairment than women in a nonvictimized group (about twice as much), and about one-fifth demonstrate serious psychopathology. In other reviews, Green (1988) and Haugaard and Reppucci (1988) reached basically the same conclusions. The latter authors also proposed a model for conceptualizing the impact of incest which integrates a number of approaches. By comprehensively capturing the complexities of the families and circumstances involved, these authors have provided clinicians with tentative explanations for the different reactions seen among children who have experienced sexual abuse.

TREATMENT RESEARCH

With many types of children's difficulties, studies of treatment and treatment effectiveness lag far behind research focused on etiology, and child sexual abuse is no exception. Very little is known about the success of any intervention with child sexual abuse, because only a few studies empirically evaluating the success of any treatment have been published. One exception to this is an evaluation conducted by Kroth (1979) of the Child Sexual Abuse Treatment Program in Santa Clara, California started by Henry Giaretto. Three groups of outcome variables were employed as criteria for evaluation in addition to parental perceptions of the comprehensive treatment. Kroth found that there were marked improvements in the psychological health of the daughters, mothers, and fathers, and in their relationships with each other. However, these conclusions need to be viewed with caution since Kroth's evaluation was not well designed. One of the other evaluations available is from Sgroi (1982), who found improvement in approximately 50% of the problems treated over a 2-year period. She also discussed the difficulties involved in working with these families. Both of these programs used a comprehensive long-term (18 to 24 months) approach to treatment.

While research evaluations allow some choices to be made regarding treatment of children and other members of sexually abusive families, there are also some clinically based accounts which can provide some guidance. Among the best of these (see Hampton & Hughes, 1988) are a chapter by Porter, Blick, and Sgroi (1982), an article by Sturkie (1983), and chapters by Waterman (1986), Long (1986), and Damon and Waterman (1986). Some of the suggestions from these sources will be discussed in conjunction with the sections on planning and course of treatment. Other valuable resources include chapters in recent books by Haugaard and Reppucci (1988) and Schetky and Green (1988).

BACKGROUND INFORMATION

In order to present the history and background information in the least confusing manner, the members of the two families and their relationships are pictured in Figure 11-1. (The names have been changed to protect the confidentiality of those involved.)

Sexual Abuse Allegations

The initial contact with the R family occurred in June when Ms. R called the Psychological Services Center for an intake appointment for herself and her husband due to her feelings of anxiety and depression. She was concerned about her husband's physically abusive behavior toward her, and the lack of affection, intimacy, and communication in their relationship. At the time of the intake, which was conducted by the Center's intake worker, Mr. and Ms. R revealed that Ms. R's 9-year-old daughter, Becky, had made allegations of sexual abuse against her stepfather, Mr. R. Several nights prior to the intake, Becky had wakened tearful and distressed from a nightmare. While she was being comforted by her mother, Becky told her that her stepfather had been touching and kissing her genital area, plus rubbing his penis against her for a long time. In the intake Mr. R denied perpetrating any sexual abuse with Becky, although both Mr. and Ms. R agreed that the proper social service agency should be contacted, and they expressed the desire to cooperate. As part of the Child Protective Services (CPS) investigation, Mr. and Ms. R and Becky were interviewed several days later by a social worker from the CPS. Since it was the worker's judgment that enough evidence was present, the sexual abuse allegation was substantiated, and charges were pressed against Mr. R. Shortly after the abuse allegation was substantiated, Becky went to live with one of her mother's sisters in a nearby town for approximately 1 month.

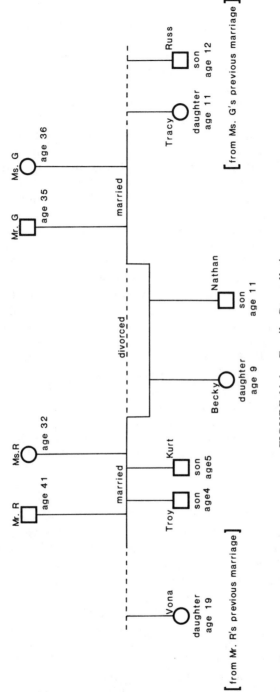

FIGURE 11-1. Family Constellation.

Mr. R continued to deny during several treatment sessions that he had molested Becky, although he did admit that he had had intercourse with his daughter, Vona, when she was 15. Mr. and Ms. R's explanation of this event was that Vona had "seduced" Mr. R to break up their marriage while he was under the influence of alcohol. They stated that at that point they had sought marital counseling at a local mental health center, although Ms. R described the three sessions as "only making things worse."

When Becky returned to the R's home after a month, she received a psychological evaluation at the local mental health center in order to obtain additional information relevant to charges being filed against Mr. R (more detail will be presented in the assessment section). It was interesting to find that a previous psychological evaluation of Becky's functioning had been conducted 2 years earlier because her first grade teacher had recommended retention due to daydreaming and noncompletion of work. At that time, Becky's abilities were found to be generally within the average range. However, a human figure drawing which Becky had completed during that previous evaluation, when she was in first grade, prompted the examiner to suspect sexual abuse, and the examiner spoke to Ms. R about that possibility. During that feedback session Ms. R told the examiner she had noticed Becky's unusual sexual interest and sexualized behavior, and said she suspected some molestation while Becky was visiting her biological father, Mr. G. Ms. R had no such suspicion regarding Mr. R at the time of that first evaluation. In this more recent assessment, however, Becky reported that the sexual abuse had begun when she was in first grade (the time of the first assessment), and had continued until the point at which she had told her mother. Becky remained with Mr. and Ms. R for about a month until Mr. and Ms. G sued for temporary custody in August, at which point Becky and Nathan went to live with their natural father, Mr. G, and their stepmother.

The R Family

The R household contained seven people: Mr. R (age 41); Ms. R (32); Vona (19), Mr. R's daughter from an earlier marriage; Becky (9) and Nathan (11), children from Ms. R's first marriage; and Tony (4) and Kurt (5), Mr. and Ms. R's biological children. The family had lived in a one-room trailer for a period of time before moving into their partially finished house on the same property. Mr. and Ms. R had married 7 years earlier, after Mr. R's release from prison and Ms. R's divorce from Mr. G. Ms. R was unemployed and Mr. R had a low-paying job, thus their financial situation was poor. Mr. R had been laid off for 2 years, had a part-time job off and on, then had been recently fired. Ms. R had injured her back several years earlier, and had not been able to work, although she did some babysitting in their home occasionally.

The history of both Mr. and Ms. R revealed long-standing difficulties. Ms. R is the middle child in a family with two sisters and her natural parents. She reported being physically abused by both of her parents, and sexually abused by her father from age 6 to 9 years. Her father threatened to kill her if she revealed the abuse, and she did not do so until 4 years prior to the contact with the Psychological Services Center. At that point her father confessed to his wife, but shortly thereafter "disowned" her. Ms. R had had little contact with her parents until recently, at the time of Becky's sexual abuse allegation. Mr. R's history is one of minimally adequate adjustment. He left home at the age of 16; spent some time in the military; and had a series of low-paying jobs. He married at the age of 20 and had one daughter, Vona. He spent 6 years in jail for cattle rustling, and met Ms. R while out on parole.

Additional information, which was revealed by Becky's brother Nathan to Ms. R when he was told of the situation between Becky and her step-father, was that he had seen Becky's grandfather (Ms. R's father) molesting Becky during a visit to the grandparent's house. During the recent psychological evaluation Becky admitted that her grandfather had also sexually abused her on several occasions.

The G Family

In August, when Mr. and Ms. G learned of the sexual abuse allegations made against Mr. R, they sued for temporary custody of Nathan and Becky. At that time Becky and Nathan went to live with Mr. and Ms. G, whom they had been visiting every other weekend for the past 4 years. Mr. and Ms. G both worked in a factory, and lived in a three-bedroom trailer along with Ms. G's children, Tracy and Russ, from a previous marriage. Just before school began in the fall, Mr. and Ms. G brought both Becky and Nathan to the Psychological Services Center upon the recommendation of their lawyer. In addition to the fears they voiced regarding the impact of sexual abuse on Becky, they were concerned about the children's emotional development since both children reported harsh physical punishment from the Rs. Behaviors which they described as problematic with regard to Becky included nightmares, fear of the dark, moodiness, stubbornness, and disobedience.

According to the usual procedures of the Center, Nathan was assigned to one graduate student/faculty clinician team for assessment, while Becky was assigned to me (a clinical child psychologist) for treatment. (Additional information will be provided in the Assessment section.) No intervention was recommended for Nate, while Becky began short-term, problem-focused treatment. In October, the Gs obtained permanent custody of Nate and Becky.

ASSESSMENT

Previous Assessment at the Mental Health Center

In July, shortly after Becky returned to the Rs after a stay with her aunt, an assessment was conducted by a clinician from the local mental health center to provide additional information for the court since charges against Mr. R were being pressed by the prosecuting attorney. At that time the examiner had conducted separate clinical interviews with Becky and the Rs and also used the Kinetic-Family-Drawing Test, the Draw-A-Person Test, and the Thematic Apperception Test (TAT) in her assessment. The results from that evaluation are summarized as follows.

During the clinical interview after rapport was established, the evaluator introduced three anatomically correct dolls (a large male doll, a smaller male doll, and a female doll) which she described as her friends and helpers. The examiner noted that Becky seemed embarrassed about handling the dolls, although they were fully clothed, preferring to verbally describe her sexual experience with her stepfather. With some encouragement she was able to demonstrate to the examiner with the dolls what had taken place. Becky described digital, oral, and penile contact with her vaginal area. She reportedly was made to touch her stepfather's penis with her hand but refused to put her mouth on it as he had instructed. Several times her stepfather put his penis between her legs and attempted intercourse, but Becky said she jerked away because it hurt. Becky also reported that he rubbed his "important part," as she referred to his penis, while he was on top of her.

According to Becky, the sexual abuse began when they were living in the trailer on their property, although most of it occurred while they were living in the house they built on that land. The abuse progressed from oral to digital to penile contact. On all occasions Ms. R was out of the house, and Mr. R told the other children to go outside. Most of the oral and digital contact occurred while Becky was seated in a large chair and Mr. R was on his knees in front of her. Penile contact was made while Becky lay on one of her brother's beds. Becky said she had to look out a window or door and watch for the others to return. According to the examiner, Becky had commented that her mother might not really believe her, since Ms. R would not think she was gone long enough. Becky also reported that Mr. R had said it was a secret between them.

Additional information from that evaluation included results from the drawings and the TAT. According to the examiner at that time, Becky's drawings reflected feelings of hostility and anxiety associated with sexuality or body integrity, while her family drawing was simplistic and generally unremarkable except for suggestions of possible lack of closeness with Mr. and Ms. R or current uncertainty about their acceptance of her. Becky's

TAT stories reflected an understanding of conventional social standards and an absence of antisocial tendencies, with a respect for authority and reliance on adults in evidence. The examiner's interpretations were that Becky was likely to deny personal difficulties, and to handle them by regressing into silliness. At the same time, Becky appeared to be able to see humor in difficult situations, had a positive outlook on life, and wished to lead a normal life patterned after conventional role expectations and gender-role models. She was thought to be somewhat unrealistic in her understanding of social interactions, and possibly too trusting. Her view of males and females was to see males as dominant and females as submissive and in need of rescuing or protecting. In addition, she perceived powerful females as excessively punitive.

Overall, the test results, interview data, and behavioral observations led the examiner to conclude that Becky had adequate reality contact and ability to develop social relationships. In general, Becky appeared to the evaluator to be well adjusted although she was experiencing mild emotional distress associated with her sexual abuse experiences. The clinician also reported that she thought that Becky was experiencing insecurity and feelings of vulnerability, possibly due to her mother's ambivalence and the disruption in family life engendered by her disclosure of sexual abuse. In addition, the examiner's clinical impression was that Becky had experienced sexual abuse by her stepfather and possibly her maternal grandfather. Recommendations made for Becky were to receive short-term counseling to deal with her feelings of responsibility and to improve her self-esteem. Marital counseling was recommended for Mr. and Ms. R.

Evaluation of Becky at the Psychological Services Center

Since Becky had received the previously described evaluation in July, I did not repeat any of the assessment procedures when she entered treatment in August. I did want to obtain a rough baseline report of difficulties Becky was experiencing, so Ms. G was asked to complete the Child Behavior Checklist (CBCL; Achenbach, 1981; Achenbach & Edelbrock, 1983). According to her stepmother, Becky's behavior problems were within the clinical range, with a Total Behavior T score of 70 (98th percentile). The T scores for Internalizing and Externalizing Behavior were 66 and 72, respectively. The profile scales which were elevated above a T score of 65 (90th percentile) were Depression 65, Social Withdrawal 75, Somatic Complaints 65, Hyperactivity 72, Aggressiveness 75, and Delinquency 65. Her social competence scales were close to the range of clinical concern (i.e., T score 20, 2nd percentile), with Activities and School receiving T scores of 30 and of 20. Based on information from the previous assessment and on Ms. G's report on the CBCL, I gave her two Axis I diagnoses according to the third edition of the *Diagnostic and Statistical Manual of Mental Disorders* (DSM-III;

American Psychiatric Association, 1980), with one being, Adjustment Disorder with Disturbance of Emotions and Conduct, and the second, Other Specified Family Circumstance (Incest).

The Teacher Report Form (TRF) of the CBCL was obtained from Becky's teacher in September. She reported no behavioral or academic difficulties with Becky and stated that she was surprised to find that Becky was receiving psychological treatment. While the teacher described Becky as shy and quiet around other children, she expressed no concern regarding Becky's social relationships. In my clinical experience, this reaction from a teacher is not unusual. Frequently, teachers have no idea that any abuse is occurring, unless they notice a sudden change in a child's behavior. Changes in a child's behavior or performance, whether abrupt or gradual, are more likely to occur at the time the sexual abuse begins (Becky's first grade teacher had noticed changes), rather than while it is ongoing or after it has ceased.

Evaluation of Nathan at the Psychological Services Center

The evaluation that Nate received included separate diagnostic interviews with Mr. and Ms. G and with him, the TAT, the House-Tree-Person, and a sentence completion test. According to the examiner, who met with Nate and the Gs, Nate's intellectual abilities appeared evenly developed within the average range. However, he seemed to experience difficulty with reading and comprehension, which was consistent with reports from school indicating a reading ability 1 year below grade level.

In the area of personality functioning, Nathan demonstrated a reasonably personable manner of interpersonal interaction. According to the examiner, Nathan's mistrust of others and guardedness of emotional expression seemingly frustrated his personal needs for prestige, dependency, and affiliation. While he wanted to feel close to people, he seemed not to feel close to anyone. His need for prestige and positive recognition appeared strong, and those areas of his self-concept seemed tenuous. In general, the examiner felt that Nate had achieved an adaptive level of defensive personality functioning that very likely interfered with meeting his personal needs.

Recommendations made included suggesting that (1) the likelihood of reading difficulties be evaluated in more depth and (2) praise and encouragement be provided for effort in school. Since no psychopathology was seen, no recommendation for treatment for Nathan was made. Rather, the examiner explained to Mr. and Ms. G that Nathan's emotional guardedness and mistrust could be modified by experiences characterized by emotional sharing and acceptance, and by predictable outcomes in his relationships with important others. It was emphasized that Nate's development of trust would be facilitated by a stable, "normal" homelife. The clinician also recommended a structured daily routine with predictable punishment for unacceptable behavior and familiarity with the motives of the others with whom Nate lives.

While Mr. and Ms. G seemed to understand the feedback, they did express their surprise at the fact that the examiner could not attribute any cause to Nathan's current level of functioning. After further discussion, they did accept the explanation that the test results reflected Nate's current transitional status, not his long-term functioning. They stated that they planned to continue setting limits on his temper outbursts and talking with him about his mistrust of others.

CASE FORMULATION AND PROPOSED TREATMENT

Due to the complexities involved in this case, especially because two families were involved, the formulation of the intervention will be discussed in terms of contact with those two families, in chronological order. Another complicating factor was that within the structure of the Psychological Services Center, in addition to my involvement with the families, other faculty and several graduate students were part of the treatment teams as well.

At the point that the families initially entered treatment (June, 1984), few sources for guiding the treatment were available, as stated previously. I consulted various sources, with Sgroi et al. (1982) and Porter et al. (1982) being the most comprehensive and practical materials available. Sgroi (1982) emphasizes that each clinician undertaking the treatment of a child and family dealing with sexual abuse is "a pioneer exploring uncharted territory" (p. 6), due to the paucity of research evaluations of different types of interventions. I certainly was no exception.

Porter et al. (1982) divide the treatment of a sexual abuse victim into three phases: (1) crisis intervention, (2) short-term therapy (lasting 6 months to 1 year), and (3) long-term therapy (lasting up to 2 years or more). They point out that each family is automatically involved in the crisis intervention aspect of treatment which begins at the point of exposure of abuse. During this phase, the child and family often require what Porter et al. call "'total life support'—a mixture of concrete environmental services and intensive day-to-day support and guidance" (p. 138). At the same time, case management takes place in which the tasks of reporting, investigation, validation, child-protection assessment, and initial management planning must be accomplished by the mandated social services personnel.

After the crisis intervention phase, therapy can begin. Porter et al. recommend making efforts to involve the entire family but acknowledge that clinicians may need to work just with the child, depending on the receptivity of the other family members. They also specify criteria for either short- or long-term treatment of the child, depending upon the degree of trauma to the child, the level of support for the child, and whether the perpetrator is still in contact with the child. A number of clinicians recommend that treatment begin with individual therapy for all family members, and possibly therapy in peer groups as well (Giaretto, 1982; Sgroi et al., 1982). After a period of time in individual and group treatment, family dyads may then be formed.

My plan initially was to provide support and crisis intervention services to Mr. and Ms. R while the investigation by social services was conducted. Because Becky was placed with her aunt in another town, only the parents were available for intervention. Under the supervision of another faculty member, Mr. and Ms. R were seen twice for marital therapy, then transferred to two different graduate student clinicians under my supervision, when it became apparent that Becky's mother and stepfather both had a number of issues which could be more productively dealt with in individual therapy. As recommended by Porter et al. (1982), the plan was to see the parents individually in short-term treatment (or long-term if they were willing) after the crisis intervention phase had passed.

When Becky was brought to the Psychological Services Center in late August by Mr. and Ms. G, the family circumstances had changed from when she was living with the Rs. Although she was currently in a stable environment, her symptoms at that point probably were related to the disruption in her life that had occurred after she had revealed the incest, which included two changes in residence and attending a new school, as well as to the experience of sexual abuse. It seemed likely that she was feeling insecure and vulnerable, at least partially as a result of her mother's ambivalent reaction to the sexual abuse. In addition, according to her stepmother's report on the CBCL, Becky was expressing her distress through both Internalizing and Externalizing behaviors, with Becky described as being depressed and socially withdrawn as well as hyperactive, aggressive, and disobedient. Since she was neither in the home with the perpetrator nor in foster care, some of the issues with which she had to deal were somewhat different from those of girls who are in one of those situations.

Regardless of the current circumstances, Becky did have to confront a number of issues which are common to all girls who are victims of child sexual abuse, especially intrafamilial. Several authors have presented discussions of what they call "impact issues," considerations which they recommend addressing with the girls (e.g., Finkelhor & Browne, 1986; Porter et al., 1982; Sturkie, 1983). Each of those authors label these considerations a little differently, although they are all basically discussing issues which (1) are reactions to related events or circumstances and (2) are feelings associated with the experience.

Impact issues delineated by the previously mentioned authors include (1) believability, (2) betrayal, (3) guilt and responsibility, (4) disempowerment, (5) bodily integrity and protection, (6) secrecy and sharing, (7) court attendance, (8) role confusion, and (9) pseudomaturation. Some of the feelings which likely accompany the experience of sexual abuse and the aftermath of revelation of the abuse which also need to be dealt with are anger, fear, and depression. The previously mentioned authors also discuss treatment implications for each of those considerations, and how the issues vary in salience for particular children, depending on their situation. Porter et al. state that the treatment of a child sexual abuse victim may be a lengthy process, with the key issue not being simply the sexual abuse itself. They conceptualize the intervention process as "strengthening the child's ego to help improve self-image, to learn to trust others, and to begin to feel secure" (p. 128).

Since the initial crisis period had passed, the original plan for intervention with Becky was short-term play therapy (6 or so months) on an individual basis. Also, based on her DSM-III diagnosis of Adjustment Disorder, short-term intervention seemed appropriate. If a group for other female survivors of sexual abuse Becky's age had been available, I probably would have recommended participation in it, in addition to the individual treatment.

COURSE OF TREATMENT

Mother

During the crisis intervention phase, both Mr. and Ms. R were seen by two graduate clinicians, first together in marital therapy for two sessions, then individually for supportive, problem-oriented treatment. Mr. R showed little interest in either the marital or individual treatment, stating that he was attending therapy only because Ms. R wanted him to, and denying sexual abuse of Becky. After two individual sessions during which Mr. R continued to externalize his difficulties, he discontinued treatment. Ms. R attended seven sessions from June to August (although she did not "officially" terminate treatment until October). Intervention issues that were focused upon during the initial phase included her response to her daughter's allegations, her relationship with Becky, and her feelings toward her husband, in addition to coping with the intervention by authorities and the disruption of her life and that of her family. The impact of Ms. R's childhood experience of being molested by her father was also explored.

According to Sgroi et al. (1982), the dynamics of child sexual abuse can be understood as consisting of five phases: engagement, sexual interaction, secrecy, disclosure, and (often) a suppression phase. The last two phases are especially relevant with regard to the intervention with Ms. R. Family reactions to disclosure are discussed by Sgroi et al. (1982) in which they point out that mothers may respond in a number of different ways. Some may cooperate fully, although the authors state that clinicians should not expect all mothers to react that way, nor should they expect that mothers who had initially reacted in a protective fashion will be able to sustain that, since self-interest and self-protection are powerful responses that must be acknowledged. Often mothers are faced with the choice of protecting the perpetrator or protecting the child. Sgroi et al. stated that it was not unusual for a mother to collapse under combined pressures from inside and outside her family, and withdraw from activities as much as possible, avoiding decision making and abandoning responsibilities.

Ms. R certainly fit the description of a mother who initially reacted very supportively toward her daughter, then collapsed under pressure. Ms. R's response to Becky's allegations was to believe that Becky had been sexually abused but pointed at both Becky's grandfather and natural father, rather than Becky's stepfather, as the perpetrator. Ms. R felt a great deal of pressure to choose between her daughter and her husband and finally "resolved" the dilemma by being supportive of both of them until the courts made the decision. Ms. R had initially expressed a desire to cooperate with the investigation with the workers from Child Protective Services (CPS) but soon became dissatisfied and angry with what she perceived as deliberate deception and manipulation by the CPS workers and lawyers. At that point, she wondered to her therapist if involving the authorities would be helpful to anyone in the long run and thought that her way of handling her own abuse (i.e., not telling) was better than dragging a family through the legal proceedings and resultant pain and disruption.

Some exploration of her feelings from childhood and ways of coping was initiated by her therapist, and she was supported in her efforts to continue to function adaptively. Sgroi et al. (1982) stated that mothers are often incest victims, and those feelings may color how they handle the situation with their own daughters. Ms. R did express her anger and feelings of betrayal toward her own mother for denying the fact of Ms. R's childhood abuse, but seemed unaware of her own denial regarding her daughter.

Another crisis occurred in August when Mr. G obtained a court order to remove his and Ms. R's biological children from her home. Ms. R became overwhelmed and suicidal. At that point the therapist was supportive and focused upon assisting her in coping with everyday tasks. During the last two sessions treatment focused on enabling her to cope with the various possible outcomes of the custody hearing (in October) and Mr. R's trial (in December). In the second to last session she was still expressing doubts about her stability, and felt that she was being pushed to the limits of her strength.

However, the next week during what turned out to be her last session with her therapist at the end of August, Ms. R felt that she was coping well, and had recovered much strength. According to her therapist, she empathized with Becky's feeling depressed and somehow to blame as she talked of her own experience of sexual abuse, and sought to reassure Becky of her love for her. Ms. R was also able to take her children's perspective by thinking of her own childhood, and realized that they might feel much safer and content in her ex-husband's home since they were removed from the turmoil of her home, plus were in a more financially stable situation. At that point her therapist felt that Ms. R seemed to be prepared for either regaining custody or being allowed visitation. Ms. R also stated that she realized the legal proceedings were going to drag out and that escape from the problems was not possible. Although Becky had been placed out of the house, and Mr. R allowed to remain, Ms. R persisted in maintaining that she had not "chosen" either individual. Possible outcomes in relation to her husband were discussed at that time, and Ms. R continued to depend on the courts to resolve her dilemma. She told her therapist that she was uncertain as to how she would respond emotionally should Mr. R be found guilty, but according to her therapist, seemed to be anticipating that he would be serving some time, and was trying to prepare for that eventuality.

Between the end of August and the end of October, Ms. R missed and rescheduled several sessions prior to termination. At the time of her last contact with her therapist, she said she had obtained employment and felt that it was too difficult to drive the 20 miles to the Center after work. She also reported that she was coping fairly well, and she discontinued services.

Child

Intervention Goals

In keeping with the original plan of short-term individual therapy, the initial treatment goals for Becky were to see her for 4 to 6 months, to focus upon: (1) the impact issues from the sexual abuse, (2) her relationships with Mr. and Ms. G and with her mother, Ms. R, (3) her adjustment in school, and (4) the stress associated with the many changes in residence. The plan was to see her in "prescriptive play therapy" (adapted from Mann & McDermott, 1983; Schaefer & O'Conner, 1983), with periodic meetings with Mr. and Ms. G, as needed. Sixteen to twenty sessions would last from the middle of September until the middle to end of January, with that time period selected initially to give Becky time to recover from the trial of Mr. R to be held the first of December, and to work through termination issues with her therapist. The actual process by which we attempted to reach those goals will be discussed in more detail in the next section.

Two other formal planning points with Becky and Mr. and Ms. G took place in treatment. At the regularly scheduled 10th session review (mid-November), the treatment goals included continuing to deal with the sexual abuse and Becky's relationship with her mother, plus preparing her to testify in Mr. R's criminal trial which was to occur approximately 3 weeks later. Another planning session was held during the sixteenth meeting, since that was the original estimate of a termination point. During that treatment planning session (in the middle of December), the agreed-upon goals for Becky were to discuss her relationship with her mother, as well as issues concerning custody and visitation.

Also, during that sixteenth session treatment review, a parent counseling focus was added with the goal of helping Mr. and Ms. G handle custody and visitation issues more effectively. As pointed out by Cantor and Drake (1983), custody and visitation can easily become problematic between ex-spouses, depending upon the amount of hostility between the two. Relevant recommendations from Cantor and Drake included first reducing the hostility that was present, then dealing with any specific issues of visitation that had not been resolved in the process. My plan at that point in mid-December was to meet with Mr. and Ms. G for four more sessions and with Becky for an additional six. The total number of sessions was 27: 20 with Becky alone, 5 with Mr. and Ms. G alone, and 2 with time divided between Becky and Mr. and Ms. G.

Intervention Process

The type of play therapy which I implemented with Becky was a combination of what Schaefer and O'Conner (1983) call "prescriptive play therapy" (p. 1) and what is labeled by Tuma and Sobotka (1983) as "structured play therapy" (p. 394). Both of these approaches are offshoots of the more traditional psychodynamically oriented or nondirective types of play therapy. In client-centered and psychoanalytically oriented play therapies, the therapist's relationship with the child is all-important, and is the primary vehicle for change, with few interpretations made to the child (Tuma & Sobotka, 1983). Generally the therapist follows the child's lead in the sessions, working with whatever material the child presents in the context of his/her play.

In contrast, in structured play therapy the clinician directs that play at times in order to focus upon conflict areas (Tuma & Sobotka, 1983). Generally the main differences with a structured approach is in the directiveness of the therapist, with the clinician taking a more active role. Other important elements of therapy such as the child's therapeutic alliance with the therapist and the interpretation of defenses are still present. Schaefer and O'Conner (1983) make the point that play therapies have become much more "prescriptive" in the last 10 years, in that clinicians attempt to individualize the treatment to fit the specific child, choosing from a variety of theories and approaches while doing so. This prescriptive individual orientation allows for flexibility in treating children, with adjunctive treatments employed as necessary.

My approach to play therapy with Becky was both prescriptive and structured, with elements of the more traditional play therapies incorporated as well. The actual course of treatment followed quite closely the three phases of psychotherapy with children conceptualized by Tuma and Sobotka (1983), consisting of an initial phase in which an assessment of the difficulties is made and a treatment contract established, a middle phase wherein the therapist and child deal with interpretations, resistance, transference, and countertransference, and a final phase of termination. Underlying the more specific goals of play therapy discussed in the previous section were the general purposes of providing Becky with a supportive, accepting relationship and enhancing her sense of self-esteem. Within each therapy session I worked in a nondirective fashion with material she provided me, as well as actively structured particular play situations when it was appropriate (e.g., playing in the dollhouse and talking about her stepfather). In addition, we engaged in purely "fun" play, talked about the play in metaphors, and talked directly about certain circumstances, depending on the phase of therapy and on the degree of distance she needed in order to handle interpretations or information I provided.

During the first five to six sessions of the play therapy, the focus of treatment was upon establishing rapport and building a therapeutic alliance, clarifying with Becky the reasons for meeting, and beginning to explore the impact issues from the incest. Becky's treatment began in a positive fashion, since she quickly established a relationship with me and seemed to clearly understand the purpose of therapy. Since a custody hearing was approximately 3 weeks away at the end of September, within each of the third to sixth sessions with Becky some issues related to visitation as well as incest were included. The sexual abuse impact issues that Becky and I dealt with first during those sessions were responsibility, believability, bodily integrity and protection, secrecy and sharing, and trust. She was told that the sexual abuse was not her fault, that people believed her, and that she did not have to tell anyone, such as the other children at school, about the abuse. Also some time was spent on whom she could tell if anyone tried to sexually molest her again. In addition, I indicated to her that her stepfather needed help, and that she was helping him get treatment.

Treatment focused upon visitation and custody during the seventh through ninth sessions, since I learned from Mr. and Ms. G that they had been awarded permanent custody, and Becky was going to visit Ms. R for the first time in several months. In talking with Becky, it was apparent that she was very concerned about fights between Nathan and Mr. G and about seeing her mother. My conversations with Becky mostly centered around feelings, including those of confusion, fear, and ambivalence. It was also clear when I met with Mr. and Ms. G during the tenth session to talk about treatment progress and goals that the focus of their interest had shifted.

They were quite concerned about Nathan, and the acting out he was doing, especially before and after visitation, rather than about Becky.

Between the tenth and eleventh sessions, I had several phone contacts with Mr. and Ms. G regarding visitation. Ms. G called to say that the two children were very upset after the visit, so I arranged an extra appointment with Mr. and Ms. G, in order to talk about the best way to handle the visitation. Between the phone call with the Gs and meeting with them, I consulted with the faculty member who had supervised the evaluation of Nathan, regarding the advisability of intervention for Nate. Based on the faculty member's opinion that it was not necessary, when I met with Mr. and Ms. G, I recommended to them that they wait 6 weeks and reevaluate the necessity for treatment at that point. I also made suggestions regarding ways that they could help keep the situation more calm. In addition, during that meeting with Mr. and Ms. G, the upcoming court trial which was approximately 2½ weeks away was discussed. I talked with Mr. and Ms. G regarding the possibility that Becky might need to testify, and that she might become more upset in the ensuing weeks before the trial.

The next three sessions with Becky were focused upon court as well as upon visitation. I read parts of the book *Carla Goes to Court* (Beaudry & Ketchem, 1982) with Becky, and explained many of the procedures, including the fact that she would talk with the prosecuting attorney and see the courtroom. At this point I also contacted the prosecuting attorney, who requested that Mr. G call him for an appointment. In the sessions with Becky, discussions focused on the visitation and her feeling torn and ambivalent, and the fact that the difficulties with visitation were not her fault. In the session just before the trial, Becky and I again read portions of *Carla Goes to Court* and talked about ways she could help herself stay calm. I reassured her again that even though it would be scary, I thought she would be able to do a good job. As occasionally happens in intrafamilial child sexual abuse cases, Becky did not have to testify, since Mr. R changed his plea to "guilty" on the morning of the trial, and received a sentence of 90 days in jail plus 5 years probation. Therefore, the focus of the treatment with Becky shifted again to visitation and repercussions from the outcome of the court sentence.

Issues that were dealt with over the next three sessions included trust, Becky's natural parents fighting over visitation, and termination. Due to the turmoil arising from Mr. R's trial and the custody issues, as well as the strength of the attachment Becky made to me, it seemed clear at that point that therapy would extend several sessions beyond the planned sixteen. Regarding the implications of the incest, I dealt with Becky's feelings that Mr. R did not receive enough punishment, and that she was afraid her mother would be angry with her. In addition, she was quite troubled by the fights between Mr. G and Ms. R, and I again reassured her that they were not her fault. At the sixteenth session the idea of ending therapy in 3 to

4 weeks was brought up, and Becky seemed quite distressed by it. Therefore, in response to both a number of telephone calls from Mr. and Ms. G, and to Becky's distress, I made a decision at that point to add ten sessions to the planned sixteen, six with Becky alone and four with Mr. and Ms. G to focus on visitation.

Regarding the therapeutic process throughout the course of treatment, Becky had been rather reluctant to talk in much detail regarding her feelings and concerns, as is often typical of children her age. Her usual defense against anxiety was to avoid the conflictual material, tactics which included ignoring the therapist's direct questions and busily playing and describing games. However, by the tenth session, she was usually able to acknowledge mild interpretations which I made, especially if they were phrased in the third person (e.g., "other girls sometimes feel . . ."). About two-thirds of the way through therapy she was also able to acknowledge the function of her defense tactic of avoiding questions which made her uncomfortable. Due to the strength of the therapeutic alliance established with Becky, and issues of security and abandonment, appropriate handling of termination was an important consideration. My approach to dealing with this phase of therapy was to begin the process early and extend the interval between sessions to every other week when there were five sessions left.

The last five sessions with Becky over the next 10 weeks focused on pointing out to her how the situation had changed, ways things were going better, and what she could do to help herself feel better. I encouraged her to talk with Mr. and Ms. G and also acknowledged the difficulty in termination. At her suggestion the last session ended with a party, which was held the middle of March of the year following the initial report. At that point, Becky and I talked again about all the things that had changed for the better, and reiterated the fact that it was difficult to say goodbye. During the last session I also gave Becky the telephone number and address of the Psychological Services Center in case she wanted to contact me.

While the approach with Becky was to "wind down" over the last five sessions, at that point intervention efforts were more intensively directed toward Mr. and Ms. G. They seemed quite committed to improving the interactions among the family members at home, although it initially appeared that it would be rather difficult for them to change their long-standing patterns, especially for Mr. G. He gave the impression of being very concrete in his thinking, with little awareness of the impact of his behavior on other people. In contrast, Ms. G seemed reasonably psychologically sophisticated and insightful, and was very interested in better understanding the feelings and motivation of her children. My approach to intervention with Mr. and Ms. G was supportive and educational, focusing upon their parenting techniques and attitudes, with discussion centering upon discipline, visitation, the incest, and improving the relationship between the two of them.

The five parenting-focused sessions allowed both parents a chance to ventilate their feelings and express their concerns. They were quite interested in the opportunity to ask questions regarding Becky's and Nate's feelings, especially related to the ways in which both children were reacting to Ms. R's actions and the court proceedings. Several discussions also centered upon Becky's and Nate's reactions to the sexual abuse, with me explaining some of the patterns and dynamics present in incest cases. Mr. and Ms. G had different methods for handling certain situations, especially regarding visitation, which needed to be worked out. The most problematic area seemed to be Mr. G's difficulties with patience and control of his temper. During the third session with them, I made several concrete suggestions to Mr. G regarding ways for him to remain in control of his temper, and his implementation of them proved to be quite beneficial to the progress of the parent counseling.

OUTCOME

With Ms. R

As previously mentioned, Ms. R chose to discontinue services in October 1984 since she was feeling better. She told her therapist that she viewed therapy as a very positive experience, and felt it had helped a great deal. It seemed likely that the therapist had been of great benefit to Ms. R during the crisis phase, even though she chose not to continue beyond that point.

With Mr. R

In cases of intrafamilial sexual abuse, "plea bargaining" for a guilty plea in exchange for a lighter sentence is not an unusual outcome. Although criminal laws regarding types of offenses and severity of the associated punishments vary from state to state, in many instances lawyers strongly suggest to their clients that they are likely to receive a lighter sentence if they plead guilty. Some states also have a "diversion" program in which offenders are court-ordered into treatment in lieu of a jail sentence. If the perpetrators do not fulfill the conditions of the intervention program, they are sent to jail. While intuitively this type of program sounds like it would be beneficial to perpetrators, Finkelhor (1986) points out that no well-conducted studies of differential outcomes exist based upon whether the offender went to jail or went into a diversion program; therefore, the effectiveness of treatment programs is, in actuality, unknown.

While no formal diversion program for offenders is established in the local area, several judges do at times order an offender to obtain counseling. As a condition of his probation, Mr. R was court-ordered to seek individual treatment. Therefore, in early January, Mr. R contacted the Psychological Services Center and requested therapy. However, the Center personnel who interviewed Mr. R assessed his motivation for treatment as being externally focused, with no real desire for changes in his behavior noted. Based upon his current low level of motivation as well as his previous failure to utilize therapy in a productive fashion, services at the Center were denied to him, and he was referred to the local mental health center.

With Becky

Improvements that were noted with Becky by the time of termination were enhanced relationships with Mr. and Ms. G and with Ms. R, a decrease in nightmares and fear of the dark, and decreased moodiness and stubbornness. In addition, it seemed that Becky had achieved increased understanding of her reactions and Mr. R's responsibility in the sexual abuse. Regarding the sexual abuse impact issues, the concerns which seemed to be most salient for Becky and provided the greatest relief when discussed were, in addition to guilt and responsibility, believability (especially regarding her mother's ambivalence), secrecy and sharing, and court attendance.

When Ms. G completed the CBCL at the end of treatment, the Internalizing, Externalizing, and Total Behavior T scores were all approximately 60. The formerly elevated narrow-band scales were T score 60 or lower, and only the Somatic Concerns and Delinquency scales remained at their previous levels of T score 65. Social competence scales of Activities and School were at T scores of 45 and 20, respectively.

With Mr. and Ms. G

In the last two sessions with Mr. and Ms. G, Mr. G reported a much better ability to control his temper, and was able to see the benefits of doing so in an improved relationship with each of his children. Other improvements I noted in the parents were more realistic, age-appropriate expectations for the children, especially with Ms. G toward Becky, and enhanced communication between the parents. During the last session (the first week of March), they expressed their satisfaction with the more pleasant, less tense atmosphere of the home, and with the improvements seen in Becky.

FOLLOW-UP

Several pieces of information are available for follow-up with these families. Approximately 1 month after termination (April, 1985), I was contacted by Mr. and Ms. G's lawyer, who explained that Ms. R had filed for custody of Becky and Nathan. Rather than testify at the custody hearing, with Mr. G's permission I wrote a letter to the court briefly describing my intervention with Becky, and stating my opinion that Becky was adjusting well in Mr. and Ms. G's home. In the letter I also pointed out that the conflict and frequent custody battles was making it more difficult for both of the children to feel secure and to be able to adjust in an optimal fashion.

Approximately 1 week later, the faculty member who had supervised Nathan's assessment was contacted by a worker at another agency who wished to obtain records of Nate's evaluation. The worker stated that their evaluation was being conducted at the request of Mr. and Ms. G, who wanted to use the information in the custody hearing.

In addition, several noteworthy events took place in 1987. Mr. R's probation was revoked in May, and he was returned to jail due to charges of cattle rustling. In July, Nathan went to live with his paternal grandparents since he and Mr. G were continuing to experience difficulties with verbal, and occasionally physical, aggressiveness.

REFLECTIONS

In addition to reflecting many of the typical dynamics seen in sexually abusive families, some of the main points illustrated by this case are the complexities of clinical work in this area, the importance of focusing upon the entire family, and the necessity of the therapist being an advocate for the child. Sgroi (1982) and Porter et al. (1982) state that in order to work effectively with a family in which there has been sexual abuse, mental health workers must be willing to be involved in the crisis intervention phase as well as the more regularly scheduled therapy sessions. Clearly in this case, the entire family needed support through the crisis, but especially Ms. R.

Keeping a "family focus" in this situation was made more complicated by the fact that two families were involved. This circumstance may be somewhat unusual, in that issues regarding custody and visitation also needed to be dealt with as well as the considerations arising from the sexual abuse. More often in these families, children remain with a relative or in foster care until a judgment is made regarding their safety. Another less frequently used approach is to have the accused perpetrator court-ordered out of the home while the child remains. Each of these situations poses different dilemmas for the clinician which must be addressed.

Another "family-focus" issue in this case relates to Nathan, the sibling of the incest victim. Due to the organization of our Center, another faculty clinician was responsible for evaluating Nate. If the decision regarding treatment for Nate had been up to me, I would have recommended a short-term, educationally oriented intervention. Information and support likely would have been helpful for Nathan so that he could better understand his role and responsibility and not feel guilty for not protecting his sister. As is sometimes the case in sexually abusive families, Nathan himself might have been abused also. In retrospect, when Mr. and Ms. G requested treatment for Nathan in January, it probably would have been helpful to provide some services to Nathan, rather than make the decision based on the earlier evaluation.

This family focus also illustrates the combination of methods for intervention. More traditional nondirective play therapy was combined with a more structured, directive approach, which was also integrated with parent counseling sessions. Each of the components was necessary for the intervention. The "family systems" aspect of the interactions also seems relevant, since it appeared that as Becky improved, Nathan became worse. In light of that, the parenting sessions probably could have lasted several more weeks in order to assist the Gs in responding to Ms. R in a way that did not escalate the conflict over custody.

Being an advocate for the child is certainly a vital task of the therapist. In most situations there are a number of people from different agencies involved, and this case was no exception. Workers from social services did the initial interviewing, a psychologist from another agency conducted an evaluation of the child, and since the court was involved, the prosecuting attorney was also part of the network. Sometimes it is necessary for one person to coordinate the effort of a number of agencies in order for the service delivery network to function smoothly, and the child's therapist is often the logical person to do so.

One issue with which therapists treating child sexual abuse victims must contend, especially if the abuse was perpetrated by a family member and the child is still in the home, is that of retraction of her/his allegation. It is not unusual for a child who is living in a family in which all members are either overtly or covertly denying that the abuse occurred to recant and change their story. Summit (1983) calls this the "child sexual abuse accommodation syndrome" and recommends specific ways that clinicians can help prevent children from retracting their allegations. Given Ms. R's ambivalence, and the fact that Mr. R remained in the home, if Becky had not been in the secure, supportive environment of the G's, there is a good chance that she might have recanted.

Another related issue of which clinicians need to be aware is demonstrated by the process of treatment and progress (or lack thereof) with these two families. No matter how "professional" we are, working with incest survivors and the other family members is difficult and can elicit a number of strong, often negative, feelings on the part of the clinician. Haugaard and Reppucci's (1988) book contains an excellent chapter entitled "Basic Issues in Treatment" in which they delineate frequent emotional pitfalls for clinicians and provide a number of suggestions for identifying and dealing with those feelings.

Although therapy for the young survivors of intrafamilial sexual abuse may prevent later severe psychological difficulties, the treatment is still after-the-fact. In order to intervene in a more preventive fashion, more effort needs to be focused at the source of the problem. According to Finkelhor's (1984) Four Preconditions Model, intervention must take place with offenders and potential offenders as well as with children in order that the perpetrator or some other factor does not undermine or overcome children's possible resistance to sexual abuse. Several chapters in books by Finkelhor (1986), Haugaard and Reppucci (1988), and Schetky and Green (1988) provide additional information regarding intervention and preventive efforts in these areas.

REFERENCES

Achenbach, T. M. (1981). *Child Behavior Checklist for Ages 4-16*. Burlington, VT: University of Vermont.
Achenbach, T. M., & Edelbrock, C. S. (1983). *Manual of the Child Behavior Checklist and the Revised Behavior Profile*. Burlington, VT: University of Vermont.
American Psychiatric Association (1980). *Diagnostic and statistical manual of mental disorders* (3rd ed.). Washington, DC: Author.
Beaudry, J., & Ketchem, L. (1982). *Carla goes to court*. New York: Human Sciences Press.
Browne, A., & Finkelhor, D. (1986). Initial and long-term effects: A review of the research. In D. Finkelhor (Ed.), *A sourcebook on child sexual abuse* (pp. 199-216). New York: Plenum.
Cantor, D. W., & Drake, E. A. (1983). *Divorced parents and their children: A guide for mental health professionals*. New York: Springer.
Damon, L., & Waterman, J. (1986). Parallel group treatment of children and their mothers. In K. MacFarlane & J. Waterman (Eds.), *Sexual abuse of young children: Evaluation and treatment* (pp. 244-298). New York: Guilford.
Finkelhor, D. (1984). *Child sexual abuse: New theory and research*. New York: The Free Press.
Finkelhor, D. (1986). *A sourcebook of child sexual abuse*. Beverly Hills, CA: Sage.
Finkelhor, D., & Browne, A. (1986). Initial and long-term effects: A conceptual framework. In D. Finkelhor (Ed.), *A sourcebook on child sexual abuse* (pp. 180-198). Beverly Hills, CA: Sage.
Giaretto, H. (1982). A comprehensive child sexual abuse treatment program. *Child Abuse and Neglect, 6*, 263-278.
Green, A. H. (1988). Overview of the literature on child sexual abuse. In D. H. Schetky and A. H. Green (Eds.), *Child sexual abuse: A handbook for health care and legal professionals*. New York: Brunner/Mazel.
Hampton, K. L., & Hughes, H. M. (1988). *Intervention with child and adolescent incest victims: A developmental approach*. Manuscript submitted for publication.
Haugaard, J. J., & Reppucci, W. D. (1988). *The sexual abuse of children: A comprehensive guide to current knowledge and intervention strategies*. San Francisco: Jossey-Bass.
Kroth, J. A. (1979). *Child sexual abuse: Analysis of a family therapy approach*. Springfield, IL: Charles C. Thomas.

Long, S. (1986). Guidelines for treating young children. In K. MacFarlane & J. Waterman (Eds.), *Sexual abuse of young children: Evaluation and treatment* (pp. 220–243). New York: Guilford.

Lusk, R., & Waterman, J. (1986). Effects of sexual abuse on children. In K. MacFarlane & J. Waterman (Eds.), *Sexual abuse of young children: Evaluation and treatment* (pp. 101–120). New York: Guilford.

Mann, E., & McDermott, J. F. (1983). Play therapy for victims of child abuse and neglect. In C. E. Schafer & K. J. O'Connor (Eds.), *Handbook of play therapy* (pp. 283–307). New York: Wiley.

Mrazek, P. J. (1983). Sexual abuse of children. In B. B. Lahey & A. E. Kazdin (Eds.), *Advances in clinical child psychology* (Vol. 6, pp. 199–216). New York: Plenum.

National Center on Child Abuse and Neglect (1978). *Interdisciplinary glossary on child abuse and neglect.* Washington, DC: U.S. Department of Education.

Porter, F. S., Blick, L. C., & Sgroi, S. M. (1982). Treatment of the sexually abused child. In S. M. Sgroi (Ed.), *Handbook of clinical intervention in child sexual abuse* (pp. 109–145). Lexington, MA: Heath.

Schaefer, C. E., & O'Connor, K. J. (1983). Major approaches to play therapy: Advances and innovations. In C. E. Schaefer & K. J. O'Connor (Eds.), *Handbook of play therapy* (pp. 1–11). New York: Wiley-Interscience.

Schetky, D. H., & Green, A. H. (1988). *Child sexual abuse: A handbook for health care and legal professionals.* New York: Brunner/Mazel.

Sgroi, S. M. (1982). Introduction: The state of the art in child-sexual-abuse intervention. In S. M. Sgroi (Ed.), *Handbook of clinical intervention in child sexual abuse* (pp. 1–8). Lexington, MA: Heath.

Sgroi, S. M., Blick, L. C., & Porter, F. S. (1982). A conceptual framework for child sexual abuse. In S. M. Sgroi (Ed.), *Handbook of clinical intervention in child sexual abuse* (pp. 9–37). Lexington, MA: Heath.

Sturkie, K. (1983). Structured group treatment for sexually abused children. *Health and Social Work, 8,* 299–308.

Summit, R. C. (1983). The child sexual abuse accommodation syndrome. *Child Abuse and Neglect, 7,* 177–193.

Tuma, J. M., & Sobotka, K. R. (1983). Traditional therapies with children. In T. H. Ollendick and M. Hersen (Eds.), *Handbook of child psychopathology* (pp. 391–426). New York: Plenum.

Waterman, J. (1986). Overview of treatment issues. In K. MacFarlane & J. Waterman (Eds.), *Sexual abuse of young children: Evaluation and treatment* (pp. 244–298). New York: Guilford.

Waterman, J., & Lusk, R. (1986). Scope of the problem. In K. MacFarlane & J. Waterman (Eds.), *Sexual abuse of young children: Evaluation and treatment* (pp. 3–14). New York: Guilford.

12
Evaluation and Treatment of Attention-deficit Hyperactivity Disorder

DALE W. WISELY

The diagnostic term Attention-deficit Hyperactivity Disorder (American Psychiatric Association, 1987) is the most recent of a historical series of terms intended to describe a disorder typically characterized by inattention, impulsivity, and hyperactivity. It is largely regarded as a childhood disorder because childhood onset is the norm; however, there is a recent trend toward increasing awareness of the adolescent and adult manifestations of the disorder (Wender, 1987). Earlier diagnostic terms and descriptions reflected an emphasis on hyperactivity as the core of the problem. Laufer and Denhoff (1957), in an early and frequently cited description of "hyperkinetic behavior syndrome," emphasized the increased motor activity displayed by children with this syndrome. In the second edition of the *Diagnostic and Statistical Manual of Mental Disorders* (DSM-II) of the American Psychiatric Association (1968) the term "hyperkinetic reaction of childhood (or adolescence)" was used to describe a disorder "characterized by overactivity, restlessness, distractibility, and short attention span" (p. 50). Ross and Ross (1976) trace the history of the term "minimal brain dysfunction," commonly used in the 1960s, to describe children with learning disorders and behavioral problems associated with vaguely defined central nervous system impairment. By the 1970s, largely in response to the work of Virginia Douglas and colleagues (Douglas, 1972, 1974; Douglas & Peters, 1980) emphasis was shifting away from hyperactivity and toward attentional deficits as the core of the disorder. This was reflected also in the third edition of the *Diagnostic and Statistical Manual of Mental Disorders* (DSM-III; American Psychiatric Association, 1980) which presented two diagnostic terms which placed emphasis on the inattentiveness of those with the disorder: Attention Deficit Disorder with Hyperactivity and Attention Deficit Disorder without Hyper-

Dale W. Wisely. The Vaughan Clinic, Birmingham, Alabama.

activity. These terms seemed to reflect the view that the attention deficit is the core of the disorder and that hyperactivity is best seen as a major symptom which may or may not be present. In the recently published revised third edition of the *Diagnostic and Statistical Manual of Mental Disorders* (DSM-III-R; American Psychiatric Association, 1987) the term "Attention-deficit Hyperactivity Disorder" (ADHD) is used to denote the common disorder in which inattentiveness, impulsivity, and hyperactivity are all present. This term is found along with "Conduct Disorders" and "Oppositional–defiant Disorder" under the category "Disruptive Behavior Disorders." A separate category, "Other Disorders of Infancy, Childhood, or Adolescence," includes the term "Undifferentiated Attention Deficit Disorder" described as a "residual category" and which is rather tentatively presented. Evidently, it is intended to label those children with developmentally inappropriate inattention who lack the impulsivity and hyperactivity of those children with ADHD. The DSM-III-R diagnostic criteria appear in Table 12-1.

TABLE 12-1. Diagnostic Criteria for Attention-deficit Hyperactivity Disorder in DSM-III-R

A. A disturbance of at least six months during which at least eight of the following are present:
   (1) often fidgets with hands or feet or squirms in seat (in adolescents, may be limited to subjective feelings of restlessness)
   (2) has difficulty remaining seated when required to do so
   (3) is easily distracted by extraneous stimuli
   (4) has difficulty awaiting turn in games or group situations
   (5) often blurts out answers to questions before they have been completed
   (6) has difficulty following through on instructions from others (not due to oppositional behavior or failures of comprehension), e.g., fails to finish chores
   (7) has difficulty sustaining attention in task or play activities
   (8) often shifts from one uncompleted activity to another
   (9) has difficulty playing quietly
   (10) often talks excessively
   (11) often interrupts or intrudes on others, e.g., butts into other children's games
   (12) often does not seem to listen to what is being said to him or her
   (13) often loses things necessary for tasks or activities at school or at home (e.g., toys, pencils, books, assignments)
   (14) often engages in physically dangerous activities without considering possible consequences (not for the purpose of thrill-seeking), e.g., runs into street without looking
B. Onset before age seven.
C. Does not meet the criteria for a Pervasive Developmental Disorder

Note. From *Diagnostic and Statistical Manual of Mental Disorders* (pp. 52–53) by the American Psychiatric Association, 1987, Washington, DC: Author. Copyright 1987 by American Psychiatric Association. Reprinted by permission.

Because of the difficulties in defining this disorder, the incidence and prevalence are not precisely known. I refer the reader to Barkley (1981) for a review of efforts to determine how many children suffer from this disorder in its various nosological incarnations. Although Barkley points out that estimates range from 2% to 20%, he concludes from his review that most investigators accept an estimate of the prevalence of this disorder of between 3% and 5% of school-aged children.

Children with ADHD may experience a range of problems in school, home, and social settings. Inattention, poor impulse control, and overactivity can seriously impair the functioning of these children in all settings. Behavioral noncompliance is a very common feature (Barkley, 1981; Forehand & McMahon, 1981) which may lead to considerable tension and even familial ill will toward these children in their families and in the school settings. Parent–child interactions are frequently affected by the disorder (Barkley & Cunningham, 1979). Academic problems are also routine in these children. Lambert and Sandoval (1980) found significant underachievement relative to grade level in their sample of hyperactive children. Although ADHD is not associated with any one of the specific learning disabilities, it is generally accepted that learning disabilities and ADHD are commonly seen together (Cantwell & Satterfield, 1978). In my experience, the presence of ADHD almost precludes the possibility of adequate educational achievement unless interventions are made.

This chapter describes the evaluation and treatment of an 8-year-old boy with Attention-deficit Hyperactive Disorder.[1] This case illustrates methods of evaluating this disorder, selecting interventions, assessing change that results from interventions, and altering interventions accordingly. It was selected because, while this child's difficulties are not especially atypical of those of other children with the disorder, there are relatively uncommon aspects of the case, including the use of imipramine as one of the interventions.

CASE BACKGROUND

The child presented in this case is an 8-year-old male referred by a friend of his family. The family is composed of the natural father who is a 35-year-old salesman of medical equipment, the natural mother, a 31-year-old receptionist at a dental clinic, a 10-year-old sister, and the patient. The patient, who will be called Jacob, a pseudonym, was in the second grade at a local

1. Although this case was diagnosed prior to the publication of the revised third edition of the *Diagnostic and Statistical Manual of Mental Disorders* (American Psychiatric Association, 1987), it is presented here with the new diagnostic terminology.

public school.[2] An intake session was conducted with the parents and with Jacob. The mother had had a normal pregnancy and a lengthy but otherwise uncomplicated labor. His medical history was unremarkable except for the presence of allergies and frequent ear infections for which he was treated by an ear, nose, and throat specialist. There was no history of serious trauma. His developmental milestones were within normal limits.

In the intake interview with Jacob present, the parents stated that they had always regarded Jacob as "hyper" and that they had been having some difficulties managing his behavior since he was a toddler. They described him as a fretful and restless baby who seemed to sleep less than most. They told me that Jacob had appeared to start the "terrible twos" early and had not yet grown out of them. They indicated that Jacob had not seemed to be a "bad child," but seemed not to listen to their instructions or to carry out their commands as they thought he should. The mother did not work for the first 4 years of Jacob's life and said that she would often spend time with Jacob in the presence of other children and their mothers. She believed that that experience allowed her to compare Jacob with other children and that she became convinced by the time Jacob was 4 that he was less cooperative, more active, and more irritable than most of his peers. By age 5, Jacob was attending a private kindergarten while both parents worked. The teacher had commented to the parents that Jacob was relatively active, but she had felt able to handle him behaviorally and, therefore, did not regard him as hyperactive. His level of achievement in the preacademic work at the kindergarten was described as average by the teacher. The mother recalls the teacher commenting that Jacob seemed intelligent but had a short attention span.

In the first grade, Jacob's parents heard frequently from his rather distraught teacher regarding his behavior. The reports generally indicated that the short-attention span continued to be a problem, but the teacher was especially concerned about his disruptive behavior and his "bad attitude." He was sometimes irritable and noncompliant and would respond to the teacher's efforts to correct him with tearful, angry outbursts. It was the parents' belief, however, that the teacher and Jacob had a personality conflict, and they stated in retrospect that they may have been inclined to blame Jacob's problems on the teacher. The parents felt that the teacher did not like Jacob and so communication with the teacher broke down during the school year. His academic performance was also poor during that year.

The second grade began somewhat more positively and both Jacob and

2. Identifying information has been changed to insure protection of the patient's identity. It is the author's opinion that this patient could not be identified by any person from this report.

his parents seemed to get along well with the teacher. For the first 6-week period of school, Jacob's conduct was improved. He was less oppositional and irritable and his academic performane was somewhat better. By the middle of the second 6 weeks, however, the parents were called in for a conference with the teacher in which she suggested that Jacob continued to be very distractible and overactive and proposed that they seek the help of their pediatrician. The pediatrician was consulted by the parents, examined Jacob in his office, and told the parents that he doubted Jacob was hyperactive. It was unclear to the parents how the doctor had reached that conclusion. He indicated to them that Jacob was probably immature and would likely grow out of his problems. By the midpoint of the second grade year, the problems persisted, and it was at that time that Jacob's parents asked us to evaluate him.

At the time of the initial interviews with the parents, Jacob seemed to be having fewer problems at home than at school. In the home setting, he was described by the parents as "whiney," "occasionally defiant," and as having "bad days when you can not get him to do anything." Both parents noted that Jacob "just doesn't listen." The father generally had the task of encouraging Jacob to do his homework and stated that he had concluded that Jacob "just doesn't care about school." The father said that it was a struggle to get Jacob to sit still for his homework. When I made a comment about attention span, the father said that Jacob seemed to have "plenty of attention span" when involved in an enjoyable activity such as watching television or playing video games.

Jacob was also continuing to sleep poorly. Bedtime routine was usually stressful because Jacob resisted going to bed. He sometimes would tell his parents that he was afraid of robbers and kidnappers. His sleep was somewhat disturbed in that he reported frequent nightmares, tossed and turned in his sleep, would shout and mumble unintelligibly, and would often awake during the night and ask his parents to allow him to sleep with them. They generally would decline and put him back in his own bed.

Jacob's parents said that they found him to be a generally cheerful child except during the times that the parents would try to persuade him to do tasks such as homework or chores and when they struggled over bedtime routine. They were not having any particular problems with aggression, lying, stealing, or destructiveness.

At the time of this initial interview, Jacob was pleasant, cooperative, and only slightly fidgety in the office, although the restlessness increased steadily as the interview progressed. When I spoke with him alone and asked him why he thought his parents had brought him to me he alluded to "being scared at bedtime" and "not doing my work at school and having homework problems." As he warmed up to the interview, he was quite verbal and rather excitedly changed the subject frequently, interrupting on several occasions. His range of affect was normal.

ASSESSMENT

During the initial interview, I presented to the parents a plan for assessing Jacob's problems. I recommended deferring formal intellectual and educational testing. Although formal testing is a very frequent procedure with these children, it is my opinion that it is often unnecessary and difficult to justify in terms of costs and benefits. I typically schedule testing when it is strongly suspected that subaverage intellectual functioning or learning disability is a major factor. However, in cases in which ADHD is suspected, I prefer to evaluate and intervene for that first and then to do intellectual and educational testing as a subsequent step when needed. I also do not rely on individual sessions with the child as a diagnostic method. I typically will see such children for one or two sessions to get to know them and to do clinical interviews: however, I do this in the hope of collecting some information which will contribute to the process of making a differential diagnosis. I have not found a child's office behavior to be a reliable source of information regarding ADHD (or other problems of children). When significant hyperactivity is present in the office setting, that may be diagnostically helpful; however, its absence in the office is not meaningful. Undoubtedly, many cases of ADHD have gone undetected because of the belief by some health professionals that if a child is calm and still in the novel environment of the clinician's offices he/she could not have ADHD. My goal in individual assessment meetings with the child is to look for the presence of other contributing emotional problems such as depression, serious anxiety, worry about specific matters, abuse or neglect, family concerns, and peer problems. I also try to establish the beginnings of a helping relationship with the child by reassurance, nonthreatening conversation, or game playing, and by addressing any of the child's concerns about what will occur in the assessment and treatment processes.

At the close of the initial interviews with Jacob and his parents, each parent was asked to complete the Conners Parent Symptom Questionnaire (Goyette, Conners, & Ulrich, 1978), and the Achenbach Child Behavior Checklist (Achenbach, 1978). They were also asked to deliver to Jacob's second-grade teacher a packet of assessment instruments consisting of the Conners Teacher Rating Scale (Goyette et al., 1978), and the School Situations Questionnaire (Barkley, 1981). The packet contains a cover letter to the teacher seeking help in evaluating the child and a form with questions regarding the child's academic performance. (As this report is being prepared, our clinic is also incorporating the teacher version of the Achenbach Child Behavior Checklist into the teacher package we send out.)

All of the rating scales sent out were returned completed, except that the father had not completed his copy of the Child Behavior Checklist. On the Achenbach Child Behavior Checklist, scores are derived on nine factors labeled Schizoid or Anxious, Depressed, Uncommunicative, Obsessive-

Compulsive, Somatic Complaints, Social Withdrawal, Hyperactive, Agressive, and Delinquent. The scores on these factors based on the mother's responses were within the normal range (T score less than 70) except for Schizoid or Anxious ($T = 72$) and Hyperactive ($T = 75$). The reader is referred to the current manual for this instrument for information about these factors (Achenbach & Edelbrock, 1983). On the Conners Parent Symptom Questionnaire completed separately by the parents, I scored these instruments for the five factors of Learning Problems, Impulsive–Hyperactive, Conduct Problems, Psychosomatic, and Anxiety. Barkley (1981) and Kerasotes and Walker (1983) discuss the scoring of these instruments and the use of the normative data. My usual procedure is to regard as significant only those scores exceeding two standard deviations above the mean for the child's gender and age group. The mother's responses to the scale yielded scores above this level on the two factors of Learning Problems and Impulsive–Hyperactive. Scores below this level were for the Conduct Problems, Psychosomatic, and Anxiety factors. Scoring of the father's questionnaire yielded similar results except that the Inattentive–Hyperactive score fell just short of the two standard deviations mark.

The teacher information packet included written comments from the second-grade teacher regarding Jacob's short attention span and poor academic performance "for a boy of normal intelligence." She also wrote that she was most concerned about his lack of interest in his homework and his classroom assignments. Her responses to the Conners questionnaire yielded scores one standard deviation above the mean for the Conduct Problems and Inattentive–Passive factors and two standard deviations above the mean for the Hyperactive factor. I do not normally use the Hyperactivity Index on the Conners, but for interested readers the teacher's ratings of Jacob did fall above the two standard deviations cutoff. The teacher also completed the School Situations Questionnaire (Barkley, 1981). Jacob's teacher indicated problems with Jacob's behavior in 5 out of 12 of the items on the instrument, which falls short of the criterion of 50% of the items which Barkley has recommended.

CASE FORMULATION AND TREATMENT PLANNING

I prefer, when considering a diagnosis of ADHD, to use all of the following criteria:

1. Meets current DSM diagnostic criteria (see Table 12-1).
2. Score at least two standard deviations above the mean on Impulsive–Hyperactive factor of Conners Parent Symptom Questionnaire.
3. Score above $T = 70$ on Hyperactivity factor of Achenbach Child Behavior Checklist (parent).

4. Score at least two standard deviations above the mean on either Hyperactivity or Inattentive–Passive factor of Conners Teacher Rating Scale.
5. Clinical interview data consistent with ADHD.

In regard to the DSM criteria, Jacob's behavior did meet the DSM-III criteria for Attention Deficit Disorder with Hyperactivity at the time of the initial evaluations. When the data of his case are now reviewed with the new DSM-III-R criteria in effect, his behavior meets those criteria as well. Referring again to Table 12-1, Jacob would satisfy criteria B and C based on history as obtained in the intake interview. Criterion A lists 14 symptoms and requires 8 for diagnosis. Jacob would meet those numbered 1, 2, 3, 5, 6, 7, 8, 10, 11, and 12. Regarding my second personal criterion noted previously, ratings of Jacob's behavior were greater than two standard deviations above the mean on the Impulsive–Hyperactive factor of the Conners completed by the mother, but not on the one completed by the father. For my third criterion, the ratings were above the $T = 70$ level on the Hyperactivity factor of the Child Behavior Checklist completed by the mother. The fourth criterion is met by virtue of the high rating scores on the Hyperactivity factor of the Conners as completed by the teacher. In addition, in my opinion, his history as provided by the parents in the interview is consistent with ADHD.

Therefore, treatment was proposed with ADHD as the primary diagnosis. It is also significant, however, that this child was displaying considerable evidence of anxiety manifested, in part, by the sleep difficulties. The following initial treatment interventions were recommended in consultation with the parents:

1. Referral to a child psychiatrist for evaluation of the use of medication.
2. A behavioral program to promote greater effort with schoolwork and more appropriate classroom behavior.
3. Parent training regarding behavioral management at home.
4. Reassessment and additional treatment planning as needed when the three interventions were implemented.

COURSE OF TREATMENT

Jacob was seen by a child psychiatrist at the same clinic in which the author practices. (This is a very convenient arrangement which is not available to most psychologists in private practice, so I will discuss consultation issues of relevance to this and similar cases in the final section of this chapter.) The psychiatrist concurred with the diagnosis of ADHD and also noted the anxiety-related symptoms. At that time, we discussed the possibility of beginning with a trial of the tricyclic antidepressant imipramine. In his 1987 review of the use of tricyclic antidepressants in the treatment of children with ADHD, Steven Pliszka concludes that, while most literature suggests that stimulants are generally superior to imipramine in the treatment of ADHD, a subgroup of children with ADHD, characterized by higher levels of anxiety and depression may respond better to imipramine than to stimulants. This viewpoint has also been expressed by Russell Barkley (personal communication, May, 1987).

For most ADHD cases, the psychiatrists with whom I work generally suggest a trial of stimulants first, followed by a trial of imipramine in those cases in which it seems appropriate and in which stimulant therapy was less than successful. In Jacob's case, the recommendation was to follow our usual procedure and begin with a stimulant trial. The use of stimulants in the treatment of ADHD is well established in clinical practice and in the literature (Barkley, 1977; Cantwell & Carlson, 1978; Hinshaw, Henker, & Whalen, 1984; Rapport et al., 1987). The positive effects of stimulants on attention, impulsivity, and disruptive conduct are well documented. The use of stimulants, however, is not without controversy. Some researchers have advocated a more behavioral and less pharmacological approach (O'Leary, Pelham, Rosenbaum, & Price, 1976; Rosenbaum, O'Leary, & Jacob, 1975). Furthermore, there is presently a trend toward greater controversy regarding alleged overuse and misuse of stimulants. There have been numerous news accounts (Lacetti, 1987; Viadero, 1987) of political and legal actions by groups of concerned parents and professionals who contend that disruptive students are being too quickly referred by teachers to physicians for medication and that physicians have been too quick to medicate such children without proper evaluation.

Our procedure for stimulant trials in children who meet criteria for ADHD is (1) to gather baseline data, typically the Conners Parent and Teacher Rating Scales, (2) begin the medication, usually methyhenidate (Ritalin) at a low dose (typically 5 or 10 mg morning and noon) for 2 weeks, and (3) repeat the Conners scales and meet with the patient and parents to consider the next step. This meeting involves reviewing the repeated scales from the teachers and/or parents, discussing any possible side effects that may have been noticed, and discussing both positive and negative effects with the child and his/her parents. Depending upon what is found during this process, we may recommend continuing with the medication at original dose level if the results are clearly positive, doing an additional 2-week trial at a higher dose if the results have been disappointing but no side effects have been noted, or switching to a second medication (e.g., another stimulant or a tricyclic antidepressant) if unwanted side effects have been noted. Because methylphenidate is a very short-acting medication that does not require the maintainance of a therapeutic blood level, we typically ask the parents to give the medication only during school days and to not administer the medication on weekends and school holidays. In many cases, particularly when ADHD-related conduct problems at home are significant, we recommend daily use of the medication once established as helpful.

Because of the utility of this approach, the decision was made to evaluate the effectiveness of stimulants before doing an imipramine trial, and Jacob was prescribed methylphenidate (5 mg) to be taken twice a day, morning and noon. The parents called a week later to say that they had noted a slight increase in his attention span but that his moodiness and irritability seemed increased at home. At the conclusion of the 2-week trial of stimulants, I met with the parents and Jacob. There was no significant change in the Conners rating scales which the parents had completed on the previous day. The scores on the Conners Teacher Scale were also unchanged in that his behavioral ratings were still significantly high in the same areas. The teacher included a note in which she stated that she thought she had noted a positive change in his attention span and activity level but that it was "not dramatic."

During that visit, I consulted again with the psychiatrist who recommended that we discontinue stimulants and do a trial of imipramine. Because the effects of imipramine are somewhat slower to establish, we usually recommend somewhat longer trials, generally about 1 month, before any firm decision is made regarding the continued use of the medication. Jacob was prescribed an initial dose of 25 mg to be taken at bedtime. We explained to the parents that, unlike methylphenidate, patients maintain a blood level of imipramine and that it is more effective taken on a daily basis, including weekends and holidays. We went over some of the potential side effects such as dry mouth, fine motor tremor, and orthostatic hypotension, but added that these side effects seem uncommon with such small doses.

During this visit, we also began working on behavioral aspects of our treatment plan. I typically start by assigning reading to the parents. I routinely ask parents to read materials on behavioral management and find this often to be a very helpful early step in the process. The reading acquaints the parents with the basic concepts and vocabulary of behavioral management and is a far less costly method of learning the basics than is direct instruction from a therapist in a private practice. Furthermore, I have found that with carefully selected materials some parents are able to implement behavioral procedures such as timeout and token reinforcement with very little direct assistance from me. Although we have a number of materials which we often use, I most commonly assign *Living With Children* by Patterson and Gullion (1976), Appendix C of *Helping the Noncompliant Child* by Forehand and McMahon (1981), *Surviving with Kids* by Bartz and Rasor (1978), and/or Appendix B in Barkley's *Hyperactive Children: A Handbook of Diagnosis and Treatment* (Christophersen, Barnard, & Barnard, 1981). In Jacob's parents' case, I assigned Patterson and Gullion (1976). I selected this text because I believed they would be able to complete a full text rather than the other shorter selections. At the time I made the assignment, I discussed with the parents the importance of implementing behavioral management in the treatment plan, and the lack of wisdom in relying entirely on medication, even if it proved to be helpful. I also asked them to go to Jacob's teacher to seek her help and to specifically ask her to send home weekly, or preferably daily, reports to the parents on Jacob's behavior, level of attention, and effort in the classroom. I provided them with some simple forms on which the teacher could note Jacob's behavior and whether his classwork is done in a satisfactory manner. I asked the family to return in 2 weeks for follow-up regarding medication and to discuss behavioral management.

Two weeks later, the parents cancelled their appointment and rescheduled for 1 month after the meeting described previously. When the mother called to cancel because of a conflict in schedules, she indicated that they had noted some positive changes in Jacob. He was much more willing to go to bed at his bedtime and was complaining less of his nighttime anxieties. She said she had found him less moody and that the teacher had told her that she found him easier to manage. The mother reported no undesirable side effects to the imipramine.

When we met 1 month after having started the imipramine and assigned the reading material, the parents had completed the Conners checklists again, as had the teacher. The results of these are summarized in Tables 12-2 and 12-3.

These tables illustrate considerable improvement in both the teacher's and the parents' ratings of Jacob's behavior. Although the use of these checklists is our usual procedure and is a common clinical procedure for evaluating treatment effectiveness, it has obvious weaknesses. It by no means constitutes a blind study since patient, parent, and teachers are aware, in most cases, that treatment is being employed. The Conners, for example, has become such a popular instrument for assessing ADHD children that most teachers have filled them out many times for their students and are then quite aware of what is being assessed. The clinician has to be aware of this methodological weakness and interpret this kind of clinical data with caution.

Both parents reported being pleased with the apparent results of the imipramine, as had the mother when she had previously telephoned. They said that he continued to go to sleep more readily and that he was "far less moody" during the day. They indicated that they had more recently observed Jacob to be less restless and "hyper" and that he did not seem to be sedated by the medication. I pointed out to them that his greater cooperation at bedtime was likely related to drowsiness children often experience shortly after taking imipramine. Overall, the parents reported being most pleased with Jacob's progress.

TABLE 12-2. Scores on Conners Parent Symptom Questionnaire Completed by Parents before Treatment and after 1-Month Treatment

Factor	M	SD	Before treatment	After treatment
Completed by mother				
Conduct Problems	0.50	0.40	1.17[a]	0.75
Learning Problems	0.64	0.45	2.50[b]	1.25[a]
Psychosomatic Problems	0.13	0.23	0.00	0.00
Impulsivity–Hyperactivity	0.93	0.60	2.25[b]	1.00
Anxiety	0.51	0.51	1.00	0.75
Completed by father				
Conduct Problems	0.50	0.40	0.83	0.67
Learning Problems	0.64	0.45	2.00[b]	1.25[a]
Psychosomatic Problems	0.13	0.23	0.20	0.00
Impulsivity–Hyperactivity	0.93	0.60	2.00[a]	1.00
Anxiety	0.51	0.51	1.25[a]	0.50

Note. From "Normative data on revised Conners Parent and Teacher Rating Scales" by C. H. Goyette, C. K. Conners, and R. F. Ulrich, 1978, *Journal of Abnormal and Child Psychology, 6,* pp. 221–236. Copyright 1978 by Plenum Press. Reprinted by permission.

[a]Exceeds one standard deviation above the mean.

[b]Exceeds two standard deviations above the mean.

The mother said that she had read the assigned book, and the father indicated that he had read parts of it. They already had occasion to employ in informal ways some of the methods Patterson and Gullion (1976) describe, such as having used a timeout procedure on a few occasions when Jacob had been noncompliant. Fotunately, the teacher had cooperated fully in sending home daily reports, and the parents had established a simple contingency system wherein Jacob was permitted to watch television on Saturdays (a preferred activity of Jacob's) only when he brought home a favorable weekly report from the teacher. After reviewing the situation with the parents, I made some fairly direct recommendations to tighten up the behavioral methods they were using. I advised them to implement a simple token system in which Jacob could earn and lose points based on the teacher's report, daily performance of chores, compliance with parental instructions, and going to bed without arguing. I discussed with them the importance of routine reinforcement of Jacob's desirable behavior and explained to them the observation that children with ADHD will respond to reinforcement but often seem to require more frequent and regular reinforcement than most children. They agreed to implement my suggestions.

TABLE 12-3. Scores on Conners Teacher Questionnaire Completed before Treatment and after 1-Month Treatment

Factor	M	SD	Before treatment	After treatment
Conduct problems	0.32	0.43	0.88[a]	0.88[a]
Hyperactivity	0.60	0.65	2.00[b]	0.86
Inattention–passitivity	0.76	0.74	1.87[a]	0.88

Note. From "Normative data on revised Conners Parent and Teacher Rating Scales" by C. H. Goyette, C. K. Conners, and R. F. Ulrich, 1978, *Journal of Abnormal and Child Psychology, 6*, pp. 221–236. Copyright 1978 by Plenum Press. Reprinted by permission.
[a]Exceeds one standard deviation above the mean.
[b]Exceeds two standard deviations above the mean.

Over the subsequent 4 months, I saw Jacob and his parents five times. After the first 2 months of treatment with imipramine, the parents indicated that the teacher had told them that Jacob seemed slightly more restless and overactive again, although she had noted that he had not returned to levels of behavior prior to treatment. In consultation with the psychiatrist, the imipramine dose was increased to 50. The parents telephoned 2 weeks later and indicated that the teacher had reported improvement. During those 4 months of follow-up, the parents reported that they continued to use behavioral methods; although they did not formalize the programs. When I asked them about this, they indicated that they felt Jacob was doing much better and that they did not want to "make the cure worse than the disease." They said that they thought that Jacob's behavioral problems were no longer so severe as to warrant an extensive, formal behavioral system in the home. They continued to make use of timeout and simple contingency programs. During those follow-up visits, I typically spent about 20 to 30 minutes alone with Jacob. He continued to display normal affect, was appropriately verbal for an 8-year-old, and said of his progress that he was "doing better on school work and minding more." When I asked him about his nighttime anxieties, he indicated that he was bothered less by them, and he told me on one occasion that he thought he was "growing up a little."

OUTCOME AND DISCUSSION

As this chapter is prepared, our most recent contacts with Jacob and his parents suggest that he continues to respond well to his medication and to alterations the parents made in their child management practices. I had a discussion with the parents about his learning difficulties. Toward the end of his second-grade year his grades were somewhat improved, but his teacher had indicated that he continued to do less well than she hoped. After some discussion with the parents, we decided to proceed with an educational evaluation. It was scheduled to occur prior to commencement of Jacob's third grade year. However, when the third grade year began, the mother called to report that Jacob was doing well academically and that she preferred to hold off on the evaluation.

This case is typical in some regards and less typical in others. In my opinion, this child's clinical presentation was very much like other ADHD children we have seen in the way the attentional problems impacted on his school performance and behavior and also on his behavior in the family context. His mother's description of his behavioral characteristics in infancy and early childhood was also rather typical. The more unusual features of this case are the considerable anxiety symptoms and the more favorable response to imipramine than to stimulants. I believe it illustrates reasonably well the integration of medically oriented treatment with psychological/ behavioral treatment. I recognize and respect the plurality of opinion among psychologists regarding the use of medication in treating this disorder and have already noted the resurgence of controversy over this issue. Although my own background includes considerable behavioral influence, my opinion is that when a child is adequately assessed and found to have this disorder, medication will almost always be a part of an effective treatment approach. The more I work with these children, the more I become convinced that those who have true attention deficit can rarely demonstrate their maximum functioning without some assistance from medications. I also believe, however, that ADHD children who receive no treatment other than medication are usually unable to reach their best level of functioning. Furthermore, these children often have interpersonal difficulties, family problems, and personal insecurities which need to be addressed with nonmedical clinical interventions. Educational planning and liaison are routinely needed. Therefore, the prudent psychologist, in my opinion, recommends and coordinates a treatment plan which includes multiple components.

There can be a number of impediments, however, to the implementation of some or all of the components of the treatment plan. I will discuss two of the most common. First, I find that parents, and perhaps to a lesser extent, the ADHD patients themselves, often resist aspects of recommended treatment. Parents are often most anxious about the use of medication, but I have found that their anxieties are often based on misinformation. They may, for example, group all medications prescribed by psychiatrists into a category of "nerve medicine" and then recall a relative's terrible experiences with antipsychotics in a state psychiatric hospital. They may be concerned about stimulants' effects on growth, the potential for addiction, or whether medication will incline their child toward drug abuse in the future. I find that education about medication can be extremely helpful in helping parents with their fears. When medication is used and is helpful, psychologists may discover that parents are resistant to other components of treatment. Buying and administering the medication is discovered to be more convenient and to require far less effort, attention, and thought than behavior modification or alteration of their parenting methods. The temptation then becomes to keep their child on medication and to neglect other aspects of the treatment plan. Very frequently in our practice, clinicians and office staff have to deal with telephone calls requesting medication refills from parents of patients who are long overdue for office visits. These situations can be avoided, to some extent, by "selling" the parents early in the process on the multiple-component treatment approach.

A second common problem for the psychologist who evaluates and treats ADHD patients (or any patients for whom medication seems appropriate) is finding an adequate consulting relationship with a physician. This is especially problematic for the independently practicing psychologist or one who works in a setting that does not include psychiatrists. I encourage psychologists starting new practices to devote all the necessary energy toward establishing a good consulting relationship with a physician. Some will find it advisable to make appointments with prospective consultants to talk over clinical and medication issues and to assess the feasibility of a working relationship. Psychologists who work in rural areas may have a difficult time finding a consultant nearby and may have to look to the nearest urban area. Some child psychologists I know work directly with pediatricians who feel comfortable prescribing stimulants, antidepressants, and/or other medications for their patients. While this can be adequate for some patients, most psychologists will find it advisable to involve psychiatrists in many cases.

My usual procedure with cases like Jacob's is to see them on a regular basis, usually monthly to make certain the medication continues to be helpful and to monitor for any potential problems with it. I arrange for medication checks with the consulting psychiatrist, usually on a quarterly basis. I also prefer to review periodically with parents the methods they are using to respond to behavior at home. We often find that we continue working with these families for years, monitoring medication, taking telephone calls about specific situations, revising behavioral programs, assisting with educational planning, and similar activities. We find that we rarely get to the point of a discrete termination of the case.

REFERENCES

Achenbach, T. M., & Edelbrock, L. (1983). *Manual for the Child Behavior Checklist and Revised Child Behavior Profiles.* Burlington, VT: University of Vermont.

Achenbach, T. M. (1978). The Child Behavior Profile: I. Boys 6–11. *Journal of Consulting and Clinical Psychology, 46*, 478–488.

American Psychiatric Association. (1968). *Diagnostic and statistical manual of mental disorders* (2nd ed.). Washington, DC: Author.

American Psychiatric Association (1980): *Diagnostic and statistical manual of mental disorders* (3rd ed.). Washington, DC: Author.

American Psychiatric Association. (1987). *Diagnostic and statistical manual of mental disorders* (3rd ed., revised). Washington, DC: Author.

Barkley, R. A. (1977). A review of stimulant drug research with hyperactive children. *Journal of Child Psychology and Psychiatry, 18*, 137–165.

Barkley, R. A. (1981). *Hyperactive children: A handbook of diagnosis and treatment.* New York: Guilford.

Barkley, R. A., & Cunningham, C. (1979). The effects of Ritalin on the mother–child interactions of hyperactive children. *Archives of General Psychiatry, 36*, 201–208.

Bartz, W. R., & Rasor, R. A. (1978). *Surviving with kids: A lifeline for overwhelmed parents.* San Luis Obispo, CA: Impact Publishers.

Cantwell, D. P., & Carlson, G. A. (1978). Stimulants. In J. Werry (Ed.), *Pediatric psychopharmacology* (pp. 171–207). New York: Brunner/Mazel.

Cantwell, D. P., & Satterfield, J. H. (1978). The prevalence of academic underachievement in hyperactive children. *Journal of Pediatric Psychology, 3*, 168–171.

Christopherson, E. R., Barnard, S. R., & Barnard, J. D. (1981). The family training program manual: The home chip system. In R. A. Barkley, *Hyperactive children: A Handbook of diagnosis and treatment* (pp. 437–448). New York: Guilford.

Douglas, V. I. (1972). Stop, look, and listen: The problem of sustained attention and impulse control in hyperactive and normal children. *Canadian Journal of Behavioral Science, 4*, 159–182.

Douglas, V. I. (1974). Sustained attention and impulse control: Implications for the handicapped child. In J. A. Swets & L. L. Elliot (Eds.), *Psychology and the handicapped child.* Washington, DC: U. S. Office of Education.

Douglas, V. I., & Peters, K. G. (1980). Toward a clearer definition of the attentional deficit of hyperactive children. In G. A. Hale & M. Lewis (Eds.), *Attention and the development of cognitive skills* (pp. 259–282). New York: Plenum.

Forehand, R. L., & McMahon, R. J. (1981). *Helping the noncompliant child: A clinician's guide to parent training.* New York: Guilford.

Goyette, C. H., Conners, C. K., & Ulrich, R. F. (1978). Normative data on revised Conners Parent and Teacher Rating Scales. *Journal of Abnormal and Child Psychology, 6*, 221–236.

Hinshaw, S. P., Henker, B., & Whalen, C. K. (1984). Cognitive–behavioral and pharmacologic interventions for hyperactive boys: Comparative and combined effects. *Journal of Consulting and Clinical Psychology, 52*, 739–749.

Kerasotes, D., & Walker, C. E. (1983). Hyperactive behavior in children. In C. E. Walker & M. C. Roberts (Eds.), *Handbook of clinical child psychology* (pp. 498–523). New York: Wiley.

Lacetti, S. (1987, November 29). Ritalin: Miracle or Nightmare? *The Atlanta Constitution,* pp. 1D, 4D–5D.

Lambert, N., & Sandoval, J. (1980). The prevalence of learning disabilities in a sample of children considered hyperactive. *Journal of Abnormal Child Psychology, 8*, 33–50.

Laufer, M. W., & Denhoff, E. (1957). Hyperkinetic behavior syndrome in children. *Journal of Pediatrics, 50,* 463–473.

O'Leary, K. D., Pelham, W. E., Rosenbaum, A., & Price, G. H. (1976). Behavioral treatment of hyperkinetic children: An experimental evaluation of its usefulness. *Clinical Pediatrics, 15,* 510–515.

Patterson, G. R., & Gullion, E. (1976). *Living with children-revised: New methods for parents and teachers.* Champaign, IL: Research Press.

Pliszka, S. R. (1987). Tricyclic antidepressants in the treatment of children with attention deficit disorder. *Journal of the American Academy of Child and Adolescent Psychiatry, 26,* 127–132.

Rapport, M. D., Jones, J. T., DuPaul, G. T., Kelly, K. L., Gardner, M. J., Tucker, S. B., & Shea, M. S. (1987). Attention deficit disorder and methylphenidate: Group and single-subject analyses of dose effects on attention in clinic and classroom settings. *Journal of Clinical Child Psychology, 16,* 329–338.

Rosenbaum, A., O'Leary, K. D., & Jacob, R. G. (1975). Behavioral intervention with hyperactive children: Group consequences as a supplement to individual contingencies. *Behavior Therapy, 6,* 315–323.

Ross, D. M., & Ross, S. A. (1976). *Hyperactivity: Research, theory, and action.* New York: Wiley.

Viadero, D. (1987, October 21). Debate grows on use of Ritalin in schools. *Education Week,* pp. 1–4.

Wender, P. H. (1987). *The hyperactive child, adolescent and adult: Attention deficit disorder through the lifespan.* New York: Oxford University Press.

13
Feeding and Eating Disorders in Young Children

DANITA CZYZEWSKI

Psychologists, especially those in pediatric settings, are increasingly asked to treat infants and children with behavioral feeding disorders. The assessment and treatment of infant and toddler eating disorders presents a chance to integrate behavioral, developmental, physiological, and interpersonal aspects of feeding. Operant and classical conditioning paradigms that attend to the myriad of individual factors which vary to effect the onset, maintenance, and remediation of these feeding problems have earned an important place in the treatment of these disorders (Handen, Mandell, & Russo, 1986; Palmer, Thompson, & Linscheid, 1975; Riordan, Iwata, Finney, Wohl, & Stanley, 1984; Siegel, 1982; Thompson, Palmer, & Linscheid, 1977).

Linscheid's (Linscheid & Rasnake, 1984) conceptualization of two types of feeding disorders, also referred to as nonorganic failure to thrive (FTT), provides a useful introduction to the types of cases presenting for treatment. Type I nonorganic FTT may also be viewed as an attachment disorder. The infant's failure to gain weight, to achieve normal developmental milestones in many areas, and to respond appropriately to human contact is thought to reflect the dysfunctional nature of the caregiver–infant relationship. The blatant nature of the thin, listless infant and the absent or dyssynchronous mother–child interaction in Type I FTT makes the identification of this pattern fairly obvious to the well-trained pediatric professionals in the hospital in which I practice. Furthermore, the infant generally responds quite rapidly to the consistent caregiving in the hospital, and the long-term treatment goal of reintegrating the child into the natural home becomes a social as well as a psychological problem. Therefore, this type of FTT will

Danita Czyzewski. Department of Psychiatry, Baylor College of Medicine, Texas Children's Hospital, Houston, Texas.

not be a focus of this chapter. (See Drotar, 1984; Roberts & Maddux, 1982; and Showers, Mandelkorn, Coury, & McCleery, 1986, for more information on the identification and treatment of these patients.)

In contrast to Type I FTT children, Type II FTT children are more likely to be thriving quite well in most developmental and social areas and generally have pleasant interactions with their caregivers. However, they fail to take in sufficient nutrients and, therefore, fail to grow properly. Meals are characterized by food refusal with or without tantrums, a very limited range of acceptable food textures and tastes, delayed self-feeding, long durations of feeding sessions (up to several hours), and unusual parental attempts at feeding ("his father sings and dances around the room while I try to sneak food into his mouth"). Linscheid sees this problem developing in the second 6 months after a period of normal intake and weight gain in the first half year of life. The introduction of solids and the development of more independent feeding behavior in ages 6 to 12 months may set the stage for the development of the unhealthy feeding interaction. Egan, Chatoor, and Rosen (1980) speculate that the feeding interaction becomes the major area of the infant's struggle for autonomy from the parents.

The development of this eating disorder may occur during the introduction of solids as an autonomy struggle or may develop out of the parents' negative reaction to the 1-year-old child's normal decrease in appetite and variability in food preference. In a pediatric setting it is also common to see young children who for various medical reasons have been delayed in the introduction of solid foods beyond a critical period (probably 7 or 8 months), or have been fed for prolonged periods via other than the oral route (i.e., nasogastic tube, gastrostomy tube, or hyperalimentation), therefore disrupting the normal development of the feeding–eating process. Other children may have had physical disorders which resulted in pain during or after eating, (e.g., gastroesophageal reflux), therefore making eating a punishing event. In children with a physical disorder interfering with eating, feeding problems prior to 6 months of age are not uncommon.

The maintenance of this maladaptive feeding pattern is conceptualized to be largely through social reinforcement. Although, in general, these children do not lack social stimulation in their lives, feeding becomes an intense social interaction. Observation of the situation reveals a very high rate of parental verbal interaction including coaxing, cajoling, and attempting to verbally distract from the feeding situation. As the child begins to talk, he or she may begin asking questions or making comments about the food or anything else, to which the caregiver will inevitably respond verbally. Not infrequently the mealtime interaction looks quite pleasant, although little food is consumed. Despite the highly verbal nature of the interaction, praise for eating is frequently absent. It appears that when the child actually exhibits the behavior that the caregivers have been coaxing the child to do, the caregivers hold their breath and pray it will continue, instead of praising the child.

Another factor in the maintenance of the child's food refusal or other negative eating behaviors is the effective escape from the aversive situation. The feeding situation may have become aversive because of the coercive style which has developed between the parent and child or because of previous experiences with discomfort during or after eating. Many parents report that each meal inevitably ends when the child is crying and screaming, sometimes distressed to the point of vomiting.

From a physiological point of view, the hunger drive is frequently severely blunted by the unusual feeding pattern of the child. When the child does not eat meals, food or drink is offered continually throughout the day with the child ingesting just enough to blunt hunger for a meal. Breakfast is frequently reported to be the "best" meal of the day because it is the only time when the child has gone hours without small amounts of food. Another physiological consideration is the development of ketosis. While the parents may have been naively counseled that the "children will eat when they become hungry enough," the breakdown of fats as the body tries to compensate for continued underconsumption of calories may result in decreasing, rather than increasing, the appetite.

The social and interpersonal context of the feeding situation may help perpetuate the poor feeding interaction. In my experience, most parents believe that the feeding process should be simple, natural, and rewarding. When feeding problems arise, they view the problem as a threat to their basic worth as parents, as well as to the health of their children. Those feelings of distress are not helped by grandmothers who often may criticize the parent's behavior or child's growth, or pediatricians who advise parents to "just relax during feeding," while reminding the parent that the child's weight has dropped below the third percentile. Since mothers are frequently the primary caregivers, they often feel blamed or resentful of the unpleasant situation they find themselves in with the child and unsupported or not understood by their husbands. These various feelings of failure, anger, or desperation do not help the caregiver to either problem solve or act in a consistent manner during feeding.

While Type I FTT will frequently be diagnosed Reactive Attachment Disorder of Infancy, Type II FTT feeding disorders do not lend themselves easily to the revised third edition of the *Diagnostic and Statistical Manual of Mental Disorders* (DSM-III-R) diagnosis. Three possible places where these problems may be classified by DSM-III-R are Parent–Child Problems, Psychological Factors Affecting Physical Condition, and Atypical Eating Disorder. Parent–child problems may be appropriate because these children usually cannot be said to display overt psychopathology, and the parent–child interaction that has developed around eating is generally important to the maintenance of the problem behaviors. Because these children often have a demonstrable physical condition—failure to gain weight as expected—Psychological Factors Affecting Physical Condition may also be quite appropriate. This diagnosis, along with a medical diagnosis reflective of the child's condition, may be looked upon more favorably than the other two diagnoses mentioned by third-party reimbursers. Atypical Eating Disorder is a wastebasket category that can also be used for notational purposes, but will add nothing to the understanding of the condition.

GENERAL GUIDELINES FOR ASSESSMENT AND TREATMENT

Throughout this chapter I refer to the "treatment team." This team is not a definite, set group of professionals, but varies given the setting, the interest of various professionals in feeding problems, and even within the same setting, based upon the needs of the patients. In a pediatric setting where I worked previously, I carried out treatments for feeding problems after referral from a pediatrician. The pediatrician generally followed the weight and intake, and I developed the behavioral feeding protocol and taught the nurses to carry it out. In my current setting, the occupational therapists are very interested in infant feeding and are frequently called to feed infants who have physical problems which make chewing or swallowing difficult, or who have been fed through other than oral means for much of their lives. We began coordinating our efforts working with children whose feeding/ eating problem had a strong behavioral component. In these cases, the occupational therapists rather than staff nurses do the feeding if alternative feeders are indicated. In this setting, I also work with the pediatric nutrition and gastroenterology physicians and dieticians. We even have the luxury of a nurse clinician who coordinates our activities. Overall, however, the people who make up the team are less important than their ability to coordinate closely and present a consistent plan to the family.

The purpose of the assesement is to determine the pattern of physiological, behavioral, and interpersonal factors that are maintaining a poor hunger satiety cycle, inappropriate eating behaviors, or behaviors incompatible with eating. An understanding of the factors that contributed to the onset of the feeding problem is optional, but not always possible and not necessary for treatment. Because of the many factors which may be contributing to the disorder, the assessor must have a thorough understanding of behavior analysis (see Gelfand & Hartmann, 1984; Ollendick & Hersen, 1984; Mash & Terdal, 1981) and approach each case individually. The following guidelines will prove useful in most cases, but should not be considered exhaustive.

The assessment of the eating problem frequently begins with a thorough developmental feeding history that includes not only a month-by-month account of what the child ate, how vigorously he/she ate, how hungry and satisfied he/she appeared to be, and by whom he/she was fed, but also the parental expectations or evaluations of the child's eating behavior, as well as any medical problems in the child or disruptions in the family or routine. Several days of food records, including the length and distribution of meals, help provide a baseline for intake, as well as assess whether a pattern of hunger and satiety is being impeded. Observation of the feeding interaction in as natural a setting as possible is important to assess the caregiver and child behaviors that are maintaining each other. Further, an observation of the parent–child interaction outside of the feeding situations helps assure that this is a fairly circumspect problem and not part of a overall parent–child interaction problem.

Medical reasons for the feeding disorder should be ruled out, treated, or understood (as in the case of a now resolved medical problem that resulted in aversive conditioning of eating behavior) in the course of the assessment. However, care should be taken not to diagnose behavioral feeding disorders by exclusion of obvious physical conditions. Attempting to diagnose by exclusion alone is not only unsound conceptually, but also practically, where the practice may result in delaying further medical or psychological evaluation that may reveal the problem. The pattern of eating disorder should be explainable by some classical or operant behavioral conceptualization before proceeding with behavioral treatment.

The behavioral treatment program may be undertaken on an inpatient or outpatient basis. Several factors mitigate for inpatient treatment, at least at the beginning of therapy. If the child is severely malnourished, alternative means of feeding may be necessary to achieve a healthier weight and some nutritional reserve. Nasogastric feedings may be undertaken initially as a continuous drip and later changed to bolus feedings to help the child grow accustomed to the feelings of hunger and satiety and fullness in the stomach. I have frequently seen anxious parents calmed by the expertise of the hospital environment and able to give up the burden of worrying whether their child will become further malnourished or dehydrate if they do not get the next meal into the child. Further, many parents are so frustrated by the months of negative feeding experiences that they find it impossible to change to the more neutral stance required by the behavioral treatment without some period of respite.

The treatment of the feeding problem with very young children is intensive, and staying in the hospital may be more convenient than making one or more trips per day to the hospital. In children who have unusual food preferences or who refuse certain textures, but whose caloric intake is roughly adequate, one treatment meal per day under the therapist's supervision has been effective in changing the pattern (Palmer et al., 1975; Thompson et al., 1977). Therefore, this type of problem is more easily and probably more appropriately treated as an outpatient. However, if food refusal is more pervasive, weight is very low, and/or parents are very anxious, the practice of the negative meal patterns must be eliminated entirely. To do this, nonoral feedings must be instituted and/or all meals must be administered under therapeutic guidelines. This typically requires inpatient treatment, generally with nonparent feeders.

The general treatment plan focuses on maximizing the hunger drive, reinforcing appropriate eating behaviors, and extinguishing inappropriate eating behaviors or behaviors incompatible with eating. Each child's treatment plan is individually designed, of course, although some procedures are relatively constant. Meals are scheduled and the duration of meals is limited, often to 20 to 30 minutes. Between-meal snacks are eliminated. Often water is withheld 1 hour before meals. Since most of these children take liquids more readily than solids, liquids may be offered near the end of the meal or in small amounts as rewards for eating solids. Shaping approximations to eating may be necessary in some cases. Punishment, generally in the form of a sharp "no" for gagging or attempts at self-induced vomiting, has been necessary in some cases.

Reinforcement in the form of social attention is most often used to reward appropriate eating behavior. Because social reinforcement is most easily administered, most readily available, and least intrusive, it is preferable over tangible reinforcers. For many of the children, reinforcement with a preferred food is impossible since they prefer no foods. The feeder gives a limited number of prompts to eat, waits a short interval silently, then, depending upon the child's response, either verbally reinforces the child for eating or withdraws social attention by turning away from the child, diverting eyes and/or being silent. Occasionally the child's chair is turned to face a wall to prevent the child from distracting himself/herself with other interesting visual diversions. Withdrawal of attention may last for a certain interval or until the child responds as prompted.

In order to increase the salience of the social reinforcers, some environmental manipulation may be useful. The child should be fed in a quiet, nonstimulating environment with the food and the feeder as the primary focuses of interest. For this reason I have not found toys, in general, to facilitate eating, although some have used short periods of access to toys as reinforcers. In some children, social interaction may be limited for a short time prior to meals.

The following cases illustrate the development of treatment programs and the ongoing assessment of two young children with feeding/eating disorders. The first case is fairly typical of feeding disorders maintained by parental anxiety. The second case is more complex, involving many medical factors, and illustrates the process of ongoing assessment and ongoing communication between medical and psychological services.

CASE EXAMPLE

Katie was an 8-month-old female infant hospitalized for evaluation and treatment of a feeding disorder. Since Katie's birth, Mrs. W had actively sought help for Katie's feeding problems. While this included one brief hospitalization in another hospital at 6 weeks of age and one or more visits with seven pediatricians and a developmental specialist, Mrs. W still felt that "no one had helped because no one really understood the problem." She reported that Katie had been very difficult to feed from birth and that even the newborn nursery nurses could not get her to take bottles. She described current feeding difficulty as continual screaming and crying thoughout the feeding process, necessitating "force feeding" to ensure intake of food. Because of the difficulty with intake, Mrs. W offered Katie food continually throughout the day, and Katie reportedly accepted food five to six times per day. Despite the feeding difficulties, the child's height and weight were both at the 25th percentile.

Background

Katie was the only child of her 28-year-old father and 24-year-old mother. Both parents were high school graduates. Mr. W was a factory worker and Mrs. W had been employed in a bank before Katie's birth. Mrs. W had no plans to return to work, although she reported that she had enjoyed working and felt isolated and lonely at home.

Mrs. W reported that she had married a man to whom she was not particularly attracted, to escape from a critical, depressed mother and an absent father. The first years of the marriage had been satisfactory as both partners worked and saved toward building a house. While Mrs. W believed that having children was an implicit agreement of the marriage, when she brought up the subject after 4 years of marriage, Mr. W announced that he wanted no children. Mrs. W "begged and pleaded" with her husband, and he finally consented to her becoming pregnant. However, according to Mrs. W, after Katie was born, Mr. W did not become involved with the child and was quite annoyed even at the fact that his wife no longer cooked hot lunches and dinners for him because of her time with the baby. At the time of hospitalization Mr. W played no part in feeding or diaper changing.

The couple had planned to have house construction completed before the baby was conceived and when that did not happen Mrs. W worried about the inconvenience of the house not being finished, as well as about the teratologic effects of the fumes from paint, adhesive, insulation, etc. Mrs. W gained 70 pounds during her pregnancy, reportedly eating "only junk food." Although her weight at the time of referral was 40 pounds greater than her prepregnancy weight, she said she "did not care" about her current state of obesity, but wondered if the junk food had adversely effected the child. Mrs. W had preeclampsia, but labor and delivery were reportedly normal.

Assessment

The admitting pediatrican determined that despite the fact that this child was thriving physically and had no medical basis for hospitalization, the feeding disorder could not be treated as an outpatient. His judgment was based largely on the mother's anxious presentation, as well as on her statements that 8 to 10 other professionals had failed to help her child. The pediatrican had agreed to evaluate and treat the child only if this was done in the hospital with the mother present and if a psychologist was involved. At the time of admission the pediatrician called me and asked me to become involved in the case, and I agreed to evaluate the feeding problem.

The goals of the psychological assessment were to (1) understand the feeding problems and (2) understand why previous attempts at treatment had apparently failed, in order to prevent replication of unsuccessful efforts.

My assessment of the feeding disorder was made through review of records, interview with mother, observation of the mother–child play interaction, and observation of the nurse–child feeding interaction.

Unlike some parents, Mrs. W did not object to the involvement of a psychologist and talked freely about her experiences with Katie. She was an extremely anxious young woman with very low self-esteem, who had fantasized that both her husband and parents "would love her" when they saw what a wonderful mother she was to her infant. These fantasies had been dashed by the reality of a poorly feeding baby. Mrs. W described herself as a "great worrier," reported that she was becoming increasingly withdrawn and depressed, avoiding friends and spending all her hours at home attempting to feed Katie and worrying. She reported feeling increasingly dissatisfied with her marriage.

Hospital records from the newborn period revealed that Katie was a child who had some difficulty taking a bottle, but the notes contradicted mother's contention that Katie had taken "nothing" in the newborn nursery. Mrs. W reported that from birth Katie never liked being fed lying in her arms, but did not mind being on her shoulder. Furthermore, Mrs. W reported that initially it took 1½ to 2 hours to feed Katie an ounce or two of formula. Kate was hospitalized at 6 weeks because of the feeding difficulties and, according to Mrs. W, was discharged without a definite plan except that mother should remain calm. Immediately following the hospitalization, the child was sent to the maternal grandmother's house for a week to see if grandmother could feed her. Grandmother did no better with feeding, but discovered that the child took a bottle better while sleeping. This ploy was attempted for awhile, until Katie was no longer successfully drinking in her sleep.

Mrs. W described feeding during the period from 2 to 7 months as consisting of hours of offering food to Katie, refusal by screaming, crying, and back arching by Katie, and then literally forcing a spoon, syringe, or bottle into Katie's mouth. Mrs. W reported that she did not "yell" at Katie during these feeding interactions because she realized yelling could be very detrimental to her. With this "force-feeding" method, Katie was eating pureed food, often by syringe, and taking formula from a bottle. However, Mrs. W reported that Katie "gagged" on pureed meats if they were too thick and "gagged" on milk if she "drank too fast." Mom described "gagging" as a frightening event to be avoided.

At 2 months of age, Katie was evaluated and followed in the developmental clinic. According to clinic records she was found to have a poor ability to suck and an equivocal neurological exam, normal weight gain, and excessive irritability, perhaps due to pain related to eating. She was given medication for colic, but no diagnosis of colic or any other gastrointestinal condition was made. Mom was again advised to "relax" during feedings, to not awaken her child for nighttime feeding, and to begin to introduce solid foods. Although Mrs. W continued to bring Katie to the developmental clinic for developmental assessments, she did not follow through with any of the recommendations, but apparently began actively seeking different pediatric opinions about possible organic problems. Extensive medical evaluations revealed no neurologic, metabolic, or toxic condition present in Katie. It was at that time that she was referred to the pediatric gastroenterologist who hospitalized Katie.

My observation of the child and review of the developmental clinic records revealed a child with gross motor and adaptive behavior development within normal limits for her age. Katie was active and alert, and mother–child play interactions appeared generally normal and pleasant.

I observed Katie being fed by a nurse who was experienced in feeding infants, but not trained in behavioral methods for problem feedings. Initially Katie sat cooperatively in the high chair, playing with keys while the nurse offered her baby food from a syringe. Katie did not appear interested in the food, but appeared to enjoy the social interaction and took food in response to the nurse's cajoling. After several minutes of cooperation, Katie frowned and refused to open her mouth for more food. In the next 15 minutes she accepted food intermittently and swallowed the food when she had it in her mouth, but began to protest more and more until she was crying loudly 20 minutes into the meal. The meal was then terminated.

In this case, I varied my typical approach to assessment in two significant ways. First, I did not interview the father. I made repeated attempts to arrange interviews with Mr. W, but he provided a myriad of excuses to make himself unavailable throughout Katie's hospitalization. He visited only two to three times during the 30 days of hospitalization. My working assumption based upon this lack of response was that Mr. W was as uninvolved with Katie and as unsupportive of Mrs. W as Mrs. W described. The reasons for this from Mr. W's perspective remained unknown to me.

The second variation from my usual procedure in the evaluation of a feeding disorder was my decision *not* to observe the parent–infant feeding interaction. In this case, observation of this interaction was not done for several reasons. The feeding situation had been observed by the pediatrician and occupational therapist in the developmental clinic, albeit several months earlier, and described in the same manner as the mother described the situation. Second, when the child was fed by the nurse, she exhibited the same behaviors the mother described, although not to the extreme the mother described. Perhaps the most important consideration was the mother's description of the anxious coercive feeding interaction. Her anxiety describing the situation was so severe that it seemed highly likely this would occur in the situation. Furthermore, Mrs. W felt so defeated and incompetent in the feeding situation, I saw no reason to have her do it again, especially if data on the child's behavior could be gathered in another manner.

Formulation and Proposed Treatment

Katie's feeding disorder was conceptualized as a problem in the mother–child interaction around feeding. It is likely that Katie was initially somewhat difficult to feed and that her weak suck caused great anxiety in this new mother for whom the feeding situation had much surplus meaning. To Mrs. W, problems in feeding not only meant she was a bad mother and unable to appropriately love Katie, but also that she was less likely to be the "wonderful mother" who would be esteemed and loved by her husband and parents. Mrs. W's anxiety was further raised by any indication of a physical problem causing or resulting from the feeding problem. She used this anxiety as a reason to make no change in her management in the eating situation (e.g., "Could this be the result of brain damage?" or "What if she doesn't get enough fluids and becomes dehydrated?"), although she also expressed dread, anxiety, and some realization that her behavior did have a negative impact on Katie's eating. On the other hand, Mrs. W's negative feeding style was reinforced by the fact that Katie did eat food intermittently while screaming and protesting and was taking in enough nutrients to keep her at the 25th percentile. Initial admonishments to "relax" during feeding were unable to be followed for all the previously mentioned reasons; anxiety about physical disorder, ambivalence about accepting maternal role in the problem, and evidence that the coercive feeding style was successful on some level. Because Katie was doing fine medically and nutritionally, the focus of treatment was on the behavioral psychological aspects of feeding.

The initial treatment plan was designed to interrupt the coercive feeding interaction characterized by very frequent feeding attempts which ended with Katie screaming and mother frustrated, and to promote periods of hunger followed by pleasant eating experiences and satiety in Katie. The treatment plan took into account the fact that Katie did intake sufficient nutrients to thrive, and at least for the early part of the meal did so in a cooperative manner. Temporary separation of infant and mother during feeding was planned. While it was initially planned to have mother in the room observing the feeding, this was changed after only 1 day of treatment. It was noted that when mother was in the room during feeding, she would talk anxiously and continually try to clean up the child's "messiness." Therefore, mother was asked to leave the hospital room during feeding. Katie's consistent feeders were to be the occupational therapist, and several nurses, one of whom would be present on all shifts. Feeding was to be limited to 1 hour per meal (I do not remember why we decided on such a long meal) and terminated whenever Katie finished her food or began to verbally protest while eating. In infants and children who are refusing food to the extent they fail to grow (unlike Katie), meal termination could be conceptualized as negative reinforcement for protest. However, I felt that Katie experienced some drive to eat and found food reinforcing, and therefore would experience early meal termination as time out from positive reinforcement.

Food was to be offered only four times per day, to promote periods of hunger followed by satiation. Formula was to be offered toward the end of the meal. Because Katie had had such early negative experiences with bottles, and because she was developmentally able to use a cup, the initial plan was to terminate the use of the bottle and use only a cup. Mrs. W disagreed with discontinuing the bottle, but agreed to compromise by using a bottle for two meals and using a cup for two. The use of the syringe was discontinued because it was unnecessary and seemed to make eating an unpleasant medical experience.

One of the most important parts of the treatment plan was to give Mrs. W a conceptualization of the feeding problem that would allow her to see the need for change in her behavior during the feeding interaction, but not become overwhelmed with guilt that she had caused the problem. It was clear from past efforts that whenever the mother felt blamed she quickly began looking for obscure medical problems in the child. The conceptualization I gave stressed the interactive nature of the feeding situation, highlighting the fact that Katie had been difficult to feed at birth due to her weak suck, although this difficulty was not a sign of great or generalized pathology, and that mom's inexperience and anxiety over feeding and lack of support had not helped Katie learn that feeding could be a pleasant experience. Furthermore, the continual offering of food had never allowed Katie to feel really hungry so that she vigorously sought food. Mrs. W was commended for her attention to Katie's nutritional state, but advised that Katie was taking in adequate calories and fluids, and therefore, unless she was ill it would not be necessary to be concerned about dehydration and malnutrition. However, I reassured her that Katie's nutritional state would be carefully monitored in the hospital while new eating patterns were being established. It was explained that other caretakers would be feeding Katie for a while because Katie would not have had long-term negative feeding experiences with them and, therefore, could begin to form new eating patterns more quickly. Mrs. W was assured that as soon as a more positive feeding pattern was developed, she would be reintroduced to the situation, and could begin to experience a more pleasant feeding interaction with Katie.

Course of Treatment

The treatment plan was instituted after a treatment team (in this case pediatrician, pediatric intern, psychologist, occupational therapist, nurses) meeting to agree on specifics and feedback to the mother. The dietary service was consulted to keep daily calorie counts and monitor daily weights. Caloric intake, Katie's behavior during feeding, and mother's attitude toward feeding were all monitored for signs of treatment effectiveness.

By design, the feeding plan decreased protesting during meals by terminating meals after only a few protests. Therefore, screaming, back-arching tantrums were immediately eliminated. Positive feeding behaviors were also noted. For example, after several days Katie became interested in finger foods, and initiated some self-feeding. Despite the behavioral changes during meals, daily caloric intake for the first 3 days of treatment was approximately one-half of that required, and intake did not reach estimated daily requirement until day 5, and then dropped to one-half of needs at least once in the next 5 days. Weight fluctuations roughly paralleled the caloric fluctuations.

Although Katie's eating behavior was improving as planned, Mrs. W's acceptance of the changes was more tumultuous. Aware of the inadequate caloric intake and early weight loss, Mrs. W repeatedly asked or attempted to feed Katie at other than meal times. Each attempt was met with a reassurance that Katie's nutritional state was being monitored and that the program must be followed as prescribed, that is, mom does not feed, and food is only given at meal times. After several days of patient reassurance, the admitting pediatrician told Mrs. W that if she could not or would not follow the treatment plan, we could not help Katie and her, and Katie would be discharged.

Mrs. W responded to this firm directive and made no further attempts (known to us) to subvert the feeding schedule. However, several days later she was found to be diffusely anxious, depressed, and angry, and an unforeseen glitch in the feeding function was revealed. While we made great efforts to explain the feeding disturbance as an interactive problem, and refrain from blaming the mother, the feeders' verbal behavior was not consistent with this conceptualization. Meals and feeding behavior were constantly described to Mrs. W as "great," "no problems." The fact that these terrible feeding problems could apparently be so easily reversed when mom did not feed, only reinforced mom's idea that she was inadequate as a mother. On the other hand, her anger and anxiety resulted from her knowledge that Katie was losing weight, and if that was "great," maybe we did not know what we were doing. Feeders were quickly advised to give only descriptive feedback on meal behavior and intake, and have only one person, the pediatrician, give daily evaluative feedback on the treatment progress. After these interventions, the feeding team was able to work very cooperatively and consistently and resist reacting to one more assertion by Mrs. W that "nothing will ever change." On about day 8 of the feeding program, Mrs. W spontaneously noted that she could now tell when Katie was hungry—"I hadn't let her get hungry before." This recognition was particularly important given Mrs. W's initial concern that Katie's lack of hunger was due to brain damage. She also agreed that she needed some psychological help for herself—apart from the problems she was having with Katie. Mrs. W felt comfortable with me, and we began exploring some of her individual issues while Katie was hospitalized and made plans to continue after discharge.

On day 9, after Katie's feeding behavior was quite cooperative—finger feeding was increasing, and intake was fairly stable and generally meeting caloric needs—mom was asked to begin observing meals. I asked the feeders to describe Katie's behavior and their response to her behavior in order to help mom learn the feeding techniques, and I also sat in on some feeding sessions and explained the process to Mrs. W. Mrs. W was noted to be much more cooperative and happier in general after she began sitting in on meals. It was planned that after 3 days of observing, mom would begin feeding Katie herself.

The day before Mrs. W was to begin feeding, Katie developed a fever and diarrhea and was subsequently diagnosed with a viral gastroenteritis. While Katie remained playful and happy, her oral intake dropped 60% to 80%. Plans to have mom feed were postponed since a failure experience was guaranteed given the gastroenteritis. Not surprisingly Mrs. W became very anxious, once again reinforced in her previously waning belief that Katie was very vulnerable physically and would remain so. While the regular treatment team had gained her trust through great consistency and confidence that we knew what Katie's problem was and could treat it, a weekend call staff of all unfamiliar persons (who apparently did not read very closely the treatment plans and strategies) created chaos when they violated every tenet of the treatment. They let mom attempt to feed when the child was very distressed and unwilling to take liquids from anyone; they let mom decide whether Katie needed an IV or nasogastric tube to rehydrate her; and they speculated about a chromosomal anomaly in Katie. Happily, the regular treatment team quickly regained Mrs. W's confidence, and 1 week after the onset of the viral illness, Mrs. W began feeding Katie under the observation of a nurse or occupational therapist. The feeding interaction was very appropriate with no force-feeding by mom, and no violent reactions by Katie. Unfortunately, Katie's intake was still low following the effects of the illness. Mrs. W appeared to understand the reason for the low intake. After 3 days of feeding by mom, Katie was discharged from the hospital. While she had fairly well recovered from the viral illness, ideally we would have sought more time to solidify the feeding interaction. However, Katie had been hospitalized for a month, and Mrs. W was anxious to take her home.

Outpatient plans included follow-up with a pediatrician who had been involved in the hospital treatment and psychotherapy for mom. Mrs. W planned to continue feeding Katie according to a schedule as had been established in the hospital. Further, Mrs. W reported she was going to enroll Katie in a "Mother's-day-out" program several mornings a week and also find a regular babysitter so that she and her husband could spend some time alone together.

Follow-Up

Mrs. W did not return for outpatient psychotherapy, ostensibly because of her husband's concern over the cost. About 1 month after discharge she reported by telephone that Katie was continuing to eat on schedule and beginning to eat table foods. Mrs. W was very pleased with her progress. Pediatric records revealed Katie's weight was between the 30th and 50th percentiles at from 12 to 18 months of age. At 4 years Katie's weight and height were both greater than the 95th percentile (wgt/hgt 70%) when she was treated for a twisted ankle hurt while ice skating. While Mrs. W voiced some strange concerns during the pediatric visits (e.g., "Does she need a spinal tap?" when brought in for an earache), there was no evidence of pediatrician visits which were not appropriate (i.e., factitious symptoms, lack of appropriate follow-up by mother), and mother's concerns were fairly easily allayed.

Reflections

This case is a very good illustration of the interactive nature of feeding disturbances in infants and young children and their caregivers. With a more experienced or confident mother, Katie's early weak suck may never have developed into 8 months of screaming and refusing food. On the other hand, with a normally vigorous feeder, Mrs. W may have been able to more closely fulfill her fantasy of a loving, nurturing feeding experience. The lack of fit between Katie and her mother was much more blatant than that which is evident in many feeding disturbances.

Can the outcome of the case be considered a success? In terms of the specific goal of hospitalization, to reduce the negative feeding interaction and establish developmentally normal eating patterns, the treatment was a success. Some might question whether Katie's weight-for-height percentile of 70% at age 4 represented overfeeding by Mrs. W. The meaning of this single datum point is unknown, although the pediatrician, usually attuned to issues of over-weight, registered no concern in her chart notes. The inability to engage Mr. W in treatment or engage Mrs. W in psychotherapy were obvious areas of failure, although not at all unpredictable. It was hoped that Mrs. W felt fairly and consistently treated by the treatment staff and reinforced for her considerable changes, (perhaps for the first time in her life) and may at some later time have felt comfortable seeking psychotherapy for herself. Follow-up pediatric visits did reveal Mrs. W as an anxious mother, but not the overwhelmed mother she had been upon presentation. When Katie was 18 months old, Mrs. W told the pediatrician that she was feeling increasingly comfortable as a mother as Katie grew older and that babies were very difficult for her to understand.

This case illustrates the need for very tight coordination and consistency among members of the treatment team, as well as the myriad of ways inconsistency can be manifested, and the many problems inconsistency can cause. Katie was one of the first children treated by such an organized approach in this hospital, but the staff felt good about our coordinated efforts and eager to work together again on infant feeding disorders. On subsequent experiences, the team avoided many of the pitfalls of thinking of mom as bad, competing with mom for feeding success, and answering questions which should most appropriately (and consistently) be handled by the designated spokesperson for the treatment team.

CASE EXAMPLE

Lisa was hospitalized by a pediatric gastroenterologist for evaluation and treatment of a feeding disorder when she was 10 months old. Two months earlier, Lisa had been diagnosed with mild gastroesophageal reflux for which she took medication prior to meals. However, her pediatric gastroenterologist did not believe that reflex accounted for her current poor eating behavior or her failure to thrive and asked for a psychological evaluation to evaluate the feeding from another perspective. At the time she was hospitalized, Lisa had had feeding problems for 8 months. Lisa's weight was in the 5th to 10th percentile, her height in the 95th percentile, her weight-for-height ratio and her triceps skinfold were less than the 5th percentile. These anthropometrics were thought to indicate chronic malnutrition.

Background

Lisa was the third child of her 36-year-old mother and 38-year-old father. Both parents were college graduates. Her father had a doctorate and was employed as a research chemist; her mother did not work outside the home. Lisa's 9-year-old sister and 5-year-old brother had had no eating problems as infants and were considered to be without behavioral or emotional problems.

Lisa, like her siblings, was the result of a planned pregnancy and was initially breast fed. Unlike her siblings, Lisa was unwilling to occasionally take a bottle if her mother was not available to nurse her. At 2 months of age, Lisa began vomiting and stopped gaining weight. According to Mrs. M, the pediatrician suggested discontinuing breast feeding entirely at that time. Mrs. M was very hesitant about this, but when a second pediatrician suggested the same strategy at 3 months, she complied. At this time, Lisa did not increase the amount of formula taken by bottle, but continued to ingest very small amounts of formula, regardless of the interval between meals, and began to sleep a great deal. Mrs. M reported that her pediatrician was concerned about a brain problem accounting for Lisa's feeding difficulty, but at 4 months of age a developmental evaluation revealed Lisa to be ahead of developmental norms. In general, she was thought to be a smart, strong-willed infant who was happy as long as she was not being fed.

Between 4 and 10 months, Lisa refused to take formula from anyone but her mother. Mr. M, as well as family friends, had attempted to feed Lisa with no success. At the time of hospitalization she was taking 4 ounces of formula at a time. If attempts were made to feed her more than 4 ounces, she would begin gagging and look like she was going to vomit. Lisa had made some tentative attempts at self-feeding and was taking a very limited variety of strained foods, mostly vegetables and meats, and cereal. She did not appear to like strained fruits.

Assessment

An occupational therapist experienced in feeding problems and I observed Mrs. M feeding Lisa both the bottle and solid foods. Mrs. M's approach to feeding Lisa while Lisa sat in the high chair appeared quite appropriate. She occasionally held Lisa's head gently in order to put the spoon in and generally praised her or verbalized when Lisa ate. At times Mrs. M talked more and seemed to distract Lisa from the eating. Lisa was easily distracted during eating. She was observed to be highly attentive to voices outside the room, even when she was sucking on the bottle. While sitting on her mother's lap to take her bottle, Lisa never looked as if eating was her primary interest. Her hands moved around, she played with her hair, and despite the fact that she sucked vigorously for 10 minutes and took 5 ounces, she never seemed settled into the eating. Mother appeared calm while she fed Lisa, despite Lisa's lack of settling into the process.

In the course of the assessment, I interviewed Mr. and Mrs. M about Lisa's developmental and feeding history, as well as their expectations and reactions to feeding, and general aspects of family functioning. I also observed Mrs. M playing with Lisa. Mrs. M reported that Lisa ate even more poorly than usual when there was another person besides herself in the room. When her siblings were present during meals, Lisa would interact with them rather than eat. Mrs. M worried that Lisa was unable to take food from anyone but herself. Because her two older children had been much more adaptive in their eating habits, Mrs. M wondered if Lisa's behavior reflected a pathological relationship between the two of them. However, there appeared to be no evidence which reflected a mother–child interaction problem. Lisa was wary of strangers, which was appropriate at her age, but was comfortable with others when her mother was present. Lisa was also very adept at entertaining herself. Mrs. M's expectations for Lisa's feeding seemed very reasonable given Mrs. M's previous experiences and usual feeding patterns.

Conceptualization and Recommendations

In general, Mrs. M seemed to know her child quite well and to have basically good skills in feeding her. While a description of the child's behavior alone was similar to the behavior of children with behavioral feeding disorders (i.e., little interest in food, social priorities during meals, some initial acceptance of food), neither the mother–child interaction nor the mother's expectations or perceptions of feeding were like those of feeding problems with a strong parent–infant interaction component. In fact, Mrs. M fed Lisa as if she had already been trained in behavioral feeding techniques. Mrs. M's anxiety about Lisa's feeding situation was quite apparent as Mrs. M described the problems, but not while she fed Lisa. It appeared that much of Mrs. M's confidence in mothering, which she had achieved with the other two children, had been eroded by Lisa's different style, and also by what Mrs. M felt were communications from her pediatrician that she was not mothering Lisa well and that someone else should take care of Lisa for a while.

Prior to discharge from the hospital, the dosage of Lisa's reflux medication was increased. I told the family and the pediatrician that I had no clear behavioral or psychological conceptualization to account for Lisa's feeding problem, but would offer some behavioral guidelines to optimize cooperation during feeding and prevent the development of inappropriate feeding interactions.

Mrs. M was given a set of specific instructions to help her understand and consistently maintain the positive manner in which she fed Lisa and to increase Lisa's acceptance of a wider variety of mealtime environments. These included: (1) having Lisa sit in the high chair while the rest of the family ate and providing her with finger food; (2) having another family member present while Lisa was being fed, at least one meal a day; (3) enrolling Lisa in day-care for several hours, several times a week, in order that she see other children eat; (4) continuing to feed Lisa quickly, holding her head gently, and focusing her attention on the spoon, reducing coaxing, and verbally reinforcing Lisa during and after bites; and (5) gradually introducing more variety into Lisa's meals, by combining small amounts of nonpreferred foods such as fruits with preferred foods such as meats and vegetables.

Follow-Up

Mr. and Mrs. M returned with Lisa to see me several weeks after hospitalization. They reported that they had carried through with all the feeding suggestions and were feeling satisfied with the progress Lisa was making in her eating. I felt that no further psychological follow-up was necessary at that point.

However, when Lisa was 13 months of age she was again hospitalized for failure to thrive, with her weight below the 5th percentile and her height falling to the 80th percentile. A tentative request for psychological consultation was made, but after briefly conferring with Mrs. M, I told the new pediatric gastroenterologist that I had no clear evidence for a behavioral feeding problem initially and that since the family had followed through reliably with the few suggestions I did make and had seen some increase in food intake, I had no further suggestions, and did not think further psychological evaluation or treatment would be useful. While I remained supportive to this mother, who was frustrated and anxious about her child's failure to thrive, I made it clear that psychological explanations were not sufficient to explain Lisa's FTT.

During this hospitalization, several astute pediatric diagnosticians, through interview and review of Lisa's dietary history presented to the hospital dietician, noticed that Lisa's food preferences and dislikes were unusual. Specifically, Lisa liked many sour foods which young children do not typically prefer (e.g., pickles, tomato juice) and intensely disliked many sweet foods, such as chocolate and many fruits. Lisa was tentatively diagnosed with hereditary fructose intolerance. This rare (1 in 40,000) autosomal-recessive disorder of metabolism is generally manifested with very severe symptoms of jaundice, hepatomegaly, vomiting, lethargy, irritability, and convulsions (Behrman & Vaughan, 1987), but the pediatricians believed that in Lisa's case the recognition of the disorder may have been more difficult because of the milder symptoms of refusal to eat foods containing fructose and increased sleeping after ingestion of fructose-containing foods.

Lisa was given a fructose-free diet via a nasogastric tube and in about a week had gained a pound and a half. She was discharged on a fructose/sucrose-free diet, and the pediatricians planned to readmit her in 3 to 4 weeks for a fructose challenge which would confirm the diagnosis. I was in contact with the family at this time only to provide emotional support and to assess and facilitate their understanding of the hospital process, although in my frequent contacts with the pediatric Nutrition/GI staff I heard some details of Lisa's medical progress. Occasionally Mrs. M would call me on her own and report on Lisa's progress.

At 14 months of age the fructose challenge was performed with equivocal results; however, the family was advised to keep Lisa on a fructose/sucrose-free diet. However, at 16 months, Lisa was again admitted for a vomiting and food refusal which had resulted in a 2-pound weight loss in a month. The etiology of her failure to thrive was again unclear, and once again the pediatricians speculated the cause was emotional. Once again, after a brief interview with the now very familiar family, I found no basis for a psychological conceptualization. The anxiety and frustration exhibited by the mother and shown very readily to the pediatricians were most parsimoniously explained as a reaction to the inability to find a consistent cause to account for her child's failure to thrive, and not *the* cause for the child's FTT.

Because of the lack of progress in weight gain, nasogastric tube feedings of Isocal, a liquid nutritional formula without fructose, were begun in the hospital, and Lisa was discharged with nighttime tube feedings. Her parents were told by the pediatricians to encourage oral intake during the day, and I clarified with the parents ways to do this without overattending to eating. However, it seemed clear that since Lisa would be getting all her caloric needs met by tube feedings and the reason for food refusal remained elusive, oral food intake would not improve with this plan. The primary purpose of the tube feeding was to improve Lisa's nutritional state, and in the next few months this occurred, despite the fact that, as predicted, she took in very little orally.

The parents initiated contact with the occupational therapist and myself after Lisa had been receiving nasogastric tube feedings for several months, because they were concerned about the lack of oral intake. At the time, Lisa ate only chicken. She would suck on pretzels and crackers for long periods of time, but would refuse or eventually spit out all other foods but chicken. Despite cautions to the parents, they had begun to overattend to oral intake. Because Lisa was hoarding foods in the mouth, the parents were concerned about choking and would do periodic "mouth checks." This behavior, along with much coaxing to eat, was the first observed parental behaviors which could maintain a feeding disorder. The parents were advised that Lisa had a healthy gag response and that choking on hoarded pretzels or crackers was not a problem. They were advised to avoid mouth checks, except if they were unclear about food in her mouth prior to sleep. They were also once again asked to avoid coaxing Lisa to eat and counseled to offer food when others ate and not attend to eating other than that. Furthermore, they were told that after Lisa's nutritional status was stable, we would recommend bolus tube feedings for a period of time and then attempt to reintroduce oral intake in a systematic manner.

Isocal tube feedings proceeded without incident for 3 months, beginning when Lisa was 16 months old. At 19 months, the formula was changed to Similac, and Lisa lost weight despite a constant volume of formula. Because of the father's job change, the family was now seen for medical treatment in an health maintenance organization. The new HMO pediatrician suggested that the weight loss had a psychological basis. By this time, Mrs. M was becoming somewhat sensitive to the inference that the problem was psychological whenever a medical explanation was not readily apparent. However, the family cooperated with an evaluation by a child psychiatrist affiliated with the family's HMO who found nothing unusual in the family's interaction or the child's emotional state. Weight gain commenced after Isocal was once again used in the tube feedings, and Mrs. M reported that she had sarcastically asked the pediatrician if Lisa had had a psychological problem with Similac.

The experience with Similac gave yet a third gastroenterologist (again the change was necessitated by the switch to the HMO) another idea about Lisa's underlying physical disorder. The pediatrician noted that Similac contained lactose while Isocal did not. At 2 years of age, Lisa was hospitalized for evaluation of lactose intolerance (Behrman & Vaughan, 1987). During that hospitalization, lactose intolerance was confirmed. Lisa had been previously evaluated for lactose intolerance and found able to digest lactose-containing foods. The gastroenterologist believed that Lisa had subsequently acquired this condition after bouts of gastroenteritis probably brought home from school by Lisa's siblings. Also during that hospitalization, further evaluation of Lisa's sugar metabolism produced a diagnosis of congenital sucrose–isomaltase deficiency (Behrman & Vaughan, 1987), a problem with sucrose metabolism rather than fructose metabolism as earlier believed. Finally, there appeared to be a solution which accounted for the many episodes of food refusal and failure to thrive that Lisa had experienced—congenital sucrose–isomaltose deficiency *and* acquired lactose intolerance, not "psychological problems."

Reconceptualization and Treatment

The events in the 14 months since the initial contact could be understood using the new diagnostic information. The initial behavioral suggestions, and more likely the support for Mrs. M's mothering ability, had improved the feeding briefly because they had reduced the minor behavioral components of the feeding problem. The consistent feeding program may have even resulted in an increase in fructose intake, resulting in poorer nutritional status several months later. The fructose-free diet worked relatively well until Lisa began to eat and drink more milk products. Her vomiting and weight loss were likely caused by lactose intolerance at that time and, without diagnosis, were inadvertently remedied by nasogastric feedings of a lactose-free formula. Growth proceeded normally until a lactose-containing formula was started by tube; normal growth returned when the lactose-free formula was reintroduced.

The complicated diagnosis was a great relief to the parents. They were finally able to stop worrying that no one would ever really understand what was happening to their child. However, the many months of unclarity had resulted in some feeding practices and behaviors which were problematic from a psychological perspective. The parents remained very anxious about oral intake, and they frequently described Lisa's unwillingness to cooperate in eating as "fear." They felt the introduction of new foods would cause more fear. Although they had stopped doing "mouth checks," they continued to coax Lisa to eat, almost always without success. Furthermore, now that Lisa had an unusual combination of diagnoses, they started to refer to her as "special," frequently with the implication that the expectations and requirements for her behavior were different from that of other children.

For 4 months after the last hospitalization, Lisa's tube feedings were gradually changed from nighttime continuous drip to bolus feeding four times per day. After the bolus feedings were tolerated, the occupational therapist and I met with Lisa and her parents to begin the transition to oral feeding. The observed feeding consisted of pureed chicken and green beans. Mrs. M attempted to feed these to Lisa since no self-feeding—except finger foods—had been established. Mrs. M's rate of verbal interaction with Lisa was very high. Lisa refused the green beans but took a bit of the chicken after several prompts. Very soon after the bite she coughed, then gagged and vomited. Mrs. M appeared very concerned at the first gag and felt further feeding would not be successful at that time. Since Lisa's vomiting did not look clearly volitional, we agreed to terminate the feeding at that time, check with the gastroenterologist, and proceed with the treatment once gastrointestinal reasons for vomiting had once again been ruled out. However, the parents reported that while there was intermittent and unpredictable vomiting with tube as well as spoon feeding, Lisa continued to gain weight. Therefore, the gastroenterologist suggested keeping accurate records of the vomiting, but proceeding with the feeding program. Because Lisa's oral intake was so limited, and she was not responsive to parental requests to taste or eat foods, we (psychologist, occupational therapist, pediatrician) decided to maintain full nutrition via bolus feeds, while we attempted to increase Lisa's eating behaviors. Because Lisa did not vomit regularly with spoon feeding, we established an initial goal of having Lisa accept tastes of a few new foods offered by her mother. These tastes were to be reinforced by bites of chicken, and practice sessions were to occur one time per day before a bolus feeding. Since Lisa was receiving her full caloric needs via tube so there was no expectation for oral caloric intake, just accepting tastes.

The family returned in several weeks with many excuses for not practicing the treatment plan (i.e., Lisa had "refused" to eat for 1 week after vomiting in the session and later Lisa had a virus for 10 days). However, some progress had been made; Lisa was putting rice and cucumbers in her mouth and had eaten one shredded wheat.

The next step was to have Lisa comply more readily with requests to take bites of food by allowing participation at family meals only if she accepted one bite every 5 minutes (she seemed to like sitting at the table interacting with her family, but not eating). The parents were asked to keep records of her intake and return in a month. Again we expected little caloric intake, merely the acceptance of eating, not just social interaction, at meals.

The family again returned with excuses for not following through reliably on the prescribed feeding program. They were again concerned with vomiting; they wondered whether an allergy was causing the vomiting. This concern over physical disorders despite reassurances seemed to be another remnant of their experience with over a year of unclear diagnosis. However, the family had been unable to produce records of vomiting which convinced the gastroenterologist that there was treatable organic pathology. They were advised to ignore any vomiting that might occur and to definitely avoid acting in a way to anticipate vomiting. Observation of the feeding revealed that the family was not using the approach recommended to reinforce eating behavior in Lisa. Instead of allowing normal social interaction contingent upon appropriate eating behavior, the parents tried to coax Lisa to eat by playing games such as "feed the dolly," by telling Lisa stories prior to eating, and in many other ways inadvertently reinforcing food refusal. The feeding interaction now looked clearly like a behavioral feeding problem, and the family was confronted with this fact. After all these months, Lisa now had a strong psychological component to her food refusal, clearly understandable and learned through her very unusual eating experiences.

The parents acknowledged the behavioral component of the food refusal (although they saw Lisa as "frightened" of food), but felt unable to enforce any behavioral contingencies around eating. They explained that they had been permissive in their childrearing practices with all of their children. The children went to bed when they wanted to, went to school because they wanted to, and presumably ate and did not eat when and what they wanted to. While this permissive style had worked well with the children in virtually all situations but Lisa's eating, they were now unable to conceptualize privileges or loss of privileges contingent upon eating behavior as anything but "force." Mrs. M repeatedly said she would feel too guilty is she "forced" Lisa to eat, but she would be willing to have Lisa hospitalized and have a behavioral feeding program carried out by the staff.

Before planning a hospital-based treatment, we (psychologist, occupational therapist, and pediatrician) acquiesced to mom's request to remove the tube and see if Lisa ate on her own at home. Since Lisa had some nutritional reserve, this appeared to be a reasonable approach. While her parents had no behavioral control over Lisa's eating, it was hoped that Lisa would be motivated by hunger to eat sufficient quantities. Foods which she could not tolerate (i.e., those with high lactose, fructose, or sucrose content) would be kept from Lisa's sight so her parents would not have to take forbidden foods from her, although in practice it was felt she would not initially eat enough of these to cause problems.

After the tube was removed, Lisa was offered Isocal to drink approximately every half-hour. Foods were also offered, but Isocal was stressed. Lisa was so unaccustomed to maintaining her nutrition through oral intake, that the first consideration was to prevent dehydration, and second, to promote adequate caloric intake. The first 10 days were quite rocky. Lisa's intake of Isocal dropped off greatly, and she became quite irritable and refused to separate from her mother. During short frequent (several times a week) outpatient visits and phone calls, both the pediatrician and I spent time supporting the family and encouraging tolerance of a trial without the tube long enough to ascertain whether or not oral intake would return. Lisa's weight was monitored daily in the pediatric Nutrition/GI clinic, so that everyone's anxiety could be contained. By the end of 8 days, the intake of Isocal was increasing. Mom was encouraged to resume a more normal schedule, leaving Lisa with the babysitter 3 hours per day. Return to the babysitter was fairly easily accomplished. By day 11, Lisa's weight had stopped dropping. She nibbled on crackers or chips all day long. By day 13 she had begun to gain weight and was eating crackers and drinking Isocal without prompting.

Shaping her to eat different tastes and textures and eat meals instead of snacks proceeded quite rapidly. Lisa generally led the way by asking for and eating a greater variety of foods, but about 5 weeks after the nasogastric tube was removed, Mom was instructed to begin restricting the number of times per day food was prepared for Lisa. Six weeks after the tube was removed, Lisa was feeding herself entirely, eating when her mother was not around, and tending to eat more at meals than snacks. She was eating meats but still liked salty or sour foods like olives.

I observed an interesting change in parental attitude when Lisa returned to the hospital to repeat the lactose tolerance test several weeks after she began eating and gaining weight. The lactose tolerance test requires the patient to ingest several ounces of lactose-containing liquid. I was visiting with the family in the clinic when the nurse brought in the liquid. No amount of coaxing by Lisa's parents could persuade Lisa to drink the required fluid; therefore, a nasogastric tube was passed and the fluid was poured into the tube. Although they soothed Lisa's distress, Lisa's parents told her that the tube was the consequence she had to endure since she refused to drink the liquid. The parents did not express concern about fear or psychic trauma as they frequently did while Lisa's eating was still tenuous.

Follow-Up

Seven months after the tube was removed, when Lisa was 39 months old, I called Mrs. M to ask about Lisa's progress. She reported that Lisa had continued to grow and develop and had begun preschool the week before with no problems. Lisa was eating a variety of foods, including meats and breads, although Mrs. M felt she got a disproportionate amount of calories from milk (she was no longer lactose-intolerant). Lisa loved fruits but had to be quite restricted in her ingestion of them because of her sugar intolerance. (She had once eaten 10 grapes and had diarrhea for 2 weeks.) Mrs. M appeared fairly calm about Lisa's eating behavior and general development. While she thought that her new school schedule and the opportunities to eat with other toddlers might increase Lisa's intake at meals, she was able to see that Lisa's intake and eating style was not atypical for a toddler.

Reflections

Like the previous case, understanding and treating Lisa's FTT required fairly intensive interdisciplinary coordination. Lisa's long and complicated course illustrates also two important points especially pertinent for mental health providers working in a medical setting. The first point is the tendency for psychologically less sophisticated personnel to try to diagnose psychological disorders on the basis of exclusion. If nothing can be found medically to cause the disorder, the cause must be psychological. The psychological diagnosis may be especially likely if the personnel find the family difficult or anxious. In this case I frequently felt pressured to uncover some esoteric psychological "cause" for Lisa's FTT, but had no sound conceptualization for the onset or maintenance of the feeding disorder based upon psychological or behavioral principles. It might be argued that I never should have made feeding suggestions upon first consultation, albeit to prevent future feeding problems. However, in reviewing the file it was clear that the parents, as well as the pediatrician, understood that I could not explain this feeding disorder on a psychological basis. During the period of diagnosis my primary purpose was to support the family and to keep rejecting attempts to make this a behavioral problem.

The second point, ironically related to the first, is that behavioral feeding problems may very well develop after long periods of organic feeding problems. In Lisa's case, as is fairly typical, this feeding problem was related to the conditioning aspects of organic illness, that is, Lisa felt ill after eating certain foods, and the parental anxiety and expectations which developed around feeding. The basic soundness of the parent–child relationship was illustrated by the return of normal parental expectations and attitudes toward Lisa as normal eating patterns were developed. This normalization of the relationship appears to be typical in cases of a circumscribed feeding problem.

REFERENCES

Behrman, R. E., & Vaughan, V. C. (1987). *Nelson textbook of pediatrics.* Philadelphia: Saunders.

Drotar, D. (Ed.). (1984). *New directions in failure to thrive: Implications for research and practice.* New York: Plenum.

Egan, G., Chatoor, I., & Rosen, G. (1980). Non-organic failure to thrive: Pathogenesis and classification. *Clinical Proceedings of Children's Hospital National Medical Center, 36,* 173-182.

Gelfand, D. M., & Hartmann, D. P. (1984). *Child behavior analysis and therapy.* New York: Pergamon.

Handen, B. L., Mandell, F., & Russo, D. C. (1986). Feeding induction in children who refuse to eat. *American Journal of Diseases of Children, 140*(1), 52-54.

Linscheid, T. R., & Rasnake, L. K. (1984). Behavioral approaches to the treatment of failure to thrive. In D. Drotar (Ed.), *New directions in failure to thrive: Implications for research and practice,* (pp. 279-294). New York: Plenum.

Mash, E. J., & Terdal, L. G. (Eds.). (1981). *Behavioral assessment of childhood disorders.* New York: Guilford.

Ollendick, T. H., & Hersen, M. (Eds.). (1984). *Child behavioral assessment.* New York: Pergamon.

Palmer, S., Thompson, R. J., & Linscheid, T. R. (1975). Applied behavior analysis in the treatment of childhood feeding problems. *Developmental Medicine and Child Neurology, 17,* 333-339.

Riordan, M. M., Iwata, B. A., Finney, J. W., Wohl, M. K., & Stanley, A. E. (1984). Behavioral assessment and treatment of chronic food refusal in handicapped children. *Journal of Applied Behavior Analysis, 17,* 327-341.

Roberts, M. C., & Maddux, J. E. (1982). A psychosocial conceptualization of nonorganic failure to thrive. *Journal of Clinical Child Psychology, 11*(3), 216-226.

Showers, J., Mandelkorn, R., Coury, D. L., & McCleery, J. (1986). Non-organic failure to thrive: Identification and intervention. *Journal of Pediatric Nursing, 1*(4), 240–246.

Siegel, L. (1982). Classical and operant procedures in the treatment of a case of food aversion in a young child. *Journal of Clinical Child Psychology, 11*(2), 167–172.

Thompson, R. J., Palmer, S., & Linscheid, T. R. (1977). Single-subject design and interaction analysis in the behavioral treatment of a child with a feeding problem. *Child Psychiatry and Human Development, 8*(1), 43–53.

14

A Case Study of a Family with Four Nocturnally Enuretic Children

GARY R. GEFFKEN
SUZANNE BENNETT JOHNSON

INTRODUCTION

The diagnostic criteria for functional enuresis set forth by the revised third edition of the *Diagnostic and Statistical Manual of Mental Disorders* (DSM-III-R; American Psychiatric Association, 1987, p. 85) include:

A. Repeated voiding of urine by night or day into bed or clothes, whether involuntary or intentional.
B. At least two such events per month for children between the ages of five and six, and at least one event per month for older children.
C. Chronologic age at least five, and mental age at least four.
D. Not due to a physical disorder such as diabetes, urinary tract infection, or a seizure disorder.
Specify primary or secondary type.
Primary type: the disturbance was not preceded by a period of urine continence lasting at least one year.
Second type: the disturbance was preceded by a period of urinary continence lasting at least one year.
Specify nocturnal only, diurnal only, or *nocturnal and diurnal.*

In a study of 1,129 enuretics, Forsythe and Redmond (1974) reported that primary enuresis is far more common than secondary enuresis and that nocturnal enuresis is more common than nocturnal plus diurnal enuresis. Diurnal enuresis without nocturnal enuresis is quite rare. The incidence of

Gary R. Geffken and Suzanne Bennett Johnson. Departments of Psychiatry, Pediatrics, and Clinical and Health Psychology, University of Florida Health Science Center, Gainesville, Florida.

nocturnal enuresis is higher in boys while the incidence of nocturnal plus diurnal enuresis is higher in girls. A review of relevant literature (Johnson, 1980) suggests that whether a child is a primary or secondary enuretic does not seem to be related to treatment success or failure.

Some research has suggested that the prevalence of psychopathology is greater in enuretic individuals than in the general population (Rutter, Yule, & Graham, 1973), while other sources find the data equivocal (Johnson, 1980). However, it is generally agreed that the majority of children with enuresis do not manifest significant psychopathology (APA, 1987; Johnson, 1980; Rutter et al., 1973; Schwartz & Johnson, 1981). However, children with enuresis are often ashamed of their wetting and may avoid situations (e.g., overnight visits with friends) with potentially embarrassing consequences. In addition, there may be problems with self-esteem resulting from rejection and punishments by caretakers and/or peers (American Psychiatric Association, 1987). Readers interested in overviews of literature on enuresis may refer to Johnson (1980) and Kolvin, MacKeith, and Meadow (1973).

CASE BACKGROUND

The case study to be reviewed in this chapter involves treatment of four children with nocturnal enuresis, all residing within the same middle-class family.[1] The E family was self-referred to the Department of Psychiatry's Enuresis Clinic at the University of Florida's Health Science Center. The mother of the children had initially responded to a newspaper article describing the behavioral treatments offered through this clinic. The family included two caucasian boys, 13-year-old Alvin and 3-year-old David, both biological offspring of the E's marriage. In addition, the family included two adopted Hispanic girls, 7-year-old Beda and 5-year-old Cathy. When the family initially came to the clinic, we considered 3-year-old David too young for treatment. However, 1 year later, treatment was initiated with this child as well. All children exhibited primary nocturnal enuresis without diurnal enuresis at the time of presentation. They had not received prior treatment for this disorder.

ASSESSMENT

Physical Examination

The pretreatment assessment for all the children included a physical examination by a licensed physician to rule out any organic basis for the bed-

1. Clinically insignificant aspects of the case have been changed to preserve the confidentiality of the family members.

wetting. These physical examinations were conducted through the Department of Pediatric's Diagnostic Outpatient Clinics at the University of Florida's Health Science Center and included urinalysis to rule out infection; high glucose; blood or other abnormalities in the urine; an external examination of the genitalia; an examination for normal sensation in the saddle area; and a neurological screening. No demonstrable organic basis for these children's bedwetting was found. In our experience, children's bedwetting is rarely organically induced, although a physical exam should always be conducted to confirm a diagnosis of functional enuresis.

Psychological Battery

The psychological assessment conducted through the Enuresis Clinic included a clinical interview, a measurement of the child's functional bladder capacity, an assessment of the child's self-concept and attitudes toward enuresis, and a brief screening of the youngster's receptive language ability. The child's mother also completed paper-and-pencil measures tapping her attitudes toward enuresis, as well as a behavior problem screening questionnaire. Each of these measures is described in more detail subsequently. A 2-week baseline of wetting was also collected for each youngster prior to the initiation of treatment: Each morning Mrs. Edwards was asked to record which child's bed was dry or wet.

Clinical Interview

An interview was conducted with Mrs. E and the four children. Mr. E, who was employed in real estate, did not participate. Mrs. E, a homemaker, reported adopting the Hispanic children after the birth of her first child. The E's youngest child was born after the adoptions. Mrs. E described herself and her husband as fairly conservative, with a strong religious affiliation. Neither she nor her husband had a history of bedwetting as a child.

All of the E children had primary enuresis. Mrs. E sometimes awakened her children to go to the bathroom prior to retiring to bed, but this approach had not successfully eliminated the problem. She had not tried restricting fluids after supper. Neither parent used punishment in response to the children's bedwetting. Overall, Mrs. E appeared nonpunitive toward her children's bedwetting and supportive of treatment to help arrest the wetting. We advised her not to use either nightime awakening or fluid restriction during the baseline data collection or treatment phases, as our goal was to have the children arrest wetting while under normal drinking and sleeping patterns.

A review of the children's school functioning found them to be performing well with the possible exception of the older boy, Alvin, who had some grades of Cs and Ds. However, none of the children had ever repeated a grade, and none were described as having significant behavior problems either at home or at school.

Functional Bladder Capacity

Measures of bladder capacity in children with enuresis have been reported by a number of researchers (Starfield, 1967; Starfield & Mellits, 1968; Vulliamy, 1956; Zaleski, Gerrard, & Shokier, 1973). Investigations have consistently found that enuretic children have smaller maximum functional bladder capacities (MFBC) than nonenuretic children (Muellner, 1960; Starfield, 1967; Zaleski et al., 1973). The method used to assess MFBC in our Enuresis Clinic requires each child to drink 500 ml of water and then to inhibit urination until no longer comfortably possible (Zaleski, et al., 1973). The child makes two consecutive voids into a "urine hat," a plastic basin placed on the toilet to collect the child's urine specimen. Each of the child's two voids is measured; the larger specimen is taken as the MFBC. On the side of each urine hat are calibration strips indicating liquid volumes marked in 2-ounce and 50-cc intervals, permitting an observer to quickly measure the volume of the urine specimen. Stable test–retest measures of bladder capacity for a group of enuretics have been reported by Harris and Purohit (1977).

The oldest children in this family, Alvin and Beda, had pretreatment MFBCs of approximately 11 ounces. The next youngest child, Cathy, had a 9-ounce pretreatment MFBC. Compared with other enuretic children their own age, Alvin, Beda, and Cathy all had large MFBCs. In contrast, the fourth child, David, had a pretreatment MFBC of 4 ounces, which is small compared with other 5-year-old enuretic children (no norms are available on children less than 5 years old).

Piers–Harris Children's Self-Concept Scale

The Piers–Harris Children's Self-Concept Scale (Piers & Harris, 1969) is an 80-item child self-report measure presented in a yes/no format. It is appropriate for children from grades 3 through 12, and scores may be referenced against a normative sample. Bentler (1972) reported reliability coefficients ranging between .71 and .93. The measure is positively correlated with other measures of self-concept and inversely correlated with measures of anxiety. Although this measure is susceptible to social desirability effects, Piers and Harris (1969) maintain that in applied use, a low score (indicative of a negative self-concept) should be of concern to the clinician. The E's children's scores on this measure were all within normal limits.

Child Attitude Scale

The Child Attitude Scale (Wagner & Geffken, 1986) provides comparative data, based on a sample of 100 enuretic children who answered yes or no to 25 statements tapping four basic constructs: the child's knowledge about enuresis, the child's feelings about enuresis, current child enuresis-related behaviors, and the child's perception of significant others' reactions to enuresis. It is similar to the Nuisance and Tolerance Scales for Enuresis developed by Morgan and Young (1975) for parents of children with this problem.

The youngsters in the E family displayed attitudes toward enuresis similar to the majority of respondents in this initial sample of 100 enuretic children. They all expressed a willingness to participate in treatment and a desire to stop wetting.

Peabody Picture Vocabulary Test—Revised (PPVT-R)

The PPVT-R is a measure of an individual's hearing vocabulary for American English (Dunn & Dunn, 1981). Although the test is not timed, it usually requires about 10 to 15 minutes to complete. The examiner orally presents a word, and the child is asked to select the picture that best corresponds to the word from four pictorial choices. Words of increasing difficulty are presented until six errors occur in eight consecutive responses. The child's total score is then referenced against a normative sample. In our experience, this brief screening test constitutes an adequate assessment of the child's receptive language abilities. All of the E children scored in the average- to high-average range on the PPVT-R, indicating adequate receptive language abilities to understand and follow our intervention protocol.

Tolerance and Nuisance Scales

The Tolerance Scale (Morgan & Young, 1975) is a brief questionnaire administered to a parent of a child with enuresis. It assesses a dimension of tolerance or intolerance toward enuresis, which its authors believe may be related to parental cooperation or compliance with treatment. Each of 20 items on this scale has been assigned a value on the basis of ratings by 40 independent judges. The parent's score is then calculated as the median value of all items answered "yes"; higher scores indicate greater intolerance. Morgan and Young (1975) reported a split-half reliability coefficient of .43, but provided no test-retest reliability data. In two studies (Morgan & Young, 1975; Wagner, Johnson, Walker, Carter, & Wittmer, 1982), mothers who withdrew their children prematurely from treatment had higher tolerance scale scores (i.e., were more intolerant) than mothers who stayed in treatment. However, this finding failed to be replicated in a third investigation (Geffken, Johnson, & Walker, 1986).

The Nuisance Scale was also developed by Morgan and Young (1975) to assess parental attitudes towards enuresis. It consists of a checklist of 25 childhood behavior problems. Parents are asked to check all problems they consider to be worse than bedwetting. Morgan and Young (1975) have reported the frequencies of checked behaviors for 108 mothers of enuretic children seen in treatment. However, there are no data available on the reliability of this instrument.

The responses of Mrs. E to these scales indicated that she was quite tolerant of enuresis. She viewed enuresis as a problem not under her children's control and perceived her children as needing help and sympathy. She did not endorse the use of punishments for bedwetting and rated bedwetting as easier to deal with than quite a number of other behavior problems. Mrs. E's nonpunitive and constructive attitude toward her children's bedwetting suggested to us that she and her children might be ideal candidates for treatment.

Behavior Problem Checklist (BPC)

The Behavior Problem Checklist was developed by Peterson (1961) to assess problem behaviors occurring in childhood and adolescence. It consists of 55 common behavior problems which the parent rates as either no problem, a mild problem, or a severe problem. Peterson generated the checklist by examining the most frequently mentioned problems seen in a large child guidance clinic. Subsequent factor analyses of the BPC have consistently reported four factors: Conduct Disorder, Anxiety–Withdrawal, Inadequacy–Immaturity, and Socialized Aggression (see Quay, 1986, for a review). There are also a few items which screen for childhood autism and psychosis. Norms are available in the manual for each of the four factor-derived subscales (Quay & Peterson, 1975). Split-half reliabilities ranged from $r = .92$ for the Conduct Problem subscale to $r = .26$ for the Inadequacy–Immaturity subscale. Reliability estimates determined by the Kuder–Richardson formula 20 ranged from .89 for the Conduct Problem subscale, to .68 for the Inadequacy–Immaturity subscale. We use the BPC as a clinical screening instrument. Mrs. E rated all four of her children as having low levels of behavior problems.

Case Study Assessment Summary

The brief physical screenings found no demonstrable organic basis for wetting in any of the E's children. Baseline wetting frequencies collected for 2 weeks prior to the initiation of treatment showed Alvin and David each had 13 wet nights, while Beda and Cathy each had 9 wet nights. Alvin, Beda, and Cathy all had large MFBCs compared with other enuretic children their own age, while David had a small MFBC. Hence, David was the only child in the family for whom supplemental treatment using retention control training in addition to the urine alarm was indicated.

All of the E children scored in the average to high average range on the PPVT-R, indicating that these children had the necessary receptive language skills for instruction in a behavioral treatment for enuresis. They also displayed high motivation for treatment. They readily acknowledged their desire to stop wetting, to participate in treatment, and viewed their parents as supportive of their effort to stop wetting.

As indicated earlier, Mrs. E's responses suggested that she was quite tolerant of and nonpunitive toward her children's bedwetting. She also rated her children as having low levels of behavior problems both at home and at school. Mrs. E's nonpunitive and constructive attitude toward her children's bedwetting as well as her children's low levels of behavior problems made them suitable candidates for a behavioral intervention approach to their enuresis.

TREATMENT

Treatment Options

There are a number of available treatments for enuresis. We considered each in terms of the probability of success with the E children. Medication, most notably Tofranil or imipramine, offered the easiest form of treatment. Blackwell and Currah (1973) suggest that imipramine, a tricyclic antidepressant, relaxes the bladder wall muscle and increases the tone of the vesicular outlet. This, in turn, permits increased urine volume in the bladder prior to the induction of the stretch reflex resulting in bladder contraction and voiding. Tricyclics are the only drugs demonstrated to be consistently superior to placebos for the treatment of enuresis. The effect of medication is usually seen in the first week of treatment, although total remission of involuntary wetting occurs in less than half the patients. Patients typically relapse to pretreatment levels of wetting as soon as the medication is withdrawn (see Blackwell & Currah, 1973; Johnson, 1980, for reviews). Drug treatment of enuresis, although relatively easy to administer, does not offer a high likelihood of success. Consequently, we considered other treatment options for the E family. All of these options were behaviorally based due to the superior results demonstrated in empirical and case research.

The urine alarm was originally popularized by Mowrer and Mowrer (1938) and has had a long history of success in the treatment of enuresis. This battery-powered alarm is connected by wires to two foil pads which are separated by an insulating pad. The pads are placed on the bed of the enuretic child beneath the bottom sheet (see Figure 14-1). When the youngster has an accident, the insulated pad becomes wet, completing the circuit between the foil pads and sounding the alarm.

A number of theoretical rationales have been offered to explain the effectiveness of the urine alarm. Mowrer and Mowrer (1938) believed that the principles of respondent conditioning were involved: The alarm served as an unconditioned stimulus producing an unconditioned response, waking. After repeated pairing of full-bladder sensations with the alarm's sounding and the child's waking, bladder distention became a conditioned stimulus, waking the child prior to urination and the alarm's sounding. Of course, operant and social learning principles may also contribute to the treatment's efficacy (Johnson, 1980; Ross, 1981). The aversive qualities of the alarm and having to get up in the middle of the night may result in avoidance learning and negative reinforcement for learning the desired response of staying dry. The practice of recording wet and dry nights and familial involvement may further contribute by positively reinforcing the learning process.

Johnson (1980), in summarizing her comprehensive review of the controlled and uncontrolled studies using the urine alarm, suggested that most children will benefit from the urine alarm, but as many as half who achieve initial arrest will eventually relapse. Two studies (DeLeon & Mandell, 1966; Werry & Cohrssen, 1965) found the urine alarm to be superior to psycho-

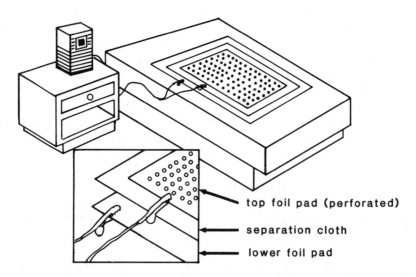

FIGURE 14-1. Urine alarm properly positioned on a bed. (Adapted from instructions for use of the "Wee Alert" distributed by Sears, Roebuck & Company.)

therapy. One study, (Wagner et al., 1982) found the urine alarm to be superior to imipramine. Representing a combined total of 740 subjects using the urine alarm in controlled investigations, Johnson (1980) reported that most of these studies cited arrest rates of over 60% with relapse rates ranging from 15% (McConaghy, 1969) to 80% (DeLeon & Mandell, 1966).

Although the urine alarm is the most thoroughly investigated behavioral treatment for enuresis, other behavioral treatments are available. A number of investigators (Muellner, 1960; Paschalis, Kimmel, & Kimmel, 1972; Starfield & Mellits, 1968) have suggested that some enuretic children may show improvement as a result of bladder-stretching exercises. Bladder-training exercise, also called retention control training (RTC), requires the child to hold their urine during the day beyond the initial urge to void. Children are shaped to hold their urine for successively longer periods of time, up to 45 minutes after the initial urge to urinate. Some researchers include increased fluid intake as a part of this procedure (Harris & Purohit, 1977; Muellner, 1960), while others leave fluid intake unrestricted (Paschalis et al., 1972; Starfield & Mellits, 1968). The results of studies using RTC are not particularly impressive. Starfield and Mellits (1968) found 66% of their patients had decreased wetting, but only 19% were cured. Other studies (Doleys, Ciminero, Tollison, Williams, & Wells, 1977; Harris & Purohit, 1977) have found no significant RTC-related decrease in enuresis. Paschalis et al. (1972) did report that 45% of their RTC-treated sample attained 1 continuous week without bedwetting while no children in their control group achieved this criterion. However, Paschalis et al.'s results appear to be the exception rather than the rule. More recent research has suggested that RTC may be most helpful when used in conjunction with the urine alarm. Geffken et al. (1986) found that RTC had significant salutary effects when used with small MFBC-enuretic children who were also receiving treatment with the urine alarm.

Dry-bed training is another behavioral approach that includes both bladder training components and the urine alarm in its multiple-component treatment protocol first outlined by Azrin, Sneed, and Foxx (1974). The procedure begins with one night of intensive training administered by an outside trainer, in which the child is given extra fluids before retiring and is then required to perform 20 trials of positive practice. One trial of positive practice involves lying in bed and then going to the bathroom to try to urinate and then returning to bed. During this night of intensive training, the child is awakened every hour, taken to the bathroom, and asked to inhibit urination, for which the child is praised. The child is again given fluids at every hour's wakening. The urine alarm is also placed on the child's bed. When the child does wet and the urine alarm sounds, the child is required to engage in 20 additional trials of positive practice and cleanliness training. Cleanliness training requires the child to change bed sheets and bed clothes, and wash up after a wetting accident. Twenty positive practice trials are again required before bedtime on the evening following each accident. Positive verbalizations were given contingent upon success in meeting the program's goals.

Following the night of intensive training, posttraining supervision is implemented. Increased fluids are discontinued and nighttime awakening is faded, but the urine alarm, the cleanliness training, positive practice, and social contingencies remain in effect.

Azrin et al. (1974) and Bollard and Woodroffe (1977) reported dramatic 100% arrest rates using this procedure with relapse rates of 17% to 29%. However, not all researchers have been able to replicate this high-success rate. Doleys et al. (1977), for example, achieved an arrest rate of only 38%. It is also unclear which of the multiple components are critical to the success of this procedure, when success does occur (Johnson, 1980; Ross, 1981). Azrin and his colleagues (Azrin, Hontos, & Besalel-Azrin, 1979; Azrin & Thienes, 1978) report successful treatment outcome when dry-bed training is conducted without the urine alarm, but other investigators (Bollard & Nettlebeck, 1981; Bollard & Woodroffe, 1977) have been unable to achieve arrests without the urine alarm in place. Caceres (1982) conducted a comparison between dry-bed training including the urine alarm and the urine alarm alone with a small sample of children ($N = 14$). More youngsters reached the 2-week arrest criterion in a shorter time using the urine alarm alone than when the urine alarm was used as a component of the more involved dry-bed training.

The available literature suggested to us that the urine alarm is the most well-documented, successful treatment for enuresis. Consequently, all of the E children were treated with the urine alarm. Because the three older children, who were treated first, all had large MFBCs, RTC was not viewed as a potentially helpful treatment addition. However, for the smallest child, David, who had a small MFBC, RTC was used along with the urine alarm. Of course, social reinforcement and other operant procedures were liberally applied to help maintain compliance with the treatment procedure. Examples of these are provided in the following section on treatment process and progress.

Cast Study Treatment Process and Progress

Having completed the assessment of the children in the E family, one of the first questions we addressed was whether to treat one child at a time or to treat multiple children at the same time. The treatment of choice, a behavioral intervention program using the urine alarm, is labor-intensive and fairly disruptive, requiring considerable time investment by the parent. Table 14-1 shows detailed instructions which were provided to Mrs. E and her children (Johnson, 1983). Because the parent may be required to arise for each wetting episode at night, depending on the child's age and coopera-

TABLE 14-1. Instructions for Using the Urine Alarm

General Instructions:

1. Your child's bed should be as firm as possible. This may require the use of a "bed board" beneath the mattress.

2. It is important that the perforated foil pad be placed on top with the solid pad and cloth layer underneath. Be certain that the cloth layer completely eliminates any direct contact between the foil pads.

3. Center the pads in the middle of the mattress in the area where your child is most likely to wet.

4. When the wire clips are attached to the foil pads, be sure the clips are placed at least 6 inches apart on the side of the pad adjacent to the bedside unit.

5. Cover the pads with a sheet. It will help to tuck the sheet tightly under the mattress in order to keep the foil pads in place. Do not have your child sleep directly on top of the foil pads.

6. It will help if your child sleeps without pajama bottoms.

7. On a weekly basis it will be necessary to test the strength of the battery in the bedside unit. Do this by turning the switch on the unit to "ON" and then touch the two wire clips together to get a sound.

8. Turn on a dim night light each evening in your child's bedroom if your child has any problems with darkness.

Before the child retires:

9. Make certain that a change of dry sheets is available in the room.

10. Make certain that a place is designated for the disposal of any wet sheets that might result during the night.

11. Check the foil pads to make certain that the pads are completely separated by the cloth layer. Make sure that the wire clips are attached to the pads and are at least 6 inches apart from each other.

12. Place the regular flat sheet on the mattress and tuck it under tightly.

13. Switch the buzzer unit to "ON."

14. Have the child go to bed, lying down on the mattress.

When the child wets, he or she should:

15. Awaken, when the alarm sounds, STAND UP alongside the bed, and turn on a bedside lamp before turning the alarm switch to "OFF."

16. Go to the lavatory and splash water on his or her face to be sure of actually being awake.

17. Walk to the toilet and finish urinating.

18. Return to the bedroom, remove the wet sheet from the bed, and place the sheet in the designated place.

19. Separate the foil pads, and remove the wet cloth layer.

20. Take a dry cloth and wipe any moisture from the foil pads.

21. Replace the bottom foil pad on the mattress, insert a new layer of dry cloth, placing the perforated foil pad on top. Be sure the foil pads are not touching.

22. Attach a wire clip to each pad. Be sure the clips are at least 6 inches apart.

23. Place a dry sheet over the foil pads and tightly tuck under the mattress.

24. Turn the alarm switch to "ON."

25. Return to bed and lie on the mattress.

Note. From S. B. Johnson (1983). The treatment of enuresis. In P. Keller & L. Ritt (Eds.), *Innovations in clinical practice: A source book,* p. 94. Sarasota, FL: Professional Resource Exchange. Copyright 1983 by Professional Resource Exchange. Reprinted by permission.

tion, it is useful to look at baseline data. On the basis of pretreatment wetting for all three children, we advised Mrs. E that she or her husband should probably arise approximately 14 times per week during the initial weeks of treatment, or 1 to 3 times per night. The treatment decision was left with the mother, who in this case decided that she wanted all three children treated at the same time. This involved treatment sessions occurring every 1 to 2 weeks with all the children present. We typically schedule initial sessions on a weekly basis. However, once we are confident that a family is compliant with treatment procedures, appointments are stretched to once every 2 weeks, with resumption of more frequent sessions if problems occur. The children in the E family were quite active, which led to somewhat chaotic sessions at times.

The urine alarm that was used with these children consisted of a battery powered alarm that was contained in a small box with an on/off switch. The alarm was purchased from a local J. C. Penny Department Store. The alarm made a loud sound when activated. Extending from the alarm were two wires which were clipped onto foil pads. The foil pads were placed one over the other on top of the bed mattress and underneath the bottom sheet (see Figure 14-1). The top foil pad was perforated while the bottom foil pad was solid. The foil pads were separated by an insulation cloth which was larger in length and width than the foil pads. When the alarm was switched on, the dry insulation pad prevented an electrical circuit from being completed between the foil pads, which were connected to the alarm. When the insulation cloth became wet, the electrical circuit between the foil pads was completed, resulting in the alarm sounding. Children feel no physical sensation when alarm units like this sound. The alarm unit can be switched off to discontinue the alarm.

The treatment with the urine alarm was initiated with the three older children. Like many children we have treated, the Edwards children found the initial presentation of the alarm apparatus quite exciting. Figure 14-2 provides a graphic display of weekly wetting frequency data before, during, and after treatment. Treatment was terminated only after 14 consecutive dry nights. The 7-year-old girl Beda was able to terminate treatment relatively quickly, after 4 weeks. The second child to achieve treatment success was 13-year-old Alvin, who achieved dryness after 8 weeks of treatment. The quicker success of the younger sister represents an interesting dynamic when more than one child in the same family is treated at the same time. When one child achieves success prior to another, it may induce some competition and/or jealousy in the child taking longer. We were concerned about how Alvin, the oldest child, might view his younger sister's treatment success. Alvin seemed to view it as a challenge and was the second E child to become dry. The 5-year-old girl Cathy was the last of the three children to achieve treatment success. She took 13 weeks to achieve 2 consecutive weeks of dry nights. At the midpoint of treatment, this child began displaying uncooper-

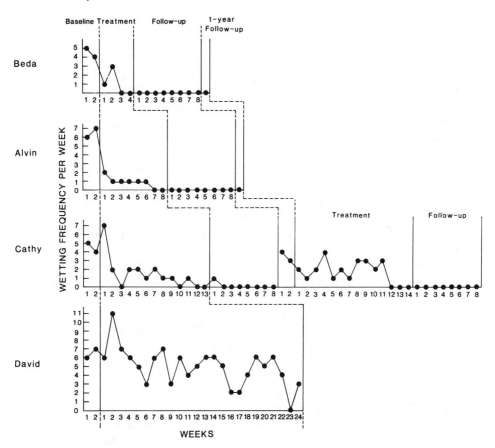

FIGURE 14-2. Weekly frequency of wetting during baseline, treatment, and follow-up.

ative behavior, including difficulty awakening and irritability. It is not
uncommon that when treatment extends beyond 2-months that the initial
excitement for the treatment wanes as the drudgery of nightly awakening
continues. A simple operant program was instituted to elicit adequate
compliance with the nighttime procedures. The mother and child generated
a list of reinforcers (hair barrettes, pencils with cartoon characters on them,
time playing with mother, etc.) which were administered by the mother on
the day following a wetting episode when Cathy awakened and cooperated
with the nightime procedures. Cathy, like many other children, found the
incentives to be a source for renewed enthusiasm for the program. Generating the list of reinforcers is often a very positive experience for children.
Occasionally, we ask the child and parent to measure the size of the wet
spots. Even when weekly wetting frequency is not decreasing, families are

often encouraged by a decrease in the size of the wet spot, a concrete sign of treatment progress.

As shown in Figure 14-2, a routine 8 weeks of follow-up data were collected, although appointments were not scheduled for a child not in treatment. Mrs. E also was advised to recontact the clinic if one of her children relapsed. We define relapse as the occurrence of 3 wet nights in a 2-week period. We have selected this relatively liberal criterion, based on our experience that many children may wet once without developing a full-blown relapse with multiple wetting episodes.

At 1-year posttreatment, the oldest boy and the 7-year-old girl had not relapsed. However, at that time Mrs. E recontacted the clinic because Cathy had relapsed. Mrs. E also was interested in treatment for her youngest son who was now 4 years old. Treatment was initiated for both of these children. Since David had a small MFBC, he received RCT as a supplement to the urine alarm treatment.

During Cathy's second treatment, the simple operant reward system was reimplemented. A phenomenon was observed that we have occasionally observed in other young children treated with incentive programs to increase compliance with the urine alarm procedures. During week 4, Cathy voiced that she received more rewards when she wet than when she was dry. Care must be taken to amply reward children for dry nights as well as for compliance with the nighttime procedures on wet nights. This will greatly reduce any motivation by a child to wet in order to receive rewards. After 14 weeks, Cathy had achieved the arrest criterion. However, after a period of 22 weeks, David, the youngest boy, was not showing gains in treatment. David's success with the RCT was limited. The duration of his holding his urine beyond the initial urge was only 10 to 15 minutes. Like many other very young children, David displayed a limited capacity to identify the need to void prior to having a sense of urgency. Mrs. E elected to terminate treatment for her youngest child, even though a period of 10 consecutive dry nights was observed during the last several weeks of treatment. Mrs. E admitted that her compliance with the nighttime and daytime procedures had diminished as her motivation for continued treatment had dwindled. It appeared that the process of working with her three older children had exhausted Mrs. E as far as getting up at night to comply with the nighttime urine alarm procedures. Mrs. E expressed gratitude for assistance with all her children, and appeared relieved when we gave her permission to discontinue treatment with her youngest child.

The unique nature of this case report is that it involved a number of children from the same family treated at the same time. Although the treatment sessions were relatively chaotic with numerous lively young children in the same room at once, the process of treatment was easier for us because Mrs. E faithfully attended sessions and, at least for the three older children, was compliant with treatment procedures and record-keeping.

Parents who do not ensure appointments are kept and procedures are followed decrease the likelihood of treatment success. As well, parents who are less tolerant and patient than Mrs. E require close monitoring and counseling to assure that a nonaversive approach is taken to their child's wetting.

The treatment of the children in the E family demonstrates several key points about the use of the urine alarm for children with nocturnal enuresis. Many if not most of these children, like the E youngsters, exhibit no signs of significant psychopathology. The urine alarm is an effective treatment for most, but not all, childhood bedwetters. In the case of David E treatment failure, the age of the child and the decreased parental motivation were thought to be critical factors. Based on our experience, we do not recommend routine behavioral treatment of enuretic children under the age of 5 years; very young children do not appear to have the physical and cognitive maturity to benefit quickly from treatment. Relapse of wetting is common when treating children with the urine alarm. The 33% relapse rate found in the E family is consistent with rates cited in the literature. However, it is important to note that the retreatment of Cathy, like other children who have relapsed, typically results in a lasting arrest of wetting.

REFERENCES

American Psychiatric Association (1987). *Diagnostic and statistical manual of mental disorders* (3rd ed., revised). Washington, DC: Author.

Azrin, N. H., Hontos, P. T., & Besalel-Azrin, V. (1979). Elimination of enuresis without a conditioning apparatus: An extension by office instruction of the child and parents. *Behavior Therapy, 10,* 14–19.

Azrin, N. H., Sneed, T. J., & Foxx, R. M. (1974). Rapid elimination of childhood enuresis. *Behavior Research and Therapy, 12,* 147–156.

Azrin, N. H., & Thienes, P. M. (1978). Rapid elimination of enuresis by intensive learning without a conditioning apparatus. *Behavior Therapy, 9,* 342–354.

Bentler, P. M. (1972). A review: the Piers–Harris Children Self-Concept Scale. In O. K. Buros (Ed.), *The seventh mental measurement yearbook* (Vol. 1, pp. 306–307). Highland Park, NJ: The Gryphon Press.

Blackwell, B., & Currah, J. (1973). The psychopharmacology of nocturnal enuresis. In I. Kolvin, R. Mackeith, & S. Meadow (Eds.), *Bladder control and enuresis, clinics in developmental medicine,* (Nos. 48/49, pp. 231–257). Philadelphia: Lippincott.

Bollard, R. J., & Nettlebeck, T. (1981). A comparison of dry-bed training and standard urine alarm conditioning treatment of childhood bedwetting. *Behavior Research and Therapy, 19,* 215–226.

Bollard, R. J., & Woodroffe, P. (1977). The effect of parent administered dry-bed training on nocturnal enuresis in children. *Behavior Research and Therapy, 15,* 159–165.

Caceres, J. (1982). Enuresis: Cortical control or social reinforcement? *The Behavior Therapist, 8,* 65–67.

DeLeon, G., & Mandell, W. (1966). A comparison of conditioning and psychotherapy in the treatment of functional enuresis. *Journal of Clinical Psychology, 39,* 226–230.

Doleys, D. M., Ciminero, A. R., Tollison, J. W., Williams, C. L., & Wells, K. D. (1977). Dry-bed training and retention control training: A comparison. *Behavior Therapy, 8,* 541–548.

Dunn, L. M., & Dunn, L. M. (1981). *Peabody Picture Vocabulary Test—Revised.* Nashville, TN: American Guidance Services, Inc.

Forsythe, W. I., & Redmond, A. (1974). Enuresis and spontaneous cure rate: Study of 1129 enuretics. *Archives of Diseases of Childhood, 49,* 259–263.

Geffken, G. R., Johnson, S. B., & Walker, D. (1986). Behavioral interventions for childhood nocturnal enuresis: The differential effect of bladder capacity on treatment progress and outcome. *Health Psychology, 5,* 261–272.

Harris, L. S., & Purohit, A. P. (1977). Bladder training and enuresis: A controlled trial. *Behavior Research and Therapy, 15,* 485–490.

Johnson, S. B. (1980). Enuresis. In R. Daitzman (Ed.), *Clinical behavior therapy and behavior modification* (Vol. I, pp. 81–142). New York: Garland.

Johnson, S. B. (1983). The treatment of enuresis. In P. Kellar & L. Ritt (Eds.). *Innovations in clinical practice: A source book* (pp. 86–100)). Sarasota, FL: Professional Resource Exchange.

Kolvin, I., MacKeith, R., & Meadow, S. (1973). *Bladder control and enuresis, clinics in developmental medicine* (Nos. 48/49, pp. 95–101). Philadelphia: Lippincott.

McConaghy, N. (1969). A controlled trial of imipramine, amphetamine, pad-and-bell conditioning and random awakening in the treatment of nocturnal enuresis. *Medical Journal of Australia, 2,* 237–239.

Morgan, R. T., & Young, G. C. (1975). Parental attitudes and the conditioning treatment of childhood enuresis. *Behaviour Research and Therapy, 13,* 197–199.

Mowrer, O. H., & Mowrer, W. M. (1938). Enuresis—A method for its study and treatment. *American Journal of Orthopsychiatry, 8,* 436–459.

Muellner, S. R. (1960). Development of urinary control in children. *Journal of the American Medical Association, 172,* 1256–1261.

Paschalis, A. P., Kimmel, H. D., & Kimmel, E. (1972). Further study of diurnal instrumental conditioning in the treatment of enuresis nocturna. *Journal of Behavior Therapy and Experimental Psychiatry, 3,* 253–256.

Peterson, D. R. (1961). Behavior problems of middle childhood. *Journal of Consulting Psychology, 25,* 205–209.

Piers, E. V., & Harris, D. B. (1969). *The Piers–Harris Children's Self-Concept Scale.* Nashville, TN: Counselor Recordings and Tests.

Quay, H. C. (1986). Classification. In H. C. Quay & J. W. Werry (Eds.), *Psychopathological disorders in childhood* (pp. 1–34). New York: Wiley.

Quay, H. C., & Peterson, D. R. (1975). *Manual for the behavior problem checklist.* Unpublished manuscript, University of Miami, Coral Gables, FL.

Ross, A. O. (1981). *Child behavior therapy: Principles, procedures, empirical basis.* New York: Wiley.

Rutter, M., Yule, W., & Graham, P. (1973). Enuresis and behavioral deviance: Some epidemiological considerations. In I. Kolvin, R. MacKeith, and S. Meadows (Eds.), *Bladder control and enuresis, clinics in developmental medicine* (Nos. 48/49, pp. 137–150). Philadelphia: Lippincott.

Schwartz, S., & Johnson, J. H. (1981). *Psychopathology of childhood: A clinical-experimental approach.* New York: Pergamon.

Starfield, B. (1967). Functional bladder capacity in enuretic and non-enuretic children. *Journal of Pediatrics, 70,* 777–781.

Starfield, B., & Mellits, E. D. (1968). Increase in functional bladder capacity and improvements in enuresis. *Journal of Pediatrics, 72*(4), 483–487.

Vulliamy, D. (1956). The day and night output of urine in enuresis. *Archives of Disease in Childhood, 31,* 439–443.

Wagner, W. G., & Geffken, G. R. (1986). Enuretic children: How they view their wetting behavior. *Child Study Journal, 16*(1), 13–18.

Wagner, W. G., Johnson, S. B., Walker, D., Carter, R., & Wittmer, J. (1982). A controlled comparison of two treatments for nocturnal enuresis. *Journal of Pediatrics, 101,* 302–307.

Werry, J. S., & Cohrssen, J. (1965). Enuresis—an etiologic and therapeutic study. *Journal of Pediatrics, 67,* 423–431.

Zaleski, A., Gerrard, J. W., & Shokier, M. H. (1973). Nocturnal enuresis: The importance of a small bladder capacity. In I. Kolvin, R. MacKeith, & S. Meadow (Eds.), *Bladder control and enuresis, clinics in developmental medicine* (Nos. 48/49, pp. 95–101). Philadelphia: Lippincott.

15
Multidisciplinary Treatment of Encopretic Children

STEVEN C. PARKISON
PATRICK C. KELLY

Functional encopresis is a common childhood condition occurring in approximately 3% of the general pediatric population (Levine, 1975). It can have devastating effects on a child's psychological development, and yet, the vast majority of children with encopresis can be quickly and effectively treated with a proper combination of medical, psychological, and dietary interventions. In this chapter we will define the disorder, explain our approach to encopretic children, and then describe the treatment of two children.

Functional encopresis as defined by the revised third edition of Diagnostic and Statistical Manual of Mental Disorders (DSM-III-R) is the "repeated passage of feces into places not appropriate for that purpose (e.g., clothing, floor) whether involuntary or intentional" (American Psychiatric Association, 1987, p. 83). This definition is much improved over the one given in DSM-III which emphasized an intentional or voluntary etiology for encopresis. Current pediatric and psychological literature strongly suggests that voluntary soiling is, at best, highly unusual. Doley's (1979) definition remains the most consistent with the current literature: "the passage of fecal material of any amount or consistency into clothes or other generally unacceptable areas in the absence of any organic pathology beyond the age of three years" (p. 186).

Steven C. Parkison. Clinical Psychology Service, Department of Psychiatry, Madigan Army Medical Center, Tacoma, Washington.

Patrick C. Kelly. Department of Pediatrics, Developmental Pediatrics Section, Madigan Army Medical Center, Tacoma, Washington.

This paper was submitted when the authors were at the Exceptional Family Member Department, Department of Army, 97th General Hospital, Frankfurt Army Regional Medical Center, Frankfurt, West Germany.

Some clinicians further define a primary and secondary encopresis (Anthony, 1957; Doleys, Schwartz, & Ciminero, 1981), the former applied to children past the age of 4 years who have not had 1 year of bowel continence and the later applied to children past 4 who have had a year of bowel control. In clinical practice these distinctions are arbitrary, and there is little research support that this distinction aids in designing a specific treatment program. Encopresis is reported to be more common in boys than girls by a 6:1 ratio (Levine, 1975; Newson & Newson, 1986).

The primary etiology of encopresis, while a matter of extensive speculation by various disciplines, remains unclear. The suggested initiating factors range from major to minor psychological, anatomical, physiological, and dietary abnormalities. The most likely explanation is that the causes of encopresis are multifaceted and interrelated.

The physiological basis of encopresis is chronic, or intermittent, retention of feces, resulting in distension of the rectum and colon leading to a lack of sensitivity for the defecation reflex. The absorption of water from the fecal material is increased and the stools become large and hard. Attempted passage of the stools often results in pain and toilet avoidance, which worsens the situation. Long-standing problems lead to rectal impaction, and the watery contents of the higher colon are passed around the retained stool resulting in involuntary soiling. The loss of sensory feedback from the bowel makes the child unaware that he/she is about to pass fecal material. This soiling is generally represented by liquid staining of the underwear rather than complete bowel movements and may at times be difficult to distinguish from poor bathroom hygiene. A discussion with the child and parent regarding what actually is occurring usually resolves this issue. The approach to intervention is to ensure that the colon is allowed to remain undistended for sufficient time to restore normal tone and defecation reflexes. While the initiating factor may be of emotional, physical, nutritional, or multiple etiologies, in most cases it is indeterminable at the time of presentation.

Several excellent treatment protocols have appeared in the research literature, beginning with a pediatric approach to encopresis by Davidson (1958). Davidson's program involves a daily dose of mineral oil with increases in this dose until normal bowel function is restored. Additionally, Davidson recommended alterations in diet by increasing fruit and decreasing dairy products such as milk and cheese. This program was shown to be highly effective in the treatment of 119 encopretic children with 90% of the children considered treatment successes (Davidson, Kugler, & Bauer, 1963).

Levine and Bakow (1976) followed 110 encopretic children utilizing a program involving enemas and suppositories for a clean out period, followed by daily doses of mineral oil and scheduled toilet sitting twice a day. At 1 year follow-up, 80% of the children were either markedly improved or showed some improvement. Wright (1973) and Wright and Walker (1977) have described a slightly different approach to the treatment of encopresis with a program involving the use of positive reinforcement for unassisted bowel movements after an initial clean-out period. Bowel accidents are punished with such things as loss of privileges or time-out. Other programs utilizing similar behavioral steps have placed a much greater emphasis on the dietary changes that facilitate regular bowel functioning (Christophersen & Berman, 1978; Christophersen & Rainey, 1976; Christophersen & Rapoff, 1983). The issue of symptom substitution, considered by some clinicians as problematic in directly treating conditions such as encopresis, was addressed by Levine, Mazonson, and Bakow (1980). This study compared a group of children whose encopresis was successfully treated with another group who were refractory to treatment. It was clearly demonstrated on 3-year follow-up that encopresis can be directly treated with little fear of symptom substitution.

Functional encopresis frequently has devastating effects on a child's self-esteem and peer interactions. Encopretic children feel guilt and shame at their lack of control over their own bowel function. They constantly fear discovery of their problem by their peers as they very often become the focus of ridicule both in the school and in their neighborhood. This leads to the child's being excluded from important peer interactions. In our experience, children with encopresis frequently develop problems such as depression, low self-esteem, and poor academic performance.

Our developmental disabilities clinic is the largest and most specialized of the three which comprise the Exceptional Family Member Department of the United States Army's Regional Medical Center in Frankfurt, West Germany. The clinic is comprised of 11 co-located health care sections including developmental pediatrics, pediatric psychology, child psychiatry, social work, occupational therapy, physical therapy, community health nursing, dietary–nutrition, optometry, audiology, and speech and language pathology. Pediatric neurology and orthopedics are actively involved on a regular basis but are not located within our clinic. Services are available to children from birth to 21 years of age with mild to severe handicapping conditions of a physical, developmental, behavioral, emotional, or educational nature. Referrals are accepted from health care providers, schools, child development centers, and parents. There are currently over 2,000 active cases with approximately 30,000 visits per year. Evaluations are conducted in a multidisciplinary fashion involving all sections when deemed appropriate and include a staffing (professional group discussion) of each case to ensure overall direction and prioritization of therapeutic interventions. Each child and family is assigned a case manager who acts as a liaison between the patients and the parents and other medical or educational professionals. All disciplines function in the role of case managers. Treatment is given in the clinic, hospital, child development centers, homes, and in the 29 Department of Defense Dependent Schools serviced by the department.

The departmental philosophy is one of "lively professional argument" with all disciplines participating equally. We strongly encourage that individuals in such a setting display an attitude of respect for the opinions of professionals in other disciplines and be capable and willing to aggressively convey their own findings and suggestions to the other team members. The close association of the various medical specialties has led to the development of many specialized multidisciplinary treatment programs such as the one for encopresis presented in this chapter.

We utilize a team approach in treating the encopretic child. The team consists of a developmental pediatrician, pediatric psychologist, and a registered dietitian, with the pediatric psychologist usually acting as the primary therapist and case manager. It is emphasized to the parents and child that there is a primary therapist with the other professionals functioning in important, but supportive roles. The amount of professional time spent on evaluation and program initiation may seem extensive; however, if one examines this cost against inefficient and ineffective splintered approaches to encopresis treatment, our team method appears to be cost-effective. Our case reports illustrate this multidisciplinary approach.

During initial evaluation the physician obtains a complete medical history and performs a thorough physical and neurological examination, including a digital rectal examination. This evaluation is used to elicit signs and symptoms consistent with a diagnosis of functional encopresis and to ascertain the likelihood of previously unrecognized organic pathology. Constipation and resultant encopresis may be due to defective rectal filling or emptying and the differential diagnosis among other disorders includes: hypothyroidism, medication usage (e.g., opiates), bowel obstruction by structural anomaly, or Hirschsprung disease (Hamilton, 1983). Such definable organic causes are in our experience rarely encountered in the school-aged child. While Hirschsprung disease is frequently discussed in the differential diagnosis, the clinical presentation of these two disorders is quite different. Patients with Hirschsprung disease have a history of soiling difficulties dating from birth or the first weeks of life with symptoms of intestinal obstruction such as vomiting, abdominal distension, and failure to pass stool. Later in life these children display chronic constipation and on rectal examination have tight anal tone without large amounts of feces in the ampulla. Conversely, children with functional encopresis usually do not have symptoms early in life and characteristically display patulous anal tone and an ampulla packed with feces.

An excellent comparison of Hirschsprung disease and encopresis is presented by Levine (1981). Patients with ultrashort-segment Hirschsprung disease may demonstrate the clinical features of functional encopresis and, while a more complete discussion of this controversial disorder is beyond the scope of this chapter, we view a 3-month trial of our program in the school-aged chronic encopretic prior to consideration of ultrashort-segment Hirschsprung disease as entirely appropriate.

The psychologist interviews the parents and child to determine whether the child displays evidence of a significant emotional disturbance, toileting fears such as avoidance of public facilities (Gavanski, 1971), past history of sexual abuse, or family problems which may interfere with conducting the treatment program. Reports of classroom attitude, behavior, and performance are routinely obtained from standard departmental teacher questionnaires, often supplemented by direct teacher contact or indirectly from departmental personnel working with the child in the school. Despite the fact that most of the children referred to this clinic have long-standing encopresis which has been refractory to prior treatment, it is the exception to find a serious emotional etiological component to the problem.

The nutritionist interviews the parents, obtains a dietary history, and develops nutritional goals. The direct participation of a dietitian is perhaps a unique feature of this program when compared with other published reports of encopresis treatment. Although many authorities consider diet a frequent contributory component, the inclusion of a registered dietitian on the treatment team is unusual in the approaches we have reviewed. The typical approach involves a clinician (usually physician or psychologist) utilizing a dietary handout with, we suspect, little information regarding prior family dietary practices and little discussion of the importance of this aspect to the protocol. In our experience poor dietary practices are frequently encountered in the encopretic children referred to our program.

At our clinic, all involved health care providers hold the same basic view of the physiology and treatment of encopresis, and we find this critically important in order to avoid giving the parents or children conflicting advice. The parents and children are told that we understand the problem and can help resolve it in a relatively short period of time. All professionals reinforce the idea that the family has come to the right place.

While we have emphasized that most children presenting with encopresis do not have significant emotional problems, we have had selected cases in which this did appear to be the case, for example, sexual abuse. Under these circumstances, it has been our practice to refer the family to the child psychiatry service in our clinic for evaluation and treatment of the emotional problems, rather than instituting the encopresis program. The psychotherapist will then assume the role of case manager and refer the patient back to our encopresis treatment program when they have determined that the child has been adequately prepared for this type of intervention. While these children require more extensive therapy and a more cautious approach, the underlying anatomical and physiological basis as explained previously does not change, and we do not alter the essential elements of our treatment approach. In these limited number of cases we have been successful in resolving the encopresis, and this appears to have made an important contribution to the overall therapeutic effort. Additionally, children with clearly organic etiologies, for example, myelomeningocele, respond quite well to our approach. Clearly an explanation of the physiological aspects in such cases must be altered. We have also successfully employed this program with very little modification in children with mild to moderate mental retardation.

Another observation is the frequency of the coexistence of functional encopresis and enuresis. In some cases the enuresis appears to be a secondary problem apparently related to limited bladder capacity as a result of pressure on the bladder produced by distension of the rectum and colon by retained feces. Our approach as been to medically evaluate the problems individually, but given a work-up which does not suggest an organic defect for either the encopresis or enuresis, we choose to defer intervention for the enuresis, pending the completion of the program for encopresis. In some cases the encopresis program resolves the enuresis, but others require a separate program for the urinary accidents.

Clearly, the physiological aspects of encopresis make the soiling episodes involuntary; however, the majority of patients appear to have residual bowel sensations, and we speculate that most childhood environments (school and playground) do not allow adequate time for an appropriate response. A limited number of children display such severe and long-standing impaction and dilatation as to require hospitalization for bowel evacuation in a program such as that described by Levine (1983).

For the initial session we ask both parents to attend, a requirement we consider important for several reasons. First, it allows the clinicians the opportunity to obtain information from both parents and to assess their views and opinions on the subject. Second, it is important that both parents hear our explanation of encopresis and the physiological basis for the problem so that we avoid problems of miscommunication between parents. Third, it allows us the opportunity to ally the family in the total treatment process which becomes particularly critical when dealing with older children who are uncomfortable with the administration of an enema or suppository by the opposite-sexed parent. Additionally, we obtain a complete history of prior attempts at treatment. We have found this practice produces a wealth of information about what has or has not worked in the past, and also reveals information about parental compliance with previous interventions.

Following this data gathering, the physiology of encopresis is explained to the parents and the child. Most parents seen in our program find this quite helpful because in the past they have not had anyone who explained why their child was soiling. We explain to the parents that their child's soiling is due to long-standing constipation that has led to an enlarged bowel and loss of the sensation and urge to have a bowel movement. Additionally, we utilize drawings and diagrams to further illustrate to the child and parents the anatomical–physiological mechanisms of the distended bowel. Levine (1983) has commented on how helpful this demystification process can be in furthering the treatment goals, and we utilize this explanation to answer a question that parents of encopretic children almost universally ask: "How can my child have an accident and not feel it until it is already in their pants?" Providing a physiological explanation for this question does a great deal to reduce the parent's anger at a child who they have felt was either lying about the accident or deliberately doing it to "get back" at them. We have also been impressed that the vast majority of children seen in our program do not know or have not heard of another child who has a soiling problem, and much like Levine (1983), we work to reduce the feelings of isolation this causes the child. After completing this explanation and allowing the parents and child an opportunity to ask questions, the program steps are explained to the parents and child.

The dietary portion of the program involves direct parent–child instruction supplemented with printed material. Suggested meal planning involves daily limitation of milk intake to three cups, elimination of cheese, four to six servings of high-fiber foods, and eight glasses of liquid. A well-balanced diet is explained and encouraged as well as physical exercise and adequate rest.

The medical/behavioral aspect of the program is a two-step approach to encopresis similar to that of Wright (1973) and Wright and Walker (1977). The initial step is to completely evacuate the child's bowel of impacted fecal material. To ensure completion of this procedure, we use a regime of daily enemas twice a day for 3 days with parents instructed in the proper administration of the enemas and then directed to give one in the morning and evening for 3 consecutive days. The quantity of solution given as an enema depends on the age and size of the child, with most children above age 8 years being given one hypophosphate enema (Fleets Adult) twice daily.

We have found that parents report the evacuation of a large amount of fecal material during the first day but even a larger amount the second day. While this clean-out period is longer than some others reported in the literature (Christophersen & Rapoff, 1983; Wright, 1973; Wright & Walker, 1977), it is our experience that it ensures a higher probability of success with the refractory encopretic child. We do not routinely utilize a pre- and postevacuation abdominal radiograph as suggested by some protocols (Barr, Levine, & Wilkinson, 1979; Levine, 1983). In cases in which the parents seem skeptical about the physiological explanation, the pediatrician has the parent repeat the digital rectal examination which demonstrates the markedly dilated ampulla packed with an impressive amount of hard stool. This graphically demonstrates to the parents that the physiology we have explained indeed applies to their child.

The second step is to establish normal bowel habits. During this phase of the program we request that the child attempt to have an unassisted bowel movement in the toilet in the morning. If the child is able to accomplish this task, we have the parents heavily reinforce the event. The parents are directed to lavishly praise the child for success and are instructed to give the child an individually wrapped reward (e.g., a small toy car). We have found that individually wrapping the rewards increases their power as reinforcers, and letting the child pick one from a group increases their power even further. If the child is unsuccessful in having a bowel movement after 5 minutes of sitting on the toilet, the parents are advised to insert a glycerin suppository and wait for up to 45 minutes for the suppository to stimulate a bowel movement. During this period the child can get dressed and eat breakfast. If the child successfully defecates with the aid of a suppository, he/she is praised by the parents and allowed to select a smaller individually wrapped gift. We generally recommend a value of approximately $1.00 for the larger gifts and 50¢ for the smaller gifts. Because parents frequently report having difficulty finding items that are rewarding and still cost 50¢, we advise them to buy larger items such as a bag of toy soldiers and divide the bag so the child receives one each time. If the child is unsuccessful with the previous steps, we instruct the parents to administer an enema and give no rewards. If the child does have a soiling accident we instruct the parents to help the child rinse out their underwear and pants and hang the items up to dry. We have not found the use of punishment for soiling accidents particularly helpful in resolving the problem.

An important aspect of our program is that of continued monitoring of the children. As a rule, if the child has not made significant gains (near or complete resolution in 3 months), further evaluation of the case is in order. We feel that careful follow-up is a more effective approach than the routine use of unpleasant, costly, and generally unnecessary medical and psychological tests prior to the institution of therapy.

Another issue to be faced is that of compliance. Our program is designed to ensure compliance from the outset and to continue the psychologist's supervision of the parents and children to verify that they strictly adhere to our directives. Even under these circumstances some parents will not comply, and this possibility must be constantly considered. A more easily resolved issue is that of professional compliance with our own program. Despite our familiarity with the problem of encopresis and our standardized approach, we recognize that at times there is a tendency to take shortcuts, for example, failure to emphasize the use of rewards or to make telephone contacts. Once a treatment approach has been designed, we strongly encourage that professional compliance be an integral part of an internal monitoring program.

While the program is largely standardized, it is not rigid as we can and do make appropriate alterations in individual cases and feel that our multidisciplinary approach makes this important feature possible. In addition, the parents are advised from the outset that although we have every confidence in resolving the problem, there is a possibility of relapse, and this must be accepted and appropriately treated if it occurs.

The following are two case reports of encopretic children seen in our clinic. These cases were selected to display some of the typical features and possible pitfalls that health care professionals will face in the treatment of this disorder. Both of these children's initial evaluations were similar, but diametrically different in their treatment courses. Debbie, in the first case, illustrates a more typical experience of ours. Ronny, in the second case, illustrates a less frequently encountered situation, but one which displays features with which the clinician should be familiar. The coexistent medical, psychological, academic, dietary, and family problems in these cases are not unusual and actually an underestimation of the typical referral case to this clinic. Both authors have worked in less specialized settings accepting primary psychological and general pediatric referrals and feel that these cases represent a common experience for clinicians in such settings. We have altered the names and histories in order to protect the identities of the children, but the significant events in evaluation and treatment remain intact.

CASE EXAMPLE

Debbie was a 9-year-old girl referred to our encopresis program with a chronic history of soiling that had been refractory to past treatment interventions. At the time of the referral Debbie was soiling twice a day.

Debbie was the product of a full-term pregnancy complicated in the seventh month by maternal hypertension. Her delivery was by cesarean section due to failure of progression during the labor. She had a birth weight of 9 pounds, 10 ounces and Apgar scores of 9 at both 1 and 5 minutes. Debbie's neonatal period was uneventful, but in her first year of life she was noted to be mildly anemic and was treated with supplemental iron until age 4 years. At age 6 Debbie was found to have a bilateral sensorineural hearing loss of undetermined etiology and was fitted with hearing aids. The child had no hospitalizations, serious injuries, known allergies, and was taking no medications at the time of evaluation. Her early developmental milestones were reportedly in the normal range.

Debbie was toilet trained for both bowel and bladder at approximately 2 years of age. The parents noted no particular problems with her toilet training and felt she achieved this milestone rather easily, although her mother reported that she was frequently constipated and required periodic laxatives. Debbie began daily soiling at age 5 and was seen by a physician who told the parents that she would probably outgrow the problem. However, her encopresis continued to worsen until age 7 when she was soiling twice daily. She was again seen by a physician who treated her with mineral oil, and while she showed improvement on this regime for 2 to 3 weeks, she later resumed soiling one to two times per week. She continued on the mineral oil regime for 6 months, until her mother returned to the physician who told her that Debbie's soiling was probably due to a psychological problem, and referred them to a psychiatrist. The psychiatrist, by the parents' report, felt that Debbie's encopresis was related to her low self-esteem and hearing loss, and followed her for 6 months in individual child psychotherapy. Debbie's encopresis continued, and she was withdrawn from treatment when the family moved to another area. Shortly after the family arrived in this area, Debbie was seen by a physician who referred her to our clinic.

Academically, Debbie had been doing quite poorly in school. She was in the third grade and doing below average work. Debbie had not attended a preschool and had started kindergarten at age 5. She had progressed satisfactorily until the present school year when her teacher began to note her declining academic performance. Her teacher reported on our school referral report that Debbie was self-conscious of her bowel accidents at school, and would be very embarrassed when the other children remarked about her smelling bad. Her behavior was appropriate, and other than the encopresis, she did not represent a problem to the school. The audiological section of our clinic was involved with this child and assured us that her current audiological therapy and academic placement were appropriate.

Psychologically, Debbie was noted to be a shy child who did not interact well with other children and had few friends. Her mother reported that this behavior began when she was 8 years old and had gradually increased over the past school year. Her parents had encouraged her to go out and play with other children in her neighborhood, but Debbie increasingly preferred to stay at home in her room. No history of sexual abuse was given, and she reportedly did not show any unusual fears of toileting facilities. In talking to Debbie without her parents present, it was clear to us that she had a very low self-concept as she tearfully expressed the belief that there must be something very wrong with her because she was so "fat," had to wear hearing aids, and could not control her bowels.

Her nutritional history was significant for a poor diet and minimal physical exercise. She was also found to be 12 pounds overweight. Debbie had frequent snacks of cookies, cheese, and milk and her fiber intake was felt to be inadequate. It appeared that her weight problem, lack of physical exercise, and poor diet were contributing not only to her encopresis, but also to her low self-concept.

On physical examination the developmental pediatrician noted Debbie had a mildly distended abdomen, patulous anal tone, and a dilated rectal vault containing a large amount of fecal material.

Debbie's case, while typical, displays several significant features. First, her encopresis had been long-standing, and although there were periods of reduced soiling, it is very likely that she had been chronically constipated. The use of an iron supplement from 1 to 4 years may have contributed to this problem. She had been evaluated by several professionals and had failed prior attempts at intervention. Finally, Debbie's hearing impairment was a coexisting feature.

In formulating a treatment strategy for this case, there were several areas of particular importance. The parents were convinced that Debbie was willfully soiling and until this view of her problem could be changed and the tension it created in the family reduced, there was a high probability that parental compliance would be low. The parents had previously tried a laxative treatment program that had failed, and we hypothesized they were likely to assume that we were employing a previously unsuccessful protocol. In addition, the parents and Debbie appeared to be quite demoralized by her problems.

Both parents attended the initial evaluation and were given a complete explanation of the physiological basis of Debbie's encopresis. We provided information and written material for dietary alterations, and they acknowledged understanding of the instructions. Debbie and her parents were receptive and anxious to begin, with Debbie electing to have the suppositories and enemas administered by her mother. The 3-day clean-out was explained, and Debbie's parents were then instructed to begin the behavioral program on the morning of the fourth day. The behavioral program consisted of the following steps. Debbie would be awakened 1 hour earlier, and when fully awake, be asked to sit on the toilet and try to have a bowel movement. She would be required to sit on the toilet no more than 5 minutes, and if she was able to produce approximately one-half a cup of feces, she received a reward. If she was unsuccessful, her mother would insert a glycerin suppository, and Debbie could continue to get dressed for school or play. If during this period she was successful in having a bowel movement of the amount previously stated, she would receive a small reward. If after 45 minutes she had not had a bowel movement, she was to be given an enema and would receive no reward. As the pediatric psychologist on the team, I (S. P.) was assigned as case manager and continued to follow Debbie.

Four days after the session I (S. P.) contacted Debbie's mother to check on her progress. We believe phone calls to be a valuable part of the treatment program, and informal parent feedback has substantiated that the phone calls accomplish two things. The first and most obvious is that we have an opportunity to answer any of the parents' questions and correct any errors they may be making in implementing the treatment program. The second is that it communicates to the parents that we are genuinely interested in their child's problem and committed to assisting in resolving it. Many parents, when questioned at the termination of treatment, have stated that the telephone calls were very important in successfully completing the program, stating that having the doctor make an unsolicited call to check their child's progress was a real morale boost.

In Debbie's case the mother reported that the 3-day clean-out period had gone well and that they had been impressed with the amount of fecal material evacuated. The morning before the parents were contacted, Debbie had begun the behavioral program, and although she had been unable to have a bowel movement on her own, she had been successful with the use of a suppository.

I met with the family for the second session in the clinic 4 days after the phone call, and the mother reported that there had not been any soiling since we began the program. Debbie had been able to have bowel movements 2 mornings on her own and had required a suppository on the other mornings. She was producing more than a cupful of feces with the suppositories and had not required any enemas after the clean-out period. Debbie and her parents were satisfied with these results. The family met briefly with the dietitian and further alterations to Debbie's diet were suggested. I again emphasized to her parents that it requires time for a child's bowel to regain its normal tone and that they had done a very good job following our instructions. They were instructed to continue the program and return in 1 week.

For the next 2 weekly sessions Debbie and her parents reported that she had stopped soiling, and required suppositories only infrequently. One enema had been given during this period when Debbie had been unsuccessful with the suppository. Dietary changes had been implemented by the family, and Debbie had adapted to these changes very well.

At the fifth session, 2½ months after her initial clean-out, the parents reported to me that Debbie had been successful in having unassisted bowel movements for the last 2 weeks. Debbie told me that for the first time she could feel the sensations associated with having a full rectal vault and the urge to defecate. Her parents were excited about this development and happy that there had not been a soiling episode since they had started the program. Debbie appeared more animated than in her past sessions, and she showed me the numerous Smurfs (small plastic miniatures of cartoon characters) that she had earned as rewards for her successes. Our dietitian reviewed Debbie's diet and felt that Debbie was now consuming more appropriate foods less likely to contribute to her constipation. The parents also reported that she was spending more time outside and getting much more exercise. I congratulated Debbie and her parents on their success and directed them to continue with the program.

By the sixth session, 3 weeks later, Debbie had still not soiled, and she was having two bowel movements a day. The Smurfs were beginning to mount up, and Debbie appeared to be a happier child. Her distended abdomen had disappeared and the parents were delighted with her progress. Debbie's mother remarked in this session that it was like she had her "old Debbie back." A report from the school revealed that her academic performance had improved, and her parents reported that she now had a girlfriend with whom she spend considerable time playing outside the house.

Debbie continued to progress and 6 months later she was doing very well with establishment of normal and regular bowel habits and no resumption of the soiling. Debbie's psychological state had continued to improve, and the concerns we initially had about her adjustment were no longer present. In addition, Debbie's diet was now considered quite good and her weight was gradually returning to normal limits for her height. Her interest in receiving the rewards had waned soon after the sixth session, and she no longer received rewards for her bowel movements. We have found that interest in material rewards for successful bowel movements fades out independently, and we advise that the parents allow this to occur rather than abruptly discontinue the reinforcers and risk a conflict with the child.

Debbie's treatment course is representative of those of the vast majority of children treated in our program. The parents were compliant in following instructions and the family was functional and supportive of Debbie. In analyzing her past treatment failures, we feel that previous intervention plans were incomplete and/or lacked consistent follow-up. Over the past few years we have come to appreciate the critical nature of these factors.

CASE EXAMPLE

Ronny was an 11-year-old boy referred to our clinic and presenting with a chronic history of fecal soiling dating from 4 years of age. He had been refractory to a number of interventions in the past and at the time of referral was soiling four to five times a day. Past medical evaluations had proved negative for any disease process that would account for his encopresis.

Ronny was the product of a normal pregnancy, labor, and delivery. His birth weight was 9 pounds, 12 ounces, and Apgar scores were unknown. While his neonatal period was uneventful, he had one hospitalization at 30 months after a toxic ingestion of iron tablets for which he spent 1 day in intensive care and 3 days on the pediatric ward. His follow-up from this incident was normal with no long-term effects noted. Ronny had no other hospitalizations, serious injuries, or significant illnesses and was taking no medications at the time of referral. His early developmental milestones were reportedly in the normal range.

Ronny was toilet trained for bowel and bladder at approximately 2 years of age, and his parents reported no problems with his achieving this milestone. His mother became concerned about Ronny's toileting at 4 years of age, when she noted daily soiling, and he was subsequently seen by a physician who placed him on a daily regime of mineral oil, which was continued for 1 year with little improvement. This treatment was discontinued when the family moved from the area, but at age 6 the mother again consulted a physician, and was instructed to institute a program very similar to our own. She reported that Ronny did achieve cessation of the soiling and resumption of regular bowel habits for a 2-month period, but he tired of the program and resumed soiling. At a follow-up visit the physician told the mother that he felt the encopresis was a psychological problem and directed Ronny to a psychologist, but the mother did not follow through on this referral. When Ronny was 8 years old, the mother once again sought the advice of a physician who began a regime of oral laxatives and directed the mother to punish Ronny with loss of privileges or time-out when he soiled. The mother reported that this attempt only made Ronny angry, and she discontinued it after a short period.

Ronny's academic performance had always been marginal, but he had done particularly poorly in the past school year. Our standard school report revealed that Ronny was refusing to turn in homework and had been openly defiant toward his teachers. The school had recently completed a psychoeducational assessment to determine if he might have a learning disability, but his test scores did not support this possibility. His mother blamed the school for much of Ronny's problems and contended that the teachers had been picking on him.

The physical examination during the initial visit to our clinic was remarkable only for patulous anal tone and a dilated rectal vault with a large amount of fecal material. However, while this and previous medical evaluations had failed to reveal a specific organic defect, the mother maintained that an unidentified disease process might be the etiology of her child's current problems.

Psychologically, Ronny presented as a rather sullen, withdrawn youngster who initially spoke very little. His mother reported that he had difficulty making friends, and when he did play with other children that frequently ended in a fight. This behavior had apparently worsened over the last several years, and Ronny's mother felt these problems were due to the other children teasing him about his soiling. No history of sexual abuse was given, and he reportedly did not show any unusual fear of toileting facilities. In talking with Ronny alone, it was quite apparent to me (S. P.) that he was unhappy. He was very reluctant to discuss any of his problems, preferring to blame his difficulties on others. It took considerable time during this session before he would acknowledge his soiling, but when he did it was clear he wanted to cooperate in resolving his encopresis. While I did not feel Ronny had a significant emotional disorder as such, it did appear he was having considerable emotional distress, and I felt his encopresis was a major contributory factor to his problems.

His nutritional history was significant for a low intake of fiber and fluids, but his intake of dairy products was considered normal. His weight was appropriate for his height, and although his mother reported that he was not very active, he did manage to get what was considered adequate exercise.

Following our protocol, it had been requested that both parents attend the initial evaluation, but only Ronny and his mother appeared because the father had reportedly been called away that morning. Rather than reschedule the meeting, we agreed to see them because they had driven a considerable distance.

The team presented the mother with the results of the evaluation and explained the physiological basis of Ronny's problem. The mother was receptive to our conceptualization, and both she and Ronny voiced their willingness to begin treatment. After explaining the entire program to Ronny and his mother, Ronny was asked whom he preferred to administer the enemas and suppositories. After considerable discussion it was decided that his mother would perform this task. Due to the mother's work schedule, a follow-up appointment with the pediatric psychologist was scheduled in 2 weeks and a telephone call in 1 week. Additionally, we requested that the father be present for the follow-up visit.

In formulating our treatment strategy for Ronny we felt that there were several important areas to consider. Ronny, like Debbie, had been through three previous treatment programs which had failed, and we speculated that at least part of the reason was a lack of compliance by the parents. If our program was to be successful, we had to ensure that the parents continued the program for at least 3 months. Another area of concern was the mother's view of the problem as a disease process, and until this perception could be changed it was likely that parental compliance would be problematic. We also considered the potential problem of having the mother administer enemas to her 11-year-old son. Generally by this age, boys prefer to have the enemas administered by their fathers, but when asked whom he preferred to administer the enemas, Ronny said that it did not matter to him.

As the pediatric psychologist and case manager, I (S. P.) contacted the mother by telephone after 1 week for a progress report. She reported that the initial clean-out period had gone well, but felt Ronny was not making further progress. While Ronny had not soiled in the last 3 days, he still had not had an unassisted bowel movement. In reviewing the program the mother reported that she was giving the enema immediately after Ronny had failed to have an unassisted bowel movement and then giving a suppository after the enema. The mother's misunderstanding of the sequence of suppository then enema administration was discussed, and she was assured that the 3 days without soiling represented progress. Ronny's mother reported that she had decided to give him money as a reinforcer for successful toileting. In my experience, money is frequently not as powerful a reinforcer as the wrapped gifts because often after accumulating a few dollars, children "retire" and lose interest in money as a reinforcement. I discussed this with the mother, but she felt this would not be the case with Ronny. The dietary alterations were also discussed, and the mother reported that she had managed to increase Ronny's intake of fiber; but he still was resistant to the increases in fluid such as fruit juices that the dietitian had suggested. She was instructed to continue the program and bring the family in for their scheduled appointment.

The mother and Ronny returned to the clinic 2 weeks into the treatment program. The mother again explained that the father had planned to come to the appointment but had been called away that morning. The second failure for the father to appear was troublesome, but the nature of our clinic's population does not make such an occurrence particularly unusual in that soldiers in Europe are frequently called for field duty on very short notice. Initially Ronny's mother reported that he had made no progress, but upon further interview, she noted that he had not soiled in the last 10 days. The mother seemed to reluctantly view this as progress but maintained that he still had not had an unassisted bowel movement or a bowel movement with just the suppository. I (S. P.) reviewed the program, including dietary interventions, with the mother and it appeared that she was following our instructions. Time was spent with Ronny alone discussing the program and how he thought he was progressing. Ronny felt that he was doing better and reported that while he did try to have a bowel movement, he was unable to defecate either on his own or with the suppository. I still felt that the lack of soiling was a positive sign and warranted continuation of the program. We scheduled the next appointment 2 weeks later with instructions to the mother to call if she had any questions or felt that the program was not progressing.

Ronny's mother called 2 days before the next appointment and reported that Ronny had 5 days of soiling episodes. She reported that he had been unable to have a bowel movement either on his own or with the suppository, and the enemas had produced very little material. I requested that the parents and Ronny come in for their appointment the next day to discuss this development. Only Ronny and his mother came to this appointment, and it was immediately clear that Ronny was back to daily soiling. I explained that I could not understand why the child had continued to soil despite daily enemas, and when confronted, the mother revealed that the enemas had been given infrequently and only when she felt they were necessary. The pediatrician and nutritionist at my request reevaluated Ronny during this visit and a restaffing of his case was performed. The team decided that since the rectal examination was still positive for impaction, the clean-out procedure should be repeated for 2 days and the program restarted. The mother agreed to this, and after all aspects of the program were explained again, another appointment was scheduled in 2 weeks. A call to Ronny's mother after 4 days revealed that the clean-out had gone well and Ronny had again stopped soiling.

During the next appointment with the psychologist the mother reported that there still had not been an unassisted bowel movement but did report three bowel movements with the appropriate use of the suppositories.

She reported three bowel accidents in the last 2 weeks, but attributed these to a viral illness. I felt that Ronny was once again making progress and congratulated both Ronny and his mother on their hard work.

During the fifth session, 2 months after the initial evaluation, the family was scheduled to see both the psychologist and the nutritionist. The father again failed to make the appointment, and during the sessions the mother gave conflicting accounts to the nutritionist and psychologist on how well Ronny was doing on the program. She reported to the psychologist that Ronny was doing quite well, but told the dietitian that the diet was a failure because Ronny was continuing to soil. The mother continued to question the possibility of an unrecognized organic factor and further questioned the possible need of other medical approaches even in the absence of organic pathology. The pediatrician was alerted to this development and, after a third staffing of the case, the team felt that rather than confront the mother again a thorough medical work-up should be completed to definitively rule out an organic basis for the soiling. The mother and child were advised of this, and all agreed that given an unrewarding evaluation the program would be reinstituted and strictly followed.

Another consideration at this point could have been a brief hospitalization for a clean-out period as described by Levine (1983). In Ronnie's case this appeared inappropriate in that the clean-out seemed to have been effective, and the issue was one of unidentified organic pathology versus lack of compliance with the follow-up program. Although we do not dispute the need for inpatient clean-outs in selected cases, we feel that these cases are extremely rare. We have utilized this method and caution that the staff of the pediatric ward must understand the problem and the treatment program to fully support the approach. In the absence of this type of setting, we consider hospitalization as generally ill-advised.

As part of the subsequent outpatient evaluation a barium enema was obtained. This study was interpreted as essentially normal, but the radiologist did note that the mucosal pattern in the rectosigmoid colon was suspicious for shallow ulcerations which are often seen in children with chronic constipation or mechanical trauma (enemas and other manipulations); however, other causes for these findings, such as inflammatory bowel disease, could not be ruled out. The likely etiology of these findings was explained to the mother by the pediatrician (P. K.), but she expectedly, and probably reasonably, requested further subspecialty opinion on her son's condition. Ronny was then referred to a university-based pediatric gastroenterologist.

After extensive medical evaluation this specialist concluded that there was no evidence of organic pathology and suggested to the mother that she was obstructing the resolution of her child's encopresis and that our instructions should be strictly followed. The mother returned to our clinic in tears, complaining to the psychologist about the rude physician, but after calming, she no longer questioned the possibility of an undetected medical problem. Another appointment was scheduled for the next week, and for this session I (S. P.) absolutely required that the father be present.

For this session both parents and Ronny were present. I (S. P.) reviewed the treatment to date and my opinion that Ronny's problems were quite possibly functional in the family. This was my first meeting with the father, and in observing his interactions with his wife and Ronny it was obvious that he was very detached from his family. His concern with Ronny's problems seemed superficial, and he was extremely distant from his wife. Ronny's mother became quite angry with her husband for what she perceived as abandonment of both herself and Ronny and, as the session progressed, it was clear that the family dynamics, specifically the marital conflict and the father's detachment, would have to be addressed before progress on the encopresis could be made. While marital conflict had been denied in the initial evaluation, it was now clear that the family was quite dysfunctional. With some difficulty I was able to convince the parents that family therapy was the next appropriate step in treatment and referred them to a therapist in our clinic.

Over the course of the next few months the family engaged in therapy and was gradually able to resolve many problem issues. Briefly, the family therapist felt that Ronny and his mother were using Ronny's problems in an attempt to draw the father into the family. The harder they tried to draw the father in, the more he distanced himself from Ronny and a wife he felt was smothering. At the request of the therapist, I (S. P.) restarted the encopresis program 2 months into family therapy, but this time placed the father in charge of the treatment. Within 2 months Ronny had ceased soiling and was having regular unassisted bowel movements. Follow-up 6 months after the last treatment session revealed that Ronny was toileting appropriately with no resumption of his soiling.

We feel this case is an excellent example of what may first appear to be a straightforward case which can represent into something much more involved. In analyzing this case we feel we made an error in violating our protocol by not insisting that the father attend all sessions. When the father did participate, the family and marital conflicts were evident and appeared resolvable. On the other hand, we have had numerous successful cases with the involvement of a single well-motivated parent, and we feel that the clinician must make an individual determination on the difficult issue of one involved and one distant parent. We do, however, encourage the clinician to make direct contact with the uninvolved or unavailable parent; this may provide better direction to the treatment program. In Ronny's case a telephone call to the father after he failed to come to the first or second session could have furnished us with invaluable information to more appropriately plan our treatment strategy. Our eagerness to help a child in distress led us to attempt a rapid but perhaps ill-advised intervention.

Another equally critical factor was that our treatment team did not give up on Ronny when we began to encounter difficulties. Levine (1983) has appropriately noted the importance of clinical tenacity in resolving encopresis. We felt committed to helping the child resolve his problem and were willing to continue the steps necessary to see that we fulfilled our commitment. When treating a child with refractory encopresis we feel that clinicians must be persistent in their approach or risk repeating a cycle of failure that is harmful to the patient and demoralizing to the family.

Our clinic provides an opportunity for medical professionals to work together daily and to exchange information and ideas on a regular basis. We fully realize that this type of association does not routinely occur in common practice. It is not our intent to imply that a multidisciplinary approach is the only way to properly treat children with functional encopresis; however, all health care providers need to recognize that the parents of children with developmental/behavioral problems seek treatment from a multitude of health care professionals. Our view is that there must be some degree of commonality of opinions regarding etiology and treatment of these children for an approach to be successful.

With the institution of this program we have been surprised by the large number of children of late pre- and early adolescence who have continuing problems with encopresis. It appears that the availability of a treatment program encourages health care providers to inquire about symptoms and that parents who have long ago ceased to seek medical advice on this issue report encopresis when they are given the hope of possible resolution. We have received numerous requests from pediatricians, psychiatrists, neurologists, parents, and others to evaluate children with long-standing encopresis, and we speculate that a critical element in treating what in many cases has become a family secret, is to offer a program with a reasonable chance of success and to demonstrate a strong desire to be given the opportunity to employ our therapy.

While we view encopresis as a problem which is usually not associated with a significant organic defect or serious emotional maladjustment, our experience is that it frequently coexists with other low-severity high-incidence developmental/behavioral disorders of childhood, such as poor academic performance, attention deficit disorders, enuresis, low self-esteem, social avoidance, and family dysfunction. It is difficult to separate the primary, secondary, or unrelated aspects of these problems; however, the knowledgeable clinician should be aware of the likelihood of the need to broaden the treatment regime.

Encopresis is a common childhood problem with potentially devastating effects. The etiology is controversial but likely involves multiple factors, including individual and family psychological functioning, anatomical and physiological considerations, and dietary practices. As such, the evaluation and treatment of this disorder requires that all factors be considered and addressed. We have found that this is best accomplished through the participation and cooperation of health care providers from a variety of fields working together to resolve the problem. The appropriate treatment of encopresis offers the opportunity for medical professionals to make an extremely important contribution to a child's development and enjoyment of life.

REFERENCES

American Psychiatric Association (1980). *Diagnostic and statistical manual of mental disorders* (3rd ed.). Washington, DC: Author.

American Psychiatric Association (1987). *Diagnostic and statistical manual of mental disorders* (3rd ed., revised). Washington, DC: Author.

Anthony, E. J. (1957). An experimental approach to the psychopathology of childhood: Encopresis. *British Journal of Medical Psychology, 30,* 146-175.

Barr, R. G., Levine, M. D., & Wilkinson, R. H. (1979). Occult stool retention: a clinical tool for its evaluation in school-aged children. *Clinical Pediatrics, 18,* 674-679.

Christophersen, E. R., & Berman, R. (1978). Encopresis treatment. *Issues in Comprehensive Pediatric Nursing, 3*(4), 51-66.

Christophersen, E. R., & Rainey, S. (1976). Management of encopresis through a pediatric outpatient clinic. *Journal of Pediatric Psychology, 1,* 38-41.

Christophersen, E. R., & Rapoff, M. A. (1983). Toileting problems of children. In C. E. Walker & M. C. Roberts (Eds.), *Handbook of clinical child psychology* (pp. 593-615). New York: Wiley.

Davidson, M. (1958). Constipation and fecal incontinence. *Pediatric Clinics of North America, 5,* 749-757.

Davidson, M., Kugler, M. M., & Bauer, C. H. (1963). Diagnosis and management in children with severe and protracted constipation and obstipation. *Journal of Pediatrics, 62,* 261-275.

Doleys, D. M. (1979). Assessment and treatment of childhood encopresis. In A. J. Finch & P. C. Kendall (Eds.), *Treatment and research in child psychopathology* (pp. 679-710). New York: Spectrum.

Doleys, D. M., Schwartz, M. S., & Ciminero, A. R. (1981). Elimination problems: enuresis and encopresis. In E. J. Mash & L. G. Terdal (Eds.), *Behavioral assessment of childhood disorders* (pp. 679-710). New York: Guilford.

Gavanski, M. (1971). Treatment of non-retentive secondary encopresis with imipramine and psychotherapy. *Canadian Medical Association Journal, 104,* 227-231.

Hamilton, J. R. (1983). The gastrointestinal tract. In R. E. Behrman & V. C. Vaughan (Eds.), *Nelson: Textbook of pediatrics* (12th ed., pp. 887-891). Philadelphia: Saunders.

Levine, M. D. (1975). Children with encopresis: A descriptive analysis. *Pediatrics, 56,* 412-416.

Levine, M. D. (1981). The schoolchild with encopresis. *Pediatrics in Review, 2*(9), 285-290.

Levine, M. D. (1983). Encopresis. In M. D. Levine, W. B. Carey, A. C. Crocker, & R. T. Gross (Eds.), *Developmental-behavioral pediatrics* (pp. 586-595). Philadelphia: Saunders.

Levine, M. D., & Bakow, H. (1976). Children with encopresis: A treatment outcome study. *Pediatrics, 58,* 845–852.

Levine, M. D., Mazonson, P., & Bakow, H. (1980). Behavioral symptom substitution in children cured of encopresis. *American Journal of Diseases of Children, 134,* 663–667.

Newson, J., & Newson, E. (1968). *Four-year-old in the urban community.* London: Allen & Unwin.

Wright, L. (1973). Handling the encopretic child. *Professional Psychology, 4,* 134–144.

Wright, L., & Walker, C. E. (1977). Treatment of the child with psychogenic encopresis. *Clinical Pediatrics, 16,* 1042–1045.

16
Comprehensive Treatment of the Child with Cancer

DONNA R. COPELAND
EDWARD R. DAVIDSON

INTRODUCTION

Cancer and its treatment have significant and frequently insidious psychosocial sequelae affecting the individual child and the family. Adjustment to the disease is variable as shown in research by O'Malley, Koocher, Foster, and Slavin (1979), who found that 59% of a sample of children surviving malignant neoplasms exhibited mild to marked psychological maladjustment. Early in treatment, overt behavior may be inhibited, and the child may show signs of withdrawal and regression or behavioral avoidance and noncompliance. Emotional separation and loneliness commonly follow alterations in family interaction patterns. There may be a decline in academic performance and school attendance as a consequence of extended and intensive treatment.

A simple but useful way to describe the medical treatment of the child with cancer is to differentiate three phases: (1) initial diagnosis and treatment planning, (2) initiation of active treatment, and (3) follow-up post-treatment. Within each phase, there are important psychological issues to be considered in response to the physical illness (Moos, 1982). During the initial diagnosis and treatment planning phase, situational crises are common. Hospitalization may be imminent, separation from family and friends is likely, and the patient's body is assaulted with various diagnostic testing procedures. Essential tasks for the individual are to learn to deal with illness-related symptoms, to establish rapport and a working alliance with members of the health care team, and to learn hospital and treatment

Donna R. Copeland and Edward R. Davidson. Department of Pediatrics, The University of Texas, M. D. Anderson Cancer Center, Houston, Texas.

routines and procedures. During the second phase, active treatment and developing a sense of continuity and emotional equilibrium is essential. Adaptive tasks to be accomplished include creating an existential meaning for the illness with a sense of competency and, ideally, mastery; to develop flexibility about future goals; and to initiate new, normative patterns of family life while functioning under the spector of cancer. Finally, in the posttreatment, chronic phase of illness, further developing a sense of identity without feeling victimized by cancer is the essential task.

In this chapter, we report on the case of John D, an adolescent whose personal and family history was complex even prior to the diagnosis of cancer (the names of the family have been changed for their privacy). He and his family were followed by the authors for 2½ years. D.R.C. was a staff psychologist and director of the Mental Health Section in the Department of Pediatrics. E.R.D. was initially a clinical psychology fellow and later appointed to a staff position.

During the active medical treatment phase (approximately 1 year), John D was hospitalized once for surgery and numerous times for chemotherapy. Chemotherapy treatments involved hospitalization for approximately 1 out of every 3 weeks. In this phase of treatment, he and his mother were seen for individual psychotherapy sessions on a frequent basis (once or twice a week) and occasionally for joint sessions when John was in the hospital.

Following medical treatment, when John returned to the hospital for checkups, the Ds were seen less frequently (about once a month). This follow-up period was approximately 18 months. John and his mother were seen individually during this period of time, and when Mr. D was present at the hospital, six marital sessions took place. At his request, Mr. D was seen individually about four times.

Although not all children with cancer will present with the characteristics of John and his family, they are likely to share a great deal in common. Aspects of this case that will be of interest to clinicians working with children with cancer include effects of cancer treatments, frequent hospitalizations, a preexisting learning disability, a moderate degree of psychopathology, socioeconomic constraints, adolescent issues, fluctuations in the family system, and staff–family interactions.

The pediatric oncology literature relevant to this case ranges from studies conducted on children with cancer and their families during the diagnostic phase (Kupst & Schulman, 1980b; Spinetta, 1978, 1980; Spinetta & Maloney, 1978), during treatment (Copeland, Pfefferbaum, & Stovall, 1983; Deasy-Spinetta, 1981; Desmond, 1980; Goggin, Lansky, & Hassanein, 1976; Kagen, 1976; Kashani & Hakami, 1982; Kellerman & Katz, 1977; Kellerman, Zeltzer, Ellenberg, Dash, & Rigler, 1980; Kirten & Liverman, 1977; Kupst & Schulman, 1980a; Kupst, Schulman, Honig, Maurer, Morgan, & Fochtman, 1982; Kupst, Schulman, Maurer, Honig, Morgan, &

Fochtman, 1984; Kupst, Schulman, Maurer, Morgan, Honig, & Fochtman, 1983; Lansky, Smith, Cairns, & Cairns, 1983; Schowalter, 1977; Schulman & Kupst, 1980; Spinetta, 1977; Spinetta & Deasy-Spinetta, 1981; Zeltzer, 1980; Zeltzer, Kellerman, Ellenberg, Dash, & Rigler, 1980), and posttreatment and long-term follow-up (Copeland & Van Eys, 1987; Foster, O'Malley, & Koocher, 1981; Kagen-Goodheart, 1977; Katz, 1980; Kemler, 1981; Koocher & O'Malley, 1981; Koocher, O'Malley, Gogan, & Foster, 1980; O'Malley et al., 1979). The most recent reviews of these phases of childhood cancer and its treatment and the effects on the family are by Michael and Copeland (1987) and Van Dongen-Melman and Sanders-Woudstra (1986). For a review of research on the emotional, social, and behavioral functioning of learning disabled children, see Porter (1980).

DIAGNOSIS

Diagnostic criteria for use in the treatment of the child with cancer have a lengthy tradition in physical medicine. A careful, systematic assessment using diagnostic radiology, surgery, and biochemistry determines the stage of the disease and the presence and absence of favorable or unfavorable prognostic factors. Similarly, using the third revised edition of the *Diagnostic and Statistical Manual of Mental Disorders* (DSM-III-R; American Psychiatric Association, 1987) operational criteria, the psychologist can precisely describe symptomatic behaviors to establish a diagnosis and prescribe treatment modalities. With a treatment plan implemented, the psychologist may confirm, refute, or modify the diagnosis and, subsequently, the treatment.

Based on clinical interviews with John and staff and parent reports, the diagnosis of Oppositional Defiant Disorder (DSM-III-R, 313.81) was established. According to the diagnostic manual, the essential features of this disorder are a pervasive opposition to authority regardless of self-interest, argumentativeness, and unwillingness to respond to reasonable persuasion. Behaviorally, the individual may be oppositional even with respect to his/ her own desires or preferences. Negativism, stubbornness, and blocking of communication are typical mechanisms employed by individuals with this disorder.

Oppositional defiance is typically directed toward family members, particularly parents, but may also be present in interactions with school authorities and, less frequently, with peers. Generally, the disorder is pervasive with well-established patterns of conflict. The individual shows little insight regarding his/her contributions to conflict, and instead blames problems on the unreasonable demands of others. Consequently, this disorder may cause more distress to those around the individual than it does to the individual.

Developmental Reading Disorder (DSM-III-R, 315.00) had been recognized by John's school prior to the diagnosis of cancer. Routine neuropsychological assessment with a comprehensive test battery at the cancer treatment center confirmed this diagnosis. The essential features of this disorder are significant impairment in the development of reading recognition and comprehension skills not due to mental retardation or an inadequate education. Associated behavioral problems are common. At the time of diagnosis, John was in the sixth grade, as he had previously failed a grade.

Assessment of family members of children with an oppositional disorder is essential. Mrs. D, the parent who most often accompanied John to the hospital, was predisposed to a mood disorder, which was diagnosed as Cyclothymic Disorder (DSM-III-R, 301.13). This disorder consists of alternating periods of depression and hypomania that are not of sufficient severity or duration to meet the criteria for a full affective syndrome. Characteristic features during affective periods include symptoms associated with depression and hypomania. The most common are elevated mood, expansiveness, and irritability during hypomanic phases, and loss of interest or pleasure in activities, appetite and sleep disturbances, distractibility, and feelings of worthlessness during depressive phases. This is a chronic disorder without psychotic symptoms such as delusions, hallucinations, incoherence, or loosening of associations. Among outpatients, cyclothymic disorder is common, and impairment in social and occupational functioning is usually moderate, although it may be severe without treatment.

CASE BACKGROUND

John D was 12 years old when his illness was diagnosed as osteosarcoma of the left proximal tibia. Approximately 2 to 3 months prior to the diagnosis, he reported pain in his leg and was seen by a physician who referred him to the cancer center for evaluation and treatment. After confirmation of the diagnosis, a series of treatments was planned, consisting of seven doses of high-dose cisplatin, a highly emetic drug administered intraarterially after the patient is completely anesthetized. After four treatments, however, John developed hypertension and renal problems, and his compliance with these treatments was variable. Because he was too young for a limb salvage procedure (resection of tumor and insertion of a metal prosthesis) and more physical growth was anticipated, the physician suggested that the family consider amputation. They agreed, and amputation was performed. He tolerated the surgery well which was followed by chemotherapy (methotrexate, Adriamycin, and cisplatin) administered intravenously. John was treated for approximately 18 months, and he has remained free of disease for over 2 years following the termination of treatment. He and his family were followed by one, then two psychologists (the authors) from the time of diagnosis to the posttreatment follow-up period (approximately 3 years total).

John's family consisted of his mother, his stepfather, and a half-sister 8 years younger than he. John had had no contact with his natural father for more than 10 years. He used his stepfather's surname, although he was not officially adopted until he was 14 years old. The adoption had been post-poned to allow John the opportunity to make his own decision. The family lived in a small town in Texas where John's stepfather was employed in the construction business. Shortly before diagnosis of John's illness, Mr. D had suffered a back injury at work and had been unemployed for a short period of time. Upon recovery, he was able to resume work in the construction business; however, these jobs were usually out of state because the area in which he lived was in an economic slump. Thus, he was away from home for extended periods.

This case report focuses on John and his mother, because they were the family members most consistently present at the hospital. Mr. D and John's sister were seen only on occasion.

ASSESSMENT AND CASE FORMULATION

The assessment and classification of children with severe chronic illness helps the clinician devise effective strategies for dealing with clinical prob-lems. Three dimensions comprise the context in which children cope with and adapt to the disease. These are interrelated and include: (1) the individ-ual child who experiences the disease; (2) the family system that responds to illness on a day-to-day basis; and (3) the psychosocial dimensions of the hospital system where much of the medical treatment occurs.

Patient

Psychological consultation was requested by the attending physician soon after diagnosis when John began refusing treatment procedures, was oppo-sitional to his mother and to the staff, and threatened self-harm. Initially, my (D. R. C.) assessment was limited to parent–child interviews, and inter-vention was directed toward discouraging acting-out behaviors. Following this brief intervention, John's behavior improved, and he was fairly com-pliant during the period of amputation of his leg and recovery. However, soon after this he began to resist ward schedules and staff directives, and became more verbally aggressive. He was not interested in working with the psychologist to develop a plan that would be beneficial to him.

John's pattern of behavior and attitude toward authority figures are consistent with the diagnosis of oppositional defiance disorder. Opposition to authority figures was noted at home, in school, and at the hospital.

Temper outbursts, arguing with adults (especially his mother), and defying adult requests or rules were apparent and acknowledged by John. Differential diagnosis of conduct disorder was ruled out because a pattern of problems in violation of the basic rights of others was not present.

Verification of John's learning disability was made as a result of his participation in my (D. R. C.) longitudinal study of the neuropsychological effects of cancer treatment on children. The evaluation was conducted just after diagnosis and then repeated at annual follow-up. The test battery consisted of 14 measures assessing general intelligence, memory, language, academic achievement, visual–spatial/constructional skills, tactile–perceptual skills, and fine-motor skills (see Table 16-1).

TABLE 16-1. Neuropsychological Test Battery Listing Tests by Cognitive Domain

Cognitive domain	Test
General intelligence	Wechsler Intelligence Scale for Children—Revised (WISC-R) (Wechsler, 1974)[a]
Memory	Verbal Selective Reminding Task (Buschke, 1974)
	Nonverbal Selective Reminding Task (Fletcher, 1985)
Language	Rapid Naming (Denckla & Rudel, 1974)
	Word Fluency (Gaddes & Crockett, 1975)
	Peabody Picture Vocabulary Test—Revised (PPVT-R) (Dunn & Dunn, 1981)
Academic achievement	Wide Range Achievement Test (Jastak & Jastak, 1978)
	Arithmetic Test
	Spelling Test
	Peabody Individual Achievement Test (Dunn & Markwardt, 1970)
	Reading Recognition
	Reading Comprehension
Visual–spatial/constructional	Recognition-Discrimination (Small, 1969)
	Beery Test of Visual–Motor Integration (Beery & Buktenica, 1967)
Tactile–perceptual	Benton Stereognosis Test (Benton et al., 1983)
Fine motor	Trailmaking Test, Parts A and B (Reitan, 1969; Spreen & Gaddes, 1969)
	Finger Tapping (Reitan, 1969)
	Grooved Pegboard Test (Trites, 1977)

[a] Excluding Vocabulary and Picture Arrangement.

At the time of diagnosis, John's general level of intelligence was within the normal range (Full scale IQ = 100). His perceptual–motor abilities (Performance IQ = 105) were found to be superior relative to verbal skills (Verbal IQ = 95). His scores on the Wechsler Intelligence Scales for Children—Revised (Wechsler, 1974) revealed weaknesses on the subtests of Arithmetic, Coding, Information, and Digit Span, which indicates distractibility (Kaufman, 1979).

Academically, John performed significantly below grade level on spelling, reading recognition, and reading comprehension. On timed arithmetic tests, he performed below grade level as well. However, when he was given unlimited time to complete the math tests, his performance improved to grade level.

In language, John's performance was variable. Expressive language was at age level; however, phonological processing of verbal information was significantly impaired, which undermined his performance in spelling and reading. Marked deficits in auditory processing, particularly for encoding and decoding consonant blends, were observed. In his favor, John could comprehend words and sentences at age level, once he had thoroughly learned the words, and his memory for verbal material was age-appropriate. Memory for verbal and nonverbal material was at age level or above. On perceptual-motor, fine-motor, and visual–spatial tasks, John's performance was within the normal range.

These findings of average intellectual level in the presence of distractibility and significant impairment in academic achievement and specific language tasks are characteristic of language-based or generalized learning disabilities. Following this assessment, a report with the following recommendations was put in John's medical chart and sent to his school. We advised hospital staff and teachers to give John instructions in simple statements. He could be told to write the instructions down in his own words or to repeat them verbally to ensure that he understood. We also suggested that they reinforce John only for socially appropriate behaviors and to reward him for trying, as much as for achievement of tasks. Because he had difficulty predicting future events and interpreting social situations, we recommended that John be told of his daily schedule in home, hospital, and school settings to provide more predictability. We suggested that the consequences for misbehavior be stated clearly prior to an activity. Resource learning in reading and math were recommended to the school.

Family System

The nature of a family's functioning as a system will promote or inhibit interactions with staff. Family processes have been described by principles of homeostasis, with the network of interpersonal relationships serving as a dynamic unit in which every member of the family is simultaneously organizing and being organized by others to achieve balance and equilibrium (Bateson, 1972; Jackson & Weakland, 1961). The most successful family systems are those that respond to change with flexibility and structural growth. Family patterns are developed over a long period of time and are fairly resistant to change. Consequently, the family system that presents for treatment in the cancer center brings with it a history of problem solving and methods for maintaining equilibrium. Thus, the illness quickly becomes embedded in already existing mechanisms available to the family.

The initial impact of the diagnosis of cancer on the D family was intense agitation and disruption, which is a common reaction. The D family initially demonstrated hypersensitivity to the distress of individual family members, difficulties in conflict resolution, and diffuse boundaries between parents and children.

Treatment Setting

Patients' reports of environmental stresses in the cancer treatment setting are consistent with a body of literature that describes how social environmental characteristics organize and influence the behaviors of individuals within the setting (Moos, 1977). Although physical components, such as the structure and design of the treatment unit, are frequently identified as key factors, more often, personal relationships exert greater influence on satisfaction with the treatment center.

Our evaluations of our own treatment environment using the Ward Atmosphere Scale (Moos, 1974) indicate that patients, family members, and staff have significantly different perceptions of the environment (Davidson, Copeland, Dowell, Riggert, & Mize, 1987). Significant differences were reported in relation to the treatment program and its ability to encourage self-sufficiency and expression of anger. Compared with their parents and staff, patients perceived higher degrees of staff control and viewed the treatment environment as less open to direct expressions of anger. These findings are important to consider in the treatment of the cancer patient, because such factors mediate patient compliance with treatment. As such, the social environment functions as an interactive ground that may enhance the expression of problematic individual or family behaviors.

COURSE OF THERAPY

Referral and Establishment of Therapeutic Relationships

John was referred for psychological intervention when he resisted treatment for cancer and threatened to "put a pencil in my ears." His resistance persisted even when it was carefully explained to him that the consequences of treatment refusal would most likely be pain and even death. In my (D. R. C.) interview with her, Mrs. D reported that she felt John was attempting to deny his illness and that he did not fully appreciate the consequences of treatment refusal. She observed that because he was learning disabled, he had difficulty adjusting to change. Mr. and Mrs. D agreed that John should be treated for cancer despite his objections, just as they had insisted on other types of interventions for him in the past.

After conferring with John and with the agreement of the physician, I (D. R. C.) recommended that the administration of intra-arterial cisplatin be postponed until the following day. At that time, John would be heavily sedated, as he requested, and I would accompany him to the treatment room. Because John had made several threats to harm himself, suicidal precautions were instituted as outlined in the hospital patient care manual for nurses. These included psychiatric consultation, one-to-one attendance of a specified family member or nurse, removal of sharp objects, open door to room, observation of medication intake, and documentation of all suicidal remarks and gestures. John was not considered to be at great risk; these precautions were meant to increase structure and give him a sense of support, thus aiding him in regaining control over his impulses. Mrs. D was in complete agreement. I remained available at all times through the hospital paging system.

After conferring together, the treatment team (medical, nursing, and mental health staff) decided that it would be advantageous for the family to return home and consider carefully the various options for treatment. (At that time, the limb salvage procedure, amputation, and chemotherapy were being considered.)

When John and his parents returned to the hospital several days later, they announced that an amputation was their treatment choice. The decision was based partly on its being a more standard treatment; but in addition, compared with a limb salvage procedure, amputation would allow John to continue his participation in the type of sports he favored (e.g., running, skiing). With a metal prosthesis, these activities would be prohibited. Continuing treatment with systemic chemotherapy was planned, which would require John to be hospitalized 1 week out of every month for the next 12 to 18 months. The amputation was performed, and psychological intervention consisted of short visits for emotional support.

Problems emerged again several months later when John became resistant to following the daily schedule for patients in the hospital and began having temper outbursts. At that time, he was once again given the choice of talking with me (D. R. C.), which he declined. As an alternative approach, I began developing a therapeutic relationship with his mother. Because my impression was that John's acting-out behavior was at least partially related to adjustment to the recent amputation of his leg, Mrs. D was advised to reduce her pressure on John and allow him more opportunity to bring his behavior under control on his own. At the same time, I made a similar recommendation to staff; that is, to relax the schedule involving school, physical therapy, and eating. Because the end of the school year was approaching and school was another arena for tension and frustration, John was "excused" from attending until the following fall semester. These recommendations were made with the intent of giving John a sense of "winning" and to increase his sense of control in situations where he was feeling helpless.

In sessions with Mrs. D, I (D. R. C.) encouraged her to allow John more opportunities for making decisions and taking steps toward increasing his independence. For example, one day when he proposed going on his own for lunch to a nearby hospital in his wheelchair, I suggested that his mother grant him permission. It was a difficult task, but John managed it and was very proud of his accomplishment. At the same time, because it was very difficult, it allowed him to test his own limits of ability.

This sequence of events illustrates repeated patterns throughout the course of John's treatment: (1) John's resistance to a treatment recommendation evidenced by outright refusal and/or temper outbursts; (2) our (D. R. C., E. R. D.) recommendation to the mother and staff to relax pressure and allow John more opportunity to make his own decisions; and (3) John's compliance with treatment.

During her psychotherapy sessions with me (D. R. C.), Mrs. D began discussing her relationship with her husband and her friends at home. Six months into John's treatment, she was becoming aware of how the experience was changing her perspective on life and strengthening her values. A positive working alliance with me gave her an opportunity to explore freely her thoughts and feelings in a nonjudgmental context and to review her own history from a new perspective. Her previous experience had shown her that others often did not take her seriously and regarded her as somewhat limited in her problem-solving skills, reliability, and consistency. Contrary to this image, I observed Mrs. D to be insightful, practical, and thoughtful in her approach to child-rearing and creative in her ideas for managing difficult situations. More problematic were her modes of relating to other people, her self-image, and her tendency toward emotional lability. She came for her therapy sessions regularly and used the time productively. As a result, I took an insight-oriented approach to the therapy and permitted Mrs. D to focus on her own concerns and self-development. This included her personal history as well as her current family relationships and her relationships with me and other hospital staff. Her movements toward individuation and self-assertion were validated and reinforced on a consistent basis.

In her psychotherapy sessions, Mrs. D began to identify areas of conflict such as dependency versus independence, her marriage, her relationships with authority figures at the hospital and at John's school, and parental responsibilities. Identity issues assumed more prominence as she realized that her children were growing older, and that she would need to develop a better understanding of herself and her goals in the near future. She used the therapy sessions for validating herself and her ideas and for testing her construction of reality with respect to John and hospital staff. For instance, she found that her judgment of where to set limits with John was accurate, so she could confidently follow through with contingencies on a consistent basis. In relation to staff, she found that she could be upset about a matter, confront staff on the issue, and, as often as not, find her position to be realistic. In many respects, the hospital environment served as a "training ground" for Mrs. D to examine her relationships with others, test her newly acquired assertiveness in relation to authority figures, and develop a more clearly defined sense of self and purpose in life.

In addition to acquiring information from hospital staff, Mrs. D extended her reading on learning disabilities and parenting techniques to the literature on cancer and its treatment and self-development. She quickly assimilated this information and applied it to life situations. After reading a book on parenting, she reported "I used the same strategies on other people besides my kids, and it works!" What she learned from her therapy and from her reading, Mrs. D applied to situations in her home community, specifically at John's school, where she had met with resistance in trying to arrange for appropriate instruction for John. After informing herself about children's right to an education under Public Law 94-142 (Education for All Handicapped Children Act, 1975) and provisions for appeal, she arranged for admission, review, and dismissal (ARD) meetings with school officials. Over time, her skills in negotiating reflected higher-level coping strategies and defenses. She began to develop more tolerance for frustration and a better sense of timing with respect to assertiveness and patience. Staff provided support to her when she was rehearsing a strategy, sent neuropsychological evaluations and recommendations to the school, and communicated with the school directly via telephone. Her husband was supportive as well, and frequently attended school meetings with her. The D's were aware that school officials were often more responsive to Mr. D than to Mrs. D.

Despite these efforts and Mrs. D's improvements, John continued to exhibit problematic behavior. For example, he resisted regular school attendance and compliance with medical instructions such as dental appointments and collection of urine. Increasing structure and reinforcing the mother's assertiveness were only partially successful. Hence, a male psychologist (E. R. D.) was asked to see John and engage him in a therapeutic relationship. John responded reluctantly and with ambivalence, but he did talk with me (E. R. D.) about his current interests in football and model cars. I established immediate goals of developing a therapeutic relationship and regular school attendance with appropriate contingencies. Toward these goals, John explored his feelings and considered strategies in therapy that he could use to cope with medical treatments. He demonstrated his capacity for insight when he associated the depression he felt to resistance to instructions in the form of "pitching a fit." Additionally, he began to see that he had developed a bad reputation at the hospital, which interfered with the staff's recognition of the improvements he made. Similarly, I helped him consider the changes in family relationships at home and in his self-perception subsequent to his illness and treatment. These appeared to concern him, and he stated flatly, "I ain't gonna be no handicapped person in a wheelchair." John was invited to attend the hospital's annual ski trip for amputees, which he eagerly anticipated. However, some of the staff for the ski trip expressed their concern about his conduct. In response, I (E. R. D.) developed a behavioral contract with John for him to follow during the trip. The contract was then presented to the staff, who made recommendations, and then we refined it accordingly. John's behavior during the ski trip was exemplary. He was one of the best skiers and was observed to be very helpful and supportive of those who skied less well.

During this period, John participated in individual therapy sessions, although sometimes reluctantly. He began to learn better means of communicating with staff and coping with anger through assertiveness and impulse control, and consequently developed a better sense of his own responsibility and effectiveness in solving problems.

During the course of therapy, Mrs. D consulted with each of us in the management of John's behavior at home and at school. She continued to learn how and where to set limits and to develop more confidence in her parenting skills. Gradually, she reported to us that John's behavior had greatly improved, particularly at school. At this point, approximately 1 year from diagnosis, John was nearing the completion of his active medical treatment, and Mrs. D expressed her concern about maintaining the progress they had achieved when they would be coming to the hospital less frequently.

We then began planning for the termination phase of medical treatment with John and his mother. Since it was agreed that continued psychological follow-up was desirable, two options were considered. John and Mrs. D could return to the hospital for therapy sessions, or they could be referred to a mental health agency nearer their home. Mrs. D decided to return to the hospital for therapy during John's monthly medical checkups.

Anxiety in mother and son grew as the date for termination of the cancer treatment neared, as shown by their nervousness and increased conflict with staff. The issue seemed to be related as much to separation from the hospital environment as it was to termination of treatment for cancer. Over 1 weekend, a conflict developed between John and the nurses regarding the proper use of a room and bedtime. We met with John, Mrs. D, and the staff to discuss the issues involved. John was helped to see the advantages of cooperation with medical procedures and hospital rules. Staff were supported in their reinforcement of the bedtime curfew. Staff had erred in calling the father at home during the evening in question, rather than calling the mother who was in town, a mistake that had angered her. To address this problem, the mother's telephone number was then attached to the front of John's medical chart. Consultation was provided to the nursing staff concerning strategies for obtaining adolescents' compliance. Additionally, they were reminded that they could call us any time they desired psychological assistance in dealing with compliance problems.

Considering the attachment and long-term relationship that had developed between this family and hospital staff and the family's anxiety about separation, we arranged for a staffing conference (Copeland, 1988; van Eys & Copeland, 1984), a multidisciplinary review of treatment with the family present. The purpose was to reflect on the main events that occurred during the treatment period and the substantial changes John and his mother had made in their interpersonal relationships, their strategies for coping, and their self-images. The family agreed and attended the meeting; however, Mrs. D was quieter than usual, which was attributed to tension about the news that another patient had relapsed.

During the conference, staff reported on their work with John, and Mrs. D and John shared their thoughts about ending treatment. Their concerns centered primarily on separating from the people they had come to know at the hospital. Nevertheless, they looked forward to being home more and resuming contact with friends on a more regular basis. Mrs. D was looking forward to relaxing more and increasing her involvement in her own activities.

The evening following the conference, Mrs. D felt ill and requested medical assistance. After some difficulty in getting staff's attention, she was escorted to a general hospital in the medical center. There, she evidenced heightened anxiety, confusion, suspicious ideation, reduced concentration, and emotional lability. She called me (D. R. C.), and I met with her in the emergency room. A medical workup indicated that she had an electrolyte imbalance that had resulted from an inadequate diet; however, the possibility of a manic episode was considered as well. Mrs. D remained in the hospital for several days, during which time her symptoms cleared. She experienced a similar episode several weeks later at home but has had no difficulties of the same degree since that time.

Following these events, the family decided Mrs. D needed extra support, so Mr. D began accompanying her and John to the hospital. This provided the opportunity for family therapy sessions to address family system dynamics and the changes that had occurred as a result of John's illness and treatment and his and his mother's individual psychotherapy.

The parents agreed to participate, although Mrs. D was somewhat reluctant. Even though she appreciated her husband's assistance, she was ambivalent about his taking an active role in the context in which she had begun to actualize her potential for leadership and self-assertion. John declined to attend the meetings.

In the marital sessions, Mr. and Mrs. D reflected on their experience of extended treatment for their son (e.g., separation of family members, increased demands on individuals), their methods of coping with frustration and family disagreements, and management of John's behavior. They had recently devised strategies for dealing with some of these problems, and it was apparent to both of us that they took pride in what they had done on their own. Therefore, we as therapists reinforced their approaches. One of these consisted of a five-point plan for John when he tested limits. He was progressively denied privileges as his behavior escalated, until the fifth denial was reached. The fifth denial prohibited him from attending an event such as a football game. Additionally, we encouraged the parents to use incentives (e.g., riding in his four-wheeler) to shape John's behavior.

Agitation about separation was heightened by Mr. D's absence from home when he had to travel for construction jobs. Furthermore, John was more difficult for Mrs. D to manage when Mr. D was away from home. We noticed that the parents felt resentful about their circumstances but seldom shared their feelings about it or expressed sympathy to one another. We encouraged them to share more of their feelings during the sessions and express sympathy and empathy more frequently.

Consultation on school issues continued throughout the treatment termination period. John's behavior at school was inconsistent but generally improved. He sometimes had difficulty understanding instructions, a problem attributed to the learning disability and to some of the teachers' reluctance to follow the plan officially agreed upon in the individualized education program (IEP). Mr. and Mrs. D received little support from the school principal, so they requested a second ARD conference, which was held shortly thereafter. Later, Mrs. D reported success with the school's compliance to the IEP agreement, specifically with respect to special education requirements. Subsequently, John's behavior improved, and he became increasingly more skilled in identifying the sources of his problems at school. With these improvements, Mrs. D was encouraged to set limits on her involvement in John's affairs in the hope that he and his teachers would be able to function independently of her.

From time to time during the course of therapy, Mrs. D expressed various concerns about her daughter Karen, which related to the possibility of a learning disability, psychosomatic complaints, separation anxiety, and problems with limit setting. To allay the mother's fears about having another child with a learning disability, the neuropsychology staff administered a screening battery,[1] the results of which showed that Karen was functioning normally. Mrs. D consulted the therapists on ways to manage Karen's frequent somatic complaints and distress about being separated from her mother. Mrs. D found it helpful to set aside specific times to be with her daughter and give her attention and to institute the same limit-setting techniques that she was using with John. Occasionally, Mrs. D would bring Karen along to the hospital for John's treatment, which also helped. I (D. R. C.) suggested to Mrs. D that she could regard the times when she and John came to the cancer center as opportunities for Karen to feel closer to her father. This did indeed occur with time, and Karen did well, earning high grades after she started school.

Critical Incidents in Medical Treatment

The first critical incident occurred at the beginning of treatment when amputation was being considered, and John demonstrated resistance to treatment and behavior problems that were typical of him prior to diagnosis. Referral for psychological intervention was made to assist the family in decision making as well as to help them learn better management techniques. Family members subsequently remained confident of their decision, and the parents felt supported in their efforts to obtain the best treatment possible for John. Treatment compliance was achieved primarily through the staff's support of the parents' strong stand and the parents' ability and willingness to try suggestions made by the staff.

The second critical incident occurred when Mrs. D experienced a reaction either to an electrolyte imbalance and/or to impending separation from the hospital as a "second home." Prompt treatment at a nearby hospital and an established, positive therapeutic relationship lessened the impact of this incident and allowed Mrs. D to resume her daily activities.

Critical Incidents in Psychological Intervention

Many of the issues confronting the clinician proposing psychotherapy to the adolescent cancer patient have their roots in general developmental themes such as independence and autonomy in relation to parental/authority figures (Blos, 1962). For John, accepting the recommendation to begin therapy represented an unreasonable effort by authority figures to control, dominate, and discipline him. In his mind, implicit in the recommendation for psychotherapy was the assumption that he was basically deficient and needed improvement. Thus, addressing the resistance to therapeutic help was essential for engaging him in therapy.

[1]The screening battery consisted of selected items from the tests shown in Table 16-1.

After John initially declined treatment with one therapist (D. R. C.), another (E. R. D.) was suggested when John continued to resist following instructions. Subsequently, when he was approached to schedule an initial appointment, he loudly protested that he did not need to see a psychologist because he was not crazy. He saw no reason to meet since he perceived there were no problems. I (E. R. D.) agreed that he was not crazy; however, I noted that John did have a problem, which seemed to be others' perceptions that he needed psychotherapy. I proposed to him that we begin therapy with trying to discover why other authorities believed that he had a problem. The goal of therapy would be to convince hospital staff that John should quit therapy. This technique was successful because it circumvented his preparation to resist my influence as a therapist. I maintained the symptom (John has a problem) but redirected the locus to someone else (hospital staff) and proposed a benefit (quitting therapy) that assumed compliance (accepting the recommendation for therapy).

At this point in therapy, the goal was to move from a stance of opposition and distrust to one of possible cooperation and alliance. This was accomplished by minimizing attention to the presenting problem (John's noncompliance) and reframing his actions in a more positive light, and conveying a nonjudgmental, caring attitude. My sharing with him experiences of similar struggles by other adolescents seemed to normalize this issue and set the stage for successful resolution. Finally, when I responded to him in a genuine manner regarding information about myself, John recognized that I was understanding and positively inclined toward him.

The ability to demonstrate an awareness of the interests of adolescents is essential in establishing rapport. Throughout these initial appointments, I (E. R. D.) focused John's attention on his reactions to chemotherapy and his expectations regarding future treatments. This technique of interspersing easily identifiable therapeutic issues with my ability to attend to contemporary interests and develop the relationship played a critical role in reducing resistance and establishing a working alliance. After John had established a rapport and a working alliance with me, the therapy could focus on maintaining continuity in the medical treatments.

A second set of critical incidents in psychological intervention was the expanded focus from the patient-as-problem to an appreciation of the broader context of family- and hospital-related variables that were problematic for John. The marital/parental subsystem was strengthened to meet increased demands associated with managing adolescent noncompliance. Insight-oriented psychotherapy for the mother improved her concept of herself as an effective individual and parent, thus making it possible for her to become more assertive with her children and with hospital and school staff.

Intervention at the hospital community level was necessary as well. The influence of the hospital social system on John's behavior was illustrated in the nursing staff's somewhat ineffective efforts to reduce symptoms by increasing control, discipline, and restrictions. To a large extent, success in resolving the stalemate that resulted was a function of refocusing attention on the shared goals of the psychology and nursing staff. Scheduling patient care conferences and planning for impromptu consultations with the nurses to review their behavior management strategies and to educate them regarding the oppositional adolescent provided this sense of shared goals. Also, it encouraged the nurses to consult with us before attempting to institute behavioral contracts and contingencies.

Therapeutic Decision-Making Process

John was unusually resistant to establishing a therapeutic alliance. Thus, he was engaged on his terms, which allowed him to maintain a sense of control in the immediate situation but also to maintain his identification with a strong, independent father figure and to differentiate and separate from his mother.

Although the initial sessions with the family centered around medical treatment considerations and were crisis oriented, the therapy gradually emphasized personal growth and development. A combination of treatment approaches was selected, depending on the needs of the family at different times. For instance, John's resistance to therapy made it necessary to consult with the mother on child management in the beginning rather than working with John directly. Mrs. D agreed to this arrangement, which also preserved her authority as a parent and allowed her to discover new approaches to child-rearing. Once she achieved a greater sense of parental control, and the generational boundaries became more firmly established, it was easier for John to develop a relationship with his therapist.

In John's therapy, indirect paradoxical strategies were effective in achieving a therapeutic rapport. I (E. R. D.) used humor and sometimes exaggerated it to extremes to reduce or inhibit anger and to promote therapeutic rapport. Rogerian person-centered therapy with an emphasis on helping John identify his feelings and providing caring and sensitive, nonjudgmental understanding were particularly helpful. Cognitive–behavioral strategies were designed to help him achieve better impulse control, negotiate better relationships with peers and authority figures, and solve problems more rationally. It was especially helpful for him to learn how to predict consequences of his and others' actions.

In Mrs. D's case, an object–relations approach in therapy was helpful in restructuring her perceptions of herself and others and in developing more mature relationships with other adults. In these endeavors, my (D. R. C.) positive, accepting, and supportive stance enabled Mrs. D to examine her life and her relationships with her family, her friends, and staff, and to try new approaches without fear of criticism. She was permitted to talk about any subject she chose during the sessions and was encouraged to use her own creativity and common sense in solving problems. My role was primarily one of guidance and support, with occasional observations about Mrs. D's self-concept and processes and patterns in her relationships with the therapist and significant others.

The changes that occurred because of medical and psychological treatment were substantial and, not surprisingly, had an impact on a family system that was already at risk for serious problems. Consequently, marital therapy sessions and occasional individual sessions with Mr. D were offered to help improve communication between husband and wife and to develop a more unified approach to managing John's behavior. Mr. D needed reassurance that the therapists respected him and that they considered him a good husband and father. Although he appreciated the positive changes in his wife and son, these required a certain amount of adaptation on his part. Individual and marital sessions helped him identify the changes and their implications for him and discuss ways in which he could adjust to them in a positive manner.

Interventions extended beyond the child and family to the home community. John had a history of problems at school predating the diagnosis of cancer. Prior to, but especially during his illness, Mrs. D had some difficulty convincing school authorities that it was important for John to maintain his academic efforts. Toward the end of the treatment period, and as John remained disease-free, the school community began to realize that John would have a future and that careful preparation and planning for an occupation were just as important for him as for any other child. They became more receptive to implementing the recommendations suggested in the neuropsychological reports. At the same time, it was clear that Mrs. D preferred negotiation with the school officials on her own as much as possible. In fact, to some extent, she used this as an opportunity to enhance her own personal development and effectiveness in managing adult conflicts. In circumstances such as these, therapists must gauge their level of activity based on the parents' capabilities and preferences.

Treatment Summary

The course of therapy was a complex mosaic as reflected by the interactive effects of the treatment environment, the family system, and the individuals' level of functioning. Individual psychotherapy sessions were used for personal development and to aid in achieving better differentiation among overly enmeshed family members. Family therapy was essential to promote pleasurable relationships and productive activities at home and at school. Particular emphasis was placed on enhancing parental communication and collaboration and teaching the parents to use limit-setting and consistency in their management of the children. Broadening psychological intervention with children and families to include hospital and school systems may be necessary when they hamper the family's adjustment to the cancer experience.

OUTCOME AND FOLLOW-UP

In the case presented here, psychological follow-up after termination of medical treatment was indicated because of the developmental nature of the presenting problems—problems that existed before the diagnosis and were exacerbated by the illness and treatment. Termination is a sensitive time because it evokes memories of previously experienced separations and losses. Therefore, thoughtful planning for this phase is important, as it helps the child and family make a smooth transition from the dependency created by the treatment to relatively autonomous functioning at home.

In a setting in which a child's life-threatening illness has been cured, families frequently express anxiety associated with the withdrawal of medical and psychological support (Alby, 1980; Lewis & LaBarbera, 1983). In this case, we planned the termination phase with John and his mother by establishing a termination date, scheduling follow-up sessions, exploring their thoughts and feelings about separation, and discussing the progress made and goals achieved.

The primary theme explored during the termination phase was family members' feelings about separation and loss. They were readily able to describe their ambivalence, that is, sadness about leaving long-term friends made during hospitalizations and their eagerness to resume regular, uninterrupted contact with hometown friends. Feelings about these issues were sharpened by the deaths of other children at the hospital and the loss of staff members due to job changes. Expressions of grief and anger about these situations provided a parallel context in which to explore similar feelings related to psychotherapy. Additional themes addressed during termination included identification of John's academic goals, the impact of continuing employment problems on the marriage, and recommendations for continued psychotherapy for John and his parents.

In recommendations for follow-up during termination, practical considerations of time, finances, and geographic distance often dictate compromises (Strupp & Binder, 1984). Another is the clinically recognized but poorly understood attachment that develops as a family shares their problems and finds support from the hospital-based staff during a life crisis. Although the hometown community mental health facility was recommended for follow-up psychotherapy, the D's elected to receive follow-up treatment on a continuing basis from us at the medical center. This appeared to be a function of the family's difficulty in locating good sources of therapy in their small hometown and the solid working alliances that had developed with the hospital staff. Because the frequency of medical check ups was adequate to serve the needs for follow-up therapy, we agreed to this arrangement. Now, 3 years postdiagnosis, John and his parents are seen by us (D. R. C., E. R. D.), primarily for progress reports and brief consultations.

REFLECTIONS

Although complex, this case involved aspects at diagnosis and during treatment that are very common in families of children with a chronic illness that at times may be life-threatening. These include: (1) resistance of a family member to psychological intervention; (2) the referral of the child as the identified patient; (3) staff–patient–parent miscommunication; (4) periodic episodes of stress; and (5) the occurrence of a learning disability in a child with cancer.

Resistance

The true basis for resistance to psychological intervention may not be easily discernible, although it is commonly observed in families of childhood cancer patients. For some families who expect only "medical" treatment, it may seem like an intrusion or perhaps an undeserved luxury. Many families have to be convinced of its usefulness and its relationship to medical treatment. In this case, the child, rather than the parents, was resistant. We assumed that John needed to identify with the strength and independence he perceived in his father and to differentiate and separate from his mother, with whom he had had a close attachment before the diagnosis of cancer. Mrs. D had worked diligently to help him learn at school despite his disability which had required spending hours on homework each evening after school. Consequently, a dependent relationship tinged with hostility had developed between them. John was understandably averse to establishing a therapeutic relationship with another mother figure who he anticipated would likewise try to control him. In this case, a male therapist who John perceived would approach him on common ground and allow him to set the pace was much more agreeable. Additionally, John was probably apprehensive about psychotherapy because of society's assumption that therapy is for "crazy" people; therefore, if a person is in therapy, he or she must be "crazy." His mother's willingness to participate in therapy and the improvement he saw probably made it easier for John to accept psychotherapy later.

The Child as the Identified Patient

Identifying a child who needs psychotherapeutic intervention and support is usually only the first step in the therapeutic process in a pediatric treatment setting. This case is typical in that respect in that John's behavior problems represented a composite of interrelating factors in family dynamics and structure.

Communication

When families arrive at the pediatric treatment center, the quality of their communication with one another will to some extent determine the level of communication with staff. As with this family, it may be necessary to work with them on improving communication among themselves and to encourage them to approach staff openly and on an equal footing. Sometimes, they may need help in learning the art of negotiation and compromise. Clearly, psychologists are in a position to serve as advocates for children and parents in a medical setting; it is usually more beneficial, however, to teach them how they can communicate more effectively. Often, the psychotherapy setting provides the first opportunity for them to practice greater assertiveness in communicating with hospital staff. Because family members are not typically assertive in their interactions with medical personnel, medical and nursing staff may not be prepared to relate to them on this basis. Therefore, when psychologists encourage families to participate more in the child's care, it will be necessary to prepare staff and advise them of the benefits of this approach and coach them in positive responses.

Periodicity of Stress

Another commonly observed aspect of this case is the periodicity of stress episodes. Psychologists working with families may elect to use medically quiescent periods to allow the family to function independently and regard the psychologist as a resource person or consultant. In some cases, however, the psychologist and family may decide to use these periods to work on chronic problems in family functioning or on personal development of individual family members. Both methods were applied in this case due to John's resistance to therapy, the geographic distance of the family's home, and the mother's receptiveness to dynamically oriented psychotherapy. That is, John's treatment was more sporadic than the mother's by his own choice, but the mother's treatment had to be interrupted when she could not afford the time or money to travel to the treatment center from home.

Learning Disability

With regard to John's learning disability, we are reminded that learning disabilities are not uncommon among children with cancer (Copeland & Dowell, 1987; Powazek, Kennelly, Imbus, & Rosen, 1983), and that it compounds the risk for social and emotional difficulties. Although psychosocial problems are not inevitable in children with learning disabilities, they frequently occur (Ozols & Rourke, 1985; Porter & Rourke, 1985).

SUMMARY

The main points illustrated by this case include: (1) the necessity of well-coordinated and integrated multidisciplinary approaches; (2) the importance of identifying preexisting problems and their manifestation in the family's adjustment to the cancer experience; and (3) the importance of recognizing and managing fluctuations in the family's adjustment as a function of personality styles, course of cancer treatment, and life events.

Multidisciplinary Treatment

Cancer is a complex illness requiring long-term and sometimes very difficult treatments. The psychologist works closely with the physicians and nurses in managing the interactions that occur between psychological variables and medical requirements. A staffing conference (Copeland, 1988; van Eys & Copeland, 1984) provides the opportunity for the parents and all disciplines involved in the child's care to formulate a comprehensive plan. With a large team, fragmentation of treatment, overlap in services, and inefficiency can be avoided by specifying goals, frequent communication, and a unified approach to achieving stated goals. In this case, we worked closely with the parents and medical and nursing staff to improve compliance with the medical treatment; with the parents, we worked with the hospital and home schools to minimize the effects of treatment for a child already at risk for school failure.

Problem Identification

From the beginning of treatment, it was apparent that John's typical responses to anxiety and uncertainty would be manifested in the treatment setting and take the form of testing limits and opposing the authority of his parents and the hospital staff. Whereas this behavior was previously irritating and frustrating, in the cancer treatment setting it became life-threatening. Similarly, the D's marriage was problematic, and with the increased stress and the amount of time they were separated, problems in this area were intensified as a function of the cancer experience. Prompt identification of children and families at risk for various types of problems and timely interventions can help prevent medical failures, academic failures, and family problems that might otherwise occur. The treatment team's ability to predict difficulties ahead of time and its prompt attention to adverse responses will also minimize cancer treatment effects. For instance, children like John respond much better when procedures are explained beforehand and measures are taken to assure that they have completely understood the information presented to them. When this is not possible, such as in an emergency situation, providing extra emotional support will be helpful. Furthermore, the treatment team can help smooth the transition by being aware that for some families the termination of treatment is highly stressful, causing feelings of loss of protection as well as loss of support from treatment team members. At such times, it is helpful to make the family aware of these feelings ahead of time and plan with them the ways in which they and the treatment team can minimize the stress.

Case Management and the Therapeutic Process

The problems in this case are related to preexisting characteristics of the child and the parents, characteristics of the illness and its treatment, and characteristics of the treatment community. Psychologists working with children with cancer will provide better service if they are able to offer a broad range of techniques that include behavioral, psychodynamic, marital, and family systems approaches, as well as consultation to medical and nursing staff and to schools. Additionally, the task of organizing and coordinating the services of many disciplines in the hospital is frequently assumed by the psychologist who has developed skills in organizational consultation and the art of diplomacy. In complex cases such as this one with multiple interacting factors, we suggest the following:

1. *Two therapists.* The therapists may work independently or as co-therapists, depending on the therapeutic approach needed at different times. Male–female therapy pairs are advantageous from a family therapy standpoint (Keith & Whitaker, 1983) and, as in this case, when the child would work better with a therapist of one gender or the other.

2. *Flexibility.* The psychologists should be flexible in using a variety of treatment techniques, and in altering or blending approaches when it becomes apparent that one is not effective. Similarly, in consulting, compromise and negotiation are required to formulate plans that are agreeable to all concerned. The therapists should be flexible, as well, in the degree of assistance offered to the family.

3. *Treatment at a cancer center.* The advantages of a cancer center over a local mental health center include the variety of mental health disciplines working closely together (e.g., psychologists, child life specialists, social workers, and psychiatrists), continuity of care, and coordination of medical and psychosocial treatments. Furthermore, the cancer center professionals' knowledge of cancer and its effects on children and families is helpful in determining the sources of problems and in deciding whether they are cancer-related and physiologically based or due to other factors.

An alternative to consolidated treatment is the referral of the family to local health service providers. The advantages of this approach are the greater convenience to families and the greater opportunity for them to have frequent, regular sessions nearer their home.

4. *Pacing therapy with resistance.* Resistance to psychological treatment is not uncommon in settings where people have come for medical treatment. The psychologist must be attuned to resistance of all types and be able to gauge the extent to which families or individual family members are prepared to develop a therapeutic relationship. In this respect, accurate timing and creativity in approaching families will facilitate therapeutic work and neutralize the resistance.

5. *Assessment.* Prompt identification of families' needs will make it easier to plan their treatment, give them a better sense of support from the treatment team, and allow the institution of preventive measures.

Acknowledgment. We wish to express our sincere appreciation to the D family for allowing us to describe our association with them. They were delightful to work with, and we learned a great deal from their experiences.

REFERENCES

Alby, N. (1980). Ending the chemotherapy of acute leukemia: A period of difficult weaning. In J. L. Schulman & M. J. Kupst (Eds.), *The child with cancer* (pp. 175–182). Springfield, IL: Charles C Thomas.

American Psychiatric Association (1987). *Diagnostic and statistical manual of mental disorders* (3rd ed., revised). Washington, DC: Author.

Bateson, G. (1972). *Steps to an ecology of the mind.* New York: Ballantine.

Beery, K., & Buktenica, N. (1967). *Developmental Test of Visual–Motor Integration.* Chicago: Follet Education Corp.

Benton, A. L., Hamsher, K. D., Varney, N. R., & Spreen, O. (1983). *Contributions to neuropsychological assessment.* New York: Oxford University Press.

Blos, P. (1962). *On adolescence.* New York: Free Press.

Buschke, H. (1974). Components of verbal learning in children: Analysis by selective reminding. *Journal of Experimental Child Psychology, 18,* 488–496.

Copeland, D. R. (1988). The staffing conference as a demonstration of integrated care. In B. Pack & D. R. Copeland (Eds.), *The nurse as person* (pp. 85–96). Houston, TX: University of Texas M. D. Anderson Hospital and Tumor Institute.

Copeland, D. R., & Dowell, R. E. (1987). Cognitive and social problems in children who survive. *Proceedings of the Fifth National Conference on Human Values and Cancer* (pp. 79–84). New York: American Cancer Society.

Copeland, D. R., Pfefferbaum, B., & Stovall, A. J. (1983). *The mind of the child who is said to be sick.* Springfield, IL: Charles C Thomas.

Copeland, D. R., & Van Eys, J. (Eds.). (1987). Childhood cancer survivors: Living beyond cure. *The American Journal of Pediatric Hematology/Oncology, 9,* 56–118.

Davidson, E. R., Copeland, D. R., Dowell, R. E., Riggert, S. C., & Mize, M. M. (intr.

by J. van Eys). (1987). Staff perceptions of ward atmosphere in a pediatric oncology unit. *Clinical Research, 35*(1), 73A.

Deasy-Spinetta, P. (1981). The school and the child with cancer. In J. J. Spinetta & P. Deasy-Spinetta (Eds.), *Living with childhood cancer* (pp. 153–168). St. Louis, MO: Mosby.

Denckla, M. B., & Rudel, R. (1974). Rapid "automatized" naming of pictured objects, colors, letters, and numbers by normal children. *Cortex, 10*, 186–202.

Desmond, H. (1980). Two families: An intensive observational study. In J. Kellerman (Ed.), *Psychological aspects of childhood cancer* (pp. 100–127). Springfield, IL: Charles C Thomas

Dunn, L. M., & Dunn, L. M. (1981). *Peabody Picture Vocabulary Test—Revised.* Circle Pines, MN: American Guidance Service.

Dunn, L. M., & Markwardt, F. C., Jr. (1970). *Peabody Individual Achievement Test.* Circle Pines, MN: American Guidance Service.

Education for All Handicapped Children Act of 1975, 20 U.S.C. § 1401 (1975).

Fletcher, J. M. (1985). Memory for verbal and nonverbal stimuli in learning disability subgroups: Analysis by selective reminding. *Journal of Experimental Psychology, 40*, 244–259.

Foster, D. J., O'Malley, J. E., & Koocher, G. P. (1981). The parent interview. In G. P. Koocher & J. E. O'Malley (Eds.), *The Damocles syndrome* (pp. 86–100). New York: McGraw-Hill.

Gaddes, W. H., & Crockett, D. J. (1975). The Screen-Benton Aphasia Tests, normative data as a measure of normal language development. *Brain and Language, 2*, 257–280.

Goggin, E. L., Lansky, S. B., & Hassanein, K. (1976). Psychological reactions of children with malignancies. *Journal of the American Academy of Child Psychiatry, 15*, 314–325.

Jackson, D. D., & Weakland, J. H. (1961). Conjoint family therapy: Some considerations on theory, technique, and results. *Psychiatry, 24*, 30–45.

Jastak, J. F., & Jastak, S. (1978). *Wide Range Achievement Test—Revised Edition.* Wilmington, DE: Jastak Associates, Inc.

Kagen, L. B. (1976). Use of denial in adolescents with bone cancer. *Health and Social Work, 1*, 71–87.

Kagen-Goodheart, L. (1977). Reentry: living with childhood cancer. *American Journal of Orthopsychiatry, 47*, 651–658.

Kashani, J., & Hakami, N. (1982). Depression in children and adolescents with malignancy. *Canadian Journal of Psychiatry, 27*, 474–477.

Katz, E. R. (1980). Illness impact and social reintegration. In J. Kellerman (Ed.), *Psychological aspects of childhood cancer* (pp. 14–46). Springfield, IL: Charles C Thomas.

Kaufman, A. S. (1979). *Intelligent testing with the WISC-R.* New York: Wiley.

Keith, D. V., & Whitaker, C. A. (1983). Co-therapy with families. In B. B. Wolman & G. Stricker (Eds.), *Handbook of family and marital therapy* (pp. 343–355). New York: Plenum.

Kellerman, J., & Katz, E. R. (1977). The adolescent with cancer: Theoretical, clinical and research issues. *Journal of Pediatric Psychology, 2*, 127–131.

Kellerman, J., Zeltzer, L., Ellenberg, L., Dash, J., & Rigler, D. (1980). Psychological effects of illness in adolescence—I. Anxiety, self-esteem and perception of control. *Journal of Pediatrics, 97*, 126–131.

Kemler, B. (1981). Anticipatory grief and survival. In G. P. Koocher & J. E. O'Malley (Eds.), *The Damocles syndrome* (pp. 130–143). New York: McGraw-Hill.

Kirten, C., & Liverman, M. (1977). Special educational needs of the child with cancer. *Journal of School Health, 47*, 170–173.

Koocher, G. P., & O'Malley, J. E. (Eds.). (1981). *The Damocles syndrome.* New York: McGraw-Hill.

Koocher, G. P., O'Malley, J. E., Gogan, J. L., & Foster, D. J. (1980). Psychological adjustment among pediatric cancer survivors. *Journal of Child Psychology and Psychiatry, 21*, 163–173.

Kupst, M. J., & Schulman, J. L. (Eds.). (1980a). *The child with cancer.* Springfield, IL: Charles C Thomas.

Kupst, M. J., & Schulman, J. L. (1980b). Family coping with leukemia in a child: Initial reactions. In J. L. Schulman & M. J. Kupst (Eds.), *The child with cancer* (pp. 111–128). Springfield, IL: Charles C Thomas.

Kupst, M. J., Schulman, J. L., Honig, G., Maurer, H., Morgan, E., & Fochtman, D. (1982). Family coping with childhood leukemia: One year after diagnosis. *Journal of Pediatric Psychology, 7*, 157–174.

Kupst, M. J., Schulman, J. L., Maurer, H., Honig, G., Morgan, E., & Fochtman, D. (1984). Coping with pediatric leukemia: Two-year follow-up. *Journal of Pediatric Psychology, 9*, 149–162.

Kupst, M. J., Schulman, J. L., Maurer, H., Morgan, E., Honig, G., & Fochtman, D. (1983). Psychosocial aspects of pediatric leukemia: From diagnosis through the first six months of treatment. *Medical and Pediatric Oncology, 11*, 269–278.

Lansky, S. B., Smith, S. D., Cairns, N. U., & Cairns, G. F. (1983). Psychological correlates of compliance. *American Journal of Pediatric Hematology/Oncology, 5*, 87–92.

Lewis, S., & LaBarbera, J. D. (1983). Terminating chemotherapy: Another stage in coping with childhood leukemia. *The American Journal of Pediatric Hematology/Oncology, 5*(1), 33–37.

Michael, B. E., & Copeland, D. R. (1987). Psychosocial issues in childhood cancer: An ecological framework for research. *The American Journal of Pediatric Hematology/Oncology, 9*, 73–83.

Moos, R. H. (1974). *Evaluating treatment environments: A social ecological approach.* New York: Wiley.

Moos, R. (1977). A social ecological perspective on mental disorders. In E. Wittkower & H. Warnes (Eds.), *Psychosomatic medicine: Its clinical applications.* New York: Harper & Row.

Moos, R. (1982). Coping with acute health crisis. In T. Millon, C. Green, & R. Meagher (Eds.), *Handbook of clinical health psychology* (pp. 129–151). New York: Plenum.

O'Malley, J. E., Koocher, G., Foster, D., & Slavin, L. (1979). Psychiatric sequelae of surviving childhood cancer. *American Journal of Orthopsychiatry, 49*, 608–616.

Ozols, E. J., & Rourke, B. P. (1985). Dimensions of social sensitivity in two types of learning-disabled children. In B. P. Rourke (Ed.), *Neuropsychology of learning disabilities* (pp. 281–301). New York: Guilford.

Porter, J. F. (1980). Identification of subtypes of learning disabled children: A multivariate analysis of patterns of personality functioning. *Dissertation Abstracts International, 41*, 1125B.

Porter, J. E., & Rourke, B. P. (1985). Socioemotional functioning of learning-disabled children: A subtypal analysis of personality patterns. In B. P. Rourke (Ed.), *Neuropsychology of learning disabilities* (pp. 257–280). New York: Guilford.

Powazek, M., Kennelly, D., Imbus, C., & Rosen, R. (1983). Neuropsychological and neurological functioning of children surviving acute lymphocytic leukemia (ALL). *Proceedings, American Society of Clinical Oncology, 2*, 73.

Reitan, R. (1969). *Manual for administration of neuropsychological test batteries on adults and children.* Bloomington, IN: Indiana University Press.

Schowalter, J. E. (1977). Psychological reactions to physical illness and hospitalization in adolescence: A survey. *Journal of the American Academy of Child Psychiatry, 16,* 500–516.

Schulman, J. L., & Kupst, M. J. (Eds.). (1980). *The child with cancer.* Springfield, IL: Charles C Thomas.

Small, N. (1969). *Levels of perceptual functioning in children: A developmental study.* Unpublished masters thesis, University of Florida, Gainesville.

Spinetta, J. J. (1977). Adjustment in children with cancer. *Journal of Pediatric Psychology, 2,* 49–51.

Spinetta, J. J. (1978). Communication patterns in families dealing with life-threatening illness. In O. J. Z. Sahler (Ed.), *The child and death* (pp. 43–51). St. Louis, MO: Mosby.

Spinetta, J. J. (1980). Disease-related communication: How to tell. In J. Kellerman (Ed.), *Psychological aspects of childhood cancer* (pp. 257–269). Springfield, IL: Charles C Thomas.

Spinetta, J. J., & Deasy-Spinetta, P. (1981). *Living with childhood cancer.* St. Louis, MO: Mosby.

Spinetta, J. J., & Maloney, L. J. (1978). The child with cancer: Patterns of communication and denial. *Journal of Consulting and Clinical Psychology, 46,* 1540–1541.

Spreen, O., & Gaddes, W. H. (1969). Developmental norms for 15 neuropsychological tests, age 6 to 15. *Cortex, 5,* 171.

Strupp, H. H., & Binder, J. L. (1984). *Psychotherapy in a new key.* New York: Basic Books.

Trites, R. L. (1977). *Neuropsychological test manual.* Ottawa, Ontario, Canada: Royal Ottawa Hospital.

Van Dongen-Melman, J. E. W. M., & Sanders-Woudstra, J. A. R. (1986). Psychosocial aspects of childhood cancer: A review of the literature. *Journal of Child Psychology and Psychiatry, 27,* 145–180.

van Eys, J., & Copeland, D. R. (1984). The staffing conference in pediatric oncology. In A. E. Christ & K. Flomenhaft (Eds.), *Childhood cancer: Impact on the family* (pp. 87–103). New York: Plenum.

Wechsler, D. (1974). *Wechsler Intelligence Scale for Children—Revised.* New York: The Psychological Corporation.

Zeltzer, L. K. (1980). The adolescent with cancer. In J. Kellerman (Ed.), *Psychological aspects of childhood cancer* (pp. 70–99). Springfield, IL: Charles C Thomas.

Zeltzer, L., Kellerman, J., Ellenberg, L., Dash, J., & Rigler, D. (1980). Psychologic effects of illness in adolescence—II. Impact of illness in adolescents. Crucial issues and coping styles. *Journal of Pediatrics, 97,* 132–138.

17
Bone Marrow Transplantation in Children: A Case Study

ANDREW S. BRADLYN
STEPHEN R. BOGGS

INTRODUCTION

Over the past 30 years, the prognosis for pediatric cancer patients has improved dramatically. For example, 30 years ago the median length of survival for children with acute lymphoblastic leukemia (ALL) was 6 months postdiagnosis. Contrast this with the fact that 70% of the children who began treatment in 1978 for ALL were alive in 1985 (Hammond, 1986). Similar findings have been reported for other neoplastic diseases (e.g., Young, Gloeckler, Silverberg, Horm, & Miller, 1986). These improvements are the result of improved diagnostic and treatment procedures, for example, the advent of central nervous system (CNS) therapy for ALL patients (Siegel, 1980).

However, for those patients who do not respond to standard treatment protocols, bone marrow transplantation (BMT) is an accepted therapeutic option. The bone marrow is the cellular material in the central portion of the bone; red blood cells, white blood cells, and platelets are manufactured by the marrow. Parkman (1986) notes that BMT is the treatment of choice for ALL patients with a second remission, first remission acute myelogenous leukemia (AML) patients, and chronic myelogenous leukemia (CML) patients. Additionally, BMT may be used to treat patients diagnosed with relapsed non-Hodgkin lymphoma and some solid neoplasms (Parkman, 1986; Quinn, 1985). The prognosis for transplanted patients varies and is

Andrew S. Bradlyn. Department of Behavioral Medicine and Psychiatry, West Virginia University Health Sciences Center, Morgantown, West Virginia.

Stephen R. Boggs. Department of Clinical and Health Psychology, University of Florida, Gainesville, Florida.

somewhat dependent upon the ability to find a suitable donor, the specific disease, number of previous relapses, and type of transplant performed.

BMT is a relatively straightforward procedure. Patients are typically admitted to the hospital to undergo a conditioning regimen that may include intensive chemotherapy and total body irradiation to destroy malignant cells and to suppress the immune system in order to ensure that the new marrow is not rejected. Additionally, a central venous line is placed in the child for transfusing blood products, nutrition, and the new marrow itself.

Following these treatments, the new bone marrow is infused through the central line. This process appears identical to the manner in which blood products are infused. The new marrow may come from the patient himself/herself (autologous), an identical twin (syngeneic), or from a genetically nonidentical donor such as a sibling (allongenic). The remainder of the hospitalization entails evaluation and monitoring of the engraftment process and treatment of any medical complications. The average stay is from 6 to 8 weeks duration. As a result of the conditioning regimen, patients are hospitalized in laminar airflow rooms that provide an environment protected against bacteria and germs. These rooms are relatively small and contain a bed, a toilet, exercise equipment (e.g., stationary bicycle), and a television. Everyone entering the room must wear a gown and wash his/her hands prior to entry. Visitors are not allowed to stay overnight. While hospitalized, the patients are given a low-bacteria diet and drink bottled water. Most importantly, patients are not allowed to leave their room until discharge. Families are asked to remain in the local community for up to 3 months after the discharge in order for follow-up care to be provided.

There are a number of areas of potential stress associated with a BMT. From a medical standpoint, a variety of complications may result, including the failure of the transplanted marrow to engraft, opportunistic infection, pneumonia, graft-versus-host disease, and the possibility of recurrent malignancy (Quinn, 1985).

From a psychosocial perspective, the potential stressors are numerous. In an early study of seven pediatric patients, ages 4 to 15 years, undergoing BMT, Gardner, August, and Githens (1977) administered a variety of objective and projective measures and identified five problem areas: (1) anxiety and depression associated with the painful procedures and fears of death; (2) overly dependent behavior that is related to feelings of helplessness; (3) anger toward staff and parents; (4) diminished tolerance for medical procedures; and (5) periodic refusal to cooperate. Similar findings, in part or in whole, have been reported by a number of other authors (Holland, Plumb, Yates, Harris, Tuttolomondo, Holmes, & Holland, 1977; Patenaude & Rappeport, 1982; Patenaude, Syzmanski, & Rappeport, 1979).

It is important to note however, that at least two investigations have provided data indicating that negative behavior changes in protected environments such as the laminar airflow room are transitory. Kellerman and his colleagues (Kellerman, Rigler, & Siegel, 1979; Kellerman, Rigler, Siegel, McCue, Pospisil, & Uno, 1976) examined the effects of protected environments on intellectual and behavioral observation measures collected on 14 and 7 children, respectively, who were between the ages of 2 and 16 years of age. Nurses provided daily behavior ratings of children's behavior on a number of psychosocial dimensions, including appetite, sleep, physical discomfort, affect, activity, and social–interpersonal. The authors reported that no generalized pattern of decrement was found on test-retest administrations of standardized intellectual measures. Additionally, these investigators reported that the behavioral changes noted by the nursing staff were largely transitory in nature and no long-term or severe psychological disturbances were observed. These studies can not be considered completely naturalistic, however, as the children who were investigated participated in a comprehensive psychosocial program that may have served to attenuate many of the negative aspects of the transplant process.

Without question, an overwhelming majority of authors have stated the importance of providing psychosocial care to these children. Kellerman et al. (1976, 1979) outline a program of pre- and postdischarge orientation, ongoing therapy, continuous measurement, evaluation of cognitive functioning, and intense play therapy as being important components of a program that aims to provide psychological evaluation and management of these children. In a more recent article, Linn, Beardslee, and Patenaude (1986) outline one such puppet therapy program, although no data are provided to support its effectiveness.

The following case illustrates the psychological evaluation, treatment, and consultation associated with the bone marrow transplantation of a 10-year-old female with Ewing sarcoma, a highly malignant bone tumor. This case illustrates the functions of a psychologist who is routinely involved in the psychosocial care of these patients. Additionally, the use of a standardized daily monitoring assessment completed by the nurses is described to highlight the importance of frequent and efficient data collection. Interventions designed to improve adjustment and reinforce compliance with treatment regimens are also illustrated.

CASE BACKGROUND

At the time of admission to the Bone Marrow Transplant Unit (BMTU), Sheila M was 10 years old. She lived with her natural mother (aged 35 years), her father (aged 37 years), and one older brother (aged 12 years). Both the mother, Jacqui, and the father, Jim, were employed. Jacqui was a full-time secretarial supervisor at an accounting firm, and Jim was a self-employed plumber. Sheila's brother John had just entered the seventh grade and was described as well-behaved and understanding of the parental time involved in his sister's medical treatment. The paternal grandmother and one paternal aunt lived in the family's community and provided assistance with child care when necessary. Both the grandmother and aunt had agreed to help the Ms with transportation and domestic arrangements during Sheila's hospitalization.

Sheila's early development was unremarkable; her mother related that all developmental milestones were reached on time. The parents stated that Sheila was quite sociable throughout her life, had numerous friends her own age, and most enjoyed outdoor activities such as bike riding, skateboarding, and swimming. Sheila's behavior at home presented no difficulties for the family. Although she was occasionally noncompliant and "stubborn," the Ms were not concerned about these infrequent problems. Sheila had successfully completed the fourth grade of elementary school and had begun the fifth grade year on homebound instruction. Her school performance was average, and her mother noted that no significant behavior problems were ever mentioned by her teachers.

Sheila's medical history to this point had been short but traumatic. Nine months prior to her transplantation admission, she had had an accident on her skateboard that resulted in a painful back injury. She was taken to her local pediatrician and treated for muscle strain for several weeks. When her pain did not diminish, the physician ordered a routine x-ray which suggested a lesion on one rib. She was immediately referred for further evaluation to a major medical center 200 miles from her home, where a CAT scan revealed the presence of a large tumor involving her rib and causing displacement of her liver and kidney. There was no evidence of metastases. A biopsy the next day led to the diagnosis of Ewing sarcoma, 8 weeks after her initial discomfort began.

Ewing sarcoma is a highly malignant tumor of the bone that primarily affects children and young adults. The disease usually presents in the extremities and in flat bones such as the pelvis and ribs (Mankin, 1985). Because Ewing tumors are at high risk for local recurrence and metastases, such patients are candidates for bone marrow transplantation, in order to potentially increase long-term survival. For Sheila, this treatment included intensive chemotherapy, total body irradiation, and an autologous bone marrow transplant.

After diagnosis, the M family traveled weekly for 6 months to the medical center for outpatient radiation and chemotherapy. The side effects of these treatments included persistent alopecia (hair loss), episodes of nausea and vomiting, and general malaise. Twice during these 6 months of therapy, Sheila was hospitalized for 4- to 5-day periods because of infections caused by decreased immune system functioning resulting from these treatments. During these hospitalizations, Sheila would become somewhat withdrawn and irritable, but was reported to have cooperated readily with medical personnel and her parents.

As a part of the routine procedure for patients admitted to the BMTU, Sheila was referred to the medical center's pediatric psychology service by her attending physician. A psychological evaluation was requested to assist the BMTU medical personnel in planning for her stay in the intensive care environment. It was also requested that psychological intervention and support be provided as needed.

ASSESSMENT

Sheila and her family were contacted by us the day after admission. We explained that the pediatric psychology service was routinely involved in the care of BMTU patients, and that we would like to gather information to assist the staff in Sheila's care and the day-to-day management of her psychosocial needs. The family consented to provide this information and, subsequent to an initial interview, an assessment battery was administered in order to gather a broad range of information regarding Sheila's current social and emotional adjustment. Additionally, we were interested in assessing Sheila's ability to understand procedures related to bone marrow transplantation.

The data gathered indicated that Sheila was functioning in the average range of intellectual abilities [Wechsler Intelligence Scale for Children— Revised (WISC-R)] and was achieving in school at a level consistent with her grade placement and intelligence test performance. Based on these data, we believed that Sheila could be expected to understand many instructions related to the complex daily regimens that would be required of her once treatment began.

Jacqui completed the Achenbach Child Behavior Checklist (Achenbach, 1979) during Sheila's assessment. It was evident from this measure that outside of an expected elevation on a scale measuring somatic complaints, Jacqui perceived Sheila's behavior as within normal limits for girls this age on measures of both Internalizing and Externalizing behavior problems. In addition, the Social Competence scale results indicated good social adaptation prior to hospitalization.

Sheila's responses to a variety of self-report questionnaires were similarly unremarkable. She did not report significant pretransplant levels of depression (Children's Depression Inventory; Kovacs, 1981) or anxiety (Children's Manifest Anxiety Scale—Revised; Reynolds & Richmond, 1978), and endorsed items suggesting that her perceived self-concept was generally positive (Piers–Harris Children's Self-Concept Scale; Piers, 1984). However, some responses to individual items on the checklists were of concern. On the Piers–Harris, for example, Sheila endorsed several items relating to being excessively worried and nervous. When queried about these answers, she stated that she was afraid of the strange people at the hospital and was unhappy that she was different from other people. She also remarked that she did not understand the transplant process and was "scared about getting sick again."

Together with the interviews with Sheila and her parents, the assessment procedures suggested that Sheila was a well-behaved girl who was adjusting to her illness. She was experiencing some anxiety specific to her disease and its treatment and appeared fearful about unknown aspects of this final phase of treatment. Jacqui and Jim did express some concern that after Sheila became sick and irritable it might be difficult to gain her compliance with the various procedures of the transplant (e.g., mouthcare, exercise), and the parents were quite interested in input from the pediatric psychology service with regard to maximizing Sheila's adjustment while hospitalized.

CASE FORMULATION AND PROPOSED TREATMENT

Sheila's premorbid adjustment had been quite good, and she continued to be socially responsive and generally cooperative with her family and health care providers after the rapid onset of her illness. During past hospitalizations for infections, however, she had tended to become irritable, withdrawn, and occasionally oppositional. She also reported fear and uncertainty with regard to the upcoming medical procedures.

We developed an initial treatment plan that would be minimally intrusive, allow careful monitoring of Sheila's mental status and behavioral adjustment, and permit quick response to any emerging emotional/behavioral problems. Specifically, the plan involved the following:

1. Encouraging medical staff to explain carefully the procedures involved in the transplant process so that Sheila and her parents would be better able to predict the course of her treatment and her possible reactions to various components of the transplant regimens. Because of Sheila's fears concerning unknown aspects of the treatment, care was taken to answer her questions about any procedures using vocabulary she could easily understand. Additionally, the nursing staff was asked to give Sheila choices regarding her treatment whenever possible in order to increase her perceived control over events occurring during her hospitalization. For example, nurses were to give Sheila a choice of times for exercise rather than imposing strict schedules.

2. Providing frequent supportive contacts to Sheila and her parents which would serve to maintain a positive relationship with the family and provide a context for possible psychological intervention should such a need arise.

3. Implementing a daily monitoring system using nurses' ratings of Sheila's compliance, activity level, social interactions, and emotional adjustment. The results of these ratings could be graphed and visually inspected for trends suggestive of developing problems.

The monitoring system designed was based on previous research conducted by Kellerman and his colleagues (e.g., Kellerman et al., 1979; Kellerman, Rigler, & Siegel, 1977). Forty-three items were generated for a nurses' rating scale that covered such areas as compliance with routine care (e.g., oral hygiene, exercise, bathing); presence of physical symptoms (e.g., nausea, vomiting, headaches); emotional/social responses (e.g., anger, fear, withdrawal, happiness, friendliness); and activity level (e.g., time spent watching television, playing, reading, talking). Each item permitted a rating by the child's nurse on a four-point Likert scale (1 = "never" to 4 = "always"). A final item asked the nurse to rate the child's overall mood during the shift from 1 = "very negative" to 5 = "very positive." In addition, critical events such as "receiving chemotherapy" or "total body irradiation" were noted in a space for comments at the bottom of the form. The form was completed daily by the nurse, and each item was graphed daily in an individual time series allowing quick inspection of the nurses' perception of Sheila's performance on the various items over time. Figure 17-1 presents the daily monitoring form completed by the nurses.

COURSE OF THERAPY

We informed Sheila and her parents of the proposed treatment plan soon after the assessment was completed. Medical personnel were individually approached by the psychology intern (S. B.) and requested to complete the daily monitoring form and to provide Sheila with more detailed information about her medical treatment during their many daily interactions with her.

The psychology intern assigned to this case met with Sheila individually several times during the 2 days prior to the beginning of her medical treatment. Sheila was noted to maintain a high rate of positive interactions with staff, and she seemed friendly and cheerful at most times.

During the next 4 days, Sheila received intensive chemotherapy and total body irradiation. Her physical condition rapidly declined. She experienced severe vomiting and nausea, mucositis, and fatigue. Due to the intensity of mouth sores and nausea, Sheila could no longer eat and was maintained nutritionally with hyperalimentation through her central line. As could be expected, Sheila's behavioral functioning also showed dramatic changes. Nurses' ratings of predominant mood fell from an average of 4.3 (range 4–5) prior to treatment to an average of 3.1 (range 1–5) after treatment but prior to transplant, indicating that the nurses perceived Sheila's overall mood to be more negative in comparison with her presentation at admission.

PROTECTED ENVIRONMENT DAILY RATING SCALE

Patient:_____ Date:_____
Shift: 7-3   3-11   11-7   Nurse:_____

Please rate this child's behavior <u>for your shift</u> on the following dimensions:

```
 1. Food refusal.........................1....2....3....4....NA
 2. Appetite loss........................1....2....3....4....NA
 3. Restless sleep.......................1....2....3....4....NA
 4. Need for sedation....................1....2....3....4....NA
 5. Nightmares...........................1....2....3....4....NA
 6. Nocturnal enuresis...................1....2....3....4....NA
 7. Headache.............................1....2....3....4....NA
 8. Nausea/emesis........................1....2....3....4....NA
 9. Other physical discomfort...........1....2....3....4....NA
10. Cheerfulness.........................1....2....3....4....NA
11. Cooperativeness......................1....2....3....4....NA
12. Sociability..........................1....2....3....4....NA
13. Happiness............................1....2....3....4....NA
14. Friendliness.........................1....2....3....4....NA
15. Activity.............................1....2....3....4....NA
16. Aggressiveness.......................1....2....3....4....NA
17. Whining/complaining..................1....2....3....4....NA
18. Anger................................1....2....3....4....NA
19. Fear.................................1....2....3....4....NA
20. Withdrawal...........................1....2....3....4....NA
21. Crying...............................1....2....3....4....NA
22. Auditory/visual hallucinations......1....2....3....4....NA
23. Confusion/disorientation............1....2....3....4....NA
24. Self-stimulatory behavior...........1....2....3....4....NA
25. Time in bed..........................1....2....3....4....NA
26. Time watching TV.....................1....2....3....4....NA
27. Time listening to music.............1....2....3....4....NA
28. Time on telephone....................1....2....3....4....NA
29. Time reading.........................1....2....3....4....NA
30. Time playing.........................1....2....3....4....NA
31. Time sleeping........................1....2....3....4....NA
32. Time in conversation.................1....2....3....4....NA
33. Management problem w/oral meds......1....2....3....4....NA
34. Management problem w/IV inject......1....2....3....4....NA
35. Management problem w/eat or drink..1....2....3....4....NA
36. Management problem w/exercise.......1....2....3....4....NA
37. Management problem w/baths..........1....2....3....4....NA
38. Management problem w/toileting......1....2....3....4....NA
39. Management problem other............1....2....3....4....NA
40. Talking about illness...............1....2....3....4....NA
41. Request for physical care...........1....2....3....4....NA
42. Request for emotional support.......1....2....3....4....NA
43. Positive response to visitors.......1....2....3....4....NA
```

Predominant Patient Mood This Shift:
```
     1          2          3          4          5
   very     positive   neutral    negative     very
  positive                                    negative
```

<u>Comments</u>:

FIGURE 17-1. Nurses' daily rating form.

The most significant specific changes, as reflected in the nurses' ratings of behavior were food refusal, nausea/emesis, decreased activity level, and decreased social behaviors (e.g., "cheerful," "friendly," "positive response to visitors").

The nausea and emesis, although a predictable side effect of the aggressive chemotherapy and radiation, presented a particular problem for Sheila and her caregivers. Vomiting was occurring more frequently than expected, despite the painful effect that the emesis had on Sheila's mouth sores. It was noted that Sheila appeared to be very aware of her nauseous feelings and seemed to focus exclusively on these sensations. When she was awake, she spent most of her time sitting in bed leaning over an emesis basin cradled in her lap. She appeared to be watching television on occasion during these times, but her attention was primarily directed toward her physical condition. In order to relieve discomfort and prevent as much vomiting in response to nausea as possible, we decided, in consultation with the medical team, that Sheila might benefit from learning strategies that would increase her attention to the unpleasant physical sensations of nausea and thus increase the length of time between vomiting episodes.

We suggested a distraction/relaxation procedure that involved Sheila placing her emesis basin on the bedside table, leaning back on her pillows, closing her eyes, and imagining herself engaged in one of her favorite activities. The intern (S. B.) met with Sheila and explained to her that the frequent vomiting was something that might prevent her from getting well quickly and that other children with the same problem had found it fun and helpful to try "not paying attention" to their bad feelings by using their imaginations to forget their nausea. Sheila was skeptical about the idea that she could control her vomiting, but was willing to try. The intern (S. B.) then spent time discussing possible "pleasant dreams" with Sheila. Her favorite activities were used to develop scenarios involving swimming in a pool, roller skating, and lying on the beach in the sun. Sheila practiced imagining these scenes with S. B. coaching her and guiding her imagery with verbal descriptions. After this session, Sheila was asked if she noticed any change in how sick she felt while she was "relaxing and imagining." Her response was a firm "no," but the intern observed that during the 45 minutes they had been talking and practicing that Sheila had not vomited or complained of nausea at all. Although she remained unconvinced, Sheila did agree to try these techniques at least twice each day. The mother and the nurse were asked to prompt Sheila's use of the strategy as well. Jacqui also began attempting to distract Sheila with games and television programs. Nursing progress notes and ratings of vomiting frequency from the daily monitoring system support general observations of a rapid decrease in emesis episodes over the next 2 days ($M = 3.2$, range 1–4 prior to transplant; $M = 2$, range 1–3 following transplantation).

On the seventh day after admission, Sheila received an autologous bone marrow transplant. The transplant itself involved infusing bone marrow through her central line and resulted in no pain or discomfort. Medical treatment posttransplant involves monitoring the patient's marrow recovery, prevention of infection, and supportive treatment. The patient must remain in the isolation room continuously until his/her marrow has recovered enough to allow discharge, often remaining 6 to 8 weeks after the transplant has occurred.

The posttransplant period of "waiting" can be very stressful for the patient and family. The patient's physical condition improves only gradually, and complications may occur such as excessive bleeding, infections, and rejection of the bone marrow graft. The day-to-day routine of uncomfortable medical procedures and limited availability of social interactions and entertainment may result in boredom, irritability, noncompliance, withdrawal, and/or depression. For the family, the posttransplant hospitalization period represents a continued disruption of family routine. It usually involves the prolonged absence of at least one parent from the family home, financial strain on the family's resources, and continual emotional stress for each family member.

In Sheila's case, medical complications during this period were relatively minimal compared with other children. At no time during her recovery phase did life-threatening events occur. She experienced frequent pain and discomfort from the treatment of mouth sores and unpleasant side effects resulting from antibiotics and antifungal medications. Her behavior during this period reflected her physical distress. Compliance to medical regimens decreased over this time, and it became more and more difficult for her caregivers to elicit cooperation with routine care. The time series data from the nurses' rating scales indicated that soon after transplant, management problems began emerging in oral care, food consumption, and exercise.

These problems were discussed with Sheila, her family, and the nursing personnel in order to specify clearly what was expected in each of these areas. A sticker chart was constructed that listed the important components of daily routine, and the chart was placed in Sheila's room. The caregivers were instructed to award brightly colored stickers each time a task was completed for the day. Items were included that reflected required regimens such as riding the stationary bicycle, bathing, and mouth care. Sheila was included in most discussions regarding the sticker chart and appeared excited about the system. She helped to set the daily goals for earning stickers and chose various backup rewards that could be earned through accumulating specified numbers of stickers. The effectiveness of the intervention was assessed through the ongoing nurses' rating system. Scores on items related to compliance with the regimens gradually increased over the

next few days and weeks, indicating that Sheila was increasingly cooperative in routine care activities.

At approximately 3 weeks posttransplant, the nurses caring for Sheila
began to express concern that she was unusually irritable and angry. Although she continued to cooperate with daily care and had begun eating
small amounts of food, the staff felt she had become "more negative and
hostile" than previously.

Responding to these comments, we consulted those data plotted during
Sheila's hospitalization that related to social interaction. It was noted that
during the early days of Sheila's hospital stay, she was rated very highly on
items related to positive interactions with staff ($M = 16$, range 6-20).
She was seen as outgoing, cheerful, and happy. Over the same period, base
rates of negative social behaviors such as whining, complaining, crying,
and verbal aggressiveness were low ($M = 7.8$, range 6-9). However, such
behaviors were indeed occurring regularly from the onset of her hospitalization. Since the posttransplant stage had begun, the rate of positive social
interactions had significantly decreased ($M = 10$, range 7-14), but the
nurses' ratings of frequency of negative social behaviors had increased only
slightly.

Given these data, we hypothesized that the nurses' perception of an
increase in negative social behavior were actually controlled more by the
decline from baseline of prosocial behavior than an increase in disruptive,
negativistic behavior. These data had important impact in developing
an intervention; because it was determined that Sheila was only infrequently emitting positive social behaviors, a strategy for increasing pleasant
events and positive stimulation was implemented as opposed to a decel-
erative strategy targeted toward negative social interaction. These data
were presented to the treatment team, and a general plan was implemented
that involved positive social response (e.g., special attention, playing
new games) to any socially positive initiation by Sheila. Gradual increases
in Sheila's positive interactions were reported via the daily monitoring
system.

OUTCOME

Sheila was discharged from the BMTU 6 weeks after admission. Postdischarge, she was seen several times weekly for a period of 5 weeks in the
pediatric oncology outpatient clinic to monitor her physical recovery. After
this monitoring period, less frequent follow-up was scheduled. At present
(2 years posttransplant), Sheila remains disease-free.

Sheila was also seen during her outpatient visits by S. B.; her psychosocial adjustment postdischarge was similarly uneventful. As Sheila's health
gradually returned to normal, so did her day-to-day behavioral functioning.

Although she remained on homebound instruction throughout her fifth-grade year, she returned to school in the sixth grade, and her parents report that she earns above average grades.

REFLECTIONS

This case illustrates many of the typical problems that we have encountered in our work with children hospitalized for BMT. The information gathered prior to, during, and following hospitalization supports the conclusions of other workers; that is, that these children generally do not demonstrate either severe or long-term psychological disturbance. The patient in this case did demonstrate noncompliant behavior in regard to self-care activities; however, they were effectively dealt with by means of a contingency management/point system. Her gradual decrease in positive social interactions was targeted for intervention using social reinforcement contingent upon prosocial interactions.

Perhaps the most important issues in this case involve the *process* by which consultation or management services are provided by psychologists and other mental health professionals. In our experience, it is critical that a mental health professional be an active member of the treatment team. This generally allows for earlier entry in the patient's evaluation and care, and relieves the physician of the responsibility of having to decide when a consultant should be called. It is our belief that transplant centers that include trained mental health professionals in the initial workup and on an ongoing basis throughout the patient's care are able to better meet the psychosocial needs of their patients. This identified professional can then manage the ongoing data collection procedures and be responsible for ensuring that the physicians responsible for the child's care are aware of problems as they develop.

Clearly, one must choose carefully the measures to be used for evaluating behavioral and cognitive functioning. In intensive settings such as a BMTU, there are a number of practical constraints and limitations that must be recognized. These include the large number of activities and interruptions during the conditioning regimen and the uncertainties of medical complications. Another factor that moderates the work of the psychologist is the fact that these children are seriously ill and may not have the energy or motivation to participate in lengthy assessments. Thus, it is important to balance the specificity of information needed against the demands made on the child. We have since questioned the utility of obtaining a complete intellectual and academic achievement battery, and presently use only gross measures of overall abilities (e.g., Vocabulary and Block Design subtests of the WISC-R; Wide Range Achievement Test—Revised).

The psychology staff involved in the case maintained daily contact with the child and/or the staff. Contacts with the patient could be as brief as

5 minutes or as lengthy as several hours, depending on the needs at that time. Additionally, the psychology staff attended the morning staffing rounds, during which time the medical and psychosocial needs of the patients were discussed and treatment personnel could be brought up-to-date on status changes.

The use of the daily nurses' ratings provided some of the most worthwhile information. This data collection method has the advantage of being frequent, allowing for problems to be identified as early as possible. Additionally, having a format such as this ensures that certain information is collected routinely, and thus one does not have to rely on the vagaries of perceptual biases and varying levels of tolerance for specific behaviors. The nurses' ratings do not require a great deal of time to complete, and can be easily incorporated into the charting routine, thereby providing a cost-effective method of collecting standardized information.

This case had a positive outcome. Unfortunately, not all transplants are successful. In those instances, continued contact with the family may be beneficial. The follow-up care of these patients has not been well investigated, and it is probably an area in which we are not as effective as we might be. It is our feeling, however, that contact must be maintained with the family to monitor the child's adjustment. We would encourage workers in this area to adopt the orientation that these children are "normal people in an abnormal situation" and not by default, psychopathological.

REFERENCES

Achenbach, T. M. (1979). The child behavior profile: An empirically based system for assessing children's behavioral problems and competencies. *International Journal of Mental Health, 7*, 24–42.

Gardner, G., August, C., & Githens, J. (1977). Psychological issues in bone marrow transplantation. *Pediatrics, 60*, 625–631.

Hammond, G. D. (1986). The cure of childhood cancers. *Cancer, 58* (Suppl. 2), 407–413.

Holland, J., Plumb, M., Yates, J., Harris, S., Tuttolomondo, A., Holmes, J., & Holland, J. F. (1977). Psychological response of patients with acute leukemia in germ-free environments. *Cancer, 40*, 871–879.

Kellerman, J., Rigler, D., & Siegel, S. E. (1977). The psychological effects of isolation in protected environments. *American Journal of Psychiatry, 134*, 563.

Kellerman, J., Rigler, D., & Siegel, S. E. (1979). Psychological response of children to isolation in a protected environment. *Journal of Behavioral Medicine, 2*, 263–274.

Kellerman, J., Rigler, D., Siegel, S. E., McCue, K., Pospisil, J., & Uno, R. (1976). Psychological evaluation and management of pediatric oncology patients in protected environments. *Medical and Pediatric Oncology, 2*, 353–360.

Kovacs, M. (1981). *The Children's Depression Inventory: A self-rated depression scale for school-aged youngsters.* Unpublished manuscript, University of Pittsburgh, Pittsburgh, PA.

Linn, S., Beardslee, W., & Patenaude, A. F. (1986). Puppet therapy with pediatric bone marrow transplant patients. *Journal of Pediatric Psychology, 11*, 37–46.

Mankin, H. J. (1985). Bone tumors. In J. B. Wyngaarden & L. H. Smith (Eds.), *Cecil textbook of medicine: Seventeenth edition* (pp. 1466–1468). Philadelphia: Saunders.

Parkman, R. (1986). Current status of bone marrow transplantation in pediatric oncology. *Cancer, 58*, 569–572.

Patenaude, A. F., & Rappeport, J. M. (1982). Surviving bone marrow transplantation: The patient in the other bed. *Annals of Internal Medicine, 97*, 915–918.

Patenaude, A. F., Szymanski, L., & Rappeport, J. (1979). Psychological costs of bone marrow transplantation in children. *American Journal of Orthopsychiatry, 49*, 409–422.

Piers, E. V. (1984). *Piers-Harris Children's Self-Concept Scale: Revised manual, 1984.* Los Angeles: Western Psychological Services.

Quinn, J. J. (1985). Bone marrow transplantation in the management of childhood cancer. *Pediatric Clinics of North America, 32*, 811–833.

Reynolds, C., & Richmond, B. (1978). What I think and feel: A revised measure of children's manifest anxiety. *Journal of Abnormal Child Psychology, 6*, 271–280.

Siegel, S. E. (1980). The current outlook for childhood cancer—the medical background. In J. Kellerman (Ed.), *Psychological aspects of childhood cancer* (pp. 5–13). Springfield, IL: Charles C Thomas.

Young, J., Gloeckler, L., Silverberg, E., Horm, J., & Miller, R. (1986). Cancer incidence, survival, and mortality for children younger than age 15 years. *Cancer, 58*, 598–602.

18

Cognitive–Behavioral Treatment of Pediatric Cancer Patients' Distress during Painful and Aversive Medical Procedures

LYNNDA M. DAHLQUIST

Pediatric cancer treatment involves a number of diagnostic and therapeutic procedures which are invasive and can be extremely distressing to child patients. For example, many chemotherapy protocols involve intravenous infusions, intravenous and/or intramuscular injections, and finger sticks at daily, weekly, or monthly intervals over several months and sometimes several years. Over time, the venopuncture process can become increasingly stressful. Local complications such as inflammation can develop, thus necessitating the use of veins that are more difficult and painful to access (Plumer, 1975). In addition, the chemotherapy itself causes significant aversive side effects including nausea, vomiting, diarrhea, immunosuppression, and hair loss.

Bone marrow aspirations (BMAs) are among the most traumatic of the diagnostic procedures frequently used with children with leukemia. BMAs involve the insertion of a needle into the child's hip bone. The marrow is then removed with a syringe and examined for presence or absence of cancer cells. The BMA procedure involves sharp, stinging pain as the needle pierces the skin; pain and heavy pressure as the needle penetrates the bone; and intense pain as the marrow is aspirated into the needle and syringe (Jay, Ozolins, Elliott, & Caldwell, 1983). Children with active disease may undergo BMAs as often as weekly or biweekly. Other patients may receive BMAs at 2- to 6-month intervals.

Severe anxiety often is associated with chemotherapy and diagnostic procedures. Patients may exhibit nausea, vomiting, skin rashes, insomnia,

Lynnda M. Dahlquist. Department of Psychiatry and Behavioral Sciences, Baylor College of Medicine, Houston, Texas.

and crying both immediately and several days before the procedure is scheduled (Jay et al., 1983; Katz, Kellerman, & Siegel, 1980). Because of the repeated nature of both diagnostic and chemotherapy procedures, the risk of developing conditioned anxiety reactions is great. In a recent survey of 68 pediatric oncology patients and their parents at Texas Children's Hospital, we found that 47% reported some anticipatory nausea and 29% reported anticipatory vomiting (Dahlquist, Cox, & Fernbach, 1986). These anticipatory symptoms can be embarrassing, unpleasant, and stressful for the child, parent, and medical staff. In addition, parent–child conflicts can easily arise if the child is reluctant to go to the clinic.

The traumatic, aversive nature of cancer treatment is significant for several additional reasons. It has been estimated that 20% of adult cancer patients drop out of treatment because of the aversive side effects of chemotherapy (Morrow, 1982). In children, the rate of noncompliance due to aversive aspects of treatment has been estimated at 30%, and may be even higher in adolescents.

Anxiety-related behaviors also can affect the safety of the medical procedure itself. For example, vomiting which occurs at the start of chemotherapy administration can compromise the sterility of the procedure. In addition, young children may exhibit extremely negative behavioral reactions, such as kicking, screaming, and resistance to such a degree that actual physical restraint by several adults may be necessary (Jay et al., 1983). The random, jerking, and flailing movements of the distressed child make the procedure more difficult to perform, prolong it, and, most importantly, increase the risk of unintentional injury to the child.

In summary, extreme distress during painful or aversive medical procedures can significantly increase the risk of physical and emotional harm to the child. The need for intervention to deal with this problem is clear. However, the psychological study of the difficulties faced by children undergoing repeated painful medical procedures is relatively new. As a result, the empirical literature offers only general conceptual and procedural guidelines for the clinician. Thus, the clinician must rely on fundamental theoretical principles, studies with adults, and his/her own creativity to address the practical problems involved in applying the empirical literature to a specific child.

A brief overview of the research and clinical literature will be presented as an introduction to the case material which follows.

OVERVIEW OF THE LITERATURE

The majority of studies employing psychological procedures to relieve children's distress during medical procedures have involved single stressful events of relatively brief duration, such as hospitalization, surgery, and dental restorations (Elkins & Roberts, 1983). Information about the procedure; observation of another child coping adaptively with the procedure (modeling); and training in cognitive–behavioral coping skills, such as relaxation and imagery, have all been demonstrated to decrease children's distress during such stressful medical procedures (see Elkins & Roberts, 1983; Melamed & Siegel, 1975).

However, closer examination of the literature, as well as the results of more recent studies, suggests that these approaches are not equally effective with all patients (Dahlquist, Gil, Armstrong, DeLawyer, Greene, & Wuori, 1986). Modeling and information appear to be most useful for naive, inexperienced patients, whose anxiety appears to be based on their unfamiliarity with the medical procedure. "Experienced" children, who have already undergone the procedure in the past (and particularly those patients whose past experiences have been negative), may not benefit at all (Klorman, Hilpert, Michael, LaGana, & Sveen, 1980), or may even become sensitized when exposed to modeling and/or information programs (Dahlquist et al., 1986; Faust & Melamed, 1984; Melamed, Dearborn, & Hermecz, 1983). Therefore, it has been recommended that experienced children may benefit the most from preparation that includes specific training in ways to cope with the procedure (Faust & Melamed, 1984).

Only a few researchers have attempted to teach specific coping strategies to children undergoing repeated, painful invasive medical procedures. For example, Elliott and Olson (1983) used a cognitive–behavioral program to decrease distress behaviors in children undergoing burn treatment. Patients were taught the following skills: (1) attention–distraction techniques (ways to attend to stimuli not associated with the medical procedure); (2) relaxed breathing (deep inhalation followed by slow exhalation); and (3) emotive imagery (heroic and relaxing scenes). Subjects received rewards for using the coping techniques during the burn treatment.

By means of a well-controlled multiple-baseline design, Elliott and Olson (1983) demonstrated that all four subjects trained in the coping strategies showed 25% to 52% decreases in behavioral distress. However, treatment effects did not generalize to burn treatment periods in which the therapist was not present to coach the child. When the coach was absent, all subjects returned to approximately baseline levels of behavioral distress, suggesting that the presence of the therapist was a crucial factor in decreasing the children's distress.

Similar cognitive–behavioral coping strategies were employed by Jay, Elliott, Ozolins, Olson, and Pruitt (1985) to reduce the distress of pediatric cancer patients undergoing BMAs and lumbar punctures (LPs). Patients were taught deep-breathing exercises and emotive imagery techniques involving superheros. For example, they imagined that they were Superman and were undergoing a painful experience in order to rescue someone in distress. Three behavioral rehearsal sessions were conducted in which the child and therapist pretended to perform the medical procedure and practiced appropriate coping. In addition, patients were shown a 12-minute modeling film in which a child goes through the coping strategies training program and eventually copes effectively with a BMA and a LP. Patients received trophies if they remained still and practiced the breathing exercises during the medical procedure. The subjects in this multiple-baseline study demonstrated approximately 50% decreases in observed distress following intervention.

Cognitive–behavioral coping strategies also have been shown to decrease children's distress during venopunctures for chemotherapy (Dahlquist, Gil, Armstrong, Ginsberg, & Jones, 1985). Dahlquist et al. (1985) taught pediatric cancer patients cue-controlled muscle relaxation, relaxing deep-breathing exercises, pleasant imagery, and positive self-talk coping strategies during four, 45-minute training sessions. The therapist reviewed the coping strategies with the child prior to each chemotherapy administration and coached the child through the actual venopuncture. Videogame playtime was provided as a reward for listening to relaxation tapes and using the coping procedures during the venopunctures. A multiple-baseline design demonstrated 46% to 68% reductions in observed distress and lower self-reported levels of distress following intervention.

The following two cases are examples of cognitive–behavioral treatment of children's distress during painful medical procedures. Both of these children appeared to be well-adjusted in their social, academic, and family functioning. Their revised third edition of the *Diagnostic and Statistical Manual of Mental Disorders* (DSM-III-R) diagnoses of "psychological factors affecting physical condition" (316.0) reflected the circumscribed nature of their difficulties, which was limited to the aversive aspects of their medical treatment. These particular cases were selected because they illustrate the problem-solving strategies the therapist must employ when the available empirical literature does not provide adequate direction for all aspects of intervention. For example, adapting therapeutic approaches designed for adults to the problems children face during medical treatment can be difficult. The clinician must also adjust to the practical constraints of his/her setting, which may include space and scheduling problems as well as financial realities. And finally, the individual needs of the patient must be taken into account. This requires a flexibility in one's approach to treatment, constant monitoring of treatment effectiveness, and creative problem solving when treatment does not work as expected.

CASE 1

BACKGROUND INFORMATION

Chris, an 8-year, 6-month-old boy, was diagnosed as having acute lymphocytic leukemia (ALL) at 5 years of age. After completing 2½ years of a 3-year chemotherapy protocol, he was found to have central nervous system relapse (leukemia cells were found in his spinal fluid). He subsequently underwent a 2-month course of radiotherapy and began a new chemotherapy protocol, which was scheduled to last 2 years. He reportedly responded well to treatment and quickly went into remission.

His mother described his first years of treatment as "easy." He was sick only a few times after chemotherapy and had little difficulty with aversive procedures such as BMAs, LPs, or venopunctures. However, he began experiencing more difficulty after his relapse. He developed what appeared to be a conditioned nausea and vomiting reaction during radiotherapy. He would vomit at the stoplight in front of the hospital as they drove in for his radiotherapy sessions. His anticipatory vomiting was controlled with Phenergan, an antiemetic, which his mother said "left him so sleepy that he did not vomit."

He developed chemotherapy-related anticipatory nausea and vomiting approximately 2 months after radiotherapy, following an adverse reaction to one of his chemotherapy medications, L-asparaginase. A small percentage of children treated with intravenous L-asparaginase have anaphylactic reactions ranging from skin rashes to bronchial constriction and cyanosis (Suto, Fernbach, & Vietti, 1984). During his L-asparaginase treatment, Chris's blood pressure dropped, and he reported feeling very hot, sensing that his heart was racing, and feeling extremely frightened. Since this anaphylactic reaction, nursing personnel reported that Chris had vomited before each chemotherapy administration as the IV needle was being inserted.

His mother also noticed that Chris had become much more apprehensive about treatment. He did not cry during painful procedures but did attempt to stall and delay the start of procedures. He cried each time he vomited during the initiation of chemotherapy. His mother noticed that he seemed more calm during procedures when he was distracted by computer game play prior to BMAs and LPs. She also noted that his postchemotherapy nausea and vomitting was less intense when he had an enjoyable activity planned after treatment.

Chris was the oldest of two children. His father worked as a teamster; his mother was recently laid off from a clerical position. The family's insurance had covered most of the expenses of Chris's medical care, thus keeping financial stresses to a minimum. Chris's mother said that they had tried to maintain as normal a life-style as possible during his illness, despite their concern and disappointment over his relapse. In addition, they attempted to find special activities for his younger sister so that she could also be the focus of attention and thereby minimize jealousy between the children. Both parents participated in his medical care.

Chris was described as a "straight A" student at the time of referral. He had just completed an advanced second-grade class (an intermediate placement between regular and gifted classes), where he excelled with little effort and little concern about grades or tests. Chris also was active in several organized sports, in which he also excelled, and had friends in the neighborhood and at school. No home or school behavioral problems were reported, except for occasional attempts to use illness complaints to get out of responsibilities, which his mother reported handling firmly.

ASSESSMENT

In the initial session, Chris and his mother were interviewed individually. The history presented previously was obtained from his mother. Chris initially was quiet and shy in the interview, but quickly warmed up. He enthusiastically discussed his sports interests in a friendly, socially appropriate manner. His vocabulary and verbal expression seemed at least average for his age. He did not appear anxious during the interview, but he did acknowledge feeling worried and nervous before chemotherapy. He said he "tried not to vomit" when his chemotherapy infusion was started, but that he "couldn't help it."

Chris obtained a State Anxiety score of 27 and a Trait Anxiety score of 31 on the State–Trait Anxiety Inventory for Children (Spielberger, Edwards, Lushene, Montuori, & Platzek, 1973). His scores fell around the 21st percentile for his age, suggesting that he did not have a pervasive anxiety disorder. His mother obtained a State Anxiety score of 31 (41st percentile) and a Trait Anxiety score of 30 (29th percentile) on the State–Trait Anxiety Inventory (Spielberger, Gorsuch, Lushene, Vagg, & Jacobs, 1983). She appeared to have a moderate amount of anxiety associated with Chris's medical treatments.

The intake interview was conducted immediately prior to a scheduled chemotherapy administration, which allowed for more direct measurement of Chris's reaction to chemotherapy. Chris was asked to rate how sick he had felt (1) the previous night, (2) when getting up that morning, (3) in the car, on the way to the hospital, and (4) before going to the clinic to receive chemotherapy. He also was asked to estimate how sick he expected to become that day. He also rated how sick he felt at the start of chemotherapy and again 10 minutes into chemotherapy.

Chris indicated his ratings on a visual analog scale consisting of a drawing of a 10-mm-long thermometer, anchored from "not at all sick" to "the sickest I've ever felt." He colored in the thermometer to indicate how "sick" he was feeling. The height of his colored-in "mercury" was then measured. His baseline subjective reports of nausea were:

1. Last night   0.4 mm
2. This morning   0.8 mm
3. Driving to hospital   0.4 mm
4. Before chemotherapy   0.7 mm
5. Expected degree of nausea   2.0 mm
6. Start of chemotherapy   0.7 mm
7. 10 minutes into chemotherapy   1.2 mm

Chris also was observed while receiving chemotherapy. He vomited about 75 ccs of emesis approximately 1 minute after the needle was inserted, while the nurse was taping the needle down. Such a quick vomiting response was assessed by the medical staff to be too soon to be due to the toxic effects of the drug. Chris was withdrawn and lethargic after vomiting. The nurse rated the severity of his vomiting as "1" on a scale of 1 to 10, anchored "mild" to "very severe." She described the vomiting episode as "much less severe" than his previous episodes.

Chris completed the same visual analog self-report ratings of nausea for each subsequent chemotherapy treatment throughout the course of psychological intervention. The nurse also recorded the time of IV needle insertion and the time vomiting began, estimated the amount of emesis, and rated the severity of the vomiting episode on the 10-point scale for each chemotherapy treatment.

CASE CONCEPTUALIZATION AND PROPOSED TREATMENT

Chris appeared to be a well-adjusted child who had developed a circumscribed conditioned anxiety reaction to chemotherapy. It was speculated that his nausea and vomiting had become classically conditioned to the environmental stimuli associated with chemotherapy, particularly to the insertion of the IV needle. Many of the medications he received as part of his chemotherapy protocol caused severe nausea and vomiting. These drugs were also paired with a number of "neutral" environmental stimuli, including the sight of the needle and sensations associated with the injection. Over time, these neutral stimuli had become conditioned and now elicited the nausea and vomiting. His traumatic experience with L-Asparaginase appeared to have enhanced the development of the conditioned response because of the extreme anxiety he experienced during the anaphylactic reaction, and his subsequent apprehension regarding chemotherapy.

Although there was no available literature at the time pertaining to the treatment of anticipatory nausea and vomiting in children, studies with adults suggest that progressive muscle relaxation training can be used in a counterconditioning paradigm (Lyles, Burish, Krozely, & Oldham, 1982).

Therefore, the initial treatment plan involved (1) training in progressive muscle relaxation and (2) home practice with relaxation tapes.[1]

COURSE OF THERAPY

Chris was seen in psychological therapy for 21 sessions over the course of 14 months. In the initial therapy session (Session 2), classical conditioning was explained to Chris and his mother. Chris was assured that we believed he was not vomiting volitionally and that he had been actively trying not to vomit. Appointments were scheduled at approximately 2-week intervals and were conducted in the therapist's office the hour prior to chemotherapy administration. This procedure differed from procedures reported in the literature with adults, in which the therapist typically conducted the relaxation training in the actual clinic treatment room. However, our hematology clinic facilities were too busy and too cramped to allow for comfortable relaxation therapy. Therefore, a different site was employed.

In this session, Chris was taught a condensed version of Bernstein and Borkovec's (1973) tension-release progressive relaxation procedure involving eight muscle groups. This condensation of the traditional 16 muscle groups was based on my clinical experience with children who tended to become bored and restless if the relaxation procedure took too long and was too detailed. A deep-breathing procedure was incorporated into the relaxation instructions. Chris was told to take a deep breath while tensing a muscle group and to exhale slowly while releasing the muscle group. An image of a peaceful scene was incorporated at the end of the relaxation sequence. (For example, Chris imagined he was outdoors by a lake on a sunny day.) Chris cooperated with the relaxation induction and appeared very relaxed at the end of the initial relaxation session. The relaxation training session was audiotaped. Chris was given the tape and instructed to practice relaxing at home twice a day.

In Session 3, Chris reported practicing relaxation four times the first week following training, and only one time during the next week. Therefore, a poster was made reminding Chris to practice his tape. Relaxation training was continued in Session 4.

As illustrated in Figure 18-1, Chris initially appeared to benefit from relaxation training. His vomiting latency increased to 3 minutes in the first chemotherapy treatment following training, which actually may have rep-

1. In a recent study, Redd, Jacobson, Die-Trill, Dermatis, McEvoy, and Holland (1987) found that videogame play during chemotherapy-related procedures resulted in lower self-reported anticipatory nausea in pediatric cancer patients. Their findings suggest that cognitive distraction may be an effective treatment for conditioned nausea and vomiting reactions in children.

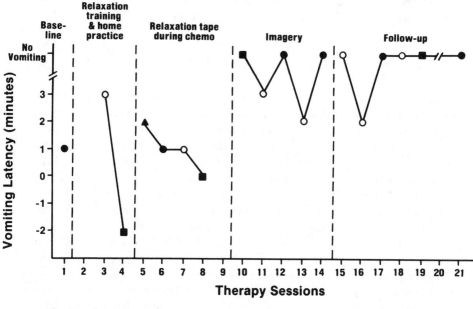

FIGURE 18-1.   Vomiting latency over the course of therapy. *Note*: 0 = the start of chemotherapy. Negative values indicate vomiting that occurred *before* the start of chemotherapy; positive values indicate vomiting that occurred *after* the start of chemotherapy.

resented a drug-induced effect, rather than an anticipatory response. However, he showed a dramatic deterioration in the subsequent chemotherapy administration; he vomited 2 minutes before the IV was even inserted.

Although Chris reported minimal compliance with home practice, he appeared quite skilled in the relaxation procedure during the therapy sessions. He remembered the tension-release exercises and appeared to be very relaxed at the end of the sessions. Therefore, his continued difficulties during chemotherapy did not appear to be attributable to an inability to relax. I hypothesized that the delay between relaxing in my office and receiving chemotherapy was too long. The delay might have provided him with too much time to think about the upcoming treatment and become anxious again before the chemotherapy started. Furthermore, I speculated that he might have difficulty relaxing in the clinical setting while receiving chemotherapy without some sort of external structure. However, it was extremely difficult to schedule his medical procedures so that I could be present during the chemotherapy administration. Therefore, an attempt was made to employ the relaxation tapes in place of my active participation.

In Session 5, I instructed him to listen to the tape in the clinic waiting room before chemotherapy, as well as at the start of chemotherapy. (He continued to receive relaxation instruction from me prior to each chemotherapy administration.) However, Chris was highly variable in his compliance with this recommendation. He used the tape only two times (Sessions 5 and 7) during actual chemotherapy administrations. As Figure 18-1 illustrates, the use of the relaxation tape before chemotherapy initially appeared to have a slightly beneficial effect, but his vomiting quickly returned to near baseline levels.

Several hypotheses were generated to account for the failure of this intervention: (1) Chris's difficulties might be due to his failure to listen to the tapes during chemotherapy administration. However, the vomiting data obtained when he *did* use the tapes did not provide convincing evidence that the tapes were effective. (2) The tapes might not have interrupted his anxious thoughts about the chemotherapy and therefore did not adequately serve as a competing response. (3) The tapes may have been boring. (4) The incentives might be inadequate.

Therefore, his treatment program was changed. A guided imagery component was added on the assumption that negative cognitions were not being affected by the progressive muscle relaxation alone. Chris provided the therapist descriptions of special places where he had felt comfortable and peaceful or happy in as vivid detail as possible. I incorporated these scenes into the end of each relaxation session, which was audiotaped.

The following is a paraphrase of one of the imagery instructions used with Chris.

> Imagine you are out in the boat with your grandfather, fishing for catfish. It's late in the afternoon on a hot summer day. You're both sitting quietly in the boat, trying hard not to make a sound that might scare the fish. Picture the boat. See the stringer with a couple of fish on it. You can see the sun way down low as it's starting to set. 'It almost looks like the sun is right on the lake' [his words]. Notice how pretty the sky looks as it starts to change colors. You feel a soft warm breeze on your face and the gentle rocking of the boat. The only sounds are the gentle plop, plop of the shrimp as you throw them into the water and the waves gently hitting the side of the boat. Off in the distance you hear a soft splash as a fish jumps and the faint chirping of a cricket. You quietly take a sip of the nice cold drink your grandmother sent along for you and wonder if a fish is coming up to your shrimp.

In Sessions 10 to 14, the combined relaxation and imagery exercise was conducted in the therapist's office. Chris then walked to the hematology clinic. I joined him when he was taken into the treatment room. He was instructed to lie down on the examining table and close his eyes. I then began describing the relaxing scene. When he appeared relaxed (i.e., no obvious muscle tensing, regular slow respiration rate), I signaled the nurse to begin the venopuncture. Meanwhile, I continued describing the relaxing scene.

A chart was developed to record Chris's progress. The theme of the chart was designed to fit his interests. For example, for the first chart Chris drew a football field marked off in yard lines. He pretended it was the fourth quarter of the playoff game between Chicago and LA; LA was ahead 14 to 9. For every minute Chris did not vomit during the start of chemotherapy, he was allowed to advance a football marker on his chart 1 yard. Whenever he did not vomit at the start of chemotherapy (which was defined as more than 3 minutes after the needle was inserted), he was allowed to advance the marker 15 yards. His parents planned special activities for him on days he did not vomit at the start of chemotherapy (such as a special purchase of clothes, a small toy, or a pizza lunch).

His subsequent improvement is dramatically illustrated in Figure 18-1. For the first time in more than 5 months, he did not vomit at the start of his treatment. Only three more episodes of anticipatory vomiting were reported. One incident occurred when he said he felt as though he were getting the flu (Session 13), and another incident occurred when the clinic was very busy and he was not given any time to relax before they began his infusion (Session 16).

The final phase of data collection presented in Figure 18-1 (Sessions 15 to 21) represents follow-up. Chris met with the therapist before each chemotherapy session and discussed his progress. Neither relaxation training nor in vivo coaching was conducted.

Chris's self-report of nausea also improved over the course of treatment. During follow-up, the following average self-report scores were obtained:

1. Last night   0.2 mm
2. This morning   0.2 mm
3. Driving to hospital   0.2 mm
4. Before chemotherapy   0.2 mm
5. Expected degree of nausea   1.1 mm
6. Start of chemotherapy   0.3 mm
7. 10 minutes into chemotherapy   0.3 mm

Therapy was terminated when Chris completed his chemotherapy protocol. For approximately 1 year following therapy termination, Chris and his mother contacted the therapist in conjunction with 1- to 3-month medical checkups. No subsequent problems were reported.

REFLECTIONS

This case illustrates the practical problems the clinician can encounter when trying to apply therapeutic techniques reported in the literature to the clinical setting. In our hematology clinic, the treatment rooms were heavily scheduled, noisy, and lacked comfortable furniture. Therefore, relaxation training had to be conducted away from the clinic. Second, the clinic schedule was very unpredictable. In order for a therapist to be present during actual chemotherapy administration, a minimum of 3 hours of therapist time would need to be left unscheduled. This can be very costly in a clinical setting where income generation is important. The compromise selected (i.e., using relaxation tapes in the place of live coaching) was hoped to be a more cost-effective method of intervention. In retrospect, this strategy was a poor choice. The live coaching component appeared to be essential for clinical improvement.

My experience with Chris proved very valuable in designing a treatment program for the case which follows. I developed a streamlined version of the live coaching program that was effective with Chris, in the hope of producing more rapid behavior change. However, this child was much younger than Chris and, therefore, required an intervention approach that was tailored to his developmental level and his interests. Finally, I attempted to reduce the cost of psychological intervention by actively involving his mother in the treatment process.

CASE 2

BACKGROUND INFORMATION

Alex, a 5-year, 5-month-old boy, was diagnosed as having leukemia at 17 months of age. He had completed a 3-year treatment protocol and had been off treatment for 6 months when he relapsed. At the time of referral, he had been involved in a new, very intensive chemotherapy protocol for approximately 6 months. His new protocol required one to three treatments per week in the clinic, in addition to medication at home. Most of the drugs he received reportedly made him either very ill with nausea and vomiting, or gave him flu-like symptoms, including fever, muscle aches, and lethargy.

Alex was referred for psychological treatment because he had become increasingly distressed during his medical procedures over the previous 2 months. For example, nurses reported that he became very tense when receiving intramuscular injections. When his leg was tense, the injections were quite painful for him. In addition, he had vomited two times in anticipation of receiving his IV medications. His crying also had increased during procedures, and he had begun to try to delay the initiation of procedures. His mother said that she used to be able to calm him by holding him and talking to him, but her efforts no longer were effective. Although she was able to keep from crying in his presense, she indicated that she felt upset and anxious when he became distressed.

Alex was the only child of parents in their late 20s. Alex's father was a computer technician and his mother was an administrative assistant. His mother described the first year after Alex's diagnosis as "stressful." She said that she and her husband coped differently with the disruption in their family schedule and with their concerns about his survival, which resulted in some marital tension that was subsequently resolved. His mother handled the majority of his medical care and medical visits and relied on family members to help care for Alex only on days he was sick from his treatments. Alex was scheduled to begin kindergarten the following year.

ASSESSMENT

The above history was obtained through an interview with Alex's mother. Alex also was interviewed individually. He was a charming, cute boy with a delightful sense of humor. His vocabulary was advanced for his age, and he showed a surprising openness in describing his problems with medical procedures.

During the interview, he said that he did "OK" with finger sticks, but that he got "nervous" when he saw the needles for shots, venopunctures, and BMAs. He said he felt scared when getting IVs and BMAs and that he felt like he wanted to move, but knew he was not supposed to do so. When he got that scared feeling, he said he felt like "throwing up." Then he looked up at me and calmly said, "All this talking stuff makes me want to throw up!" However, he continued to cooperate with the interview and was able to discuss his cat, his parents, and school without difficulty.

I observed Alex in the hematology clinic while he received two medications through intravenous injections in his hand. These medications reportedly had caused him significant nausea and vomiting in the past. The Observation Scale of Behavioral Distress (OSBD; Jay et al., 1983) was used to provide a quantifiable index of his level of distress during the procedure. This scale consists of 11 verbal, vocal, and motoric behaviors indicative of pain and anxiety in children, which are then weighted according to intensity. The occurrence of distress behaviors was coded in 15-second continuous intervals cued by tape-recorded signals. A total OSBD score was calculated by computing the average incidence of each distress behavior per 15-second interval, multiplying the average by the appropriate weight, and summing the values for all the distress behaviors. Thus, the final OSBD score represented a weighted mean distress score.

Alex's OSBD score for the baseline observation was 5.19 (see Figure 18-2). He cried, requested emotional support, and was visibly rigid during approximately half of the injection period, which lasted 7½ minutes. He screamed and verbalized pain during about one-fourth of that time period. At the end of the injection he asked for an emesis basin in case he needed to vomit.

CASE FORMULATION AND PROPOSED TREATMENT

Alex appeared to have a conditioned anxiety reaction to his chemotherapy. His level of anxiety during chemotherapy was quite high. He also was experiencing very severe side effects from the chemotherapy, which probably were frightening to him. He also appeared to be in the early stages of developing a conditioned nausea and vomiting reaction.

Based on the experience with the child in Case 1, it was decided to proceed directly to in vivo coaching in relaxation coping strategies during chemotherapy. Because of his young age, a very simplified relaxation procedure involving relaxing breathing was chosen, rather than a more elaborate progressive muscle relaxation. To combat anxious cognitions, guided imagery was used. A reward program also was included.

COURSE OF THERAPY

I saw Alex for 10 psychological therapy sessions which took place during the actual chemotherapy administration. Because he was scheduled for several treatments a month, we were able to practice coping skills frequently.

In the first session, I explained to Alex how anxiety affects the pain and discomfort associated with chemotherapy. He was asked to demonstrate tensing his leg during a shot. His tense leg muscle was used to illustrate how difficult and painful it would be to get a needle into the muscle. I then asked him to relax his leg to illustrate nice, soft muscles, in which it would be easier to stick a needle.

A similar analogy was used to explain his nausea. I explained that when he was nervous his stomach muscles got tight and felt bad and that made his stomach feel like he needed to vomit. He needed to learn to keep all his muscles nice and relaxed so that his stomach would feel better and the chemotherapy procedures wouldn't hurt as much. We also discussed how scared and worried thoughts made it hard for his body to stay relaxed, and that he would learn ways to think happy thoughts and help his body stay calm. To ensure he did not develop unrealistic expectations, I told him not to expect totally painless procedures, but rather to expect that each time he tried to relax, it would get a little easier for him.

I taught Alex a deep-breathing exercise similar to that used by Elliott and Olson (1983). First, he imagined he was a big bicycle tire being pumped up with air as he inhaled. To illustrate slow exhalation, he then pretended that the tire had a tiny pinhole in it and practiced letting the air leak out of the tire slowly with an audible hissing sound. He also pretended there was a huge hole in the tire to illustrate rapid exhalation, to remind him of what he should *not* do during painful procedures. Slow, relaxing breathing was practiced several times.

We developed a reward system involving a special toy goal. A picture of the toy was drawn and then divided into several sections. Alex was allowed to color in a part of the picture each time he closed his eyes and tried to relax during a procedure. When the entire picture was colored, he was able to buy the toy. In addition, I provided a surprise sticker at the end of each medical procedure as a reward for trying to relax. I decided to reward effort, rather than actual accomplishment of no vomiting or no crying, for two reasons: (1) to avoid unrealistic expectations for immediate mastery over pain or distress, and (2) because it was uncertain how well he would be able to use the relaxation strategies or how much improvement would be reasonable to expect. My objective was to avoid the possibility of a failure experience.

About 10 minutes before each medical procedure, Alex entered the treatment room and positioned himself in preparation for the injection. He typically sat on his mother's lap. Although the possibility existed that this position would make it more likely that any anxiety his mother might experience would be communicated to him, he was so upset by the prospect of not sitting on her lap that it appeared less distressing to proceed with this arrangement. I instructed him to close his eyes and take slow deep breaths. As he began to appear relaxed, I began describing a relaxing scene. In the first few sessions, the therapist provided the imaginary scene (e.g., floating on a cloud above his neighborhood). Later in therapy, he provided his own content for the scenes.

After 10 to 15 minutes of relaxing imagery, the nurse or physician entered the room. Alex was told what procedure was going to be done and was instructed to close his eyes again, take deep breaths, and imagine the relaxing scene. I provided an ongoing description of the scene and prompted him to take deep breaths when he appeared tense.

During the initial therapy sessions, Alex was reluctant to close his eyes. He became very upset when he thought he would not know what was being done to him. He repeatedly asked questions such as, "What are you doing? Is the needle in yet?," which interfered with the imagery. His mother and the nurses attempted to answer his questions and reassure him, which appeared to further distract him from relaxation efforts. In addition, his questions served to delay the procedure.

Therefore, the following changes were made. Alex was allowed to ask the nurses two questions prior to the procedure. He was reminded that no more questions were allowed, and that I would tell him when the needle was going in. Instructions to close his eyes and breathe deeply were repeated and the relaxing scene was described. When he appeared calm, I told him that the needle was going to be inserted and instructed him to take a deep breath. Relaxing imagery was continued for about 1 minute following needle insertion.

During a few of the initial sessions, Alex complained of needing to vomit, and asked for an emesis basin. Rather than bring him the basin and thereby communicate the expectation that he would indeed vomit, I told him to take deep breaths and relax his tummy. In this manner, he was able to successfully inhibit vomiting.

Alex seemed to enjoy the imagery work a great deal. He would often interject details he wanted included in the image as he was relaxing. For example, he often invited the staff in the room to join him in his fantasy trip, telling them where to sit on his magic cloud or flying dragon, etc.

At the end of the session, he often suggested an image he wanted to imagine in the next appointment. Sometimes his ideas taxed my creativity. For example, he once requested a fantasy ride on the back of a great big shark. It was a real challenge to make a shark ride a soothing, relaxing experience, but I was able to create an image of a benign somewhat sluggish shark, who liked to float and rock on the waves and visit interesting sea creatures.

Whenever possible, the actual sensory experience of the venopuncture was incorporated into the imagery as a transformed, nonthreatening stimulus. For example, one image involved a walk in the woods and the discovery of a tree covered with bright red cardinals. As Alex stood very still, taking slow deep breaths to keep from frightening the birds, one little bird hopped on his hand. The bird dropped a red berry on his hand and then pecked at his hand, trying to get the berry. I told Alex to imagine the bird pecking his hand as the IV needle was inserted. He seemed to enjoy this reconceptualization of the painful stimulus and later spoke of a speck of blood on his hand as "berry juice." (See Turk, Meichenbaum, & Genest, 1983, for an excellent overview of cognitive pain-management strategies.)

RESULTS

Alex's overt distress during chemotherapy venopunctures decreased dramatically once the "two question" rule was instituted. Limitation of the amount of delaying conversation appeared to help him focus on the relaxing imagery. He was able to remain still and calm throughout most of the subsequent chemotherapy treatments. Because of his cooperation, the venopunctures and injections also were conducted more quickly and with less apparent difficulty in accessing the veins.

After the third or fourth chemotherapy session, Alex told me, "You were right. It does get a little easier each time." He seemed proud of his mastery of the situation and bragged about his success to several of the medical staff members after each session, which resulted in considerable praise and attention. His mother reported that she felt much more relaxed during the chemotherapy procedures as well. Her decreased anxiety probably also contributed to the success of the intervention.

Psychological treatment was terminated when Alex was able to undergo a BMA without crying or interfering with the procedure. His cooperation during the BMA was seen as a good test of the generalization of the intervention, because he had a history of difficulty with BMAs and because he described the BMA himself as the most difficult of his medical procedures. Alex's mother had been present during all of his therapy sessions, and appeared to have a good understanding of the deep-breathing and imagery techniques. At termination, she planned to continue coaching him in the coping strategies. Alex was observed by my research assistant (who was unaware of his baseline distress scores and had been trained to a level of 85% agreement with my OSBD scores) at 9, 10, and 13 weeks after termination of psychological treatment while receiving two separate chemotherapy treatments and an LP. His resulting OSBD scores are presented in Figure 18-2 and represent 70% to 87% reductions from his baseline distress levels.

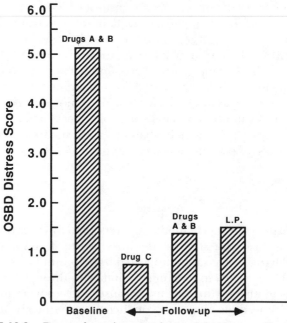

FIGURE 18-2.   Pre- and postintervention weighted mean distress scores.

A follow-up telephone call to his mother 4½ months after termination indicated that Alex continued to handle medical procedures without difficulty. Thus, the therapy effects appeared to generalize across medical procedures and to maintain following treatment.

REFLECTIONS

Several factors appeared to contribute to the success of this case. First, Alex received very frequent chemotherapy treatments. Although this was very stressful for him and may have contributed to the original development of his conditioned anxiety reaction, the frequency of his treatments also facilitated progress in therapy. It allowed for repeated, massed practice of coping skills, and therefore may have helped with the acquisition of the coping skills as well as the extinction of the anxiety response. Alex's sense of humor and vivid imagination also served to make the imagery process enjoyable for him (and for me). He also was very responsive to social reinforcers. Finally, his mother was bright and interested in his therapy. She appeared to use the coping strategies herself and most likely was an excellent coach. In fact the success of this case has prompted us to design a larger-scale study examining the effectiveness of training parents to serve as their child's coach during painful medical procedures.

This case also taught me a valuable lesson about the impact of painful medical procedures on caretakers. During one of Alex's chemotherapy treatments, his mother had to leave the room, so he sat on my lap during the procedure. I attempted to coach him as usual, but found myself becoming increasingly emotionally upset and tense when the venopuncture did not proceed smoothly, and he began to cling to me in search of comfort. This experience provided me with a small-scale, first-hand experience of the distress and sense of impotence parents must experience every time they must watch their child undergo a painful procedure. It is my clinical impression that some sort of "distance" is necessary if one is to be an effective coach. Something as simple as placing a child next to, instead of on the lap of, a parent may provide such a distance and help the parent function in the role of a coach.

The cooperation of the hematology medical staff also was crucial to the success of both Alex's and Chris's treatment. The nurses, in particular, were very helpful. They allowed us access to treatment rooms before procedures and were willing to rearrange their very busy schedules and wait patiently to allow time for relaxation exercises. The physicians and nurses also provided a great deal of praise for the children's successful coping efforts. Their cooperation may have been enhanced by my efforts to involve them in the assessment and treatment process by asking for their impressions frequently and by checking out treatment ideas with them ahead of time to make sure the intervention strategies were practical.

Finally, it should be noted that because of the designs of both case studies presented in this chapter, one cannot determine which specific aspect of the treatment package was the effective ingredient. Imagery, in vivo therapist coaching, and reinforcement all were introduced at the same time. Any one or all of these procedures may have resulted in the observed clinical improvement. Further research is needed in which the effectiveness of the individual components (progressive relaxation, deep breathing, imagery, reward systems, and in vivo coaching) in reducing children's distress during painful medical procedures is studied independently.

REFERENCES

American Psychiatric Association. (1987). *Diagnostic and statistical manual of mental disorders* (3rd., revised). Washington, DC: Author.

Bernstein, D. A., & Borkovec, T. D. (1973). *Progressive relaxation training: A manual for the helping professions.* Champaign, IL: Research Press.

Dahlquist, L. M., Cox, C. N., & Fernbach, D. (1986, March). *Correlates of anticipatory nausea in pediatric cancer patients.* Paper presented at the meeting of the Society for Behavioral Medicine, San Francisco, CA.

Dahlquist, L. M., Gil, K. M., Armstrong, F. D., DeLawyer, D. D., Green, P., & Wuori, D. (1986). Preparing children for medical examinations: The importance of previous medical experience. *Health Psychology, 5,* 249–259.

Dahlquist, L. M., Gil, K. M., Armstrong, F. D., Ginsberg, A., & Jones, B. (1985). Behavioral management of children's distress during chemotherapy. *Journal of Behavior Therapy and Experimental Psychiatry, 16,* 325–329.

Elkins, P. D., & Roberts, M. C. (1983). Psychological preparation for pediatric hospitalization. *Clinical Psychology Review, 3,* 275–295.

Elliott, C. H., & Olson, R. A. (1983). The management of children's distress in response to painful treatment for burn injuries. *Behaviour Research and Therapy, 21,* 675–683.

Faust, J., & Melamed, B. G. (1984). Influence of arousal, previous experience, and age on surgery preparation of same day of surgery and in-hospital pediatric patients. *Journal of Consulting and Clinical Psychology, 52,* 359–365.

Jay, S. M., Elliott, C. H., Ozolins, M., Olson, R., & Pruitt, S. (1985). Behavioral management of children's distress during painful medical procedures. *Behaviour Research and Therapy, 23,* 513–520.

Jay, S. M., Ozolins, M., Elliott, C. H., & Caldwell, S. (1983). Assessment of children's distress during painful medical procedures. *Health Psychology, 2,* 133–147.

Katz, E. R., Kellerman, J., & Siegel, S. E. (1980). Behavioral distress in children undergoing medical procedures: Developmental considerations. *Journal of Consulting and Clinical Psychology, 48,* 356–365.

Klorman, R., Hilpert, P. L., Michael, R., LaGana, C., & Sveen, O. B. (1980). Effects of coping and mastery modeling on experienced and inexperienced pedodontics patients' disruptiveness. *Behavior Therapy, 11,* 156–168.

Lyles, J., Burish, T., Krozely, M., & Oldham, R. (1982). Efficacy of relaxation training and guided imagery in reducing aversiveness of cancer chemotherapy. *Journal of Consulting and Clinical Psychology, 4,* 509–524.

Melamed, B. G., Dearborn, M., & Hermecz, D. (1983). Necessary considerations for surgery preparation: Age and previous experience. *Psychosomatic Medicine, 45,* 517–525.

Melamed, B. G., & Siegel, L. J. (1975). Reduction of anxiety in children facing hospitalization and surgery by use of filmed modeling. *Journal of Consulting and Clinical Psychology, 43,* 511–521.

Morrow, G. R. (1982). Prevalence and correlates of anticipatory nausea and vomiting in chemotherapy patients. *Journal of the National Cancer Institute, 68,* 585–588.

Plumer, A. D. (1975). *Principles and practice of intravenous therapy.* Boston: Little, Brown.

Redd, W. R., Jacobson, P. B., Die-Trill, M., Dermatis, H., McEvoy, M., & Holland, J. C. (1987). Cognitive/attentional distraction in the control of conditioned nausea in pediatric cancer patients receiving chemotherapy. *Journal of Consulting and Clinical Psychology, 55,* 391–395.

Spielberger, C. D., Gorsuch, R. L., Lushene, R. E., Vagg, P. R., & Jacobs, G. A. (1983). *Manual for the State-Trait Anxiety Inventory.* Palo Alto, CA: Consulting Psychologists Press.

Spielberger, C. D., Edwards, C., Lushene, R., Montuori, J., & Platzek, D. (1973). *Preliminary manual for the State-Trait Anxiety Inventory for Children.* Palo Alto, CA: Consulting Psychologists Press.

Suto, W. W., Fernbach, D. J., & Vietti, T. J. (1984). *Clinical pediatric oncology.* St. Louis: Mosby.

Turk, D. C., Meichenbaum, D., & Genest, M. (1983). *Pain and behavioral medicine: A cognitive-behavioral perspective.* New York: Guilford.

19
Behavioral Management of Chronic Back Pain in Children and Adolescents

LEONARD S. MILLING
WILLIAM J. SHAW
KAREN DURNIAT

INTRODUCTION

Chronic back pain is one of the most common health problems in Western society. Approximately 50% to 80% of the population will at some time suffer from back pain (Dehlin, Hedenrud, & Horal, 1976; Hirsch, Jonsson, & Lewin, 1969; Horal, 1969; Hult, 1954; Hult, 1965; Lawrence, 1969). A wealth of literature has addressed the etiology, assessment, and treatment of chronic back pain among adults (Flor & Turk, 1984; Stanton-Hicks & Boas, 1982; Turk & Flor, 1984). However, there have been few, if any, documented accounts of this problem among pediatric populations.

DEFINITION AND CLASSIFICATION

Our understanding of chronic back pain (CBP) has been hampered by the lack of a standard definition for this problem. Traditional distinctions between acute and chronic pain, as well as between organic and psychogenic pain have been blurred in descriptions of CBP. The distinction between acute pain and chronic pain is primarily a temporal one. That is, pain that lasts for less than 6 months is said to be acute, whereas pain that persists for more than 6 months is considered to be chronic. Acute pain

Leonard S. Milling. Department of Psychiatry, Medical College of Ohio, Toledo, Ohio.
William J. Shaw. Oklahoma City Clinic, Oklahoma City, Oklahoma.
Karen Durniat. Department of Nursing, Medical College of Ohio, Toledo, Ohio.

functions to focus attention on the injured or diseased tissue and is often associated with anxiety. Chronic pain no longer serves a warning function, may cause the affected individual to become dysfunctional, and is often associated with depression.

Distinctions between organic and psychogenic pain address the etiology of the problem. Organic pain is defined as pain having a known physiologic etiology. Psychogenic pain is diagnosed in the absence of an identifiable pathophysiologic cause and in the presence of contributing psychological factors. Consequently, both acute pain and chronic pain may be exclusively organic or exclusively psychogenic. Alternatively, each kind of pain may combine organic and psychogenic etiologies. Unfortunately, in the absence of a standard definition, many studies of CBP have failed to distinguish between patients suffering from long-term back pain primarily organic in nature and those experiencing long-term back pain primarily psychogenic in nature. It should be noted that, in practice, our ability to distinguish between organic and psychogenic pain is limited. However, CBP that is primarily organic may respond very differently to treatment interventions than will CBP that is psychogenic in origin.

Utilizing these distinctions, chronic psychogenic back pain can be defined as back pain of 6 months or longer duration that is primarily psychogenic in nature. Originally, the back pain may have had an organic etiology (i.e., identifiable disease or injury), but later came to be maintained by psychological factors. Alternatively, the back pain may always have had a psychologic etiology. This definition would be consistent with a diagnosis of Somatoform Pain Disorder according to the third revised edition of the *Diagnostic and Statistical Manual of Mental Disorders* (DSM-III-R; American Psychiatric Association, 1987, pp. 264–266). The diagnostic criteria are preoccupation with pain for at least 6 months when there is no organic pathology or when there are complaints of pain or disability grossly exceeding what would be expected from physical findings of organic pathology.

Varni, Katz, and Dash (1982) have grouped children's pain problems into four categories: (1) pain associated with an observable injury or trauma such as burns or fractures; (2) pain associated with a disease state such as hemophilia or sickle-cell disease; (3) pain associated with invasive medical procedures such as bone marrow aspirations or lumbar punctures; and (4) pain not associated with a disease state or identifiable physical trauma, such as recurrent abdominal pains or headaches. According to this schema, psychogenic CBP can be classified in the fourth category.

PREVALENCE

As previously suggested, there have been few, if any epidemiologic studies of chronic back pain among children and adolescents. However, reports of other chronic pediatric pain problems not associated with a disease state or identifiable injury, such as headaches, limb pains, and recurrent abdominal pains have appeared in the literature (Apley, 1975; Levine & Rappaport, 1984; Oster, 1972; Passo, 1982; Schechter, 1984). This observation may indicate that CBP is relatively uncommon compared with other chronic pediatric pain problems. Indeed, Oster (1972) examined the prevalence rates of recurrent headaches, limb pains, and abdominal pains in an 8-year longitudinal study of youngsters aged 6 to 19. Abdominal pains were found among 14.4% of the children, limb pains were found among 15.5% of the children, and headaches were found among 20.6% of the children. Undoubtedly, pediatric CBP, in particular, is a far less common disorder than other pain problems.

With regard to the adult population, over 18 million Americans experience persistent back pain (Bonica, 1980). As noted earlier, about 50% to 80% of the population suffers from back pain at some time in their lives and 3.9% of the population is permanently disabled by back pain (U.S. Vital and Health Statistics, 1974). The incidence rates are highest for the 20- to 30-year-old age group, whereas the prevalence rates are highest for the 40- to 60-year-old age group, with an equal number of men and women affected (Hirsch et al., 1969; Horal, 1969; Lawrence, 1969). CBP patients at multidisciplinary pain clinics have been estimated to comprise about 30% to almost 100% of clinic populations (Cinciripini & Floreen, 1982; Hallett & Pilowsky, 1982; Keefe, Black, Williams, & Surwit, 1981; Pinsky, 1983). It is interesting to observe that CBP is probably one of the least common chronic pain problems among children, but it is one of the most common chronic pain problems among adults.

RELATED DISORDERS

Back pain in children typically suggests significant underlying organic pathology (Behrman & Vaughan, 1983). Before a diagnosis of psychogenic CBP can be established, a thorough medical examination must be undertaken to rule out known pediatric pathophysiologic conditions, such as Scheuermann disease, spondylolisthesis, osteoid osteoma, infection of the vertebral bodies, or narrowing of the disc space indicative of an adjacent bony infection. Scheuermann disease is an irregularity of the growing areas of the vertebral bodies. Spondylolisthesis is a slipping of one vertebral body on the one below it in the lower spine. Osteoid osteoma is a benign tumor that occurs in the middle, softer portion of a bone. All of these conditions are associated with persistent pediatric back pain. *Nelson's Textbook of Pediatrics* (Behrman & Vaughan, 1983) provides a complete description of these conditions.

On the other hand, in a review of the adult literature on CBP, Flor and Turk (1984) note that numerous medical terms have been associated with the symptom of back pain (e.g., lumbosacral strain, lumbar disc disease, sciatica, lumbago, spondylosis, osteoarthritis, spinal stenosis, myofacial pain syndrome, sacroiliac sprain, myalgia, fibrositis, and degenerative disc disease). They point out that these terms are descriptive of pain symptoms rather than explanations of the etiology of the pain, and they conclude that little is known about the physiologic causes of adult CBP.

Generally, the following approach to diagnosis and classification seems reasonable. After identifiable pathophysiologic conditions have been ruled out by a qualified physician, a psychogenic component in the etiology of the pain can be entertained. Care should be taken to distinguish between medical terminology explaining the etiology of the pain that would tend to rule out or diminish psychological factors and medical terminology merely describing the pain symptoms that would not rule out psychologic factors. Thereafter, a qualified mental health professional can assess whether indicators of a psychological etiology are present.

THEORIES OF ETIOLOGY

In their review of CBP, Turk and Flor (1984) grouped the suspected psychological etiologies of this problem into six categories: (1) psychoanalytic approaches; (2) family system approaches; (3) respondent conditioning model; (4) operant conditioning model; (5) observational learning model; and (6) diathesis–stress model.

Psychoanalytic Approaches

According to psychoanalytic theorists, psychogenic back pain is suggestive of unconscious conflict or underlying personality disorder. For example, Freud conceptualized nonorganic somatic symptoms as a hysterical neurosis in which the affect associated with a traumatic event is not discharged at the time of the event, but rather is converted into physical symptoms. These symptoms are thought to represent some aspect of the trauma (Nemiah, 1980). Engle (1959) characterized chronic psychogenic pain as a form of hypochondriacal reaction. He described the "pain-prone" patient as a guilty, defeated individual evidencing fears of loss and unmet aggressive needs. For these patients, chronic pain is said to represent an expression of unresolved psychic pain.

Family Systems Approach

Family systems theory views the family as a homeostatic entity in which symptoms are assumed to maintain or to be maintained by family transactions (Minuchin, 1974). For example, chronic back pain may cause the identified patient to reduce family conflict by maintaining a focus on medical problems or to diffuse the boundary between parent and child subsystems by having the child be responsible for the care of a disabled parent. In particular, Minuchin and his colleagues have described family processes promoting the development of psychosomatic illness in children that can be applied to pediatric CBP (Minuchin, Baker, Rossman, Liebman, Milman, & Todd, 1975). More specifically, enmeshment, overprotection, rigidity, lack of conflict resolution, and detouring of conflict through the child, in combination with the child's physiologic vulnerability would be a precursor to pediatric CBP.

Respondent Model

Gentry and Bernal (1977) have hypothesized that a debilitating pain–tension cycle may be created when pain, tension, and avoidance of movement are classically conditioned during an acute pain episode. Accordingly, movement becomes paired with pain immediately following injury or disease. The pain causes the patient to avoid movement, resulting in muscle tension and atrophy. With time, the patient's fear of movement leads to a progressive cycle of pain, immobility, muscle atrophy, and finally greater pain. This model is thought to apply not only to CBP, but to all forms of chronic pain.

Operant Model

According to Fordyce, pain behaviors (e.g., complaining, inactivity, etc.) during an episode of acute pain receive positive reinforcement through increased access to desirable consequences such as attention, as well as negative reinforcement through avoidance of aversive consequences such as going to work (Fordyce, 1976). Eventually the pain behaviors are maintained by external consequences alone and occur independently of the original injury or disease process. Moreover, when pain behaviors receive more reinforcement than well behaviors (e.g., positive statements about wellness, activity, etc.), the pain behaviors tend to persist and the well behaviors become extinguished. Thus, in the case of pediatric CBP, a child's complaints of back pain and disability may be positively reinforced by increased parental attention and negatively reinforced by school avoidance.

Observational Learning

Behaviors (including pain behaviors) may be learned when they are modeled by others in the environment (Bandura, 1969). Consequently, when a parent or sibling receives reinforcement for pain behaviors, an observing child may acquire similar behaviors. Turk and Flor (1984) speculate that the pain site may be determined by modeling factors.

Diathesis–Stress Model

A comprehensive biopsychosocial model of CBP integrating a number of etiologic factors has been suggested by Flor (1982). Accordingly, CBP occurs when environmental events interact with predisposing organic or psychological factors. An individual is vulnerable to CBP when three conditions are met. First, the individual must be exposed to aversive situations that engender chronic stress. Second, the individual must lack adaptive coping abilities to deal with the stressors. Finally, the individual must characteristically respond to stress through hyperactivity of the back muscles. This characteristic mode of responding to stress may be the result of genetic predisposition, injury, or observational learning. At first, situational stressors may initiate muscle hypertension and pain. Thereafter, pain may act as an additional stressor, further increasing muscle tension and pain. Accompanying pain behaviors can be increased by environmental reinforcers. Eventually, an accelerating cycle of chronic tension and pain evolves.

Evaluation of Etiologic Theories of CBP

According to Turk and Flor (1984), empirical support for most etiologic models of CBP is scarce. In particular, there is little evidence to validate psychoanalytic, family systems, respondent, and observational models of CBP. The diathesis–stress model is a relatively new theory possessing only preliminary evidence of empirical confirmation. Support for an operant conceptualization of CBP is provided by research demonstrating the utility of operant procedures in modifying pain behaviors. However, chronic pain behaviors may be only one component of chronic pain, thus leaving many aspects of CBP unexplained. It should be noted that studies of the etiology of CBP have focused exclusively on adults and have unknown relevance for pediatric populations. Moreover, theorists are implored to remember that chronic pain is a symptom that may be the "final, common pathway" of a variety of disorders, each with unique etiologies. Finally, as suggested by the diathesis–stress model, it may be that a number of etiological factors interact to produce CBP.

CLINICAL ASSESSMENT

A thorough clinical assessment should be performed in order to better understand the child experiencing persistent pain, to identify potential treatments, and to evaluate the effectiveness of the treatments. A comprehensive assessment could include physiologic, self-report, and behavioral methods to assess aspects of pain perception and pain behavior. Masek, Russo, and Varni (1984) advocate that the pain behavior assessment should attempt to describe the behaviors of the child when in pain, to identify the functional limitations on daily activities imposed by the pain, and to ascertain the reinforcers maintaining pain behavior. Also, these authors suggest that pain perception assessment should attempt to discover the relationship between the child's perception of pain and the resulting behaviors. Specific types of information to be obtained from each of the important methods of measurement are detailed subsequently.

Physiologic Component

A thorough medical examination should be performed by a qualified physician in order to rule out known pathophysiologic conditions requiring further medical attention (e.g., bone tumor, infection, etc.). Furthermore, when a pain problem combines organic and psychogenic etiologies, it may be useful for a physician to estimate the extent of organic factors contributing to the pain in order to set realistic behavioral goals for the patient. A medical assessment might include a physical examination, x-rays, CAT scan, radionuclide bone scan, and roentgenography. Finally, most behavioral approaches to chronic pain advocate reducing or eliminating medication by placing it on a time-contingent schedule rather than on a pain-contingent schedule. The physician prescribing the medication should always be involved when a pharmacologic regimen is modified.

In addition to a medical examination, other physiologic measures may provide a useful baseline of functioning prior to treatment. For example, galvanic skin response, heart rate, frontalis electromyograph, and palmar sweating have been used as generalized biologic markers of pain or distress (Harpin & Rutter, 1982; Holzman, Turk, & Kerns, 1986). Also, site-specific electromyography can be used to provide an index of local muscle tension in the affected area of the back.

Self-Report Component

Clinical interviews and objective questionnaires can be used to assess chronic pain patients. Perhaps the best known objective questionnaire in this area is the McGill Pain Questionnaire (Melzak, 1975) which assesses sensory, affective, and evaluative aspects of adult pain. A downward extension of this instrument utilizing developmentally appropriate questions has been created for children (Tesler, Ward, Savedra, Wegner, & Gibbons, 1983). Similarly, Varni and Thompson (1985) developed the Pediatric Pain Questionnaire that measures pain intensity, as well as sensory, emotive, and affective qualities of pain. Child and parent versions of the scale are available to permit convergent validation of pain reports, and a family history section taps information about the pain history of the entire family. There are several simple measures of pain intensity presented in a visual format that make them easier for children to use than a verbal analogue scale (Jay, Ozolins, Elliott, & Caldwell, 1983; Stewart, 1977). Finally, Eland and Anderson (1977) and Scott (1978) have developed visually oriented measures in which the child selects a color to indicate the intensity of the pain.

In addition to assessing the patient's general psychosocial functioning, a clinical interview should attempt to describe several pain-specific processes. First, the clinician should obtain information about potential reinforcers of pain behaviors, such as the use of medication, avoidance of undesired school, family, and social responsibilities, as well as increased attention and nurturance from others. Also, the child's attitudes, beliefs, and expectations about the pain should be assessed. In particular, excessive focus on the pain and bodily processes, unrealistic fears and worries, as well as passivity and helplessness should be noted. The presence or absence of these factors can be corroborated by interviewing the child's parents.

Behavioral Component

Informal observation of the child provides the clinician with information about verbal and nonverbal pain behaviors, such as reports of pain, facial grimaces, compensatory posturing, restricted movements, and the absence of developmentally appropriate well behaviors. Also, watching the child interact with his/her family may provide clues as to operants reinforcing the child's pain behavior.

Several formal behavioral observation rating scales have been developed to assess children's pain behavior (Jay et al., 1983; Katz, Kellerman, & Siegal, 1980; LeBaron & Zeltzer, 1984). However, these scales are research instruments designed to assess distress during painful medical procedures. Thus, it is questionable whether they would be valid or useful as clinical measures of children's chronic pain.

TREATMENT

There have been few, if any, reports in the literature of case studies or controlled research on treatments for pediatric CBP. However, there have been some studies of treatments for adult CBP, other adult chronic pain problems, as well as pediatric pain problems including those not associated with a known disease or injury. Efforts in these areas can serve as a guide in designing and evaluating potential interventions for pediatric CBP.

Numerous medical and psychologic treatments have been attempted with adult CBP. In their review of the literature on CBP, Turk, and Flor grouped these treatments into five categories: (1) medical treatments, (2) operant treatments, (3) respondent treatment, (4) hypnosis, and (5) cognitive–behavioral treatments (Flor & Turk, 1984; Turk & Flor, 1984).

Medical Treatments

A range of somatic therapies have been used to treat adult CBP, including: medications; surgeries; physical therapy; manipulation, traction, and supports; steroid therapy and nerve block; and hyperstimulation (i.e., electrical nerve stimulation). Generally, Flor & Turk (1984) concluded that none of these treatments have been shown to be of long-term value in alleviating CBP and that some of these interventions were dangerous or exacerbated pain problems.

Operant Treatment

This approach, developed by Fordyce (1976), utilizes the principles of operant conditioning to extinguish pain behaviors (e.g., complaining, inactivity, etc.) and to increase well behaviors (e.g., positive statements about wellness, exercise, etc.). Accordingly, pain behaviors are extinguished by reducing positive reinforcers such as attention and by reducing negative reinforcers such as avoidance of school. Simultaneously, well behaviors are reinforced through praise, attention, or concrete reinforcers. Well behaviors are often shaped by graduating them into steps that increasingly approximate normal functioning. Medications are gradually withdrawn or administered on a time-contingent schedule rather than on a pain-contingent basis to avoid inadvertently reinforcing pain behaviors. Also, medications are delivered in a "pain cocktail" in which the amount of active medication is gradually reduced. Traditionally, operant programs have been conducted in inpatient settings because of the enhanced control of contingent reinforcers. Family involvement in such programs is used to assure generalization of behavior changes to the patient's natural environment.

Reviews of studies of the operant approach have suggested that it is a useful treatment for increasing physical activity and decreasing medication use among adult sufferers of CBP, as well as other forms of chronic pain (Roberts, 1986; Turk & Flor, 1984; Turner & Chapman, 1982b). With pediatric populations, there is preliminary evidence that operant treatment may be effective in reducing pain behaviors associated with migraine headaches (Masek et al., 1984), recurrent abdominal pains (Miller & Kratochwill, 1979; Sank & Biglan, 1974), and burn injuries (Varni, Bessman, Russo, & Cataldo, 1980).

Respondent Treatments

Respondent approaches to CBP, such as biofeedback and progressive muscle relaxation, are based on the premise that pain and tension become paired in an accelerating cycle. Respondent treatments attempt to break the pain cycle by teaching the patient to relax the back muscles rather than allowing the muscles to become increasingly tense (Gentry & Bernal, 1977).

Biofeedback helps patients to monitor their physiologic processes and to produce responses incompatible with pain and tension. Four types of biofeedback can be used to treat CBP patients: thermal biofeedback, electro-encephalogram biofeedback, electromyograph biofeedback, and site-specific electromyograph biofeedback. Thermal biofeedback teaches the patient to increase finger temperature by increasing blood flow to the periphery of the body, resulting in a generalized state of relaxation. Electroencephalogram (EEG) feedback trains the patient to generate alpha brain waves associated with general relaxation. Electromyograph (EMG) feedback applied to the frontalis muscle (i.e., muscles of the forehead) reduces muscle tension and increases relaxation. Finally, site-specific EMG feedback can be used to reduce tension among the affected muscles in the back itself.

Progressive muscle relaxation training is another technique used to reduce general muscle tension associated with pain. The patient is coached to focus on individual muscle groups throughout the body (e.g., chest, back, stomach, etc.) and to reduce tension by alternately tensing and then relaxing them. After one muscle group is relaxed, the patient proceeds to the next group until the entire body is relaxed. Eventually, the patient learns to achieve the relaxed state without a coach, thereby enabling him/her to decrease discomfort at will.

Reviews of research investigating biofeedback suggest that it is an effective treatment for reducing adult pain associated with tension head-aches, migraine headaches, and temporomandibular joint dysfunction (Belar & Kibrick, 1986; Keefe, 1982; Turk & Flor, 1984; Turner & Chapman, 1982a). Similarly, research reviews have concluded that progressive muscle relaxation training is useful for treating problems such as headaches and myofacial pain (Turk, Meichenbaum, & Berman, 1979; Turner & Chapman, 1982a). Furthermore, these reviews questioned whether biofeedback is any-more effective than relaxation training in treating adult pain problems. As for children's pain problems, reviews of studies of pediatric chronic pain treatments have suggested that biofeedback or biofeedback in combination with progressive muscle relaxation is useful in reducing the distress asso-ciated with pediatric migraine (Lavigne, Schulein, & Hahn, 1986; Varni, Jay, Masek, & Thompson, 1986; Varni et al., 1983).

Hypnosis

Hypnotherapy has long been employed to treat chronic pain, although there is little agreement as to how hypnosis achieves its effect (Bandler & Grinder, 1975; Barber & Hahn, 1962; Crasilneck & Hall, 1975; Hilgard & Hilgard, 1975; Kirsch, 1985). Traditionally, most approaches to hypnother-apy utilize a combination of relaxation, focused attention, and imagery, as well as direct or indirect suggestions for pain control. Accordingly, hyp-notic trance, thought to be a state of heightened concentration, relaxation, and suggestability, is achieved by focusing attention on a visual, auditory, or kinesthetic image, ideomotor phenomena (in which the patient is instructed to focus on a motor movement and then to allow the movement to occur), eye fixation phenomena (in which the patient focuses on a visual stimulus), or progressive muscle relaxation. Thereafter, the patient is given suggestions for analgesia, anesthesia, dissociation of the painful body part, or distraction. Procedures for utilizing hypnotherapy with children have been described in great detail by Gardner and Olness (1981).

A technique related to hypnosis is imagery (Elliott & Ozolins, 1983). Typically, imagery incorporates muscle relaxation with instructions for visual, auditory, and kinesthetic images. The imagery is designed to be highly absorbing by associating it with relaxation (e.g., bathing in a warm tub of water), competency (e.g., achieving mastery over a problem situation), or pleasurable activities (e.g., playing with a cuddly puppy). Patients are usually instructed to experience the images as if they were actually occurring, and they are typically given some control over the direction of the imagery. The difference between imagery and hypnosis is unclear. Both techniques appear to share in common heightened attention and relaxation, as well as visual, auditory, and kinesthetic images. Hypnosis may be distinguished by its use of suggestion for dissociation, analgesia, or anesthesia, as well as by an expectancy effect created through the use of the term "hypnosis."

According to reviews of studies of hypnotherapy of adult chronic pain, almost all of the research consists of uncontrolled case studies or studies of experimental pain having little relevance to clinical pain. Consequently, no conclusions can be drawn about the effectiveness of this treatment with adults (Turk & Flor, 1984; Turner & Chapman, 1982b). On the other hand, there is preliminary evidence that hypnosis is an effective treatment for reducing children's distress associated with painful medical procedures such as bone marrow aspirations and lumbar punctures (Hilgard & LeBaron, 1984), as well as with burn injuries (Wakeman & Kaplan, 1978). With regard to imagery, a recent review of this technique as a treatment for children's psychological and medically related problems concluded that it may be of great benefit as an intervention, but that it lacked empirical validations (Elliott & Ozolins, 1983).

Cognitive–Behavioral Treatments

The cognitive-behavioral approach to chronic pain control comprises a wide range of loosely unified interventions based on the theory that cognitions mediate affect, behavior and, ultimately, pain symptoms. The Melzak and Wall pain-gate theory proposes that the pain experience is a function of a variety of factors including cognitive variables (Melzak & Wall, 1965). Following from this theory, it has generally been accepted that aversive mental states (e.g., anxiety, depression, etc.) can exacerbate pain perception (Varni, 1983). Cognitive–behavioral techniques designed to treat pain are grounded in these premises, and they include reframing of pain, education, relabeling of pain sensations, distraction, monitoring of pain behaviors, coping skills training, modeling, behavioral rehearsal, and homework (Holzman et al., 1986; Turk & Flor, 1984; Turner & Chapman, 1982b; Varni et al., 1986). These terms are somewhat arbitrary, and similar interventions have been given diverse labels by different authors.

In "reframing," patients are helped to modify their thinking from a belief that pain is uncontrollable to a view of pain as being controllable or at least partially controllable through various psychological interventions. As a result, patients are presumed to decrease the feelings of depression and helplessness thought to be associated with aversive, uncontrollable events and to increase their sense of mastery. "Education" refers to providing patients with information about the nature of pain so as to increase their sense of control. "Relabeling" is designed to prevent chronic pain patients from becoming preoccupied with pain sensations by assisting them to find, where possible, other, less noxious descriptors (e.g., a tickling feeling) for the sensations. A related technique is "distraction" in which attention to bodily sensations is replaced by a focus on external events. "Monitoring" helps patients to recognize pain-arousing thoughts, feelings, behaviors, and situations, thereby enabling them to substitute more adaptive responses. In "coping skills training," patients are taught to self-administer a variety of interventions described earlier (i.e., hypnosis, imagery, progressive muscle relaxation, etc.) as a way of intervening with the pain on their own. Also, they are trained in such skills as assertiveness that may help them to more effectively handle life problems associated with pain exacerbations. A therapist may help a patient to acquire new skills by "modeling" their correct use. To promote the generalization of responses to the patient's natural environment, "behavioral rehearsal" is used to anticipate real-world problem situations associated with the pain and to roleplay interventions for them. Finally, "homework" may be prescribed where patients are instructed to practice pain regulation techniques and other coping skills in their natural environments.

Reviews of research examining the effectiveness of cognitive–behavioral interventions have generally concluded that, although they tend to lack empirical validation, these techniques hold much potential for treating a variety of adult chronic pain problems such as migraine and tension headaches (Turner & Chapman, 1982b), as well as CBP (Turk & Flor, 1984). Similarly, a recent review of case studies of cognitive–behavioral interventions for pediatric pain suggests the potential of this modality for treating pain associated with chronic disease and invasive medical procedures (Varni et al., 1986).

CASE EXAMPLE: PSYCHOGENIC CBP IN
A 15-YEAR-OLD MALE

The following case history illustrates how many of the assessment and intervention concepts presented earlier can be integrated into the treatment of an adolescent with CBP. Robert S, a 15-year-old white male, suffered from persistent back pain for 12 months duration. No organic basis had been established for the back pain despite the numerous medical tests and examinations that had been conducted during the year preceding his referral for psychological intervention. Robert was in the 10th grade, having sustained his back problem shortly after making the transition from junior high school to high school. Robert's pain was sufficiently disabling to prevent him from attending school, and he had received homebound instruction for most of the 9th grade and all of 10th grade up to the time of his referral for psychological intervention.

Robert came from an intact middle-class family that lived in a rural area of a large midwestern state. Robert's father, Mr. S, 41, was successfully employed as a welder for a large manufacturing company. His wife, Mrs. S, 39, was a housewife. Robert had an older brother, Richard, 17, who attended the 11th grade and a younger sister, Rachel, 14, who attended the 9th grade. The family did not evidence any unusual medical or psychiatric history. However, Mr. and Mrs. S felt significant financial pressure resulting from the numerous medical bills that had been incurred as a result of Robert's back pain.

Before the onset of the back pain, Robert had felt in good health. He had been hospitalized previously for a tonsillectomy at age 4 and for an appendectomy at age 11. Also, he experienced seasonal asthma that was controlled by the use of an inhaler. He had been attending school regularly and participated in the sport of wrestling. Immediately prior to the onset of the back pain, Robert recalled engaging in a wrestling match, but without memory of a specific injury occurring during the event.

Robert underwent thorough medical examinations and several medical treatments prior to referral for psychological intervention. Initially, the back pain was treated by the family physician as a thoracic sprain, and symptomatic relief measures were suggested (e.g., analgesic medication). However, the pain persisted and intensified for the next 3 months. Robert was reexamined by an orthopedic specialist, and he was subsequently admitted to a general hospital for treatment and evaluation.

This first hospitalization employed extensive physical examination, x-rays, and laboratory studies. Pathological abnormalities were not revealed. Robert was treated with cervical traction during his 8-day admission to the hospital and during an additional 17 days at home. Adjunctive treatment consisted of whirlpool baths and hotpacks. None of these treatments were successful in resolving the pain.

This unsuccessful outcome prompted further evaluation and alternative treatment measures. A bone scan was performed to determine bone formation and density. This examination revealed no significant findings. The treatment of choice then seemed to be total rest for the painful area. Consequently, Robert was placed in a body cast that extended from his neck to his pelvis and he was followed in the orthopedic outpatient clinic of the general hospital.

Approximately 1 month after being treated with the body cast, only marginal improvement had been noted, and an additional consultation was sought from the rheumatology clinic. The rheumatologist suspected that Robert suffered from Scheuermann disease, a vertebral deformity of the midthoracic region that results in curvature of the spine. The deformity usually occurs during adolescence and presents clinically as back pain on exertion that is relieved by rest. Robert reported that his pain increased with activity and was somewhat relieved by rest. (However, both the referring physician and the rheumatologist agreed that there was little evidence from physical examination or x-ray studies to support a diagnosis of Scheuermann disease.) Robert described his pain as sharp and nonradiating. There was no associated weakness or paresthesia (numbness) in his back or extremities. The physician fitted him with a kyphosis brace (a back brace covering the entire torso used to treat curvature of the spine).

Robert was seen on a outpatient basis every 6 weeks for a period of 5 months. During this time, he wore the kyphosis brace, limited his activity, and took oral medication (a mild analgesic) for pain relief. He did not attend school and received homebound academic instruction. There was no significant improvement or deterioration during this time and few if any other medical complaints. Upon returning to school in the fall, Robert began to experience extreme back pain. The intensity of the pain necessitated reinstitution of homebound instruction, an increase in pain medication to a moderate analgesic with codeine, and rehospitalization.

Again, Robert underwent a thorough examination and testing to rule out possibly physical abnormalities, including laboratory tests, x-rays, bone scan, and a CAT scan of the thoracic spine. All tests were negative for pathology, and he was discharged from the hospital. At this point, the physicians did not have new treatment plans unless new symptoms presented. They began to consider the possibility of a psychogenic etiology for the pain. Consequently, they referred Robert to the adolescent outpatient medical clinic of a regional teaching hospital for psychological consultation.

Following a routine screening by one of the clinic's pediatrics residents, a referral was made for psychological evaluation and intervention through the hospital's consultation and liaison service. Robert was accompanied by his parents to the initial interview with two of us (W. J. S. and L. S. M.). He presented as a somewhat overweight teenager who appeared to be younger than his chronological age. Robert was neatly dressed for the interview, he moved slowly and stiffly, and it was readily apparent that he was wearing a kyphosis brace under his shirt. During the interview, Robert related in a quiet, withdrawn manner. He avoided eye contact, offered no spontaneous verbalizations, and provided short answers to questions. Robert's verbal responses were difficult to understand because of a pronounced speech defect. Indeed, he seemed quite comfortable allowing his parents to speak for him. Robert reported that he had a few close friends, but upon further questioning, it became apparent that most of his social interaction occurred at home with his family. He suggested that his school performance was average, and he indicated that he had been on homebound instruction since the onset of the pain. Throughout the interview, Robert's affect was somewhat flat and dysphoric. On several occasions during the interview, he verbalized a wish to recover from his back pain.

Mr. and Mrs. S were pleasant, extremely polite people who seemed highly concerned about the welfare of their son. Mr. and Mrs. S stated that Robert was the "baby" of the family. As Mr. and Mrs. S described typical family interactions, we detected that Robert was infantilized and overprotected by other family members. Mr. and Mrs. S confirmed that most of Robert's social interaction took place within the family and that his brother and sister tended to intervene on his behalf in social situations at school. Furthermore, we learned that family members tended to respond to Robert's complaints of pain by increasing their attention to him, for example by spending extra time with him and by sympathizing with his pain. Mr. and Mrs. S reported that Robert wore his back brace throughout the day, removing it only for sleep. Finally, they noted that Robert spent most of his free time at home.

Generally, we viewed Robert as a somewhat depressed, dependent, socially awkward teenager whose back pain was reinforced by family attention and avoidance of peer interaction at school. Robert was a withdrawn youngster whose capacity for social interaction was limited by his physical immaturity, lack of social skills, and perhaps most significantly by his pronounced speech defect. Indeed, Robert's interpersonal difficulties probably became more apparent when he made the transition from junior high school to the more socially demanding environment of high school. Whereas Robert seemed to feel isolated from and rejected by peers at school, he appeared to be very comfortable with and accepted by parents and siblings at home. Overall, we conceptualized Robert's back pain and consequent disability as being positively reinforced by an increase in pleasant family interactions at home and negatively reinforced by a decrease in aversive peer interactions at school.

Robert and his parents were seen by one of us (L. S. M.) for approximately 20 bimonthly treatment sessions. The great distance (100 miles) between the family's residence and the hospital prevented a more frequent schedule of meetings. However, as Robert began to make steady improvement, a bimonthly schedule of sessions appeared to be appropriate for his rate of progress. That is, as Robert and his parents began to master the behavioral techniques presented in early sessions, bimonthly sessions were sufficient to monitor changes in Robert's condition and to make the necessary adjustments in the intervention program. The typical format for my contacts consisted of a brief meeting with Robert's parents without Robert (15 to 30 minutes), followed by a longer meeting with Robert alone (30 to 60 minutes) in which a range of interventions were employed, including biofeedback, progressive muscle relaxation, and imagery.

Operant Treatment Through Family Therapy

As part of family treatment, I saw Mr. and Mrs. S to modify their tendency to reinforce Robert's pain behavior (i.e., complaints of pain, physical disability, etc.). Since operant treatment is one of the few interventions for chronic pain possessing solid empirical evidence of effectiveness, I considered this approach to be necessary to achieve a successful outcome. Robert's brother and sister were not seen because they would have missed a full day of school in order to attend our sessions. Generally, Mr. and Mrs. S were amenable to a psychological explanation for Robert's pain behavior, including how such behavior could be reinforced by attention. In discussing the possible etiologies of the back pain, I assured Mr. and Mrs. S that Robert's perception of pain was very real, regardless of the degree to which it was psychogenic versus organic in nature. Furthermore, family counseling sessions tended to minimize the importance of identifying the etiology of Robert's pain sensation and rather focused on ways of gaining operant control of his pain behavior and disability.

During our initial meetings, I coached Mr. and Mrs. S to redirect their attention from Robert's pain behaviors to his well behaviors. I instructed Mr. and Mrs. S to praise Robert for positive self-statements about wellness (e.g., "I feel well today" or "I did not have any pain this afternoon," etc.), as well as for behaviors incompatible with pain and disability (e.g., physical exercise, out-of-home activities, etc.). Also, I directed the parents to extinguish Robert's complaints about pain. For example, I told them to briefly sympathize with Robert's complaints and then to change the topic of conversation. Alternatively, they could send him to his room to listen to a relaxation and imagery tape until the pain abated. Finally, I advised Mr. and Mrs. S to work with Robert's brother and sister in order to prevent them from reinforcing Robert's pain behavior and to encourage them to reinforce his well behaviors.

As our contact proceeded and Robert made steady progress, it seemed that a formal behavior management program and attendance at family sessions by Robert's brother and sister would not be necessary. Parent meetings began to focus on more general issues regarding Robert's independence from the family. In particular, I reframed encouraging a teenager's independence as an important function of a good parent. Thereafter, Mr. and Mrs. S attempted to identify ways in which they could promote Robert's autonomy, including supporting him in a decision to take a driver's education course. Driving a car was an enjoyable activity that provided Robert with greater mobility and independence from home.

Individual Therapy

Whereas family therapy sessions tended to focus on operant reinforcement of pain behavior, my individual sessions with Robert emphasized behavioral techniques designed to reduce his perception of pain. I utilized such techniques as relaxation, imagery, and biofeedback to reduce Robert's muscle tension and anxiety level. These procedures were implemented within the context of a therapeutic relationship. Although Robert's poor verbal skills and resistance to insight made him a poor candidate for psychotherapy, a trusting relationship with me was a necessary prerequisite for the success of the behavioral procedures. Robert appeared to enjoy my attention, and he responded well to praise for his compliance with treatment procedures and for his therapeutic gains.

At the outset of our work, I offered Robert a psychological explanation for the etiology of his pain. As with his parents, I assured Robert that the pain he experienced was real, not made up, regardless of its etiology. Also, I described the various behavioral procedures as ways of increasing relaxation and reducing or eliminating pain sensations. Little, if any, discussion was devoted to the family's role in reinforcing Robert's pain behavior. This was done to avoid creating resistance to the operant program by posing a threat to reinforcers for the pain behaviors. However, it should be pointed out that a noted expert in the field believes that the operant treatment of patients such as this one can be facilitated rather than hindered by discussing with them the details of an operant intervention (W. O. Fordyce, personal communication, September 24, 1987).

Progressive Muscle Relaxation and Imagery

From the outset of our contact, I trained Robert in the use of progressive muscle relaxation and imagery. As part of the preliminary assessment, I identified potential topics for imagery by inquiring about Robert's favorite movies and television programs, pleasurable leisure activities, and favorite foods. Also, I administered to Robert the Stanford Hypnotic Clinical Scale for Children (Morgan & Hilgard (1978/1979), which revealed that he was relatively nonresponsive to hypnotic suggestions. Since Robert seemed to be a poor candidate for hypnosis, the imagery techniques were not framed as "hypnosis," and direct suggestions for analgesia and anesthesia were not employed to avoid what almost certainly would have been a failure experience for him.

I taught Robert standard progressive muscle relaxation in which I instructed him to relax individual muscle groups throughout his body in a systematic manner. Robert did not appear to have any problems relaxing his back muscles during this procedure. Thereafter, I suggested pleasant imagery to Robert, including scenes of relaxing in a warm tub of water, resting in a country meadow on a sunny day, and going on an adventure with the "Dukes of Hazard" in which he drove the "General Lee" across the surface of a giant cheeseburger as he was pursued by "Sheriff Roscoe." Several principles were employed to enhance Robert's response to the imagery. First, I instructed Robert to participate in his visual, auditory, and kinesthetic images as if they were occurring in the present moment (e.g., "and now you are noticing the warm water against your body . . . how is it feeling against your skin?"). I thought that "here and now" activation of the imagery would make the experience more involving for Robert. Second, I helped Robert to take an active role in determining the direction of his imagery as much as possible. This role was initially difficult for a passive, dependent youngster like Robert. However, with practice, Robert was able to take increasingly greater responsibility for directing the imagery. Finally, rather than relying on traditional imagery topics, our imagery work tended to emphasize topics generated from Robert's interests and leisure activities that were combined in novel and unexpected ways (i.e., Dukes of Hazard, cheeseburgers, etc.) since I thought these would be more intrinsically interesting to Robert and therefore more rewarding to practice over a long period of time.

I made a relaxation and imagery audiotape based on our work during the sessions. I instructed Robert to listen to the tape at home upon awakening in the morning and before going to sleep in the evening, as well as whenever he experienced pain during the day. Additionally, during our sessions, I taught Robert to associate the self-prompt "relax" with the heightened state of comfort achieved through the relaxation and imagery. At times when Robert experienced discomfort, but when listening to the audiotape would have been impractical (e.g., at school), I directed Robert to do deep breathing and to employ the self-prompt as a way of reducing his anxiety and pain.

Self-Monitoring of Pain Sensation and Behavior

Throughout treatment, Robert kept a daily diary in which he monitored his pain. Each evening, he rated the frequency, duration, and severity of the pain along five-point scales ranging from the worst he had ever experienced to none at all. These ratings were arithmetically combined (frequency $\times$ duration $\times$ severity) to provide a weekly metric of his discomfort. This information provided a longitudinal measure of Robert's progress in treatment. Also in his diary, Robert wrote about the circumstances in which his pain episodes occurred. I used these descriptions to clarify potential precipitants and reinforcers for his pain episodes.

Thermal Biofeedback

Approximately halfway through the treatment process, I introduced thermal biofeedback as a method of facilitating general relaxation. I explained the basic rationale of the treatment to Robert, and he was amenable to the process. I used the biofeedback in combination with the relaxation and imagery. Each biofeedback session began with a brief baseline period (30 seconds) in which Robert received continuous feedback. Typically, Robert was able to achieve significant increases in skin temperature during the baseline period. Thereafter, the relaxation and imagery instructions were provided, resulting in additional large increases in temperature. Finally, I instructed Robert to utilize self-prompts to further enhance relaxation, typically resulting in small skin temperature increases.

In addition to formal biofeedback training during our sessions, Robert carried a small card that measured skin temperature in order to generalize adaptive responses to his natural environment. (This device was a credit-card-sized instrument with a window on the face. In order to use the card, the patient holds his thumb against the window for 10 to 20 seconds. The card turns one of four colors—black, red, green, or blue—depending on the temperature of the patient's thumb, thereby providing a gross measure of relaxation level.) Robert carried the card with him throughout the day and took readings of his skin temperature at 10:00 A.M., 2:00 P.M., 4:00 P.M., and 8:00 P.M. These times were selected to enable Robert to monitor his relaxation level throughout the day, including several assessments during school hours. Whenever Robert observed that his level of comfort was less than optimal, as measured by the card, he was instructed to employ the relaxation self-prompts for about 5 minutes, followed by retesting with the card. Typically, Robert reported that he was able to use the self-prompts to increase his skin temperature, thereby enhancing his level of relaxation.

Shaping of Well Behaviors

At approximately the sixth session, Robert began reporting improvements in his back. Up to this point, Robert had been wearing the kyphosis brace throughout his waking hours. This brace seemed to prevent Robert from engaging in normal activities. Also, it appeared to be a cue for pain behavior as well as for reinforcement of the pain behavior from the environment. In order to gradually fade Robert's use of the brace, I initially instructed him to remove it 15 minutes before retiring to bed during the following 2 weeks.

At the next session, no significant problems were reported, thus for the following 2 weeks I instructed Robert to remove the back brace 30 minutes before bed. Thereafter, I increased the amount of time between removing the back brace and retiring, first in 30-minute intervals and later in increasingly larger amounts of time. At each session, I assessed Robert's discomfort without the brace in order to regulate the speed of the fading process. By about the 16th session, Robert was no longer wearing the brace.

As Robert's discomfort decreased, his interest in returning to school increased. At around the 15th session, Robert and his parents approached me about the possibility of Robert attending regular classes at his high school. Together, we agreed on a schedule for gradually returning Robert to full-time attendance at school. During the first week that Robert returned to school, he attended only 2 hours of classes each day. Some minor increases in pain were reported. However, Robert was eager to continue at school and in particular to go to a driver's education course. Mr. and Mrs. S were supportive of this interest and, after receiving his learner's permit, Robert began driving the family car under his brother's supervision. Robert's use of the car seemed to reflect his growing psychological independence from home. The number of classes that Robert attended was gradually increased over the next several sessions. His remaining reports of pain diminished dramatically, and he soon began carrying a full load of classes each day. By our last meeting at the 20th session, only minor and infrequent complaints of pain were reported.

Reflections

A range of behavioral interventions, commonly used to treat chronic pain problems in children and adults, were adapted to successfully treat CBP in a 15-year-old adolescent male. Of course, as an uncontrolled case study, it is impossible to determine which treatments were necessary or sufficient to produce complete resolution of the pain. Furthermore, it is impossible to know whether any of these interventions would benefit other pediatric CBP patients. In particular, one may question whether these interventions would help a much younger child (e.g., elementary school age) or a child suffering from CBP having a significant organic component. In any event, the case example illustrates intervention strategies that may be of potential benefit in treating similar cases of pediatric CBP.

One of the distinguishing factors about the case example was the patient's rapid response to treatment. Unlike many other chronic pain patients with whom I have worked, Robert made very steady progress and suffered only a few, minor setbacks throughout the course of therapy. In large measure, I suspect this was due to the unflagging cooperation of Robert's parents with the operant component of therapy. Mr. and Mrs. S attended sessions regularly, were amenable to a psychological explanation of Robert's problems, demonstrated good understanding of operant principles, and seemed to follow through with operant interventions in a consistent and appropriate manner. Such consistent compliance may not be typical of all patients and their families. However, with a broad array of potential treatments and a high level of patient adherence, pediatric CBP appears to be responsive to behavioral interventions.

REFERENCES

American Psychiatric Association (1987). *Diagnostical and statistical manual of mental disorders* (3rd ed., revised). Washington, DC: Author.

Apley, J. (1975). *The child with abdominal pains* (2nd ed.). Oxford: Blackwell.

Bandler, R., & Grinder, J. (1975). *Patterns of the hypnotic techniques of Milton H. Erickson, M.D.* (Vol. I). Cupertino, CA: Meta Publications.

Bandura, A. (1969). *Principles of behavior modification.* New York: Holt, Reinhart & Winston.

Barber, T. X., & Hahn, K. (1962). Physiological and subjective responses to pain producing stimulation under hypnotically suggested and waking-imagined "analgesia." *Journal of Abnormal and Social Psychology, 65,* 411–418.

Behrman, R. E., & Vaughan, V. C. (1983). *Nelson textbook of pediatrics.* Philadelphia: Saunders.

Belar, C. D., & Kibrick, S. A. (1986). Biofeedback in the treatment of chronic back pain. In A. D. Holzman & D. C. Turk (Eds.), *Pain management: A handbook of psychological treatment approaches* (pp. 131–150). New York: Pergamon.

Bonica, J. J. (1980). Pain research and therapy: Past research, current status and future needs. In L. Ng & J. J. Bonica (Eds.), *Pain discomfort and humanitarian care* (pp. 1–46). New York: Elsevier.

Cinciripini, P. M., & Floreen, A. (1982). An evaluation of a behavioral program for chronic pain. *Journal of Behavioral Medicine, 5,* 375–389.

Crasilneck, H. B., & Hall, J. A. (1975). *Clinical hypnosis: Principles and applications.* New York: Grune and Stratton.

Dehlin, O., Hedenrud, B., & Horal, J. (1976). Back symptoms in nursing aids in a geriatric hospital. *Scandinavian Journal of Rehabilitation Medicine, 8,* 47–53.

Eland, J. M., & Anderson, J. E. (1977). The experience of pain in children. In A. Jacox (Ed.), *Pain: A source book for nurses and other professionals* (pp. 453–473). Boston: Little, Brown.

Elliott, C., & Ozolins, M. (1983). Use of imagery and imagination in the treatment of children. In C. E. Walker & M. C. Roberts (Eds.), *Handbook of clinical child psychology* (pp. 1036–1049). New York: Wiley.

Engle, G. L. (1959). Psychogenic pain and the pain prone patient. *American Medicine, 137,* 899–918.

Flor, H. (1982). *The psychophysiology of back pain.* Unpublished manuscript, Yale University, New Haven, CT.

Flor, H., & Turk, D. C. (1984). Etiological theories and treatment for chronic back pain. I. Somatic models and interventions. *Pain, 19,* 105–121.

Fordyce, W. E. (1976). Behavior concepts in chronic pain and illness. In P. O. Davidson (Ed.), *The behavioral management of anxiety, depression and pain* (pp. 147–188). New York: Brunner-Mazel.

Gardner, G. G., & Olness, K. (1981). *Hypnosis and hypnotherapy with children.* Orlando, FL: Grune and Stratton.

Gentry, W. D., & Bernal, G. A. A. (1977). Chronic pain. In R. B. Williams & W. D. Gentry (Eds.), *Behavioral approaches to medical treatment* (pp. 173-182). Cambridge, MA: Ballinger.

Hallett, E. C., & Pilowsky, I. (1982). The response to treatment in a multidisciplinary pain clinic. *Pain, 12,* 365-374.

Harpin, V. A., & Rutter, M. (1982). Development of emotional sweating in the newborn infant. *Archives of Disease in Childhood, 57,* 691-695.

Hilgard, E. R., & Hilgard, J. (1975). *Hypnosis in the relief of pain.* Los Altos, CA: Kaufman.

Hilgard, J. R., & LeBaron, S. (1984). *Hypnotherapy of pain in children with cancer.* Los Altos, CA: Kaufman.

Hirsch, C., Jonsson, B., & Lewin, T. (1969). Low back symptoms in a Swedish female population. *Clinical Orthopedics, 63,* 171-176.

Holzman, A. D., Turk, D. C., & Kerns, R. D. (1986). The cognitive behavioral approach to the management of chronic pain. In A. D. Holzman & D. C. Turk (Eds.), *Pain Management: A handbook of psychological treatment approaches* (pp. 31-50). New York: Pergamon.

Horal, J. (1969). The clinical appearance of low back disorders in the city of Gothenburg, Sweden. *Acta Orthopaedica Scandinavica, 118*(Suppl.), 8-73.

Hult, L. (1954). Cervical, dorsal and lumbar spinal syndromes. *Acta Orthopaedica Scandinavica, 17*(Suppl.), 7-102.

Hult, L. (1965). The munkfors investigation. *Acta Orthopaedica Scandinavica, 16*(Suppl.), 1-76.

Jay, S. M., Ozolins, M., Elliott, C. H., & Caldwell, S. (1983). Assessment of children's distress during painful medical procedures. *Health Psychology, 2,* 133-148.

Katz, E. R., Kellerman, J., & Siegal, S. E. (1980). Behavioral distress in children with cancer undergoing medical procedures: Developmental considerations. *Journal of Consulting and Clinical Psychology, 48,* 356-365.

Keefe, F. J. (1982). Behavioral assessment and treatment of chronic pain: Current status and future directions. *Journal of Consulting and Clinical Psychology, 50,* 896-911.

Keefe, F. J., Black, A. R., Williams, R. B., & Surwit, R. S. (1981). Behavioral treatment of chronic pain: Clinical outcome and individual differences in pain relief. *Pain, 11,* 221-231.

Kirsch, I. (1985). Response expectancy as a determinant of experience and behavior. *American Psychologist, 40,* 1189-1203.

Lavigne, J. V., Schulein, M. J., & Hahn, Y. S. (1986a). Psychological aspects of painful medical conditions in children. I. Developmental aspects and assessment. *Pain, 27,* 133-146.

Lavigne, J. V., Schulein, M. J., & Hahn, Y. S. (1986b). Psychological aspects of painful medical conditions in children. II. Personality factors, family characteristics and treatments. *Pain, 27,* 147-169.

Lawrence, J. S. (1969). Disc degeneration—its frequency and relationship to symptoms. *Annals of Rheumatic Disorder, 28,* 121-136.

LeBaron, S., & Zeltzer, L. (1984). Assessment of acute pain and anxiety in children and adolescents by self-reports, observer reports and a behavior checklist. *Journal of Consulting and Clinical Psychology, 52,* 729-738.

Levine, M. D., & Rappaport, L. A. (1984). Recurrent abdominal pain in school children: The loneliness of the long distance physician. *Pediatric Clinics of North America, 31,* 969-991.

Masek, B. J., Russo, D. C., & Varni, J. W. (1984). Behavioral approaches to the management of chronic pain in children. *Pediatric Clinics of North America, 31*, 1113–1131.

Melzak, R. (1975). The McGill Pain Questionnaire: Major properties and scoring methods. *Pain, 1,* 277–299.

Melzak, R., & Wall, P. D. (1965). Pain mechanisms: A new theory. *Science, 150,* 971–979.

Miller, A. J., & Kratochwill, T. R. (1979). Reduction of frequent stomachache complaints by time-out. *Behavior Therapy, 10,* 211–218.

Minuchin, S. (1974). *Families and family therapy.* Cambridge, MA: Havard University Press.

Minuchin, S., Baker, L., Rossman, B., Liebman, L., Milman, L., & Todd, T. C. (1975). A conceptual model of psychosomatic illness in children. *Archives in General Psychiatry, 32,* 1031–1038.

Morgan, A. H., & Hilgard, J. R. (1978/1979). The Stanford Hypnotic Clinical Scale for Children. *The American Journal of Clinical Hypnosis, 21,* 148–169.

Nemiah, J. C. (1980). Somatoform disorders. In H. I. Kaplan, A. M. Freedman, & B. J. Sadock (Eds.), *Comprehensive textbook of psychiatry* (pp. 1525–1544). Baltimore: Williams & Wilkins.

Oster, J. (1972). Recurrent abdominal pain, headache, and limb pain in children and adolescents. *Pain, 50,* 429–436.

Passo, M. H. (1982). Aches and limb pain. *Pediatric Clinics of North America, 29,* 209–219.

Pinsky, J. A. (1983). Psychodynamic understanding and treatment of the chronic intractable benign pain syndrome—treatment outcome. *Seminars in Neurology, 3,* 346–354.

Roberts, A. H. (1986). The operant approach to the management of pain and chronic disability. In A. D. Holzman & D. C. Turk (Eds.), *Pain management: A handbook of psychological treatment approaches* (pp. 10–30). New York: Pergamon.

Sank, L. I., & Biglan, A. (1974). Operant treatment of a case of recurrent abdominal pain in a 10-year-old boy. *Behavior Therapy, 5,* 677–681.

Schechter, N. C. (1984). Recurrent pains in children: An overview and an approach. *Pediatric Clinics of North America, 31,* 949–968.

Scott, R. (1978). It hurts red: A preliminary study of children's perception of pain. *Perceptual and Motor Skills, 47,* 787–791.

Stanton-Hicks, M., & Boas, R. A. (1982). *Chronic low back pain.* New York: Raven Press.

Stewart, M. L. (1977). Measurement of clinical pain. In A. Jacox (Ed.), *Pain: A sourcebook for nurses and other health professionals* (pp. 107–137). Boston: Little, Brown.

Tesler, M., Ward, J., Savedra, M., Wegner, C. B., & Gibbons, P. (1983). Developing an instrument for eliciting children's description of pain. *Perceptual and Motor Skills, 56,* 315–321.

Turk, D. C., & Flor, H. (1984). Etiological theories and treatments for chronic back pain. II. Psychological modesl and interventions. *Pain, 19,* 209–233.

Turk, D. C., Meichenbaum, D. H., & Berman, W. H. (1979). Application of biofeedback for the regulation of pain: A critical review. *Psychological Bulletin, 86,* 1322–1338.

Turner, J. A., & Chapman, C. R. (1982a). Psychological interventions for chronic pain: A critical review. I. Relaxation training and biofeedback, *Pain, 12,* 1–22.

Turner, J. A., & Chapman, C. R. (1982b). Psychological interventions for chronic pain: A critical review. II. Operant conditioning, hypnosis and cognitive-behavioral therapy. *Pain, 12,* 23–46.

United States Vital and Health Statistics (1974). *Limitation of activity due to chronic conditions* (Series 10. No. 111). Washington, DC: United States Department of Health, Education, and Welfare.

Varni, J. W. (1983). *Clinical behavioral pediatrics: An interdisciplinary biobehavioral approach.* New York: Pergamon.

Varni, J. W., Bessman, C. A., Russo, D. C., & Cataldo, M. F. (1980). Behavioral management of chronic pain in children: A case study. *Archives of Physical and Medical Rehabilitation, 61,* 375–379.

Varni, J. W., Jay, S. M., Masek, B. J., & Thompson, K. L. (1986). Cognitive-behavioral assessment and management of pediatric pain. In A. D. Holzman & D. C. Turk (Eds.), *Pain management: A handbook of psychological treatment approaches* (pp. 168–192). New York: Pergamon.

Varni, J. W., Katz, E. R., & Dash, J. (1983). Behavioral and neurochemical aspects of pediatric pain. In D. C. Russo & J. W. Varni (Eds.), *Behavioral pediatrics: Research and practice* (pp. 177–224). New York: Plenum.

Varni, J. W., & Thompson, K. L. (1985). *The Varni/Thompson Pediatric Pain Questionnaire.* Unpublished manuscript, University of Southern California, Los Angeles.

Wakeman, R. J., & Kaplan, J. Z. (1978). An experimental study of hypnosis in painful burns. *American Journal of Clinical Hypnosis, 22,* 3–12.

20
Treating Anorexia Nervosa: Diagnostic Dilemmas and Therapeutic Challenges

DARLENE M. ATKINS

Anorexia nervosa has been a recognized clinical entity for only the past 100 years. Prior to that time there had been but a few isolated reports of "nervous consumption," such as a classic 1694 paper by Richard Morton (Andersen, 1985). In 1874, Sir William Gull coined the term "anorexia nervosa." The term has persisted, although not without controversy regarding its accuracy. Rather than being without appetite as the term suggests, patients with anorexia nervosa have been found to be intensely preoccupied with food, while denying and disowning their hunger. Although psychological factors were recognized early on, the theory of a pituitary origin (i.e., Simmond disease), became popular in the early 1900s and persisted for several decades (Bruch, 1973). During the 1930s the concept of a psychogenic form of anorexia nervosa was introduced. In subsequent years, the emphasis shifted to the intrapsychic and early developmental aspects of the disorder. Specific diagnostic criteria were proposed by Russell (1970) and by Feighner, Robins, Guze, Woodruff, Winokur, and Munoz (1972). These criteria have been criticized (Rollins & Piazza, 1978), but they continue to be cited for their clinical contributions. Currently, the criteria used most widely for the diagnosis of anorexia nervosa are those contained in the third revised edition of the *Diagnostic and Statistical Manual of Mental Disorders* (DSM-III-R), published by the American Psychiatric Association (1987). They are as follows:

Darlene M. Atkins. Departments of Adolescent Medicine and Psychiatry, Children's Hospital National Medical Center, George Washington University Medical School, Washington, D.C.

A. Refusal to maintain body weight over a minimal normal weight for age and height, e.g. weight loss leading to maintenance of body weight 15% below that expected; or failure to make expected weight gain during period of growth leading to body weight 15% below that expected.
B. Intense fear of gaining weight or becoming fat, even though underweight.
C. Disturbance in the way in which one's body weight, size, or shape is experienced, e.g. the person claims to "feel fat" even when emaciated.
D. In females, absence of at least three consecutive menstrual cycles when otherwise expected to occur (primary or secondary amenorrhea). (p. 67)

While the DSM-III-R criteria combine some of the essential features proposed by Russell and Feighner et al., they too are weak in several respects. The difficulty most relevant to the present chapter is the specific weight loss criteria. Younger patients (e.g., preadolescent, prepubertal) often do not lose sufficient weight to meet the criteria, especially in this age of increased public awareness resulting often in early detection. Irwin (1981, 1984) argued that the earlier DSM-III (American Psychiatric Association, 1980) criteria were not appropriate for preadolescent youngsters who, having less total body fat to begin with, would be more emaciated than teenagers who lost the same percentage of total body weight. While the DSM-III-R has liberalized the weight loss criterion from 25% to 15% of body weight, this may still be too restrictive for the younger patient population.

The first reports of anorexia nervosa in children began to appear in the literature in the 1960s (Blitzer, Rollins, & Blackwell, 1961; Kyger, 1966; Lesser, Ashenden, Delruskey, & Eisenberg, 1960; Warren, 1968). Although additional studies were published in the 1970s dealing with child anorectics (Goetz, Succop, Reinhart, & Miller, 1977; Poznanski, 1970; Reinhart, Kenna, & Succop, 1972), until quite recently anorexia nervosa was viewed as a disease of older adolescents and young adults. Two outcome studies, one a review of earlier reports (Hawley, 1985; Swift, 1982), have refuted earlier claims that childhood-onset anorexia nervosa is a milder disease with a more favorable prognosis. On the contrary, young anorexic patients often exhibit marked physiological, nutritional, psychological, and familial problems necessitating intensive intervention and even hospitalization. Fosson, Knibbs, Bryant-Waugh, and Lask (1987) described 48 children with a mean age of onset of 11.7 years and found significant wasting, and a high incidence of depression and distorted family interactions. Silber and Atkins (1986) also found depression to be a predominant component of anorexia nervosa in childhood, along with separation anxiety and overanxious disorder. Also of note is the fact that, in their preliminary study, one-half of the patients had experienced early physical maturation which they felt ill-equipped to handle. They expressed extreme fearfulness about leaving childhood and facing demands for more autonomous functioning. Several patients developed their eating disorder at the time of transition from elementary to junior high school.

The onset of anorexia nervosa does occur most commonly during the adolescent years and approximately 95% of those affected are female, and are from the upper socioeconomic classes. Estimates of prevalence are as high as 1 in 100 females between 12 and 18 years (DSM-III-R; American Psychiatric Association, 1987) or 1% of middle-class adolescent females (Andersen, 1985). Certain athletic, social, or professional groups that demand low body weight have even higher rates of anorexia nervosa. Mortality rates have been estimated to be as high as 18% (DSM-III-R; American Psychiatric Association, 1987), with deaths resulting from suicide, effects of starvation, and electrolyte imbalance. Andersen's (1985) description of the epidemiology of anorexia nervosa also includes the increased incidence of depression and eating disorders in the families of anorectic patients, and the increased incidence of anorexia nervosa during stressful life events (e.g., school change, family move). The specific prevalence of anorexia nervosa in pre-adolescent youngsters has not been reported, but all indications suggest an increased number of cases in this as well as in the older age groups.

Anorexia nervosa often begins as an attempt to lose 5 to 10 pounds. Overall caloric intake is steadily decreased while intense strenuous exercise is often steadily increased. Even after passing his/her weight goal, the individual continues to pursue thinness and to view himself/herself as fat. Food obsessions are common, as are peculiar behaviors such as hoarding and concealing food, preparing elaborate meals for others, and paranoia regarding possible disguised calories. Some of the ideation and associated behaviors are clearly secondary to the effects of starvation. Hyperactivity and restlessness are often observed as are social withdrawal, anhedonia, and cognitive constriction. Anorexic youngsters have been described as having characteristic underlying developmental and personality disturbances which predispose them to the development of the disease. Hilde Bruch (1973, 1978, 1980, 1982) has offered the clearest and most in-depth understanding of anorectic patients. She describes them as generally overly compliant, perfectionistic, self-critical youngsters who feel helpless and ineffective in conducting their own lives. While "model children," their lack of initiative and self-regulation is incompatible with the developmental challenges of adolescence. Their social relationships are often quite immature as they continue to function with the morality, cognitive style, and rule-governed behavior of much younger children.

There is greater consensus on how anorectic patients think and behave than on the causes of their pathology and the preferred methods of treatment. After the early zealous search for physiological causes, the psychoanalytic view became quite popular during the 1940s and 1950s. Within this perspective, the focus centered on the "oral" component, with anorexia nervosa seen as a form of conversion hysteria and a repudiation of oral impregnation fantasies (Bruch, 1982). The treatment of choice was, and for some practitioners still is, classical psychoanalysis. More recent advances have deepened our understanding of the intrapsychic elements as well as extended our treatment of eating disorders into a wider interpersonal arena. Developmental theories and self-psychology have been especially helpful in this regard. The rising popularity of communications and systems theories have expanded mental health professionals' interpersonal thinking to include the patient's family in views on etiology and treatment. I will now briefly review four major theories of etiology—sociocultural, familial, developmental, and self-psychological—with an emphasis on the latter two. Although described separately, these etiological viewpoints are not mutually exclusive. Theorists today generally recognize anorexia nervosa as a complex, multidetermined disorder, although most espouse a particular set of beliefs about primary etiology which then guides their treatment approach.

The sociocultural theory of the etiology of anorexia nervosa stems largely from the work of David Garner and Paul Garfinkel in Canada (Garner & Garfinkel, 1980; Garner, Garfinkel, & Bemis, 1982). They postulate that sociocultural pressures for women to be thin represent at least one important predisposing factor leading to the development of eating disorders. While Garner and Garfinkel view anorexia nervosa as multidetermined, their focus rests largely on sociocultural influences. Treatment from their perspective utilizes cognitive behavioral techniques to help patients modify distorted thinking patterns and to challenge unrealistic and potentially unhealthy cultural ideals. Cognitive restructuring involves confronting the patient's faulty logic, practicing new behaviors through behavioral exercises, and didactic teaching about weight and nutrition.

Family systems theorists focus less on the broad societal context and more on disturbed family functioning to explain and treat anorexia nervosa. The following predominant dysfunctional patterns have been described in families with an anorexic youngster: enmeshment, overprotectiveness, rigidity, lack of conflict resolution, and involvement of the sick child in unresolved parental conflict (Minuchin, Rosman, & Baker, 1978). Family therapy is aimed at changing the behavior of all family members and is designed to reorganize the family by limiting disturbed patterns of interaction and encouraging healthier alternatives (Sargent, Liebman, & Silver, 1985). Therapy within this framework includes fostering more direct communication, clarifying family roles, encouraging individuation, strengthening the parental dyad, and extricating the anorexic patient from the special position of parental mediator or confidant.

The developmental model proposed by Hilde Bruch (1980, 1982) links anorexia nervosa to disturbances in the early parent–child interaction with specific deficits in the responses to child-initiated cues. According to Bruch, this mismatch between the child's cues and the parents' responses causes confusion and mistrust of the self. As a result of not being responded to consistently and contingently, the child fails to develop an accurate sense of her own internal experiences (e.g., the ability to differentiate between her own physiological and emotional need states). She remains closely tied to the parent, is deficient in her sense of separateness, and feels helplessly controlled by outside forces and her own bodily urges. Three specific areas of psychological dysfunction described by Bruch are the disturbance in body image; the disturbance in perceiving stimuli arising in the body (e.g., hunger and fatigue are often denied); and the paralyzing sense of ineffectiveness. Bruch views anorexia nervosa as a misguided attempt at autonomy in an overly compliant youngster who has had no effective practice with separation and individuation. Treatment may include individual as well as family therapy. The therapeutic aim is to encourage initiative and autonomy in the patient and to help her know herself well enough to differentiate emotions from bodily experiences. A combination of empathy and cognitive behavioral techniques is used in an active approach to uncover and correct early developmental deficits which have led to faulty assumptions and years of "faked existence." Bruch advocates nutritional rehabilitation as an integral first step so that the patient can participate fully in the treatment process.

The self-psychological perspective, a view closely related to Bruch's developmental theory, describes anorexia nervosa as a major form of self pathology. Drawing largely on the work of Heinz Kohut, self-psychological theorists (Geist, 1985; Goodsitt, 1985) propose that anorexia nervosa represents a deficit in the organization of the self which stems from chronic failure in the empathic connection between the child and parent. As Geist (1985, p. 274) points out, "The anorexic patient is not lacking in good enough mothering; she experiences a distortion of a very specific aspect of mothering—empathic mirroring." Empathic mirroring refers in part to a type of healthy, fine-tuned interaction whereby the caregiver responds to the child's various needs by accurately reading the child's subtle cues (e.g., indicating whether she is hungry, wet, or just wants to be held). The infant's experience of having her needs responded to appropriately helps her to gradually recognize and differentiate between her own need states. An example of this would be that the infant is comforted when she signals fear rather than, for instance, being misinterpreted and fed. Without such mirroring, there is inner fragmentation, a distorted sense of self, and a split between the bodily sense of self and the psychic sense of self (Rizzuto, Peterson, & Reed, 1981). During the first few years of life when the foundation for important ego structures is laid, the anorexic patient may have been responded to in terms of isolated parts of her, rather than her whole self; as an extension of the parent rather than as a unique individual with needs for both autonomy and dependency; or by an emotionally unavailable caregiver (e.g., one who was depressed). Insufficient empathic mirroring results in failure to internalize and develop critical self-regulatory functions and leads to defensive identification with the parent and heightened compliance and pseudomaturity. Lacking the ego structures necessary to calm herself, to guard against overstimulation, and to regulate self-esteem, the anorexic feels rigidly dependent upon and controlled by others. Because of the inability to integrate bodily, cognitive, and affective experiences into a core sense of self, initiative is severely impaired (Goodsitt, 1985; Lerner, 1983). While Bruch's view underscores disturbances in separation/individuation, the self-psychological perspective focuses more on early failures in parental empathy and mirroring. This subtle distinction has important treatment implications.

Within the self-psychological model, psychotherapy is aimed at establishing an idealized transference whereby the patient takes in the therapist's soothing presence and utilizes the therapist as a "transitional object" in Winnicott's terms or a "selfobject" in Kohut's terms (Geist, 1985; Goodsitt, 1985). This empathic contact is viewed as the foundation for internal structure building and a beginning integration of the self. The therapist strives to maintain an empathic bond and avoids unempathic responses such as confrontation and behavioral manipulation. Rather than confront the patient's distorted perceptions and provocative behavior, the therapist explores the patient's feelings of being misunderstood and of needing to engage in fierce struggles for power and control. By consistently affirming the patient's emerging self, the therapist becomes internalized in such a way as to heal internal fragmentation, and thus to decrease the patient's defensive stance and her need for omnipotent control (Geist, 1985).

The following case example of a young anorexic patient illustrates a dynamic formulation and treatment approach based upon developmental and self-psychological theory. The self-psychological perspective seemed particularly applicable given this patient's core disturbances in self-regulation and identity formation. Although cognitive restructuring and behavioral techniques were used by the physician and nutritionist, the aim of individual psychotherapy was structural change and personality development. Dieting and weight loss were the arena in which the patient's deeper psychological deficits were manifested. Thus, correcting her malnutrition was necessary but not sufficient to build internal structures which would aid her overall development. Similarly, changing family patterns seemed beneficial but not without also addressing the patient's poorly integrated sense of self.

CASE BACKGROUND

Anne, a 12-year-old white female, was referred to the Eating Disorders Program at Children's Hospital National Medical Center by her pediatrician following a 2-month history of increasing preoccupation with food and dieting and a 6-pound weight loss during her stay at an overnight summer camp. During the previous school year, Anne had become a bit zealous in her avoidance of sweets, but she did not actually diet or lose weight. At camp, she intentionally set out to lose weight for the first time. When she returned home, her parents became concerned about her compulsive exercising and her restricted intake of both food and liquids. Mealtime battles quickly ensued. Significant stressors at the time of referral included Anne's transition from elementary to junior high school; increased peer difficulties and social isolation; and her mother's return to full-time employment. Psychological evaluation was requested to assess for possible anorexia nervosa as well as for depression.

Anne presented as a pale, withdrawn youngster who appeared anxious and hypervigilant. In the initial interview, she described her inability to eat more than 500 calories per day, stating that she heard a voice telling her not to eat. She expressed intense feelings of guilt and worthlessness to the extent that she felt she did not deserve to eat, to sleep in a bed, or to wear attractive clothes. Her parents confirmed that she had been sleeping on her bedroom floor. She felt unworthy in all respects and stated firmly her readiness to be "a nobody." She admitted that obsessive thoughts about food and weight were severely impairing her sleep and concentration and, for these reasons, she was not resistant to seeking help. Sleep disturbance consisted of difficulty falling asleep and early morning awakening. Her teachers observed marked problems with attention and concentration which hampered her adjustment to the new junior high school environment. They described her as having inordinate difficulty organizing her materials and completing even basic homework tasks the first few weeks of school. Anne's parents found her to be sad, tearful, and drained of all life or enthusiasm. She expressed self-deprecating thoughts in the initial interview, but she denied any depression or suicidal ideation. At the time of referral, Anne's parents reported feeling terrified about her condition but helpless to do anything about it. They saw her as having deteriorated rapidly into an empty shell of her former self. Her refusal to eat shocked them, given her previously compliant nature. They feared not only for her physical health but that she might be having some form of mental breakdown.

Developmental History

The history given by Anne's parents was that she was born following a full-term uncomplicated pregnancy and delivery. Developmental milestones were within normal limits. Anne was described as an easygoing, compliant baby who was always eager to please. She demonstrated no temper tantrums or willful behavior. Her mother served as primary caretaker throughout her preschool years. She was quite close to her mother and had marked difficulty with separation (e.g., when left with babysitters), as well as with any type of disruption or change. For instance, although Anne was able to adjust to kindergarten, she had a rather dramatic response to moving from kindergarten to first grade. Upon entering the first grade, she demonstrated extreme anxiety and panic which was treated with phenobarbitol and brief play therapy. Anne went on to become an excellent student, and she continued to excel in school over the years. She was quite perfectionistic with regard to her academic work, and she completed assignments thoroughly and ahead of schedule.

Anne's parents described her as having a long history of emotional difficulties consisting mainly of her being socially awkward and somewhat isolated from peers. According to their description, she often missed nuances and social cues. Her thinking was quite literal and concrete and her behavior was often abrupt. In focusing on minor details, she missed the overall complexity of social interactions. Even as a young child, she tended to misread others' reactions as well as to perseverate on concrete, nonessential content to the exclusion of any affective experience or process. Anne's mother poignantly illustrated this narrow focus on details with the example that if you told Anne someone had been hit by a car, her first response would be to ask what type of car it was. Overall, Anne was presented by her parents as a rather "economical" youngster who tended to compartmentalize and to express only those needs which she could not fulfill herself. She had difficulty adapting to any change and she lacked spontaneity. During childhood, she generally had one friend at a time and remained rather oblivious to larger peer-group dynamics. Her parents and teachers both noted that as she grew older, she increasingly became the victim of teasing because of her intellectual zeal and her moralistic, rule-governed attitudes and behavior.

Family History

Anne was an only child from an intact, upper middle-class family. Her parents were both professionals with graduate educations. This was a close-knit, geographically stable, nuclear family, actively involved in community activities.

When Anne's father was in his teens, he was involved in psychotherapy because of difficulty expressing emotion. He found the experience helpful and was functioning well at the time of Anne's referral. Anne's mother had a history of chronic, treatment-resistant depression. She had terminated psychotherapy after several years and was maintained on tricyclic antidepressants. She appeared to be a characteriologically depressed woman with very poor self-esteem. She had had a particularly severe bout of depression at the time when Anne left home to enter school. At the time of referral, she was returning to full-time employment for the first time since Anne's birth. Her depressive episodes, which consisted of sleep disturbance and extreme self-doubt, had interfered at times with even part-time career pursuits, and also strained the marital relationship which seemed otherwise firmly based. At the time of Anne's referral, her mother's depression appeared to be marginally under control.

In addition to depression in her mother, Anne's family history was significant for depression in her paternal grandmother and depression and bulimia in her maternal grandmother.

ASSESSMENT AND DIAGNOSTIC IMPRESSIONS

The multidisciplinary assessment team consisted of a clinical psychologist (D. A.), an adolescent medicine physician, and a nutritionist. The outpatient evaluation procedure routinely utilized by the Eating Disorders Program was completed in a rapid, abbreviated manner because of the level of the family's distress. Over the course of a week, the patient was evaluated medically and nutritionally, and psychological data were obtained through interviews with the patient and her parents, separately and together. The patient also completed the Diagnostic Interview Schedule for Children (DIS-C), a computer-scored assessment tool which generates DSM-III diagnostic categories (Herjanic, Puig-Antich, & Connors, 1981). A live interview with the patient was conducted by a consulting child psychiatrist, with members of the larger multidisciplinary team observing through a one-way mirror. In the interest of time, the following typical components of the eating disorders evaluation were omitted: the self-administered Eating Disorder Inventory (Garner, Olmstead, & Polivy, 1983); the self-administered Somatopsychological Differentiation Scale (Chatoor, Atkins, Bernard, & Rohrbeck, 1987); the patient's drawing of herself and ideal self; and a family interview session.

The first diagnostic question was whether or not Anne's symptomotology met the criteria for a diagnosis of anorexia nervosa. The presence of the essential features of distorted body image, intense fear of becoming obese, refusal to maintain normal body weight, and no known physical illness to account for the weight loss, was established through psychological and medical evaluation. Anne was an otherwise physically healthy, slim youngster who reported feeling preoccupied with the size of her stomach and thighs and was intensely fearful about the possibility of gaining weight. At the time of referral, she was premenarchal, but breast development was significant. Anne's parents had responded quickly to early signs of an eating disturbance, and they sought medical attention after only 6 pounds had been lost. She thus did not meet the DSM-III-R criterion of loss of 15% of original body weight or even of 15% loss of combined body weight plus projected weight gain expected from growth charts. From my interviews with Anne, it became clear that she would have eventually lost enough weight to meet this diagnostic criterion had she been permitted to continue her restrictive dieting and compulsive exercise. Her responses on the DIS-C were also consistent with the diagnosis of anorexia nervosa, as she positively endorsed those items which tap the DSM-III diagnostic criteria.

In addition to her eating disorder symptomatology, Anne demonstrated severe psychological difficulties. We raised the possibility of a thought disorder because of Anne's report of a "voice" telling her to restrict her caloric intake. Further examination revealed that the voice was internal, and it seemed more a facet of her harsh, punitive superego and an effort to exercise supreme self-control than any type of hallucination. Overall, Anne's reality testing was intact, other than her distorted perception of her own body and her refusal to take in adequate food and liquids.

Anne's poor sleep and concentration were undoubtedly related to her inadequate nutrition, but were also suggestive of a marked depression. She described loss of pleasure in all activities, feelings of worthlessness and inadequacy, irritability, and ruminating thoughts. Although she verbally denied feeling depressed, her responses on the DIS-C were indicative of the presence of an affective disorder. Thus, a dual diagnosis of anorexia nervosa and depression seemed appropriate for Anne. An association between these two disorders has been proposed increasingly in the clinical literature (Hudson, Pope, Jonas, & Yurgelun-Todd, 1983; Rivinus, Biederman, Herzog, Kemper, Harper, Harmatz, & Houseworth, 1984).

Obsessive–compulsive personality features were also evident from the history and from Anne's current presentation. She was extremely attentive to detail, she scheduled her time carefully, and she placed high value on efficiency and strict adherence to rules. Anne's focus on details interfered at times with her concentration and productivity. Her thoughts and behaviors were often perseverative, including exercising in a compulsive, driven manner. She described a fear of letting her mind wander and of being distracted by "frivolous" socializing. Her personality structure and intellectual rigidity, limited affective availability, and social awkwardness are consistent with Shapiro's (1965) description of the obsessive–compulsive neurotic style. Many anorexic patients have similarly been found to manifest obsessive–compulsive symptoms which predate and possibly predispose them to their eating disorder (Solyom, Freeman, & Miles, 1982).

FORMULATION AND RECOMMENDATIONS

Anne's development of anorexia nervosa can be understood within a developmental, self-psychological perspective. Constitutionally, Anne was a rather passive infant who did not signal her needs in a forceful, easily discernible manner. At the same time, her mother's depressive disorder likely interfered with her capacity to tune in to Anne's needs and to respond with consistent emotional availability. The early mother–child relationship seemed characterized by overinvolvement interspersed with failures in empathic connectedness. Anne became overly reliant on her mother without developing a sense of her own separateness and without taking in aspects of her mother in the formation of a rudimentary autonomous self. Her somato-psychological differentiation (Chatoor et al., 1987), or what Bruch has described as her ability to identify and separate her own physiological and emotional need states, was consequently deficient. Lacking necessary internal structures, Anne was vulnerable to later disturbances of self-regulation (namely, an eating disorder), to difficulties with management of anxiety, and to deficits in her interpersonal abilities. She relied on her mother and on others to such an extent that separations and transitions were exceedingly difficult (e.g., entering first grade, going to overnight camp, starting junior high).

Over the course of her development, Anne began to display a "contact-shunning personality," one of the three personality types hypothesized by self-psychologists (Baker & Baker, 1987) to result from consistent shortcomings in early empathic mirroring. This personality type is characteristically isolated and avoids social interaction because the individual fears that either further nonempathic mirroring will destroy her/his fragile sense of self or that she/he will be "swallowed up" altogether by others. Anne appeared to have a very low threshold for social contact, and she was described by her parents as having always been sensitive and easily overwhelmed. In her interpersonal style, she vacillated between being cautious and skittish and being overly familiar and overbearing. There was no comfortable middle ground reinforced by appropriate boundaries. Recently, Anne had become increasingly avoidant of her parents, especially her mother. The press of impending adolescence, as well as her mother's return to work, sparked a defensive pulling away and a misguided attempt at separation/individuation through food refusal and demonstrated control over her own body.

Given this conceptualization of how and why Anne developed her eating disorder, the challenge remained of how best to help her and her parents. First of all, an interpretive conference was held with them to given them feedback about her physical and psychological status. They were presented with a summary of the formulation in a manner they could understand and accept: Her anorexia nervosa was described as a developmental disorder with contributing genetic, constitutional, and interactional factors. When they requested reading material to increase their understanding, Hilde Bruch's *The Golden Cage: The Enigma of Anorexia Nervosa* (1978) was recommended.

From the time of initial referral and throughout the brief evaluation period, Anne's parents described themselves as panic stricken and at a loss with how to cope. Anne was exercising compulsively, starving herself, sleeping poorly, and not able to function in her new junior high school. Because of their level of distress, we recommended that Anne be treated on an inpatient basis, although her medical condition was not yet severely compromised. Anne's parents were frightened by and resistant to inpatient treatment, and they opted instead to first engage in an intensive outpatient program. The treatment team agreed to an outpatient approach since her condition did not seem dangerous, but they were very pessimistic about its potential efficacy in this situation. With the team's concurrence, Anne's parents withdrew her from her large public junior high school and enrolled her in a small private school willing to work with youngsters with emotional difficulties.

Medical and nutritional follow-up were scheduled on a weekly basis, and Anne's parents were encouraged to disengage themselves from the struggle to get her to eat. This incidentally is in stark contrast to other treatment approaches in which one intervention may be to have the parents take greater control of their youngster's food intake (Minuchin et al., 1978). The physician in this case assured them that her vital signs and her weight would be monitored closely, and he asked that he be allowed to assume responsibility for this aspect of Anne's care, increasingly including her as an active participant. They were to maintain all other parenting functions and to uphold expectations for Anne consistent with her age and the family's routine functioning. Both the physician and the nutritionist worked with Anne in a supportive yet firm manner. They educated her about her physiological functioning, and they utilized cognitive–behavioral techniques to challenge her distorted body image and her many misconceptions about food and weight. Their emphasis was on health and growth and they reassured her that these aims did not necessitate her becoming overweight. Whenever this rational appeal seemed insufficient (e.g., she lost weight), they were a bit more authoritative. They let Anne know that if her fears gripped her to the point of jeopardizing her health, they would have to assume control by limiting her physical activity and possibly even hospitalizing her. Had she required inpatient treatment, some additional behavioral therapy techniques would have been utilized, for example, she would have been given increased freedom and privileges as she demonstrated a greater capacity to adequately feed and care for herself. Many inpatient programs employ behavioral contingencies at least early in treatment when nutritional rehabilitation is essential (Halmi, 1985; Mitchell & Eckert, 1987).

Psychological treatment was designed to include twice-weekly individual psychotherapy and separate weekly parent counseling, both conducted by the same therapist. Individual psychotherapy was chosen to address Anne's self-deficits in the context of an empathic mirroring relationship. Specific caloric and weight requirements were issued by the physician, not the psychotherapist, so as to protect the therapist's empathic bond with Anne. As Bruch has pointed out, however, some didactic teaching about physical growth and metabolism was a necessary part of psychotherapy in order to clarify Anne's misconceptions and work on her distorted body image.

The decision to go with parent counseling rather than family therapy was a difficult and possibly controversial one. In retrospect, family therapy might have been a useful adjunctive modality, and it is one I often include, especially in the treatment of young anorexic patients. Early on, Anne's parents appeared so overwhelmed and needy themselves that therapy for them seemed imperative. I was hesitant to encourage them to express their fear and guilt in Anne's presence, given her own level of anxiety and vulnerability. I decided to work with Anne and her parents separately, assuming that their relationships with one another would ultimately benefit. Of course, failure to conduct family therapy limited my view to what Anne and her parents told me about their interactional patterns and precluded me from intervening directly in vivo. Had family therapy been utilized, however, I would have referred the family to a colleague so as to avoid any threat to the individual therapeutic relationship. Even with separate parent counseling this is a delicate issue to manage.

One other component of outpatient treatment was the use of a tricyclic antidepressant, prescribed and managed by Anne's adolescent medicine physician. Pharmacotherapy was utilized because of the level of interference caused by Anne's depressive symptoms (sleep disturbance, impaired concentration, anhedonia). Medication was introduced after several weeks of the outpatient treatment program failed to relieve Anne of her acute symptoms. The consulting child psychiatrist recommended imipramine as the specific tricylcic antidepressant, in part because Anne's mother had herself responded favorably to imipramine. The role of pharmacotherapy in the treatment of anorexia nervosa remains controversial, although less so with a patient such as Anne in whom depression is a salient feature (Garfinkel & Garner, 1987).

COURSE OF THERAPY

My first individual psychotherapy session with Anne ranks as one of my most memorable sessions with any patient. She spent the hour crying and protesting bitterly against entering psychotherapy. She expressed anxiety about not knowing what she was "supposed to" talk about during the two therapy hours per week and not knowing what I expected of her. She also verbalized a fear that once we began working together she would become desperately dependent on me and would never be able to stop therapy. Despite sobbing uncontrollably at times, Anne vehemently denied any feelings that were reflected back to her (e.g., fear, sadness). She continued this pattern of denying affect even when tearful throughout most of the first year of her therapy. From the outset, Anne professed self-sufficiency and self-denial with a fervor. Even in the first session, however, it was apparent that Anne's fears of closeness raged side by side with her fears of separation and loss. Feeling an emptiness inside, she both wished to be fulfilled through a relationship with another person, and yet feared that such closeness would jeopardize her own tenuous sense of self.

Initially, Anne demonstrated minimal capacity for insight or introspection. She spent our sessions reporting to me on her eating and her schoolwork in a methodical, dutiful manner. She reacted angrily to any probing about her peer relationships, stating that she was satisfied she was no longer being teased. She denied any desire for friends. During the early phase of treatment, I was struck continually by Anne's lack of relatedness, by her rigidity, and by the absence of an active fantasy life or any sense of internal richness. She lacked empathy, and she was also unable to tolerate any empathic expression by others. I was left feeling I must tread lightly; that I risked overwhelming her if I was warm, or disappointing her if I refrained from responding. Despite her statements to the contrary, I assumed that she did want to make contact, and I proceeded slowly and gently to intrude upon her isolated existence. Engaging her in a relationship with me was an arduous, often frustrating task. I did not interpret her difficulty establishing a relationship as "resistance" but viewed it instead as a reflection of her lack of sense of self. She was not, for instance, refusing to tell me her feelings; instead she was confused herself about her internal experience. My approach was to listen, even to her most obsessive expounding, and to convey to her the sense that I was with her, that I could tolerate the full range of her affect, and that she was a person in her own right beyond her external physical appearance. I acknowledged her wish to be slim but encouraged her to explore other possible functions of her weight loss and compulsive exercise. Beginning work on her somatopsychological differentiation involved helping her to recognize her own hunger and satiety; distinguishing these from feelings such as anxiety and anger; and unraveling with her the meaning and message underlying her refusal to eat. She came to understand her self-starvation not just as a means to stay slim but also as a way to convey a range of feelings, many of which she was either unaware of or ill-equipped to handle.

Psychotherapy and antidepressant medication served to contain Anne's acute symptomology to such an extent that she was able to function effectively. She settled in at her new school, and I initially collaborated weekly by telephone with her counselor and teachers to help them in their work with her. Anne's nutritional intake stabilized to the extent that she was able to continue treatment as an outpatient, although weight fluctuations persisted throughout the early months of therapy.

Gradually, Anne developed an increased ability to trust me and to enter into a fuller therapeutic relationship. I hesitate to call it a therapeutic alliance since she was not an active partner cognizant of her own difficulties until much later in the treatment process. During this middle phase of therapy, Anne was quite verbal, although she repeatedly reminded me that she was only in therapy under duress. She moved beyond focusing exclusively on eating and schoolwork, which allowed several significant themes to emerge. As Anne began to relax her rigid controls and hypervigilance, she expressed fears of loss of impulse control. These fears were particularly evident in her dreams, which she was increasingly willing to relate. In one dream, for example, she was angrily overturning tables of food and in another she was greedily accumulating large sums of money. Fostering Anne's acceptance of even the angry or greedy parts of herself was one of my goals during this period of our work together.

Another theme which emerged was Anne's intense anger at and disappointment in her mother. She was critical of what she saw in her mother as disorganization, emotional lability, and overall vulnerability. She was enraged whenever her mother's depression resulted in her sleeping more and participating less fully in the family and in her job. Anne did not necessarily want more time with her mother so much as she wanted to feel that her mother was strong and competent. She needed both a well-functioning female role model and reassurance that her mother was able to sustain the attention of her father in the marital dyad. Anne identified strongly with her father, and admired his intellect and his career achievements. Warm feelings toward her father or affectionate overtures by him toward her seemed increasingly frightening as she became dimly aware of her own sexuality and was simultaneously doubtful of her mother's strength and viability. As the therapy progressed, oedipal themes began to appear amid more basic, preoedipal concerns. Her dyadic relationship with me enabled Anne to progress toward these triadic issues.

Nine months into her psychotherapy, Anne's depression had improved to such an extent that her antidepressant medication was discontinued. Her weight was also stable although she continued to exercise excessively. For the first time ever, Anne joined a team. She demonstrated a growing awareness of and interest in her peers though, if this was acknowledged, she would reply that she saw this as her only way of getting out of therapy. Despite such statements, Anne appeared invested in the relationship, even to the extent of giving me a handmade "anniversary" card to commemorate 1 year of working together. One and one-half years into her treatment, however, Anne had a rather sudden deterioration, with no obvious precipitant. She appeared depressed again and her weight dropped over several weeks. After a number of tearful sessions, Anne revealed that she was angry at her parents for not recognizing her progress thus far by decreasing her therapy to once a week. She had not voiced this request but had expected that they should know her wishes. This highlighted not only her wish for mirroring and almost telepathic attunement, but also the need for further work on her reliance on food refusal to express her needs and feelings. With my encouragement Anne talked with her parents and asked that they at least discuss this issue with me. We did discuss it, decided the timing was not appropriate, and asked that Anne initiate the request verbally in the future rather than through not eating. She responded in a surprisingly calm manner, suggesting a stronger need to be heard and understood than to actually have her request filled. Six months later when she was doing quite well, Anne raised the issue in a direct manner, and the therapy was tapered to once a week.

In the later phase of therapy, the focus of treatment shifted from Anne's eating disorder to her peer relationships. She became highly concerned about her delayed interpersonal skills and set out on a mission to improve her social position. She was able to acknowledge her wish to be noticed and accepted. Her strategies included spending free periods socializing versus doing homework, getting a stylish haircut, and taking an increased interest in fashion and music. She commented frequently on my attire and appearance and seemed to be looking more closely at people than she had ever done. It appeared that Anne was entering a "love affair with the world" (Greenacre, 1957), and with more energy and enthusiasm than I had ever seen her demonstrate. Her obsessive style was still evident, however, and revealed itself in her rather driven, task-oriented approach to engaging her peers. A little over 2 years into treatment, Anne obtained a true close friend, a girl her own age who was a newcomer to the school and did not know her poor social track record. Anne began attending social activities with her and talking incessantly on the telephone. She remained on the periphery of the more popular social circles, but her new-found longing to form relationships was clearly being noticed by her peers. They not only congratulated her on her academic and athletic accomplishments, they also included her more in their lunchtime and after-school gatherings.

Anne's relationship with her mother also improved dramatically during the later phase of therapy. She continued to express irritation and disappointment in her mother at times, but overall she displayed warmer feelings and genuine caring. She accepted her mother more, disclosed more to her, and was much more physically affectionate. With increasing frequency, Anne talked with me about concerns she had already shared with her mother and her best friend. These concerns often revolved around sexuality, and boys she had crushes on. Amid Anne's intrapsychic and interpersonal growth there were still periodic reminders of the remnants of her rigid, economical personality. For example, when she had the onset of her menses, Anne handled this in a pragmatic, matter-of-fact manner, initially failing to tell even her mother. She denied any feelings about this event and would discuss it only from a rather depersonalized, intellectual stance.

Overall, Anne made enormous progress in all areas over the course of therapy. She improved significantly in her affective expression and interpersonal relatedness. She also recovered the weight she had lost; ceased her restrictive dieting and compulsive exercising; developed a more accurate body image; and thus no longer met any of the diagnostic criteria for anorexia nervosa. Now, 3 years after initial diagnosis, Anne is slowly tapering her individual psychotherapy. This separation/individuation process looks to be a successful one, as she is armed with necessary internal self-structures and the ability to mobilize external support systems.

Working with Anne's parents was likewise challenging and rewarding. The first task was to help them preserve their marriage and family life despite Anne's eating disorder and depression. As individuals, both parents had a tendency to deny their own needs. They needed permission as well as prompting to let go of their guilt and channel their energy into restoring their own sense of confidence and self-efficacy. They also needed reassurance that it was still appropriate to view Anne as a young adolescent with a developing need for autonomy, despite her seeming fragility and vulnerability. Anne had received mixed messages from her parents to on the one hand express her feelings, but on the other hand to keep her feelings toned down and well contained. Gradually, they came to recognize patterns such as the power of her anxiety to escalate their own and their tendency to dampen her expression of intense or negative affect. They feared Anne's depression and undoubtedly communicated this to her. For example, when she deteriorated midway into therapy as described, they quickly requested the reintroduction of antidepressants. Their deep caring for Anne made it intolerable for them to see her distressed. At the same time, Anne also received implicit messages to make few demands, especially when her mother was depressed.

A critical aspect of the parent work was mobilizing Anne's mother and helping her father to support his wife. He insightfully pointed out to her that she almost encouraged Anne's criticism of her by "handing Anne a loaded gun," that is, by being extremely self-critical and self-doubting. We discussed Anne's need to idealize her mother despite her mother's own feelings of unworthiness and underlying poor self-esteem. I recommended individual psychotherapy for Anne's mother on several occasions, but she refused. The parents and I continued working on both marital and parenting issues with sessions reduced from weekly to twice monthly during the first year of treatment.

As Anne began to improve, her parents found themselves having difficulty accepting her assertiveness. Instead of being defensively self-sufficient, Anne became truly able to handle more situations and decisions without feeling overwhelmed. They needed help in therapy to avoid viewing her increased independence as a rejection or personal affront. They struggled also to accept her expression of emotions and her spontaneous demonstrations of affection. As these new behaviors emerged, they were frequently unmodulated. For instance, her parents described her as overly enthusiastic at times, with a tendency to approach people and activities in a "bulldozer" fashion. Gradually, Anne improved to the point of resembling a rather bouncy, egocentric teenager, and her parents were increasingly able to view her as such. The later phase of parent counseling then moved toward focusing on normal adolescent concerns.

Anne's parents currently maintain periodic contact with me as her individual treatment nears completion. Their own progress was significant, although compromised to some degree by the mother's underlying depressive illness. They were able to make gains in their attunement with Anne, in their ability to tolerate her affect, and in their responsiveness to her needs for closeness as well as autonomy. They seemed to become closer as a couple, making more time for themselves without their feeling guilty. My continued frustration was the couple's resignation to and almost complacency with the mother's depression and poor self-esteem. Systems theorists would argue that her symptomatology must serve some stabilizing function within the dyad. Although there was definite improvement that was maintained even as Anne got better, her mother's difficulties remain an area of unfinished business.

DISCUSSION

The case presented was in some ways representative of work with anorexic patients and in other respects atypical. To begin with, the initial evaluation was more abbreviated than usual in that we omitted some evaluation tools which may have been useful (e.g., diagnostic family interview, self-report measures). We reacted to the family's level of anxiety and desperation and quickly launched treatment in an effort to stabilize the patient on an outpatient basis. Although unavoidable, this resulted in the loss of some pretreatment data which may have been useful later in assessing outcome. The utilization of collateral parent counseling was also a deviation from our typical procedure of using family therapy, especially with young anorexic patients. Of course, the multidisciplinary team approach including school collaboration would be relevant to working with nearly all anorexic patients. The complex issues raised in the use of hospitalization and inpatient treatment of anorexia nervosa were not covered in this case description but may be found in other works (Andersen, Morse, & Santmyer, 1985; Garfinkel, Garner, & Kennedy, 1985). While some programs and practitioners utilize a system whereby the psychotherapist supervises the patient's weight and caloric intake, we have found a policy of dividing these roles to be more compatible with a self-psychological approach to psychotherapy wherein the therapist strives to stay within the subjective experience of the patient.

Maintaining a stance of empathic mirroring was quite difficult at times when confronted with Anne's perseverative, quasi-delusional thinking. The choice, however, was whether to deny her internal experience and tell her how to think, or to communicate to her that I was someone who could tolerate her confusion and inner pain. Knowing that the physician and nutritionist were working with Anne to help correct her misconceptions and body image distortion freed me from my urges to do so. As her individual psychotherapist, I was able to focus more on the psychotherapy process than on the content of what was discussed. For example, instead of talking to her about the value of interpersonal relationships, I fostered the development of a relationship with me to draw her out of her isolation and to serve as a template for other relationships. Despite my best intentions, there were inevitably several breaks in my attunement and empathic connectedness with Anne. These ranged from simple misunderstandings of things she was trying to communicate to interrupting our scheduled sessions by going on vacation. Such breaks, if minor and if in the context of a fairly solid ongoing relationship can be weathered by the patient, can actually be opportunities for growth, and can be part of the curative process. Anne became attached to me, it seems, almost in spite of herself. Her trust in and desire for interpersonal contact was thereby stimulated, and she ultimately replaced me with a best friend and with a closer relationship with her mother. Her dependence on psychotherapy was thus a temporary and seemingly beneficial one.

The level of Anne's interpersonal difficulties was marked and was not characteristic of all anorexic patients. Her obsessiveness was also more pronounced than I have seen in other patients. She will no doubt retain features of an obsessive personality but may now be more able to derive pleasure from her pursuits and from interpersonal relationships. The length of Anne's treatment was significant, but not excessive, given her distraught presentation, her premorbid personality and self-deficits, and the complication of her mother's recurrent, treatment-resistant depression. Other preadolescent anorexic patients with milder psychological disturbance have required shorter courses of treatment despite more severe weight loss.

Fortunately, this family was motivated, and they had the resources to take advantage of intensive intervention. In this case, the treatment was tailored to the needs of the patient and family rather than being dictated by the constraints of insurance benefits or by a rigid therapeutic protocol. The investment was undeniably great, but the payoff also was substantial. The story does not always end so happily for many anorexic patients. A number of them do die and others remain chronically ill or marginally functional. Anne's recovery from her eating disorder symptoms seemed complete and was accomplished without hospitalization. Cases like this are the ones that sustain those of us who devote much of our professional time and energy to this challenging patient population.

REFERENCES

American Psychiatric Association. (1980). *Diagnostic and statistical manual of mental disorders*, (3rd ed.). Washington, DC: Author.

American Psychiatric Association. (1987). *Diagnostic and statistical manual of mental disorders*, (3rd ed., revised). Washington, DC: Author.

Andersen, A. (1985). *Practical comprehensive treatment of anorexia nervosa and bulimia.* Baltimore: The Johns Hopkins University Press.

Andersen, A., Morse, C., & Santmyer, K. (1985). Inpatient treatment for anorexia nervosa. In D. Garner & P. Garfinkel (Eds.), *Handbook of psychotherapy for anorexia nervosa and bulimia* (pp. 311-343). New York: Guilford.

Baker, H., & Baker, M. (1987). Heinz Kohut's self-psychology: An overview. *American Journal of Psychiatry, 144*, 1-9.

Blitzer, J., Rollins, N., & Blackwell, A. (1961). Children who starve themselves: Anorexia nervosa. *Psychosomatic Medicine, 23*, 369-383.

Bruch, H. (1973). *Eating disorders: Obesity, anorexia nervosa, and the person within.* New York: Basic Books.

Bruch, H. (1978). *The golden cage: The enigma of anorexia nervosa.* New York: Vintage Books.

Bruch, H. (1980). Preconditions for the development of anorexia nervosa. *American Journal of Psychoanalysis, 40*, 169-172.

Bruch, H. (1982). Anorexia nervosa: Therapy and theory. *American Journal of Psychiatry, 139*, 1531-1538.

Chatoor, I., Atkins, D., Bernard, P., & Rohrbeck, C. (1988). Measuring somatopsychological differentiation in anorexia nervosa: Development of a scale. Paper presented at the Third International Conference on Eating Disorders, New York.

Feighner, J., Robins, E., Guze, S., Woodruff, R., Winokur, G., & Munoz, R. (1972). Diagnostic criteria for use in psychiatric research. *Archives of General Psychiatry, 26*, 57-63.

Fosson, A., Knibbs, J., Bryant-Waugh, R., & Lask, B. (1987). Early onset anorexia nervosa. *Archives of Disease in Childhood, 62*, 114-118.

Garfinkel, P., & Garner, D. (Eds.). (1987). *The role of drug treatments for eating disorders.* New York: Brunner/Mazel.

Garfinkel, P., Garner, D., & Kennedy, S. (1985). Special problems of inpatient management. In D. Garner & P. Garfinkel (Eds.), *Handbook of psychotherapy for anorexia nervosa and bulimia* (pp. 344-359). New York: Guilford.

Garner, D., & Garfinkel, P. (1980). Socio-cultural factors in the development of anorexia nervosa. *Psychological Medicine, 10*, 647-656.

Garner, D., Garfinkel, P., & Bemis, K. (1982). A multidimensional psychotherapy for anorexia nervosa. *International Journal of Eating Disorders, 1*, 3-46.

Garner, D., Olmstead, M., & Polivy, J. (1983). Development and validation of a multidimensional eating disorder inventory for anorexia nervosa and bulimia. *International Journal of Eating Disorders, 2*, 15-34.

Geist, R. (1985). Therapeutic dilemmas in the treatment of anorexia nervosa: A self-psychological perspective. In S. Emmett (Ed.), *Theory and treatment of anorexia nervosa and bulimia* (pp. 268-288). New York: Brunner/Mazel.

Goetz, P., Succop, R., Reinhart, J., & Miller, A. (1977). Anorexia nervosa in children: A follow-up study. *American Journal of Orthopsychiatry, 47*, 597-603.

Goodsitt, A. (1985). Self psychology and the treatment of anorexia nervosa. In D. Garner & P. Garfinkel (Eds.), *Handbook of psychotherapy for anorexia nervosa and bulimia* (pp. 55-82). New York: Guilford.

Greenacre, P. (1957). The childhood of the artist: Libidinal phase development and giftedness. *Psychoanalytic Study of the Child, 12,* 27–72.

Halmi, K. (1985). Behavioral management for anorexia nervosa. In D. Garner & P. Garfinkel (Eds.), *Handbook of psychotherapy for anorexia nervosa and bulimia* (pp. 147–159). New York: Guilford.

Hawley, R. (1985). The outcome of anorexia nervosa in younger subjects. *British Journal of Psychiatry, 146,* 657–660.

Herjanic, B., Puig-Antich, J., & Connors, K. (1981). *Diagnostic Interview Schedule for Children (DIS-C).* Working draft. Rockville, MD: National Institute of Mental Health.

Hudson, J., Pope, H., Jonas, J., & Yurgelun-Todd, D. (1983). Family history study of anorexia nervosa and bulimia. *British Journal of Psychiatry, 142,* 133–138.

Irwin, M. (1981). Diagnosis of anorexia nervosa in children and the validity of DSM-III. *American Journal of Psychiatry, 138,* 1382–1383.

Irwin, M. (1984). Early onset anorexia nervosa. *Southern Medical Journal, 77,* 611–614.

Kyger, K. (1966). Pre-pubertal anorexia nervosa. *Journal of the Tennessee Medical Association, 59,* 865–870.

Lerner, H. (1983). Contemporary psychoanalytic perspectives on gorge-vomiting. *International Journal of Eating Disorders, 3,* 47–63.

Lesser, L., Ashenden, B., Delruskey, M., & Eisenberg, L. (1960). Anorexia nervosa in children. *American Journal of Orthopsychiatry, 30,* 572–580.

Minuchin, S., Rosman, B., & Baker, L. (1978). *Psychosomatic families: Anorexia nervosa in context.* Cambridge, MA: Harvard University Press.

Mitchell, J., & Eckert, E. (1987). Scope and significance of eating disorders. *Journal of Consulting and Clinical Psychology, 55,* 628–634.

Poznanski, E. (1970). Functional anorexia in school-age children. *Clinical Pediatrics, 9,* 115–117.

Reinhart, J., Kenna, M., & Succop, R. (1972). Anorexia nervosa in children—Outpatient management. *Journal of the American Academy of Child Psychiatry, 11,* 114–131.

Rivinus, T., Biederman, J., Herzog, D., Kemper, K., Harper, G., Harmatz, J., & Houseworth, S. (1984). Anorexia nervosa and affective disorders: A controlled family history study. *American Journal of Psychiatry, 141,* 1414–1418.

Rizzuto, A., Peterson, R., & Reed, M. (1981). The pathological sense of self in anorexia nervosa. *Psychiatric Clinics of North America, 4,* 471–487.

Rollins, N, & Piazza, E. (1978). Diagnosis of anorexia nervosa: A critical reappraisal. *Journal of the American Academy of Child Psychiatry, 17,* 126–137.

Russell, G. (1970). Anorexia nervosa. In J. H. Price (Ed.), *Modern trends in psychological medicine* (pp. 131–164). New York: Appleton-Century-Crofts.

Sargent, J., Liebman, R., & Silver, M. (1985). Family therapy for anorexia nervosa. In D. Garner & P. Garfinkel (Eds.), *Handbook of psychotherapy for anorexia nervosa and bulimia.* New York: Guilford.

Shapiro, D. (1965). *Neurotic styles.* New York: Basic Books.

Silber, T., & Atkins, D. (1986, July). *Pre-pubertal anorexia nervosa.* Paper presented at the XVIII International Congress of Pediatrics, Honolulu, HI.

Solyom, L., Freeman, R., & Miles, J. (1982). A comparative psychometric study of anorexia nervosa and obsessive neurosis. *Canadian Journal of Psychiatry, 27,* 282–286.

Swift, W. (1982). The longterm outcome of early onset anorexia nervosa. A critical review. *Journal of the American Academy of Child Psychiatry, 21,* 38–46.

Warren, W. (1968). A study of anorexia nervosa in young girls. *Journal of Child Psychology and Psychiatry, 9,* 27–40.

21
Multicomponent Inpatient Approaches with an Impulsive, Noncompliant Male Delinquent

STEVEN THURBER
LAURA J. HEWETT

A variety of descriptive terms and verbal labels have been applied to poorly controlled, antisocial behaviors that occur during the adolescent developmental period: conduct disorder, delinquent, sociopath, externalizing-antisocial personality, psychopath. The common behavioral elements that seemingly occur across those diagnostic labels include (1) repetitive and persistent patterns of direct violations of the rights of others (e.g., violence, thefts); (2) interpersonal manipulations—using the emotional needs and weaknesses detected in others to satisfy one's own personal ends; and (3) attempts to maximize personal gains through inflicting pain or loss on others (see Loeber, 1982).

The third edition of the *Diagnostic and Statistical Manual of Mental Disorders* (DSM-III; American Psychiatric Association, 1980) uses the phrase "Conduct Disorder, Aggressive Subtype" with reference to undercontrolled action combined with person-centered hostility occurring among children and adolescents (pp. 45–50). If the individual classified as displaying an aggressive conduct disorder shows evidence of a capacity for establishing and maintaining interpersonal attachments (e.g., a friendship of 6 months or longer), an additional subclassification of "socialized" is inferred. The term "undersocialized" is used to describe individuals lacking compunction for inappropriate actions and who display little concern for other people. The revised third edition of the *Diagnostic and Statistical Manual of Mental Disorders* (DSM-III-R; American Psychiatric Association,

Steven Thurber and Laura J. Hewett. Psychology Department, Northwest Passages Adolescent Hospital, Boise, Idaho.

1987) uses the label "Conduct Disorder, Solitary Aggressive Type" with reference to similar symptomatology (p. 59).

The adolescent classification "Conduct Disorder, Aggressive, Undersocialized" resembles the criteria for "Psychopathic Personality" or what the DSM-III now calls "Antisocial Personality." According to Cleckley's (1976) dicta, the following traits characterize the psychopathic (antisocial) syndrome: (1) an inability to develop warm, genuine relationships with others; (2) a lack of empathy; (3) callous disregard for the rights and feelings of others; (4) unstable life style with an absence of long-term plans and commitments.

Despite the DSM-III caveat against classifying youngsters under 18 in the antisocial (psychopathic) diagnostic category, empirically based diagnostic systems suggest covariations among adolescent behavioral problems corresponding to Cleckley's notions concerning adult psychopathy (Achenbach, 1982). Factor analytic research of Quay (1964) supports a consistency between certain patterns of adolescent delinquent behavior and the antisocial personality diagnosis and suggests the appellation "unsocialized, psychopathic delinquency."

Whatever diagnostic label is ascribed, there can be no question that antisocial behavior among adolescents has significant clinical and societal ramifications. Such behaviors show a relatively stable developmental course, for example, with a trend from frequent, low-intensive actions to less frequent but more intensive antisocial activities over time (Patterson, 1982). Antisocial (particularly aggressive) actions occurring in childhood and adolescence appear strongly related to antisocial behaviors later in life (Loeber, 1982; Robins, 1978). In terms of criminal acts alone, there has been a dramatic upsurge in juvenile crimes in the United States, reflected in part by a 131% increase in property crimes and a 293% increase in violent juvenile crimes between the years 1960 and 1974 (Shamsie, 1981). From one-third to one-half of clinical referrals involve antisocial behaviors (Kazdin, Esveldt-Dawson, French, & Unis, 1987).

This chapter describes the assessment, diagnosis, and inpatient treatment of an adolescent male with a history of antisocial, impulsive behaviors together with strong inclinations not to adhere to formal therapeutic interventions.

BACKGROUND INFORMATION

James was a 16-year-old male raised predominantly by his mother. His parents were divorced when he was about 1½ years of age. Although James's mother never remarried, she reported that he was exposed to positive male models during his early development (maternal grandfather, mother's boyfriends). James's father had difficulties with drugs and alcohol and was placed in treatment facilities on approximately six occasions. The father lived with his parents throughout most of his adult life, was diagnosed as sociopathic, and served time in prison on drug charges. Following a cold winter's evening in which James and his father ingested a variety of illicit drugs and alcohol, James awakened to find his father in the family automobile, dead of exposure secondary to excessive chemical usage.

James's mother became pregnant and married at the age of 17. She reported using drugs and alcohol as a teenager but only having an occasional beer during pregnancy. She had a normal pregnancy and delivery and reported no problems with James during his infancy and early childhood. She supported herself and James as a licensed practical nurse. When James's problems became evident, she reportedly "rescued" him with geographic moves, compromises with school officials, and by allowing him to reside in her home while continuing to use drugs.

James's adjustment problems first became evident when he was in the fifth grade; at the age of 10 years, he was caught in possession of marijuana and referred to a counselor. Later, he was expelled from junior high school for behavior problems and expelled again during his junior year of high school. At that time he was referred for outpatient chemical dependency treatment. He reportedly participated in the treatment program but failed to abstain from chemical usage. Subsequently, he attended a new high school but was expelled after 3 weeks. At this time his mother described him as "out of control" as evidenced by James's apprehension by the police for drinking, theft, and acts of vandalism. A psychiatric evaluation concluded that he was of no danger to himself. Therefore, James was again referred to a counselor, but failed to keep his appointment and was placed in a juvenile detention center. The maternal grandparents "rescued" him from this situation, and he moved into their home. His lying, stealing, and drug usage soon became evident, and the grandparents asked him to leave after only 3 months.

James's mother reported that he frequently sold his possessions for money, never held down a job, and received illicit chemicals from his father. She described him as "guiltless"; he never expressed feelings of remorse or apologized for his behavior. He saw himself as a victim and a martyr. She believed her relationship with James began to deteriorate when she stopped "rescuing" him; she joined a "Tough Love" organization composed largely of parents of out-of-control teenagers. The goals of the organization involve mutual support, establishing rules of deportment, and strict adherence to established behavioral contingencies within the home environment.

Shortly after his father's death, James was again placed in the juvenile detention facility for shoplifting. During his stay at the center, he was involved in numerous incidents resulting in his being physically restrained. He evidently kept other adolescents in a constant state of agitation: He challenged rules, made verbal threats, and instigated escape plans and staff "takeovers." As a result, James stayed only 22 of the planned 30 days and was transported in handcuffs (actually carried by two police officers) to the adolescent psychiatric hospital.

At the time of his hospitalization, James's mother was cooperative, supportive, and willing to participate in any suggested activities.

It is important to note that James's antisocial behaviors showed a pattern predictive of long-term chronicity. His deportment problems were occurring at high frequency rates across several environmental settings and began early in life, all factors suggesting the likelihood of antisocial progressions into adulthood (Koller & Gosden, 1980; Mitchell & Rosa, 1981; Patterson, 1982).

ASSESSMENT AND DIAGNOSIS

The Child Behavior Checklist (CBCL; Achenbach & Edelbrock, 1983), completed by parents or other adult caregivers, was the primary assessment instrument used for the diagnosis and planned interventions.

As perceived by his mother, the rated intensity and extensity of James's problems were in the clinical range with a T score of 73. Whereas he manifested some internalizing problems (especially uncommunicativeness), only the total externalizing score was significantly elevated (T score = 77). James was found to have clinically relevant elevations (T score above 70) on the externalizing subscales: Aggressive (impulsivity, temper tantrums, arguments, threats), Delinquent (lying, alcohol–drug usage, stealing), and Hyperactive (nail-biting, disobedience at school, nervousness, showing off). His pattern of behavioral problems was most similar to the profile typologies "Uncommunicative–Delinquent" (intraclass correlation = .661) and "Delinquent" (intraclass correlation = .516).

James, then, showed a strongly externalizing (poorly controlled) constellation of disordered behaviors. It is also noteworthy that his antisocial actions apparently occurred in the absence of anxiety or remorse, according to his mother's ratings. In terms of a distinction to be made later in the chapter, James's delinquent behaviors included both clandestine and overt components.

The CBCL findings, together with James's history of illegal, antisocial actions and an apparent incapacity for establishing enduring relationships, suggest conformance with the *Diagnostic and Statistical Manual of Mental Disorders* classification "Conduct Disorder, Undersocialized, Aggressive" (DSM-III; American Psychiatric Association, 1980, p. 47) or the revised designation "Conduct Disorder, Solitary Aggressive Type" (DSM-III-R, American Psychiatric Association, 1987, p. 59).

Because there appears to be a congruence between these diagnostic categories and the designations "psychopathic," "antisocial personality," and the empirically derived "unsocialized psychopathic delinquency," these terms are viewed as functionally equivalent and will be used interchangeably throughout the chapter.

Observations of James's behaviors during the first week of hospitalization suggested a diagnostic picture highly congruent with a traditional psychopathic designation. First, he repeated acts that led to recurrent lost privileges or isolation in the "closed" unit. He punched holes in the walls of his room; he broke mirrors; and he frequently threatened staff members and other residents with physical violence. It is noteworthy that the hospital program is structured to accelerate learning: Consequences for inappropriate actions are immediate and predictable. Moreover, James expressed verbally and behaviorally (by crying) that isolation was a most aversive consequence. Yet, he was apparently limited in his capacity to moderate behaviors accordingly. Second, treatment approaches would initially appear to be effective, but it seemed that when the novelty wore off, unacceptable actions returned. Third, despite generally impulsive irrational actions, James would occasionally display behaviors described by staff observers as highly controlled and calculating for the apparent purpose of achieving personal advantages and special privileges. At these times, his demeanor would change from a glaring, threatening posture to one of smiling, ingratiating charm. At the same time James was conforming to hospital rules, interacting cordially with staff, and beginning to advance in the privilege level system, he wrote the following letter to an acquaintance in the county juvenile detention center. (It should be noted that it is the policy of the center to withhold mail from juveniles only when there is evidence to suspect illegal intent of the communication such as a planned escape strategem. The unopened letter was given to James's mother by the center's administrator. It was presented by the mother to hospital personnel in the hope of facilitating understanding of James's continuing antisocial thinking in spite of ostensive improvements in behavioral functioning.)

Dear —————,

Hey dude, how's it going: I'm in this mother-fucking hellhole of a hospital for a little over 2 weeks. It's shittier than detention here. I got kicked out of detention for leading a riot; it was a killer. One dude broke his cell door window with his fist and ripped his mattress open and shoved the insides down the toilet till it flooded the whole cell-block. Another dude tried kicking nigger Robert's ass. Another one took on three staff at once, and I took six for a while until they cuffed me. Everybody was trying to kick their cell doors open. The next day, they brought me here to the hospital. The two cops that tried to drag me down the halls of the hospital didn't last long. They each tried bending my arms behind my back, but I wouldn't let them. I kicked one pretty close to the balls, and he doubled over and the other one let go. Then I

*turned around and headed for the door and four hospital dudes grabbed
me while a nurse shot me up with a huge dose of hypnotics, that was all
she wrote. I woke up strapped to a bed on my stomach with my arms
strapped to my sides and my legs strapped down. It freaked the hell out
of me. I stayed that way till Tuesday. Man, the drug was so strong all I
could do is keep sleeping.*

*I should be out of here by the end of _____; please wait for me
before you leave; don't leave me in this hellhole. We can start our trip
going through _____; we can grab a job on a fishing boat for a couple
of weeks to replenish our money. I'm going to borrow a few grand from
a friend on the condition that I'll pay him back when my mom gives me
my Social Security checks. By law, she don't have to till I'm 18, but
that's cool anyway. In a couple of weeks I'll be able to have 3-hr., then
6-hr., then 10-hr. passes on Saturdays and Sundays. I'll get hold of you
and we can discuss all this over some beer. Man, I hope you don't leave
me here.*

*When I or we get to another state I'll get emancipated so I can
collect my checks. Dude, I think I'm going to be totally insane when I
get out but that's okay because I'll have more fun out there that way. It
wouldn't be too hard for me to run away from here and if I did, I'd go to
my dad's friend's, you know _____ house. But then I'd have to haul ass
out of the state because they'd call me an escaped runaway mental
patient. I'm seriously thinking about it. But I'd need a little help from
you, like on the canal that runs behind the hospital, there's a 10-foot
fence that has loose boards. If you broke a hole in it from the outside and
waited out on the road in your car, I could kick the back door open,
crawl through the fence and run and jump in the car. I'll talk to you
about it on the phone.*

*Oh yeah, my mom's so dumb she and the insurance company are
spending _____ for 4 weeks of this. It's a good thing she got the stupids
in the family and not me, huh. Well, I'll talk to you on the phone.
See ya.*

The contradictions between overt, ingratiating behaviors and the
general tone of the letter suggest that James was engaging in the "fundamental psychopathic maneuver," attempting to manipulate via conformance and charm with the objective of personal benefits and potential
humiliation of the hospital staff and programs.

Perhaps the most prominant behavioral problem shown by James
during the first week of hospitalization was failure to evaluate the consequences of his actions. He would yell obscenities and threaten to hurt
personnel. He shared a prescription medication with another resident leading to a strong adverse reaction. He made verbal commitments that were not
fulfilled. James seemingly centered his thinking on personal benefits and
was not able to orient himself in relation to negative social reactions to his
noncompliant, aggressive actions. Characteristically, following unaccept-

able deportment, James would inundate staff members with apologies and promises for revolutionary changes. He often would say, "This time, I've really learned my lesson."

ETIOLOGICAL CONSIDERATIONS

Unsocialized psychopathic delinquency is presumed to involve multiple causation. From a sociocultural point of view, political and societal events themselves may create or aggravate deviant social behavior. The Vietnam war, for instance, flooded young people with televised visual imagery of violence, perhaps preconditioning or disinhibiting aggressive acts by children (Nichtern, 1982). A variety of psychodynamic interpretations have been profferred, usually centering on defensive reactions or psychosexual fixations. One common psychodynamic explanation for aggressive, antisocial deportment in the male is the symbolic reenactment of the oedipal struggle. The young child's wish to discredit and destroy his father is transferred symbolically to others in authority positions (see Alexander & Staub, 1956).

The search for causal factors in relation to psychopathy and delinquency has included possible genetic predispositions. Cotwin research, for instance, suggests stronger concordance rates for identical than fraternal twins (Cloninger, Christiansen, Reich, & Gottesman, 1978). Furthermore, Hook (1973) reported the presence of an extra "Y" chromosome at a higher frequency among institutionalized criminals in comparison with the general population. In a related area of investigation, disorders in the structure and functions of certain brain mechanisms have been posited. Tucker (1981), for example, reports asymmetrically low left hemisphere arousal among persons with antisocial personality classifications. This suggests that such individuals may be deficient in certain language processes important in behavioral regulation and self-control.

The hypothesis that the psychopath may have a functionally hyporesponsive autonomic nervous system leading to problems in learning and possible arrested development has been the object of much research activity over the years (see Eysenck, 1957; Lykken, 1957). Nevertheless, there seems to be a current consensus that persons classified as antisocial personalities are capable of normal autonomic nervous system responses. In fact, such individuals may actually be more responsive autonomically than normals and may generally be in an overaroused condition. Consistent with this theorizing, Hokanson, Megargee, O'Hagen, and Perry (1976) posit that the impulsive actions of the psychopath are reinforced by the most rapid and available means of arousal reduction.

Quay (1965) was the first theorist to suggest that the psychopath may have an intolerance for repetitive, redundant stimuli. More succinctly, the psychopathic individual is easily bored. The result may be that stimuli that function to exercise control over behavior will, with satiation, rapidly lose that capacity. The outcome may be the oft-recorded erratic behavior of persons with antisocial personalities: She or he may evince appropriate, "stimulus-controlled" behavior under conditions of salience and novelty, but when the newness wears off and satiation occurs, disturbing behaviors are emitted.

An approach that analyzes the antisocial personality relative to possible arrested cognitive development was recently discussed by Kegan (1986). To Kegan, the psychopathic individual is seemingly caught, via developmental delay or fixation, between the extreme egocentricism of the young child and the more flexible "sociocentric" thinking of older children and adolescents. The individual is unable completely to orient himself/herself to the point of view of others. Hence, interpersonal relationships are shallow and nonreciprocal, often defined in terms of self-centered benefits. However, the psychopath is seen as possessing rudimentary empathic skills sufficient enough to discern how other people might be "used" instrumentally. The individual has just enough understanding of others for discovering vulnerabilities that allow him/her to concoct strategies for social manipulation. But the basic childlike egocentrism precludes an anxious anticipation of how important others will respond to antisocial actions.

Investigations of family dynamics associated with antisocial behaviors began in the 1920s (see Partridge, 1928). Recent theorizing distinguishes two subsets of conduct disorders that may differ with respect to child-rearing antecedents. The "covert" or clandestine subtype involves the more underhanded, concealed antisocial behaviors such as noncompliance and illicit drug usage. The "overt" conduct disorder classification includes the more aggressive, confrontive activities (Loeber, 1982; Patterson, 1986). The covert form of psychopathy mainly appears to be associated with inadequate parental monitoring and unskilled child-rearing as precursors (Kazdin, 1985; Loeber, 1982).

TREATMENT MODALITIES

Individualized treatment approaches for James were superimposed on a general psychiatric inpatient treatment program for adolescents. Included were various group therapies (e.g., one group focused on the acquisition of interpersonal skills, another emphasized emotional states), day-to-day contact with a "primary caregiver" (a member of the nursing staff), occupational and recreational modalities, and individual therapy provided by a licensed clinical psychologist. The therapists provided documentation of each session including topics covered, strategies, a summary of what took place, and any progress noted. The overall program was consistent with Bloor (1980): That is, a variety of treatment approaches are implemented that are found variously effective by different patients.

The interpersonal group therapy was designed fundamentally to reduce social deficiencies and engender skills for initiating and maintaining friendships. This included social sensitivity skill acquisition (e.g., accurate observation and assessment of a given social situation), judgment (e.g., accurate prediction of the effects of one's own actions on others), and self-control (e.g., regulation of behaviors appropriately relative to social feedback). For James, this component of treatment stressed role taking, or the accurate perception and understanding of another person's perspective in a given social situation.

Another important group therapy modality centered on negative affective conditions and associated behavioral manifestations using a cognitive-behavioral framework (see Beck, 1976). For James, this group stressed the development of skills for understanding and controlling hostility and aggression. First, an educational component is presented, beginning with Schachter and Singer's (1962) approach in relation to emotionality. Schachter and Singer's (1962) original research on the nature of affective arousal was followed by Schachter's (1964) elaboration of a two-factor theory of emotional experience. Briefly stated, one's awareness of adrenalin-based, physiological arousal (trembling hands, increased respiration, pounding heart) combines with a simultaneous evaluation of social cues (how others are reacting emotionally in a specific situation) to produce a given emotional experience. The physiological component is assumed to be nonspecific and common to the various emotional states. It is the social appraisal that yields a cognitive label and a distinctive emotional experience. From a treatment perspective, procedures designed to reduce physiological arousal (e.g., relaxation training) or to improve the accuracy of labeling can potentially have an impact on negative emotional conditions such as depression and hostility. For most patients, a modification of cognitions and beliefs was required in which cathartic release was devalued as an effective therapeutic modality. The Schachter–Singer approach further emphasized the role of relaxation skills involving responses that are incompatable with aggression and hostility. Second, methods for inhibiting anger expressions are presented: Patients practice reassigning causal intent for irritating behaviors of others and develop their own self-statements concerning possible adverse consequences of aggressive actions. Next, patients imagine actual situations in which they have behaved aggressively and are asked to record reasonable, nonaggressive alternatives. This also extends to in vivo "homework" assignments given occurrences of anger and aggression in the hospital setting. Finally, patients practice covert reinforcement (self-praise) for actual instances of inhibited aggression and for behavioral expressions that are incompatable with aggressiveness.

Individual therapy involved hourly sessions, two to three times a week for the 60-day hospitalization period. It was geared toward the general facilitation of adherence to treatment regimens and to the development of a quality, therapeutic relationship. I did not accede to the position that James had an incapacity for establishing a stable, reciprocal attachment to another human being. I tried initially to fulfill the role of an empathic listener who accepted, in a nonjudgmental manner, James's explanations of the injustices to which he was continuously subjected. I gradually attempted to "engage" James emotionally by appealing to his narcissistic desires. For example, I defined the major goal of therapy as the development of skills in James that would help him to increase rewarding experiences while reducing punishment and pain. This seemingly was a goal that appealed to his egocentric orientation. As therapy proceeded, we emphasized that rational, socially responsible actions constituted the only way to achieve this goal in the long term. Over time, the individual sessions were progressively saturated with therapeutic exercises for improving James's ability to "decenter" from himself and to think and feel sociocentrically. For example, at first I asked James if he were at all curious as to what I thought of him. This apparently appealed to James's curiosity motive and eventually progressed to having James predict my thoughts and estimate how I was feeling based on vocal patterns and nonverbal signals.

The Privilege Level System

It has been posited that individuals who later become delinquents repeatedly experience social reactions indicating they do not matter as persons and that their behaviors are inconsequential (Ullmann & Krasner, 1975). From a learning theory perspective, the psychopathic delinquent has experienced schedules of reinforcement and punishment so intermittant and variable that "contingency cognitions" (thoughts concerning behavior–outcome relationships) do not develop adequately. Accordingly, the fulcrum of a treatment model advocated by Yochelson and Samenow (1977) is the patient's rational apprehension of the consequences of actions.

In the hospital setting, a privilege level system was designed to generate awareness of a consistent, predictable contingency between positive behaviors and commensurately positive outcomes. The patient enters the program at level zero and progresses through successive steps (four levels) as specified criteria are met. Successive levels require more sophisticated, mature behaviors, while yielding increasingly attractive reinforcers.

Within the levels program is a point system. Each level attained is determined by the number of points earned each day. Points are earned in 13 areas important in hospital management, physical hygiene, and interactions among patients and staff. Additionally, points are given for progress observed in relation to therapeutic goals targeted individually for each patient.

The privilege level system is designed to engender positive anticipatory-arousal motivation by providing attractive incentives contingent upon progressive improvements in behavior. Nevertheless, punishments are also a part of the program and range from mild social reprimands to point losses, level reductions, and closed unit confinement. Punishments are administered for violations of "community" rules (e.g., dress code standards, inappropriate physical contact, contraband possessions), failure to make reasonable therapeutic progress, and displays of verbal and physical threats and aggression.

Treatment Course

James's treatment plan was formulated with combined input from representatives of the various mental health disciplines: psychology, psychiatry, social work, nursing, education, and occupational and recreational therapies. Each professional conducted an independent evaluation of James. The obtained information was then shared and integrated in a multidisciplinary "treatment team" meeting leading to an overall treatment strategy with short-term objectives and long-range treatment goals. For James, treatment centered on impulse control and reduced aggressiveness. On a weekly basis, the treatment team met to discuss James's progress (or lack of the same) from the perspective of each discipline, with the view of implementing different approaches if warranted.

James's hospital treatment began with tranquilizing medications (Thioridazine) and physical restraints, hardly the most propitious beginning. The restraints were removed in about 1 hour.

The next day, James had evidently resigned himself to hospitalization, stating that it was at least better than juvenile detention. He was informed that he could determine his own destiny in the adolescent hospital by working through the four tiers of a privilege level system via displays of progressively mature, responsible behaviors. It was explained that potential outcomes (e.g., points, privileges) were unambiguous, fair, and waiting to be earned. Hospital rules were likewise discussed in terms of expected deportment and automatic sanctions for violations (e.g., point losses).

James indicated an understanding of the privilege level system and corresponding rules and standards and expressed willingness to enter the treatment program. Accordingly, a behavioral contract was completed, stipulating that rewards and privileges were to be granted James given the attainment of increasingly complex, responsible behavioral criteria, and for genuine involvement in the therapeutic regimens.

During the initial phases of treatment (during weeks 1 through 3), James's actions might be best described as erratic. He would sometimes conform to treatment requirements and hospital rules while at other times show passive resistance or hostile aggressiveness (see subsequent material). He periodically offered constructive comments in group therapy sessions and, later, inexplicably shift to verbalizations that were caustic and denigrating to peers and staff members. As his point earnings began to decline, James would accuse personnel of being unfair in point allotments and would display threatening, hostile behaviors.

Chart entries of James's behaviors during the first few days of hospitalization may convey some of the challenging problems encountered by staff persons (presented in chronological order):

> "He worked to put staff members in uncomfortable positions."
>
> "Patient leaned over desk and in a smiling, persuasive manner stated 'Don't tell me you never drink.'"
>
> "Much pacing, frowning: 'I don't think I can maintain control much longer.'"
>
> "Patient confronted by peers for writing profanities on door. He just sat there with arms folded, feet on table, smiling."
>
> "What would happen if I punched you in the face: Would you shoot me up with drugs and put me in restraints?"
>
> "Patient returned to closed unit for aggression."
>
> "Shared prescription pain killers (Tylenol-3 for wisdom teeth extractions) with other patients."
>
> "Patient's request for narcotics refused; he flew into rage, pounded walls and furniture; escorted bodily to seclusion room."

At the end of the second week of James's inpatient treatment, he began repeatedly to express disdain for the undeserved, unfair sanctions (e.g., loss of privileges) he was receiving together with statements about staff members who were intentionally "impeding his therapeutic progress" by irritating him to the point that he committed aggressive acts. At this time he wrote the first of several letters to the hospital's administrator asking for an authoritative intervention in his behalf:

Dear _____,

> *I wish this could be a more formal letter but I only know you as my friend and the administrator. I have a reasonable request to make of you, the administrator. One of the attendants found a personal stereo and headphones in my room, and I lost 50 points for not following community guidelines (having personal stereos is against the rules). I'll enclose a copy of the community guidelines for your consideration; I'm sure you'll see they are not fair; I feel that listening to music is therapeutic for me. I'd like you to find a way that we could have our stereos without getting in trouble. I'd also like you to help me get back the points which were taken wrongfully. Thank you for your help and friendship. Love, James.*

During week number 3 in James's hospitalization, information was shared among the multidisciplinary members of the treatment team suggesting that James was attempting to cause dissension in the organization by creating animosity between certain key personnel. He would go to the director of nursing, for instance, and explain that the clinical director had expressed concern about the ineptness of the nursing staff in program implementation. Later, James met with the clinical director regarding the poorly trained nurses, and how they were incapable of carrying out his program directives.

Another noteworthy trend involved his reactions to frequent confinements following violations of cardinal hospital rules. On one occasion James was discovered defacing hospital property by writing profanities on a glass door with a grease pen. As he was escorted to the closed unit (the automatic consequences for this violation), he uttered softly and repeatedly, "You guys don't care about me." Later, he approached personnel in the restricted unit with tear-filled eyes and stated, "You might as well give me a razor blade, and I'll get rid of all your problems." Then, typically, James would seemingly gain rational control, say that he had learned his lesson, and solemnly promise to become the ideal patient "if only he were returned to open unit privileges." Over time, James's approach (some would call it manipulation) often "worked," and he was granted attenuated aversive consequences for rule violations. When his emotional appeals were not effective, James would show signs of foreboding physical aggressiveness (e.g., pacing back and forth with clenched fists) while uttering a variety of expletives.

A very obvious pattern emerged in which James would display conforming, appropriate actions for a period of time followed by some grievous hospital violation and loss of privileges. This led to histrionic displays of remorse and the promise that complete repentance would be forthcoming. In addition to his alternating, contrasting actions, an evaluation of possible midhospitalization (30 day) CBCL changes indicated nothing in the way of overall improvements. (The CBCL was completed by his assigned primary caregiver.) Instead James was fluctuating between frequent minor gains and subsequent regressions. It seemed to the staff that a drastic, innovative approach was required, potentially to generate more stable progression in his hospital treatment program.

A "Drastic" Treatment Alternative

An underlying problem for persons classified as psychopathic delinquents may be a failure to evaluate consequences. On the other hand, there may be an arena for such individuals with highly predictable consequences where the psychopath can anticipate consistent, sometimes intense, social impact. In her/his quest for a stable interpersonal environment, the psychopath may use the weaknesses, emotional reactivity, and vulnerabilities in others to obtain personal benefits and influence the social environment. This socially manipulative behavior may take the form of charm and ingratiation, or the psychopath may engage others emotionally via effusive apologies for unacceptable actions. The control of the social environment may also involve the use of weakness and vulnerabilities for the purpose of humiliating people of authority and power (see Person, 1986).

It can be reasonably argued that interpersonal manipulation only occurs effectively under conditions of predictability. Manipulative actions seemingly require reliable estimates regarding how the "manipulatee" is likely to respond given, for instance, charm, apologies, or threats.

From a hospital treatment standpoint, there is a dilemma. On the one hand, a highly structured, predictable approach is advocated to produce meaningful, responsible actions (Leschiad, Jaffe, & Stone, 1985). Yet the predictability itself may encourage and facilitate manipulation of personnel for self-aggrandizement and advantages within such a treatment environment. If this proposition has credence, it might be possible for James to "learn the words but not the music," to emit socially desirable actions sufficient to progress through the levels system without making genuine changes that would persist over time. A related consideration involves the premise that the psychopathic delinquent is in something of a manipulative "rut." The habitual "engagement" and control of others through ingratiation and charm may require extinction before effective treatment can take place (see Beier, 1966).

A drastic and, to the staff, novel approach to treatment was implemented, designed (1) to appeal to James's presumed egocentric grandiosity and (2) to be unpredictable and hence less subject to manipulative control.

An individualized privilege level system was established for James alone; no other patient received an analogous treatment approach. James was told he was a special person and therefore required special treatment modalities. Instead of a levels system by numbers, James was given his own program with letter designations. However, the order inherent in the alphabet did not correspond to the ordering of the levels. Thus, James began arbitrarily at level "B," progressed to level "A," and later advanced to level "D." Because James was a special person, he was allowed, within the confines of hospital rules, personally to develop his own list of privileges associated with each level. However, at the discretion of the clinical treatment team, the privileges for two selected levels might be unpredictably interchanged (sometimes from 1 hour to the next) or privileges at a certain level deleted.

For a 2-week time period (from the 30th day to the 45th day approximately), James had his own levels system but still endured predictable, automatic closed unit isolation for specified violations of hospital rules. As previously discussed, closed unit confinement led to signs of grievous remorse and solemn promises that if confinement were cut short, he would work assiduously on therapeutic goals with the promise that rule violations would not recur. James's signs of repentance and remorse were often effective. When his emotional appeals failed to produce the desired impact, he tended to resort to aggressive and accusative strategies (e.g., "staff members have no authentic concern for patients; they just want to hurt and punish").

We decided that a possible solution was a randomized procedure for determining when James could leave confinement. The "decision" was based solely on the selection of one predetermined ticket from among five multicolored tickets. At the end of each hour of confinement, James made his selection. Leaving or remaining on the closed unit was now governed by the laws of probability, not by "incompetent" hospital personnel. The result was a reduction to near zero of behaviors ostensibly calculated to manipulate himself off the closed unit (this followed more than 20 instances of isolation contingencies). There was simply no payoff for such actions.

Attempts to escape punishment via the emotional control of caregivers were dramatically affected by a randomized, unpredictable procedure. However, the special, individualized levels program, which reduced the possibility of manipulative action–outcome relationships, was notably ineffectual. In fact, the approach was associated with increases in James's aggressiveness, including, in the main, noncompliance and verbal threats. During the implementation of this program, for instance, he compiled a list of staff names and addresses with the expressed commitment that everyone on this "hit list" would be "eliminated" when he left the hospital. James would also typically pace back and forth in his room threatening that he was on the verge of violent loss of control. Eventually James's individualized levels program was expunged, and he returned to the hospital's standard, predictable privilege levels system.

Treatment of Aggression

During the first few weeks of treatment in particular, James's main inpatient problem was recurrent expressions of verbal and physical aggression. That is, he displayed numerous actions intended to irritate or harm other persons (see Eron, 1987).

Although the scientific study of human aggression has not supported a cathartic model, the notion that emotional release is a necessary aspect of effective therapy for aggressive behavior may still persist (Feshbach, 1984). Moreover, as judged by the espoused beliefs of most staff persons in the adolescent hospital, the idea of catharsis has apparently become thoroughly ingrained in conventional wisdom.

Those members of the hospital nursing staff spending the most daily time with James, seemed to accept and promulgate the cathartic approach. When James showed actions assumed to be precursors to hostile aggression, he was often directed by staff to enter a "catharsis room." Thereupon, he was given a pillow and encouraged to take out his wrath by hitting, kicking, and screaming. During this period, James could be heard releasing aggression on that pillow for upwards of 3 hours per cathartic "session."

According to the monitoring by nurses, the cathartic interventions were exceedingly successful. This was gauged by the observation that following cathartic release, James would often refrain from physical and verbal aggression for several hours consecutively. The efficacy of this method was simply obvious to the frontline personnel: It worked.

Unquestionably, frequency counts of James's aggressive actions indicated a significant decline following catharsis. The problem was that day-by-day indexes of aggressiveness suggested increases in overall frequency and intensity. A reasonable hypothesis, therefore, was that James's cathartic expressions were enervating, culminating in fatigue sufficient to briefly inhibit his hostile actions. However, the cathartic release itself was associated over longer time periods with increased hostile actions.

Criticizing the cathartic model likely borders on unwarranted desecration with those who truly believe. Nonetheless, inservice training was undertaken in which important studies were detailed, showing how the therapeutic "release" of aggression seems to increase aggressive actions in the future (e.g., Mallick & McCandless, 1966). Furthermore, discussions centered on how, in uncontrolled settings, observers can be deceived by fatigue effects into believing the inference that catharsis actually works.

It apparently requires more than didactic information to modify strongly engrained, intuitively obvious belief systems. Nursing staff members continued tacitly to advocate and encourage catharsis for James and other patients. Meanwhile, what might be termed a "wave of catharsis effects" was occurring on the unit. Associated with cathartic therapy were dramatic increases in property destruction (e.g., mirror, furniture damage), verbal hostility toward staff, and patient-to-patient aggression. Patients were increasingly being placed in closed unit restriction and, on occasion, in leather restraints for hostile acts.

Eventually, the general escalation of aggressive, sometimes violent, behaviors across patients was too salient to ignore; the nurses were ready for change. They began to encourage activities and specific responses considered incompatible with aggression. In particular, given signs of mild aggressiveness, patients were instructed to engage in relaxation exercises ("you can not be aggressive and relaxed simultaneously") and to monitor hostility inducing thoughts. When instances of aggressive outbursts took place, the parties involved were assigned to record and ponder alternative, more constructive ways of acting. Moreover, staff members focused on, and attempted to reinforce, manifestations of prosocial behaviors (helping, cooperating).

The evident result of this approach was an almost complete extinction of aggression and a marked increase in prosocial behaviors among patients, especially James

Resistance to Treatment

Adherence to prescribed treatment modalities was a major problem for James during initial phases of treatment. Consonant with the notions of Turk, Meichenbaum, and Genest (1983), noncompliance was seen as resistance to treatment stemming, in part, from a lack of understanding. James understood neither the severity nor the possible developmental course of his constellation of problems. Additionally, he did not see a connection between the presenting problems and the treatment interventions.

A first step in addressing noncompliance was to convey information concerning the nature, severity, and the possible course of antisocial behaviors into the adult years. The "match" between James's problems as theoretically conceptualized (e.g., a failure to develop language controls over behavior) and the various treatment procedures (e.g., generating and practicing coping self-statements) was emphasized.

I promoted adherence in individual therapy by following the advice of Marlatt (1985). I tried to establish a solidarity (equal status) relationship in which James was treated as a coinvestigator, a collaborator, with me in a mutual search for problem solutions. James's evaluation of his individual therapy (using the patient evaluation form of Kazdin et al., 1987) indicated that I treated him as a worthwhile person, deserving of respect. Such perceptions have been found to be associated with adherence to treatment (Turk et al., 1983).

Emphasis across all therapeutic modalities was on a logical step-by-step presentation of material tailored to James's capacity for understanding. Target goals were broken down into small, easily accomplished objectives; I tried not to push him into trying to achieve too much too quickly (see Marlatt, 1985).

Treatment Evaluation

CBCL Data

A CBCL assessment completed by James's designated "primary caregiver" (the member of the nursing staff who spent approximately 3 hours per day with James) within the hospital setting indicated essentially no change after 1 month of hospitalization. This same measure was completed at the end of 60 days of treatment. Comparison between the latter assessment and CBCL findings at the beginning of hospitalization indicated a reduction in total behavioral problems from 72 to 22, a change in the Externalizing score from 47 to 15, and a reduction in the Internalizing score from 22 down to 2.

In order to control for pretest–posttest regression effects and as a method of estimating the clinical meaningfulness of treatment impact, reliability change indexes (Jacobson, Follette, & Revenstorf, 1984) were computed for the total CBCL change score as well as for externalizing and internalizing changes. The results approximated the normal distribution and suggested highly significant, clinically relevant improvements. The reliable change index (RC) for the total was 7.49 ($p < .01$); the RC's for Externalizing and Internalizing change scores were, respectively, 12.65 ($p < .01$) and 6.43 ($p < .01$).

Therapist's Rating of Treatment

The therapist evaluation form developed by Kazdin et al. (1987) is a 15-item, 5-point Likert scale containing two a priori (intuitively derived) subscales: (1) the child or adolescent's progress in therapy (receptivity to treatment, understanding of strategies used, degree of learning that took place) and (2) the likelihood that improvements will be maintained across environmental settings in areas of interpersonal problems and self control. In the only study on the validation of the scale, Kazdin et al. found significant correlations between the therapist's predictions of maintenance of improvements following therapy and reduced deviant behaviors at a posttreatment period and a 1-year follow-up for 51 children treated in a psychiatric hospital.

James's mean score of 3.3 across the Receptivity to Therapy Items indicated that I perceived a moderate to strong therapeutic impact. His score of 24 on the Maintenance of Improvement subscale is higher than the mean (20.6) for a treatment contact control group in Kazdin et al., suggesting that I, as the therapist, foresaw a fair to good chance that therapeutic gains would be maintained for a reasonable period following hospitalization.

Peer Interaction and Social Functioning Observation Form

James was unobtrusively observed interacting in a variety of situations including group therapy settings, recreational activities, and more spontaneous transactions. The rating form developed by Michelson and Dilorenzo (1981), standardized in a psychiatric hospital setting, was used to code interpersonal behaviors. Periodically, on a daily basis, James would be observed for 1 minute on a 10-second observe, 5-second record schedule. This occurred five times per day at varying time intervals throughout the course of treatment.

During the initial days of hospitalization, ratings of James's transactions with peers were dominated by entries in the categories (1) maladaptive interactions and (2) solitary behaviors, the combined frequencies accounting for over 90% of total entries. Over time, there was a gradual change in the direction of adaptive interactions (e.g., cooperative vocalizations, maintaining facial attention, listening to others speak). During the final week of inpatient treatment, virtually all ratings were of an adaptive variety.

Levels System Performance

Another method of estimating the extent of James's improvements during the 60-day treatment period involved his performance in relation to the privilege level program. Beginning with defiant noncompliance (he set a record for number of closed unit confinements unlikely to be surpassed), James progressed to earning an incremental number of points for cooperative interchanges with professional personnel and other residents, obeying community guidelines, actual demonstrations of acquired therapeutic skills (e.g., presumed honest expressions of feelings in acceptable ways, thought analysis, thought stopping, relaxation), and for being an effective role model for other patients. The fact that James was able to proceed through all levels and "graduate" (based on a consensus of staff judgments vis-a-vis point allotments) suggests that important therapeutic improvements were being made. His progression in the levels program required deferring impulse gratification, working effectively toward relatively long-term therapeutic goals, completion of therapeutic "homework" assignments, contributing in a constructive manner in the various group therapy modalities, and, perhaps most importantly, exercising rational control over adverse emotional expressions. Furthermore, James had to show the capacity to regulate his behaviors appropriately, according to the reactions of others.

Thought Monitoring

James's eventual responsiveness to the many components of inpatient treatment can also be appraised by considering actual exemplars of his thought monitoring at three time periods during hospitalization (all patients were asked to record verbatim their main covert self-statements on an hourly basis): (1) the first week of treatment; (2) at approximately the midpoint of hospitalization; and (3) just prior to discharge.

1. *First Week*
   I feel anger.
   I feel explosive.
   I hate _____ (staff member).
   I feel like fucking shit.
   I need to cry; it's the only thing I can do when I have no control and
   I'm being treated shitty.

I'd like to hit the bastard that keeps me from doing better; I should only have had one Goddamn community violation; I shouldn't have to go to the closed unit. I hate it; it pisses me off. Fuck it!

2. *Midtreatment*

I'm worried about getting community violations.
I want to go out and see for myself how my life will be changed.
I hope tonight I will have no conflicts.
I want to go to the next level; I wonder if I'll make it tomorrow.
I feel a sense of accomplishment; it makes a good feeling inside me that I don't really understand.
I feel like a failure because of the amount of time I've been here.
I hate _____ (professional staff member); he's a scumbag wimp; I'd like to punch him out right in front of everybody.

3. *Termination*

I'm so scared.
I want out.
I wish I had someone close who I could talk to.
I wish I had all the answers.
I feel bad. I don't know why. I wonder maybe I know why but I'm not comfortable writing it down.

If these words accurately reflect what was going on "in James's head," they suggest a diminution of hostile, aggressive thinking and a reduction in narcissism and self-centeredness. A more humble willingness to admit and explore personal weaknesses and problem areas may also be indicated.

DISCHARGE CRITERIA

Brief mention should be made of an issue producing justifiable concern among mental health professionals. Private psychiatric inpatient treatment programs for adolescents are expensive; most caregivers can not afford such multidisciplinary, medically based interventions independent of health insurance coverage. One result of this may be that the duration of inpatient treatment is dictated more by the availability of insurance funds than by clinically germane criteria. In this context, it should be then noted that James's treatment took place in a facility with explicit discharge criteria; the patient is discharged only when these criteria are met. If third-party coverage has terminated prior to fulfilling these standards, treatment continues, often at the hospital's expense. The discharge criteria include (1) completion of all stages of the privilege level system; (2) demonstrated significant changes in presenting problems and symptoms such that the patient is not considered a threat to himself/herself, to other people, or to society; (3) the presence of home and family environment judged adequate for maintenance of hospital gains; and (4) a developed after-treatment program that typically includes weekly attendance at a relapse-prevention group, weekly meetings with other hospital "graduates" as a support group, continuing family and individual therapy, and an aftercare behavioral contract specifying sanctions for adherence and violations.

AFTERCARE

It is noteworthy that James independently developed an after-discharge plan for the expressed purpose of maintaining inpatient gains. This additionally suggests that James was no longer avoiding problems but was facing them directly and taking responsibility for reducing relapse probabilities:

1. Narcotics Anonymous: Attend at least 4 hours of meeting attendance per week for at least 3 months.
2. Work: Look for a job 2 hours per day Monday through Friday; at least two personal contacts per day until I find a job.
3. Education: With GED, I can enroll at _____ University. I will initially take six semester units in field of communication
4. Home responsibility: Make time for activities with Mom (i.e., movies, meal preparations). Work to keep living space in clean and good condition.
5. Support system: Have daily contact with N.A. people; spend daily time with peers committed to abstinence.
6. Attend Dr. _____ weekly group therapy to keep aggression under control and prevent relapse; weekly individual therapy with Dr. _____ for at least 3 months.
7. Amends to family: Help repay my family for problems I've caused them; take time away from leisure activities as needed.

IN RETROSPECT

Perhaps the unpredictable environment implemented early in James's hospital program contributed to the eventual "success" of the predictable system used later (e.g., through an extinction of manipulative behaviors). Nonetheless, the unpredictable approach was correlated with escalations in unacceptable actions and in retrospect led to more problems than benefits.

The importance of a united, mutually supportive treatment staff can not be overly emphasized in the hospital treatment of psychopathic delinquents. The skilled manipulator may attempt successfully to divide the staff by creating factions, pitting one professional staff person against another, or by making emotional appeals to individuals possessing higher organizational power.

In a multidisciplinary setting, a variety of theoretical positions may be extant that differ with respect to practical implications. This was shown to be a problem in the treatment of James's aggressiveness. Although the clinical decision had been made to strengthen prosocial responses incompatible with aggression and to engender controls over aggressive urges through cognitive–behavioral techniques, staff personnel responsible for implementation held firmly to the catharsis model. The results were undoubtedly a sense of confusion for James, together with attenuated therapeutic progress. It was unfortunate that these conflicting orientations were not recognized earlier in the treatment process and that a more concerted treatment effort depended on the actual observed failure of the cathartic approach. In retrospect, formal professional staff training should have preceded the self-control methods with emphasis on the necessity for an effective alternative to catharsis.

Of the various theoretical positions on psychopathic delinquency, two accounts, in particular, seem especially apt with respect to James's presenting problems and observed changes. The first involves the possible developmental arrest leading to generally egocentric thought patterns. During the beginning of treatment, James's interpretations of experiences and anticipated consequences tended not to include the reactions of others and were predominantly self-centered. As treatment progressed (especially individual and interpersonal therapies), he evinced an improved perspective-taking capacity that appeared strongly associated with demonstrated behavioral changes.

The second explanation includes how so-called psychopaths respond to environmental stimuli, especially the rapid satiation hypothesis. Over time, it was gradually recognized that effective treatment required a variety of reinforcing contingencies together with periodic changes in the nuances of existing treatment modalities. Without some degree of novelty, James would rapidly lose interest and fail to adhere to the treatment regimen.

It has been assumed that psychopathic individuals are not able to establish authentic, nonmanipulative relationships. The consensus of hospital personnel was that although difficult and protracted, the reactions of peers and adult caregivers did become important to James (maybe his thinking became more sociocentric), and he began to moderate his actions according to expectations of others and deport himself appropriately. It could be argued that his behaviors only became "meaningful" once other people began to matter to James.

ADDENDUM

James's aftercare program provided for frequent returns to the hospital, including weekly involvement in group therapies centering on aggression control and abstinence from illicit drug usage. In addition, he continued weekly individual therapy sessions. His apparent motivation for and commitment to maintaining treatment-related changes can be seen by his desires for improving himself educationally. Having obtained a GED, James was able, at age 17, to enter the local university in the field of communications.

James faithfully adhered to what might be considered a very rigorous posthospitalization schedule. A month after discharge, his mother's posthospitalization CBCL ratings indicated that treatment gains were, in fact, being preserved in the home environment.

It was not until the third month following hospital discharge that James missed his first therapy session. He explained that he was feeling somewhat ill but would certainly attend the subsequent week. At about this same time, James's mother reported that, although he was still deporting himself well in the home, the amount of time James was spending preparing for classes and completing homework assignments was dissipating. She expressed concern about potential relapse.

James showed a gradual, insidious decline in conforming to his aftercare program by failing to attend sessions while offering effusive apologies and promises. He dropped out of school; did not return telephone messages; and eventually left home, his whereabouts unknown.

Recently (7 months after discharge), James's mother contacted the hospital, indicating that James was incarcerated in the state facility for juvenile offenders; he had been sentenced to serve 6 months. Just the other day James wrote the hospital's clinical director stating that after completing his sentence, he hoped to continue university studies and return to his aftercare program.

REFERENCES

Achenbach, T. M. (1982). *Developmental psychopathology* (2nd ed.). New York: Wiley.

Achenbach, T. M., & Edelbrock, C. S. (1983). *Manual for the Child Behavior Checklist and Revised Child Behavior Profile.* Burlington, VT: University of Vermont, Department of Psychiatry.

Alexander, F., & Staub, H. (1956). *The criminal, the judge, and the public: A psychological analysis.* Glencoe, IL: Free Press.

American Psychiatric Association (1980). *Diagnostic and statistical manual of mental disorders* (3rd. ed.). Washington, DC: Author.

American Psychiatric Association (1987). *Diagnostic and statistical manual of mental disorders* (3rd ed., revised). Washington, DC: Author.

Beck, A. T. (1976). *Cognitive therapy and the emotional disorders.* New York: International Universities Press.

Beier, E. C. (1966). *The silent language of psychotherapy.* Chicago: Aldine.

Bloor, M. J. (1980). A report on the relationship between informal patient interaction and the formal treatment programme in a day hospital using therapeutic community method. *Institute of Medical Sociology Occasional Paper, No. Four.* Aberdeen, Scotland: Institute of Medical Sociology.

Cleckley, H. (1976). *The mask of sanity* (5th ed.). St. Louis, MO: Mosby.

Cloninger, C. R., Christiansen, K. O., Reich, T., & Gottesman, I. I. (1978). Implications of sex differences in the prevalence of antisocial personality, alcoholism, and criminality for familial transmission. *Archives of General Psychiatry, 35,* 941–951.

Eron, L. D. (1987). The development of aggressive behavior from the perspective of a developing behaviorism. *American Psychologist, 42,* 435–442.

Eysenck, H. J. (1957). *The dynamics of anxiety and hysteria.* New York: Praeger.

Feshbach, S. (1984). The catharsis hypothesis, aggressive drive, and the reduction of aggression. *Aggressive Behavior, 10,* 91–101.

Hokanson, J. E., Megargee, E. I., O'Hagan, S. E., & Perry, A. M. (1976). Behavioral, emotional, and autonomic reactions to stress among incarcerated, youthful offenders. *Criminal Justice Bulletin, 3,* 203–234.

Hook, E. B. (1973). Behavioral implications of the human X Y Y genotype. *Science, 179,* 139–150.

Jacobson, N. S., Follette, W. C., & Revenstorf, C. (1984). Psychotherapy outcomes research: Methods for reporting variability and evaluating clinical significance. *Behavioral Therapy, 15,* 336–352.

Kazdin, A. E. (1985). *Treatment of antisocial behavior in children and adolescents.* Homewood, IL: Dorsey.

Kazdin, A. E., Esveldt-Dawson, K., French, N. H., & Unis, A. S. (1987). Problem-solving skills training, and relationship therapy in the treatment of antisocial child behavior. *Journal of Consulting and Clinical Psychology, 55,* 76–85.

Kegan, R. S. (1986). The child behind the mask: Sociopathy as developmental delay. In W. H. Reid, D. Dorr, J. I. Walker, & J. W. Bonner (Eds.), *Unmasking the psychopath: Antisocial personality and related syndromes* (pp. 47–55). New York: Norton.

Koller, K. M., & Gosden, S. D. (1980). Recidivists: Their past and families compared with first time only prisoners. *Australian and New Zealand Journal of Criminology, 13,* 117–123.

Leschiad, A., Jaffe, P., & Stone, G. (1985). Differential response of juvenile offenders to two detention environments as a function of conceptual level. *Candian Journal of Criminology, 27,* 467–477.

Loeber, R. (1982). The stability of antisocial and delinquent child behavior: A review. *Child Development, 53,* 1431–1466.

Lykken, D. F. (1957). A study of anxiety in the sociopathic personality. *Journal of Abnormal and Social Psychology, 55,* 6–10.

Mallick, S. K., & McCandless, B. R. (1966). A study of catharsis of aggression. *Journal of Personality and Social Psychology, 41,* 591–596.

Marlatt, G. A. (1985). Lifestyle modification. In G. A. Marlatt & J. R. Gordon (Eds.), *Relapse prevention* (pp. 280–344). New York: Guilford.

Mitchell, S., & Rosa, P. (1981). Boyhood behavior problems as precursors of criminality: A fifteen year follow-up study. *Journal of Child Psychology and Psychiatry, 22,* 19–33.

Michelson, L., & Dilorenzo, T. M. (1981). Behavioral assessment of peer interaction and social functioning in institutional and structured settings. *Journal of Clinical Psychology, 37,* 499–503.

Nichtern, S. (1982). The sociocultural and psychodynamic aspects of the acting-out and violent adolescent. *Journal of Adolescent Psychiatry, 10,* 140–146.

Patterson, G. R. (1982). *Coercive family process.* Eugene, OR: Castalia.

Patterson, G. R. (1986). Performance models for antisocial boys. *American Psychologyst, 41,* 432–444.

Partridge, G. E. (1928). A study of 50 cases of psychopathic personality. *American Journal of Psychiatry, 7,* 953–973.

Person, E. S. (1986). Manipulativeness in entrepreneurs and psychopaths. In W. H. Reid, D. Dorr, J. I. Walker, & J. W. Bonner (Eds.), *Unmasking the psychopath: Antisocial personality and related syndromes* (pp. 256–273). New York: Norton.

Quay, H. C. (1964). Personality dimensions in delinquent males as inferred from the factor analysis of behavior ratings. *Journal of Research in Crime and Delinquency, 1,* 33–36.

Quay, H. C. (1965). Psychopathic personality as pathological stimulus-seeking. *American Journal of Psychiatry, 122,* 180–183.

Robins, L. N. (1978). Study of childhood predictors of adult antisocial behavior: Replication from longitudinal studies. *Psychological Medicine, 8,* 611–622.

Schachter, S. (1964). The interaction of cognitive and physiological determinants of emotional state. In L. Berkowitz (Ed.), *Advances in experimental social psychology* (Vol. 1 pp. 49–80). New York: Academic.

Schachter, S., & Singer, J. (1962). Cognitive, social, and physiological determinants of the emotional state. *Psychological Review, 69,* 379–399.

Shamsie, S. J. (1981). Antisocial adolescents: Our treatments do not work—where do we go from here? *Canadian Journal of Psychiatry, 26,* 357–364.

Tucker, D. M. (1981). Lateral brain function, emotion, and conceptualization. *Psychological Bulletin, 89,* 19–46.

Turk, D. C., Meichenbaum, D., & Genest, M. (1983). *Pain and behavioral medicine.* New York: Guilford.

Ullmann, L. P., & Krasner, L. (1975). *A psychological approach to abnormal behavior* (2nd ed.). Englewood Cliffs, NJ: Prentice-Hall.

Yochelson, S., & Samenow, S. E. (1977). *The criminal personality: Vol. 2. The change process.* New York: Aronson.

Author Index

Subject Index